# INTRODUCTORY REGRESSION ANALYSIS

This text is designed to help students fully understand regression analysis, its components, and its uses. Taking into consideration current statistical technology, it focuses on the use and interpretation of software, while also demonstrating the logic, reasoning, and calculations that lie behind any statistical analysis. Furthermore, the text emphasizes the application of regression tools to real-life business concerns. This multilayered, yet pragmatic approach fully equips students to derive the benefit and meaning of a regression analysis.

This text is designed to serve in a second undergraduate course in statistics in which regression and its component features are the main focus. Although previous exposure to statistical concepts would prove helpful, it is possible to achieve a full understanding of regression and the many ways it can be used from a thorough reading of this text alone.

**Allen Webster** is a Professor at Bradley University. He gained his Ph.D. in Economics from Florida State University, and both an M.S. and B.S. in Economics from Fort Hays State University.

# INTRODUCTORY REGRESSION ANALYSIS

## With Computer Application for Business and Economics

**Allen Webster**

Routledge
Taylor & Francis Group
NEW YORK AND LONDON

**FIRST INDIAN REPRINT, 2014**

First published 2013
by Routledge
711 Third Avenue, New York, NY 10017

Simultaneously published in the UK
by Routledge
2 Park Square, Milton Park, Abingdon, Oxon OX14 4RN

*Routledge is an imprint of the Taylor & Francis Group, an informa business*

*Library of Congress Cataloging in Publication Data*
Webster, Allen.
Introductory regression analysis: with computer application for business and economics / Allen Webster.
p. cm.
Includes bibliographical references and index.
1. Commercial statistics. 2. Economics—Statistical methods. 3. Regression analysis. I. Title.
HF1017.W435 2012
519.5′36—dc23
2012007399

ISBN13: 978-0-415-89932-1 (hbk)
ISBN13: 978-0-415-89933-8 (pbk)
ISBN13: 978-0-203-18256-7 (ebk)

Typeset in Times New Roman
by Book Now Ltd, London

Printed and bound in India by Nutech Print Services

Please visit the eResources Website at www.routledge.co.uk/9780415899338

**FOR SALE IN SOUTH ASIA ONLY.**

To Mona:
With love and deep devotion –
because of who you are

# TABLE OF CONTENTS IN BRIEF

# TABLE OF CONTENTS
# IN BRIEF

## INTRODUCTORY REGRESSION ANALYSIS

# TABLE OF CONTENTS IN DETAIL

# PREFACE

With the advancing level of technology available to business analysts that, willing or otherwise, has been thrust upon us, the acquisition and examination of vast amounts of data have become increasingly straightforward. It is now possible to compile large data sets that offer valuable insight into many issues decision-makers face on a daily basis. Based on this collection of vital information powerful statistical tools can be brought to bear in efforts to develop optimum solutions to complex problems. Only the most naïve bureaucrat would attempt to direct any commercial effort without first giving serious consideration to the multitude of effective statistical tools currently at his or her disposal.

This text explores the essential fundamentals of one of the most compelling statistical tools available to those charged with the responsibility of making consequential decisions that have a direct bearing on the course of their professional endeavors. That tool is regression analysis. Perhaps no other statistical procedure is as universally applicable to so many commercial tasks as is regression and its statistical extensions.

Reliance on analytical methods of decision-making that have consistently proven useful is essential to any serious effort to effectively manage a dynamic organization. Therefore, this book places a strong emphasis on realistic business applications of statistical tools to common questions that arise on a daily basis.

Developments in modern computer software and its almost universal presence throughout progressive organizational structures make data management a practical goal for all those concerned with effective management. Given the overwhelming array of information and resources that lie at our disposal, only with the aid of powerful computers is it possible to fully avail ourselves of the advantages data analysis can provide. The reader is therefore shown how computers can be used to facilitate the task of data manipulation. This book demonstrates both when and how computer technology can be used to further business aspirations.

However, such effort is of no benefit if the significance and import of this analysis is not fully understood. It is crucial that a clear perception of the results of our analysis be achieved. Only in this manner can the full benefit of statistical analysis be applied. Recognizing the critical need for total understanding and complete comprehension of the outcome of intensive data analysis, this book provides a lucid description of the interpretation and meaning of the statistical findings.

# Chapter 1

# A REVIEW OF BASIC CONCEPTS

## INTRODUCTION

This first chapter provides an important overview of the fundamental concepts relevant to a thorough understanding of statistical analysis. Basic terms and definitions that are commonly used in statistical studies are presented. These definitions are crucial to a complete understanding of what statistics is and what it can do for you. It is important for you to distinguish between populations and samples and to identify various types of variables used in statistical analysis.

The specific steps that should be taken in any statistical analysis are examined. This "statistics process" affords an organized and analytically structured procedure that can be followed to minimize the chance of error and ensures that all phases of a statistical study are completed.

Numerous types of data and the different ways in which they can be measured are presented. The levels of complexity and scale of refinement of data display must be considered in their analysis. Using data to draw conclusions for which they may be unsuitable is a common blunder committed by uninformed analysts. Many research efforts are impaired and the results corrupted by the improper use of data.

It is essential that researchers understand the concept behind the statistical procedures they perform. Without a full conceptual appreciation of statistical tools their use is severely limited. This text emphasizes the interpretation and application of statistical analysis as well as the mathematical process analysts must complete.

> A conceptual understanding of the results of any statistical study is of paramount importance to the interpretation and application of statistical analysis. Merely "crunching the numbers" or performing the simple mathematical computations is of limited value.

## 1.1 THE IMPORTANCE OF MAKING SYSTEMATIC DECISIONS

As the business world becomes increasingly complex, so does the process of decision-making. As times have changed, so has the manner in which intelligent and informed choices must be made. No longer is it possible to continue some policy simply because "that's the way we've always done it" or "it's worked that way in the past." Today it is necessary to decide courses of action only after a careful evaluation of all potential alternatives and the outcomes these options offer.

This thorough assessment requires a more systematic and analytical approach to the decision-making process. Flipping a coin simply isn't going to work. An examination of alternative procedures must involve the informed use of statistical tools that provide analytical insight into problem-solving. Only with the aid of rational thought offered by a statistical investigation can the decision-maker feel confident of his or her work. Through statistical analysis we are able to decrease the level of uncertainty and risk associated with the decision-making process.

This is true regardless of the field of study. Marketing executives must determine the potential for consumer acceptance of any new product they wish to introduce into the marketplace. The effort to market a new product that ultimately proves to be a failure can be quite disastrous. Many companies have suffered serious damage to their "bottom line" by rushing an untested product to market before fully evaluating its potential for market success. This unfortunate turn of events could have been avoided by a coherent review of market conditions.

Business managers must often decide which training program is optimal for their employees, what is the best form of transportation for their final product, and what are the desired levels of inventory that should be maintained. They face a wide array of crucial decisions that could be made more prudent through some form of statistical analysis.

Financial analysts are often faced with alternative sources of investment funds that can be used for various purposes. They must carefully evaluate different capital budgeting procedures to decide the most desirable method to finance their firm's operations.

Corporate accountants concern themselves with the relative effectiveness of different audit procedures. They frequently wish to identify the most effective method of drawing information from financial statements and evaluating the results of earlier corporate decisions. Economists must often estimate product demand, perform crucial cost analysis, and measure levels of competition within domestic as well as foreign markets. Estimating the shelf-life of their perishables, examining production schedules, and researching the character of competitive markets also fall within the scope of economists' daily tasks.

The applications of statistical analysis to the business decision-making process are unlimited. No aspect of business behavior escapes the vital scrutiny that can be provided only through a formal and detailed statistical process. The tools and techniques that make up statistical analysis allow businesses to derive vital and meaningful information from data they have collected for just that purpose. Making any consequential business decision in the absence of a statistical study is a hazardous prospect at best.

## 1.2 THE PROCESS OF STATISTICAL ANALYSIS

The statistical process takes on several clearly identifiable steps. We can examine each briefly in turn.

### ● Data Collection

Data may be collected either internally or externally. Internal data are taken from within the organization for which the researcher works. Company production and sales records can serve as a plentiful source of valuable data. Accounting records, employee files, and customer profiles also provide an abundant wealth of information. Data pertaining to inventory control, quality management, tax records, and a whole host of privileged information can be obtained from company sources.

External data may be acquired from government agencies, industry associations, and special interest groups. Popular business publications including *The Wall Street Journal*, *Business Week*, and *Forbes*, to name only a few, now maintain divisions within their corporate structure for the sole purpose of maintaining data bases. In many cases these data can be freely obtained by interested parties while in other instances it may be necessary to pay a small fee to acquire the data. Moody's Industrials, Dun and Bradstreet, Robert Morris Associates, and Dow Jones specialize in maintaining data bases that can be used for business and economic research. Even the Internet now serves as a data source of growing importance. Given advances in communication technology and information systems over the past few years data are readily available from any number of sources.

### ● Organizing the Data

Once the data have been collected you may feel overwhelmed by the mass of numbers that form the data set. In self-defense you must devise some method of organizing and presenting the data in a more concise manner so that pertinent information becomes readily apparent. Simply staring at a bunch of numbers jotted down on seemingly endless pages from a yellow legal pad or a computer printout does very little to generate any useful information. You must somehow gain a perception of the general nature of all these numbers staring back at you. There are many ways in which you might manage the data set and bring it into focus.

You could prepare graphs and pictorial displays that summarize the data in a single image. Pie charts, bar graphs, frequency tables, and other diagrams are all very useful in providing a quick characterization of the data. By merely calculating an average you can get a more clearly defined impression of what the data are like. Many of these organizational methods are discussed in this text. But in some way it is critical that you begin your task of data analysis by gaining some idea of the nature and disposition of the data.

● **Analyzing the Data**

After organizing the data you can now begin the true process of data analysis. This involves the application of the many statistical tools that lie at your disposal. Statistical tests such as confidence intervals that allow you to estimate unknown values with a specific degree of assurance are often applied at this point. Hypothesis tests permit you to test an assumption about some unknown level of business activity important to your organization. Regression models that identify relationships between various measures of economic activity and correlation analysis that can measure just how strong those relationships might be are invaluable in your study. These are the tools of statistical analysis that are examined in this text.

● **Interpreting the Results**

Given the outcome of your analysis, what can you conclude from your findings? What does your analysis tell you? If your original intent was to examine the impact of national tax policies on your sales levels or how international exchange rates might affect your import/export operations, what inference can you now draw? Based on the results of your work you are now able to evaluate the relative wisdom of anticipated policy changes and decisions that will determine the direction your organization should take.

● **Prediction and Forecasting**

Statistical analysis can also act as a "crystal ball" by allowing you to actually look ahead and predict future developments with some degree of accuracy. If you have done your work correctly you can now forecast impending events. Next year's sales levels, changes in foreign exchange rates, demands that will be placed on next quarter's inventory levels, and many more trends can be foreseen through the use of statistical analysis. The ability to predict what's going to happen in the future makes decision-making today a whole lot easier!

## 1.3 OUR "ARABIC" NUMBER SYSTEM

The number system used in the Western world consisting of the integers 0 through 9 is often referred to as the Arabic number system. However, it is not really Arabic in origin. It was first developed by the Hindus in India in the third century BCE. It wasn't adopted into the Arab world until around the seventh or eighth century CE (formerly AD). When Europeans finally embraced the scheme in 976 CE they were unaware of its Hindu origin and inappropriately called it the Arabic system.

The Hindus used different symbols than those we currently employ, but the application of the ten characters is essentially the same. Our number system, whatever you choose to call it, is most often categorized into *real* numbers, *imaginary* numbers, and *complex* numbers.

1.  Real numbers contain integers, rational numbers, and irrational numbers.

    A.  Integers are simply *whole* numbers. There are positive integers, negative integers, and the integer 0, which is neither positive nor negative. Thus, numbers such as 5, 39, –254, 73, –10, and 5,710 are all integers.

    B.  Rational numbers are fractions or *ratios*. Numbers such as 3/4, 2/5, and 6/5 are examples. Actually, integers are rational numbers in that 5 can be expressed as 5/1. When expressed as decimals, rational numbers are either "repeating," such as 3/9 = 0.33333~, or "terminating," such as 5/2 = 2.5.

    C.  Irrational numbers are not expressed as ratios. Examples include $\sqrt{2}$ and $\sqrt{5}$. When expressed as decimals they are *not* repeating or terminating. For example $\sqrt{39}$ = 6.244997998~.

2.  An imaginary number is the square root of a negative number such as $\sqrt{-4}$. Imaginary numbers are often indicated by the lower case "*i*." We say $i^2 = -1$ and thus $\sqrt{-1} = i$. Then, $\sqrt{-4}$ can be written as $\sqrt{4} * \sqrt{-1} = 2i$.

3.  Complex numbers are numbers that contain both a real component and an imaginary component. For example, given the quadratic equation

$$X^2 + 4X + 8 = 0$$

we get the "solution"

$$-2 + \sqrt{-4} \quad \text{and} \quad -2 - \sqrt{-4}$$

If, as noted above, we let

$$\sqrt{-4} = \sqrt{4}\sqrt{-1}$$
$$= 2\sqrt{-1}$$
$$= 2i$$

the solution is then $-2 + 2i$ and $-2 - 2i$.

Thus, imaginary numbers allow us to derive a solution to quadratic equations without real roots.

A prime number, although not a specific category in our number system, is a number that is evenly divisible by only 1 and itself. Examples include 2, 3, 5, 7, 11, 13, etcetera. Prime numbers carry a special place in calculations in that they form the building blocks for our number system.

## 1.4 SOME BASIC DEFINITIONS

To fully understand the application of statistical analysis to the decision-making process we must acquire a coherent meaning of some fundamental statistical terms and the manner in which those terms are used in the analytical process. Without these clear distinctions any discussion of the statistical process loses all meaning and proves to be of little use.

## ● Populations and Samples

Perhaps most importantly, we must distinguish between *populations* and their *parameters* and *samples* and their *statistics*. The population is the entire set of *all* individual observations of interest to our study. If our study centers on our company's operations with our foreign customers, then *all* overseas companies to whom we have sold products constitute the population. A physical list of each observation in the population is called the *frame*.

> A population is the entire set of all observations of interest to our study.

A *parameter* is a descriptive measure of the population. For example, the average dollar sales to *all* our foreign customers or the proportion of *all* late payments received from overseas sales are parameters. They detail some aspect of all observations in the study—that is, the entire population. Remember, a parameter describes some characteristic of the population. Parameters are indicated by Greek letters—that is, letters from the Greek alphabet.

> Parameters describe populations. They are indicated by letters from the Greek alphabet.

However, populations are generally too large to study in their entirety. We simply don't have the time, money, or resources to undertake an examination of the entire population. Therefore, although it is the population in which we are interested, we are often forced to select a smaller, more manageable subset of the population called a *sample*. Of importance, that sample must be *representative* of the population. In our study of our foreign customers we can't merely select for our sample only those European firms with which we have dealt. European firms may have a larger (or smaller) average purchase than Asian companies or those firms that have purchased from us in other parts of the world. Perhaps European firms are more likely (or less likely) to pay on time than other buyers. In each of these cases a sample of only European firms would prove to be misleading in our efforts to obtain some perception of our world-wide business operations. Thus, it is essential that the sample we use in our study accurately depicts the population in which we are interested.

There are many sampling techniques that should be used to ensure the sample you select is indeed representative of your population. These sampling practices are beyond the scope of this text and the reader is advised to consult sources that adequately demonstrate how to collect a representative sample.

> A sample is a scientifically selected *representative* subset of the population.

Samples are described by *statistics*. Our average sales to just the foreign firms in our sample and the proportion of just those firms selected in our sample that pay late are examples of statistics. Statistics are obtained from samples and are indicated by Latin letters—letters from our alphabet.

Statistics describe samples and are indicated by Latin letters.

The population mean (average) is a parameter and indicated by the Greek letter $\mu$ (mu, read "mew"). The mean of a sample is a statistic and indicated by $\bar{X}$. It is the Latin letter $X$ with a bar above it and is read as "X-bar." Further, the size of a population is indicated by $N$, which is the Greek letter "nu" (read "new"), while the size of a sample is indicated by the lower case Latin letter $n$. Note, in all cases the parameters are Greek letters and the statistics are Latin letters.

As noted above, the examination of entire populations and the calculation of their parameters is often too time-consuming and costly. We are seldom able to compute the parameters of any population. Instead, we must obtain a representative sample and calculate its corresponding statistics. These statistics then serve as estimates of the parameters we would really prefer to know if we had sufficient resources.

For example, we may wish to verify the mean number of days it takes for our outbound shipments to reach all of our international customers. That is, we wish to determine the mean transit time for the entire population of all customers—that's the parameter $\mu$. However, since there have been so many shipments over the past several quarters we can collect data for only a small number, a sample, of those customers. We can then compute mean transit time for that sample—a statistic $\bar{X}$. That sample mean then serves as an estimate of the unknown population parameter. If $\bar{X}$ is found to be 9.4 days, then that is our estimate of $\mu$. The $\bar{X}$ is called the *estimator* and 9.4 is said to be the *estimate*.

There is a difference between a sample and the observations in a sample. If you were to take a sample of $n = 100$ observations, you do *not* have 100 samples. You have only one sample with 100 observations.

● **Sampling Error**

In estimating the parameter we are likely to suffer *sampling error*. Sampling error is simply the difference between the sample statistic and the unknown population parameter it is intended to estimate. The sampling error is expressed as the difference between the sample mean and the unknown population mean ($\bar{X} - \mu$).

You're right. We will never be able to actually calculate the sampling error because we will never know the value of the parameter. If we did we wouldn't have to take a sample in an effort to estimate it. Nevertheless, you must be aware of the fact that a sampling error is likely to occur.

● **Sources of Sampling Error: Sampling Bias and Plain Bad Luck**

Sampling errors arise primarily from two sources. Failure to collect a representative sample will produce *sampling bias* that can distort results. Sampling bias results from a sampling scheme that tends to favor the selection of certain sample elements at the expense of others. The illustration above recognizing the hazards of selecting only European firms in our study of late payments is an example.

The classic illustration of bias sampling is found in the effort by *Literary Digest*, a popular publication of the time, that attempted to predict the winner of the 1936 presidential election between the Democratic candidate, Franklin Delano Roosevelt, and the Republican representative, Alf Landon. The magazine took a survey by randomly selecting names from the telephone book. Regrettably, only wealthier people less affected by the Great Depression could afford a telephone. Since the general public, rightly or wrongly, blamed the Republicans for the depression, those voters most likely to cast favor with FDR were not included in the sample. The magazine unwittingly biased its sample by selecting respondents who were more inclined to vote Republican at the exclusion of FDR's supporters and boldly predicted a Republican victory. We all know how that election turned out.

A second source of sampling error stems from simple misfortune. Even if all precautions are taken to ensure a representative sample, it is still possible to unknowingly select atypical sample elements that misrepresent the population simply due to the "luck of the draw." In the effort to estimate the population mean for example it is possible to select observations that are unusually large, thereby over-estimating the population mean. On the other hand, misfortune might result in uncharacteristically small observations that under-estimate the parameter. In either case, sampling error has occurred.

The only way to combat this problem is to increase the size of your sample. Presume you want to estimate the mean of a population of size, say, $N = 10,000$. Which do you think would cause you to suffer a larger sampling error, a sample of size $n = 350$ or a sample of size $n = 9,999$? Taking a larger sample will obviously tend to reduce our sampling error. Of course, the drawback to this "solution" is an increase in time, resources, and cost of collecting the larger sample.

> Sampling error can result from sample bias due to a non-representative sample or simply bad luck in selecting sample observations.

## ● A Sampling Distribution

It is possible to get many different samples of a given size from any population. Each sample will have its own mean. Take the ridiculously small population of 2, 4, 6, and 8. Obviously, the population mean is $\mu = 5$. But pretend for a moment we don't know that and wish to estimate it by taking a sample of size 2. We could randomly select any one of the six possible samples as seen in Table 1.1. We might, for example, select the first two values of 2 and 4 for our sample. The sample mean would then be $\bar{X} = 3$. Or we might have selected the sample elements 2 and 6, in which case $\bar{X} = 4$. All six possible samples shown in Table 1.1 constitute a *sampling distribution* in that it lists all possible samples of size two and the means of all six samples.

A sampling distribution is simply a list of *all* possible samples of some given size that can be randomly chosen from a population and the mean of each of those samples.

■ **Table 1.1**   A Sampling Distribution of Sample Size Two

| Sample | Sample Elements, $X_i$ | Sample Mean, $\bar{X}$ |
| --- | --- | --- |
| 1 | 2,4 | 3 |
| 2 | 2,6 | 4 |
| 3 | 2,8 | 5 |
| 4 | 4,6 | 5 |
| 5 | 4,8 | 6 |
| 6 | 6,8 | 7 |

Notice that some of the samples report a mean that differs from the "unknown" population mean of 5. If you were to select one of those samples you would experience sampling error. For example, if you were to randomly select the fifth sample, which produces a sample mean of 6, you will have unwittingly over-estimated the population mean of 5.

Notice also that the "mean of the sample means," which can be displayed as $\mu_{\bar{x}}$, is equal to the mean of the original population. That is, if we were to find the mean of all six sample means we would have

$$\mu_{\bar{x}} = \frac{3+4+5+5+6+7}{6} = 5 = \mu$$

The number of samples that make up a sampling distribution can be determined by calculating the *combination* of those samples. This is done using Equation (1.4.1), where $N$ is the size of the population and $n$ is the sample size. $N!$ (read "N factorial") is the product of all numbers from 1 through $N$. For example, 5! is $1 \times 2 \times 3 \times 4 \times 5 = 120$.

The number of samples of some given size that can be obtained from a population can be determined by

$$C_n^N = \frac{N!}{n!(N-n)!} \tag{1.4.1}$$

where $N$ is the size of the population and $n$ is the sample size.

In our present case of the sampling distribution above we have

$$C_2^4 = \frac{4!}{2!(4-2)!} = \frac{1 \times 2 \times 3 \times 4}{1 \times 2(1 \times 2)} = 6$$

If a more realistically large sample were used rather than the mere 2, 4, 6, and 8 shown above, a much more extensive sampling distribution would have resulted. Consider the sales manager who wants to estimate the mean value of shipments to his overseas customers. There have been $N = 750$ sales over the time period in question so the manager selects a random sample of $n = 75$ shipments. The sampling distribution for this experiment would therefore contain $C_{75}^{750} = 373,315,824$ E+96 possible samples. You can see now why it was necessary to use such a small population of only $N = 4$ to illustrate the process of forming a sampling distribution.

### ● Types of Variables

In addition to populations and samples we must also distinguish among the numerous variables commonly encountered in any statistical study. A *variable* is simply the characteristic of the population we wish to examine. It might be the sales revenues, tax payments, factory output, or our amount of accounts receivable. The list of potential characteristics which we may wish to study is virtually unlimited.

Variables may be either *quantitative* or *qualitative*. A quantitative variable is measured numerically. The rate of return on investors' portfolios, the dollar volume of sales, production levels measured in tons, or the prices of inputs are examples. A qualitative variable is measured non-numerically. The types of industries of our customers or the countries in which they are located are often of interest in a statistical examination of our business transactions. The color of our best-selling product and whether our customers tend to buy on credit or pay cash are qualitative observations.

> A quantitative variable is measured numerically, while a qualitative variable is expressed as some non-numeric physical characteristic, such as color, gender, or type of corporate stock.

Quantitative variables can be mathematically manipulated. They are subject to all forms of mathematical calculations. They can be added, subtracted, or subjected to any arithmetic treatment as may be desired.

Qualitative variables, on the other hand, are not expressed numerically. They cannot be arithmetically analyzed. Qualitative variables can be summarized or described only through pictorial displays such as bar charts.

A *continuous* variable can take on any value within a given range, including fractional values. It is the result of measurement. For example, if a stockbroker executes a sale (or purchase) for his client, it may take one minute for the order to complete. Or, on a heavily traded stock, the wait time may be 1.5 minutes. Perhaps the order is finalized in 1.74 minutes. If you are manufacturing building products, a length may be cut to 7 ft 10 in., or conceivably, measurements may be sufficiently critical that a length of 7 ft 10.5 in. is necessary. In measuring continuous variables, no matter how close two observations might be, a third can be found that falls between the first two if the instrument used in the measurement is precise enough. The weight of shipments measured in pounds is an example. One shipment might weigh 50 pounds, another 51 pounds, and a third might weigh 50.5 pounds or 50.25 pounds.

*Discrete* variables can take on only certain values, usually whole numbers. They are the result of counting. The number of customers, the number of cars sold at a car lot, and the number of births at a local hospital qualify as discrete.

> Continuous variables, the result of measurements, can take on any value within a specific range, including fractional values. Discrete variables can assume only certain values, usually whole numbers, and result from simply counting the number of observations.

## 1.5 LEVELS OF DATA MEASUREMENT

Data can be classified on the basis of their level of measurement. Some are considered more refined or advanced forms of data than others. The manner in which they are categorized impacts the way in which we can use them. Data that are more developed can be used in more advanced applications than those restricted to lesser levels of refinement. In this regard, data may be nominal, ordinal, interval, or ratio.

### ● Nominal Data

*Nominal data*, or categorical data, merely divide data into separate and distinct categories. Nominal data can consist of a list of types of food such as "dairy, meat, fruits, and vegetables." Classifying stocks as "blue chip, penny stocks, growth stocks, income stocks, or value stocks" or identifying nations as "developed" or "emerging" creates nominal data. Viewers' favorite television shows such as *Desperate Housewives*, *Twenty-Minutes*, *Monday Night Football*, *Days of Our Lives*, and *The Big Bang Theory* are nominal data. Countries you intend to visit on your vacation may include Great Britain, Spain, Italy, and Germany. All can be listed in your itinerary.

It's important to recognize that nominal data are qualitative (not quantitative) data. As such, none of the mathematical operators such as addition, subtraction, multiplication, or division can be applied to nominal data. The TV shows could be identified as simply 1, 2, 3, 4, and 5. But these numbers merely serve to indicate the categories and carry no numerical meaning. They could also be identified by colors for that matter. Again, they carry no mathematical significance.

### ● Ordinal Data

*Ordinal data* are also categorical but are a bit more sophisticated than nominal data. Ordinal data use a Likert scale to *rank* the observations. Consumers might be asked to rank a product on a scale from 1 to 5, with 5 being the best ranking. Service at a plush resort might be graded as "good, better, or best" compared with other vacation sites. Unlike nominal data, the order of the rankings is important. The TV shows above could be listed in any order. The arrangement wouldn't matter. But it would be illogical to list the service as "good, best, better" or a scale such as 1, 4, 3, 5, and 2. Here the order of the rankings carries consequential meaning.

Again, with ordinal data none of the mathematical operators can be applied. Averaging the rankings of a Likert scale is pointless. The rankings for the TV shows could consist instead of 10, 20, 30, 40, and 50 yielding a far different average even if the same viewers were surveyed. The average obviously carries no meaning. Many inexperienced and poorly informed data analysts try to mathematically manipulate ordinal data. It can't be done with any logical or meaningful outcome. A TV show ranked "2" is not twice as good as one ranked "1." The difference between "1" and "2" is *not* the same as the difference between "2" and "3." The analogy of a horse race is often applied. The distance between the first and second horses may not be the same as the distance between the two horses that finish second and third. Only the order of their finish is significant.

● **Interval Data**

*Interval data* are measured only numerically. They can be added and subtracted, but not multiplied or divided. Temperature is one of the few unequivocally interval measures. The temperature in Chicago may be 25 degrees while Cincinnati basks in 50-degree weather. We can subtract the difference and say the temperature is 25 degrees warmer in Cincinnati. But to divide the values and contend it is twice as warm in Cincinnati is baseless. Or to claim that it is twice as cold in Chicago is baseless. This is due to the fact that with interval data the value of zero is arbitrarily chosen. This is evidenced by the fact that we have two *different* measures of "zero" with respect to temperature—Fahrenheit and centigrade. Unlike the horses, if Miami is 75 degrees the difference of 25 degrees between Chicago and Cincinnati *is* the same difference as that between Cincinnati and Miami.

Scholastic Assessment Test scores (SATs) are another accepted example of interval data. If three students were to score 1052, 907, and 875 they could be ranked from best to worst. In addition, the difference between the first two is $1052 - 907 = 145$, while there is difference of $907 - 875 = 32$ between the second and third students. Measuring the differences in this manner is meaningful unlike the difference between the first and second horses and the difference between the second and third horses.

● **Ratio Data**

*Ratio data* represent the highest evolution of numerical measures. Most business and economic data are ratio data. Production levels, profits, prices, stock values, and most other variables pertinent to business data are rational in nature. All four mathematical operators are applicable. In all of these cases zero is a meaningful value. To say we have zero profits means there are no profits. A temperature of zero degrees does not mean we have no temperature.

If two business firms have profits of $100 million and $200 million, we can say that the second firm is twice as profitable. In contrast, recall we cannot conclude that Cincinnati is twice as warm as Chicago.

---

### EXAMPLE 1.1: Trimming The Bloated Heifer

**Problem Statement:** Facing Chapter 11 bankruptcy[1] the CEO for The Bloated Heifer, a nation-wide restaurant chain offering a wide variety of beef dishes and other gastronomic indulgences, requires a complete analysis of business operations. Data are collected for a large number of variables and measures that describe the nature of previous business operations. These variables include:

- *Sales Revenues*—weekly receipts measured in dollars;

- *Number of Patrons* on a weekly basis;

- *Levels of Employee Training* measured as years of experience and whether the employee had received in-house training;

- *Most Popular Items on the Menu* measured by customers marking a ballot for their favorite and by the number of times each item is ordered;

- *Customer Ratings* on a Likert scale.

Before the analysis can begin it is necessary to identify the type of variable the researcher will work with in order to determine exactly what information that variable might reveal.

**Solution:** Sales revenues clearly constitutes ratio data. A value of zero has meaning and all four mathematical operators can be applied. Mean weekly receipts can be computed and receipts from one week can be compared with those in another week. The same is true for the number of patrons who enter the restaurant each week.

The level of employee training is also a ratio variable when measured as the number of years of experience. But when recorded as to whether an employee has received in-house training it becomes a nominal variable. The employee either received the training or did not receive the training. Thus, the employee falls into one category or the other much like the TV shows cited above.

This is also true of the most popular menu items when gauged by the ballot process. Again, the process is identical to the selection of favorite TV shows. However, when measured by the number of times an item is requested, it becomes ratio data. All operators can be applied, average orders per week (or day or month) can be meaningfully computed, and zero carries significance.

Customers' rating using a Likert scale is a clear use of ordinal data. A Likert scale is a psychometric scale named after its inventor, psychologist Rensis Likert, that employs a sliding scale allowing the respondent to choose his or her level of agreement with a question posed for an expressed purpose to elicit information about a specific concern. Possible responses commonly offered are Strongly Disagree, Disagree, Neither Agree Nor Disagree, Agree, and Strongly Agree.

Obviously, no mathematical calculations are possible. The results may be summarized graphically as a pie chart or bar chart. Even if the scaling is done with numerical values such as 1 through 5, mathematical calculations are meaningless. The numbers are nothing more than placeholders. An average of the responses is pointless. If the scale ranged from 10 through 50, any average would be entirely different. In addition, while the difference between sales revenue of $1 and $2 is the same as the difference between $2 and $3, such is not the case with a Likert scale. A rating on the 1-through-5 scale of 1 may be many times better than a rating of 2 in the minds of the respondents, while the difference between 2 and 3 may be quite slim. An analogy is generally offered that the Likert scale is like a horse race. The distance between the two horses that finished first and second may not be the same distance as that between the second- and third-place winners.

**Interpretation**: Determining the nature of the variables is essential to ensuring that the results of the study carry a proper interpretation. Sometimes faulty research is worse than no research at all.

## 1.6 PROPERTIES OF GOOD ESTIMATORS

The need to estimate parameters requires that we identify the characteristics of good estimators. Since we can only approximate the value of a parameter we want to ensure that our approximation is as accurate as possible. This section examines the four primary characteristics estimators must have in order to adequately fulfill this need.

### ● A Good Estimator Is Unbiased

An estimator is unbiased if the mean of the sampling distribution equals the corresponding parameter. Recall our earlier discussion of the sampling distribution of sample means for the population consisting of only the values 2, 4, 6, and 8. It was shown that if we take all six possible samples, the mean of those six sample means is equal to the population mean of 5.

Thus, if repeated samples are taken, the mean of those sample means (i.e., 5) will approach the mean of the population (i.e., $\mu = 5$). The more samples that are taken the closer the mean of

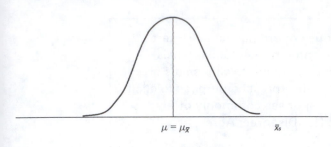

■ **Figure 1.1**    A Distribution of Sample Means

those sample means is to the unknown population mean. It is said that the *expected value* of the sample mean, written $E(\overline{X})$, equals the value of the unknown parameter $\mu$. The sample mean is therefore an unbiased estimator of the population mean.

Figure 1.1 displays this principle. Its horizontal axis shows the variation of the sample means, $\overline{X}s$, above and below the population mean, $\mu$. The *Central Limit Theorem*, an important concept we will examine in greater detail later on, assures us that under the proper set of circumstances these sample means will be *normally distributed* around the unknown population mean and form the bell-shaped curve shown in the figure.

It can be seen in Figure 1.1 that some of the sample means are below the population mean while others are above it. Look at Table 1.1 discussed earlier. However, note that the mean of the sample means, $\mu_{\overline{X}}$, equals the population mean, $\mu$.

> An estimator is considered unbiased if the mean of its sampling distribution equals the mean of the population from which the sampling distribution was formed.

### ● A Good Estimator Is Efficient

The efficiency of an estimator depends on its variation around its mean. Keep in mind that a sampling distribution contains many samples with different means. Again, see Table 1.1. The less each of those sample means varies from the population mean, the more efficient the estimator proves to be.

Let $\Omega$ (the Greek letter omega) be the parameter we wish to estimate. Two potential estimators are to be considered, $\hat{\Omega}_1$ (read "Omega hat one") and $\hat{\Omega}_2$. The estimator with the smaller variation above and below $\Omega$ is more efficient.

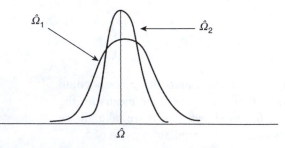

■ **Figure 1.2**    A Comparison of Two Potential Estimators

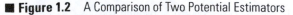

Consider Figure 1.2. It shows the distributions of each of the potential estimators, $\hat{\Omega}_1$ and $\hat{\Omega}_2$. As you can see, both are indeed unbiased in that their means equal the mean of the unknown parameter, $\Omega$. However, $\hat{\Omega}_2$ is the more efficient estimator since its dispersion above and below $\Omega$ is less than that of $\hat{\Omega}_1$. $\hat{\Omega}_2$ is more compact. The chance of getting more extreme estimates farther above or farther below $\Omega$ is less than if $\hat{\Omega}_1$ were used as the estimator.

> An estimator is efficient if its variation around (above and below) the parameter is small.

### ● A Good Estimator Is Consistent

An estimator is consistent if its value approaches the value of the unknown parameter as the sample size increases. This means that if a larger sample is taken the statistical estimate more closely approximates the unknown parameter.

Furthermore, the variation of a consistent estimator approaches zero as larger samples are chosen. If many samples of size 500 are selected to estimate the population mean the variation among those sample means would be more than if many samples of size 1,000 were taken. This is *not* to imply that a researcher would ever take more than one sample. You only get one chance to take a representative sample. This feature of a good estimator is discussed here only to note the importance of a consistency in the estimation process, not to suggest that you waste time taking a second sample and comparing it with the first.

> An estimator is consistent if it yields less sampling error as the sample size increases.

### ● A Good Estimator Is Sufficient

This simply means that a sufficient estimator takes into consideration all relative information about the parameter. Nothing more can be learned about the parameter by using a different estimator.

## 1.7 OTHER CONSIDERATIONS

Statistical analysis can be either descriptive or inferential in nature. *Descriptive* statistics is used to summarize a large data set in a concise and succinct manner. As noted earlier, once you have collected all the data to be used in the study it is easy to become overwhelmed by the vast display of numbers. It is helpful, and even necessary, to gain some impression or perspective as to the general nature of the data. This is done by organizing the data in some meaningful manner. The use of charts and graphs can provide the analyst with a general impression of the basic nature of the data. By calculating certain descriptive statistics such as the average the researcher can get a preliminary idea as to just what kind of numbers he or she is working with.

*Inferential* statistics is considered a higher form of statistical analysis. Here the researcher uses the data to draw some kind of inference or conclusion about what information the data might reveal. Statistical tools such as confidence intervals and hypothesis tests, both of which are examined thoroughly in later chapters, can be used in this effort.

By the way, the term "data" is plural. That is, we must say "the data *are*..." To say "the data is ..." is incorrect and analogous to saying "they is." Thus, it is proper to say "The data are 4 and 7." The singular form of the word is "datum." "The datum is 4."

Distinguishing between *time series* data and *cross-sectional* data is also important. Time series data are data that are collected for some series (some variable) across several time periods such as weeks or months. Monthly sales for January 2011 through August 2012 are an example. Quarterly depreciation levels for the last several years is another illustration. In both cases, data have been gathered for specific sequential time periods.

Table 1.2 displays monthly time series data for the U.S. unemployment rates for the years 2008 through 2010. Notice that the data reveal unemployment rates for successive time periods (months) and thus comprise time series data.

■ **Table 1.2** Monthly Unemployment Rates for the United States

| Year | Jan | Feb | Mar | Apr | May | June | July | Aug | Sept | Oct | Nov | Dec |
|------|-----|-----|-----|-----|-----|------|------|-----|------|-----|-----|-----|
| 2008 | 5.0 | 4.8 | 5.1 | 5.0 | 5.4 | 5.5 | 5.8 | 6.1 | 6.2 | 6.6 | 6.9 | 7.4 |
| 2009 | 7.7 | 8.2 | 8.6 | 8.9 | 9.4 | 9.5 | 9.4 | 9.7 | 9.8 | 10.1 | 10.0 | 10.0 |
| 2010 | 9.7 | 9.7 | 9.7 | 9.9 | 9.7 | 9.5 | 9.5 | 9.6 | 9.6 | 9.6 | 9.8 | 9.9[a] |

Source: U.S. Department of Labor—Bureau of Labor Statistics. Extracted from http://data.bls.gov/cgi-bin/surveymost. Dec 2010.
[a] Estimate.

Cross-sectional data are data that have been collected for a specific time period for several observations. For example, if you were to compile data for income levels of 1,000 families for the year 2011 you would have a cross-sectional data set. In collecting the data you have cut *across* the income-spectrum including poor families, medium-income families, and the more fortunate families at a *single* point in time. Figure 1.3 provides levels of per capita Gross National Product for several countries for a single time period—the year 2008. As such, it constitutes cross-sectional data in that it includes different strata of national wealth.

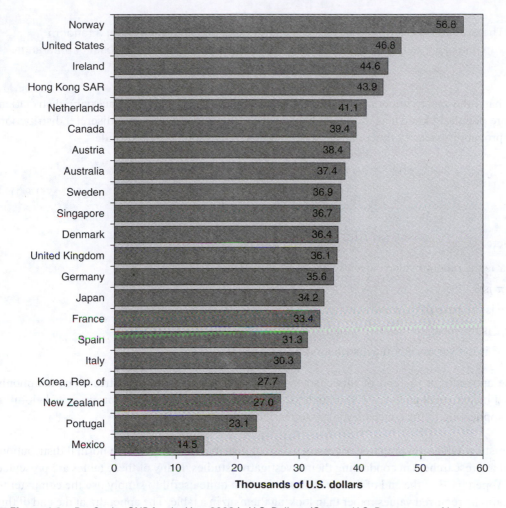

■ **Figure 1.3** Per Capita GNP for the Year 2008 in U.S. Dollars. (Source: U.S. Department of Labor—Bureau of Labor Statistics. From http://www.bls.gov/fls/chartbook/section1.htm#chart1.1, December 2011.)

## 1.8 PROBABILITY DISTRIBUTIONS

The discrete and continuous variables described earlier in this chapter can be defined by *probability distributions*. These statistical "blueprints" identify the possible values of those variables and the probability of occurrence for each of those values. The probability distribution may be presented by a table, a graph, or a formula. It identifies either the probability of each value of a random variable when the variable is discrete, or the probability the value will fall within a particular interval if the variable is continuous.

> The probability distribution describes the range of possible values that a random variable can attain and the probability that its value is within some subset of that range.

Perhaps the most common probability distribution is the normal (or Gaussian)[2] distribution. More popularly known as the "bell-shaped curve" it is a continuous (not discrete) distribution. Its probability density function is described by the rather foreboding formula

$$f(x) = \frac{1}{\sqrt{2\pi\sigma^2}} e^{-\frac{(x-\mu)^2}{2\sigma^2}}$$   (1.8.1)

where:

$x$ is the random value currently under examination;

$\pi$ is 3.14;

$e$ is the base of the natural log of 2.718;

$\mu$ is the mean of the distribution;

$\sigma^2$ is the variance of the distribution.

The appendix at the end of this chapter reviews certain probability distributions commonly used in statistical analysis. A thorough examination of this material will prove quite helpful in its application to the concepts you are to master in this text.

Statistical tables are prepared for many different distributions, such as the normal distribution, that aid researchers in conducting their investigative studies. Many of these tables are presented in Appendix B at the end of this book. But it is often quite useful to simply use the computer to obtain the required values rather than looking them up in a table. The appendix at the end of this chapter contains many of the commands that can be used with Excel to obtain critical values for several important probability distributions. You are encouraged to review these commands as well as acquaint yourself with the use of the statistical tables.

## 1.9 THE DEVELOPMENT AND APPLICATION OF MODELS

Much of the discussion above implies that the potential application of statistical analysis is widespread. Much of the statistical work that is done uses mathematical or econometric *models*. These models are attempts to explain some aspect of the prevailing environment and are based on some insightful, rational perception of actual real-world phenomena. A classical illustration is the standard demand curve which postulates a relationship between the price of a commodity and the quantity purchased. Another might depict the standard consumption function which characterizes the response of personal consumption of goods and services to changes in personal income. Still others can be extended to studies of crime rates, national poverty levels, crime prevention, economic growth, and an entire realm of socio-economic issues. Models can be used to examine physical relationships such as those between temperature and pressure that physicists might want to investigate or the deteriorating effect weathering has on our planet's surface with which geologists are so concerned. The application extends over an almost limitless multitude of interesting and valued studies.

Based on these models, researchers can perform many analyses that broaden our knowledge base and shed light on critical matters that populate our way of life. As a result, decision-making becomes more accurate and solutions to pressing problems appear more obvious. Some of the direct applications of statistical studies include:

- **Hypothesis Testing:** A hypothesis is merely an educated guess or assumption about some prevailing condition. Business endeavors to which hypothesis testing can be applied are virtually unlimited. A business firm might hypothesize, for example, that the funds they spent on advertising have increased sales. Given the enormous expense associated with advertising a firm's product or service it is only prudent to ensure that the money was well spent. If the hypothesis that the advertising is precipitating new sales is correct, the practice should perhaps be suspended.

  A student currently contemplating attending graduate school may want to test the hypothesis that a degree in one area of study results in greater income than in another area. The results of these findings would have a pronounced impact on the decision as to which major to pursue.

  Does inflation result from rising wages or does higher pay follow intense inflationary pressures? This question has plagued economists for years.

  Purchasing agents for large international business concerns may want to test the comparative cost of acquiring raw materials from different suppliers around the globe. Hypothesis testing is crucial to such a study.

  A hypothesis regarding the results of expanding output at a steel plant is a fundamental aspect of decisions concerning production levels. If the hypothesis that output expansion would likely result in increased profits is rejected, perhaps the current level of activity should be maintained.

  With only a bit of imagination it is easy to determine that wise business decisions rely heavily on simple hypothesis tests offered by fundamental statistical methods. The value of hypothesis testing is immeasurable.

- **Public Policy Formation:** The same can be said for governments' determination of national policy. The colossal impact government strategy can have on its citizenry should not be implemented without a thorough study of its impact on the economic and social status of the nation.

  The question of what will result from a change in the tax policy is of critical importance in forming revenue plans. Any attempt to alter the tax code will inarguably affect the economy in a most pronounced manner. Tax policy must therefore be enacted only after stringent statistical examination.

Welfare plans, economic controls placed on businesses, manipulations of the interest rate, maintaining appropriate levels of competition in the economy, and the passage of laws that direct our social and political course are all an essential feature of government's responsibility. Again, none of this can be effectively accomplished without an analytical examination of the prevailing conditions.

■  **Forecasting:** The ability to build a crystal ball that would allow us to look into the future would be of immense benefit. If we know what tomorrow holds, making decisions today becomes much easier and more devoid of risk and uncertainty.

Imagine a world in which you can peer into the future and clearly discern what will transpire. How intelligent would you seem to others if you could forecast and predict the future with alarming accuracy? Statistical models can be used to do just that.

If you know what sales for your firm will be next month or next quarter, that tells you a lot about what you should be doing today. Many business decisions depend on sales. Inventories, raw materials, storage and transportations costs, and required levels of employment all expand and contract with sales levels.

The ability to predict interest rates in the near future would simplify decisions as to whether to conduct your business using internal capital or base operations on borrowed funds. The impact on the firm's bottom line would be unmistakable.

Developments in the stock market, movements in exchange rates, and the future course of market trends all present pronounced implications for business patterns. Advanced knowledge of these matters would prove of immense benefit.

The issues regarding social, governmental, and economic matters that can be explored using fundamental statistical procedures are limited only by the researcher's knowledge and understanding of the mathematical tools available at his or her disposal. As researchers expand their knowledge base of quantitative analysis, they become better equipped to work effectively in their chosen fields. Without a firm foundation in statistical procedures, a research can do little more than hazard an uninformed guess as to the outcome of any decision.

## 1.10 "IN GOD WE TRUST—EVERYBODY ELSE HAS TO BRING DATA"

This quote is often attributed to Williams Edwards Deming (1900–1993), the father of modern quality control. Deming is most noted for his work in Japan to improve product quality and combat defective manufacturing processes. Quality control, or "total quality management" (TQM), is intended to improve product design and overall product quality. Highly data-driven, TQM is credited with raising the Japanese standard of manufacturing and allowing Japan to attain a strong foothold in the global export market. The practice has spread throughout the world to many businesses and commercial concerns that strive to ensure that manufacturers' standards for quality across all areas of production and sales are maintained.

The concept of quality management brought to the forefront the recognition that data analysis is essential to commercial achievement and financial success. Now, undeniably, it is generally accepted that most jobs in business and industry require a firm grasp of statistical processes. Without an understanding of how quantitative measures can be applied to many business conditions and aid in the formulation of effective policy, the decision-maker faces a severe handicap in the attempt to attain commercial success.

## CHAPTER PROBLEMS

CHAPTER PROBLEMS
1

1. Identify a common business problem from the popular business press or from your own personal experience. How do you think statistical analysis might help you approach that problem in your search for a solution? In what way would a more analytical solution prove more advantageous than merely "spit-balling" a potential solution?

2. Given the problem you defined in the first question, how would you complete the five basic stages of a statistical process? How would you go about collecting the data? Would it be necessary to take a sample? Why? What organizational feature would you use to characterize the data set? How would you go about using the data to analyze the problem you face? What interpretations of your results could you use to devise potential solutions to the problem? In what way would you apply these interpretations to any effort to predict or forecast future events?

3. How would you use the results of the first two questions above to make better business decisions?

4. Identify each of the numbers below as to the type of number it is, based on the Arabic system in use in the Western world.

   A. $\sqrt{12}$
   B. $\sqrt{-12}$
   C. 4/5
   D. 6/18
   E. $56i$
   F. 4
   G. −5
   H. 0

5. Distinguish between a population and a sample; between a parameter and a statistic.

6. What is the difference between an estimator and an estimate?

7. Define a continuous variable and a discrete variable. How do they differ? Cite several examples of each.

8. What is sampling bias? Give an example. What generally causes it? What problem is it likely to cause?

9. What is sampling error and how does it arise in a statistical study? What causes sampling error?

10. Define and give examples of the four levels of data measurement. Why can you not mathematically manipulate the first two types?

11. Distinguish between descriptive statistics and inferential statistics as to their general purpose. Explain how each type might be performed. Give your own original examples.

12. Is the sample mean an unbiased estimator of the population mean? Explain.

13. What is the difference between cross-sectional data and time series data? Give your own original examples.

14. What is meant by a sufficient estimator? Do you think the sample mean is a sufficient estimator of the population mean? Explain your answer.

15. Discuss why you think it's important for an estimator to be efficient.

16. What does it mean for an estimator to be consistent? Why do you think this is important and what does it have to do with the variation in the value of the estimate?

APPENDIX<br>1

## APPENDIX: EXCEL COMMANDS AND COMMON PROBABILITY DISTRIBUTIONS

In probability theory, a probability mass, probability density, or probability distribution is a function that describes the probability of a random variable taking certain values. A probability distribution simply lists all the possible outcomes of an experiment and the probability associated with each outcome. For example, the experiment of rolling a die has six possible outcomes. These outcomes and their associated probabilities are listed in the table shown here.

■ A Probability Distribution for the Experiment of Rolling a Die

| Outcome ($X_i$) | Probability of Outcome P($X_i$) |
|---|---|
| 1 | 1/6 |
| 2 | 1/6 |
| 3 | 1/6 |
| 4 | 1/6 |
| 5 | 1/6 |
| 6 | 1/6 |

Notice that the outcomes are listed in the first column and the probability of each outcome is shown in the second column. This is referred to as a *uniform* probability distribution because all the probabilities are the same.

There are many other types of probability distributions in addition to the uniform, but in general we can distinguish between two forms: discrete and continuous. With a discrete probability distribution the variable itself is discrete as defined earlier in this chapter. That is, the variable can take on only certain values—usually whole numbers. As you might expect, the continuous probability distribution uses continuous data.

This appendix examines some of the more common probability distributions and the Excel commands that can be used to access them. We began with perhaps the most common probability distribution—the normal distribution.

## ● The Normal Distribution

The normal distribution is a continuous distribution and was introduced in Figure 1.1 earlier in the chapter. Sometimes referred to as the Gaussian distribution, the normal distribution is perhaps more commonly known as the bell-shaped curve. The normal distribution is extremely useful in finding the likelihood or probability that a particular observation will fall within some specified range.

That probability is simply the *area* under the curve within that range. That is, if we know area we will know probability. To illustrate, presume you have a target, one-third of which is painted yellow, the remaining two-thirds of which is painted red. You are going to shoot at the target and you have an equal probability of hitting any one spot as you do any other spot. That is, you are not shooting at the bull's-eye in the center. The probability you hit yellow is one-third. Why? Because one-third of its area is yellow. Since we know area we know probability.

### The =NORMSDIST Command

There are many instances in which we want to find the *area* under the curve between two values of concern that we call "Z-values." We will see later how to apply these Z-values in our analysis. We will find that the Z-values have a mean of zero and will be normally distributed above and below zero. Values to the left will be negative and those to the right will all be positive. One-half (50%) of the area under the curve is to the right of $Z = 0$ and the other half to the left.

This Z-value (or normal deviate) is calculated as

$$Z = \frac{X - \mu}{\sigma}$$

where $X$ is some value of interest, $\mu$ is the population mean, and $\sigma$ is the population standard deviation. The Z-values are graphed on the horizontal axis as shown in Figure Appendix 1. Suppose you want to find the area under the normal curve to the left of $Z = 2.14$. In any cell in an Excel worksheet simply enter the command

=NORMSDIST(2.14)

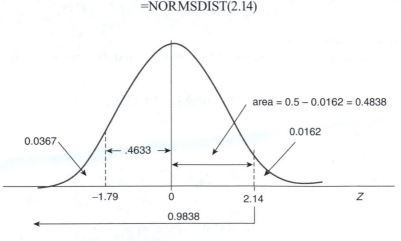

**■ Figure Appendix 1**   The Normal Distribution

Excel responds with 0.9838 as seen in Figure Appendix 1. This is the entire area under the curve to the *left* of $Z = 2.14$. Thus, of the total area under the distribution, 98.38% is to the left of 2.14 and $1 - 0.9838$, or about 0.016177 (1.6%), is above that point. Since 50% of the area under the curve is below zero and 50% is above zero, the area between zero and $2.14 = 0.50 - 0.0162 = 0.4838$.

If a $Z$-value of $-1.79$ is of interest,

$$=NORMSDIST(-1.79)$$

yields 0.0367. This is the area (again) to the *left* of $-1.79$. Thus, the probability the value for $X$ is less than $-1.79$ is 3.67%. Since one-half of the area under the curve is less than zero, the probability the value for $X$ is between $-1.79$ and zero is $0.50 - 0.0367 = 0.4633$.

Identifying these areas is often essential. They reveal *probabilities* that a value for $X$ will fall within some bound. That is, if we find area, we will know probability. As still another example, the probability a value for the $X$ variable is between 0 and 2.14 is $P(0 \leq X \leq 2.14) = 48.38\%$. Knowing the probability some event may occur is often indispensable in making decisions and formulating strategy for future courses of action.

## The =NORMDIST Command

Suppose the $Z$-value is unknown but we do have the parameters for the population mean of $\mu = 22$ and the population standard deviation $\sigma = 1.402$. We are interested in the probabilities associated with a value of $X = 25$. We could use the Excel command

$$=NORMDIST(25,22,1.402,TRUE)$$

Notice this is NORMDIST *without* the "S" used in the previous illustration above. Excel responds to the command with 0.9838. This represents the area under the curve to the left of $X = 25$ (Figure Appendix 2). As such it reveals the probability that a randomly selected value will be less than 25.

This should come as no surprise. From the formula for $Z$ given above, you can see that if $\mu = 22$ and $\sigma = 1.402$, $Z = 2.14$.

## The =NORMINV Command

If, on the other hand, we have the areas and we want to find the corresponding $X$ value, we would use the command

$$=NORMINV(0.9838,22,1.402)$$

which yields $X = 25$.

## The =NORMSINV Command

Finally,

$$=NORMSINV(0.9838)$$

produces $Z = 2.14$.

These Excel features are very helpful and quite convenient when tackling many of our statistical issues. You are encouraged, however, to use the statistical tables in Appendix B to verify the findings revealed here.

### ● Student's t-Distribution

Another continuous distribution we will frequently encounter is the t-distribution. The t-distribution is also symmetrical around a mean of zero like the Z-distribution. The t-distribution

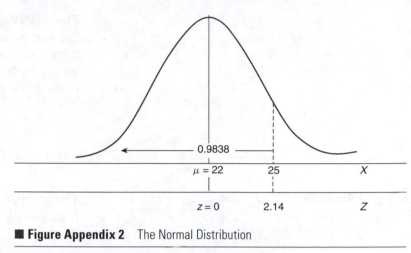

**■ Figure Appendix 2** The Normal Distribution

has a larger variance than the Z-distribution and its graph would be "squashed down" and spread out more than the normal curve above. The t-distribution is most often used if the sample size is small, defined as $n < 30$. If $n > 30$ the Z-distribution can be used. This is allowed because the Z-table is easier to read than the t-table. Given the nature of the tables and our human frailties, resorting to the Z-table in the presence of large samples simply makes life easier. However, computers do not suffer from these same human limitations and will always report the t-values.

### The =TDIST Command

Suppose we are given a t-value of 1.746. The command

$$=TDIST(1.746,16,2)$$

can be entered into any cell in the Excel worksheet. The reply of $0.09998 \approx 0.10$ means that about 10% of the area under the curve is evenly divided in the two tails: 5% in each tail (Figure Appendix 3). The 16 is the number of degrees of freedom and the 2 is for a two-tailed test. The $0.099998 \approx 10\%$ is the p-value of a hypothesis test.

### The =TINV Command

The command =TINV(0.10,16) returns the t-value. In this case the response would be 1.746.

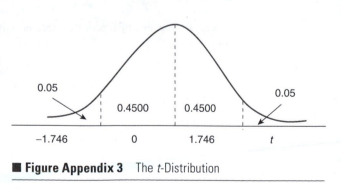

**■ Figure Appendix 3** The t-Distribution

### ● The F-Distribution

Unlike the Z-distribution and the t-distribution, the F-distribution is not symmetrical but is highly skewed right as seen in Figure Appendix 4 over page. It too is used in many statistical applications and Excel offers many advantages in its application. As we will find, as a ratio, the F-distribution carries two "degrees of freedom"—one for the numerator and one for the denominator.

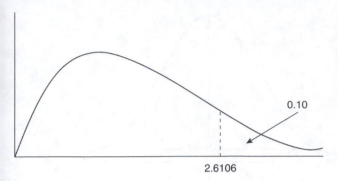

**Figure Appendix 4**   The *F*-Distribution

### The =FINV Command

Suppose we wish to find a certain *F*-value given an "alpha" value of 10% and the degrees of freedom of 5 for the numerator and 9 for the denominator. The proper Excel command is

$$=FINV(0.10,5,9)$$

which yields $F = 2.6106$.

### The =FDIST Command

If we have the *F*-value and want to find the associated *p*-value, use

$$=FDIST(2.6106,5,9)$$

where 2.6106 is the *F*-value calculated from the sample data set. It results in a *p*-value of 0.10.

#### ● The Chi-Square Distribution

### The =CHIINV Command

This command yields a critical value for chi-square ($\chi^2$). If we select an alpha-value of 5% with 10 degrees of freedom, the command

$$=CHIINV(.05,10)$$

produces a value of 18.30704 as seen in Figure Appendix 5.

Given 10 degrees of freedom, there is only a 5% chance your data will yield a chi-square value above 18.30704.

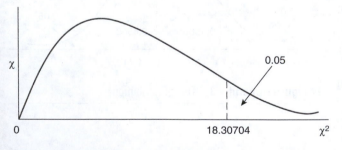

**Figure Appendix 5**   The Chi-Square Distribution

### The =CHIDIST Command

This command yields the area beyond some $\chi^2$ value. Given 10 degrees of freedom, if you calculate $\chi^2 = 18.30704$, the area can be found as

$$=CHIDIST(18.30704,10)$$

Excel responds with 0.05.

These Excel features are very helpful and quite convenient when solving many of our statistical issues. You are encouraged, however, to use the statistical tables in Appendix B to verify the findings revealed here.

*Chapter 2*

# AN INTRODUCTION TO REGRESSION AND CORRELATION ANALYSIS

## INTRODUCTION

This chapter examines two of the most powerful statistical techniques that can be used to deal with common business problems: regression and correlation analysis. They recognize that we can identify and quantify functional relationships between two or more variables. We can say, for example, that "$Y$ depends upon $X$." This is written as $Y = f(X)$ and read "$Y$ is a function of $X$." $Y$ is identified as the *dependent* or *response* variable. The $X$ variable, or right-hand-side (RHS) variable, is the *independent* or *explanatory* variable. $Y$ is also called the *regressand*, while $X$ is the *regressor*. It is said that you "regress the dependent variable on the independent variable." You do not regress "$X$ on $Y$."

Although most often used in conjunction, regression and correlation are two separate and distinct tools. The purpose of regression is to determine the basic nature of the relationship between $X$ and $Y$. It addresses the issue as to whether $X$ and $Y$ are directly related in that they both move in the same direction, or whether they are indirectly (inversely) related so that one goes up when the other goes down. Correlation, on the other hand, measures the strength of that relationship. Is there a strong relationship between $X$ and $Y$ or is the relationship weak and of little vivacity?

The fundamentals of regression were first explored by Sir Francis Gaulton (1822–1911) in his now famous study of heredity. He began by observing the growth pattern of sweet pea plants. He noticed that plants that were particularly tall produced plants that were also taller than the average plant. The same pattern persisted with smaller plants. However, in both cases Gaulton found that subsequent generations of plants tended to "regress" back to the height of the average sweet pea plant. He soon extended his observations into the growth trends of humans and found much the same result. From this humble beginning of horticulture spawned the universal applications of perhaps the most dominant instruments of statistical analysis.

Jointly, regression and correlation are designed to explain changes in the dependent variable. Moreover, they are intended to explain changes in the dependent variable *from its mean*. Note, this is *not* to say that regression and correlation explain *why* $Y$ changes. Regression and correlation cannot identify cause-and-effect relationships or model causal linkage. They merely explain the manner in which $Y$ responds when $X$ changes.

Regression determines the *basic nature* of the relationship between $X$ and $Y$. That is, whether $X$ and $Y$ are directly related in that they move together or whether one increases when the other decreases evidencing an indirect or inverse relationship. Correlation measures just how strong that relationship is.

> Regression determines the basic nature of the relationship between $X$ and $Y$, while correlation measures the strength of that relationship. Their intent is to explain changes in the dependent variable from its mean.

*Simple regression* employs only one RHS independent, explanatory variable. A *multiple regression* model uses two or more explanatory variables and is expressed as $Y = f(X_1, X_2 \ldots X_k)$ in which the model incorporates $k$ RHS variables as explanatory factors.

We should also distinguish between linear regression and curvilinear regression. *Linear regression* describes the relationship between $X$ and $Y$ with a straight line. In a general sense it can be expressed as

$$Y = \beta_0 + \beta_1 X \qquad (2.1.1)$$

A general linear model where $\beta_0$ is the vertical intercept and $\beta_1$ is the slope of the line.

The slope of the regression line, $\beta_1$, measures the change in $Y$ given a one-unit change in $X$. In a linear model the change in $Y$ is constant. Equation (2.I.1) is said to be *exact* or *deterministic* in that given a value for $X$ we can easily determine the value of $Y$.

Presume we have the model $Y = 5 + 2X$ shown in Figure 2.1. The vertical intercept is seen to be 5 with a slope of 2. Since it's a positive relationship, every time $X$ increases by one unit $Y$ will increase by two units.

The second model in Figure 2.1 shows a negative relationship. The variables move in opposite directions. Each time $X$ goes up by one unit $Y$ decreases by two units.

A non-linear (or curvilinear) model might be expressed as the quadratic equation $Y = 5 + 2X^2$. As seen in Figure 2.2 the change in $Y$ is *not* constant as with a linear function, but the change in $Y$ increases as $X$ increases.

Our focus in this chapter is on simple, linear regression. Models of a more involved nature are explored in subsequent chapters.

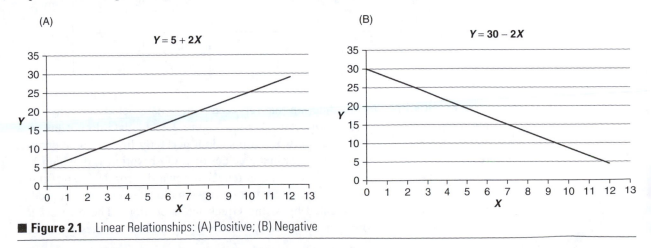

■ **Figure 2.1**  Linear Relationships: (A) Positive; (B) Negative

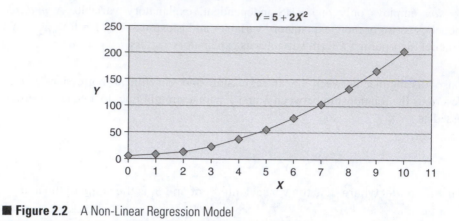

■ **Figure 2.2**   A Non-Linear Regression Model

## 2.1 THE SIMPLE REGRESSION MODEL

In developing a linear model we must recognize that the real world is not perfectly linear. Any effort to estimate a relationship with a linear expression will therefore invariably suffer some error. Suppose we were to collect data for paired observations for $X$ and $Y$ as seen in Table 2.1 and plot them in a scatter diagram as in Figure 2.3. Each of the dots in the scatter diagram represents one of the actual values for $Y_i$ such as $Y_1 = 25$ and $Y_4 = 15$.

■ **Table 2.1**   Paired $X$–$Y$ Data

| Observation | $X_i$ | $Y_i$ |
|:---:|:---:|:---:|
| 1 | 5 | 25 |
| 2 | 6 | 10 |
| 3 | 2 | 17 |
| 4 | 9 | 15 |
| 5 | 7 | 19 |
| 6 | 1 | 4 |
| 7 | 5 | 12 |
| 8 | 10 | 32 |

We now want to "fit a line" to this diagram that represents these data better than any other line we might envision. However, as you can see from Figure 2.3, the data do not fall in a straight line since relationships in the real world are seldom perfectly linear. Some error is going to result in our attempt to explain or estimate values of $Y$. Observation 1, in which $Y_1 = 25$, and observation 4, in which $Y_4 = 15$, reflect that tendency toward error. Neither of those points lie on the regression line. If we were to use our regression model to estimate or predict $Y$ we would suffer some error indicated by $\varepsilon$ (the Greek letter epsilon). These errors are found to be random in that sometimes we over-estimate $Y$ ($Y_4$) and sometimes we under-estimate $Y$ ($Y_1$).

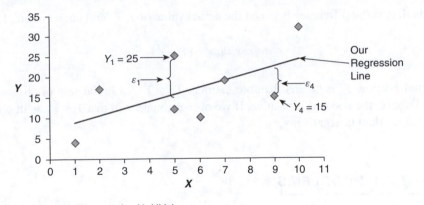

**■ Figure 2.3** A Scatter Diagram for $X$–$Y$ Values

The deterministic form of Equation (2.I.1) must be altered to account for this random (or stochastic) error, $\varepsilon$. At the population level it takes the form of Equation (2.1.1) in which $\beta_0$ and $\beta_1$ are the vertical intercept and the slope of the population regression line.

$$Y = \beta_0 + \beta_1 X + \varepsilon \qquad (2.1.1)$$

$\varepsilon$ is the error that results in the effort to model the true relationship.

Equation (2.1.1) represents the expression for the entire population. $\beta_1$ and $\beta_2$ are parameters. The exact value of $Y$ will equal the deterministic portion of Equation (2.1.1), $\beta_0 + \beta_1 X$, plus any error that results from the non-linear nature of the relationship. However, since that error, $\varepsilon$, is random and unpredictable, the exact value of $Y$ can never be precisely determined.

Further problems arise in that, as we noted earlier, populations are too large to study in their entirety. We can only develop a model based on sample data. The sample model is expressed as

$$Y = b_0 + b_1 X + e \qquad (2.1.2)$$

Sample regression line in which $e$ reflects any error in the estimation effort

where $b_0$ and $b_1$ are statistics for the intercept and slope at the sample level. They are the statistical estimates of the unknown population parameters, $\beta_0$ and $\beta_1$, respectively. $e$ is the *residual* that serves as the estimate of the error term, $\varepsilon$.

There is a technical difference between the "error," which pertains to the use of population data, and "residual," which is the term that should be used when discussing sample data. In popular usage the two terms have become interchangeable and you may see $e$ carelessly referred to as the error in common literature. Nevertheless, the distinction remains.

But like the error term, $\varepsilon$, the residual, $e$, is random and unpredictable. So Equation (2.1.2) can never be calculated. The best we can do is estimate $Y$ using Equation (2.1.3).

$$\hat{Y} = b_0 + b_1 X \qquad (2.1.3)$$

$\hat{Y}$ is read "$Y$-hat" since anything under a hat is being estimated.

The residual, $e$, is the difference between the actual value of $Y$, $Y_i$, and our estimate, $\hat{Y}$.

$$e = residual = \left(Y_i - \hat{Y}\right) \qquad (2.1.4)$$

If the actual $Y$-value, $Y_i$, is greater than our estimate $(Y_i > \hat{Y})$, as in the case of observation 1 in Figure 2.3 above, the residual is positive. If we over-estimate $Y$ in that $Y_i < \hat{Y}$, as in observation 4 above, the residual is negative.

## SECTION 2.1 PROBLEMS

1.  A regression model is found to be $\hat{Y} = 2.3 + 4.5X$. Draw a graph depicting the model. What happens to the estimated value of the response variable as $X$ increases by one unit? By two units?

2.  Given the data seen here presume the regression model reports to be $\hat{Y} = 1.7957 + 1.2241X$.

    A. Provide a scatter diagram of the data.
    B. Compute the estimated values for $Y$.
    C. Calculate the residuals. Find the sum of the residuals.

| X | Y |
|---|---|
| 5 | 10 |
| 9 | 12 |
| 1 | 3 |
| 8 | 11 |
| 0 | 1 |
| 6 | 11 |
| 8 | 12 |
| 6 | 7 |

3.  A chemical is added to the harvest of eight loads of fresh vegetables to preserve their freshness during transit. Agricultural economists wish to characterize the relationship between the preservative and the amount of produce lost to spoilage. They want to determine if the amount of the chemical applied to the crop seems to affect the loss. The resulting pounds of spoilage are to be regressed on the units of chemical added to estimate the effect of the chemical. The regression model was determined to be Pounds = 15.489 – 2.0326 (Units). This indicates that for every one additional unit of chemical added to the harvest, spoilage will decrease by 2.0326 pounds. Given the data opposite

    A. Provide a scatter diagram of the data.
    B. Compute all the estimated values for $Y$ at all eight values of $X$.
    C. Calculate the residuals. Find the sum of the residuals.

| Units (X) | Pounds (Y) |
|---|---|
| 2 | 10 |
| 3 | 8 |
| 1 | 15 |
| 6 | 2 |
| 5 | 3 |
| 8 | 2 |
| 2 | 12 |
| 1 | 15 |

4.  What is the difference between an error and a residual? Explain and give an example.

5.  What is the purpose of regression analysis and how does it differ from correlation analysis?

## 2.2 ESTIMATING THE MODEL: ORDINARY LEAST SQUARES

Our purpose in estimating the regression model is to "fit a line" to the data. That is, to find a line that fits the data better than any other line we might draw. The process to do this is called *ordinary least squares* (OLS). We'll find out why it's called OLS later. Right now, let's concentrate on *how* it's done.

Arco Industries has collected data for their exports to 12 foreign countries across the globe. They intend to estimate a regression model using the customer nations' gross domestic products (GDP) as a predictor of export levels. The data are shown in Table 2.2. The second column shows the nations' world rankings in terms of size based on GDP. The GDP for each nation is measured in trillions of U.S. dollars (column 3) and exports are shown in thousands of dollars (column 4).

■ **Table 2.2**  Arco Exports to 12 Nation-Customers

| (1) Country | (2) Rank | (3) GDP in Trillions ($X$) | (4) Exports in Thousands ($Y$) |
|---|---|---|---|
| France | 5 | 2.58 | 13.7 |
| Russia | 11 | 1.47 | 7.5 |
| Turkey | 17 | 0.742 | 8.6 |
| Canada | 9 | 1.57 | 14.2 |
| Ireland | 43 | 0.204 | 8.2 |
| Slovakia | 60 | 0.086 | 2.1 |
| Italy | 8 | 2.06 | 13.6 |
| China | 2 | 5.88 | 13.2 |
| Finland | 36 | 0.239 | 6.9 |
| Egypt | 40 | 0.218 | 6.1 |
| Norway | 25 | 0.414 | 9.2 |
| United Kingdom | 6 | 2.25 | 15.6 |
| Means | | 1.476 = $\bar{X}$ | 9.908 = $\bar{Y}$ |

Taken from the International Monetary Fund, World Economic Outlook Database, April 2011: Nominal GDP list of countries. Data for the year 2010. http://en.wikipedia.org/wiki/List_of_countries_by_GDP_(nominal)

Remember, the purpose of regression is to explain changes in $Y$ from its mean. Thus, we begin by finding the means of the $X$-values ($\bar{X}$) and the $Y$-values ($\bar{Y}$). These means are $\bar{X} = 1.476$ and $\bar{Y} = 9.908$. Then, the first step in completing OLS is to calculate the *sums of the squares* and *cross-products* using Equations (2.2.1), (2.2.2), and (2.2.3).

The sum of squares for the $X$-values, $SS_X$, is found by summing the squared differences between each individual $X$-value ($X_i$) and the mean of all $X$-values ($\bar{X}$). That is, subtract the mean value of $X$ from each $X$-value, square the differences, and sum the squared differences.

$$SS_X = \Sigma(X_i - \bar{X})^2 \tag{2.2.1}$$

*where $X_i$ is each individual value of the explanatory variable.*

Table 2.2 shows the first value of $X$ to be 2.58. Therefore, the first calculation for $SS_X$ is $(2.58 - 1.476)^2 = 1.219$. The remaining values for $SS_X$ are found in the same manner.

The sum of squares for the $Y$-values, $SS_Y$, is found by summing the squared differences between each individual $Y$-value ($Y_i$) and the mean of all $Y$-values ($\bar{Y}$).

$$SS_Y = \Sigma(Y_i - \bar{Y})^2 \tag{2.2.2}$$

For the first observation of $Y$ we have $(13.7 - 9.908)^2 = 14.377$. All remaining values for $SS_Y$ are calculated using Equation (2.2.2).

The sum of the cross-products between $X$ and $Y$ is calculated as seen in Equation (2.2.3):

$$SS_{XY} = \Sigma(X_i - \bar{X})(Y_i - \bar{Y}) \tag{2.2.3}$$

For the first observation for France we have $(2.58 - 1.476)(13.7 - 9.908) = 4.187$. Table 2.3 displays all the values for $SS_X$, $SS_Y$, and $SS_{XY}$.

It only remains now for us to calculate the intercept and the slope of the estimated regression line, $b_0$ and $b_1$. The slope coefficient is

$$b_1 = \frac{SS_{XY}}{SS_X} \tag{2.2.4}$$

The intercept is

$$b_0 = \bar{Y} - b_1\bar{X} \tag{2.2.5}$$

Based on these data, Arco finds

$$b_1 = \frac{48.913}{29.892} = 1.636$$

and

$$b_0 = (9.908) - (1.636)(1.476) = 7.493$$

■ **Table 2.3** Finding the Sums of Squares and Cross-Products

| GDP ($X$) | Exports ($Y$) | $(X - \bar{X})^2$ | $(Y - \bar{Y})^2$ | $(X - \bar{X})(Y - \bar{Y})$ |
|---|---|---|---|---|
| 2.58 | 13.70 | 1.219 | 14.377 | 4.187 |
| 1.47 | 7.50 | 0.000 | 5.800 | 0.014 |
| 0.742 | 8.60 | 0.539 | 1.712 | 0.960 |
| 1.57 | 14.20 | 0.009 | 18.418 | 0.404 |
| 0.204 | 8.20 | 1.618 | 2.918 | 2.173 |
| 0.086 | 2.10 | 1.932 | 60.970 | 10.852 |
| 2.06 | 13.60 | 0.341 | 13.628 | 2.157 |
| 5.88 | 13.20 | 19.397 | 10.835 | 14.497 |
| 0.239 | 6.90 | 1.530 | 9.050 | 3.721 |
| 0.218 | 6.10 | 1.582 | 14.503 | 4.870 |
| 0.414 | 9.20 | 1.127 | 0.502 | 0.752 |
| 2.247 | 15.60 | 0.595 | 32.395 | 4.389 |
| **Sums** | | $SS_X = 29.892$ | $SS_Y = 185.108$ | $SS_{XY} = 48.913$ |
| **Means** | 1.476 | 9.908 | | |

With $\widehat{Ex}$ ("exports-hat") as the estimated level of exports, their regression model is

$$\widehat{Ex} = 7.493 + 1.636(\text{GDP})$$

The *regression coefficient* of 1.636 means that for every one-unit increase in a nation's GDP ($1 trillion), exports to that nation will go up by 1.636 units ($1,636).

> The regression coefficient measures the change in the dependent variable given a one-unit change in the independent variable.

Given the GDP for any country, Arco can now estimate the amount of exports it might ship to that country. The same IMF data source cited above for Table 2.2 recorded the GDP for Spain (the 12th largest economy in the world) to be $1,400,000 million. Since the GDP data used to estimate the model are based in units of trillions of dollars that would be $1.4 trillion. Arco's exports to Spain can be now estimated to be $\widehat{Ex} = 7.494 + (1.636)(1.4) = 9.7854$. Since exports were measured in units of thousands of dollars that export value is $9,785.

## EXAMPLE 2.1: Do Sales Explain Inventory Levels?

**Problem Statement:** In an effort to control costs associated with inventory management the National Retailers Association undertook a study of the relationship between sales and inventory levels. Data were collected for selected years starting in the 1990s and are recorded in the table below in billions of dollars. The study involved regressing inventories on sales to determine if there might be some optimum relationship that should be maintained.

**Solution:** $SS_X$, $SS_Y$, and $SS_{XY}$ are first calculated as seen here. The model is then estimated by computing $b_0$ and $b_1$. An interpretation of the findings is provided below.

| Year | Sales ($X$) | Inventories ($Y$) | $(X-\bar{X})^2$ | $(Y-\bar{Y})^2$ | $(X-\bar{X})(Y-\bar{Y})$ |
|------|-------------|-------------------|-----------------|-----------------|---------------------------|
| 1992 | 151.3096667 | 261.369 | 10096.951 | 18080.228 | 13511.298 |
| 1993 | 161.854 | 279.526 | 8089.069 | 13527.024 | 10460.451 |
| 1994 | 175.8350833 | 305.442 | 5769.644 | 8170.305 | 6865.839 |
| 1995 | 185.2086667 | 322.925 | 4433.507 | 5315.392 | 4854.465 |
| 1996 | 197.2220833 | 333.926 | 2978.013 | 3832.32 | 3378.269 |
| 1997 | 206.1669167 | 344.609 | 2081.763 | 2623.769 | 2337.106 |
| 1998 | 215.5920833 | 357.269 | 1310.525 | 1487.085 | 1396.016 |
| 1999 | 234.0463333 | 384.963 | 314.953 | 118.129 | 192.887 |
| 2000 | 249.063 | 406.73 | 7.454 | 118.772 | −29.755 |
| 2001 | 255.64375 | 394.554 | 14.826 | 1.633 | −4.92 |
| 2002 | 261.1935 | 415.977 | 88.365 | 405.832 | 189.37 |
| 2003 | 272.3193333 | 432.084 | 421.32 | 1314.227 | 744.117 |
| 2004 | 289.9828333 | 461.253 | 1458.444 | 4279.942 | 2498.41 |
| 2005 | 308.1358333 | 472.038 | 3174.486 | 5807.395 | 4293.657 |
| 2006 | 323.4643333 | 486.502 | 5136.744 | 8221.097 | 6498.436 |
| 2007 | 333.7706667 | 498.302 | 6720.296 | 10500.155 | 8400.247 |
| 2008 | 329.92975 | 478.823 | 6105.312 | 6887.55 | 6484.646 |
| 2009 | 305.9320833 | 429.149 | 2931.013 | 1110.04 | 1803.758 |
| 2010 | 327.4019167 | 455.362 | 5716.67 | 3543.852 | 4501.004 |
| **Sums** | 4784.071833 | 7520.803 | 66849.355 | 95344.747 | 78375.301 |
| ***n* =** | 19 | | $SS_X$ | $SS_Y$ | $SS_{XY}$ |
| **Means** | 251.7932544 | 395.8317368 | | | |

Data measured in billions of U.S. dollars. From Statistical Abstract of the U.S.: http://www.census.gov/compendia/statab/cats/business_enterprise/economic_indicators.html

$$SS_X = \Sigma(X_i - \bar{X})^2 = 66849.4$$

$$SS_Y = \Sigma(Y_i - \bar{Y})^2 = 95344.7$$

$$SS_{XY} = (X_i - \bar{X})(Y_i - \bar{Y})^2 = 78375.3$$

$$b_1 = \frac{SS_{XY}}{SS_X} = \frac{78375.3}{66849.4} = 1.172$$

$$b_0 = \bar{Y} - b_1(\bar{X}) = 395.83 - 1.172(251.79) = 100.732$$

$$\hat{I} = 100.732 + 1.172$$

**Interpretation:** Since the data are measured in billions of dollars, the results reveal that for every one billion dollars (one unit) by which sales increase, inventories will increase by 1.172 billion dollars (1.172 units). Businesses can use this information to aid in the decisions regarding how much inventory they should stockpile, as well as other issues concerning many of their business matters.

## ● Multiple Regression: A Look Ahead

We should not conclude from this work that exports will indeed prove to be $9,785 for any nation with a GDP of $1.4 trillion. There are many factors that might influence Arco's exports to a country other than GDP. International trade policies imposed by the country's government, currency exchange rates, diplomatic relations, and national inflation rates are but a few influences on Arco's exports. All might serve as additional explanatory variables in a multiple regression model that we will examine in later chapters.

## ● Calculating the Residuals

In addition, it must be remembered that the estimate is based on a linear model and, as noted above, real-world phenomena do not usually follow a strict linear pattern. The estimate will likely differ from the actual exports. This difference between the actual level of exports, $Y_i$, and the estimate, $\hat{Y}$, is the *residual*. Table 2.4 illustrates the calculation of these residuals for Arco. The $\hat{Y}$-estimates of the exports based on the regression model are recorded in column (4). The residuals, $(Y_i - \hat{Y})$, and the residuals squared, $(Y_i - \hat{Y})^2$, are seen in columns (5) and (6). Notice that the residuals sum to zero. The significance of that fact is discussed in the next section.

■ **Table 2.4**   Arco's Residuals

| (1) Country | (2) GDP | (3) Exports | (4) $\hat{Y} = b_0 + b_1 X$ | (5) Residual = $(Y_i - \hat{Y})$ | (6) Residual$^2$ |
|---|---|---|---|---|---|
| France | 2.58 | 13.7 | 11.71 | 1.98527 | 3.94129 |
| Russia | 1.47 | 7.5 | 9.90 | −2.39879 | 5.75419 |
| Turkey | 0.742 | 8.6 | 8.71 | −0.10780 | 0.01162 |
| Canada | 1.57 | 14.2 | 10.06 | 4.13761 | 17.11983 |
| Ireland | 0.204 | 8.2 | 7.83 | 0.37236 | 0.13865 |
| Slovakia | 0.086 | 2.1 | 7.63 | −5.53459 | 30.63171 |
| Italy | 2.06 | 13.6 | 10.86 | 2.73598 | 7.48559 |
| China | 5.88 | 13.2 | 17.11 | −3.91347 | 15.31524 |
| Finland | 0.239 | 6.9 | 7.89 | −0.98490 | 0.97002 |
| Egypt | 0.218 | 6.1 | 7.85 | −1.75054 | 3.06439 |
| Norway | 0.414 | 9.2 | 8.17 | 1.02881 | 1.05844 |
| United Kingdom | 2.25 | 15.6 | 11.17 | 4.430052 | 19.62536 |
| Sums | | | | 0.00 | 105.073 |

## SECTION 2.2 PROBLEMS

1.  In the effort to establish selling prices for new homes, a real-estate agent in New Hampshire estimates a regressing model using square footage as a predictor of price. The model is based on the data seen below. Use OLS procedures to produce the model. Interpret the results. What would you estimate the average price to be for a house with 1,750 square feet? Prices are in thousands of dollars.

| Sq. Footage ($X$) | Price ($Y$) |
|---|---|
| 1150 | 87.4 |
| 1800 | 123.8 |
| 1047 | 78.6 |
| 1099 | 84.5 |
| 1147 | 87.2 |
| 998 | 79.9 |
| 1058 | 82 |
| 2011 | 145 |
| 1489 | 114 |
| 2354 | 125 |
| 1166 | 88.7 |

2. International trade has become more precarious due to terrorist activities and other global threats. A transit company that specializes in international shipping collected the data shown here in the effort to estimate a model that uses distance (D) measured in hundreds of miles to estimate total cost of shipment measured in hundreds of dollars. Compute and interpret the model. What would be your estimate of the average cost of a shipment covering 12 (1,200) miles?

| Distance | Cost |
|---|---|
| 14.2 | 52.3 |
| 8.3 | 47.3 |
| 3.6 | 32.8 |
| 15.4 | 48.86 |
| 25.3 | 57.77 |
| 19.3 | 50 |
| 14.6 | 48.2 |
| 20.1 | 53.09 |
| 12.8 | 46.52 |

3. A firm in Leon, France sends many of its executives to meetings with their counterparts in Paris to co-ordinate business planning. Some questions arise in the firm's upper management as to the benefit of such trips. Data are collected to record the number of employees making the journey each month for nine months and the resulting sales in thousands of euros that can be attributed to those trips. The intent is to judge whether the number of executives dispatched to Paris can be justified on the basis of the sales.

Estimate the equation relating the two variables. What is your conclusion regarding the wisdom of sending personnel to Paris?

| Executives (X) | Sales (Y) |
|---|---|
| 10 | 34 |
| 15 | 26 |
| 8 | 33 |
| 9 | 35.3 |
| 15 | 15.6 |
| 12 | 26.5 |
| 14 | 28 |
| 20 | 15.3 |
| 12 | 32.9 |

4. Research and development expenditures by Wiltshire Ltd in southern England are intended to generate international patents for the company's exclusive use. Use the data here to determine if these annual expenditures measured in thousands of British sterling pounds translate into registered patents. How might expenditures explain patents?

A. Compute the model and interpret the results.
B. Calculate the residuals and plot them. Sum the residuals.

| Expenditures | Patents |
|---|---|
| 5 | 8 |
| 6 | 9 |
| 9 | 12 |
| 3 | 7 |
| 7 | 15 |
| 2 | 5 |

5. It has long been argued that education and income are directly related. To support this contention data from a recent U.S. census are reported in the table seen here.

Education is measured in years and income in thousands of dollars.

| EDU | INC |
|---|---|
| 10 | 24.9 |
| 12 | 32.8 |
| 14 | 40.7 |
| 16 | 56.1 |
| 18 | 75.1 |

Data extracted from:
http://soc101.wordpress.com/2009/02/10/education-pays-income-by-education-level-2009-update/

A. Estimate the model.
B. Plot the residuals. Sum the residuals.
C. What is your estimate of the average income earned by someone with 13 years of education?

## 2.3 WHY THE PROCESS IS CALLED ORDINARY LEAST SQUARES

The procedure described above to estimate the regression model produces the "line of best fit." It will generate a line that goes right through the middle of all the data points in the scatter diagram. Figure 2.4 plots the data for Arco from Table 2.4 and demonstrates how the $\hat{Y}$-regression line comes closer to all the data points than any other line we might draw. The residuals are measured by the vertical distance (difference) between the actual values for the exports, $(Y_i)$, and the $\hat{Y}$-regression line. Thus, the residual is $(Y_i - \hat{Y})$.

Since the line falls squarely in the middle of the data plot the sum of those residuals will be zero as indicated by Equation (2.3.1). These calculations can be seen in Table 2.4.

$$\Sigma\left(Y_i - \hat{Y}\right) = 0 \qquad (2.3.1)$$

The values sum to zero because the residuals are positive when the model under-estimates the actual value of $Y_i$ $(Y_i > \hat{Y})$. However, the residuals are negative if the model over-estimates the true value for exports as $(Y_i < \hat{Y})$.

For example, Figure 2.4 shows the actual exports to Canada were $Y_c = 14.2$ thousand. The model estimates the level of exports to be

$$\widehat{EXP} = 7.493 + 1.6364(GDP) = 7.493 + 1.6364(1.57) = 10.063 \text{ thousand}$$

The residual is $(14.2 - 10.063) = 4.14$.

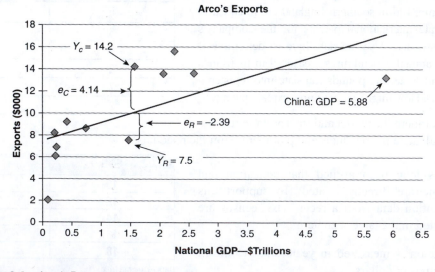

**Arco's Exports**

■ **Figure 2.4**   Arco's Regression Line

Conversely, while the actual exports to Russia were $Y_R = 7.5$ thousand, the estimated exports were

$$\widehat{EXP} = 7.493 + 1.6364\,(\text{GDP}) = 7.493 + 1.6364\,(1.47) = 9.89 \text{ thousand}$$

The residual is $(7.5 - 9.89) = -2.39$.

If these calculations are made for all observations in the data set, the positive and negative residuals cancel out and the residuals sum to zero.

But if the residuals are squared, as shown in Equation (2.3.2), the negative values disappear and no longer cancel out the positive values. The sum of the *residuals squared* is, however, minimized. Thus, the sum of the squared residuals, $\Sigma(Y_i - \hat{Y})^2$, will be minimized. That is, using the OLS procedure described here, the sum of the squared residuals will be smaller than that produced by any line other than the one OLS provides. Hence, the term "ordinary least squares." It is the sum of the squared residuals that is "least." From Table 2.4 we see the sum of the residuals squared is 105.073.

That the squared residuals sum to the least possible amount testifies to the soundness of the OLS process. If you can construct a model so that the residuals sum to zero and the residuals squared are minimized it would bear witness to the model's reliability.

$$\Sigma(Y_i - \hat{Y})^2 = \text{minimum} \qquad (2.3.2)$$

The sum of the residuals for any and all models will always be zero because of the cancelation process. The sum of the residuals squared will vary among models but it will always be less than that reported by any regression model developed by any other procedure.

## 2.4 PROPERTIES AND ASSUMPTIONS OF THE OLS MODEL

At this point it would serve us well to examine the properties and assumptions upon which the OLS model is based. Properties are conditions that we know hold true. For example, just by the arithmetic mechanics of the OLS procedure we can be assured that the sum of errors is zero. This result is a certainty and serves as the first property of the OLS model. The second property states that the sum of the *squared* errors is a minimum value. This too is a certainty and is taken as the second property of the model. These points were demonstrated in the previous section using the sample data from Arco.

Assumptions are conditions that we hope are true and to the extent they are not our model suffers in its accuracy and reliability. Let us examine each in turn.

### Assumption 1: The Error Terms Are Random and Normally Distributed

Given any value for $X$ we could get many different $Y$-values. If there were several countries with the same GDP it's unlikely Arco would export the exact same amount to every country. In fact, given the same value for $X$ (GDP) many times we could get an entire distribution of different $Y$-values (exports). It is assumed that these $Y$-values are normally distributed.

But wait. If there are different $Y$-values for any given value of $X$ how do we use the regression model to estimate $Y$? Actually, we don't. The model estimates the *mean*, or expected value, of all those different $Y$-values.

At one point, long ago, the regression line was called the "mean line." It will always pass through the point $(\overline{X}, \overline{Y})$. The value of $\hat{Y}$ used in the model is an estimator of the expected value of $Y$ given $X$ is set equal to some value many times. This is written as $E(Y|X_i)$ and read "the expected value of $Y$ given $X$ equals $X_i$ many times."

Figure 2.5 illustrates. If several countries reported a GDP of $4.0 trillion, according to the model Arco would export a *mean* of $7.494 + 1.63(4) = 14.04$ thousand dollars to those countries. However, some countries would import more, while others would purchase less. This is shown by the distribution of $Y$-values (exports) above and below the regression line. Notice that this distribution fits a normal (bell-shaped) curve.

The same holds true if there were many countries with a GDP of $5.0 trillion. The mean export level to those countries is estimated to be $15.68 thousand, but there will reasonably occur some dispersion above and below that mean. The actual export levels, $Y_i$, would vary from that mean measured on the $\hat{Y}$-regression line.

Since the error in the estimation attempt is found as $(Y_i - \hat{Y})$, if the variation of $Y_i$ around the regression line is normally distributed, so are the error terms. OLS is thus based on the assumption that the error terms are random and normally distributed above and below the regression line.

### Assumption 2: The Error Terms Have the Same Variance
It is also assumed that error terms have the same variance. This too can be seen in Figure 2.5. Notice that the distribution of the $Y$-values around the regression line is the same when GDP = 4 as when GDP = 5. That is, the degree of dispersion in the $Y$-values, and hence in the error terms, is the same at $X = 4$ and at $X = 5$. It is said that the error terms exhibit *homoscedasticity*.

> The error terms are homoscedastic if they have the same variation, or variance, around the regression line for all values of $X$.

### Assumption 3: The Errors Are Independent of Each Other
Simply put, the error you suffer when trying to estimate $Y$ one time has nothing to do with the error you experience with any other attempt at estimation. The errors are uncorrelated or unrelated. There is no *autocorrelation* among the error terms.

> Autocorrelation means that a variable is correlated with itself. OLS assumes that the errors are not correlated with themselves.

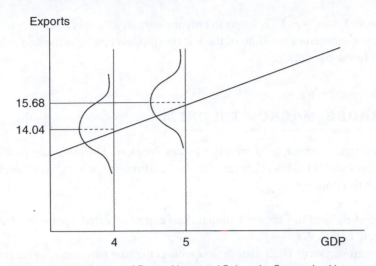

■ **Figure 2.5**  The Normal Distribution of Errors Above and Below the Regression Line

## Assumption 4: The Independent, Explanatory Variables Are Uncorrelated with the Error Terms

Again, a simple statement. The independent variable, $X$, is unrelated to the error terms. In a multiple regression model, like those we will examine in later chapters, this condition applies to all RHS variables.

## Assumption 5: No Independent Variable Is a Linear Function of Any Other Independent Variable(s)

This condition applies only in multiple regression models in which there are several RHS variables. It states that none of the independent variables can be linearly related. Thus, linear relationships such as $X_2 = 2X_3$ or $X_4 = X_3/X_2$ or $X_3 = 0.25X_2$ and so on are not permitted. If two or more RHS variables are correlated the model is said to suffer from *multicollinearity*. This can have a devastating impact on the efficacy of your model.

> Multicollinearity occurs when two or more RHS variables are linearly correlated.

## Assumption 6: The Model Is Linear in the Parameters

The model must be linear in the parameters (coefficients) but it is not necessary that it be linear in the variables. To distinguish, an equation is linear in the parameters only if the values for the parameters (the $\beta_i$) are expressed in their simplest form. For example, $\hat{Y} = \beta_0 + \beta_1^2 X$ is not linear in the parameters because $\beta_1$ is squared. On the other hand, $\hat{Y} = \beta_0 + \beta_1 X$ is linear in both the parameters and the variable $X$ since the parameters and the variable $X$ are raised only to the first power. $\hat{Y} = \beta_0 + \beta_1 X^2$ is linear in only the parameters. It is not linear in the variables, since $X$ takes on a squared value. Both of the last two models can be estimated using OLS since both are linear in the parameters.

## 2.5 THE GAUSS–MARKOV THEOREM

Given the assumptions above hold true the Gauss–Markov Theorem[1] ensures that the least squares estimators are BLUE (Best Linear Unbiased Estimators), where "Best" means minimum variance. The estimators are:

1. unbiased as defined in Chapter 1 in that their expected value equals the true value of the parameter. That is, $E(\hat{\beta}) = \beta$.
2. of minimum variance. Their distribution around the true parametric value is less than that of any other linear unbiased estimator. This too was discussed in Chapter 1.
3. consistent. As explained in Chapter 1, this means that as the sample size increases the variance decreases and the estimate approaches the true value of the parameter.
4. normally distributed and carry a given variance. This is written as $\hat{\beta} \sim N(\beta, \hat{\sigma}^2)$. As a result of the normality in the distribution of the estimators it is possible to base hypothesis tests and other statistical procedures on a normal distribution.

## 2.6 MEASURES OF GOODNESS OF FIT

Now that we have used OLS to establish the line of best fit the question arises as to just how good that "best" is. Just because the model fits the data better than any other linear estimate doesn't necessarily mean it's a good fit. There are two measures of goodness of fit we can use to determine just how well our model describes the relationship between the two variables $X$ and $Y$. These are the *standard error of the estimate* and the *coefficient of determination*. In this section we will examine each in turn.

### ● The Standard Error of the Estimate

As Assumption 2 above noted, OLS presupposes the variance in the $Y$-values around the regression line is the same for all $X$-values. That is, if we examine all observations where $X = 5$ we will find an entire distribution of different $Y$-values. Those $Y$-values will have a certain variance, $\hat{\sigma}^2$. If we perform the same action for all observations where $X = 6$ (or any other value) we will find the $Y$-values will have the same variance, $\hat{\sigma}^2$. This was shown in Figure 2.5 above.

Based on this assumption of homoscedasticity, this variation of the $Y$-values around the regression line common at all $X$-values is a measure of the *standard error of the estimate*. In that manner it serves as a measure of how adequately the model measures the relationship between the dependent and independent variables.

> The standard error of the estimate reflects the standard deviation of the $Y$-values around the regression line.

The standard error of the estimate, $S_e$, is found as Equation (2.6.1). Notice that it does indeed capture the estimation error. The term in the numerator is the *sum of the squared errors* is it not? It finds our error as the difference between the actual value of $Y$, $Y_i$, and our estimate, $\hat{Y}$. It then sums those squared differences. The 2 in the denominator is the number of parameters that have to be estimated to derive the linear model. Of course, to construct a straight line we need two points. They are $\beta_0$ and $\beta_1$.

$$S_e = \sqrt{\frac{\Sigma(Y_i - \hat{Y})^2}{n-2}} \qquad (2.6.1)$$

where $n$ is the number of observations. In our Arco case there are $n = 12$ countries.

However, look at the amount of arithmetic necessary to calculate it. You must use the regression equation $n$ times to find $\hat{Y}$. You must then subtract each $\hat{Y}$ from the actual values of $Y$ to get the error. Finally, you then sum up those squared differences, divide by $n - 2$, and find the square root. That's a lot of calculations.

Equation (2.6.2) offers a simpler process since we have already computed all the terms needed to calculate it. The numerator is an easier method of finding the sum of the squared errors.

$$S_e = \sqrt{\frac{SS_Y - b_1(SS_{XY})}{n-2}} \qquad (2.6.2)$$

Equation (2.6.1) is useful to demonstrate the *concept* behind the standard error of the estimate. It shows the actual calculation of the error itself in the numerator and in doing so clearly reveals what the standard error of the estimate is actually measuring.

But Equation (2.6.2) is much more computationally convenient even though it provides little or no conceptual insight into just what $S_e$ measures.

Applying Equation (2.6.2) to our Arco data we find

$$S_e = \sqrt{\frac{185.11 - (1.636)(48.896)}{12-2}} = 3.242$$

Regression Model A                          Regression Model B

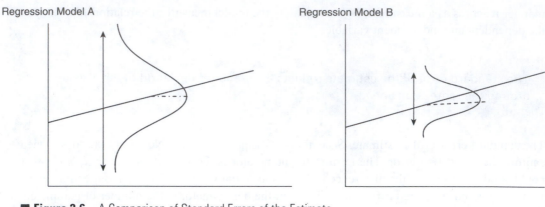

■ **Figure 2.6**   A Comparison of Standard Errors of the Estimate

Since $S_e$ is always expressed in the same units as $Y$, our standard error of the estimate is $3.242 thousand, or $3,242. This measures the degree of dispersion of the actual export levels above and below Arco's estimated regression line. It might be perceived as the "typical" error Arco will suffer in any effort to estimate exports to a given country. It's not the average (mean) error. Remember, the mean error is zero. But the standard error of the estimate reflects Arco's tendency to misjudge export levels to potential customers.

As a measure of goodness of fit, obviously the smaller the $S_e$ is, the better the fit. Is 3.242 "small"? There is no set rule to distinguish what can be classified as small or large. It's all relative—3.242 is smaller than 3.423 but larger than 3.241.

> The standard error of the estimate, $S_e$, is always expressed in the same units as the dependent variable, $Y$, and measures the tendency to err in the estimation of $Y$.

Figure 2.6 illustrates the manner in which the standard error of the estimate can vary between different regression models. In regression model A in Figure 2.6 the dispersion of the $Y$-values above and below the regression line is quite large suggesting a higher $S_e$ and a poor fit. This model will produce larger estimation errors and a less satisfactory fit. In model B we find a tighter fit with less variation in the $Y$-values and a smaller $S_e$. Estimation will prove to be more accurate in a general sense.

## ● The Coefficient of Determination

A second measure of goodness of fit is based on the principles of correlation analysis. It requires that we first calculate the *correlation coefficient* which measures the strength of the relationship between $X$ and $Y$. Symbolized with the lower case $r$ it is calculated as Equation (2.6.3):

$$r = \frac{\Sigma \left( X_i - \bar{X} \right)\left( Y_i - \bar{Y} \right)}{\sqrt{\Sigma(X_i - \bar{X})^2 \; S(Y_i - \bar{Y})^2}} = \frac{SS_{XY}}{\sqrt{\left( SS_X \right)\left( SS_Y \right)}} \qquad (2.6.3)$$

The correlation coefficient will always fall between $-1$ and $+1$; that is, $-1 \le r \le +1$. The closer it is to $-1$ or $+1$ the stronger the relationship. An $r$-value close to $-1$ indicates a strong negative relationship in which $X$ and $Y$ move in opposite directions. If $X$ and $Y$ exhibit a strong positive relationship, $r$ will approach $+1$. If $r$ nears 0, the relationship between $X$ and $Y$ is a weak one.

Using Equation (2.6.3), Arco's correlation coefficient is

$$r = \frac{48.913}{\sqrt{(29.892)(185.108)}} = 0.657$$

> The correlation coefficient measures the strength of the relationship between $X$ and $Y$. A strong positive relationship will produce a coefficient close to $+1$. A value close to $-1$ results if a strong negative relationship exists. A coefficient close to 0 indicates there is little or no relationship between $X$ and $Y$.

Does $r = 0.657$ reveal a strong association? Again, as with $S_e$, there is no decisive dividing point that differentiates a strong relationship. The closer $r$ is to $+1$ or $-1$, the better is the fit.

We can now easily compute the coefficient of determination as our second measure of goodness of fit. It is found as simply the squared value of the correlation coefficient. Indicated as $r^2$, the coefficient of determination for Arco is $r^2 = (0.657)^2 = 0.432$. The coefficient of determination measures that *portion of the change in Y that is explained by a change in X*. In our present case, about 43% of the change in exports is explained by changes in nations' GDP.

Since the coefficient of determination is a squared value it must be positive and will always fall within the interval $0 \le r^2 \le 1$. The larger $r^2$ is—the closer it is to $+1$—the more explanatory power your model possesses.

> The coefficient of determination, $r^2$, measures the percentage of the change in $Y$ that is *explained* by a change in $X$. The closer it is to 1 the more explanatory power your model has.

Notice it was not stated that 43% of the change in exports was *caused* by a change in GDP. As we noted earlier, regression and correlation cannot establish cause-and-effect relationships. They can only identify linkages.

● **How $r^2$ Can Be Used as a Measure of Goodness of Fit**

Remember, in general we are trying to explain the deviation in individual $Y$ values from its mean. In our present case for Arco we want to find what might explain the difference in the imports of a certain country from the mean of all the other nations. In that vein, the coefficient of determination measures the portion of the total deviation from the mean explained by the model.

> The coefficient of determination compares the total deviation of a nation's imports from the mean to the portion of that total deviation that the model can explain.

To understand how $r^2$ can be used as a measure of goodness of fit we must consider the *total deviation* in $Y$ from its mean. Again, recall that the intent of regression and correlation is to explain changes in $Y$ from its mean. Figure 2.7 aids in this discussion.

The total deviation (*TD*) is the amount by which a given value for $Y_i$ deviates from the mean value of $Y$, $\overline{Y}$. That is, $TD = (Y_i - \overline{Y})$.

$$TD = (Y_i - \overline{Y}) \tag{2.6.4}$$

> The total deviation of an observation is the amount by which it deviates from the mean.

As an example, Table 2.4 reveals that the actual exports to the United Kingdom were $Y_i = 15.6$. The total deviation of the UK's exports from the mean for all 12 countries of $\overline{Y} = 9.91$ is

$$TD_{UK} = (15.6 - 9.91) = 5.69$$

This is displayed in Figure 2.7.

This total deviation can be broken down into its two components: the explained deviation and the unexplained deviation. The *explained deviation* (*ExD*) is that portion of the total deviation that is explained by our $\hat{Y}$-regression model. It's the difference between what our model estimated $Y$ to be ($\hat{Y}$), and the mean value of $Y$ ($\overline{Y}$). It is found as $ExD = (\hat{Y} - \overline{Y})$. This too is seen in Figure 2.7.

This explained deviation is

$$ExD = (\hat{Y} - \overline{Y}) \tag{2.6.5}$$

> The explained deviation is the difference between our model's estimated value and the mean value for $Y$.

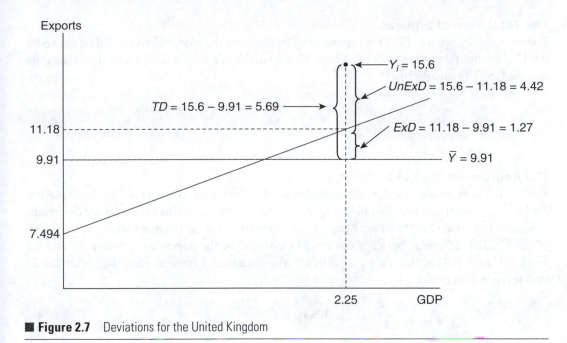

**■ Figure 2.7**   Deviations for the United Kingdom

Since the UK's GDP is 2.25, estimated exports are $\hat{Y} = 7.494 + 1.636(2.25) = 11.18$. Thus,

$$ExD_{UK} = (11.18 - 9.91) = 1.27$$

The *unexplained deviation* is that portion of the total deviation in the UK's exports that our model does not explain. It's the difference between what $Y_i$ actually was and what our model predicted. It's defined as $UnExD = \left(Y_i - \hat{Y}\right)$.

$$UnExD = (Y_i - \hat{Y}) \qquad\qquad (2.6.6)$$

The unexplained deviation is the difference between
what $Y$ was and what our model said it was going to be.

Since exports to the UK were 15.6 and our model predicted 11.18, the unexplained deviation is

$$UnExD_{UK} = (15.6 - 11.18) = 4.42$$

All of this is shown in Figure 2.7.

The next task requires calculating the *sums of squares* for all three deviations.

## The Total Sum of Squares

The *total sum of squares* (SST) is computed by performing the calculations described above for the UK for the remaining nations. These 12 deviations are then squared and the results are summed. SST is calculated as[2]

$$SST = \Sigma(Y_i - \bar{Y})^2 \qquad (2.6.7)$$

## The Regression Sum of Squares

Since it is the regression model that is explaining the deviation from the mean, the explained deviation is called the *regression sum of squares*, RSS. It is calculated as the explained deviations as seen in Equation (2.6.5) that are squared and summed up for all 12 observations. It is the sum of the squared difference between our model's estimate of the dependent variable, $\hat{Y}$ and the mean value for $Y$. This measures the portion of the change in $Y$ from its mean that is explained by our regression model:

$$RSS = \Sigma(\hat{Y} - \bar{Y})^2 \qquad (2.6.8)$$

## The Error Sum of Squares

As Equation (2.6.6) shows, the unexplained deviation is the difference between the reported value of $Y$, $Y_i$, and the value our model predicts. This, by definition, is the error. Thus, the *error sum of squares* (or sum of the squared errors), SSE, is simply the unexplained deviations from the mean after they have been squared and summed. Equation (2.6.9) illustrates:

$$SSE = \Sigma(Y_i - \hat{Y})^2 \qquad (2.6.9)$$

The coefficient of determination is then found by comparing the total amount of the deviation we need to explain, SST, to that portion that our model is indeed explaining, RSS. $r^2$ is determined as the ratio of the regression sum of squares to the total sum of squares.

$$r^2 = \frac{RSS}{SST} \qquad (2.6.10)$$

It measures what percentage of the total deviation our model explains. In that manner, it gauges the explanatory power of the model and serves as a measure of goodness of fit.

Although you can calculate $r^2$ using Equation (2.6.10), it obviously requires much less arithmetic to compute $r$ using Equation (2.6.3) and then square it to get $r^2$. Equations (2.6.7) through (2.6.10) are the conceptual formulas and explain much more clearly how and why $r^2$ is a measure of goodness of fit. They provide the intuitive insight into just what $r^2$ is and what it tells us. But Equation (2.6.3) should be used as the computational formula.

**EXAMPLE 2.2: Measuring the Strength of the Relationship Between Sales and Inventories**

**Problem Statement:** The National Retailers Association from Example 2.1 above now wants to measure the strength of the relationship between sales and inventories that has prevailed in the past. This requires that the Association calculates and interprets the coefficient of determination, $r^2$.

**Solution:** First, they compute the correlation coefficient, $r$.

$$r = \frac{SS_{XY}}{\sqrt{(SS_X)(SS_Y)}} = \frac{78375.3}{\sqrt{(66849.4)(95344.7)}} = 0.9817$$

Then, the coefficient of determination is $r^2 = (0.9817)^2 = 0.9637$.

**Interpretation:** The correlation coefficient measures how "tightly" the two variables are related. A coefficient of 0.9817 indicates a very strong positive relationship. The coefficient of determination of $r^2 = 0.9637$ reveals that 96.37% of the change in inventories is explained by changes in sales. Apparently, businesses can use sales to predict and estimate inventory levels needed to maintain business activity.

This example for the National Retailers Association reports a strong positive association between inventories and sales. The correlation coefficient can be either negative or positive depending on the nature of the relationship between the two variables under consideration. That is, $-1 \leq r \leq +1$. The coefficient of determination, $r^2$, will always be positive. That is, $0 \leq r^2 \leq +1$. Example 2.3 illustrates a case in which $r < 0$ revealing a negative relationship.

**EXAMPLE 2.3: How Does the Unemployment Rate Impact Personal Savings?**

**Problem Statement:** As national and world-wide economic conditions worsen, federal governments express serious concern over the amount of savings households are able to set aside. These savings can be used for investment purposes that can then stimulate the economy and bring it out of the recessionary doldrums. In 2009 a task force from several industrial nations was established to examine the connection between the number of employed persons and the level of national savings. Data shown here record the unemployment rates and the amount of income households are able to save. The task force has the duty to measure the manner in which unemployment is related to personal savings.

*(Continued)*

**EXAMPLE 2.3: (Continued)**

| Nation | Unemployment Rate ($X$) | Personal Savings ($Y$) | $(X-\bar{X})^2$ | $(Y-\bar{Y})^2$ | $(X-\bar{X})(Y-\bar{Y})$ |
|---|---|---|---|---|---|
| 1 | 6.2 | 257.3 | 1.604 | 343.073 | −23.461 |
| 2 | 12.5 | 225.25 | 25.334 | 183.001 | −68.09 |
| 3 | 5.9 | 240.43 | 2.454 | 2.73 | −2.588 |
| 4 | 4.6 | 243.42 | 8.218 | 21.55 | −13.308 |
| 5 | 8.3 | 234.91 | 0.694 | 14.96 | −3.223 |
| 6 | 7.5 | 236.75 | 0.001 | 4.112 | −0.068 |
| 7 | 10.6 | 229.62 | 9.818 | 83.865 | −28.694 |
| 8 | 6.8 | 238.36 | 0.444 | 0.175 | 0.279 |
| 9 | 4.8 | 242.96 | 7.111 | 17.491 | −11.153 |
| **Sums** | 67.2 | 2149 | 55.678 | 670.957 | −150.306 |
| ***n =*** | 9 | | $SS_X$ | $SS_Y$ | $SS_{XY}$ |
| **Means** | 7.466666667 | 238.7777778 | | | |

**Solution:** The correlation coefficient is

$$r = \frac{SS_{XY}}{\sqrt{(SS_X)(SS_Y)}} = \frac{-150.306}{\sqrt{(55.678)(670.957)}} = -0.777$$

Then, $r^2 = (-0.777)^2 = 0.6047$.

**Interpretation:** Thus, 60.47% of the drop in savings can be explained by rises in the unemployment rate. The negative value for $r$, −0.777, represents the inverse relationship between unemployment in a nation and the amount of money households are able to save. While that may be painfully obvious, by calculating the correlation we obtain a quantifiable measure of just how strong that relationship is.

## SECTION 2.6 PROBLEMS

1. Explain conceptually in your own words how the standard error of the estimate and the coefficient of determination can be used as measures of goodness of fit. Use all necessary graphical work in your answer.

2. Distinguish among the regression sum of squares, error sum of squares, and the total sum of squares. Use a graph to aid your answer.

3. What is meant by explained sum of squares, unexplained sum of squares, and the total sum of squares? How do they compare and what do they measure?

4. What does the standard error of the estimate have to do with the assumption of homoscedasticity? Use a graph to illustrate.

5. Given the data opposite, calculate and interpret

A. The model.
B. The total deviation using Equation (2.6.4).
C. The explained deviation using Equation (2.6.5).
D. The unexplained deviation using Equation (2.6.6).
E. The total sum of squares using Equation (2.6.7).
F. The regression sum of squares using Equation (2.6.8).
G. The sum of the squared errors using Equation (2.6.9).
H. The coefficient of determination using Equation (2.6.10).

| X | Y |
|---|---|
| 2 | 8 |
| 3 | 10 |
| 5 | 15 |
| 4 | 14 |
| 3 | 11 |
| 6 | 18 |

6. Disputes between labor and management often arise over benefits wage earners receive from management as a result of their employment. Employers are generally concerned about the labor costs they face over and above the wages they must pay. Labor argued that the issues of income should be separated from contributions employers make to workers' pension and insurance funds. The data shown here are taken from the 2010 Economic Report of the President. They record in billions of dollars the national income and employers' contributions from the years 2000 to 2008.

Does it appear from these data that labor is correct in its argument? Estimate the regression model using NI as the independent variable. Does it appear there is no relationship between these two macroeconomic measures? Comment on your findings.

| Year | NI | Emp Cont |
|------|------|----------|
| 2000 | 8938.9 | 615.9 |
| 2001 | 9185.2 | 669.1 |
| 2002 | 9408.5 | 747.4 |
| 2003 | 9840.2 | 845.6 |
| 2004 | 10534 | 874.6 |
| 2005 | 11273.8 | 931.6 |
| 2006 | 12031.2 | 960.1 |
| 2007 | 12448.2 | 993 |
| 2008 | 12635.2 | 1023.9 |

7. A candidate for political office wishes to determine if the money spent for television advertisements translates into additional votes in different political districts. Data are collected for the number of ads run on local television stations, the amount of money spent for these announcements, and the percentage of votes received by the candidate in each district. Does it appear from these data that the number of ads or the amount of money spent can be used to estimate political success in terms of votes? Use both number of ads, and, as a second model, expenditures, to estimate the percentage of votes received. Based on your results, should the candidate rely on these models to predict success at the polls? Money is in thousands of dollars. Percentage is of the total number of votes cast. Calculate the model in each case. What is your estimate of the percentage of votes the candidate will receive if Ads is 43? If Money is 38?

Evaluate each model on the basis of the measures of goodness of fit.

| District | Ads | Money | Percentage |
|----------|-----|-------|------------|
| 1 | 54 | 45 | 54 |
| 2 | 51 | 12 | 30 |
| 3 | 36 | 15 | 22 |
| 4 | 42 | 17 | 25 |
| 5 | 25 | 35 | 15 |
| 6 | 63 | 36 | 38 |
| 7 | 58 | 58 | 35 |
| 8 | 48 | 48 | 29 |
| 9 | 57 | 65 | 33 |
| 10 | 69 | 39 | 20 |
| 11 | 25 | 58 | 29 |
| 12 | 47 | 48 | 24 |

## 2.7 LIMITATIONS OF REGRESSION AND CORRELATION

As powerful as regression and correlation are they do face certain constrictions. They are, for example, unable to establish cause-and-effect relationships. They can explain changes in the dependent variable but they cannot explain *why* Y changed. A correlation between X and Y can be identified but that does not mean that the change in X caused the change in Y. Correlation does not mean causation. It may be that a third variable not included in the model is the cause of the change in both X and Y.

Nor is it wise to use the model outside the range of the independent variable. The linear relationship between GDP and exports for Arco has been estimated for GDP levels ranging from 0.086 (Slovakia) to 5.88 (China). However, nations with GDP outside those limits may behave differently in terms of their ability and willingness to import from Arco.

Finally, in using any regression model the analyst must be aware of spurious (coincidental) correlation. Any two variables, even if they are randomly chosen, will report a non-zero correlation coefficient no matter how small. There will always occur some correlation that is merely incidental and carries no meaningful statement as to any true relationship. This is why tests of statistical significance examined in the next chapter are required.

## 2.8 REGRESSION THROUGH THE ORIGIN

Some financial and economic theories postulate that in certain models the regression line passes through the origin. That is, $b_0 = 0$. A popular illustration is that of Okun's Law.[3] While serving on President's Kennedy's Council of Economic Advisors in 1962, Arthur Okun posed a relationship between changes in national output and changes in the unemployment rate.

The CEA wanted to convince Kennedy that the economy-wide gains from lowering unemployment from 7% to 4% were greater than previously imagined. Okun's Law was a major part of the empirical justification for Kennedy's tax cuts. The concept is based on data from the period between World War II and 1960.

The "gap version" of Okun's Law can be stated as

$$(Y^* - Y) = b_1(u - u^*)$$

where:

$Y^*$ is potential GNP;

$Y$ is actual current GNP;

$u$ is actual unemployment rate;

$u^*$ is the natural unemployment rate.

The natural rate of unemployment is defined by economists as that level that occurs in the long-run when the labor market is in equilibrium.

The left-hand side of the expression is the "gap" between potential output and the prevailing level of output. Since about 1955 the value of $b_1$ in the United States has typically been around 2 or 3. Thus, for every 1% by which the existing unemployment exceeds the natural unemployment rate, about a 2.5% GDP gap is predicted.

Notice the expression does not contain an intercept term. The model argues that the regression line should extend through the origin with $b_0$ set equal to zero. This is in accord with the observations made by Okun and other economists at the time.

Most computer software programs allow the option of regression through the origin by simply choosing an option. In Excel you merely check the box "Constant is Zero." After entering the commands for Minitab explained in the next section uncheck the option "Fit Intercept."

Manually, the computations are performed by calculating the coefficient using Equation (2.8.1):

$$b_1 = \frac{\Sigma(X_i Y_i)}{\Sigma X_i^2} \qquad\qquad (2.8.1)$$

Regression through the origin should be used with caution! The $r^2$ value is artificially inflated and cannot be considered reliable. Nor do the errors sum to zero as OLS otherwise promises. Furthermore, $b_1$ is not an unbiased estimate of $\beta_1$ if the intercept is set equal to zero.

## 2.9 COMPUTER APPLICATIONS

Although the mathematical calculations displayed in this chapter are generally done using computer software it was necessary to manually perform the work using raw data in order to fully understand what regression and correlation do and how they do it. This section examines the steps required to obtain the results with the welcome aid of modern software.

### ● Using Excel

Begin by entering the data from Table 2.4 for GDP and exports in the first two columns of an Excel spreadsheet as seen here:

| | A | B |
|---|---|---|
| 1 | GDP | Exports |
| 2 | 2.58 | 13.7 |
| 3 | 1.47 | 7.5 |
| 4 | 0.742 | 8.6 |
| 5 | 1.57 | 14.2 |
| 6 | 0.204 | 8.2 |
| 7 | 0.086 | 2.1 |
| 8 | 2.06 | 13.6 |
| 9 | 5.88 | 13.2 |
| 10 | 0.239 | 6.9 |
| 11 | 0.218 | 6.1 |
| 12 | 0.414 | 9.2 |
| 13 | 2.247 | 15.6 |

Then, click on Data > Data Analysis > Regression > OK. In the "Input $Y$ Range" window enter B1:B13. In the "Enter $X$ Range" window enter A1:A13. Check the Box for "Labels" and click "OK." Part of the resulting output is shown in Excel Output 1.

**Excel Output 1**

| A | B |
|---|---|
| SUMMARY OUTPUT | |
| | |
| *Regression Statistics* | |
| Multiple R | 0.657372492 |
| R Square | 0.432138593 |
| Adjusted R Square | 0.375352453 |
| Standard Error | 3.242165199 |
| Observations | 12 |

The correlation coefficient of $r = 0.657$ (here called "Multiple R") is seen as the first reported statistic. Also $r^2$ of 0.432 is shown and the standard error of $S_e = 3.242$ is revealed. All correspond to the values we computed manually. The sample size of $n = 12$ also appears.

Excel also provides the information shown in Excel Output 2. The regression coefficients reveal the model to be $\hat{E} = 7.494 + 1.636(\text{GNP})$ just as we calculated using the OLS procedure discussed in the chapter. Ignore the values in the last two columns. We will discuss them in the next chapter.

**Excel Output 2**

| 16 | | Coefficients | Standard Error | t Stat |
|---|---|---|---|---|
| 17 | Intercept | 7.493897308 | 1.281408712 | 5.8481710∃ |
| 18 | GDP | 1.635981496 | 0.593045531 | 2.758610279 |

To obtain the correlation coefficient click on Data > Data Analysis > Correlation. In the Input Range window you should highlight (or manually enter) A1:B13. Check the box for "Labels In First Row." Then click OK. Excel responds with

**Excel Output 3**

| | A | B | C |
|---|---|---|---|
| 1 | | GDP | Exports |
| 2 | GDP | 1 | |
| 3 | Exports | 0.657372 | 1 |

The correlation between GDP and exports is 0.657 just as we calculated by hand earlier.

To plot data with Excel you must place the variable you want to appear on the *vertical* axis in the *second* column as we did above. First highlight (select) the two columns with the data you wish to plot. Click on Insert > Scatter. Select the upper left diagram. The scatter plot will appear as seen in Figure 2.4. To add the trend line right-click on one of the data points, select Add Trendline and then Linear.

### ● Using Minitab

Enter the data from Table 2.4 as shown here in a Minitab worksheet:

| | C1 | C2 |
|---|---|---|
| | GDP | Exports |
| 1 | 2.580 | 13.7 |
| 2 | 1.470 | 7.5 |
| 3 | 0.742 | 8.6 |
| 4 | 1.570 | 14.2 |
| 5 | 0.204 | 8.2 |
| 6 | 0.086 | 2.1 |
| 7 | 2.060 | 13.6 |
| 8 | 5.880 | 13.2 |
| 9 | 0.239 | 6.9 |
| 10 | 0.218 | 6.1 |
| 11 | 0.414 | 9.2 |
| 12 | 2.247 | 15.6 |

Worksheet 1 ***

Click on Stat > Regression > Regression.

Highlight C2 Exports in the left portion of the drop-down window and click "Select." Enter C1 GDP in the same fashion in the "Predictors" window. Click "Storage" and "Residuals." Click "OK."

The resulting Minitab output is shown here:

```
Regression Analysis: Exports Versus GDP

The regression equation is

Exports = 7.49 + 1.64 GDP


Predictor    Coef   SE Coef    T      P

Constant    7.494     1.281  5.85  0.000

GDP         1.6360    0.5930  2.76  0.020


S = 3.24217 R-Sq = 43.2% R-Sq(adj) = 37.5%
```

The model is given in the first line as Exports = 7.49 + 1.64 GDP and agrees with our calculations. The coefficients are shown next in the output. Ignore the last three columns of the output. We will examine these data in the next chapter.

The standard error (indicated here as S) is seen to be 3.242 just as we calculated it to be. The coefficient of determination (indicated here as R-Sq) is 43.2% and agrees with our findings.

To get just the correlation coefficient in Minitab click on Stat > Basic Statistics > Correlation. Then select both variables and hit OK. Minitab reports:

```
Correlations: GDP, Exports
Pearson correlation of GDP and Exports = 0.657
```

showing the correlation to be 0.657 as we found in our hand calculations earlier in the chapter.

To plot with Minitab, click on Graph > Scatterplot > OK. Then select the variables, being careful to put the dependent variable in the $Y$-column. Click on OK.

## ● Using SPSS

Enter the data in two columns of a PASW Data Editor. You can click on the Variable View tab in the bottom left corner and enter the variable names in the NAMES column. To run the regression, click on Analyze > Regression > Linear. Enter EXPORTS in the Dependent Variable window and GDP in the Independent Variable window. Click OK. PASW responds with the output seen here. The coefficients of 7.493 and 1.636 are reported.

**Coefficients[a]**

| Model | | Unstandardized Coefficients | | Standardized Coefficients | | |
|---|---|---|---|---|---|---|
| | | B | Std. Error | Beta | t | Sig. |
| 1 | (Constant) | 7.493 | 1.281 | | 5.848 | .000 |
| | GDP | 1.636 | .593 | .658 | 2.760 | .020 |

a. Dependent Variable: EXPORTS

The correlation coefficient and correlation of determination are also reported in the Model Summary along with the standard error of the estimate.

Analyze > Correlate > Bivariate produces the correlation matrix much like the one shown above for Minitab.

## 2.10 REVIEW PROBLEMS

Pelican Press markets books and other printed materials to customers spread around the globe. The Financial Planning staff wishes to estimate a regression model to predict shipping times for their standard package as a function of distance. Such information would prove useful in establishing policy issues for future international shipments. Data are collected for a random sample of 13 previous shipments with Time in hours and Miles in hundreds with the intent of estimating the model $\hat{T} = b_0 + b_1 M$:

|  | A | B | C | D | E | F | G | H |
|---|---|---|---|---|---|---|---|---|
| 1 |  | Miles (X) | Time (Y) | (X-Xbar)^2 | (Y-Ybar)^2 | (X - Xbar)(Y - Ybar) |  |  |
| 2 |  |  |  | SSx | SSy | SSxy |  |  |
| 3 |  | 1.2 | 10 | 1.35 | 1.16 | -1.25 |  |  |
| 4 |  | 2.6 | 12 | 0.06 | 9.47 | 0.73 | n= | 13.00 |
| 5 |  | 1.6 | 7 | 0.58 | 3.70 | 1.47 | Xbar = | 2.36 |
| 6 |  | 0.23 | 3 | 4.55 | 35.08 | 12.64 | Ybar = | 8.92 |
| 7 |  | 2.5 | 8 | 0.02 | 0.85 | -0.13 |  |  |
| 8 |  | 3.5 | 10 | 1.29 | 1.16 | 1.22 |  |  |
| 9 |  | 1.6 | 7 | 0.58 | 3.70 | 1.47 |  |  |
| 10 |  | 1.8 | 7 | 0.32 | 3.70 | 1.08 |  |  |
| 11 |  | 3.5 | 12 | 1.29 | 9.47 | 3.50 |  |  |
| 12 |  | 4.2 | 15 | 3.37 | 36.93 | 11.16 |  |  |
| 13 |  | 2.9 | 6 | 0.29 | 8.54 | -1.57 |  |  |
| 14 |  | 3.5 | 9 | 1.29 | 0.01 | 0.09 |  |  |
| 15 |  | 1.6 | 10 | 0.58 | 1.16 | -0.82 |  |  |
| 16 |  |  |  |  |  |  |  |  |
| 17 | SUMS |  |  | 15.58 | 114.92 | 29.58 |  |  |
| 18 |  |  |  |  |  |  |  |  |

The means for $X$ and $Y$ are subtracted from each of the 13 respective observations and the differences are squared. Summing these squared differences produces $SS_X$ and $SS_Y$. $SS_{XY}$ is found by multiplying the individual differences. With only these three simple values the model can be developed as:

$$b_1 = \frac{SS_{XY}}{SS_X} = \frac{29.58}{15.58} = 1.899$$

and

$$b_0 = \bar{Y} - b_1 \bar{X} = 8.92 - (1.899)(2.36) = 4.44$$

The model is then $\hat{T} = 4.44 + 1.899M$. For every additional 50 miles the consignment must travel will require $(1.899)(50) = 95$ hours or about four days.

The planning staff can estimate that to ship to a customer 250 miles away will take 16.44 + 1.899(250) = 491.2 hours or about 20 days. It must be kept in mind that this is an average of the time required for many such shipments and there is no assurance any particular shipment will reach its intended destination in that amount of time.

The standard error of the estimate, $S_e$, that reflects the dispersion above and below that mean delivery time, is

$$S_e = \sqrt{\frac{SS_Y - (b_1)(SS_{XY})}{n-2}} = \sqrt{\frac{114.92 - (1.899)(29.58)}{13-2}} = 2.31 \text{ hours}$$

While the mean shipping time for a distance of 250 miles is 491.2 hours, there is a tendency for the transit time to vary by about 2.31 hours.

The strength of the relationship between time and distance is determined by calculating the correlation coefficient, $r$.

$$r = \frac{SS_{XY}}{\sqrt{(SS_X)(SS_Y)}} = \frac{29.58}{\sqrt{(15.58)(114.92)}} = 0.699$$

This represents a reasonably strong positive relationship between distance and time. To actually determine if this might be the case will require interval estimates and hypothesis tests performed in the next chapter. At this point, however, it seems the model to estimate delivery times could prove to be valuable input in establishing company policies regarding shipments.

Further, that portion of the change in time that is explained by changes in distance is given by the coefficient of determination, $r^2 = (0.699)^2 = 0.489$. Almost 50% of the change in time required to ship a cargo of materials is explained by changes in distance. There are potentially many other measures that could be used to estimate shipping times. Other explanatory variables could be chosen to form a multiple regression model that might provide even greater insight into shipping issues the company faces.

Given what seems to be a measurable explanatory relationship between these two variables, Pelican may want to consider revising their methods of shipment and the carriers they currently use. Twenty days to ship 250 miles might constitute an unacceptable delay. Customers may become unusually restless and impatient. But now Pelican personnel have a systematic and analytical tool they can use to make decisions and solve problems that commonly arise in the daily conduct of their business activities.

## CHAPTER PROBLEMS

### Conceptual Problems

1. Explain in your own words why the modeling procedure discussed in the chapter can be called ordinary least squares. Use all pertinent graphical work in your response.

2. What is meant by the statement, "the sums of the errors is zero"? Use all pertinent graphical work in your response.

CHAPTER
PROBLEMS
**2**

3. What is meant by "residual" in reference to the OLS model? Use all pertinent graphical work in your response.

4. What is the standard error of the estimate?

   A. What does it have to do with the concept of homoscedasticity? Explain what is meant by homoscedasticity. Use all pertinent graphical work in your response.
   B. How can the standard error of the estimate be used as a measure of goodness of fit? Use all pertinent graphical work in your response.

5. What is the coefficient of determination? What does it measure? How can it be used as a measure of goodness of fit? Use all pertinent graphical work in your response.

6. Discuss each of the properties and assumptions of the OLS model. What is the difference between a property and an assumption? Use all pertinent graphical work in your response.

7. Explain the Gauss–Markov Theorem. How does the acronym BLUE relate to it? Explain each of the terms.

8. A model is reported to be $Y = 15.364 + 2.54X$. Estimate $Y$ if $X = 37$. Can you be assured that $Y$ will be the amount you calculated? What connotation does $E(Y|X = 37)$ have in this model?

## Computational Problems

1. Basic Keynesian theory postulated by the noted British economist John Maynard Keynes in his famous book, *The General Theory of Employment, Interest and Money*, published in 1936, holds that consumption is a function of income. Below are data taken from the 2009 Economic Report of the President for disposable personal income and personal consumption expenditures for the years indicated in trillions of dollars.

   A. Estimate the regression model to test Keynes' theory. The theory states that the marginal propensity to consume (that portion of an extra dollar of income used for consumption purposes) is less than one. Does this appear to be the case? Comment on the regression results.
   B. Plot the data in a scatter diagram. Does it appear to be a linear model? How does your answer relate to the coefficient of determination you calculated?

| Year | Income | Cons |
|------|--------|------|
| 2001 | 7.6 | 7.1 |
| 2002 | 8 | 7.4 |
| 2003 | 8.4 | 7.8 |
| 2004 | 8.9 | 8.3 |
| 2005 | 9.3 | 8.8 |
| 2006 | 9.9 | 9.3 |
| 2007 | 10.4 | 9.8 |
| 2008 | 10.8 | 10.1 |
| 2009 | 11 | 10.1 |

Table extracted December 2011: http://www.gpoaccess.gov/eop/tables10.html

C.  Compute and interpret the coefficient of determination and the standard error of the estimate.

2.  Over a period of several years a local school district in Illinois followed their students through high school, college, and graduate school to determine the impact of education on lifetime earnings. A portion of the data collected in the study is shown here. EDU is years of education and INC is annual income measured in thousands of dollars.

| EDU | INC |
|-----|-----|
| 12  | 110 |
| 12  | 98  |
| 16  | 114 |
| 16  | 105 |
| 16  | 111 |
| 15  | 132 |
| 14  | 87  |
| 12  | 74  |
| 8   | 52  |
| 12  | 115 |
| 13  | 107 |

A.  Construct the earnings function in which income is explained on the basis of educational levels. Comment on results.

B.  What is your estimate of mean earned income for someone with (i) only nine years of education; (ii) a graduate degree consisting of four years of undergraduate schooling and a two-year master's degree?

C.  What happens to the estimated income for someone who gets one additional year of education?

3.  Given the data in the previous problem, what percentage of the change in income is explained by changes in educational levels? Calculate and interpret the standard error of the estimate.

4.  The raw data for the returns of U.S. treasury bonds and treasury bills were obtained from the Federal Reserve database in St. Louis (FRED). The treasury bill rate is a three-month rate and the treasury bond is the constant maturity 10-year bond.

Many financial analysts argue that treasury bond and bill rates closely correlate over time. Use the statistical tools discussed in this chapter to determine the validity of that claim.

| Year | T. Bills | T. Bonds |
|------|----------|----------|
| 2000 | 5.76%    | 16.66%   |
| 2001 | 3.67%    | 5.57%    |
| 2002 | 1.66%    | 15.12%   |
| 2003 | 1.03%    | 0.38%    |
| 2004 | 1.23%    | 4.49%    |
| 2005 | 3.01%    | 2.87%    |
| 2006 | 4.68%    | 1.96%    |
| 2007 | 4.64%    | 10.21%   |
| 2008 | 1.59%    | 20.10%   |
| 2009 | 0.14%    | 11.12%   |
| 2010 | 0.13%    | 8.46%    |

Table extracted December 2011: http://pages.stern.nyu.edu/~adamodar/New_Home_Page/datafile/histretSP.html

5.  Economic data for best-and-worst state economies for several states are shown below. Due to the large numbers, which are difficult to compute by hand, enter the data into an Excel, Minitab, PASW, or your preferred spreadsheet. Obtain the correlation coefficient for per capita debt and household income.

**1st: Wyoming**

Debt per capita: $4,310 (2nd)
Unemployment rate: 6.8% (8th)
Home price change (2006–2009): 23.6% (1st)
Median household income: $52,664 (19th)

**2nd: North Dakota**

Debt per capita: $5,651 (10th)
Unemployment rate: 3.7% (1st)
Home price change (2006–2009): 17.2% (4th)
Median household income: $48,827 (27th)

**3rd: Iowa**

Debt per capita: $5,138 (6th)
Unemployment rate: 6.8% (8th)
Home price change (2006–2009): 8.3% (22nd)
Median household income: $48,044 (26th)

**4th: Vermont**

Debt per capita: $6,983 (23rd)
Unemployment rate: 6% (5th)
Home price change (2006–2009): 12.1% (12th)
Median household income: $51,618 (20th)

**5th: Minnesota**

Debt per capita: $7,909 (32nd)
Unemployment rate: 7% (10th)
Home price change (2006–2009): −3.7% (41st)
Median household income: $55,616 (12th)

**6th: Utah**

Debt per capita: $6,007 (15th)
Unemployment rate: 7.4% (14th)
Home price change (2006–2009): 19.2% (2nd)
Median household income: $55,117 (14th)

**7th: Virginia**

Debt per capita: $6,939 (22nd)
Unemployment rate: 7% (10th)
Home price change (2006–2009): 3.4% (31st)
Median household income: $59,330 (8th)

**8th: New Hampshire**

Debt per capita: $7,946 (33rd)
Unemployment rate: 5.7% (4th)
Home price change (2006–2009): −1.4% (38th)
Median household income: $60,567 (7th)

Extracted from http://www.theatlantic.com/business/archive/2010/10/the-best-and-worst-performing-state-economies-in-america/64307/

A.  Do changes in income explain changes in debt levels? Does it appear that those in states with higher incomes incur more debt? Obtain the regression model that addresses that issue. Compute and interpret the standard error of the estimate.

B.  What is the correlation between these two variables? Interpret that correlation.

6.  Data for the year 2010 for 10 countries are shown in the table below. Population is in millions of people; debt and GDP is measured in trillions of U.S. dollars.

| Country | Debt | GDP | Population |
|---|---|---|---|
| Canada | 1 | 1.56 | 34 |
| UK | 8.9 | 2.26 | 62 |
| Germany | 4.7 | 3.31 | 82 |
| Russia | 0.48 | 1.48 | 143 |
| Japan | 2.2 | 5.39 | 128 |
| USA | 14.4 | 14.62 | 310 |
| France | 4.7 | 2.56 | 66 |
| Italy | 2.2 | 2.04 | 61 |
| Argentina | 0.129 | 0.35 | 40 |
| Zimbabwe | 0.0058 | 0.0056 | 13 |

Population data from http://www.census.gov/ipc/www/idb/. GDP and debt data from http://en.wikipedia.org/wiki/List_of_countries_by_GDP_(nominal)

Enter the data in your preferred software. Create another variable by calculating the percentage each country's debt is of its GDP. Create still another variable consisting of debt per capita. Keep in mind debt is measured in units of trillions of dollars and population in units of millions. Then:

A.  Determine and interpret correlation coefficients for all pairs of variables. Which variables show positive correlations and which show negative? How would you interpret the positive correlations? How do you interpret the negative correlations? Do the values and their signs make sense? Comment on the results.

B.  Estimate the regression equation for debt using population as the explanatory variable.

C.  By how much does debt change as GDP changes? This requires a regression model. Which is the dependent variable? Run the regression and interpret the results.

D.  What happens to debt as GDP increases? Provide an economic rationale for that.

E.  Discuss any economic rationale for the relationship between GDP and debt as a percentage of GDP.

F.  Do more heavily populated countries have higher per capita debt? Explain. Provide your economic rationale for this phenomenon.

7. Economic theory holds that the demand for different goods and services respond in dissimilar fashion to changes in consumers' incomes. Inferior goods are those that consumers purchase only because they cannot afford better commodities. Examples include poor cuts of meat, substandard clothing, cheap forms of transportation (buses as opposed to luxury cars), and other less desirable purchases. Normal (or superior) goods are those that consumers want to buy more of as their incomes go up. Data are provided here for the incomes of several consumers and their respective purchases of two commodities, Q1 and Q2.

| Income | Q1 | Q2 |
|--------|-----|-----|
| 1.2 | 3 | 5.8 |
| 1.3 | 3.1 | 5.1 |
| 2.5 | 4.9 | 4.5 |
| 3.6 | 6.6 | 4.3 |
| 2.5 | 4.9 | 5.2 |
| 3.5 | 6.1 | 4.7 |
| 1.9 | 4.1 | 5.3 |
| 2.8 | 5.4 | 5.1 |
| 3.5 | 6.4 | 4.7 |

A. Use two regression models to determine which might be classified as an inferior good and which as the normal good based on changes in incomes. Be careful in determining which variable is the dependent variable.

B. Calculate and interpret the correlation coefficients between Income and Q1 and between Income and Q2. Do they substantiate your conclusion from part A?

C. Graph the functions placing the dependent variable on the vertical axis. What can you conclude from these graphs and do they support your contention regarding which good is inferior?

8. Financial theory holds that there is a direct relationship between the risk associated with an investment and the rate of return it generates. Data for several heavily traded stocks on the organized exchanges are shown in the table. The Beta for a stock is the measure of its non-diversifiable risk. It measures the stock's volatility in relation to the market as a whole. The dividend yield is also shown for each investment. These data are taken from the Scott Trade web site, http://research. scottrade.com/qnr/Public/Stocks/Snapshot?symbol=hal.

A. Prepare a discussion of the results of a regression model treating Yield as the dependent variable. Do the results seem to support the theory? Why or why not?

| Stock | Symbol | Beta | Yield |
|-------|--------|------|-------|
| Exxon | XOM | 0.9 | 2.05 |
| Apple | AAPL | 1.37 | 0 |
| Chevron | CVX | 0.76 | 2.63 |

| General Electric | GE | 1.66 | 2.77 |
| Microsoft | MSFT | 1.06 | 2.45 |
| Citigroup | CVX | 2.54 | 0.36 |
| Ford | F | 2.37 | 1.59 |
| Halliburton | HAL | 1.42 | 0.75 |

B. Compute and interpret the standard error of the estimate.
C. Graph the relationship in a scatter diagram. How does it confirm the results of the regression model?

9. For over a decade, *The Wall Street Journal* and The Heritage Foundation, Washington's preeminent think tank, have tracked the march of economic freedom around the world with the influential Index of Economic Freedom. The Index has measures for 10 freedoms—from property rights to entrepreneurship—in 184 countries. Economists and international scholars place considerable importance on the level of economic freedom and its impact on economic growth and development within a nation. Nations are ranked as either (1) Free, (2) Mostly Free, (3) Moderately Free, (4) Mostly Unfree, or (5) Repressed.

Data have been collected on the Index rankings of a random sample of nations seen here and the growth rate of their GDP from 2010 to 2011. Based on these data, construct a regression model to measure whether the level of freedom can explain GDP growth rates. Comment on your findings. What conclusions can you draw?

| Nation | Type of Rating | Freedom Index[a] | GDP Growth Rate[b] |
|--------|----------------|--------------|-----------------|
| Hong Kong | Free | 89.9 | 6.8 |
| Singapore | Free | 87.5 | 15.3 |
| Italy | Mostly Unfree | 58.8 | 1.3 |
| Honduras | Mostly Unfree | 58.8 | 2.7 |
| Qatar | Mostly Free | 71.3 | 16.3 |
| Netherlands | Mostly Free | 73.3 | 1.7 |
| France | Moderately Free | 63.2 | 1.4 |
| Portugal | Moderately Free | 63 | 1.3 |
| Hungary | Moderately Free | 67 | 1.2 |
| Slovenia | Moderately Free | 62 | 1.2 |
| Iran | Repressed | 42.3 | 1 |
| Bosnia | Mostly Unfree | 57.3 | 0.8 |

[a] http://www.heritage.org/index/ranking
[b] http://en.wikipedia.org/wiki/List_of_countries_by_GDP_(real)_growth_rate

## COMPUTER PROBLEMS

1.  To compare the movement in the price of a stock with changes in the Dow-Jones Industrial Average an investment analyst collected the data contained in the data set DOW-JONES. Access the data set to determine if changes in the Dow-Jones can explain changes in the price of the stock the analyst is following. Comment on the results of the model.

2.  Realizing that customers prefer speedy service, a "hot room" at a call center considers the time in minutes callers must wait before speaking with a live person. The data set HOT ROOM provides the data to regress wait time on the number of staff on duty at the time the call is placed. Does it appear wait time can be explained by staff? Plot the residuals and comment on the results.

*Chapter 3*

# STATISTICAL INFERENCES IN THE SIMPLE REGRESSION MODEL

## INTRODUCTION

In Chapter 2 we applied OLS techniques to estimate our bivariate regression model. The relationship between the dependent and independent variables was quantified and measures of how well the model performed its prescribed duties were provided. The entire methodological foundation upon which the OLS model is structured was thoroughly examined. However, could it be that at the population level no relationship truly exists between $X$ and $Y$? Perhaps due to bias or some other distortion our sample erroneously suggests that an association prevails when in reality there is no statistical relationship between $X$ and $Y$. Perhaps our detection of a relationship resulted from an aberration based on a misleading sample. Our sample data may be lying to us!

If this is the case our model is perilously deceptive and any decision based on its outcome could result in a serious blunder. It is therefore essential that tests be conducted to determine the statistical significance of our findings. This chapter examines these tests and explores the importance and meaning of *statistical significance*. The two most common tests of significance are confidence intervals and hypothesis tests. The purpose of each test and the role each plays in the general scheme of statistical analysis are thoroughly examined in this chapter.

## 3.1 CONFIDENCE INTERVAL ESTIMATION

A primary reason to develop our regression model is to estimate and forecast values for the dependent variable. In Chapter 2 our efforts provided values for $b_0$ and $b_1$ which serve as *point* estimators for the unknown parameters $\beta_0$ and $\beta_1$. Given the model based on the Arco data, $\beta_0$ was estimated at the point $b_0 = 7.493$ and $\beta_1$ was estimated at the point $b_1 = 1.636$. But how much confidence do you have that your estimate is correct? Probably not much.

However, *interval estimates* are much more meaningful. They provide both an upper and lower bound within which we think the parameter might fall. Unlike point estimates, we can actually attach some level of confidence we have as to whether the parameter is indeed within the interval. How confident are you that $\beta_1 = b_1 = 1.636$? Not very! In fact, you are probably wrong. There was most likely some sampling error causing $b_1$ to vary somewhat from $\beta_1$. No assurance can be taken that $\beta_1$ is indeed 1.636.

But with an interval estimate a desired degree of confidence can be chosen to accompany the estimate. It is possible to stipulate a level of confidence that the unknown parameter is bounded within that specified interval. Common levels of confidence are 90%, 95%, and 99%. There is nothing special about those levels; they are merely customary. If you are less than 90% confident in your conclusion, nobody's interested. You can't be 100% confident about your findings regarding a parameter unless you examine the entire population, and we have repeatedly noted the impracticality in that effort. So stated levels of confidence between 90% and 99% are archetypal.

There are two types of interval estimates we can apply to our regression model: the *conditional mean interval* and the *predictive interval*. Let's examine each in turn.

## ● Conditional Mean Interval

If we were to examine many observations in which $X$ is set equal to some given amount we would most likely find that the corresponding $Y$-values were not all the same. Supposed Arco traded with several nations all reporting, coincidentally, the same GDP of $3 trillion. Exports to these nations would probably all be different. Sales to one nation with GDP equal to $3 trillion might be $6,000 while those to a second country with the same GDP might total $4,000. Each of the countries, all with a GDP of $3 trillion, would likely import varying amounts from Arco.

The purpose of the interval for the conditional mean is to estimate the mean of all those different $Y$-values. The intent is to estimate the mean exports to all countries on the condition that each reports a GDP of $3 trillion. The interval is formed by first finding the estimated level of exports, $\hat{Y}$, based on a GDP of $3 trillion. This serves as the point estimate of exports. A certain amount is then added to that estimate to establish the upper bound of the interval and the same amount is subtracted to form the lower bound. Equation (3.1.1) illustrates:

$$\text{C.I. for } \mu_{Y|X} = \hat{Y} \pm (t_{\alpha,df})(S_Y) \tag{3.1.1}$$

estimates the mean of the many $Y$-values that result if $X$ is set equal to some given amount many times.

The term $\mu_{Y|X}$ is read "the mean value of $Y$ given $X$." It estimates the mean value of $Y$ for all observations on the condition that their $X$-value is some specific amount. In a moment we are going to estimate the mean exports to all nations with a GDP of $5 trillion. The $t$-value in Equation (3.1.1) is derived from the *t-distribution* which is used extensively when working with small samples. A sample is considered "small" if it has less than $n = 30$ observations as does our example with Arco. Legend has it that the $t$-distribution was developed by William S. Gosset (1876–1937) in 1908 when he worked as a master-brewer for Guinness in Dublin, Ireland. He was said to enjoy "tinkering with numbers for the sheer enjoyment." His employer had other ideas. He ordered Gosset to "cease his foolishness forthwith and avoid wasting energy on trivial matters else there would be dire consequences to pay." But Gosset could not forsake his passion. When he discovered this $t$-distribution he knew he dared not share it with others under his own name for fear of dismissal from his chosen profession, so as a loving student of numerology he published his work under the name of Student. Hence the term Student's $t$-distribution.[1]

Use of the $t$-distribution requires that a level of confidence somewhere between 90% and 99% be chosen by the researcher. An *alpha-value*, $\alpha$, is then established as $\alpha = (1 - \text{confidence level})$. In addition, a number of *degrees of freedom*, *df*, must also be determined. The degrees of freedom is equal to the number of observations used in the study minus the number of values those observations must generate. Suppose we have a ridiculously small data set just for the purpose of illustration of $n = 4$ observations. These four numbers must produce a mean of, say, 10. There will be $4 - 1 = 3$ degrees of freedom. You are free to choose any three numbers you want. But once that third number is chosen the fourth number is fixed if they are to yield a mean of 10. Suppose you freely choose 11, 12, and 9. Once the 9 is selected you are not free to choose the fourth. It *must* be 8 if the four numbers are to average 10. You lost one degree of freedom because of the need to average 10.

> The degrees of freedom associated with a statistical test is the number of observations in the sample data set, $n$, minus the number of values those observations must generate.

In a *simple* regression model the *df* will always be $n - 2$. You lose two degrees of freedom since, to get the regression line, you must generate two values—one for the intercept and one for the regression coefficient (slope).

$S_Y$ in Equation (3.1.1) is the *standard error of the conditional mean*, not to be confused with the standard error of the estimate, $S_e$, we calculated in Chapter 2! It recognizes that many different samples of some given size can be taken from any population. This point was made in Chapter 1 in our discussion of *sampling distributions*. It was noted that given a population of size $N$, the equation for combinations can be used to determine how many different samples of size $n$ can be selected as

$$C_n^N = \frac{N!}{n!(N-n)!}$$

(1.4.1)

The point is, each of those samples can produce different results for $b_0$ and $b_1$. Therefore, $\hat{Y}$ will vary based on what sample we randomly selected for the study. Had Arco by chance collected different elements in their sample, the OLS procedure would have produced different values for $b_0$ and $b_1$. The $\hat{Y}$ in Equation (3.1.1) would not have been the same and a different interval estimate would have resulted. The standard error of the conditional mean takes this fact of life into consideration and measures the variation in $\hat{Y}$ from one sample to the next. Equation (3.1.2) provides the standard error of the conditional mean:

$$S_Y = S_e \sqrt{\frac{1}{n} + \frac{(X_i - \bar{X})^2}{SS_X}}$$

(3.1.2)

$S_e$ is the standard error of the estimate we calculated in Chapter 2 to be 3.242. $X_i$ is the value of $X$ at which the interval is being estimated, which is going to be set at GDP = $5 trillion in our illustration below.

Given the $\alpha$-value and the $df$, the critical $t$-value is taken from the $t$-table in Appendix B at the end of the book. Alternatively, you can use Excel to find the critical $t$-values as shown in the appendix to Chapter 1.

Returning to our Arco illustration, the Chief Financial Officer (CFO) for the company wants to estimate the mean export level to many different countries with GDP of $5 trillion. There are several potential export markets in countries with GDP in the $5 trillion range. To develop these markets, the CFO feels it useful to estimate the mean exports the company might reasonably expect to ship to these countries. A 95% level of confidence is chosen. The alpha-value is $1 - 0.95 = 0.05$ or 5%. With $12 - 2 = 10$ degrees of freedom the $t$-table reveals the proper $t$-value is $t_{\alpha,df} = t_{.05,10} = 2.2281$.

Before Equation (3.1.1) can be used to create the interval, its components must be figured. If $X = 5$ ($5 trillion), the point estimate is

$$\hat{Y} = b_0 + b_1 X$$
$$= 7.494 + (1.636)(5)$$
$$= 15.674$$

Using Equation (3.1.2) the standard error of the conditional mean is

$$S_Y = 3.242\sqrt{\frac{1}{12} + \frac{(5 - 1.4761)^2}{29.888}} = 2.289$$

Equation (3.1.1) reveals the 95% confidence interval to be

$$\text{C.I. for } \mu_{Y|X} = 15.674 \pm (2.2281)(2.289)$$
$$10.57 \leq \mu_{Y|X} \leq 20.77$$

The CFO can now be 95% confident that the average exports to countries with GDPs of $5 trillion will be somewhere between $10,570 and $20,770. Knowledge such as this will prove very insightful and quite useful in deciding whether to pursue these prospective customers and how a sales campaign should be developed.

*Interpretation of the Interval for the Conditional Mean*

The CEO can be 95% confident that the *mean* exports to those nations with GDP of $5 trillion will fall between $10,570 and $20,770.

Now the bad news. It might be decided that the interval is too wide and doesn't offer the precision needed to make important decisions regarding a marketing campaign. The interval of 10.57 to 20.77 is rather broad and perhaps not precise enough to formulate critical business resolutions.

A narrower and more exact interval might better serve the cause. However, such an interval can be extracted only at a cost in confidence. If a 90% confidence interval were estimated, the appropriate $t$-value carries an alpha-value of 10% and, according to the $t$-table in Appendix B, would be $t_{0.10,10} = 1.8125$. Substituting this $t$-value for the 2.2281 used in the 95% interval yields

$$\text{C.I. for } \mu_{Y|X} = 15.674 \pm (1.8125)(2.289)$$

$$11.53 \leq \mu_{Y|X} \leq 19.82$$

This interval is narrower and offers greater precision. However, the CFO is now only 90% confident it is correct. He has less assurance that mean sales to countries with GDPs of $5 trillion would fall within this more well-defined range. Obviously, basing decisions on interval estimates requires a trade-off between precision and confidence. If the sample size is held constant, one can be gained only at the expense of the other.

### ● The Predictive Interval

The predictive interval provides an interval estimate of a *single* Y-value if $X$ takes on a given value only *once*.

> The interval for the conditional mean estimates the mean of all the Y-values that result when $X$ is set equal to a given amount many times. The predictive interval provides an interval estimate of the single Y-value that results when $X$ is set equal to some amount only once.

The predictive interval, $Y_X$, is estimated as

$$\text{C.I. for } Y_X = \hat{Y} \pm (t)(S_{Y_i}) \tag{3.1.3}$$

> Provides an interval estimate of a single Y-value if X is set equal to some amount only once.

$S_{Y_i}$ is the *standard error of the predictive interval*. Like the standard error of the conditional mean, it captures the tendency for estimates to vary among samples. The standard error of the predictive interval is found as

$$S_{Y_i} = S_e \sqrt{1 + \frac{1}{n} + \frac{(X_i - \bar{X})^2}{SS_X}} \tag{3.1.4}$$

In Arco's case it is

$$S_{Y_i} = 3.242 \sqrt{1 + \frac{1}{12} + \frac{(5 - 1.476)^2}{29.888}} = 3.969$$

The standard error of the predictive interval will always be greater than the standard error of the conditional mean:

$$S_{Y_i} > S_Y$$

This is because it is more difficult to estimate single, individual values than it is to estimate means. Individual values of a variable can be spread about over a large range. Means are more centrally located somewhere near the middle and are more easily estimated. Thus, you will always suffer a larger error in an attempt to estimate a single value. Given any set of conditions, the standard error of the predictive interval will always exceed the standard error of the conditional mean.

If we retain the 95% confidence level the $t$-value remains $t_{.05,10} = 2.2281$. The predictive interval is

$$\text{C.I. for } Y_X = 15.674 \pm (2.2281)(3.969)$$

$$6.83 \leq Y_X \leq 24.52$$

The CFO can be 95% confident that exports to any *single* nation with GDP equal to $5 trillion will be between $6,830 and $24,520. The interval is unfortunately much wider than that developed for the conditional mean. This results from the fact that, as just mentioned, errors encountered in an effort to estimate individual values will exceed those associated with an estimate of means. Thus, if we are to retain a 95% level of confidence, our interval must be wider. Nevertheless, this information can be extremely useful in formulating business plans and designing policy to direct the pending course of company activity.

*Interpretation for the Predictive Interval*

The CEO can be 95% confident that exports to a single nation with a GDP of $5 trillion will fall between $6,830 and $24,520.

---

**EXAMPLE 3.1: Interval Estimates for National Unemployment**

**Problem Statement:** In 2012 the International Monetary Fund (IMF) undertook a study of the changes in labor productivity as it related to national unemployment levels. Productivity is generally defined as "the ratio of a volume measure of output to a volume measure of input." Due to the serious economic climate that permeated many of the industrialized nations during that time it seemed wise to examine matters related to unemployment. Selected countries involved in the study are shown in the table. A regression model must be estimated and interval estimates of unemployment prepared.

*(Continued)*

**EXAMPLE 3.1: (Continued)**

| Country | Productivity $(X)$ | Unemployment $(Y)$ | $(X-\bar{X})^2$ | $(Y-\bar{Y})^2$ | $(X-\bar{X})(Y-\bar{Y})$ |
|---|---|---|---|---|---|
| United States | 8.2 | 9.6 | 5.881 | 5.476 | −5.675 |
| Canada | 11.45 | 7.1 | 0.681 | 0.026 | −0.132 |
| Australia | 12.4 | 5.2 | 3.151 | 4.244 | −3.657 |
| Japan | 12.6 | 4.8 | 3.901 | 6.052 | −4.859 |
| France | 10.3 | 9.4 | 0.106 | 4.58 | −0.695 |
| Germany | 11.4 | 7.2 | 0.601 | 0.004 | −0.047 |
| Italy | 10.7 | 8.6 | 0.006 | 1.796 | 0.1 |
| Netherlands | 12.75 | 4.5 | 4.516 | 7.618 | −5.865 |
| Sweden | 10.85 | 8.3 | 0.051 | 1.082 | 0.234 |
| United Kingdom | 5.6 | 7.9 | 25.251 | 0.41 | −3.216 |
| | | | $SS_X = 44.148$ | $SS_Y = 31.288$ | $SS_{XY} = -23.812$ |

Data from http://www.imf.org/external/data.htm#data

**Solution:** Regressing unemployment on productivity produced the following results:

$$\hat{U} = 12.99 - 0.539(Prod)$$

$$r^2 = 0.41, \; S_e = 1.52$$

Interestingly, this shows a negative relationship between productivity and unemployment. As productivity of the labor force rises, the unemployment rates fall. At this point the researcher should ponder the logic of the findings. Does economic theory support this result? Do these findings seem logical? Can these results be used to support or contradict earlier findings by other researchers? What do you think? Does it seem rational that as labor productivity increases, unemployment will fall?

Having answered these questions, let's find the 95% confidence interval for the conditional mean value for unemployment, given productivity is set at 10 many times. First we determine the point estimate as

$$\hat{U} = 12.99 - 0.539(10) = 7.6$$

At a 95% level of confidence with 8 degrees of freedom, $t_{.05,8} = 2.306$. Using Equation (3.1.2)

$$S_Y = 1.52\sqrt{\frac{1}{10} - \frac{(10 - 10.625)^2}{44.148}} = 0.5008$$

Then,

$$\text{C.I. for } \mu_{U|P=10} = 7.6 \pm (2.306)(0.5008)$$

$$6.442 \leq \mu_{U|P=10} \leq 8.7522$$

The predictive interval is found as

$$S_{Y_i} = S_e\sqrt{1 + \frac{1}{n} + \frac{(X - \bar{X})^2}{SS_x}}$$

$$= 1.52\sqrt{1 + \frac{1}{10} + \frac{(10 - 10.625)^2}{44.148}}$$

$$= 1.6006$$

Then,

$$\text{C.I. for } Y_x = 7.6 \pm (2.306)(1.6006)$$

$$3.91 \leq Y_x \leq 11.28$$

**Interpretation:** Researchers can be 95% confident that the mean unemployment level for many countries with a productivity measure of 10 would fall between 6.442 and 8.7522, while the unemployment of any one country with that productivity measure would report an unemployment rate between 3.91% and 11.28%.

## ● Factors that Affect the Width of the Interval

Logically, the narrower the interval the more useful and meaningful it is. If the interval is extremely wide and lacks any measure of precision then it fails to provide any useful information that might be of assistance in the decision-making process. It naturally follows that anything that can be done to narrow the interval width should be explored. There are several factors that determine the width of the interval. Each is examined here.

■ The width of an interval depends in part on how close $X_i$ is to the mean value of $X$. If the interval is calculated at a value of $X$ close to its mean it will be narrower and more precise. This results from the fact that regression analysis is based on means. Recall the main purpose of regression is to explain changes in $Y$ from its *mean*. Therefore, the choice of an $X$-value near the mean of all $X$-values in the data set will produce a more accurate, narrower interval.

> If an interval is estimated at a value of $X$ close to $\bar{X}$, it will be narrower and more exact than one with the same level of confidence that is formed for a value of $X$ farther from the mean.

■ In addition, as we saw earlier, a lower level of confidence will narrow the interval. The 95% conditional mean interval for Arco proved to be 10.57 to 20.77, while the 90% interval was narrower at 11.53 to 19.82. The constricted range in the second case adds greater precision to the estimate. Of course, the bad news is that there is now less confidence that the interval is correct—that it actually contains the true value for the conditional mean.

■ A larger sample will also add precision to the interval without changing the confidence level. As the sample size increases both the standard error of the conditional mean and the standard error of the predictive interval go down. (See Equations (3.1.2) and (3.1.4).) It's only logical that a larger sample size will produce smaller errors. Do you think you could get a better estimate of the average income of a population of 10,000 people with a sample size of 200 people or with a sample size of 9,999? Obviously, the larger sample will yield an estimate of $\mu$ with a much smaller sampling error. The smaller standard errors produce a narrower interval without a loss in confidence. Again, the bad news! It's going to take more time and money to collect the larger sample.

■ You can control these first three compelling factors by choosing a larger sample, tolerating a lower level of confidence, and developing the interval estimate at a value for $X$ closer to its mean. However, this last influence is beyond the control of the analyst. It centers on the variability of the original population. The greater the variation in the population under study, the larger must be the interval at any given level of confidence. If the population is quite spread out, estimation will prove to be more difficult. A wider interval will result if the analyst wishes to retain the same level of confidence. Conversely, if the population is less dispersed, an accurate estimate is more easily attained. A narrower interval can then provide the desired level of precision without sacrificing confidence.

## ● Confidence Interval for the Population Regression Coefficient, $\beta_1$

We recognize that $b_1$ is merely the point estimate of the population regression coefficient, $\beta_1$. Oftentimes we wish to construct an interval estimate to which we can apply some level of confidence.

An interval estimate for the regression coefficient, $b_1$, is obtained in a manner similar to that for the conditional mean and the predictive interval. Beginning with $b_1$ as the point estimate of $\beta_1$, we simply add and subtract an amount to produce the interval as seen in Equation (3.1.5):

$$\text{C.I. for } \beta_1 = b_1 \pm (t)(S_{b_1}) \tag{3.1.5}$$

$S_{b_1}$ is the *standard error of the regression coefficient*. Like all standard errors it reflects the tendency for different samples to report different results. It recognizes that the regression coefficient of $b_1 = 1.636$ that we use as our starting point to form the interval would have been different if a different sample was taken. The sample that we randomly used to attain $b_1$ is not the only possible sample in the sampling distribution. Had one of the other random samples been selected, a different value for $b_1$ would have resulted. The standard error of the regression coefficient accounts for this tendency.

The standard error of the regression coefficient, $S_{b_1}$, is calculated as

$$S_{b_1} = \frac{S_e}{\sqrt{SS_X}} \tag{3.1.6}$$

For Arco, we have

$$S_{b_1} = \frac{3.242}{\sqrt{29.888}} = 0.593$$

Using Equation (3.1.5), the 95% confidence interval for the population regression coefficient, $\beta_1$, is

$$\text{C.I. for } \beta_1 = 1.636 \pm (2.2281)(0.593)$$

$$0.314 \leq \beta_1 \leq 2.96$$

The CEO can be 95% confident that the true value of $\beta_1$ is between 0.314 and 2.96.

## ● Confidence Interval for the Correlation Coefficient, $\rho$

As with the regression coefficient, it's wise to provide an interval estimate of the correlation coefficient using Equation (3.1.7):

$$\text{C.I. for } \rho = r \pm (t)(S_r) \tag{3.1.7}$$

where $r$ is the sample correlation coefficient that serves as the point estimate of $\rho$. $S_r$ is the standard error of the correlation coefficient that, like all responsible standard errors, reminds us that the $r$ we calculated in Chapter 2 for Arco of 0.657 would have been different if a different sample had served as our data set. $S_r$ is determined as

$$S_r = \sqrt{\frac{1 - r^2}{n - 2}} \tag{3.1.8}$$

Arco's value is

$$S_r = \sqrt{\frac{1-(0.657)^2}{12-2}} = 0.238$$

Thus,

$$\text{C.I. for } \rho = 0.657 \pm (2.2281)(0.238)$$

$$0.126 \le \rho \le 1.188$$

Since $\rho$ cannot exceed 100%, the interval can be adjusted as $0.126 \le \rho \le 1.00$. Arco can operate with 95% confidence that the correlation between GDP and exports is between 0.126 and 1.00.

---

### EXAMPLE 3.2: Confidence Interval for the Regression Coefficient, $\beta_1$ and the Correlation Coefficient, $\rho$

**Problem Statement**: Returning to the IMF study from Example 3.1, it is now possible to construct confidence intervals for the regression coefficient in the model relating to unemployment and productivity. The analysts for the IMF can now determine the interval estimates as follows.

**Solution**: The standard error is found as

$$S_e = \sqrt{\frac{SS_Y - b_1(SS_{XY})}{n-2}} = \sqrt{\frac{31.288 - (-0.539)(-23.812)}{10-2}} = 1.5188$$

and using Equation (3.1.6),

$$S_{b_1} = \frac{S_e}{\sqrt{SS_X}}$$

Then, at the 95% level of confidence, Equations (3.1.5) and (3.1.6) produce

$$\text{C.I. for } \beta_1 = -0.539 \pm (2.306)\left(\frac{1.5188}{\sqrt{44.148}}\right)$$

$$-1.066 \le \beta_1 \le -0.01189$$

Furthermore, using the equation for the correlation coefficient given in Chapter 2, we find in our present case that

$$r = \frac{SS_{XY}}{\sqrt{(SS_X)(SS_Y)}} = \frac{-23.812}{\sqrt{(44.148)(31.288)}} = -0.6407$$

and Equation (3.1.8) yields

$$S_r = \sqrt{\frac{1-r^2}{n-2}}$$

Based on Equation (3.1.7), the confidence interval for $\rho$ is therefore

$$\text{C.I. for } \rho = r \pm t(S_r) = -0.6407 \pm (2.306)\left(\sqrt{\frac{1-(-0.6407)^2}{10-2}}\right)$$

$$-1.266 \le \rho \le -0.0144$$

**Interpretation**: Researchers for the IMF can be 95% confident that the regression coefficient that measures the change in unemployment given a one unit change in worker productivity is between −1.066 and −0.01189. For every one unit productivity rises, unemployment will decrease between 0.01189 and 1.066 percentage points.

Furthermore, the strength of the relationship between unemployment and productivity is gauged to be between −1.266 and −0.0144. Since the correlation between any two variables cannot be less than −1.00, the lower bound on the interval for $\rho$ can be raised from −1.266 to −1.00. The coefficient of determination for the model is estimated to be $r^2 = (-0.6407)^2$ or 0.4105.

## SECTION 3.1 PROBLEMS

1. In the effort to increase agricultural yield a commercial farming cooperative seeks to examine the relationship between fertilizer use and harvest levels. Ten farms across the agricultural belt in a rural area are surveyed. The number of times a stimulant was applied to the fields and the ensuing yield per acre are recorded to determine if treatments might explain changes in crop yield. The regression procedure returns these results:

| $n =$ | 10 | $SS_X =$ | 62.9 |
|---|---|---|---|
| $\bar{X} =$ | 6.1 | $SS_Y =$ | 392.15 |
| $\bar{Y} =$ | 24.21 | $SS_{XY} =$ | 133.59 |

If the application of 6 units of the chemical produces a mean yield of around 23 bushels the cooperative will use fertilizer on all its farms. Construct a 90% confidence interval for the conditional mean value to aid in the decision.

2. Using the data above what interval estimate would you report for a single farm?

3. Rapidly increasing labor costs at an electronics firm in Kansas City raises management's concerns regarding profit levels. A 40-week study using the number of employees to predict units of output resulted in this information:

| $n =$ | 40 | $SS_X =$ | 7106.78 |
|-------|------|----------|----------|
| $\bar{X} =$ | 25.925 | $SS_Y =$ | 5412173.98 |
| $\bar{Y} =$ | 483.725 | $SS_{XY} =$ | 151265.18 |

What is your 95% interval estimate for the mean value of output if 35 employees are on staff? What is your 95% predictive interval estimate if 35 employees are working? Why is there a difference in the intervals?

4. Using the data from problem 1 compute and interpret the 95% confidence interval for the regression coefficient and the correlation coefficient.

5. Using the data from problem 3 compute and interpret the 99% confidence interval for the regression coefficient and the correlation coefficient.

6. A large retail chain throughout Great Britain requires their associates to attend a training seminar to improve their knowledge of commercial operations. A sample of 13 employees are tested before and after the training program. The improvement in their test scores and the number of hours of training are shown below.

| $n =$ | 13 | $SS_X =$ | 174.24 |
|-------|------|----------|----------|
| $\bar{X} =$ | 8.2 | $SS_Y =$ | 1888.3 |
| $\bar{Y} =$ | 34.769 | $SS_{XY} =$ | −448.4 |

A. What conclusions can you draw about the effectiveness of the training?
B. Develop 98% confidence intervals for the conditional mean and the predictive interval for 7 hours of training. Interpret the results.
C. Construct 95% intervals for $\beta_1$ and $\rho$. Interpret the results.

## 3.2 HYPOTHESIS TESTING: CHECKING FOR STATISTICAL SIGNIFICANCE

The regression coefficient for Arco's GDP/Exports model of $b_1 = 1.636$ is the statistical estimate of the unknown population regression coefficient, $\beta_1$. The non-zero value suggests that there is a relationship between a nation's GDP and its imports from Arco. But these results are based only on sample data. Could it be that at the population level there is no relationship and $\beta_1$ is actually zero? If so, perhaps sampling error has produced a misleading model and any decisions based on these results could lead to unfortunate consequences. This addresses the question posed in the introduction to this chapter as to whether our data are "lying" to us.

We must test the hypothesis that $\beta_1$ is indeed zero and no relationship exists between $X$ and $Y$. This allows us to derive some conclusion as to the significance of our findings. Sample findings are said to be *statistically significant* if they are unlikely to have occurred due to sampling error. For example, we might hypothesize that the mean income in thousands of dollars for all consumers in a market is $\mu = 90$. To test this hypothesize a sample of consumers may produce a mean of $\overline{X} = 91$. This small difference might be due merely to sampling error. It is quite possible to enter a population where $\mu = 90$ and come out with a sample mean of $\overline{X} = 91$ as a result of sampling error. Just due to the luck of the draw in collecting our sample we might have selected more consumers with incomes slightly in excess of the population mean. This difference between our hypothesized population mean of $\mu = 90$ and the sample mean of 91 is thought to be statistically *in*significant because it can be explained away on the basis of sampling error.

However, a sample mean of 95 or 99 or 110 might call into question the original hypothesis that $\mu = 90$. Such large differences are not likely to be the result of mere sampling error. They could be deemed statistically significant in that we are unlikely to suffer such a large error in the sampling process. This would lead to a rejection of the hypothesis $\mu = 90$. We might conclude that the reason the sample mean was so large is because the sample was taken from a population in which the mean was greater than 90.

> Findings are statistically significant if they are not likely to occur due to sampling error. That is, if the findings cannot be explained away on the basis of sampling error they are taken as significant. If the probability of their occurrence is too small to attribute to sampling error, they are said to be statistically significant.

With this crucial perception of "statistical significance" we can more fully appreciate the contribution hypothesis testing offers to the practice of statistical analysis. We begin with a test for the population regression coefficient.

## ● Hypothesis Test for the Population Regression Coefficient, $\beta_1$

If Arco's $\beta_1$ is zero no linear relationship exists between GDP and exports. However, the non-zero $b_1$ of 1.636 suggests that a statistical link does exist. But is this finding statistically significant? Could it be that $\beta_1$ is zero and the $b_1$ of 1.636 is due to sampling error? To answer that all-important question we must test the hypothesis that $\beta_1 = 0$ given the Arco results.

There are four steps to a hypothesis test. The first is to clearly state the set of hypotheses as:

$$H_0: \beta_1 = 0$$
$$H_a: \beta_1 \neq 0$$

"$H_0$:" is the *null* hypothesis that is being tested. It will either be (1) rejected or (2) not rejected.

"$H_a$:" is the *alternative* hypothesis and is included in the event the null is rejected.

The second step to the hypothesis test is to calculate the test statistic. In this case, the test is based on a *t*-test, since the sample is less than 30.

The *t*-test is expressed as

$$t_{test} = \frac{b_1 - \beta_1}{S_{b_1}} = \frac{b_1 - \beta_1}{\dfrac{S_e}{\sqrt{SS_X}}} \qquad (3.2.1)$$

Recall, the $S_{b_1}$ is the *standard error of the regression coefficient* and is found using Equation (3.1.6) as the standard error of the estimate divided by the square root of $SS_X$.

The third step of the hypothesis test is to formulate a *decision rule* that directs us to either reject or not reject the null hypothesis. The decision rule is based on critical *t*-values taken from the *t*-table given our chosen alpha-value, $\alpha$, and the number of degrees of freedom. The alpha-value is the *level of significance* associated with the test. These critical *t*-values are compared with the $t_{test}$ values calculated with Equation (3.2.1). Finally, the fourth and final step is to state your findings and conclusion.

You can never "accept" a null hypothesis. You can only "reject" or "not reject." Even if the sample findings exactly equal the hypothesized value of the parameter, this does not provide proof that the null is correct. Sampling error may have produced a sample value that just coincidentally happens to equal the hypothesized value of the parameter.

Testing a hypothesis is often compared to putting a person on trial. If the evidence is not strong enough to precipitate a guilty verdict, the defendant is found "not guilty." A verdict of "innocent" is never registered. In similar fashion, if the difference between the hypothesized value of the parameter and the sample findings is not sufficient to reject the null, the only conclusion is to not reject. That is, if the sample results are not statistically significant the null is not rejected.

To recap, the four steps needed to complete a hypothesis test are:

1. State the set of hypotheses.

2. Calculate the test statistic.

3. State the decision rule.

4. Note the findings and conclusion.

Let's apply these steps to the Arco example. The estimate of $\beta_1$ was $b_1 = 1.636$. We want to determine how likely it is that we could obtain these results if $\beta_1$ was zero. That is, could it be that our sample suggests a non-zero relationship between GDP and exports even though none really exists at the population level and the true beta coefficient, $\beta_1$, is actually zero?

The first step is to state the hypotheses. Since we are testing whether $\beta_1$ is zero, the hypotheses are

$$H_0: \beta_1 = 0$$

$$H_a: \beta_1 \neq 0$$

Using Equation (3.2.1), we can complete the second step of the hypothesis test by calculating our test statistic. In Chapter 2 Arco found that $S_e = 3.242$ and $SS_X = 29.888$.

Thus,

$$t_{test} = \frac{1.636 - 0}{\dfrac{3.242}{\sqrt{29.888}}} = 2.758$$

The third step of establishing the decision rule requires that we identify critical $t$-values to compare with our $t_{test}$ of 2.758 as demonstrated in Figure 3.1. These $t$-values are critical in that if the null hypothesis is true they are unlikely to occur due merely to sampling error. Suppose we decide to test the hypothesis at a level of significance of $\alpha = 5\%$. Recall that in a simple regression model the degrees of freedom are $n - 2$. In Arco's case that becomes $12 - 2 = 10$. The $t$-table in Appendix B reveals the critical $t$-values to be $t_{.05,10} = \pm 2.2281$. These values cut off $\alpha/2 = 0.025$ of the area under the curve in each tail. The decision rule is therefore:

Do not reject the null hypothesis if the $t_{test}$ value is between $\pm 2.2281$. Reject otherwise

The reasoning is simple. If the null is true and $\beta_1 = 0$, there is *only* a 5% chance the $t_{test}$ value could be less than $-2.2281$ or greater than $+2.2281$. Of all the possible samples we could take, only 5% of them would produce a $b_1$ value that would yield a $t_{test}$ outside the range of $\pm 2.2281$. So, if $t_{test}$ is greater than $+2.2281$ or less than $-2.2281$, it's unlikely $\beta_1$ is zero and the null should be rejected. That's why the areas outside $\pm 2.2281$ are marked as rejection regions in Figure 3.1 and the area within those bounds is the Do Not Reject (DNR) region.

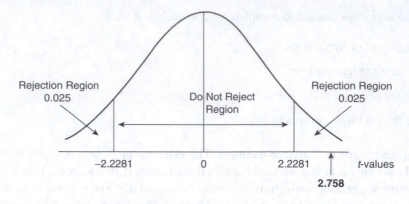

Rejection Region
0.025

Do Not Reject
Region

Rejection Region
0.025

−2.2281            0            2.2281            *t*-values

**2.758**

■ **Figure 3.1**   Hypothesis Testing Based on *t*-Values

> The decision rule for a hypothesis test is based on probability. If the probability is 'small' that the $t_{test}$ value could have been obtained if the null were true, then it's unlikely $\beta_1$ is zero and the null should be rejected.

The final stage in our hypothesis test is to note our findings and state our conclusion. Clearly, the $t_{test}$ value of 2.758 is in the right-tailed rejection region. We thereby reject the null that $\beta_1$ is zero and conclude that our model does carry statistical significance. If $\beta_1$ were zero there would be only a 2.5% chance we could take a sample that would yield a $b_1$ that would produce a *t*-value greater than 2.2281. The value of $t = 2.758$ is unlikely to occur if $\beta_1 = 0$. More likely, the reason $b_1$ was so large is because the sample was taken from a population with a $\beta_1$ greater than zero. The null is rejected and it is concluded that $\beta_1 \neq 0$. A relationship between GDP and exports does exist!

> There is *only* a 2.5% chance that if $\beta_1$ is 0 we could get a sample that could produce a $b_1$ that would yield a *t*-value from Equation (3.2.1) greater than 2.2281. Since we got a *t*-value greater than 2.2281, chances are $\beta_1$ is *not* zero and the null should be rejected.

● **The Meaning of the "Level of Significance"**

In conducting a hypothesis test there are two ways in which you may commit an error. You can (1) reject a true hypothesis or (2) fail to reject a false hypothesis. Either way you have erred.

Rejecting a true hypothesis is called a Type I error. The probability of a Type I error is the alpha-value at which the test is conducted:

$$P(\text{Type I}) = \alpha$$

Look at Figure 3.1. Assuming the null is correct and $\beta_1$ is zero, what would cause you to reject the null thereby committing a Type I error? You would do so if your $t_{\text{test}}$ was less than $-2.2281$ or more than $2.2281$. What is the probability of that happening? There is a 5% chance that if $\beta_1$ is zero you could still get a $b_1$ value that, based on Equation (3.2.1), would produce a $t$-value in either rejection region. Hence, the probability you would incorrectly reject the null is 5%— equal to the alpha-value.

The lower the alpha-value, the less likely you are to suffer a Type I error. Therefore, if you reject the null hypothesis at a low alpha-value, the probability you committed an error in doing so is small. A test that results in a rejection at a low alpha-value is said to be more significant than if the rejection occurred at a higher alpha-value because the probability of a Type I error is less.

> The *lower* the alpha-value the *more* significant your findings are. The alpha-value of a test is the probability of committing a Type I error. If the alpha-value is low, the probability of suffering a Type I error is low. Thus, if you reject a null hypothesis when $\alpha$ is set at a lower value, the more likely you are correct in doing so. That is, the more significant your findings.

## ● The Hypothesis Test for the Population Correlation Coefficient, $\rho$

The hypothesis test for the population correlation coefficient, $\rho$, is conducted in much the same manner as that for $\beta_1$. The sample correlation coefficient was $r = 0.657$, thereby suggesting a relationship between GDP and exports. But the same caution applies as in the case of $\beta_1$. Could it be that at the population level the true value of $\rho$ is zero and due to sampling error our sample is misleading?

This critical issue must be addressed by testing the hypothesis that $\rho = 0$. The same four steps are followed starting with a statement of the hypotheses:

$$H_0: \rho = 0$$
$$H_a: \rho \neq 0$$

The $t$-test is conducted using Equation (3.2.2):

$$t_{\text{test}} = \frac{r - \rho}{S_r} = \frac{r - \rho}{\sqrt{\dfrac{1 - r^2}{n - 2}}} \qquad (3.2.2)$$

$S_r$ is the *standard error of the sampling distribution*. It measures the tendency for the sample correlation coefficient, $r$, to vary from the true population correlation coefficient, $\rho$.

Based on Arco's data we have

$$t_{test} = \frac{0.675 - 0}{\sqrt{\dfrac{1 - (0.675)^2}{12 - 2}}} = 2.758$$

We get the same $t_{test}$ value as we did with the test for $\beta_1$. This will always happen with a simple regression model. However, this is not the case in the next chapter dealing with multiple regression models. So it's wise to examine both tests in preparation for the more complex application of regression and correlation.

If we retain the level of significance of $\alpha = 5\%$, the same critical $t$-values apply as those in the test for $\beta_1$. Figure 3.1 applies in this test of $\rho$ as well. The decision rule remains

Do not reject the null hypothesis if the $t_{test}$ value is between ±2.2281. Reject otherwise

As with the test for $\beta_1$, we reject the null that $\rho = 0$. We conclude that GDP serves as a predictor for exports.


## SECTION 3.2 PROBLEMS

1.  Six military teams repeatedly practice a secret operation in order to perfect their performance and minimize the time required to complete the "black ops." Below are the number of times each team carried out the operation and the time in minutes each took after their final training mission.

| Team | Number of Training Missions | Completion Times |
|:---:|:---:|:---:|
| 1 | 25 | 5.3 |
| 2 | 14 | 7.5 |
| 3 | 35 | 3.2 |
| 4 | 9 | 8.9 |
| 5 | 11 | 7 |
| 6 | 19 | 6.3 |

A.  Compute the regression model and comment on what it reveals.
B.  Compute and plot the residuals.
C.  Plot the actual completion times on the same graph as the predicted (fitted) values for completion time.
D.  Test the significance of the regression coefficient at the 5% level.

2. Employees at Dundee Products are put through a training program to enhance productivity. Given the expense of the training management wants to determine productivity levels after training. Eleven workers are subjected to the hours of training shown in the table and their levels of productivity are measured. Notice that the last four employees had the same training but their outputs varied. This denotes the tendency for $Y$ to vary around some mean, given a fixed value of $X$, as we have so often mentioned before.

| $X$ Hours | $Y$ Output |
|---|---|
| 12 | 88 |
| 14 | 101 |
| 25 | 125 |
| 32 | 198 |
| 9 | 57 |
| 18 | 135 |
| 16 | 114 |
| 14 | 101 |
| 14 | 95 |
| 14 | 110 |
| 14 | 101 |

Regressing output ($Y$) on training hours ($X$) produces these results:

| | | | |
|---|---|---|---|
| $n=$ | 11 | $SS_S=$ | 422.73 |
| $\bar{X}=$ | 16.54545455 | $SS_Y=$ | 12350.55 |
| $\bar{Y}=$ | 111.3636364 | $SS_{XY}=$ | 2127.82 |

A. Plot the data with Output on the vertical axis. Does there appear to be a linear relationship?

B. Test the hypothesis that the population coefficient for Hours equals zero at the 1% level.

3. An economist for the Federal Department of Welfare examines data for several families to identify determinants of consumption expenditures. As seen in the table, data are collected on monthly spending in hundreds of dollars along with the number of children in the family and age of the head of household.

| Children | Age | Expenditures |
|---|---|---|
| 3 | 36 | 5.2 |
| 6 | 52 | 9 |
| 0 | 47 | 3.2 |
| 2 | 32 | 5 |
| 5 | 58 | 9.5 |
| 6 | 35 | 11 |
| 1 | 21 | 3.5 |
| 0 | 19 | 2 |
| 6 | 32 | 11 |
| 3 | 39 | 6.5 |
| 4 | 41 | 8 |

Regressing Expenditures on Children produced these results:

| $n =$ | 11 | $SS_X =$ | 54.18 |
|---|---|---|---|
| $\bar{X} =$ | 3.272727273 | $SS_Y =$ | 101.56 |
| $\bar{Y} =$ | 6.718181818 | $SS_{XY} =$ | 72.25 |

The model using Age as a predictor for Expenditure resulted in

| $n =$ | 11 | $SS_X =$ | 1418.73 |
|---|---|---|---|
| $\bar{X} =$ | 37.45454545 | $SS_Y =$ | 101.56 |
| $\bar{Y} =$ | 6.718181818 | $SS_{XY} =$ | 178.71 |

Determine if either explanatory variable is significant at the 5% level. Which would you suggest be used to predict mean expenditures?

4. Given the data in problem 1 above, test the hypothesis that $\rho = 0$ at $\alpha = .05$. Compare these results to those obtained in problem 1.

5. Repeat problem 2 as a test for $\rho = 0$. Compare the results to those from problem 2. Why are the results the same?

6. Test the hypotheses for Children and Age for $\rho$ given the information in problem 3.

## 3.3 LARGE SAMPLES AND THE STANDARD NORMAL DISTRIBUTION

Gosset's $t$-distribution is used when the sample size is less than 30 and in the likely event the population standard deviation, $\sigma$, is unknown. If the sample size exceeds 30, which is a very common occurrence in statistical analysis, it is possible to use the standard normal distribution, or $Z$-distribution. This conversion can be made because as the sample size increases the $t$-distribution approaches the $Z$-distribution. Recall that the $Z$-distribution has a variance of 1, while that of the $t$-distribution is

$$\sigma^2 = \frac{n-1}{n-3}$$

As $n$ gets bigger the difference between the numerator and the denominator becomes less significant and the variance approaches 1 like that of the $Z$-distribution. Figure 3.2 shows that

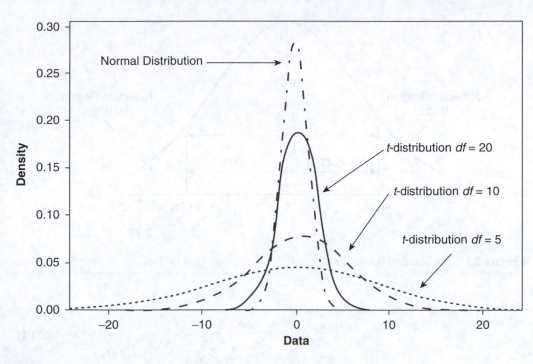

**■ Figure 3.2**   A Comparison of the Normal Distribution and the *t*-Distribution

as the sample size goes up and the degrees of freedom increase, the *t*-distribution begins to take on the same shape of that of the normal distribution. When the size of the sample reaches 30 the difference between the *t*-distribution and the *Z*-distribution is essentially inconsequential and we can use *Z*-values in our calculations.

As an illustration, presume Arco had over 30 observations instead of 12, thereby permitting use of the *Z*-distribution. The exact number doesn't matter as long as it's a "large" sample, i.e., greater than 30. Retain the $\alpha$-value of 5% to allow a comparison with the *t*-tests just completed. The standard normal distribution table in Appendix B provides the critical *Z*-values. Figure 3.3 illustrates its use. You can also use the information in the appendix to Chapter 1 to find the proper *Z*-values.

The normal distribution table in Appendix B shows values for the area under the curve from the mean to some value above or below it. Since the curve is symmetrical around the mean of zero[2] both areas are equal. If the alpha-value of 0.05 is evenly divided in the two tails of the distribution, that leaves 95% of the area in the middle. One-half of that, 0.95/2 = 0.4750, is above the mean and one-half is below the mean of zero. Since the *Z*-table in Appendix B is configured to give an area from the mean to some *Z*-value above or below it, we must look in the *Z*-table for an area of 0.4750. This entry corresponds to critical *Z*-values of ±1.96. As with the *t*-test, if $\beta_1$ is zero there is only a 5% chance our sample could yield a *Z*-value outside that range. Equation (3.3.1) is then used to compute the *Z*-test value.

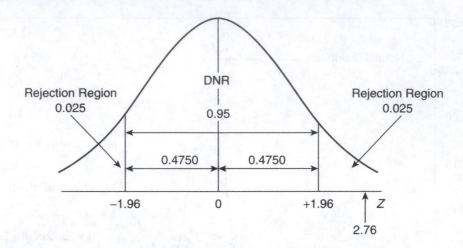

■ **Figure 3.3**  The Standard Normal Distribution

$$Z_{\text{test}} = \frac{b_1 - \beta_1}{S_{b_1}} = \frac{b_1 - \beta_1}{\dfrac{S_e}{\sqrt{SS_x}}} \qquad (3.3.1)$$

$$Z_{\text{test}} = \frac{1.636 - 0}{\dfrac{3.242}{\sqrt{29.888}}} = 2.758$$

Again, we get the same value for the test statistic of 2.758. However, now, with a large sample, the test value is compared to a critical Z-value of 1.96 rather than the t-values of 2.2281. We see from Figure 3.3 the Z-test statistic of 2.758 falls in the right-tailed rejection region just as it did with the t-test.

The test for the population correlation coefficient, $\rho$, is conducted in similar fashion. Equation (3.2.2) is used by replacing the t-values with the appropriate Z-values when working with large samples.

The reason the conversion to the Z-distribution is made is because the Z-table is easier for us to read than is the t-table. The latter is more discontinuous with large gaps requiring that approximations be made to complete the hypothesis test. It should be noted that in using computers to perform the tests, t-values are consistently reported. Computers do not suffer from human frailties, and have no trouble interpreting t-tables.

## 3.4 THE p-VALUE AND ITS ROLE IN INFERENTIAL ANALYSIS

It's often argued that the p-value is another way of testing a hypothesis. But it's more than that. The p-value of your hypothesis test tells you just how significant your findings are. It is referred to as the *significance level of your test*. The *lower* the *p*-value, the *more* significant are your findings. It measures the probability of obtaining test results at least as extreme as those that resulted from the hypothesis test if the null is indeed true. The *p*-value is:

■ the lowest level of significance (lowest alpha-value) you can set and still reject the null hypothesis;

■ found as the area under the distribution curve (*t*- or Z-curve) beyond your sample findings.

As just noted, the normal curve is a bit easier to work with since the *t*-table is so discontinuous. The large gaps in the entries in the *t*-table make it difficult to use in determining the *p*-value. Using the Z-table to introduce the *p*-value is therefore a more practical way to approach this all-important subject.

Consider Figure 3.4. To find the *p*-value it is first necessary to determine the area under the normal curve beyond the Z-test value of 2.76 produced by your sample findings. Remember, the table provides the area between the mean Z-value of 0 and some value above or below it. From the Z-table we observe that a Z-value of 2.76 carries an entry of 0.4971.

As defined above, the *p*-value is the area in the tail *beyond* our sample findings of $Z = 2.76$. Since one-half of the total area under the curve is to the right of $Z = 0$, the area in the tail beyond $Z = 2.76$ is $0.5000 - 0.4971 = 0.0029$. This value must then be multiplied by two, since this is a two-tailed test. There is a rejection region in both tails. When the rejection regions were established, the alpha-value was evenly divided in the two tails. To offset that division

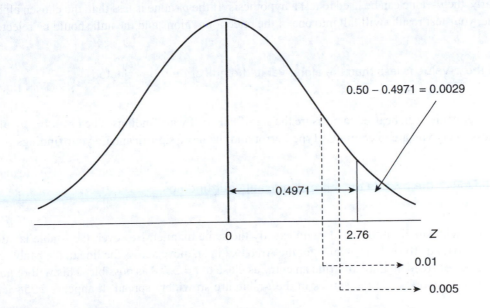

■ **Figure 3.4**  Finding the *p*-Value

we must now multiply by two. The actual $p$-value is then determined as $0.0029 \times 2 = 0.0058$, or 0.58%.

This measures the level of significance of the test. The lower the $p$-value, the more significant your findings. It is said that your findings are significant at "less than 1%." Recall that the alpha-value is the probability of committing a Type I error. In our present case with Arco, that probability is only 0.58%—less than 1%. In rejecting the null you can feel quite confident that you have not committed a Type I error.

This is also the lowest alpha-value you can set and still reject the null. You can lower the alpha-value down to less than 1% and your sample findings of 2.76 are still in the rejection region. If you were to set an alpha-value of 2%, then 1%, or 0.01, would be in the right-tailed rejection region (the other half is in the left-tailed rejection region). Since $0.01 > 0.0029$, the sample results of $Z = 2.76$ would remain in the rejection area.

If the alpha-value was lowered still further to 1%, then 0.005 would form the rejection region. Still, the findings of $Z = 2.79$ would fall in the rejection region. This would continue until the alpha-value was set so low that an area less than 0.0029 formed the right-tailed rejection region, forcing the findings of $Z = 2.76$ into the Do Not Reject region.

> The lower the $p$-value, the lower you can set the alpha-value and still reject the null. Since the alpha-value is the probability of a Type I error, the lower the $p$-value, the less likely you are to commit a Type I error and the more significant your findings when the null is rejected.

Clearly, the $p$-value can be used to test a hypothesis. If the $p$-value is less than the chosen alpha-value, your test results will fall into one of the rejection regions and the null should be rejected.

> If the $p$-value is less than the alpha-value the null should be rejected.

However, it also can be used to measure the significance of your findings. The lower the $p$-value the less likely you are to commit a Type I error and the more significant are your findings.

> The lower the $p$-value the more significant your findings.

Working with small samples is done in exactly the same manner. However, the $t$-table is more difficult to read. To find the $p$-value for the Arco example, move across the line in the $t$-table for 10 degrees of freedom until you find an entry as close to $t = 2.758$ as possible. This will require a bit of guesswork since the entries in the $t$-table are so widely spread. It appears 2.758 falls somewhere between the alpha-values shown at the top of the columns of 0.05 and 0.02—much closer to 0.02. With the small sample you can lower the alpha-value down to about 2% and still reject the null. That would mean there is a 2% chance of committing a Type I error with the small sample. There was only a 0.58% chance of doing so if you had a larger sample. The larger sample naturally offered a smaller potential for error.

Excel can be used to find the *p*-value instead of attempting to estimate using the table. Simply enter in any cell

$$=TDIST(ABS(2.758),10,2)$$

where ABS gives the absolute value of the *p*-value, 2.758 is the *t*-value, 10 is the number of degrees of freedom, and 2 signifies it's a two-tailed test. Excel responds with 0.020019 or just over 2%. If the *t*-test is used in conjunction with a large sample of say $n = 50$, we have

$$=TDIST(ABS(2.758),50,2)$$

Excel then returns 0.008100. Notice the *p*-value is lower with the larger sample. It is possible to set the alpha-value of the test at a lower level and still avoid a Type I error with a large sample.

## ● How to Detect and Interpret an Extremely Small *p*-Value

An aberration may seem to occur if the *p*-value is especially small. There may result some confusion in attempting to determine the significance of your test. Assume you are working with a sample with 15 degrees of freedom and encounter a *t*-value of, say, 3.973. To determine the *p*-value, go to the *t*-table and find the line for 15 d.f. As you move from left to right looking for 3.973 notice what is happening to the alpha-value for two-tailed tests at the top of the table. The alpha-values that measure the area in the tail of the *t*-distribution, and hence gauge the *p*-values, are getting smaller. This continues until in the last column the *t*-value is only 2.947— still short of your 3.973. But the alpha-value at the head of the column has decreased all the way down to 0.01. If we could move past that last column the $\alpha$-values would be even smaller and the *p*-value would continue its decline. Beyond an alpha-value of 0.01 we can conclude that the *p*-value is "virtually zero" and we can reject the null hypothesis with highly significant findings.

> As the *t*-value increases, the area in the tail beyond that *t*-value, and hence the *p*-value, continues to decline. Beyond an alpha-value of 0.01 the *p*-value is considered to be zero.

## SECTION 3.4 PROBLEMS

1. Use a graph to explain why the null should be rejected if the $p$-value is less than the alpha-value that was chosen to test the hypothesis.

2. Use a graph to illustrate why the $p$-value is the lowest alpha-value you can set and still reject the null. Why does a larger $p$-value indicate the null should not be rejected?

3. The $p$-value is found as the area under the curve beyond your sample finding. By means of a graph, explain how and why this statement is true.

4. Rampart Motors has estimated a model intended to explain the purchase price of a customer's new automobile on the basis of his or her income. Results of the study are shown here. Both income and price are stated in thousands of dollars.

| $n =$ | 55 | $SS_X =$ | 642067.71 |
|---|---|---|---|
| $\bar{X} =$ | 185.47 | $SS_Y =$ | 23639.66 |
| $\bar{Y} =$ | 35.5564 | $SS_{XY} =$ | 111070.93 |

A. Estimate the average price of a car for someone with an income of 120 (thousand dollars).
B. Test the hypothesis that $\beta_1 = 0$ at the 5% level. Use either $Z$ or $t$-values, since this is a large sample. What is your conclusion?
C. Calculate the $p$-value associated with the test. How does it compare with the $\alpha$-value?

5. A study by the Organisation for Economic Co-operation and Development (OECD) compared the educational achievement of students in several countries. Among others, the study acquired data from the United Kingdom, France, Germany, Italy, Brazil, the U.S., Spain, Canada, and Denmark. The entire study can be found at

   http://www.oecd.org/document/52/0,3746,en_2649_39263238_45897844_1_1_1_1,00.html

A sample of these countries was taken and their international rankings were regressed on per capita GDP. Based on the results shown here, does there appear to be a relationship between the two variables at any acceptable level of significance? What conclusion can you draw from these results?

| $n =$ | 26 | $SS_X =$ | 6440937.12 |
|---|---|---|---|
| $\bar{X} =$ | 289.731 | $SS_Y =$ | 8766.30 |
| $\bar{Y} =$ | 30.169 | $SS_{XY} =$ | 37742.38 |

6. The OECD from the previous problem also regressed educational attainment of a nation's students on the length of the school year measured in weeks. Given the results seen here, $n = 11$, $b_1 = 1.3214$, $S_{b_1} = 0.1215$, standard error of the estimate is $S_e = 1.789$, and $SS_X = 216.91$:

   A. Can you conclude at the 5% level that the longer school years are associated with higher average attainment levels?
   B. What is the lowest level of significance at which the null can be rejected?

7. An investment analyst in Madrid uses earnings per share to estimate dividend payments by 51 firms listed on the Bolsa de Madrid (Madrid Stock Exchange) and finds these results: $b_1 = 2.1013$, $S_{b_1} = 0.17299$, $S_e = 2.3183$, and $SS_X = 216.91$.

   Would you advise him to use the resulting model to estimate dividends? Why or why not?

## 3.5 COMPUTER APPLICATIONS

With the conceptual understanding of the statistical underpinnings of regression and correlation provided by the manual work performed in the chapter, we can now simplify the arithmetic task by using the computer to perform the computations. The uses of Excel, PASW, and Minitab to analyze the Arco analysis are demonstrated here.

### ● Using Excel

Follow the steps in Chapter 2 to produce Excel Output 1.

**Excel Output 1**

| 16 | Coefficients | Standard Error | t Stat | P-value | Lower 95% | Upper 95% |
|---|---|---|---|---|---|---|
| 17 Intercept | 7.493897308 | 1.281408712 | 5.84817103 | 0.00016201 | 4.638740784 | 10.34905383 |
| 18 GDP(X) | 1.635981496 | 0.593045531 | 2.758610279 | 0.020177863 | 0.314593714 | 2.957369278 |

As we saw in Chapter 2, the model is $\widehat{Ex} = 7.494 + 1.636GDP$. More to the point for our current work here in Chapter 3, Excel reports a standard error of the regression coefficient, $b_1$, of 0.593, a $t$-value of 2.7586, and a $p$-value of 0.0201, just as we calculated throughout the chapter. The 95% confidence limits for $b_1$ are shown to be 0.0202 and 2.957 and are also in accord with our earlier computations. To get other levels of confidence, check "Confidence Level" shown in the Window of Excel Output 2 and enter the desired level of confidence in the "%" window.

**Excel Output 2**

Regression

### Input

Input Y Range: $B$1:$B$13

Input X Range: $A$1:$A$13

☑ Labels ☐ Constant is Zero

☑ Confidence Level: 95 %

### Output options

○ Output Range:

● New Worksheet Ply:

○ New Workbook

### Residuals

☑ Residuals ☐ Residual Plots

☐ Standardized Residuals ☐ Line Fit Plots

### Normal Probability

☐ Normal Probability Plots

OK

Cancel

Help

● **Using Minitab**

Enter the data as seen in Minitab Worksheet 1.

### Minitab Worksheet 1

Worksheet 1 ***

| ↓ | C1 | C2 |
|---|------|------|
|   | GDP(X) | EXPORTS(Y) |
| 1 | 2.580 | 13.7 |
| 2 | 1.470 | 7.5 |
| 3 | 0.742 | 8.6 |
| 4 | 1.570 | 14.2 |
| 5 | 0.204 | 8.2 |
| 6 | 0.086 | 2.1 |
| 7 | 2.060 | 13.6 |
| 8 | 5.880 | 13.2 |
| 9 | 0.239 | 6.9 |
| 10 | 0.218 | 6.1 |
| 11 | 0.414 | 9.2 |
| 12 | 2.247 | 15.6 |

Click on Stat > Regression > Regression. Minitab Window 1 appears. After selecting the response and predictors variables, hit OK.

**Minitab Window 1**

Return to Minitab Window 1. Select "Options." Minitab Window 2 appears. To obtain interval estimates for the conditional mean and the predictive interval, check the options as

Minitab Output 1 appears showing the model with its coefficients. The standard error of the regression coefficient as we calculated it, $S_{b_1} = 0.593$, is also reported. The $t$-value and $p$-value of 2.76 and 0.020 can be seen.

**Minitab Output 1**

Regression Analysis: EXPORTS($Y$) versus GDP($X$)

```
The regression equation is

EXPORTS(Y) = 7.49 + 1.64 GDP(X)

Predictor    Coef   SE Coef     T       P
Constant     7.494    1.281   5.85   0.000
GDP(X)       1.6360   0.5930   2.76   0.020
```

Return to Minitab Window 1. Select "Options." Minitab Window 2 appears. To obtain interval estimates for the conditional mean and the predictive interval, check the options as indicated. Enter 5 in the window for "Predictions for New Observations" and 95 in the Confidence level space to match the work we did in the chapter. Other values may be entered if desired.

**Minitab Window 2**

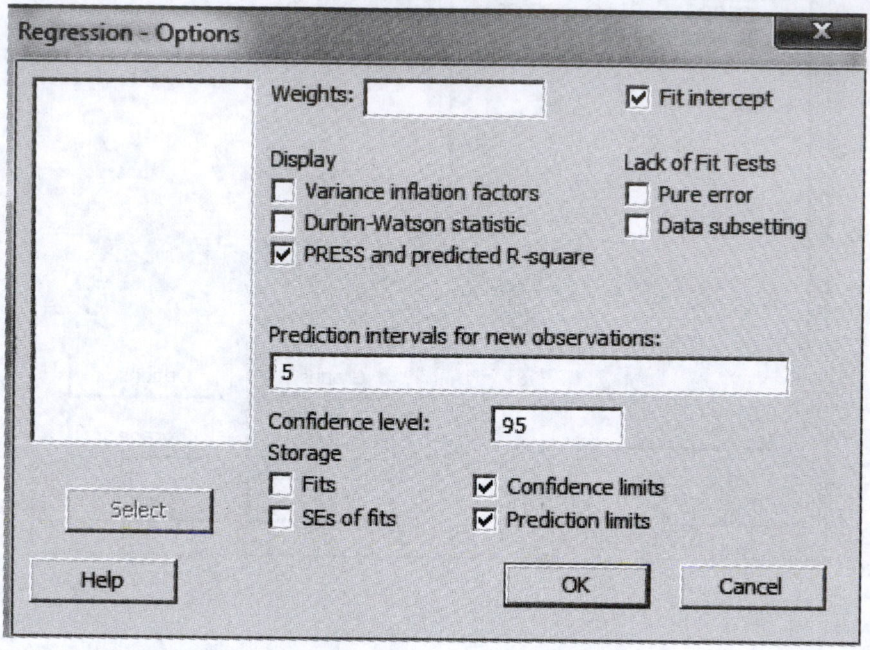

Click OK > OK. Minitab Output 2 produces the interval estimates we calculated earlier.

## Minitab Output 2

```
Predicted Values for New Observations

New Obs      Fit   SE Fit          95% CI            95% PI
1         15.674   2.290   (10.571, 20.776)   (6.830, 24.518)
```

### ● Using SPSS

Encode the data for GDP and Exports in the first two columns. Go to the bottom left-hand corner of the screen and click Variable View. Name the variables as seen here. Return to Data View.

| | | Name | Type | Width | Decimals |
|---|---|---|---|---|---|
| | 1 | GDP | Numeric | 8 | 2 |
| | 2 | EXPORTS | Numeric | 8 | 2 |

Select Analyze > Regression > Linear and enter the variables in their respective windows. Click OK. The model and the data for the hypothesis test are revealed.

**Coefficients[a]**

| Model | | Unstandardized Coefficients | | Standardized Coefficients | t | Sig. |
|---|---|---|---|---|---|---|
| | | B | Std. Error | Beta | | |
| 1 | (Constant) | 7.494 | 1.281 | | 5.848 | .000 |
| | GDP | 1.636 | .593 | .657 | 2.759 | .020 |

a. Dependent Variable: EXPORTS

To get a different confidence level, click Statistics before clicking OK and enter your chosen level of confidence.

Linear Regression: Statistics

Regression Coefficients
- ☑ Estimates
- ☑ Confidence intervals
  - Level(%): 95
- ☐ Covariance matrix

- ☑ Model fit
- ☐ R squared change
- ☐ Descriptives
- ☐ Part and partial correlations
- ☐ Collinearity diagnostics

Residuals
- ☐ Durbin-Watson
- ☐ Casewise diagnostics
  - ◉ Outliers outside: 3 standard deviations
  - ◉ All cases

Continue    Cancel    Help

You can get the mean and predictive interval for the existing values of $X$ by clicking on Save in the window below and making your choices under Predictive Intervals.

## 3.6 REVIEW PROBLEM

Throughout much of the first decade of the new century China came under international scrutiny for its manipulation of its currency, the juan, on the global market. Many popular business publications such as *The Wall Street Journal*, *Business Week*, and *Forbes* often carried articles commenting on China's efforts to control economic pressures to its advantage.

By the advent of the second decade, beginning in 2011 and well into 2012, China made further attempts to bolster national prominence by shifting world attention to the juan as an international currency. Until then it had been used primarily in its home market. Plans were set into motion that would allow the juan to "go global" as an international means of exchange.

In late 2010 and into 2011, inflationary pressures threatened the Chinese economy. Leaders began to worry that their goal to dominate the world market even further was jeopardized. To measure the impact of inflation on trade balances, data were taken from various international sources and are shown below. Trade balance surpluses are recorded as billions of U.S. dollars and the inflation rate is shown in percentage changes in domestic prices.

| Date | Inflation | Surplus |
|---|---|---|
| Sep 10 | 5.24 | 16.9 |
| Oct 10 | 1.2 | 27 |
| Nov 10 | 3.52 | 21.2 |
| Dec 10 | 6.76 | 13.1 |
| Jan 11 | 9.4 | 6.5 |
| Feb 11 | 6.3 | 3.2 |
| Mar 11 | 6.8 | 0.14 |

You are to prepare a report featuring a regression model in which inflation is used to estimate trade surplus levels. Confidence intervals and hypothesis tests are required. A complete interpretation of the results is needed.[3]

You will use the OLS principles learned in Chapter 2 and the Excel printout to complete the work.

| | A | B | C | D | E | F | G | H |
|---|---|---|---|---|---|---|---|---|
| 1 | | Inflation(X) | Surplus(Y) | (X-Xbar)^2 | (Y-Ybar)^2 | (X - Xbar)(Y - Ybar) | | |
| 2 | | | | SSx | SSy | SSxy | | |
| 3 | | 5.24 | 16.9 | 0.131665306 | 18.68709388 | -1.568579592 | | |
| 4 | | 1.2 | 27 | 19.38515102 | 208.0188082 | -63.50177959 | n= | 7 |
| 5 | | 3.52 | 21.2 | 4.338293878 | 74.35366531 | -17.96017959 | Xbar = | 5.6028571 |
| 6 | | 6.76 | 13.1 | 1.338979592 | 0.273379592 | 0.605020408 | Ybar = | 12.577143 |
| 7 | | 9.4 | 6.5 | 14.41829388 | 36.93166531 | -23.07577959 | | |
| 8 | | 6.3 | 3.2 | 0.486008163 | 87.93080816 | -6.537208163 | | |
| 9 | | 6.8 | 0.14 | 1.43315102 | 154.6825224 | -14.88903673 | | |
| 10 | | | | | | | | |
| 11 | SUMS | | | 41.53154286 | 580.8779429 | -126.9275429 | | |

The model for Surplus proves to be

$$b_1 = \frac{SS_{XY}}{SS_X} = \frac{-126.93}{41.53} = -3.06$$

$$b_0 = \bar{Y} - (b_1)(\bar{X}) = 12.58 - (-3.06)(5.6) = 29.72$$

Thus,

$$\hat{S} = 29.72 - 3.06I$$

For every one unit (percentage point) inflation increases, the surplus will decrease by 3.06 of its units (billions of U.S. dollars).

You will also need the coefficient of determination, $r^2$. But first it is wise to calculate the correlation coefficient, $r$.

$$r = \frac{SS_{XY}}{\sqrt{(SS_X)(SS_Y)}} = \frac{-126.92}{\sqrt{(41.53)(580.88)}} = -0.817$$

$r$ measures the strength of the relationship between China's trade surplus and its rate of inflation. The negative value suggests that there is a reasonably robust inverse relationship between these two important economic variables.

$r^2$ is $(-0.817)^2 = 0.668$. Thus, 66.8% of the change in China's trade surplus is explained by changes in the internal rate of inflation. The standard error of the estimate, $S_e$, is

$$S_e = \sqrt{\frac{SS_Y - (b_1)(SS_{XY})}{n-2}} = 6.213$$

The dispersion of the $Y$-values around the regression line is measured as $S_e = \$6.213$ billion (remember, the $S_e$ is measured in the same units as the $Y$-variable).

We are now ready to estimate confidence intervals, conduct hypothesis tests, and compute $p$-values. Let's begin with a 90% confidence interval for the conditional mean value of the surplus if the inflation rate is 7%. Using Equation (3.1.1) we have

$$\text{C.I. for } \mu_{Y|X} = \hat{Y} \pm (t_{\alpha,df})(S_Y)$$

$$\hat{Y} = 29.72 - 3.06(7) = 8.3$$

Equation (3.1.2) for the standard error of the conditional mean is

$$S_Y = S_e \sqrt{\frac{1}{n} + \frac{(X_i - \bar{X})^2}{SS_X}} = 6.213 \sqrt{\frac{1}{7} + \frac{(7 - 5.6)^2}{41.53}} = 2.71$$

At a confidence level of 90%, the required $t$-value is $t_{.10,5} = 2.015$. Then,

$$\text{C.I. for } \mu_{Y|X} = 8.3 \pm (2.015)(2.71)$$

$$2.84 \le \mu_{Y|7} \le 13.76$$

It can be concluded with a 90% level of confidence that if the inflation rate is 7% for many time periods the true average surplus will fall between $2.84 and $13.76 billion.

A 90% interval estimate for the predictive interval based on Equation (3.1.3) is

$$\text{C.I. for } Y_X = \hat{Y} \pm (t_{\alpha,df})(S_{Y_i})$$

where

$$S_{Y_i} = S_e\sqrt{1+\frac{1}{n}+\frac{(X_i - \bar{X})^2}{SS_X}} = 6.213\sqrt{1+\frac{1}{7}+\frac{(7-5.6)^2}{41.53}} = 6.78$$

Then,

$$\text{C.I. for } Y_7 = 8.3 \pm (2.015)(6.78)$$

$$-5.36 \le Y_x \le 21.96$$

It may be concluded with 90% confidence that given any single instance in which the inflation rate is 7%, the trade balance is in deficit by $5.36 billion or exhibits a surplus of $21.96 billion.

The point estimate for $\beta_1$ was $b_1 = -3.056$. A 95% interval estimate begins with Equation (3.1.5):

$$\text{C.I. for } \beta_1 = b_1 \pm (t_{\alpha,df})(S_{b_1})$$

where

$$S_{b_1} = \frac{S_e}{\sqrt{SS_X}} = \frac{6.213}{\sqrt{41.53}} = 0.964$$

Given $t_{.05,5} = 2.571$, we find

$$\text{C.I. for } \beta_1 = -3.056 \pm (2.571)(0.964)$$

$$-5.53 \le \beta_1 \le -0.577$$

With a level of confidence of 95% it can be said that for every percentage point by which inflation rises, the trade surplus should decrease between 5.53 and 0.577 billion dollars.

The point estimate for the correlation coefficient was $r = -0.817$. The 95% interval estimate is

$$\text{C.I. for } \rho = r \pm (t_{\alpha,df})(S_r)$$

$$= -0.817 \pm (2.571)\sqrt{\frac{1-(-0.817)^2}{7-2}}$$

$$-1.48 \le \rho \le -0.154$$

Since $\rho$ cannot be less than $-1.00$ we can say with 95% confidence that the correlation between trade balances and inflation rates is between $-1.00$ and $-0.154$.

A test of the hypothesis for $\beta_1$,

$$H_0: \beta_1 = 0$$

$$H_a: \beta_1 \neq 0$$

is based on Equation (3.2.1):

$$t_{\text{test}} = \frac{b_1 - \beta_1}{S_{b_1}} = \frac{-3.056 - 0}{0.964} = -3.170$$

The critical values for an $\alpha = 5\%$ level of significance are $\pm 2.571$. These are used to form the decision rule:

Do not reject the null if $t_{\text{test}}$ is between $\pm 2.571$; reject otherwise

This is illustrated in the graph below:

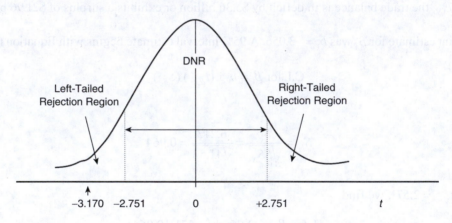

The $t_{\text{test}}$ of $-3.170$ is well inside the left-tailed rejection region. The decision is reached to reject the null. At the 5% level of significance it can be concluded that a relationship does exist between the two variables under study.

A hypothesis for $\rho$ is conducted as

$$H_0: \rho = 0$$

$$H_a: \rho \neq 0$$

$$t_{\text{test}} = \frac{r - \rho}{S_r} = \frac{-0.817 - 0}{0.258} = -3.170$$

The decision rule and conclusion are the same as those revealed by the test for $\beta_1$.

Finally, a p-value must be determined. Searching the t-table for a t-value of 3.170 (ignoring the negative sign) with 5 degrees of freedom it can be seen that the value falls between 0.05 and 0.02 for a two-tailed test. It's closer to 0.02, so let's call it a p-value of about 0.025 since the t-table is so difficult to read due to its discontinuity. An Excel printout reveals it to be 0.0248.

This p-value of 0.025 is the lowest level of significance at which the null could be rejected. If the hypothesis tests for $\beta_1$ and $\rho$ had been conducted at the 1% level the critical t-values would be ±4.032. The $t_{test}$ of −3.170 would have fallen in the Do Not Reject region leading to the conclusion that at the 1% level of significance it cannot be concluded that a relationship exists between inflation and trade balances.

# CHAPTER PROBLEMS

CHAPTER
PROBLEMS
3

## Conceptual Problems

1. Explain what is meant by degrees of freedom. Give your own example.

2. Why is the standard error of the conditional mean smaller than the standard error of the predictive interval? Explain conceptually as well as in terms of the equations.

3. What is the difference between the interval estimate for the conditional mean and the predictive interval? Under what conditions would you choose to estimate one as opposed to the other? Give real-world examples.

4. Why is the p-value the lowest level of significance you can set and still reject the null? Use a graph to fully explain.

5. Why does a low p-value indicate that your findings carry a higher level of significance?

6. What is the relationship between the alpha-value of a hypothesis test and the p-value?

7. If the regression coefficient is negative will the correlation coefficient always be negative? Explain your answer.

8. What does the standard error of the correlation coefficient measure? Why is it called a standard error?

9. What does it mean to say your findings are statistically significant?

10. Will the interval estimate for the conditional mean be wider or narrower than that for the predictive interval under the same conditions? Explain your answer.

11. If the interval estimate for the regression coefficient contains zero will the hypothesis test for its significance be rejected or not rejected? Why did you answer the way you did?

12. If the regression coefficient estimated in your model is non-zero why is it necessary to test a hypothesis about $\beta_1$?

13. Given a level of significance at which a hypothesis is to be tested will the Do Not Reject region be wider or narrower using a Z-test or a t-test? Explain.

14. Given a level of confidence, will an interval estimate be wider or narrower if you use a Z-value or a t-value? Explain.

15. Why is the decision rule in a hypothesis test a "good rule to follow"? Answer in terms of probabilities.

16. Why is the alpha-value of a hypothesis test the probability of committing a Type I error? Use a graph to fully explain.

17. Under what conditions must you use Gosset's $t$-test?

18. Why can the $Z$-distribution be used in the event of "large" samples?

19. If a coefficient is not significant at the 5% level will it be significant at the 1% level? Prove your answer with the necessary graphical work.

## Computational Problems

1. In the effort to improve gas mileage in their vehicles a domestic car-maker collected data on the weight in pounds (000s) and miles driven per gallon of fuel.

   A. Compute the model. Which do you perceive should be the dependent variable? Defend your answer.
   B. Estimate the conditional mean interval at 95% if weight is 3.2. Interpret the results.
   C. What is the 95% predictive interval for weight of 3.2 and why does it differ from the conditional mean interval?
   D. What portion of the change in mileage is explained by changes in weight?
   E. Test the hypothesis for the regression coefficient at the 1% level of significance. What do you find?
   F. Test the hypothesis for the correlation coefficient at the 1% level of significance. What do you find?
   G. How significant is the hypothesis test?

| Weight ($X$) | MPG ($Y$) |
|---|---|
| 2.2 | 39.6 |
| 3.6 | 36.2 |
| 1.6 | 41.1 |
| 4.2 | 37.2 |
| 3.9 | 36.2 |
| 3.5 | 38.5 |
| 4.6 | 37 |
| 3.8 | 35.2 |
| 2.5 | 39.3 |
| 1.6 | 40.2 |
| 5.3 | 36.2 |

2. The Environmental Protection Agency examined the impact of farming activities on water contamination in 43 localities throughout the Southeast. The tonnage of chemicals introduced by corporate farms was measured in relation to the level of contaminants in parts per million. Using chemicals as the explanatory variable test the hypothesis for the regression coefficient at the 1% level based on the preliminary computations presented here. Since this is a large sample, rely on the $Z$-test.

| | $X$ | $Y$ | | | |
|---|---|---|---|---|---|
| Sums | 139.60 | 94.74 | 53.03 | 58.93 | 19.17 |
| $n =$ | 43 | | $SS_X$ | $SS_Y$ | $SS_{XY}$ |
| Means | 3.247 | 2.203 | | | |

3. Using the data from the previous problem test the hypothesis for the correlation coefficient. How do your results compare to those in Problem 2? Explain why.

4. The National Association of Bankers completed a study of the impact of personal savings on mortgage rates in 14 states. Per capita savings in $1,000 was used as an independent variable. The results are summarized here.

| | $X$ | $Y$ | | | |
|---|---|---|---|---|---|
| Sums | 71.60 | 135.64 | 39.40 | 155.23 | 48.19 |
| $n=$ | 14 | | $SS_X$ | $SS_Y$ | $SS_{XY}$ |
| Means | 5.114 | 9.689 | | | |

A. Test the hypothesis for the significance of the regression coefficient at the 1% level. Comment on the results.

B. Test the hypothesis for the significance of the regression coefficient at the 5% level. Comment on the results.

C. Calculate and interpret the $p$-value of the test.

D. Explain the relationship between the findings in the first three parts of this problem. Do they support each other or do they contradict each other? Explain your reasoning.

5. Professor Phil Grant at Husson University in Bangor, Maine has spent much of his professional life studying the levels and determinants of employee motivation and satisfaction. In his compelling work, *The Mathematics of Human Motivation*, he examines the Law of Escalating Marginal Sacrifice. An empirical application of his principle might compare a worker's perceived marginal rewards with his or her professed output. Use the contrived data seen opposite to answer the questions posed below.

The model reports as $\hat{O} = 15.469 + 4.776MR$. Other preliminary statistics are found to be

| Marginal Rewards ($X$) | Output ($Y$) |
|---|---|
| 12 | 68 |
| 15 | 102 |
| 21 | 105 |
| 10 | 58 |
| 9 | 58 |
| 5 | 38 |
| 18 | 110 |
| 13 | 78 |
| 19 | 102 |
| 15 | 90 |

| $S_e$ | $SS_X$ | $SS_Y$ | $SS_{XY}$ |
|---|---|---|---|
| 7.82 | 218.10 | 5464.9 | 1041.7 |

Set the level of Reward at 12.

A. Compute and interpret the 95% confidence interval for the conditional mean.

B. The regional director for the firm under study is considering the promotion of a certain employee who has shown impressive managerial attributes. The director decides that if the employee's output is near 80 the promotion will be granted. Does a 95% interval estimate for this single employee suggest the promotion should be forthcoming? Explain your answer.

C. At an alpha-value of 1%, does it appear Reward is a statistically significant explanatory variable for Output?

D. Calculate the *p*-value associated with the hypothesis test in part C. How does your finding support or deny the result of your hypothesis test?

E. What portion of the change in Output is explained by changes in Reward?

6. As gas emissions from power plants around the world become an increasing threat to the environment, international agencies are examining the effect of carbon dioxide levels on smog concentration in 10 of our major cities. Preliminary calculations are shown here.

| | Emissions ($X$) | Smog ($Y$) | $(X - \bar{X})^2$ | $(Y - \bar{Y})^2$ | $(X - \bar{X})(Y - \bar{Y})$ |
|---|---|---|---|---|---|
| Sums | 137.00 | 809.00 | 218.10 | 5464.90 | 1041.70 |
| $n =$ | 10 | | $SS_X$ | $SS_Y$ | $SS_{XY}$ |
| Means | 13.700 | 80.900 | | | |
| | | | | | |
| $b_1 =$ | 4.776 | | | | |
| $b_0 =$ | 15.469 | | | | |
| $S_e =$ | 7.824167687 | | | | |

A. If the correlation coefficient proves significant at the 5% level several national governments have vowed to take action to reduce emissions. What is your recommendation to them in this regard?

B. A high-level governmental official wishes to learn how significant the findings are. What do you report?

C. Another world leader asks about the lowest level of $\alpha$ at which the null hypothesis can be rejected. What is your response?

D. As a portion of the consulting position you hold in the international community you are to test the hypothesis that the regression coefficient for the population as a whole is zero despite the study's findings. What is your response? Set $\alpha$ at 1%.

7. Founded in 1973, The Heritage Foundation is a research and educational institute with the mission to promote economic freedom and free enterprise. The Foundation provides a ranking of nations throughout the world based on their Economic Freedom Index. The EFI measures ten components of economic freedom, assigning a grade in each using a scale from 0 to 100, where 100 represents the maximum freedom. The ten component scores are then averaged to give an overall economic freedom score for each country. A total of 179 countries is typically rated (http://www.heritage.org/index/ranking).

Independently of The Heritage Foundation's ranking, the IMF projects rates of economic growth over the next two quarters. A sample of 12 nations and their EFI ratings is given in the accompanying table along with the IMF projected growth rates (PrGr).

| Nation | World Rank | EFI | PrGr |
|---|---|---|---|
| Hong Kong | 1 | 89.7 | 3.35 |
| UK | 16 | 74.5 | 3.12 |
| Finland | 17 | 74 | 3.11 |
| US | 9 | 77.8 | 3.17 |
| Japan | 20 | 72.8 | 3.29 |
| Denmark | 8 | 78.6 | 3.21 |
| Canada | 6 | 80.4 | 3.21 |
| Germany | 23 | 71.8 | 3.08 |
| Taiwan | 25 | 70.8 | 3.06 |
| Austria | 21 | 71.9 | 3.08 |
| France | 64 | 64.6 | 2.97 |
| Mexico | 48 | 67.8 | 3.02 |

The results of an OLS model are given here:

| | EFI ($X$) | PrGr ($Y$) | $(X - \bar{X})^2$ | $(Y - \bar{Y})^2$ | $(X - \bar{X})(Y - \bar{Y})$ |
|---|---|---|---|---|---|
| Sums | 894.70 | 37.65 | 467.29 | 0.134249229 | 6.7865 |
| $n =$ | 12 | | $SS_X$ | $SS_Y$ | $SS_{XY}$ |
| Means | 74.558 | 3.137 | | | |
| | | | | | |
| $b_1 =$ | 0.015 | | | | |
| $b_0 =$ | 2.019 | | | | |
| $S_e =$ | 0.056966693 | | | | |

A. An international investor conducts a hypothesis test of the regression coefficient at the 5% level to determine if there might be a statistically significant relationship. What did he learn?

B. If the 99% confidence interval for the conditional mean growth rates for nations with a EFI of 70 is above 3%, the investor in part A will begin a campaign to raise funds for future overseas investments. What will his decision be?

C. The investor wishes to determine what portion of the changes in growth rates is explained by changes in a nation's level of economic freedom. What would you tell him?

D. Now the investor has plans to expand operations in a country with an EFI of 74.6. What rate of growth can he expect with a confidence level of 99%?

8. The standard Keynesian consumption function presented by the British economist John Maynard Keynes in his 1936 opus, *The General Theory of Employment, Interest and Money*, holds that a consumer's level of spending is a function of his income. Data in thousands of dollars for income and in hundreds of dollars for consumption were collected for several consumers and the resulting OLS model was estimated.

| | X | Y | $(X - \bar{X})^2$ | $(Y - \bar{Y})^2$ | $(X - \bar{X})(Y - \bar{Y})$ |
|---|---|---|---|---|---|
| Sums | 380.00 | 665.90 | 286.24 | 2585.195151515 | 210.5606 |
| $n =$ | 80 | | $SS_X$ | $SS_Y$ | $SS_{XY}$ |
| Means | 4.750 | 8.324 | | | |
| | | | | | |
| $b_1 =$ | 0.736 | | | | |
| $b_0 =$ | 4.828 | | | | |
| $S_e =$ | 5.581818637 | | | | |

A. What is your estimated consumption if your income is 14? Now provide a 95% confidence interval for your consumption if your income is 14.

B. The coefficient of 0.736 is the marginal propensity to consume. How do you interpret the value?

C. What happens to your consumption if you receive an additional $1,000 in income?

D. How would you describe the relationship between your income and your consumption? What percentage of any change in your consumption pattern is explained by changes in your income? How do account for such a low percentage?

E. Are your findings significant at the 1% level of significance? At the 5% level?

F. What is the 92% interval estimate of consumption for a large number of people with an income of 14?

9. In 1939 the British economist John Hicks published his noted work, *Value and Capital*, describing what today serves as a foundational principle in neoclassical economics dealing with the theory of demand. He stated that the quantity purchased of a commodity is a function of its price. Based on the results shown here for $n = 120$ shoppers comment on the wisdom of that tenet. $\hat{Q} = 50 - 1.63P$, $S_e = 1.5$, and $SS_X = 4.6$. Test the hypothesis for the regression coefficient at the 5% level of significance. Find the *p*-value for the test. Compare it with the *Z*-value you calculated in the hypothesis test to comment on the results of the test.

10. The neoclassical economic theory behind supply functions holds that the price of a commodity is a direct function of the quantity available for sale. A study by the Quantitative Decision Analysis Division in your organization finds the following supply function $\hat{P} = 29.648 + 1.156Q$ and the preliminary computations shown in the table based on $n = 12$ observations.

| | | | |
|---|---|---|---|
| $SS_X =$ | 428.92 | $\bar{X} =$ | 40.083 |
| $SS_Y =$ | 1426 | $\bar{Y} =$ | 76 |
| $SS_{XY} =$ | 496 | | |

A. As part of your report to the Director of Analysis you must test the correlation coefficient for a significant linear relationship at the 5% level.

B. Does your report change if $\alpha$ is set equal to 1%?

C. You are to provide a 90% interval estimate for a single observation of price if the $Q = 40$. What are your results and how do you interpret these results?

11. Realtors in a large Midwestern town wish to base rents on apartment size. In order to devise a principle upon which to determine rents they surveyed 150 rentals. Regressing rents on square footage produced these results.

| | | | | | |
|---|---|---|---|---|---|
| $SS_X =$ | 2450 | $\bar{X} =$ | 954 | $b_1 =$ | 0.7135 |
| $SS_Y =$ | 8741 | $\bar{Y} =$ | 874 | $b_0 =$ | 193.3502 |
| $SS_{XY} =$ | 1748 | | | $S_e =$ | 7.1158 |

A. You have a single apartment with 900 square feet. What is your 92% interval estimate of the rent you can charge?

B. The city Realtors Association has asked you to provide a 98% interval estimate for apartments city-wide with 900 square feet. What do you report to them?

12. AskMen.com published statistics on the richest sports organizations in the world showing the market value and the revenues in millions of dollars in a recent calendar year. A sample taken from that list includes:

| Team | Sport | Market Values | Revenues |
|---|---|---|---|
| New York Rangers | Hockey | 272 | 113 |
| Dallas Stars | Hockey | 270 | 108 |
| Manchester United | Soccer | 312 | 177 |
| Real Madrid | Soccer | 293 | 157 |
| Ferrari | Racing | 514 | 250 |
| Toyota | Racing | 171 | 150 |
| Washington Redskins | Football | 952 | 227 |
| Dallas Cowboys | Football | 151 | 198 |

A. As a sports enthusiast you want to determine if a team's market value is related to the revenues it generates. Estimate the regression model using revenues to predict values.
B. Set $\alpha$ at 5% and determine if the model you have developed is significant.
C. Test the level of significance at the 10% alpha-value.
D. How significant are your findings? How does this relate to your answers in parts B and C?
E. In your anticipation to buy a sports team, what is your 90% confidence interval of the price you might have to pay to do so if its revenues are 200?

13. As international economic conditions worsen, ski resorts across Europe begin to notice a drop in the number of downhill racers who spend weekends and vacations on the slopes. A study covering 89 weeks compiled data for the number of guests at a ski lodge in Bern, Switzerland and the number of inches of snow each week. Treating inches of snow as a predictor of the number of "snow bunnies" resulted in the following model:

| | | | | | |
|---|---|---|---|---|---|
| $SS_X =$ | 178 | $\bar{X} =$ | 15.2 | $b_1 =$ | 2.0112 |
| $SS_Y =$ | 1201 | $\bar{Y} =$ | 847 | $b_0 =$ | 816.4292 |
| $SS_{XY} =$ | 358 | | | $S_e =$ | 2.3513 |

A. Weather forecasts for this week predict 22 inches of fine powder. At the 98% level of confidence, how many guests might the local resort prepare for?
B. What is the 95% interval estimate for the regression coefficient?

14. Shipping errors at El Dorado International have become a source of unquestioned severity. Management is considering a training program for employees who are guilty of such incompetence. However, the cost of the program is a concern. A total of 75 employees are subjected to the training and a record is kept of their subsequent errors. Data are collected on the number of hours of training and the number of errors each employee reports. Using hours of training as a regressor, the resultant model is

| | | | | | |
|---|---|---|---|---|---|
| $SS_X =$ | 417 | $\bar{X} =$ | 2.6 | $b_1 =$ | −0.3525 |
| $SS_Y =$ | 1000 | $\bar{Y} =$ | 1.3 | $b_0 =$ | 2.2165 |
| $SS_{XY} =$ | −147 | | | $S_e =$ | 3.604 |

A. Interpret the results and analyze the effect of the training on shipping.
B. Set $\alpha$ at 4% and test the hypothesis for the significance of the regression coefficient.
C. Compute and interpret the 99% confidence interval for the regression coefficient.

15. Problem 9 at the end of Chapter 2 examined the impact of measures of economic freedom on economic growth. You were asked to compute and interpret the model. However, it is now necessary to test the significance of the model using the hypothesis tests explored in this chapter. The data are repeated here for your convenience. Compute the model if you did not retain the outcome derived in Chapter 2. Test the significance of the measure of freedom as an explanatory variable. Calculate and interpret the $p$-value. Draw a graph explaining your results.

| Nation | Type of Rating | Freedom Index[a] | GDP Growth Rate[b] |
|--------|----------------|------------------|---------------------|
| Hong Kong | Free | 89.9 | 6.8 |
| Singapore | Free | 87.5 | 15.3 |
| Italy | Mostly Unfree | 58.8 | 1.3 |
| Honduras | Mostly Unfree | 58.8 | 2.7 |
| Qatar | Mostly Free | 71.3 | 16.3 |
| Netherlands | Mostly Free | 73.3 | 1.7 |
| France | Moderately Free | 63.2 | 1.4 |
| Portugal | Moderately Free | 63 | 1.3 |
| Hungary | Moderately Free | 67 | 1.2 |
| Slovenia | Moderately Free | 62 | 1.2 |
| Iran | Repressed | 42.3 | 1 |
| Bosnia | Mostly Unfree | 57.3 | 0.8 |

[a] http://www.heritage.org/index/ranking
[b] http://en.wikipedia.org/wiki/List_of_countries_by_GDP_(real)_growth_rate

## COMPUTER PROBLEMS

COMPUTER
PROBLEMS
3

1. The data set POPULATION TRENDS was extracted from http://www.census.gov/ipc/www/idb/country.php.

It contains data for a sample of 39 countries for the following variables:

■ POPULATION in thousands;

■ GROWTH: Growth rate as a percentage of the population;

■ FERTRATE: Birth rate per woman;

■ BIRTHRATE: Number of births per 1,000 population;

■ LIFEEXP: Life expectancy in years;

■ INFMORTRATE: Infant mortality rate per 1,000 people.

A.  Generate a correlation matrix for all six variables. Do any bivariate coefficients suggest a significant relationship? Do the signs make sense? Do those variables that exhibit significant correlation make sense? Explain the significant relationships you have discovered.

B.  Estimate those regression models you feel, based on the correlation coefficients in part A, that might exhibit explanatory behavior.

C.  Postulate at least three potential models you feel should prove significant. Justify your model specifications. That is, why did you choose to form the models you did? Now estimate the models and discuss the outcomes in terms of your *a priori* assumptions.

D.  Be sure to include in your discussions interval estimates and the results of hypothesis tests.

2.  The Organisation for Economic Co-operation and Development provides a wealth of data and information on a wide variety of subjects that directly affect much of the world's population. The data set Education Levels was taken from their 2010 report on the level of education in many of the OECD countries (http://www.oecd.org/dataoecd/45/39/45926093.pdf).

The data record the percentage of the population in each age group with at least a secondary education. For example, 70% of the 25- to 64-year-olds in Australia have that level of education; 82% of those in the 25–34 age group have at least a secondary education. Does there appear to be any significant correlation among the various age groups? Based on any significant correlations you uncover, estimate several regression models using one age group to explain levels in other age groups. Interpret your findings as to what they suggest in terms of educational trends.

*Chapter 4*

# MULTIPLE REGRESSION
## Using Two or More Predictor Variables

## INTRODUCTION

This chapter offers an extension of the simple regression model we examined in Chapters 2 and 3 by introducing additional explanatory variables. The use of two or more right-hand-side (RHS) variables results in a *multiple regression model*. Additional explanatory variables provide many advantages not offered by our simple, bivariate model consisting of only one RHS variable. If one independent variable proves useful in explaining changes in the dependent variable, integrating additional predictor variables could enhance the explanatory power of the model even further.

A multiple regression model allows us to control for other variables that affect the dependent variable. Rarely in business and economic matters do we find that a dependent variable is influenced by only one factor. Economic models are generally the consequence of several variables that interface to produce a combined effect. Multiple regression allows us to assimilate the aggregated results of these influential elements.

The enhanced model allows us to more decisively evaluate policy decisions and chart a more favorable course for future actions. For example, by incorporating additional explanatory variables more accurate interval estimates are possible and the viability of hypothesis tests improves. In general, our analysis becomes less equivocal and takes on a level of rigor greater than what would prevail if we restrict ourselves to only one explanatory variable.

The model no longer graphs as a line. Instead it is formed as a plane in a multidimensional space. If two RHS variables, $X_1$ and $X_2$, are used to model $Y$, we would find that a three-dimensional graph could effectively depict the relationship. The 3D surface plot in Minitab is used to create Figure 4.1. Enter the data in the first three columns of a worksheet and select Graph > 3D Surface Plot and click OK. Enter $Y$ in the $Z$-variable window and $X_1$ and $X_2$ in the two remaining windows.

### ● Additional Assumptions

Under multiple regression we must add two additional assumptions to the list that prevailed with simple regression. The first concerns the preservation of degrees of freedom. To retain at least one degree of freedom the number of observations in the data set must exceed the number of RHS variables by at least two. Remember, the degrees of freedom is found as the "number of observations minus the number of values those observations must generate." If there are, say, four RHS variables you will lose five degrees of freedom—one for each of the variables' coefficients and one for the constant in the model. Thus, if you are to have even one degree of freedom remaining the data set must contain at least six observations—two more than the number of explanatory variables. If there are $k$ RHS variables, you must have at least $k + 2$ observations. That is, where $n$ is the number of observations in the data set,

$$n \geq k + 2$$

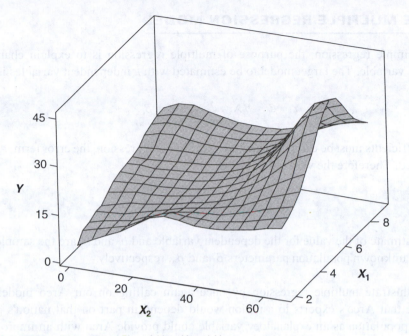

■ **Figure 4.1**    A Three-Dimensional Plot of $Y$ on $X_1$ and $X_2$

This is seldom a problem. Usually, the sample size is far in excess of the number of RHS variables contained in the model. Although a generalization is a bit perilous at this point, a model with eight or ten RHS variables is considered "large." Most models will have fewer than ten RHS variables. If too many variables are used, certain problems can beset the model that distract from its viability and efficiency. Data sets, on the other hand, can contain in some cases many hundreds of observations. So the danger this requirement is ever violated is quite small.

The second assumption associated with a multiple regression model is, however, an ever-present threat. This condition requires that there must be no linear relationships between or among the explanatory variables. If such a relationship exists, your model is said to suffer from *multicollinearity*.

Multicollinearity occurs when two or more RHS variables are linearly related.

Relationships such as $X_1 = 2X_2$, $X_3 = X_2/X_1$, or $X_4 = X_3X_2$ cannot occur. Each case represents a linear relationship among the variables and by definition constitutes multicollinearity which can have extremely deleterious effects on your model. This was not an issue with simple regression in that we had only one RHS variable. There was no chance for two or more variables to be related. We will examine this menace of multicollinearity in depth later in this chapter.

## 4.1 THE MULTIPLE REGRESSION MODEL

As with simple regression, the purpose of multiple regression is to explain changes in the dependent variable. The target model to be estimated with $k$ independent variables is

$$Y = \beta_0 + \beta_1 X_1 + \beta_2 X_2 + \cdots + \beta_k X_k + \varepsilon \qquad (4.1.1)$$

All $\beta_i$ coefficients must be estimated and, as with simple regression, the error term, $\varepsilon$, will never be observed. Therefore the working model is

$$\hat{Y} = b_0 + b_1 X_1 + b_2 X_2 + \cdots + b_k X_k \qquad (4.1.2)$$

$\hat{Y}$ is the estimate of the value for the dependent variable and $b_1$ and $b_2$ are the sample estimates of the two unknown population parameters $\beta_1$ and $\beta_2$, respectively.

We can illustrate multiple regression by once again calling on our Arco model. It seems reasonable that Arco's exports to a nation would depend in part on that nation's population. Including population as an explanatory variable could provide Arco with an improved model. The expanded model might carry greater explanatory power as evidenced by a higher coefficient of determination, $r^2$. Further, Arco may find that the standard error, $S_e$, is lower. The $p$-values may come in lower allowing Arco analysts to reduce alpha-values in their hypothesis tests. This would reduce the probability of a Type I error. All this would aid Arco's corporate planners in their efforts to establish effective sales policy.

With this in mind, data are collected for the population rounded to the nearest million of each of the countries in the sample data set. The results are shown in Table 4.1.

■ **Table 4.1**  Arco's Data Set Incorporating Population

| Nation | Exports | Pop | GDP |
|---|---|---|---|
| France | 13.7 | 66 | 2.58 |
| Russia | 7.5 | 143 | 1.47 |
| Turkey | 8.6 | 74 | 0.742 |
| Canada | 14.2 | 34 | 1.57 |
| Ireland | 8.2 | 4 | 0.204 |
| Slovakia | 2.1 | 5 | 0.086 |
| Italy | 13.6 | 61 | 2.06 |
| China | 13.2 | 1339 | 5.88 |
| Finland | 6.9 | 5 | 0.239 |
| Egypt | 6.1 | 80 | 0.218 |
| Norway | 9.2 | 5 | 0.414 |
| United Kingdom | 15.6 | 62 | 2.25 |

Population data taken from http://en.wikipedia.org/wiki/List_of_countries_by_population

The calculations for a multiple regression model are extremely tedious and quite complex. Thankfully, computers and their attendant software are capable of performing the work in quick order. We will therefore rely heavily on the computer's mathematical agility to provide the statistical output needed to complete our analysis, thereby negating the need for laborious hand calculations.

Our model can be summarized as

$$\widehat{EX} = b_0 + b_1 GDP + b_2 POP$$

It is anticipated in an *a priori* sense ("prior to" running the model) that $b_1$, $b_2 > 0$. In countries with larger populations we would expect, *ceteris paribus*, that exports would rise.

Given the data in Table 4.1, Excel Output 1 displays a portion of the results when Exports are regressed on both GDP and population. As hoped, the standard error of the estimate has decreased to $S_e = 2.099$ from that reported by the simple regression model of 3.242. Since exports are measured in thousands of dollars, and the standard error of the estimate is measured in the same units as the dependent variable, the dispersion around the mean $Y$-values is now only $2,099.

Further, the $R^2$ has risen to 0.786 from the value of 0.432 reported by the simple regression model in Chapter 2. Now, 78.6% of the change in exports is explained by the new model. This represents a substantial improvement from the simple model.

Commonly, the symbol for the coefficient of determination is $r^2$ when discussing a simple regression model, but becomes $R^2$ in a multiple regression. Generally, computer printouts will always use $R^2$ regardless.

### Excel Output 1

| Regression Statistics | |
| --- | --- |
| Multiple R | 0.886491 |
| R Square | 0.785866 |
| Adjusted R Square | 0.738281 |
| Standard Error | 2.098627 |
| Observations | 12 |

## ● The Adjusted Coefficient of Determination

Actually, in a multiple regression model, the *adjusted coefficient of determination*, $\bar{R}^2$ (read "R-bar squared"), is more closely watched than the coefficient of determination, $R^2$. This caution is taken because it is possible to artificially inflate the $R^2$ value by adding *any* explanatory variable to the model. Any two variables, regardless of whether they are truly related, will have some degree of spurious (coincidental) correlation. So including another RHS term will increase $R^2$ even if the additional term does not carry any real explanatory power. Analysts, whether by innocent naivety or purposeful and unscrupulous design, can overstate the $R^2$ and thereby bolster the presumed integrity of their model by simply adding more and more "explanatory" variables.

However, there is a cost of incorporating another RHS variable. A degree of freedom is lost every time another RHS variable is added because another coefficient must be estimated. The *adjusted* coefficient of determination will *decrease* if a variable is added to the model that does not "carry its own weight." That is, if the additional variable does not add enough explanatory power to justify the loss of the degree of freedom, $\bar{R}^2$ will go down. $\bar{R}^2$ is said to be adjusted for the loss in the degrees of freedom. It is calculated as

$$\bar{R}^2 = 1 - (1 - R^2)\left[\frac{n-1}{n-k-1}\right] \tag{4.1.3}$$

where $n$ is the number of observations and $k$ is the number of RHS variables. As $k$ goes up, the fraction in the brackets goes up and $\bar{R}^2$ decreases. The analyst, as well as those who use the results of the study, can thereby use $\bar{R}^2$ to determine if the added variable is viable and thereby measure the true explanatory power of the model.

For the Arco illustration,

$$\bar{R}^2 = 1 - (1 - 0.786)\left[\frac{12-1}{12-2-1}\right] = 0.738$$

As promised, $\bar{R}^2 < R^2$. Now 73.8% of the change in exports is explained by the model after adjusting for the degrees of freedom.

The adjusted coefficient of determination, $\bar{R}_2$, measures the portion of the change in the dependent variable explained by the model after adjusting for the degrees of freedom.

● **Analyzing the Model**

Excel Output 2 reveals additional results of the expanded regression model including the coefficients and their standard errors along with $t$-values and $p$-values for each variable.

**Excel Output 2**

|  | Coefficients | Standard Error | t Stat | p-Value |
|---|---|---|---|---|
| Intercept | 5.758852707 | 0.943638777 | 6.102815 | 0.000179 |
| Pop | −0.012969493 | 0.003364759 | −3.85451 | 0.003879 |
| GDP | 4.186217804 | 0.764835731 | 5.473355 | 0.000394 |

With *t*-values in parentheses and *p*-values in brackets, the model is

$$\hat{Ex} = 5.759 + 4.186\text{GDP} - 0.013\text{POP}$$

$$(6.10) \qquad (5.475) \qquad (-3.855)$$

$$[0.0002] \quad [0.000394] \quad [0.0003879]$$

Both variables prove to be statistically significant as revealed by extremely low *p*-values. A hypothesis test at any acceptable level of significance would result in a rejection of the null.

It should be noted at this point that a *t*-test would require $n - k - 1 = 12 - 2 - 1 = 9$ degrees of freedom. This differs from the 10 degrees of freedom used in the previous chapter because now we have two RHS variables. Now the data must generate a value for the coefficient of population so we have lost another degree of freedom.

If an alpha-value of 0.01 is selected for the tests, the critical *t*-value is $t_{.01,9} = 3.250$. The decision rule becomes

Do not reject the null if $t_{\text{test}}$ is between ±3.250; reject otherwise

Figure 4.2 illustrates the results. Clearly, both variables are statistically significant at the 1% level. This fact is also quickly revealed by merely examining the *p*-values for both variables. In both cases the *p*-values are virtually zero and the variables are significant at any chosen alpha-value.

The interpretation of the regression coefficients (now called *partial* regression coefficients, since there is more than one) is largely the same as before, with one slight, but very important, qualification. For every one unit increase in GDP ($1 trillion), exports increase by 4.186 of its units ($4,186) *assuming population is held constant*. This condition requiring other variables are held constant was not necessary in the simple regression model because there were no other variables.

Similarly, for every one unit increase in population (one million people), exports go down by 0.012969 units ($12.97), assuming GDP is held constant. This inverse relationship violates our

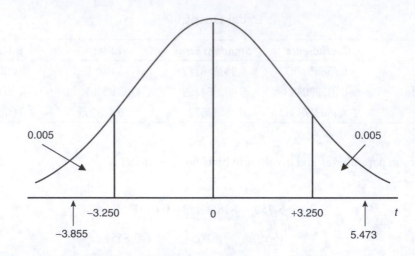

■ **Figure 4.2**  Testing the Hypotheses for Population and GDP

*a priori* assumption regarding the relationship between exports and population. We presumed a positive relationship between these two variables.

We are now obligated to explain this unanticipated result. We cannot dismiss the outcome on the argument that population is not statistically significant, which might otherwise explain its aberrant sign.

How then do we address this issue? Perhaps the negative relationship occurs because countries with larger populations have the labor resources to produce their own products and therefore don't need Arco's exports. Maybe larger nations have developed the technology to devise substitutes for Arco's output which would explain this enigma. Our model cannot answer this question. It can only report a significant negative correlation, leaving it to us to derive the explanation. But for some reason that negative correlation has been uncovered and its statistical significance necessitates an explanation if we intend to include it in the regression equation.

### ● A Change in the Coefficient for GDP

Notice that the coefficient of GDP has changed from the simple regression model of 1.636. Now that population levels have been included in the model the impact on exports of a change in GDP is no longer the same. After accounting for the effect of population, the measured influence of GDP has changed. This is to be expected. Both GDP and population bear on exports. Once population is inserted into the model, the previous balance between exports and GDP has shifted. Changes in GDP no longer register the same impact as before. It is said that "after controlling for population" the measured impact on exports of a change in GDP is different.

## EXAMPLE 4.1: Size of Bank Deposits

**Problem Statement**: The International Bankers' Association (IBA) conducted a study to model the size of personal bank account balances in 58 cities around the globe using three RHS variables thought to offer explanatory power: the value of homes in the city in question, the unemployment rate, and the level of education of the head of household. The monetary values for balances and income were measured in thousands of dollars, the unemployment rate was expressed in percentages, and education was tallied in years of formal education. The intent was to gain insight into how saving accounts might be determined.

**Solution**: Three models were estimated and summarized in the table seen here. The first model included all three variables mentioned in the problem statement. Education did not report as significant. Its $p$-value is an inflated 0.3617. Therefore, a second model was estimated without education as an explanatory variable. Finally, a simple regression model with only the value of the house was estimated.

| Coefficient | Model 1 | Model 2 | Model 3 |
|---|---|---|---|
| Constant | 5.1 | 4.7 | 1.5 |
| *t*-value | 2.03 | 1.97 | 0.73 |
| *p*-value | 0.047 | 0.0539 | 0.4684 |
| Value of House | 0.095 | 0.1002 | 0.115 |
| *t*-value | 3.85 | 2.97 | 2.14 |
| *p*-value | 0.000315 | 0.0044 | 0.0367 |
| Unemployment | −3.11 | −3.27 | |
| *t*-value | −3.29 | −3.44 | |
| *p*-value | 0.00177 | 0.0011 | |
| Education | 0.061 | | |
| *t*-value | 0.92 | | |
| *p*-value | 0.3617 | | |
| $\bar{R}^2$ | 0.597 | 0.522 | 0.332 |

Data from http://ibajapan.org/

**Interpretation**: The signs for all three variables in the first model fit *a priori* assumptions. However, education levels did not seem to explain balances held in personal bank accounts. The p-value of 0.3617 suggests the absence of any significant relationship. A second model was estimated to the exclusion of education. The results show both variables retain the expected signs and prove significant at acceptable levels. The last model used only housing values as an explanatory variable. While it reported as statistically significant it carried the lowest $\bar{R}^2$ value. The IBA can select what information they choose from these results and apply it to any analysis of banking activity they so desire.

## SECTION 4.1 PROBLEMS

1. A statistical study by an international airline is designed to model the number of miles flown by its passengers on the basis of the variables shown in the printout below. Inc is income of head of household in thousands of dollars, Age is the age of head of household, and FamilyMem is the number of family members age six and above. There were $n = 25$ observations.

| | Coefficients | Standard Error | t Stat | p-Value |
|---|---|---|---|---|
| Intercept | 50 | 26.3 | | |
| Inc | 2.25 | 1.07 | | |
| Age | 12.5 | 12.5 | | |
| FamilyMem | −1.47 | 1.02 | | |

A. Fill in the rest of the table for the $t$-values and the $p$-values. Comment on which variables are significant at various alpha-values. Would you consider removing any of the variables and running the model again?

B. What is your estimate of the average number of miles flown by a 50-year-old person with an income of $78,000 and four family members?

2. Shipping costs for a manufacturer of paper business forms in Sao Paulo, Brazil have recently risen to alarming levels. To combat this increasing burden, you have been charged with the responsibility of devising a method to estimate these costs. Your regression model incorporates a measure for distance of the shipment (*Dist*) and its weight (*Wgt*). The model reports as

$$\widehat{Cost} = 125.3 + 4.36Dist + 7.66Wgt$$
$$(2.54) \quad (3.66) \quad (5.26)$$

$t$-values are shown in parentheses. Your supervisor wants a complete explanation of the model as to what it means and what it tells you.

A. If there were $n = 22$ shipments in your sample, conduct the necessary hypothesis test on each variable. Interpret the results. Show all four steps of the hypothesis test. What is the critical $t$-value? Use any alpha-value you choose to conduct the test.

B. What are the $p$-values associated with the test for each RHS variable?

3. Economists have long held that an economy's demand for money is a function of income, the interest rate, and personal wealth. Money demand is measured by the amount of cash and other liquid assets. Cash holdings, wealth, and income are all measured in thousands of dollars in the model shown here based on 150 residents in a large metropolitan area. Complete the table and identify which variables are significant at the 5% level. Which are significant at the 1% level?

|  | Coefficients | Standard Error | t Stat | p-Value |
|---|---|---|---|---|
| Intercept | 5.55 |  | 4 |  |
| Inc | 1.635514019 |  | 2.14 |  |
| Wealth | 0.663865546 |  | 2.38 |  |
| IntRate | −1.161616162 |  | 1.98 |  |

4.  A model with 13 observations produces the following output:

|  | Coefficients | Standard Error |
|---|---|---|
| Intercept | 5.382573179 | 6.975535845 |
| X1 | 19.08475153 | 0.90783401 |
| X2 | −4.780803268 | 0.964019787 |

with a correlation coefficient of 0.9889.

A.  Calculate the *t*-values and the *p*-values. Comment on the significance of each variable.
B.  If the level of significance is set at 5%, what is the critical *t*-value for the hypothesis tests?
C.  Calculate and interpret the adjusted coefficient of determination.

## 4.2 THE ISSUE OF MULTICOLLINEARITY

As mentioned in the introduction to this chapter, multiple regression requires the additional assumption that there are no linear relationships between the independent variables. It is essential that they all be related to the dependent variable. We are trying to use them to explain changes in the dependent variable. But if two or more of the RHS variables are related to each other the debilitating problem of multicollinearity infects our model. In this section we will examine three issues dealing with this perplexing dilemma.

First, we will describe the vexing problems multicollinearity can cause and the manner in which they disrupt the model. Second, methods to detect the presence of multicollinearity will be examined. Finally, prescribed ways to treat multicollinearity will be offered.

### ● The Problems of Multicollinearity

The list of difficulties brought on by multicollinearity is quite extensive, so we will examine only a few of its more severe consequences. But even this incomplete list is enough to convince the most skeptical among us of the devastating impact multicollinearity can have.

■ Much of the trouble surrounding multicollinearity stems from the fact that it is difficult to disentangle the effects of one independent variable from that of another. If two or more RHS variables are correlated the influence of one variable may become integrated into that of another. Presume we have a model such as $\hat{Y} = 5 + 6X_1 + 7X_2 + 8X_3$ in which $X_1$ and $X_3$ are related. If $X_1$ and $X_3$ are interrelated part of the 6 attributed by the model to $X_1$ may be due to $X_3$, and part of the 8 assigned to $X_3$ may be the result of changes in $X_1$. It's not clear just what part of a variable's coefficient can be assigned to that variable. This means that coefficients are not reliable. This is quite serious. After all, the primary purpose in developing the model in the first place was to estimate the impact of a change in $X_i$ on $Y$. If the coefficients can't be believed the integrity of the entire model is called into question.

> In the presence of multicollinearity it's difficult to disentangle the impact of one RHS variable from that of another and thereby obtain an accurate measure of its impact on the dependent variable.

■ Just as damaging is the fact that multicollinearity can increase the standard error of the regression coefficients, $S_{b_i}$. This has a dual impact on the model—neither aspect of which is good. First, since the standard error measures the sampling error in the coefficients, the variation in the coefficients will become inflated. That is, the coefficients will display exaggerated variation from one sample to the next. The researcher can have little confidence that the coefficients reported by the model are close to the actual parameters they are intended to estimate. Coupled with the inability to disentangle their individual influence mentioned above, their reliability falls under further doubt.

In addition, recall that the hypothesis test for significance is based on the equation

$$t = \frac{b_i - \beta_i}{S_{b_i}}$$

If the standard error increases, the absolute value of $t$ will decrease—moving it closer to zero. This increases the likelihood it will fall in the Do Not Reject region. But if the null is not true it should be rejected. Not doing so constitutes a Type II error (not rejecting a false hypothesis). Therefore multicollinearity increases the probability of a Type II error.

> Multicollinearity can increase the probability of a Type II error by inflating the coefficient's standard error, $S_{b_i}$.

■ Multicollinearity can also cause the signs of the coefficients to report as opposite of what they actually are. An independent variable that is directly related to the dependent variable may report a negative sign, while another independent variable that is inversely related may exhibit a positive sign. Multicollinearity can cause the researcher to conclude that the relationship between two variables is exactly opposite of the true relationship. Perhaps this explains the seeming abnormality in our Arco example in which population carried a negative sign. This possibility will be addressed shortly.

Multicollinearity can also cause a RHS variable to report the wrong sign.

From this brief description it is clear that multicollinearity can drastically affect a model. Its presence can destroy its viability and usefulness. It is therefore important to prescribe ways in which multicollinearity can be detected so that it can be dealt with. This next section offers a few ways to expose multicollinearity.

## ● Detecting Multicollinearity

Specific methods have been established to reveal multicollinearity. This section discusses three of the more common approaches to detection.

### ■ The Hypothesis Test

Multicollinearity is defined as the excessive correlation between two or more independent variables. Therefore, one way to detect its presence is to conduct a hypothesis test for significant correlation between $X_i$ and $X_j$. This is accomplished in exactly the same manner as the hypothesis test for significant correlation between the dependent and independent variables carried out in Chapter 3—with one important difference. When we tested for correlation between the dependent and independent variables as $H_0$: $\rho = 0$, we hoped to reject the null. We hoped that a correlation did exist because we were trying to use $X$ to explain changes in $Y$. However, in this test for multicollinearity, we hope to not reject the null. We hope that $\rho = 0$ and that there is no correlation between $X_i$ and $X_j$. Otherwise, we must conclude that multicollinearity may be present.

The hypothesis test for correlation between two independent variables, $X_i$ and $X_j$, requires the same four steps as those carried out in any hypothesis test. The set of hypotheses is stated:

$$H_0: \ \rho_{X_i, X_j} = 0$$

$$H_a: \ \rho_{X_i, X_j} \neq 0$$

After obtaining the sample correlation between the two suspect variables, $r_{X_i, X_j}$, the $t$-test for significance is conducted. The $t_{test}$ is

$$t_{test} = \frac{r_{X_i, X_j} - 0}{S_{r_{X_i, X_j}}} \qquad (4.2.1)$$

where $S_{r_{X_i, X_j}}$ is the standard error of the correlation between $X_i$ and $X_j$. It is determined by Equation (4.2.2).

$$S_{r_{X_i, X_j}} = \sqrt{\frac{1 - (r_{X_i, X_j})^2}{n - 2}} \qquad (4.2.2)$$

As usual, a decision rule is established based on a pre-determined level of significance and, finally, a conclusion is reached regarding whether the null should be rejected.

Applying this to our Arco data, we must first find the correlation between the two independent variables, population and GDP. This can be done the same way we calculated the correlation between exports and GDP in Chapter 2. After all, it's the same concept—the correlation between two variables. The only difference here is that it involves the correlation between two independent variables.

However, in this case, we will use Minitab to obtain the bilateral correlations between each pair of all three variables. Minitab Output 1 seen here shows the correlation between population and GDP to be $r_{P,G} = 0.865$.

## Minitab Output 1

```
Correlations: Pop, GDP, Exports

             Pop         GDP

GDP        0.865
           0.000

Exports    0.270       0.658
           0.395       0.020

Cell Contents:  Pearson correlation

                P-Value
```

Then, using Equations (4.2.1) and (4.2.2),

$$t_{\text{test}} = \frac{0.865 - 0}{\sqrt{\dfrac{1 - (0.865)^2}{12 - 2}}} = 5.45$$

A warning concerning the degrees of freedom: The test of significance for an independent variable in the *entire* model carries $n - k - 1$ degrees of freedom. For our Arco example, that's $12 - 2 - 1 = 9$ degrees of freedom.

However, a test for multicollinearity requires $n - 2$ degrees of freedom. That's because here we are not examining the entire model, but only two of its RHS components. The Arco test for multicollinearity thus requires $12 - 2 = 10$ degrees of freedom.

If an alpha-value of 1% is selected for the test, a $t$-value of $t_{.01,10} = 3.169$ is used for the decision rule. Since $5.45 > 3.169$ the null is rejected and we conclude that $\rho \neq 0$. There *is* correlation between the two independent variables. Our model suffers from multicollinearity. Perhaps this explains the negative sign on population reported in the equation.

An advantage of this method of detection is that after selecting the alpha-value, there is no guesswork involved in this approach. The results are quite unequivocal. Either the $t$-test falls in the Do Not Reject region or it doesn't! This is not the case with other tests as we will discover shortly.

However, a serious drawback to this method is that it can detect multicollinearity only between two RHS variables. Only two at a time can be tested for significant correlation. If multicollinearity exists among three variables such as $X_1 = X_2/X_3$, the hypothesis test will not expose its presence.

### ■ Overlap

A quick-and-dirty way to test for multicollinearity is to search for "overlap." This occurs when the sum of the parts is greater than the whole. From Minitab Output 1 above it can be seen that the correlation between exports and population is 0.270, while that between exports and GDP is 0.658. Together they sum to 0.928. However, the model as a whole reports a correlation of only 0.886 (see Excel Output 1). Sure enough, the sum of the parts exceeds the whole. Apparently, there is some overlap. Part of the relationship that population is explaining, GDP is already explaining, and part of what GDP is explaining, population is also explaining. This redundancy can occur only if the two RHS variables are themselves somehow related. Unfortunately, there is no convenient rule of thumb that can be used to identify how much overlap is cause for concern. So this approach must be used in conjunction with others discussed here.

### ■ The Variance Inflation Factor

An all-encompassing method to detect multicollinearity is the *variance inflation factor* (VIF). Each independent variable has a VIF that measures that variable's contribution to the problem of multicollinearity.

A variable's VIF quantifies the severity of multicollinearity in an ordinary least squares regression model. It measures the extent to which a variable contributes to multicollinearity.

The VIF for $X_1$ is found by regressing $X_1$ on all other independent variables. That is, you treat $X_1$ as a dependent variable as seen in Equation (4.2.3):

$$X_1 = f(X_2, X_3, \ldots, X_k) \tag{4.2.3}$$

This may make no sense in terms of a predictive model or have any basis whatsoever in theory or practice. But that's not the purpose of the model. The intent is to obtain the $R^2$-value from Equation (4.2.3)

The VIF for $X_1$ is then calculated as

$$\text{VIF}(X_1) = \frac{1}{1 - R^2} \qquad (4.2.4)$$

Remember, the $R^2$ in Equation (4.2.4) is not the $R^2$ from the full model in which $Y$ is regressed on all RHS variables. It's the $R^2$ obtained from the abbreviated model (4.2.3) in which $X_1$ is regressed on all other independent variables.

We only want to find the correlation coefficient for the model that uses $X_i$ as a dependent variable. If the original, full model has only two RHS variables as does our Arco illustration it really isn't necessary to regress GDP on population (or population on GDP) to get the correlation coefficient. From Minitab Output 1 we find the correlation between population and GDP is 0.865. So if we were to regress GDP on population (or population on GDP) we would get a correlation of 0.865!

The VIF for GDP is therefore

$$\text{VIF(GDP)} = \frac{1}{1 - (0.865)^2} = 3.972$$

The VIF for population is also 3.972 since the correlation between GDP and population is the same as the correlation between population and GDP.

It would be necessary to run the abbreviated regression models such as Equation (4.2.3) only if you had more than two RHS variables. If the original model was $Y = f(X_1, X_2, X_3)$ you would have to regress each RHS variable on the other two to get the required correlation coefficients.

After computing the VIF, how is it used to detect multicollinearity? The rule of thumb states that multicollinearity exists if the VIF for any independent variable is greater than 10 (some use a cutoff of 5). As opposed to the hypothesis test above, this procedure suggests that multicollinearity is not a problem in our model. The VIF is only 3.972.

Some analysts (including this one) view the VIF with some degree of skepticism. Justification for the choice of a cutoff at 10 is seldom offered. Further, VIFs in excess of 10 are rarely reported even though multicollinearity is a more common problem than this test implies. In addition, while the VIF contends there is no cause for alarm, the earlier hypothesis test resulted in a rejection of the null at very high level of significance, thereby leading to the conclusion that multicollinearity was present. Furthermore, the mere observation that the correlation between population and GDP is so high at 0.865 must raise a serious question as to the presence of multicollinearity. It seems only reasonable that a correlation that elevated could signal some problem in this regard. For these reasons, the VIF exposes itself to serious criticism as a valid test for multicollinearity.

On the positive side, VIF does allow a simultaneous test for three or more independent variables. This was not the case, as you recall, with the hypothesis test.

Some computer programs provide the VIFs. Minitab can do so by choosing

Stat > Regression > Regression

After entering the appropriate variables in the "Response Variable" window and the "Predictors" window, select

Options > Variance Inflation Factors > OK > OK

The resulting Minitab Output 2 shows the VIF of 3.97.

**Minitab Output 2**

| Predictor | Coef | SE Coef | T | P | VIF |
|-----------|------|---------|---|---|-----|
| Constant | 5.7589 | 0.9436 | 6.10 | 0.000 | |
| GDP | 4.1862 | 0.7648 | 5.47 | 0.000 | 3.970 |
| Pop | −0.012969 | 0.003365 | −3.85 | 0.004 | 3.970 |

A *tolerance coefficient* can also be calculated in conjunction with the VIF as 1/VIF or 1 minus the $R^2$ from the abbreviated model. If the coefficient approaches zero, multicollinearity is considered to be a threat. If it is close to 1, the researcher can relax any fear that multicollinearity is disrupting the model. However, again there is no rule as to what "approaches zero" means or how close to 1 the coefficient must be to alleviate concern.

### ● Treating the Problem of Multicollinearity

Given the detrimental impact multicollinearity can have, the need to take action to mitigate its ill effects should be clear. There are several remedial measures that can be followed to reduce the damage it might otherwise impose.

Obviously, removing one of the offending variables would eliminate the problem. The choice as to which should be purged from the model and which should be kept must be made. The decision rests on which is more closely associated with the dependent variable. Since your goal is to explain changes in $Y$ it only makes sense to retain that variable that has the stronger correlation with $Y$.

Minitab Output 1 above revealed that GDP has a 0.658 correlation with Exports while Population reported only a 0.27 correlation coefficient. If you decide to return to a simple regression model by dropping one of the explanatory variables, the choice is clear. This may seem unfortunate since the inclusion of population provided a marked improvement in the model's standard error and coefficient of determination. But given the hazards associated with multicollinearity, can you really believe the "better" results?

> If two RHS variables are closely related the problem of multicollinearity can be eliminated by removing from the model that variable that has the weaker correlation with Y.

Another approach to reduce multicollinearity is to *combine* the offending variables if possible. Perhaps the variables giving rise to multicollinearity are of a similar nature and can be integrated into a single variable. For example, if mortgage rates and prime interest rates are parts of a regression equation to explain housing sales it's quite likely they would be highly correlated and inject multicollinearity into the model. It might be possible to eliminate the link by creating an index that would incorporate both interest rate measures into a single variable, thereby retaining the explanatory power of each and at the same time eliminating multicollinearity.

> Combining the offending variables into one single variable can often be done to mitigate the problem of multicollinearity.

Changing the form in which a variable is measured often proves cathartic. For example, personal income is used in many economic-related regressions. Any correlation with another variable can be dampened or even eliminated by expressing income in real terms rather than in current monetary terms. That is, instead of using money income, the actual amount of income earned, it is often useful to divide money income (also called current income) by a price index such as the consumer price index (CPI). Now the variable is expressed in its "real" terms. Doing so often minimizes any correlation with other RHS variables.

> Changing the manner in which a variable is measured or expressed can reduce the degree of multicollinearity.

This could apply to the use of population and GDP in Arco's model. It's possible to simply divide GDP by population and use GDP per capita in a simple regression model. Both GDP and population are thereby offered the opportunity to provide their respective contribution to the model, and multicollinearity is no longer a concern.

## SECTION 4.2 PROBLEMS

1. Define multicollinearity and give an example.

2. Why does multicollinearity increase the probability of a Type II error? Use a graph in your explanation.

3. The correlation between two RHS variables, income and wealth, in a regression model is 0.73. If there are 150 observations in the data set test the hypothesis for multicollinearity at any alpha-value you choose. What do you find? Show all four steps of the test.

4. Repeat the above problem if $n = 12$. Set $\alpha$ at 5%.

5. A PASW printout is seen here. Does multicollinearity exist between $X_1$ and $X_2$? Explain.

### Coefficients[a]

| Model | | Unstandardized Coefficients | | Standardized Coefficients | t | Sig. | Collinearity Statistics | |
|---|---|---|---|---|---|---|---|---|
| | | B | Std. Error | Beta | | | Tolerance | VIF |
| 1 | (Constant) | 44.551 | 1.104 | | 40.340 | .000 | | |
| | X1 | 5.610 | .019 | 1.001 | 290.585 | .000 | .987 | 1.013 |
| | X2 | −.045 | .027 | −.006 | −1.662 | .141 | .987 | 1.013 |

a. Dependent Variable: Y

## 4.3 ANALYSIS OF VARIANCE: USING THE *F*-TEST FOR SIGNIFICANCE

During our examination of the coefficient of determination in Chapter 2 we identified three types of sources of deviations around the mean value of Y. These deviations are reviewed here for your convenience with the aid of Figure 4.3 using $X^*$ as an illustration.

The total deviation (TD) is the difference between the actual value of Y and the mean value of Y, $(Y_i - \bar{Y})$. The total deviation is composed of the explained deviation and the unexplained deviation.

The explained deviation is that portion of the total deviation of Y from its mean that the model is able to explain. It's the difference between what the model would predict Y to be at $X^*$ and the mean value of Y, $(\hat{Y} - \bar{Y})$.

The unexplained deviation is the portion of the total deviation the model is unable to explain. It's the difference between the actual value of Y and the model's estimate, $(Y_i - \hat{Y})$. Notice that it is the measure of the error or residual.

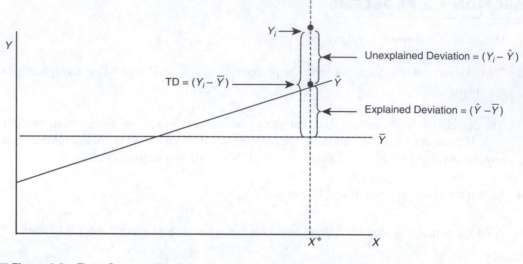

**■ Figure 4.3** Three Sources of Variation

If all three of these deviations were squared and summed for all values of $X$ (not just $X^*$), we would have the "sums of squares." The sum of the squares of the total deviation is

$$SST = \Sigma(Y_i - \bar{Y})^2 \qquad (4.3.1)$$

The deviation explained by the regression model, or regression sum of squares, is

$$RSS = \Sigma(\hat{Y} - \bar{Y})^2 \qquad (4.3.2)$$

Finally, the deviation of $Y$ from its mean that the model fails to explain, the unexplained deviation, is the sum of the squared errors:

$$SSE = \Sigma\left(Y_i - \hat{Y}\right)^2 \qquad (4.3.3)$$

It now remains only to obtain the *means* of the three sums of squares. This is done by dividing each by its respective degrees of freedom. The total sum of squares, *SST*, has $n - 1$ degrees of freedom. The mean of the total sum of squares, or mean square total (*MST*), is

$$MST = \frac{SST}{n-1} = \frac{\Sigma(Y_i - \bar{Y})^2}{n-1} \qquad (4.3.4)$$

The regression sum of squares, $RSS$, has $k$ degrees of freedom, where $k$ is number of independent variables. The mean square regression is therefore

$$MSR = \frac{RSS}{k} = \frac{\Sigma(\hat{Y} - \bar{Y})^2}{k} \qquad (4.3.5)$$

The error sum of squares, $SSE$, carries $n - k - 1$ degrees of freedom creating a mean square error of

$$MSE = \frac{SSE}{n - k - 1} = \frac{\Sigma(Y_i - \hat{Y})^2}{n - k - 1} \qquad (4.3.6)$$

The results of all this work are always summarized in an analysis of variance (ANOVA) table. A general model of an ANOVA table is seen here as Table 4.2.

■ **Table 4.2**  A Standard ANOVA Table

| Source of Variation | Sum of Squares | Degrees of Freedom | Mean Squares | F-ratio |
|---|---|---|---|---|
| Regression | SSR | $k$ | $MSR = \dfrac{SSR}{k}$ | $F = \dfrac{MSR}{MSE}$ |
| Error | SSE | $n - k - 1$ | $MSE = \dfrac{SSE}{n - k - 1}$ | |
| Total | SST | $n - 1$ | | |

These mean squares are then used to test the significance of the entire model as a whole based on an $F$-distribution. The $F$-distribution is highly skewed right as seen in Figure 4.4. Further, since the $F$-value is the ratio of squared values it is always positive. Sometimes referred to as a *global* test, ANOVA tests for the significance of all independent variables simultaneously. That is, it is said to test the *model as a whole*. The set of hypotheses is

$$H_0: \beta_1 = \beta_2 = \beta_3 = \cdots = \beta k = 0$$

$$H_a: \text{At least one } \beta \text{ is not zero}$$

If the null is not rejected, it is concluded that none of the explanatory variables used in the model offers any explanatory power. If the null is rejected we may conclude that one or more RHS variables carry significant explanatory power.

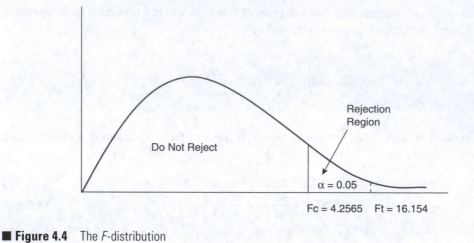

Do Not Reject

Rejection
Region

$\alpha = 0.05$

Fc = 4.2565    Ft = 16.154

**■ Figure 4.4**   The *F*-distribution

The usual four steps are taken in testing this hypothesis. After calculating the *F*-ratio, it is compared to a critical *F*-value, $F_c$, to determine if the null should be rejected. Notice the *F*-value is a ratio of *MSR* to *MSE*. The critical *F*-value is therefore based on a selected alpha-value and *two* degrees of freedom, one for the numerator and one for the denominator. The numerator in the *F*-ratio is *MSR* which has *k* degrees of freedom and *MSE* with $n - k - 1$ degrees of freedom is in the denominator. The critical *F*-ratio is thus $F_{\alpha,k,n-k-1}$.

Fortunately, this work is performed by most computer software. For Arco's ANOVA table, Excel produces Excel Output 3.

### Excel Output 3

**ANOVA**

|  | df | SS | MS | F | Significance F |
|---|---|---|---|---|---|
| Regression | 2 | 145.4710463 | 72.73552 | 16.5149029 | 0.000972933 |
| Residual | 9 | 39.63812033 | 4.404236 |  |  |
| Total | 11 | 185.1091667 |  |  |  |

Review the table and you will find the values described above and the manner in which they were computed. The *p*-value of the test, called "Significance *F*" by Excel, is much less than 1%. This reveals that some variable or variables are highly significant. It is now necessary to perform individual *t*-tests on all independent variables in the model to identify those that offer significant explanatory value.

The *F*-test calculated to be 16.514 based on the sample data is compared with the critical *F*-value that can found in an *F*-table. More conveniently, Excel permits the determination of a critical *F*-value by entering in any cell

=FINV(α, df for the numerator, df for the denominator)

If an alpha-value of 5% is selected, =FINV(.05,2,9) yields a critical value of 4.2565. The $F$-value of 16.514 falls in the rejection region as noted above. The Significance $F$ (or $p$-value) is obtained through Excel by entering in any cell

$$=FDIST(16.514,2,9)$$

Excel responds with 0.000973 as seen in Excel Output 3.

The logic behind a large $F$-value leading to a rejection of the null is simple. The $F$-value is the ratio of $MSR$ to $MSE$. If the model is able to explain a significant share of the variation in $Y$, $MSR$ will exceed $MSE$ and the $F$-ratio will be large. It is therefore likely to fall in the rejection region lending testimony to the explanatory power of the model.

In a *simple* regression model the $t$-test associated with the single explanatory variable will yield the same results as the $F$-test. If the $t$-test calls for a rejection of the null, so will the $F$-test based on ANOVA. In a simple regression model, $F = t^2$. It is only with a multiple regression model that an analysis of variance might offer additional insight into the nature of the regression model.

## SECTION 4.3 PROBLEMS

1. Given this ANOVA table:

**ANOVA**

|  | df | SS | MS | F | Significance F |
|---|---|---|---|---|---|
| Regression | 2 | 1609.740797 |  |  | 0.061443807 |
| Residual |  |  |  |  |  |
| Total | 32 | 9485.465082 |  |  |  |

   A. Complete the table.
   B. How many observations were in the data set?
   C. Are any of the variables significant?

2. Why does a "high" $F$-value result in a rejection of the null? Use a graph in your response.

3. Explain the relationship between $MSR$ and $MSE$. How and *why* do these values generate an $F$-value?

4. Complete the following ANOVA table. You may have to use the Excel feature that generates $F$-values as discussed above.

**ANOVA**

| | df | SS | MS | F | Significance F |
|---|---|---|---|---|---|
| Regression | | 1740.887461 | 870.4437307 | | |
| Residual | 21 | | | | |
| Total | 23 | 11856.66873 | | | |

## 4.4 DUMMY VARIABLES

Oftentimes we can identify variables that could prove useful in our analysis but are not expressed quantitatively. Research has shown that variables such as gender, geographical location, marital status, and whether the economy is currently in a recession offer valuable explanatory influence. Yet they are not measured numerically and in their natural form cannot be included in a quantitative model.

It becomes necessary to transform them into *dummy variables* (or indicator variables) that take on a numerical measure if we are to incorporate them into our analysis. For example, a clothing manufacturer wants to design a model that might explain body shape or weight. He recognizes that in addition to age and height, both of which can be measured numerically, gender plays an important part in one's weight. Two people of the same age and height will likely report different weights if one is male and the other female. In collecting his data the manufacturer records the weight, age, and height of the subjects. Gender is observed as male (M) or female (F). However, "M" and "F" cannot be mathematically manipulated in the OLS procedure. He must create a dummy variable for gender. This can be done by encoding "1" if male and "0" if female. We will see what happens if this order is reversed in a moment. A portion of the data set might appear as

| Weight (Pounds) | Age (Years) | Height (Inches) | Gender |
|---|---|---|---|
| 209 | 32 | 68 | 1 |
| 125 | 25 | 64 | 0 |
| 215 | 54 | 71 | 1 |
| 118 | 21 | 62 | 0 |
| • | • | • | • |
| • | • | • | • |
| • | • | • | • |

Presume the results are found to be

$$\hat{W} = 10 + 2A + 3H + 20G$$

This produces two regression models: one for males and one for females. Since "M" was recorded as a 1, the model for Male is

$$\hat{W} = 10 + 2A + 3H + 20(1)$$
$$= 30 + 2A + 3H$$

For females it is

$$\hat{W} = 10 + 2A + 3H + 20(0)$$
$$= 10 + 2A + 3H$$

Notice that the slope coefficients for age and height are the same for both males and females. It is only the intercept that is different: 30 for males and 10 for females. This reveals that if a man and a woman are the same age and height the man will weigh on the average 20 pounds more. Measuring either age or height on the horizontal axis produces the results seen in Figure 4.5. The two models, one for each gender, are clearly distinguished. They are seen to be parallel in accord with the equality in slope values of the two models and differ only in the intercept. Not surprisingly, these are referred to as *intercept dummies*.

The clothing manufacturer can now design his product for different age and height groups with gender in mind. The flexibility lends central focus to an important element in today's clothing styles based on differences in dress between men and women.

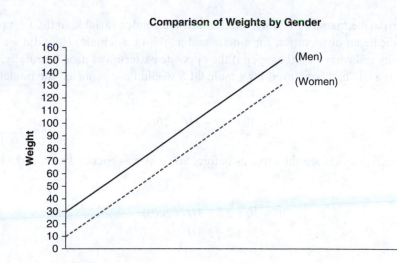

■ **Figure 4.5** Dummy Variables for Male and Female

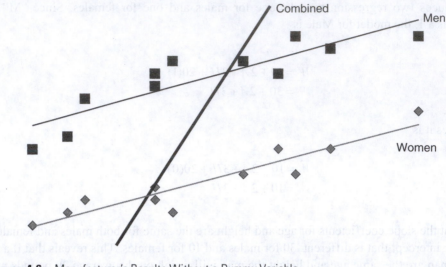

■ **Figure 4.6**   Manufacturer's Results Without a Dummy Variable

Had a dummy variable not been included in the model the results might appear as in Figure 4.6, showing the two superimposed scatter diagrams. The top scatter plot represents men and the lower is that for women. Each exhibits its own regression line, showing a reasonable fit as in Figure 4.5. Without the dummy variable generating the separate models, OLS would have tried to characterize the data by prescribing a single line through the middle of the *combined* scatter diagram shown by the bold line in Figure 4.6. Obviously, the fit is quite poor, producing a low coefficient of determination and a large standard error of the estimate.

Now let's return to the manner in which we encoded the gender variable in the first place. We used "1" to indicate an observation for a male and a "0" for a female. How did we know to record it that way and what would happen if the opposite pattern was used? Actually, it makes no difference. If a "0" had been used for a male OLS would have reported the model as

$$\hat{W} = 30 + 2A + 3H - 20G$$

The gender-specific models are the same as before. Since M was encoded as "0," the model for male is

$$\hat{W} = 30 + 2A + 3H - 20(0)$$
$$= 30 + 2A + 3H$$

which is the same as when M was encoded with a "1." The full model for females would be

$$\hat{W} = 30 + 2A + 3H - 20(1)$$

With a "1" representing females the result is

$$\hat{W} = 10 + 2A + 3H$$

It's the same as before. It's only important that you remember how you encoded the data so you can later distinguish which model is which.

How can we be so certain these results will occur? OLS is designed to model the true relationship among variables in a regression equation. The correct form will therefore be revealed regardless of how the data were encoded.

Of course, it is necessary to test the hypothesis about the coefficient for gender. If the null is not rejected, this would indicate that weight does not depend on gender, and the variables age and height could be used for both male and female. There would be no need to base a distinction on gender, and the model used to explain weight would carry only height and age as explanatory variables. Of course, logic tells us this is not the case, and a result as seen in Figure 4.6 is to be expected. Nevertheless, statistical evidence in the form of a hypothesis test is necessary.

---

**EXAMPLE 4.2: Designing Employee Salaries**

**Problem Statement**: Mona Welvaert has been Director of Human Resources for over 20 years at Quad Cities Interior Designs. Some dispute has arisen over the percentage increases in employee salaries. Data for relevant variables are collected and displayed in the table below. A dummy variable identifies those employees who have completed a training program offered to the sales staff. Training1 is encoded with a "1" if the employee completed the program and a "0" if not. Conversely, Training2 recorded the employee with a "0" if he or she completed the program.

| %Raise | Income | Education | Training1 | Training2 |
|--------|--------|-----------|-----------|-----------|
| 4.2    | 125    | 12        | 1         | 0         |
| 5.9    | 248    | 15        | 1         | 0         |
| 3.5    | 187    | 10        | 1         | 0         |
| 5.18   | 169    | 18        | 1         | 0         |
| 2.86   | 98     | 9         | 0         | 1         |
| 3.12   | 96     | 12        | 0         | 1         |
| 4.16   | 148    | 12        | 1         | 0         |
| 6.34   | 247    | 14        | 1         | 0         |
| 3.04   | 87     | 13        | 0         | 1         |
| 2.56   | 68     | 12        | 0         | 1         |

*(Continued)*

**EXAMPLE 4.2: (Continued)**

Some employees argue one method of encoding is preferred to the other. Director Welvaert insists it makes no difference. Two models are estimated using the alternative encoding schemes and a comparison is offered.

**Solution:**

■ Using Training1 in the model (those with the training were encoded with a "1") the Minitab printout reveals the results to be

$$\%Raise = -0.373 + 0.0143\ Income + 0.175\ Education + 0.199\ Training1$$

- For those with the training, the model becomes
$$\%Raise = -0.373 + 0.0143\ Income + 0.175\ Education + 0.199(1)$$
$$= -0.174 + 0.0143\ Income + 0.175\ Education$$

- For those without the training, the model becomes
$$\%Raise = -0.373 + 0.0143\ Income + 0.175\ Education + 0.199(0)$$
$$= -0.373 + 0.0143\ Income + 0.175\ Education$$

■ Using Training2 in the model (those with training encoded with "0") Minitab reports the regression equation is

$$\%Raise = -0.174 + 0.0143\ Income + 0.175\ Education - 0.199\ Training2$$

- Then, for those who have the training, the model is
$$\%Raise = -0.174 + 0.0143\ Income + 0.175\ Education - 0.199(0)$$
$$= -0.174 + 0.0143\ Income + 0.175\ Education$$

Clearly, this is the same model estimated for those with the training using Training1.

- Furthermore, the model for those without the training is
$$\%Raise = -0.174 + 0.0143\ Income + 0.175\ Education - 0.199\ Training2$$
$$= -0.174 + 0.0143\ Income + 0.175\ Education - 0.199(1)$$
$$= -0.373 + 0.0143\ Income + 0.175\ Education$$

This too is the same model as that obtained using Training1 on the RHS.

**Interpretation**: Obviously, it makes no difference to the outcome whether those with the training are encoded with a "1" or a "0." It is only imperative that Director Welvaert remembers how the data were stipulated in order to derive the proper distinction.

### ● Allowing for More Responses in a Qualitative Variable

Our gender illustration required only two categories—male and female. If there are more than two possible responses to a qualitative variable more dummy variables must be created. Suppose you wish to develop a model to estimate personal debt levels. Experience has shown that marital status is often useful in this regard. You have identified four classes for one's personal relationship: married, single, divorced, and widowed. You will need three dummy variables. In general, you must create one fewer dummy variables than there are responses to the qualitative variable. That's why there was only one dummy variable for gender in the example above—there were only two possible responses—male and female.

In this case, since there are $r = 4$ potential responses to marital status, you will require three dummy variables, one each for married, single, and divorced. If an observation fits a particular state of marriage a "1" is recorded for that category and a "0" if it does not.

A portion of the data might appear as

| Debt (Y) | Income (X₁) | Education (X₂) | Married | Single | Divorced |
|---|---|---|---|---|---|
| 5000 | 100 | 12 | 1 | 0 | 0 |
| 10000 | 75 | 10 | 0 | 0 | 1 |
| 8000 | 85 | 14 | 0 | 1 | 0 |
| 15000 | 115 | 16 | 0 | 0 | 0 |
| • | • | • | • | • | • |
| • | • | • | • | • | • |
| • | • | • | • | • | • |

The first observation is Married. A "1" was therefore recorded for "Married" and "0s" for "Single" and "Divorced." The second observation is Divorced as shown by the "1" in the Divorced column. The third observation is Single.

The fourth observation is Widowed, since a "0" is recorded for all other possibilities. A dummy variable for all four responses is not necessary. By process of elimination, if a "0" is recorded for the three dummy variables appearing in the data set, the observation must fall in the only remaining category. That is, as the fourth observation with all "0s" shows, the observation is not Married, not Single, and not Divorced. He or she *must* be Widowed. It's not necessary to have a dummy variable for Widowed.

In fact, if four dummy variables were used in the model then, taken together, they would sum to one in every case. They would be related in a linear fashion and constitute perfect multicollinearity attendant with all the damaging complications it causes.

Take a look at the partial data set seen here in which a dummy variable is created for all four categories. The data would be encoded as

| Married | Single | Divorced | Widowed |
|---------|--------|----------|---------|
| 1 | 0 | 0 | 0 |
| 0 | 0 | 1 | 0 |
| 0 | 1 | 0 | 0 |
| 0 | 0 | 0 | 1 |

Notice that now these four variables are related. They always sum to 1. Such was not the case in the encoding scheme cited above. They sometimes sum to one and other times (when the observation was Widowed) they do not.

There results then four distinct models—one for each marriage classification. This is just like the clothing example above based on differences in gender. There was only one dummy variable producing two distinct models.

## ● Using Dummy Variables to Deseasonalize Time Series Data

Dummy variables are often used to *deseasonalize* a data set consisting of time series data. Many economic variables exhibit seasonal patterns that repeat at specific times throughout the year. Consumer spending always increases around Christmas time. Gas consumption goes up around national holidays. Unemployment will rise in early spring when schools are dismissed for the summer and young workers flood the job market. These seasonal adjustments often obscure the true long-run behavior of a series. Dummy variables can be used to remove the seasonal influences and obtain a deseasonalized, or *seasonally adjusted*, measure of the variable in question.

Three years (12 quarters) of data are shown in Table 4.3 for the quarterly sales of ski equipment at Ski Masters, a sporting goods shop in Chicago. Each quarter registers three months of sales in hundreds of dollars. Data are also recorded for advertising, in hundreds of dollars, for the three quarters seen in the table. It is anticipated that sales will rise in the third quarter (months July through September) as ski enthusiasts prepare for the coming season and continue to rise in the fourth quarter as the ski season gets under way.

Quarter 1 is identified as the base response (time period in this case). Dummy variables are established for the three remaining time periods.

■ **Table 4.3**   Sales Data for Ski Masters

| Time | Sales | ADV | Q2 | Q3 | Q4 |
|---|---|---|---|---|---|
| 2009-Q1 | 89 | 4.5 | 0 | 0 | 0 |
| 2009-Q2 | 30 | 3.6 | 1 | 0 | 0 |
| 2009-Q3 | 69 | 2.6 | 0 | 1 | 0 |
| 2009-Q4 | 125 | 3.5 | 0 | 0 | 1 |
| 2010-Q1 | 74 | 1.2 | 0 | 0 | 0 |
| 2010-Q2 | 45 | 5.6 | 1 | 0 | 0 |
| 2010-Q3 | 84 | 6.9 | 0 | 1 | 0 |
| 2010-Q4 | 147 | 5.9 | 0 | 0 | 1 |
| 2011-Q1 | 68 | 4.5 | 0 | 0 | 0 |
| 2011-Q2 | 55 | 3.6 | 1 | 0 | 0 |
| 2011-Q3 | 68 | 2.5 | 0 | 1 | 0 |
| 2011-Q4 | 187 | 4.6 | 0 | 0 | 1 |

The data produce the following results with $t$-values in parentheses and $p$-values in brackets:

$$\hat{S} = 66.14 + 3.19\text{Adv} - 36.43Q_2 + 5.25Q_3 + 71.95Q_4$$

$$\begin{array}{ccccc} (4.00) & (0.864) & (-2.34) & (-0.342) & (4.52) \\ [0.005] & [0.416] & [0.051] & [0.743] & [0.003] \end{array}$$

The results of the model reveal that given a set value for advertising of, say, 10, the average sales in our base period of $Q_1$ is $66.14 + 3.19(10) = 98.04$, since the other three time periods would carry a value of zero. Since $Q_1$ was used as the base period, the coefficients for the remaining quarters give the seasonal increase or decrease in the mean values of sales for each quarter compared with $Q_1$. The coefficient of $Q_2$ of $-36.43$ indicates that the average value of sales in $Q_2$ is 36.43 ($3,643) less that in $Q_1$. Mean sales for the remaining quarters are figured in the same manner.

The deseasonalized values for Ski Masters' sales for each quarter of the years 2009 through 2011 can be found by first estimating sales levels for all 12 time periods based on the regression model. These $\hat{Y}$-values are then subtracted from the actual reported sales levels $(Y_i - \hat{Y})$. The differences are the residuals we have seen in the past. These residuals are then added to the mean value of $Y$, which is 86.75 in this case. The results are the deseasonalized sales levels for each of the 12 time periods as shown in Table 4.4.

■ **Table 4.4**  Deseasonalized Sales Values for Ski Masters

| Quarter | Sales | Advertising | Q2 | Q3 | Q4 | Predicted Sales | Residuals | Deseasonalized Sales |
|---------|-------|-------------|----|----|----|-----------------|-----------|----------------------|
| 2009-Q1 | 89 | 4.5 | 0 | 0 | 0 | 80.51337 | 8.486632 | 95.23663 |
| 2009-Q2 | 30 | 3.6 | 1 | 0 | 0 | 41.20402 | −11.204 | 75.54598 |
| 2009-Q3 | 69 | 2.6 | 0 | 1 | 0 | 69.19511 | −0.19511 | 86.55489 |
| 2009-Q4 | 125 | 3.5 | 0 | 0 | 1 | 149.2737 | −24.2737 | 62.4763 |
| 2010-Q1 | 74 | 1.2 | 0 | 0 | 0 | 69.97326 | 4.026737 | 90.77674 |
| 2010-Q2 | 45 | 5.6 | 1 | 0 | 0 | 47.59196 | −2.59196 | 84.15804 |
| 2010-Q3 | 84 | 6.9 | 0 | 1 | 0 | 82.92918 | 1.070817 | 87.82082 |
| 2010-Q4 | 147 | 5.9 | 0 | 0 | 1 | 156.9392 | −9.93923 | 76.81077 |
| 2011-Q1 | 68 | 4.5 | 0 | 0 | 0 | 80.51337 | −12.5134 | 74.23663 |
| 2011-Q2 | 55 | 3.6 | 1 | 0 | 0 | 41.20402 | 13.79598 | 100.546 |
| 2011-Q3 | 68 | 2.5 | 0 | 1 | 0 | 68.87571 | −0.87571 | 85.87429 |
| 2011-Q4 | 187 | 4.6 | 0 | 0 | 1 | 152.7871 | 34.21293 | 120.9629 |

If one of the variables for the quarters proved insignificant, we must conclude that the average sales for that quarter is the same as that for the base quarter. $Q_3$ reported a $p$-value of 0.743. There is no reason to believe that the mean sales in $Q_3$ differs from the mean sales in $Q_1$. Actually, to determine if seasonality does exist in the data set it is necessary to test the hypothesis that *all* dummy variables carry a coefficient of zero. This is accomplished using the $F$-test described in Section 4.8.

Deseasonalizing the data will also smooth out the data over the time period in question. Notice how the deseasonalized data in Figure 4.7 exhibit less variation. This also aids in analyzing the data and gaining a solid perspective on the trend and overall behavior of the variable.

● **Interpreting a Computer's Printout**

A dealer in construction machinery ships to customers on several continents around the globe. He wishes to estimate a model for shipping costs based on distance (in thousands of miles), weight (in tons), and destination. Four continents have been identified for inclusion in the study: Europe, Asia, South America, and Australia. Three dummy variables have been established for the first three destinations and the results of a Minitab computer run are shown below.

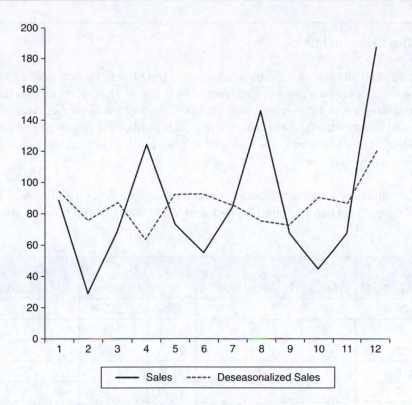

**■ Figure 4.7**    A Comparison of Actual and Deseasonalized Data

## Minitab Output 3

| Predictor | Coef | SE Coef | T | P | VIF |
|-----------|------|---------|------|-------|-------|
| Constant | 3552 | 2455 | 1.45 | 0.026 | |
| DISTANCE | 2.5650 | 0.5463 | 4.69 | 0.002 | 1.251 |
| WEIGHT | 485.9 | 497.9 | 3.98 | 0.048 | 1.036 |
| EUROPE | 2507 | 1803 | 4.39 | 0.002 | 1.884 |
| ASIA | 3175 | 1805 | 4.76 | 0.017 | 1.678 |
| SA | 3243 | 2174 | 3.49 | 0.024 | 1.460 |

Based on $p$-values all variables are judged significant at acceptable levels less than 10%. The dealer can expect the average cost of a shipment to Europe 5,689 miles away and weighing 2.3 to be

$$\hat{C} = 3552 + 2.565(5.689) + 485.9(2.3) + 2507(1) + 3175(0) + 3243(0)$$

$$= \$7,191$$

Shipments to other parts of the world would be evaluated in the same fashion. If the shipment is to Australia, "0s" would appear in the equation for the other three destinations.

## EXAMPLE 4.3: Fighting Crime in Miami

**Problem Statement**: In 2009 in an effort to combat street crime the Miami, Florida police department wished to know if a crime wave accompanied a heat wave. That is, do crimes go up with rising temperatures? There was also some question as to whether more crimes were committed near the end of the month. Government assistance is paid at the beginning of each month to welfare recipients. Does the crime rate rise later in the month—such as the third or fourth week—as welfare money runs out?

**Solution**: For the sake of conserving space, a portion of the data collected for $n = 40$ weeks is shown here. The complete data set can be found in the Excel file MIAMI CRIME. Week 1 is used as the base period.

| WEEK | CRIMES | TEMPERATURE | WEEK 2 | WEEK 3 | WEEK 4 | $\hat{Y}$ | RESIDUAL | DESEASONALIZED VALUES |
|------|--------|-------------|--------|--------|--------|------|----------|----------------------|
| 1 | 45 | 89 | 0 | 0 | 0 | 36.45 | 8.55 | 44.75 |
| 2 | 47 | 85 | 1 | 0 | 0 | 37.87 | 9.13 | 45.33 |
| 3 | 25 | 78 | 0 | 1 | 0 | 24.93 | 0.07 | 36.27 |
| 4 | 38 | 76 | 0 | 0 | 1 | 38.01 | −0.01 | 36.19 |
| 1 | 33 | 83 | 0 | 0 | 0 | 33.93 | −0.93 | 35.27 |
| 2 | 41 | 95 | 1 | 0 | 0 | 42.07 | −1.07 | 35.13 |
| 3 | 32 | 94 | 0 | 1 | 0 | 31.65 | 0.35 | 36.55 |
| 4 | 46 | 96 | 0 | 0 | 1 | 46.41 | −0.41 | 35.79 |
| • | • | • | • | • | • | • | • | • |
| • | • | • | • | • | • | • | • | • |
| • | • | • | • | • | • | • | • | • |

Regressing the number of crimes on the four RHS variables produced these results with $t$-values in parentheses and all $p$-values were virtually zero except for the constant term:

$$\hat{C} = -0.93 + 0.42T + 3.1WK2 - 6.9WK3 + 7.02WK4$$
$$(-0.15)\ (5.96)\quad (3.14)\qquad (-6.95)\qquad (7.09)$$

**Interpretation**: All four RHS variables prove to be statistically significant. Thus, the mean number of reported crimes is different in each week. If the temperature is 78 degrees, the mean number of crimes in the third week, for example, is

$$\hat{C} = -0.93 + 0.42(78) + 3.1(0) - 6.9(1) + 7.02(0) = 24.93$$

As a final and more conclusive search for seasonality the $F$-test demonstrated in Section 4.8 must be applied.

## SECTION 4.4 PROBLEMS

1. A shop owner tests the effectiveness of a training program his employees undertake by measuring their productivity in a model containing education levels and experience. The dummy variable is entered as "1" if the employee has been through the training. With $t$-values in parentheses and $n = 28$ observations the model appears as

$$\hat{P} = 12.3 + 2.3Edu + 1.58Exp + 2.54T$$
$$(2.58) \quad (2.48) \quad (1.68) \quad (2.09)$$

A. What are the equations for someone who has been through the program and for someone who has not?

B. What would be the estimated mean productivity of someone with 14 years of education and 10 years of experience who has had the training?

C. Draw a graph showing the relationships involved.

D. Are all the variables significant at the 5% level? At the 1% level?

2. Dealers in antiquities must always concern themselves with authenticity. Is the relic authentic or a fake? Certificates of Authenticity (COA) that accompany the object can often add greatly to its value. The auction price in thousands of dollars for 52 Roman artifacts was fitted to a model containing data on age (A) in centuries, a measure of condition (C), shipping costs to the winning bidder in hundreds of dollars (SC), and whether it came with a COA (encoded "1" if it did). The results of the model are shown here. Complete the table by providing the $p$-values and the coefficients.

| | Coefficients | Standard Error | t Stat | p-Value |
|---|---|---|---|---|
| Intercept | | 0.096899225 | 2.58 | |
| A | | 0.181451613 | 2.48 | |
| C | | 0.327380952 | 1.68 | |
| SC | | 0.416267943 | 2.09 | |
| COA | | 0.278309859 | 3.55 | |

A. What would be the estimated average cost of an artifact with an age of 20, a condition rating of 5, shipping costs of 25, and was complete with a COA?

B. Are all the variables significant at acceptable alpha-values?

3. Monthly data for several hundred workers are taken from http://www.bls.gov/data/#wages. Wages serve as the dependent variable in the model seen here. Gender was encoded as a "1" if male. Income is in hundreds of dollars, and experience and education are measured in years. The printout is seen here. Does there appear to be a difference in income based on gender after correcting for education and experience?

|  | Coefficients | Standard Error | t Stat | p-Value |
|---|---|---|---|---|
| Intercept | 2.14 | 0.829457364 |  |  |
| Edu | 1.05 | 0.423387097 |  |  |
| Experience | 2.69 | 1.601190476 |  |  |
| Gender | 3.2 | 2.012578616 |  |  |

4. The model in problem 3 above is expanded to include the geographical locations identified as East, South, Mid-West, and West. Each is encoded with a "1" if the observations falls in that locale. Since gender did not prove significant in problem 3 above, it has been removed from the model:

|  | Coefficients | Standard Error | t Stat | p-Value |
|---|---|---|---|---|
| Intercept | 3.55 | 1.375968992 | 2.58 |  |
| Edu | 2.58 | 1.040322581 | 2.48 |  |
| Experience | 1.54 | 0.916666667 | 1.68 |  |
| East | 1.25 | 0.352112676 | 3.55 |  |
| South | 3.2 | 0.987654321 | 3.24 |  |
| MidWest | 2.47 | 0.957364341 | 2.58 |  |

A. What variables prove significant at acceptable alpha-values?
B. What is your estimate of the average income of someone in the Mid-West with 15 years of education and 22 years of experience?

5. A "Lobster War" rages between the U.S. and Canada over fishing rights off the coast of Maine. Canadian lobster fishermen complain that U.S. boats can ply their trade year round while Canadian laws require a recess in fishing activities. Quarterly data are collected for the weight of lobsters taken by U.S. boats as seen in the table. As a spokesperson for equal treatment of the fishing boats you are to calculate and comment on the deseasonalized catch for each time period.

| Period | Catches | TEMP | Q2 | Q3 | Q4 |
|---|---|---|---|---|---|
| 2009-Q1 | 87 | 4.5 | 0 | 0 | 0 |
| 2009-Q2 | 55 | 3.6 | 1 | 0 | 0 |
| 2009-Q3 | 18 | 2.6 | 0 | 1 | 0 |
| 2009-Q4 | 68 | 3.5 | 0 | 0 | 1 |
| 2010-Q1 | 102 | 1.2 | 0 | 0 | 0 |
| 2010-Q2 | 56 | 5.6 | 2 | 0 | 0 |
| 2010-Q3 | 12 | 6.9 | 0 | 1 | 0 |
| 2010-Q4 | 98 | 5.9 | 0 | 0 | 1 |
| 2011-Q1 | 115 | 4.5 | 0 | 0 | 0 |
| 2011-Q2 | 87 | 3.6 | 0 | 1 | 0 |
| 2011-Q3 | 10 | 2.5 | 0 | 1 | 0 |
| 2011-Q4 | 98 | 4.6 | 0 | 0 | 1 |

The regression proves to be

|           | Coefficients   |
|-----------|----------------|
| Intercept | 95.39802433    |
| TEMP      | 0.905543929    |
| Q2        | −26.51922463   |
| Q3        | −7.17964566    |
| Q4        | −11.623896     |

## 4.5 INTERACTION BETWEEN INDEPENDENT VARIABLES

So far we have examined only additive models in which the variables in the equation are summed to derive the estimate. Generalized, the additive model appears as

$$\hat{Y} = b_0 + b_1 X_1 + b_2 X_2 + \cdots + b_k X_k$$

Notice that all variables are entered into the model through summation. In some models we may find *multiplicative* variables in which two or more variables *interact* in their impact on Y. The effect of one variable on Y depends on the value of another independent variable. Such variables are called *interaction terms*. The effect of $X_i$ on Y may depend on the value of $X_j$. If $X_j = 10$, the effect of a change in $X_i$ on Y may be different than if the value of $X_j$ is 12—or any value other than 10.

> An interaction term measures the way in which one independent variable affects the way another independent variable affects the dependent variable.

The interaction term is derived by multiplying two or more existing variables contained in the model. If the analyst suspects that the way in which $X_1$ affects Y depends on the value of $X_2$ he or she may introduce a third term derived as $X_1 X_2$, as seen here:

$$\hat{Y} = b_0 + b_1 X_1 + b_2 X_2 + b_3 X_1 X_2$$

The last term, $b_3 X_1 X_2$, is an interaction term in which the values for $X_1$ and $X_2$ are simply multiplied to get a third variable. The interaction term recognizes that the impact of $X_1$ on Y depends on the value of $X_2$ and vice versa.

In the model for the clothing manufacturer earlier in this chapter we included explanatory variables of age, height, and gender. Each proved significant in explaining weight. However, suppose we felt that the impact of age on weight depended to some degree on height. We might want to include in our model an interaction (multiplicative) term between age and height. Our model might appear as

$$\hat{W} = b_0 + b_1 A + b_2 H + b_3 A * H + b_4 G$$

Now $b_1$ measures the effect of age on weight, $b_2$ measures the effect of height on weight, and $b_3$ measures the way in which age affects the way in which height affects weight (and vice versa).

That is, $b_3$ reflects the way in which age and height interact in their impact on weight. Suppose we have a regression equation designed to model the number of businesses in a metropolitan area based on population, personal income, and tax rates. In an *a priori* sense we naturally anticipate a positive relationship between business starts and the two independent variables population and personal income. A negative correlation between the dependent variable and tax rates is thought likely. But we suspect that population and income might interact in their effect on new businesses. The model would be formed as

$$\hat{B} = b_0 + b_1 P + b_2 I + b_3 T + b_4 P * I$$

After running the model a hypothesis test is conducted for the significance of $b_4$. That is, the coefficient for the interaction term is subjected to the standard hypothesis test. If the null is rejected it is concluded that population not only affects business starts directly through $b_1$, but population also influences the way in which income affects business growth. The same is said for income. It has a bearing on the model via $b_2$, but it also impacts the dependent variable by influencing the way in which population affects business starts.

If $b_4 > 0$ and proves to be significant it would attest to the fact that population has a more pronounced effect on business starts at higher income levels as Figure 4.8 reveals.

Given a population level of $P_1$ it's evident from the figure that business starts are greater at higher level of income. If income is $I_2 = 20$ business starts are greater than if income is only $I_1 = 10$.

But that's not the point at the moment. Notice instead that as population increases to $P_2$ the number of business starts increases whether income is at $I = 10$ or at $I = 20$. However, and this

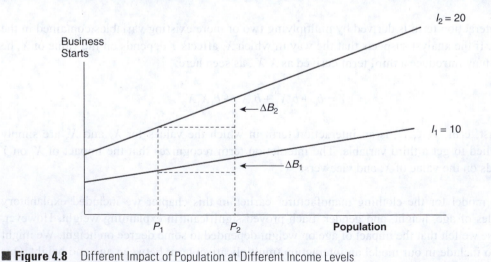

■ **Figure 4.8** Different Impact of Population at Different Income Levels

is the point, given the *same* increase in population from $P_1$ to $P_2$ the increase in business starts is greater at the higher level of income. This is evidenced by the fact that $\Delta B_2 > \Delta B_1$. A rise in population not only accelerates business growth directly since $b_1 > 0$, but population also stimulates business growth through its interaction with higher levels of income. Unlike the clothier encountered earlier, the two functions are *not* parallel. The slopes are different. The change in business starts given a change in population is not the same regardless of income.

A given increase in population from $P_1$ to $P_2$ increases business starts more at a higher level of income of 20 than it does if income is lower at 10. The impact of population on business starts depends on income. Population and income interact in their influence on business starts.

## SECTION 4.5 PROBLEMS

1. Define an interaction term and give three examples of models that could contain such RHS variables.

2. A sales manager for a large firm in the European Union wants to estimate sales ($S$) based on number of sales personnel ($P$) in a sales region, the number of new business starts ($B$), and inflation rates ($I$). There is also some interest in determining if $P$ and $B$ interact. Test for interaction and explain the consequence. Describe the full impact of $P$ on sales. Describe the full impact of $B$ on sales.

|  | Coefficients | Standard Error | t Stat | p-Value |
|---|---|---|---|---|
| Intercept | 5.71 | 2.213178295 | 2.58 | 0.0175 |
| P | 3.24 | 1.306451613 | 2.48 | 0.0217 |
| B | 6.54 | 3.892857143 | 1.68 | 0.1078 |
| I | 6.25 | 0.992063492 | 6.3 | 0 |
| P * B | 3.55 | 1 | 3.55 | 0.0019 |

## 4.6 INCORPORATING SLOPE DUMMIES

A *slope dummy* is a combination of a dummy variable and an interaction term. It's an interaction term in which one of the variables is a dummy variable. In the case of the clothing manufacturer earlier we examined the interaction between two quantitative variables, age and height.

Suppose, on the other hand, that we suspect an interaction between height and gender, the latter being a non-quantitative dummy variable. It seems reasonable that the effect of height on weight

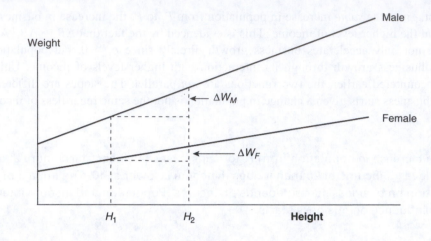

■ **Figure 4.9** Interaction Between Gender and Height

would depend on gender. That is, there is some interaction between height and gender in their impact on weight. If two people, one male and the other female, are of the same height, it seems reasonable to assume the male would weigh more despite the comparable height. If a male grew two inches it's logical to conclude that he would put on more weight than a woman who grew two inches. Given the differences in body structure, muscle mass, and other physical considerations, a change in the height of a male would likely have a different impact on his weight than would the same change in height of a female. Thus, height probably affects weight not only directly, but also through an interaction with gender.

A slope dummy could be incorporated into the model as

$$\hat{W} = b_0 + b_1 A + b_2 H + b_3 G + b_4 H * G$$

The last term is the slope dummy. It would generate a graph like that shown in Figure 4.9 in which the respective models do not produce parallel lines. Based on gender, a change in height has different effects on weight. This is much like the example of business starts cited above. That regression recognized that the effect of a change in population depended on income. Similarly, the clothier's illustration acknowledged that a given increase in height produced a bigger weight gain for men than it did for women. The only difference is that in the case of the clothier one of the interaction terms is a dummy variable.

Suppose our model in the clothier's illustration had included only age and height as predictors of weight. We could then measure only the effect of age and height without any reference to gender. Any difference between men and women would be ignored.

When the dummy variable for gender was included in the model the difference in weight based on gender became evident. But the effects of age and height were held constant between genders. That is, the effect of age and height on weight was considered the same for both males and females in our earlier model. This is why there was only a difference in the intercept of the two parallel models.

But the inclusion of the interaction term along with the gender dummy produced the model $W = f(A, H, G, H * G)$. It then became possible to examine the difference in both intercept and slope. See Figure 4.9. The change in height is held constant for both the male and female models. However, due to the inclusion of the slope dummy, $H * G$, the two models result in regression lines that are *not* parallel as opposed to Figure 4.5. Now, since $\Delta W_M > \Delta W_F$, it can clearly be seen that the same increase in height produced a larger gain in weight for males. Of course a standard hypothesis test for the interaction term is necessary to determine its significance before any conclusion can be registered.

## 4.7 CONTROL VARIABLES

We noted that a variable's coefficient will change if the composition of the model is altered. An explanatory variable may report a coefficient of some amount, but if another variable is added or removed from the model, that variable's coefficient will likely change. This happened with the coefficient for GDP in Arco's case. As the sole explanatory variable, GDP had a coefficient of 1.6364. When population was added to the mix, GDP's coefficient became 4.186. This tendency of coefficients to change given the composition of the model emphasizes the need to ensure the model is correctly specified.

There are times when a variable may not prove to be statistically significant based on the hypothesis test but should still be retained in the model. For example, fundamental economic theory dictates that the demand equation for any product must include a measure of consumer income. Income is an unequivocal determinant of market demand. If the test for income shows it to not be significant, it is still advisable to retain it as an RHS component. It becomes a *control variable* in that its retention serves to manage the coefficients of the other explanatory variables and provide a more accurate measure of their contribution to the regression equation.

> A control variable is included in the model to promote a more accurate and valid measure of the influence of other variables contained in the equation even though it may not lend any explanatory power of its own.

The analyst must decide if the variable is essential to the validity of the model's internal integrity despite its lack of explanatory power. This decision is often based on theory, common sense, and previous practice.

Another good example of a control variable can be shown with an *earnings function* often used by economists to explain wage levels. Wages are regressed on independent variables known or suspected to be related to an individual's income. In a simple case, to determine the impact of education on salaries, earnings can be regressed on education levels, yielding

$$\hat{E} = b_0 + b_1 Ed$$

However, it is generally recognized that experience, along with other demographic factors, is also related to earnings. The model might be expanded then to include a measure of experience as $\hat{E} = b_0 + b_1 Ed + b_2 Ex$. Education is still the focus of interest in our model. But the inclusion of experience allows us to more accurately capture the relationship between education and earnings after controlling for experience.

## 4.8 A PARTIAL *F*-TEST

So far we have examined two tests for our regression models: *t*-test for individual RHS variables and a global test for the model as a whole based on an *F*-test. In many cases we find it useful to test a subset of the variables contained in a regression equation. This *partial F-test* is designed to determine if the subset in question as a whole is useful in explaining variation in the *Y*-variable after controlling for the other variables. It is conducted to determine whether it is advisable to include the entire subset of RHS variables in the model.

The Marketing Director for Mid-West Manufacturing has recently developed a model to explain changes in the firm's sales (*S*) using advertising costs (*A*), local interest rates (*I*), and the number of the sales staff (*N*) at various locations. Two additional variables describing their competition are also included. They are the market share (*MS*) held by the largest competitor in the region and length of time the competition has been in business (*T*). Equation (4.8.1) is the *full* or *unrestricted* model. It contains all five RHS variables.

$$\hat{S} = b_0 + b_1 A + b_2 I + b_3 N + b_4 MS + b_5 T \tag{4.8.1}$$

The last two variables are external to Mid-West's operations. They pertain strictly to their competitors and may be referred to as *external variables*. The Marketing Director wants to determine the advisability of including this subset of external variables in the model. The hypothesis to be tested is

$$H_0: \beta_{MS} = \beta_T = 0$$
$$H_a: \text{At least one } \beta \text{ is not zero}$$

The null tests whether either of the external variables offers any explanatory contribution after inclusion of the internal factors. That is, after controlling for *A*, *I*, and *N*, does either *MS* or *T* provide further explanation for the variation in sales?

To answer this question the unrestricted model above must be compared with a model that excludes the test variables. This alternate model shown as Equation (4.8.2) is the *reduced* or *restricted* model in that it "restricts" the betas for *MS* and *T* to zero by excluding them from consideration. It assumes that the betas for $MS$ and $T$ are zero and carry no explanatory power for Mid-West's sales. That's why they are excluded from the analysis.

$$\hat{S} = b_0 + b_1 A + b_2 I + b_3 N \tag{4.8.2}$$

The decision whether to include the external variables rests on a comparison of the sum of the squared errors for the restricted model, $SSE_R$, to the sum of the squared errors from the unrestricted model, $SSE_U$. OLS is designed to minimize the SSE and when variables are removed from a model the SSE will likely rise. Therefore, since the restricted model excludes the test subset of variables, it's most likely that $SSE_R > SSE_U$.

Failure to reject the null means that the test subset provides no additional explanatory power. This decision depends on the size of the increase in the SSE suffered in moving from the full model to the reduced model. If the difference in the SSE of the unrestricted model and the SSE of the restricted model is significant the null is rejected. This would mean that $MS$ and/or $T$ offer explanatory evidence. The test subset should be included in the finished model.

Suppose the full model was revealed to be as seen here with $p$-values in brackets:

$$\hat{S} = 2.3 + 1.5A \ + \ 6.2I \ + \ 1.8\,N - 0.05\,MS - 3.7T$$
$$[0.022]\ [0.0001]\ \ [0.005]\ \ [0.211]\ \ \ [0.552]$$

It might seem simpler to test the significance of each external variable with individual $t$-tests. In which case, based on the high $p$-values for $MS$ and $T$, the null is not rejected and the variables would be excluded from the model. But this is not the intent. The Marketing Director wants to determine if $MS$ and $T$ as a single sub-group are significant. That is, the test is that *both* $\beta$s equal zero.

In a more general sense, if there are $m$ variables in the subset, the hypothesis to be tested is

$$H_0: \beta_1 = \beta_2 = \cdots = \beta_M = 0$$

If individual $t$-tests are conducted for each variable then the rejection of any one variable, even if all others were not rejected, would lead to a rejection of the hypothesis. Thus, to test this hypothesis with separate $t$-tests could produce misleading results.

Even more damaging is that the chosen alpha-value cannot be held constant. If $m$ variables are to be tested, individual $t$-tests will increase the actual alpha-value to $[1 - (1 - \alpha)^m]$. In Mid-West's case, if an alpha-value of 5% is desired, individual tests for $MS$ and $T$ will inflate the alpha-value to $[1 - (1 - 0.05)^2] = 0.0975$, well above the 5% test Mid-West preferred.

A partial $F$-test must instead be applied by comparing $SSE_R$ and $SSE_U$ from the two distinct models. The results of the unrestricted and restricted models are shown in Table 4.5.

■ **Table 4.5**  Partial ANOVA Tables for Mid-West

*Unrestricted Model:* Regression of Sales on Advertising, Interest Rate, Staff, Market Share, and Time

**ANOVA**

|  | df | SS | MS |
|---|---|---|---|
| Regression | 5 | 163.632 | 32.7264 |
| Residual | 49 | 8.102 | 0.165346939 |
| Total | 54 | 171.734 |  |

*Restricted Model:* Regression of Sales on Advertising, Interest Rate, and Staff

**ANOVA**

|  | df | SS | MS |
|---|---|---|---|
| Regression | 3 | 125.447 | 41.81566667 |
| Residual | 51 | 12.554 | 0.246156863 |
| Total | 54 | 138.001 |  |

Table 4.5 displays $SSE_R = 12.554$ and $SSE_U = 8.102$. The $F$-statistic to be used is

$$F_{test} = \frac{\dfrac{SSE_R - SSE_U}{m}}{\dfrac{SSE_U}{n - k - 1}} \qquad (4.8.3)$$

where $m$ is the number of variables removed from the restricted model (2 in Mid-West's example) and $k$ is the number of variables in the full (unrestricted) model. The $m$ and $n - k - 1$ are the degrees of freedom for the numerator and denominator, respectively, in Equation (4.8.3).

Since there were $n = 55$ observations and $k = 5$ the denominator carries 49 degrees of freedom.

The Marketing Director at Mid-West finds the $F$-statistic to be

$$F_{test} = \frac{\dfrac{12.554 - 8.102}{2}}{\dfrac{8.104}{55 - 5 - 1}} = 13.46$$

At an alpha-value of 5% with 2 and 49 degrees of freedom Excel reports the critical $F$-statistic is FINV(.05,2,49) = 3.187. The $F$-value calculated with Mid-West's data is well above 3.187, leading to the decision to reject the null. At least one of the external variables carries a non-zero $\beta$, thereby lending explanatory power to the model. The subset of external variables $MS$ and $T$ should be included in the model. That is, the full unrestricted model should be used.

This may seem surprising considering their individual $p$-values suggested the nulls should not be rejected. If tested separately $MS$ and $T$ would be excluded. But the $F$-test conducted here determined that these variables were *jointly* significant.

---

**EXAMPLE 4.4: Miami Crime Revisited**

**Problem Statement:** Applying the partial $F$-test to the Miami crime study produced values of $SSE_R = 1209.1$ and $SSE_U = 171.19$. Using Equation (4.8.3) produced the results seen here:

**Solution:**

$$\frac{\dfrac{1209 - 171.19}{3}}{\dfrac{171.19}{40 - 4 - 1}} = 70.73$$

If the hypothesis for the four weeks, $H_0: \beta_1 = \beta_2 = \beta_3 = \beta_4 = 0$, is tested at the 5% level, the Excel command =FINV(.05,3,45) = 2.874 results.

**Interpretation:** The null is rejected and it is concluded at the 5% level of significance that weekly seasonality throughout the month does prevail.

---

## SECTION 4.8 PROBLEMS

1. An analysis of subscriptions for a popular magazine produces the partial ANOVA tables below for both the unrestricted and restricted models. The publisher needs to determine if a subset of variables carries any explanatory value.

**ANOVA**

|  | df | SS | MS |
|---|---|---|---|
| Regression | 6 | 179.63 | 29.93833 |
| Residual | 143 | 21.93 | 0.153357 |
| Total | 149 | 201.56 |  |

and

**ANOVA**

|  | df | SS | MS |
|---|---|---|---|
| Regression | 4 | 164.58 | 41.145 |
| Residual | 145 | 26.63 | 0.183655 |
| Total | 149 | 191.21 | |

    A. How many variables are in the subset of interest?

    B. At the 5% level should the subset be retained as part of the model?

2. A study to determine if international shipments of cargo to foreign ports were delayed by government restrictions and red tape is conducted. A total of 23 shipments to several different countries were selected for the survey. The dependent variable was the number of days required for final delivery. Explanatory variables included the distance in miles, whether the nation's government was freely elected in a democratic manner, if the currency was allowed to fluctuate on the world market, and whether the government actively encouraged free trade. Each of the three dummy variables was encoded with a "1" if the condition prevailed.

The results were

$$\hat{D} = 8.2 + 17.3Dist + 2.1Free + 3.4Curr + 2.7Govt$$

$SSE_R = 412.5$ and $SSE_U = 79.87$. Interpret the results. At the 1% level does it appear that the three government issues impact shipment times?

## 4.9 COMPUTER APPLICATIONS

Much of the work done in this chapter can be completed with the aid of computer software. Instructions to do so are given throughout the chapter. One important feature not discussed earlier in reference to Excel is that when choosing the independent variables for a multiple regression model it is necessary that all of them are in adjacent columns.

● **Excel**

Suppose you have a spreadsheet such as that shown here and you want to regress $Y$ on $X_1$ and $X_3$. Since these two columns are not adjacent you will receive an error message, "Input Range Must Be A Contiguous Reference." You must copy and paste column D between columns B and C. Variables $X_1$ and $X_3$ are now contiguous and you can proceed with the regression as detailed in Chapter 2.

| | A | B | C | D |
|---|---|---|---|---|
| 1 | Y | X1 | X2 | X3 |
| 2 | 12 | 2 | 6 | 4 |
| 3 | 41 | 6 | 5 | 6 |
| 4 | 27 | 5 | 2 | 2 |
| 5 | 60 | 9 | 3 | 7 |
| 6 | 33 | 4 | 7 | 8 |
| 7 | 39 | 5 | 8 | 9 |
| 8 | 25 | 6 | 9 | 5 |

Choose Data > Data Analysis > Regression and enter the ranges. Check Labels and click OK. The Excel report is

## SUMMARY OUTPUT

### Regression Statistics

| | |
|---|---|
| Multiple R | 0.995534041 |
| R Square | 0.991088027 |
| Adjusted R Square | 0.982176053 |
| Standard Error | 2.013584745 |
| Observations | 7 |

### ANOVA

| | df | SS | MS | F | Significance F |
|---|---|---|---|---|---|
| Regression | 3 | 1352.693572 | 450.8978574 | 111.2085932 | 0.001424443 |
| Residual | 3 | 12.16357057 | 4.054523524 | | |
| Total | 6 | 1364.857143 | | | |

| | Coefficients | Standard Error | t Stat | p-Value | Lower 95% |
|---|---|---|---|---|---|
| Intercept | 6.23267107 | 3.728124123 | 1.671798165 | 0.193157365 | −5.63188377 |
| X1 | 3.972868269 | 0.48113725 | 8.257245239 | 0.003719607 | 2.441674805 |
| X2 | −2.41796586 | 0.41517731 | −5.823935471 | 0.010081954 | −3.739245355 |
| X3 | 3.49009295 | 0.40828922 | 8.548089891 | 0.00336411 | 2.190734432 |

Excel will not report VIFs directly. You must manually regress one RHS variable on all the others as explained in Section 4.2 and then use Equation (4.2.4) to compute the VIF.

To get an interaction (multiplicative) variable for $X_1$ and $X_3$ in Spread Sheet 1, place the cursor in cell E2 and enter "= B2*D2." Drag the entry down column E and the values will appear.

● **Minitab**

Enter the data in a Minitab worksheet as shown in the Excel illustration above. Choose Stat > Regression > Regression and enter the variables in the proper windows. Choose Options > VIF > OK > OK. The output appears as:

**Regression Analysis: C1 versus C2, C3, C4**

The regression equation is

C1 = 6.23 + 3.97 C2 - 2.42 C3 + 3.49 C4

| Predictor | Coef | SE Coef | T | P | VIF |
|-----------|------|---------|---|---|-----|
| Constant | 6.233 | 3.728 | 1.67 | 0.193 | |
| C2 | 3.9729 | 0.4811 | 8.26 | 0.004 | 1.566 |
| C3 | -2.4180 | 0.4152 | -5.82 | 0.010 | 1.676 |
| C4 | 3.4901 | 0.4083 | 8.55 | 0.003 | 1.433 |

S = 2.01358   R-Sq = 99.1%   R-Sq(adj) = 98.2%

Analysis of Variance

| Source | DF | SS | MS | F | P |
|--------|----|----|----|----|----|
| Regression | 3 | 1352.69 | 450.90 | 111.21 | 0.001 |
| Residual Error | 3 | 12.16 | 4.05 | | |
| Total | 6 | 1364.86 | | | |

● **SPSS**

After entering the data choose Analyze > Regression > Linear and enter the variables in the proper windows. Choose Statistic > Collinearity Diagnostics (which produce the VIFs) > Continue > OK. The response is

**Coefficients[a]**

| Model | | Unstandardized Coefficients | | Standardized Coefficients | t | Sig. | Collinearity Statistics | |
|-------|---|------|-----------|------|---|------|-----------|-----|
| | | B | Std. Error | Beta | | | Tolerance | VIF |
| 1 | (Constant) | 6.233 | 3.728 | | 1.672 | .193 | | |
| | X1 | 3.973 | .481 | .563 | 8.257 | .004 | .639 | 1.566 |
| | X2 | -2.418 | .415 | -.411 | -5.824 | .010 | .597 | 1.676 |
| | X3 | 3.490 | .408 | .558 | 8.548 | .003 | .698 | 1.433 |

a. Dependent Variable: Y

## 4.10 REVIEW PROBLEM

In an effort to ramp up employee productivity Webb Industries is undertaking a thorough study of their current work force. The characteristics and performance of both salaried and hourly workers are examined. Data on $n = 120$ employees are collected including variables for a measure of productivity, years of education (Edu), and if the employee has (1) no high school degree, (2) high school degree, (3) undergraduate college degree, or a (4) graduate degree. Years of experience is also included in the data set. A partial data set is shown here in an abridged Excel worksheet.

| | A | B | C | D | E | F |
|---|---|---|---|---|---|---|
| | PRODUCTIVITY | EDU | High School | College | Graduate | Experience |
| | 40 | 12 | 1 | 0 | 0 | 5 |
| | 35 | 17 | 0 | 1 | 0 | 8 |
| | 65 | 18 | 0 | 0 | 1 | 7 |
| | 57 | 10 | 0 | 0 | 0 | 6 |
| | ... | ... | ... | ... | ... | ... |
| | ... | ... | ... | ... | ... | ... |

Productivity is regressed on the independent variables generating the following output:

| | Coefficients | Standard Error | t Stat | p-Value |
|---|---|---|---|---|
| Intercept | 3.421 | 1.688715569 | 2.0258 | 0.045 |
| Edu | 2.354 | 0.719701602 | 3.2708 | 0.0014 |
| High School | 2.958 | 1.268765549 | 2.3314 | 0.0214 |
| College | 3.254 | 1.43051831 | 2.2747 | 0.0247 |
| Graduate | 3.254 | 1.672233928 | 1.9459 | 0.254 |
| Experience | 6.257 | 2.750692399 | 2.2747 | 0.047 |

Based on the p-values all variables report statistical significance at acceptable levels of less than 5% except whether the employee has a graduate degree. The question arises as to whether the model should be estimated to the exclusion of a graduate degree. Should the variable be retained as a control variable?

Aware of the many problems multicollinearity can cause, Webb Industries' management feels it advisable to test for it. The test begins with a statement of the set of hypotheses:

$$H_0: \rho_{Ex,Ed} = 0$$
$$H_0: \rho_{Ex,Ed} \neq 0$$

The bivariate correlation between the two suspect variables is 0.421. The $t$-test is

$$t = \frac{r_{Ex,Ed}}{S_{r_{Ex,Ed}}} = \frac{0.421}{\sqrt{\dfrac{1-r^2}{n-2}}} = \frac{0.421}{\sqrt{\dfrac{1-(0.421)^2}{120-2}}} = 5.01$$

The critical *t*-test at an alpha-value of 5% is 1.98. This is found using the Excel command of =TINV(.05,118). Since this is a large sample a *Z*-value of 1.96 could be used. The *t*-test value of 5.01 > 1.98 and is far into the right-tailed rejection region. Using =TDIST(5.01,118,2) reveals the *p*-value of 1.93072E-06, or 0.0000. The null is rejected and it is concluded that multicollinearity does indeed prevail.

As a further test, the VIFs for Education and Experience are determined. Regressing Education on all other RHS variables results in VIF(Edu) = 5.24, while a regression of Experience on all other RHS variables produces VIF(Exp) = 6.24.

The decision is made to remove Experience, since its correlation with productivity is lower than that of Education. Multicollinearity is eliminated.

A slope dummy is tested involving Education and Graduate. This would permit Graduate to offer any explanatory power it might possess despite its insignificant *p*-value when tested on its own. The final model becomes

|  | Coefficients | Standard Error | t Stat | p-Value |
|---|---|---|---|---|
| Intercept | 1.254 | 0.404307454 | 3.1016 | 0.0024 |
| Edu | 2.354 | 0.832567023 | 2.8274 | 0.0055 |
| High School | 2.958 | 1.268765549 | 2.3314 | 0.0214 |
| College | 3.254 | 1.43051831 | 2.2747 | 0.0247 |
| Grad*Edu | 4.23 | 1.369596892 | 3.0885 | 0.0025 |

All variables are significant and Graduate is allowed to contribute to the model. All VIFs are acceptable and hypothesis tests report no presence of multicollinearity.

# CHAPTER PROBLEMS

**CHAPTER PROBLEMS 4**

## Conceptual Problems

1.  How does the use of a multiple regression model affect the number of degrees of freedom in a regression model? Contrast your response with that involving a simple regression model.

2.  Provide an interpretation of a partial regression coefficient. What additional condition must be imposed that is not required in a simple regression model?

3.  Explain the role the adjusted coefficient of determination plays in a multiple regression model. What value does it contribute to the interpretation of the model? What does it adjust for and why is that important?

4.  Define multicollinearity. Fully describe the problems it can cause and the effect each has on the model.

5.  Discuss the various methods to detect multicollinearity. What advantages and disadvantages does each method of detection offer?

6.  How can the ill-effects of multicollinearity be mitigated? Describe each potential remedy and note the advantages and disadvantages of each.

7.  Define the Variance Inflation Factor. What function does it perform in regression analysis?

8.  Describe fully how the Variance Inflation Factor for a variable can be determined.

9.  How does the $R^2$ value found in a VIF test differ from that for the entire model?

10. What is meant by Analysis of Variance? What is its purpose? What exactly is the hypothesis in an ANOVA test? What does it mean if the null is not rejected? How do you interpret the rejection of the null?

11. How is the F-value in an ANOVA calculated? Why does a large F-value result in a rejection of the null? Use a graph in your response.

12. Clearly explain the three types of deviations as they pertain to an ANOVA test. Use a graph in the explanation.

13. What are the numbers of degrees of freedom for the regression sum of squares, error sum of squares, and the total sum of squares?

14. When must a dummy variable be used in a model? Provide your own original example of a dummy variable that might be used in a regression model.

15. A model to explain the per acre yield of grain uses rain fall, temperature, length of growing cycle in weeks, and four types of fertilizer used. Write the equation that would be used to estimate yield.

16. Distinguish between an intercept dummy and a slope dummy. Provide a definition of both and examples of models that would incorporate each.

17. When would an interaction term be incorporated into a model? Explain its intended purpose. Provide an example of a regression model that would use an interaction term. Give an interpretation of the interaction term in your model.

## Computational Problems

1.  As the product manager for a chemical company you must analyze the time required for a chemical reaction to be completed. A regression model to estimate time T measured in hours is provided here showing t-values in parentheses and p-values in brackets.

$$\hat{T} = 3.5 + 1.2X_1 + 0.54X_2 - 0.26X_3 + 2.54X_4$$
$$(0.615)\ (2.007)\ (1.828)\quad (-2.859)\quad (0.953)$$
$$[0.54]\quad [0.047]\ [0.07]\quad\ [0.005]\quad [0.35]$$

Comment on the model. Are there any changes you might make?

2. El Dorado Industries sells perishable farm products to retailers throughout its market area. Recently, losses due to spoilage have reached unacceptable levels and the Quality Control Division has been asked to explain what factors might be associated with these losses. Data for $n = 150$ observations collected on the variables seen here produce this partial printout. You are asked to fill in the missing values that somehow were not reported. You can use either $t$-values or $Z$-values given the large sample size. Excel functions of TDIST and TINV will provide much of the missing information.

| | Coefficients | Standard Error | t Stat | P-value |
|---|---|---|---|---|
| Intercept | 1.05 | | 3.1455 | |
| TEMP | 2.5 | 1.287266361 | 1.9421 | |
| DURATION | 0.354 | 0.217058066 | | 0.105 |
| SOURCE | | 0.526246547 | 2.2803 | |

3. The same study for El Dorado mentioned in the previous problem also produced the results shown below. Provide the missing values for $R^2$ and the adjusted $R^2$.

| Regression Statistics | |
|---|---|
| Multiple R | 0.739594 |
| R Square | |
| Adjusted R Square | |
| Standard Error | 1.59 |
| Observations | 150 |

4. Based on the Minitab printout of an ANOVA table from a regression model with two RHS variables:

```
Analysis of Variance

Source          DF      SS       MS       F       P
Regression       1    20.573   20.573
Residual Error  15    30.231    2.015
Total           16    50.804
```

A. Fill in the missing values. Use the FINV and FDIST Excel functions if needed.
B. How many observations were in the data set?

5. Given these results with $t$-values in parentheses for a model with 30 observations,

$$\hat{Y} = 3.2 + 6.55X_1 + 2.58X_2 + 7.66X_3 + 12.33X_4$$
$$(3.45)\ (2.022)\ \ (1.682)\ \ \ (2.403)\ \ (0.6198)$$

find the $p$-values for all variables.

6. Access the data file AIRPORT, which contains data for the number of minutes late that flights arrived at Chicago O'Hare Airport ($Y$), the number of minutes late that flights departed to Chicago ($X_1$), the number of passengers ($X_2$), whether the flight faced inclement weather ($X_3$), encoded with a "1" if it did, and miles in hundreds the departure airport was from Chicago ($X_4$).

   A. Use Excel, Minitab, or some similar software to estimate the model.
   B. Comment on the significance of each RHS variable.
   C. What are the two models that result, based on the dummy variable?
   D. How many minutes late would a flight arrive in Chicago that was 7 minutes late departing for Chicago, had 95 passengers on board, incurred bad weather, and was 530 miles from Chicago?
   E. How many minutes would the arrival time in Chicago vary from the designated time if a flight that left for Chicago 5 minutes late had 75 passengers, encountered no bad weather, and had to fly 730 miles?

7. An investment analyst wishes to explain his clients' rates of return on their portfolios using two variables measuring returns from stocks and three from bond mutuals. The results of an unrestricted model are shown here along with a reduced model with just the stock returns. Based on this information does it appear that at any acceptable alpha-value the bond funds jointly offer explanatory power after controlling for the stocks?

**ANOVA**

|  | df | SS | MS |
|---|---|---|---|
| Regression | 5 | 95.36 | 19.072 |
| Residual | 29 | 52.68 | 1.816551724 |
| Total | 34 | 148.04 | |

**ANOVA**

|  | df | SS | MS |
|---|---|---|---|
| Regression | 2 | 73.25 | 36.625 |
| Residual | 32 | 63.14 | 1.973125 |
| Total | 34 | 136.39 | |

8. Part of an ANOVA table appears as seen here. The rest was obliterated by the Division Chief when he placed his morning coffee cup on the computer printout. But now he wants to know if the model as a whole is significant at the 5% level based on a global test. Complete the ANOVA table and provide your response.

**ANOVA**

| | df | SS |
|---|---|---|
| Regression | 4 | 6585328 |
| Residual | 19 | 69524993 |
| Total | | |

9. How many observations were originally in the data set on the previous problem?

10. What is the critical $F$-value in the preceding problem at the 5% level? At the 1% level?

11. A production function for auto factories estimates output ($Q$) using as predictor variables labor ($L$), capital ($K$), and hours of training for all employees ($T$).

   A. Using your preferred software, access the file OUTPUT and estimate the model.
   B. Discuss the significance of the RHS variables.
   C. Comment on the difference between the $R^2$ and the adjusted $R^2$ values.
   D. Create an interaction term with capital and labor. Run the regression including the newly created interaction term. Discuss its significance. Would you advise retaining it in the model? Explain.

12. An investment broker is interested in predicting stock dividends based on the three variables shown below in the partial Excel output. Public is whether the company is publically or privately held. It's encoded as "1" if it's held privately. $n = 16$. Complete the table and comment on the model.

| | Coefficients | Standard Error | t Stat | P-value |
|---|---|---|---|---|
| Intercept | 0.65 | 1.153300213 | | |
| Price | 0.95 | 0.2880621 | | |
| EPS | 1.2 | 0.592709671 | | |
| Public | −0.58 | 0.268792288 | | |

13. As energy costs skyrocket, customers of Burlington Power expressed concern over their home heating bills. The staff at Burlington selects a sample of $n = 50$ home owners to form a data set regressing monthly invoices for February on family size, square footage of the home, and if the home was located in the city, a suburban locale, or rural county area. Partial results are shown here.

| | Coefficients | Standard Error | t Stat | p-Value |
|---|---|---|---|---|
| Intercept | −11.77 | 21.11589523 | | |
| FamSize | 23.61 | 11.39918888 | | |
| Footage | 0.2496 | 0.104693595 | | |
| City | 8.89 | 4.304876277 | | |
| County | −5.24 | 8.506493506 | | |

| | |
|---|---|
| Multiple R | 0.611531 |
| R Square | |
| Adjusted R Square | |
| Standard Error | 46.82 |
| Observations | |

## ANOVA

| | df | SS | MS | F | Significance F |
|---|---|---|---|---|---|
| Regression | 4 | 60243.54 | | | |
| Residual | 45 | 100845.3 | | | |
| Total | | | | | |

A. Fill in the missing values in all three output tables.

B. Which variables are significant at the 5% level? At the 1% level?

C. Compute the expected power bill if a family of three lived in the county in a 1,125-square-foot house.

D. What is the bill for same family living in same-size house in the suburbs?

14. Draw a graph depicting the three living locations in the previous problem.

15. Man's Best Friend Dog Food Company plans to market a new dry dog chow in certain test cities around the nation. Primary interest rests on the weight gain it creates in various dog breeds. Data are provided in the MAN'S BEST FRIEND data set. WEIGHT is the weight of the dog in pounds after eating the food for 12 weeks, AGE is in years, BEGWGT is weight in pounds at the start of the experiment, and three breeds were identified as SMALL, MEDIUM, and LARGE. In each case a "1" was entered if it was determined the dog fell into that category. SERVING was the number of cups feed per day. Access the data set and regress WEIGHT on all other variables.

A. Identify the significant variables. What is the level of significance for each?

B. Find the difference in weight for each dog and determine if the difference is a function of the number of cups each was fed.

## COMPUTER PROBLEM

The May 2011 issue of *Fast Company*, a popular international magazine dedicated to "the exploration of economic world-wide concerns," carried a story detailing a national restaurant chain's concern over the number of dinner reservations that were subsequently canceled or not kept. Their anxiety stemmed from the lost business they suffered due to those no-shows.

The data file RESERVATIONS contains hypothetical data that might explain the propensity for diners to alter their culinary plans. Access this data set and develop a model containing the explanatory variables you feel best fit the equation. Consider significance levels, VIFs, partial *F*-tests, and any intseraction terms you think might prove of explanatory value.

Does the dummy variable permit the inclusion of slope dummies? You will likely want to test several different models before making a final choice. Analyze the ANOVA table that results from your final model. Write a complete report detailing your findings.

The variables are:

■ Lost Reservations: The number of reservations not kept during the week the survey was taken.

■ Pop: City population in thousands.

■ PerCapInc: Per capita income in the city.

■ RestPerCap: Number of restaurants in the city per 100 people.

■ A dummy variable was included for Style that included whether the dining establishment was upscale, family-oriented, or had only private dining.

## Chapter 5

# RESIDUAL ANALYSIS AND MODEL SPECIFICATION

## INTRODUCTION

The regression model is based on several assumptions detailed in Chapter 2. Any violation of these assumptions threatens the integrity of the model. It is essential that after the model is estimated certain tests be conducted to determine if these assumptions hold. If it is decided not all assumptions are valid, some corrective action must be taken to avoid basing any policy decisions on a flawed model. These assumptions must be authenticated if the model is to command any integrity or validity.

A battery of checks on these requisite conditions can be performed using residual plots. Once the model is estimated the residuals are calculated and examined to verify whether the assumptions prevail. The residual, you recall, is the difference between the actual $Y$-value and the estimated or fitted $Y$-value, $(Y_i - \hat{Y})$. It reflects that portion of the variation in $Y$ not explained by the model.

This chapter provides a thorough discussion of the base assumptions and details the manner in which residuals can be used to test for their veracity. Numerous statistical tests can be carried out to determine if the conditions necessary to conduct OLS procedures are present. Based on the results of these diagnostics the researcher is able to proceed using the proper analytical tools with reasonable certainty that the final results offer valid conclusions.

The importance of proper model specification is also examined in this chapter. Selecting the correct variables for the regression model and ensuring that parsimony is preserved is critical to establishing a viable model. Without the appropriate RHS variables a suitable model is unlikely to result. It is therefore essential that the model contain all the explanatory variables it should and none that it shouldn't. Any bias or misspecification must be eliminated if we are to devise a suitable model. But first let's consider the ways in which residuals can be used to test the base assumptions upon which the OLS model is built.

## 5.1 USING RESIDUALS TO EVALUATE THE MODEL

A wise man learns from his mistakes. An even wiser man learns from the mistakes of others. This declaration has been attributed to many men of wisdom. So it should come as no surprise that we can gain considerable insight into our regression model by examining the residuals. Most conventional software permits the formation of residual plots so the task of probing the residuals can be quickly and easily performed. Although the plots are all too often a bit difficult to read and far from conclusive, they offer some perception as to whether the base assumptions might hold. Graphing the residuals serves as a credible launching pad for a thorough assessment of the model's reported residuals. This section examines some of the ways in which residual plots can be used to test whether certain assumptions prevail. In general, it's simply a matter of plotting the residuals after the model has been estimated and searching for certain patterns that serve as telltale signs that the violation of one or more of the fundamental assumptions has occurred.

● **A Test for Randomness**

One of the basic assumptions of the OLS model is that the error terms are random and have an expected value of zero. If any pattern can be seen in the residual plot, this assumption has likely been violated. Consider Figure 5.1. The residuals from two regression models have been plotted against one of the independent variables in Figures 5.1A and 5.1B. In both cases the residual (Res) terms clearly appear to be non-random.

In Figure 5.1A several negative residuals are followed by several positive residuals, while in Figure 5.1B the residuals change signs twice. The residuals in Figure 5.2, on the other hand, do

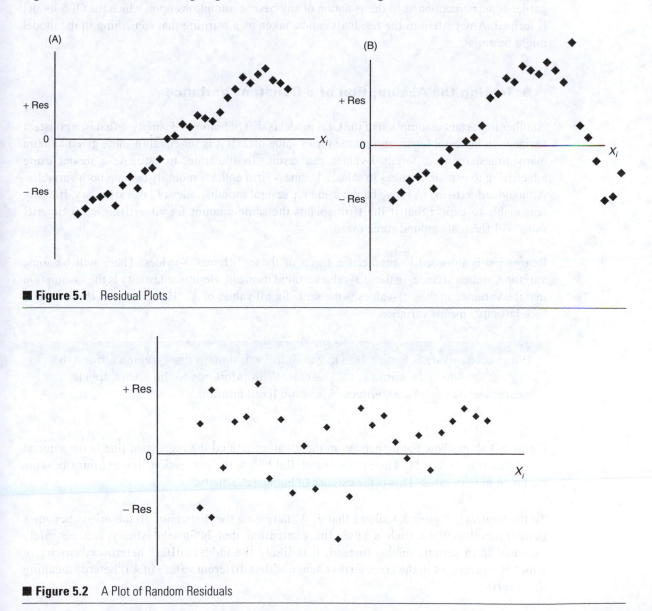

■ **Figure 5.1**   Residual Plots

■ **Figure 5.2**   A Plot of Random Residuals

appear to be random in that no pattern is visually detectable. The residuals seem to be randomly distributed around a mean of zero.

> If the residual plot exhibits any pattern the model may not meet the required assumption of random errors.

In practice the patterns, or absence thereof, are not nearly as obvious as suggested in these conveniently derived examples. But by examining residual plots the researcher is often able to garner some perception as to the violation of any basic assumptions upon which the OLS model is formed. Any pattern in the residuals can be taken as a warning that something in the model might be amiss.

## ● Testing the Assumption of a Constant Variance

Another important assumption of the OLS model is that of homoscedasticity—that is, a constant variance in the error terms around the mean value of $Y$. If $X$ is set equal to some given amount many times, many different $Y$-values can result. To illustrate, to estimate a model using advertising to explain changes in sales, a business firm collects monthly data on both variables. Although advertising ($X$) may be the same for several months, sales ($Y$) can still vary. It's only reasonable to expect that if the firm spends the same amount for advertising each time its sales will fluctuate around some mean.

Regression is intended to predict the mean of those different $Y$-values. There will be some variation, some variance, in those $Y$-values around its mean. Homoscedasticity is the assumption that the variance in those $Y$-values is the same for all values of $X$. "Homo" means *the same* and "scedasticity" means variance.

> Homoscedasticity is a condition in which the variation in the $Y$-values around the regression line is the same at all $X$-values. With reference to the errors, this is expressed as $\text{var}(\varepsilon_i) = \sigma^2$, where $\sigma^2$ is some fixed amount.

Figure 5.3 shows how the dispersion in the $Y$-values around the regression line is the same at $X = 10$ as it is at $X = 11$. The errors above and below the regression line exhibit the same variance in both cases. This is the essence of homoscedasticity.

To the contrary, Figure 5.4 shows that as $X$ increases, the dispersion in the errors becomes more pronounced. In such a case, the contention that homoscedasticity can be safely assumed is in serious doubt. Instead, it is likely the model suffers heteroscedasticity in which the variances in the error terms change across different values of $X$ ("hetero" meaning *different*).

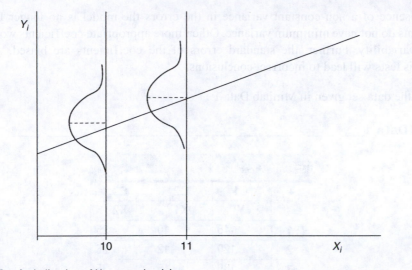

■ **Figure 5.3**    An Indication of Homoscedasticity

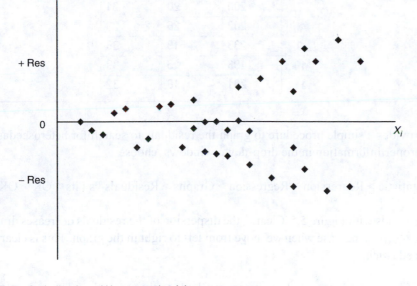

■ **Figure 5.4**    An Indication of Heteroscedasticity

In plotting the data, several variables can serve as the candidate for the horizontal axis. It is possible to plot the dependent variable of the fitted values on the horizontal axis and derive the same information. If time series data are used in the study, the errors can be plotted against time to detect non-constant variance. Methods to cope with heteroscedasticity will be examined in a separate chapter.

In the absence of a non-constant variance in the errors the model is no longer BLUE. The coefficients do not have minimum variance. Other, more appropriate coefficients would provide smaller variability. Further, the standard errors of the coefficients are biased. As a result hypothesis tests will lead to incorrect conclusions.

Presume the data set given in Minitab Data 1:

**Minitab Data 1** _____

| ▦ Worksheet 1 *** | | | |
|---|---|---|---|
| ↓ | C1 | C2 | C3 |
| | Y | X1 | X2 |
| 1 | 145 | 10 | 25 |
| 2 | 120 | 12 | 26 |
| 3 | 189 | 15 | 35 |
| 4 | 173 | 14 | 28 |
| 5 | 231 | 23 | 36 |
| 6 | 228 | 19 | 37 |
| 7 | 200 | 20 | 31 |
| 8 | 202 | 26 | 29 |
| 9 | 233 | 19 | 38 |
| 10 | 196 | 13 | 33 |
| 11 | 201 | 18 | 32 |

Minitab provides a simple procedure to graph the residuals to search for heteroscedasticity. To enter the proper information in the drop-down windows, choose

Statistic > Regression > Regression > Graphs > Residuals vs Fits > OK > OK

Minitab responds with Figure 5.5. Clearly, the dispersion of the residuals decreases dramatically as the fits ($\hat{Y}$ *values*) increase when we move from left to right in the graph. This is clear evidence of heteroscedasticity.

More specific tests for heteroscedasticity are available to the researcher. These are examined in greater detail in Chapter 7.

In the presence of unruly variances some transformation of the data may prove useful. This usually involves taking the logarithm of the dependent variable. This may alleviate the problem of out-of-control variances because logarithmic values of $Y$ are less erratic than the original values of $Y$. This may dampen the variance. The hypothetical data in Table 5.1 show that the variation in the $Y$-values is greater than that of their log values. The $Y$-values range from 2 to 15, while the log values show an interval of only 0.3 to 1.17. This practice is more fully explored in Chapter 7.

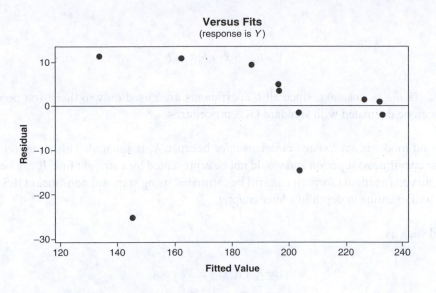

**Versus Fits**
(response is $Y$)

■ **Figure 5.5** A Graph of the Residuals Against Estimated Fits

■ **Table 5.1** A Comparison of Original Data with Their Logarithmic Values

| Observation | 1 | 2 | 3 | 4 | 5 | 6 |
|---|---|---|---|---|---|---|
| $Y$ | 2 | 4 | 5 | 9 | 10 | 15 |
| Log $Y$ | 0.30103 | 0.60206 | 0.69897 | 0.954243 | 1 | 1.176091 |

## ● The Presence of Autocorrelation

OLS presumes that the error terms are uncorrelated. That is, the error suffered in any attempt to estimate the value of the dependent variable has no relationship with that error suffered in any other estimation effort. If a relationship among error terms does exist, it is said the model suffers from autocorrelation—that is, the error terms are *autocorrelated* (or serially correlated).

Autocorrelation is particularly a problem when working with time series data. It's less likely to corrupt a model based on cross-sectional data such as those used in our Arco illustration. Therefore we will delay any detailed discussion of autocorrelation until Chapter 8.

## ● Checking for Linearity

OLS also assumes a state of linearity in the parameters (the $b$-coefficients). Models such as

$$\hat{Y} = b_0 + b_1 X_1 + b_2 X_2 + b_3 X_3$$

and

$$\hat{Y} = b_0 + b_1 X_1 + b_2 X_2 + b_3 X_3^2$$

are *linear in the parameters*, since all *b*-coefficients are raised only to their first power. Both models can be estimated with standard OLS procedures.

The second model is not *linear in the variables* because $X_3$ is squared. This equation is a non-linear (or curvilinear) function and would not be represented by a straight line. It can be graphed only as curved functional form. It *can* still be estimated using standard non-linear OLS methods that we will examine in depth in a later chapter.

A model such as

$$\hat{Y} = b_0 + b_1^2 X_1 + b_2 X_2 + b_3 X_3$$

is not linear in the parameter (but is in the variables) since one of the parameters is not expressed in its simplest form. Specifically, $b_1^2$ appears in the equation as a "squared" value. This model cannot be safely estimated with standard OLS methods.

> A model is linear in the parameters if all *b*-coefficients are taken only to the power of one. But if one of the *b*-coefficients is raised to a higher power the model is no longer linear in the parameters and OLS procedures will not provide a suitable model. A model in which one of the *X*-variables is taken to a higher power is still linear in the parameters and can be estimated using OLS techniques.

Residual plots may detect non-linearity in parameters. If a linear relationship exists the residuals should plot in a random manner like those shown in Figure 5.2. Any systematic pattern places doubt on the assumption of linearity. Minitab offers direct tests for linearity, which are examined in Chapter 6. In the absence of linearity the variables must be transformed through the use of a logarithmic model or an exponential expression. This is noted below in Section 5.3 and discussed in depth in Chapter 6.

## ● Test for Normality

The assumption that the error terms are normally distributed can also be tested with residual plots. Minitab provides a simple procedure to test the hypothesis that the residuals are normally distributed. This is done by plotting the ordered data against values that you expect if the population from which the sample was taken is normally distributed. If the population is normal, the plotted points will form an approximately straight line. Presume the data we had previously in Minitab Data 1, shown here with the estimated coefficients of the model:

## Minitab Data 1

```
The regression equation is

Y = -33.7 + 2.99 X1 + 5.49 X2

Predictor    Coef    SE Coef      T       P

Constant    -33.67     28.29   -1.19    0.268

X1           2.9920    0.8987    3.33    0.010

X2           5.4938    0.9854    5.58    0.001
```

To perform Minitab's test for normality, run the regression and save the residuals with

Stat > Regression > Regression

Enter the variables in the proper windows, then click

Storage > Residuals > OK

Next choose

Statistic > Basic Statistics > Normality Test, and select RESI1

Minitab offers three choices for the test. Using the Kolmogorov–Smirnov test produced the output seen in Figure 5.6. If the population is normal, the plotted points will form an approximately straight line.

The $p$-value of 0.055 reveals that the null hypothesis of a normally distributed residual can be rejected at the 5.5% level. There is some doubt that the residuals are normally distributed in accord with OLS requirements. Some caution should be exercised in using the model for prediction and estimation.

Actually, the condition of normality becomes critical only if we are working with small samples in which $n < 30$. If a large sample is in use the *Central Limit Theorem* assures us that regardless of the distribution of the population data, the sampling distribution of the $b$-coefficients will approach a normal distribution.

The cutoff of $n = 30$ between small and large samples is standard practice if there is only one RHS variable. As a rule of thumb it is customary to assume that an additional 20 to 25 observations are required for each additional RHS variable added to the model.

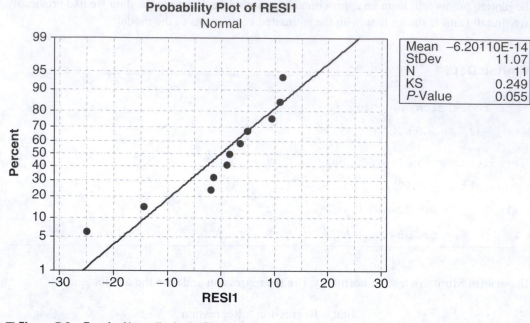

■ **Figure 5.6**  Test for Normality in the Residuals

## SECTION 5.1 PROBLEMS

1. Comment on the confidence you have that the various assumptions upon which the OLS model is based are in evidence given the residual plot seen here. Is there evidence of homoscedasticity, normality in the errors, independence of errors, and other base assumptions?

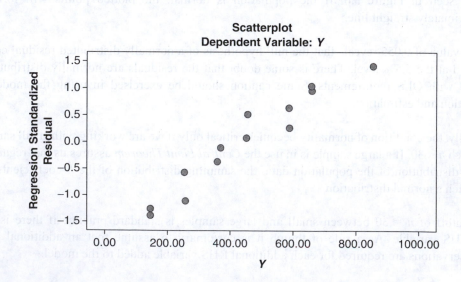

2. Repeat the first problem as stated above, given this plot:

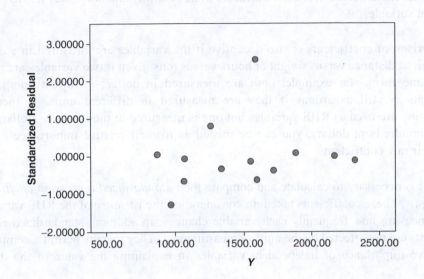

3. Discuss the assumptions upon which the OLS model is based. Explain what each means and detail the requirements they place on the data and the outcome of the model.

4. What is meant by "linear in the parameters" and "linear in the variables"? Which is a requirement of OLS procedures? Give mathematical examples of each type of linearity.

5. Describe the nature of a residual plot if heteroscedasticity is absent. What would it look like?

## 5.2 STANDARDIZED REGRESSION COEFFICIENTS

There is often the urge to judge the strength of a RHS variable's impact on the dependent variable based on the size of its coefficient. That impulse should be firmly resisted. Suppose a model is found to be

$$\hat{Y} = 5 + 10X_1 + 20X_2$$

You might be inclined to infer that $X_2$ is twice as important in determining the value of the estimated dependent variable. Such is not the case. The slope coefficients are simply not comparable. Granted, the estimated value of $Y$ will change by twice as much when $X_2$ changes by one unit as when $X_1$ changes by one unit. But that isn't the full story.

You must also consider how often $X_2$ changes. The impact of an independent variable on $Y$ depends not only on the size of its coefficient, but also on how frequently the variable changes.

If the variable doesn't change very often, the size of its coefficient is of less importance. The variable's standard deviation is a good measure of its volatility and how likely it is to impact the dependent variable.

A comparison of coefficients is also deceptive if the variables are measured in a dissimilar form, such as distance versus weight or hours versus tons. Even if two variables are measured in the same form—for example, both are measured in dollars—a direct comparison of coefficients is still hazardous if they are measured in different units. If income and consumption are used as RHS variables but one is measured in thousands of dollars and the other in hundreds of dollars, you can be misled as to their relative importance by merely citing their raw coefficients.

Instead, it is necessary to calculate and compare their *standardized regression coefficients*, or *beta weights*. These coefficients take into consideration the *variance* of the RHS variables and thereby measure how frequently each variable changes. In addition, standardized regression coefficients are not affected by the units of measurement. They thereby permit a comparison of the relative importance of independent variables in explaining the value of the dependent variable.

> The beta weight of an independent variable discussed here should not be confused with its beta coefficient, $\beta$.

The beta weight for a variable $X_i$ is defined as

$$Beta\ Weight(X_i) = \frac{b_i}{\dfrac{S_Y}{S_{X_i}}} \qquad (5.2.1)$$

where $S_Y$ is the standard deviation of the dependent variable and $S_{X_i}$ is the standard deviations of the $i$th independent variable.

If the standard deviations of $Y$, $X_1$, and $X_2$ are 21.2, 14.5, and 5.1, respectively, then based on $\hat{Y} = 5 + 10X_1 + 20X_2$ and using Equation (5.2.1), Beta($X_1$) = 6.84 and Beta($X_2$) = 4.811. After standardizing the coefficients by adjusting for their variance, $X_1$ has more influence in explaining changes in $Y$ than does $X_2$ despite the fact the latter has a larger slope coefficient.

In the matter of the tax revenues, for example, if per capita income is measured in \$1,000s, its slope coefficient, $b_1$, is an estimate of the effect on tax revenues of a \$1,000 change in per capita income holding population constant. However, if per capita income is measured in \$100s, $b_1$ would be 10 times larger and would measure the effect of a \$100 change in per capita income holding population constant. However, the beta weights wouldn't be affected by the change in the units of measure because the standard deviation of per capita income would be 10 times smaller.

Changing the units in which a variable is measured is referred to as *rescaling*. This concept is examined later in this chapter.

Many computer programs report beta weights as a part of the regression output. Suppose you have the data set in PASW Data 1 showing two RHS variables measured in significantly different units.

### PASW Data 1

|    | Y | X1 | X2 |
|----|--------|------|--------|
| 1  | 495.00 | 6.00 | 415.00 |
| 2  | 350.00 | 5.00 | 258.00 |
| 3  | 349.05 | 3.00 | 365.00 |
| 4  | 308.00 | 2.00 | 358.00 |
| 5  | 649.30 | 9.00 | 485.00 |
| 6  | 675.00 | 6.00 | 698.00 |
| 7  | 464.85 | 4.00 | 487.00 |
| 8  | 373.00 | 2.00 | 458.00 |
| 9  | 675.00 | 6.00 | 698.00 |
| 10 | 630.05 | 5.00 | 685.00 |
| 11 | 649.85 | 8.00 | 547.00 |
| 12 | 493.35 | 3.00 | 587.00 |
| 13 | 532.00 | 6.00 | 478.00 |

The output shows that the slope coefficient for $X_1$ is much greater than that of $X_2$ (36.811 > 0.650). However, the standardized coefficient for $X_2$ is greater (0.660 > 0.585), suggesting that it has more influence in impacting the value of $Y$.

### PASW Output 1

#### Coefficients[a]

| Model | | Unstandardized Coefficients | | Standardized Coefficients | | |
|-------|------------|--------|-----------|------|---------|------|
| | | B | Std. Error | Beta | t | Sig. |
| 1 | (Constant) | 1.340 | 1.837 | | .730 | .482 |
| | X1 | 36.811 | .223 | .585 | 165.082 | .000 |
| | X2 | .650 | .003 | .660 | 186.352 | .000 |

a. Dependent Variable: Y

The beta weight for a RHS variable takes into consideration its variance in determining the extent of its influence on the dependent variable. It is a better measure of the variable's impact on $Y$ than the estimated regression coefficient.

## SECTION 5.2 PROBLEMS

1.  Given the computer runs below, which variable, $X_1$ or $X_2$, has more influence on $Y$?

### Descriptive Statistics

|  | N | Minimum | Maximum | Mean | Std. Deviation |
|---|---|---|---|---|---|
| X1 | 13 | 1.00 | 22.00 | 10.9231 | 6.61389 |
| X2 | 13 | 409.00 | 459.00 | 415.5385 | 13.34551 |
| Y | 13 | 889.30 | 2258.30 | 1544.6385 | 420.80945 |
| Valid N (listwise) | 13 |  |  |  |  |

### Coefficients[a]

| Model |  | Unstandardized Coefficients | | Standardized Coefficients | | |
|---|---|---|---|---|---|---|
|  |  | B | Std. Error | Beta | t | Sig. |
| 1 | (Constant) | 34.311 | 42.290 |  |  | .436 |
|  | X1 | 64.739 | .202 |  |  | .000 |
|  | X2 | 1.933 | .100 |  |  | .000 |

a. Dependent Variable: Y

2.  Based on these results changes in which variable has a more pronounced impact on $Y$?

### Descriptive Statistics

|  | N | Minimum | Maximum | Mean | Std. Deviation |
|---|---|---|---|---|---|
| X1 | 13 | 125.00 | 985.00 | 539.3077 | 242.92673 |
| X2 | 13 | 2.00 | 9.00 | 5.4615 | 1.89804 |
| Y | 13 | 873.30 | 2317.30 | 1468.5385 | 453.47526 |
| Valid N (listwise) | 13 |  |  |  |  |

### Coefficients[a]

| Model |  | Unstandardized Coefficients | | Standardized Coefficients | | |
|---|---|---|---|---|---|---|
|  |  | B | Std. Error | Beta | t | Sig. |
| 1 | (Constant) | 37.709 | 40.752 |  | .925 | .377 |
|  | X1 | 1.972 | .039 |  | 50.280 | .000 |
|  | X2 | 67.282 | 5.019 |  | 13.405 | .000 |

a. Dependent Variable: Y

# 5.3 PROPER MODEL SPECIFICATION: GETTING IT RIGHT

Now that we know how to perform residual tests for models that may be incorrectly specified, let's spend some time learning how we might avoid the problem of misspecification in the first place. A properly specified model is simply one that contains all the explanatory variables it should contain and none that it shouldn't.

Once the proper variables are selected for inclusion in the model their functional forms must be determined. That is, should the variable be modeled as a logarithmic value such as $Y = f(\ln X_i)$, or perhaps as a squared valued $Y = f(X^2)$ creating a non-linear model in the form of a quadratic? Perhaps an exponential function $Y = f(2^x)$ or a reciprocal model such as $Y = f(1/X)$ is called for. We will leave these questions concerning the form of the function until later and concentrate in this chapter on its specification.

> The "specification" of a model deals with the selection of the proper variables to include. The "functional form" of a model focuses on the mathematical form the variables should assume.

## ● Consequences of an Omitted Variable

Suppose the *true* specification for a model is

$$Y = \beta_0 + \beta_1 X_1 + \beta_2 X_2 + \beta_3 X_3 + \varepsilon \tag{5.3.1}$$

where $\varepsilon$ is the classic error term. But if the researcher inappropriately omits a relevant variable, $X_3$, we have

$$Y = \alpha_0 + \alpha_1 X_1 + \alpha_2 X_2 + v \tag{5.3.2}$$

which specifies $v$ as the error. Notice first that the parametric regression coefficients in Equations (5.3.1) and (5.3.2) are different as suggested by the use of betas in Equation (5.3.1) and alphas in Equation (5.3.2). That's because, as we learned when the Arco model added Population as an RHS variable, thereby changing the model's specification, the coefficient of GDP changed. Thus, changing the specification of the model by adding or eliminating certain RHS variables alters the coefficients of the variables contained in the model.

But more to the point, the error term in Equation (5.3.2) becomes

$$v = \beta_3 X_3 + \varepsilon \tag{5.3.3}$$

That is, $v$ must "take up the slack" resulting from the absence of $X_3$. This is logically referred to as *omitted variable bias* due to *underfitting the model*. The coefficients as well as the constant term in Equation (5.3.2) will be bias and lead to faulty estimates.

Furthermore, it's a violation of the assumption that the sum of the errors is zero! $v$ will not sum to zero because if $X_3$ is a relevant variable, $\beta_3 \neq 0$ and hence $v \neq 0$.

But that's not all. Another basic assumption of OLS is that the explanatory variables are independent of the error terms. But, as seen in Equation (5.3.3), if $X_3$ changes so will $v$. That is, $v$ and $\beta_3$ are not independent. Thus, autocorrelation among the error terms will result.

Finally, failure to include a relevant variable is analogous to committing a Type II error—not rejecting the false hypothesis that $\beta_i = 0$. If the hypothesis is false and $\beta \neq 0$, the variable should be included in the model. Thus, omitting $X_i$ presumes incorrectly $\beta_i$ is zero and the false hypothesis is not rejected. So you can plainly see that correct specification is critical.

Of course, it is possible to include a variable which carries a $\beta = 0$. That is, to incorporate a variable into the model that has no explanatory value and should not be included. This is over-fitting the model. This results in an increase in the variances of the coefficients, $S_{b_i}$, and since

$$t = \frac{b_i - \beta_i}{S_{b_i}}$$

the absolute $t$-values of all variables, including those in which $\beta \neq 0$, will decrease toward zero and into the Do Not Reject region. Thus, you are more likely to *not* reject the null $H_0$: $\beta_i = 0$ even for those variables that do offer explanatory power. This too increases the propensity to commit a Type II error by not rejecting the false hypothesis that $\beta_i = 0$.

Relying on a variable's $t$-value to decide whether to include it can create problems of another sort. Presume a model with two RHS variables in which $X_2$ does not belong. It carries little or no explanatory value, plays no role as a control variable, and in general should not be included in the model. Due to perhaps the odd nature of your sample, the $t$-value reported by $X_2$ suggests significance and you decide to leave it in the model.

Doing so will not change the *expected value* of $b_1$. Therefore $b_1$ is not, by definition, biased in any way. It will, however, change the value of $b_1$ for any single estimate of $\beta_1$. Remember how the coefficient for GDP in our study of Arco's exports changed when Population was included. Forecasts and estimates of $Y$ are therefore unreliable.

Conversely, bias *will* result if a variable is incorrectly removed from a model. Specifically, $b_1$ will be biased by the true value of $\beta_2$ to the degree that $X_1$ and $X_2$ are correlated. Again, by definition, to say that $b_1$ is biased means that its expected value is not equal to $\beta_1$:

$$E(b_1) \neq \beta_1$$

It should be clear from this brief discussion that identifying the correct model specification is most important. Failure to do so can produce results that are less than useful and can foster misconceptions of a highly unfortunate nature.

## ● All Combinations

The benefit from any intensive effort to ensure the model is properly specified should be obvious at this point. The question is then how we successfully pursue such a vaunted goal.

Some unsophisticated researchers might approach the matter by preparing a list of all suspected explanatory variables that might lend credibility to their model. They might simply then experiment with all possible combinations of these potential variables. If they were to identify only three prospective candidates, $X_1$, $X_2$, and $X_3$, they could begin by running three simple regression models, each using a different RHS variable. This is followed with all possible pairwise models such as $X_1, X_2, X_1, X_3$, and $X_2, X_3$. Finally, an unrestricted model containing all three RHS variables might be estimated.

Their choice then depends on an evaluation of the summary statistics that result from each model. Statistics such as $R^2$, $\bar{R}^2$, $t$-values and $p$-values, the standard error of the estimate $S_e$, and other evaluative measures could be scrutinized. $F$-tests and partial $F$-tests could be considered. Residual plots could be examined for trouble signs.

However, such a tactic offers little or no regard to logic or any theoretical doctrine. It merely reports that model with the best window dressing. But in reality it may model nothing that approaches any real-world phenomenon. It just looks good statistically. If you don't have a better idea to start with as to what you should be doing other than shooting in the dark hoping to hit something, you need to do additional research of past studies and form a better comprehension of the theoretical principles you are trying to model.

## ● Backward Elimination, Forward Selection, and Stepwise Regression

Equally unscientific methods of devising a model involve allowing the computer to select which variables should be included in your model. Many software programs allow the researcher to use either a backward or forward selection process or a stepwise process.

*Backward elimination* begins by estimating the model with all possible explanatory variables included. The partial $F$-value for each independent variable is computed individually. Recall, as explained in Chapter 4, Section 4.8, that the partial $F$-value is used to determine if a subset of variables is useful in explaining variation in the $Y$-variable after controlling for the other variables. Here the subset is each RHS variable taken individually.

The variable with the *lowest* partial $F$-statistic is identified. Its $F$-statistic is compared with a critical $F$-value taken from the $F$-table based on a chosen alpha-value and the requisite numbers of degrees of freedom (remember, the $F$-value has two designated degrees of freedom—one for the numerator and one for the denominator).

If the variable's partial $F$-statistic is less than the critical $F$-value the null hypothesis that its beta-value is zero is not rejected and that variable is dropped from the model. All partial $F$-values for the remaining variables are computed and the process is repeated. This continues until all remaining variables are deemed significant. The result is the final model.

*Forward selection* works in reverse. A simple model is estimated for each RHS variable. The variable with the highest $F$-statistic (not partial $F$) is noted. If its hypothesis test reveals that variable to be significant, each remaining variable is paired with it to form all possible models with two RHS variables. The variable that produces the highest partial $F$-statistic is placed into the model and the proper hypothesis test is conducted. This continues until all variables have been introduced into the model or no more variables are deemed to have non-zero betas, at which point the selection process is terminated.

The *stepwise process* is a combination of backward elimination and forward selection. With both the backward elimination and forward selection, once a variable is rejected it never again receives consideration. Stepwise will re-evaluate the significance of each variable at each step of the process whether or not it was earlier eliminated. A variable may have been discarded in an earlier version of the model. But as the specification process continues, that variable may take on significant exploratory power. Stepwise will give that rejected variable another chance to prove its worth.

The process begins as does forward selection by running all simple regression models and selecting the most significant based on an $F$-test or a $t$-test.[1] Each of the other variables is then considered based on the partial $F$-test it produces. The variable with the highest partial $F$-test is incorporated into the model. Unlike forward selection or backward elimination, stepwise then tests the first variable that was selected for the model to see if it still offers significant explanatory power after inclusion of the second. If not, that variable is dropped. If its partial $F$-test passes, both variables are retained and a third variable is chosen based on its partial $F$-value. At this point, both of the first two RHS variables are again subjected to scrutiny. Each is either retained or rejected. This process continues until all variables have been given the opportunity to confirm their merit.

Frankly, none of these procedures is acceptable. Computers can't think. The researcher is again likely to settle for a model that reports impressive statistical results but carries no logical support or offers any theoretical insight. The final specification may violate all known theoretical precepts and simply not conform to any rational or commonsense perception.

Some experimentation in terms of trial-and-error on the part of the researcher is often productive and can provide insightful revelations that lead to new theories and ground-breaking discoveries.

Original thinking and investigative research can result in novel perceptions and innovative thought. These are the engines of progress and spawn entirely new doctrinaires. But blindly searching for a high $R^2$ is unlikely to ever produce pioneering schools of thought that advance mankind's body of knowledge. It might even be considered a bit unethical and morally unprincipled.

The researcher must instead use his or her own judgment and conceptualization to devise discerning regression models that offer the opportunity to shine new light on issues of importance to our intellectual development. Only by thorough mastery of the prevailing body of research and the acquisition of relevant analytical tools can anyone expand our understanding of the world in which we must function. These new ideas are then evaluated on the basis of residual plots, hypothesis tests, and all the other diagnostic tests at our disposal.

## SECTION 5.3 PROBLEMS

1. What problems can occur as a result of under-fitting a model? What does under-fitting mean?

2. How will under-fitting a model likely result in a Type II error?

3. Why is over-fitting a model likely to cause a Type I error?

4. What happens to the expected value of $b_1$ if:

   A. variable $X_2$ is incorrectly included in the model?
   B. variable $X_2$ is incorrectly excluded from the model?

5. Describe fully how backward elimination, stepwise regression, and forward selection work and why they are unacceptable as the means to derive a regression model.

6. Describe the dangers of misspecifying a model.

7. What conditions must exist for a model to be properly specified?

8. What is the difference between the proper functional form of a model and proper specification?

## 5.4 RESCALING THE VARIABLES

The units of measure in which the variables are expressed affect the coefficients as well as other statistics in the model. To illustrate how altering the units in which a variable is measured can affect the reported model, consider the data shown here for a model to explain the consumption of a new electronic "toy" that has recently hit the market in different geographical regions. As independent variables, the model will use mean consumer income and population in each region. Consumption is measured in units of hundreds of dollars, income is recorded as the mean in each region in thousands of dollars, and population is in millions. These data are shown in the first three columns of Table 5.2.

■ **Table 5.2**  Rescaling the Data

| Consumption (00s) | Income (000s) | Population (000,000s) | Consumption | Income | Population (1000) |
|---|---|---|---|---|---|
| 58.87 | 36.1 | 1.2 | 5887 | 36100 | 1200 |
| 97.35 | 59.5 | 2.5 | 9735 | 59500 | 2500 |
| 77.68 | 47.6 | 1.8 | 7768 | 47600 | 1800 |
| 98.6 | 65.3 | 3.5 | 9860 | 65300 | 3500 |
| 81.71 | 48.9 | 2.6 | 8171 | 48900 | 2600 |
| 74.04 | 45 | 1.9 | 7404 | 45000 | 1900 |
| 89.02 | 56.2 | 1.2 | 8902 | 56200 | 1200 |
| 102.3 | 87.3 | 0.9 | 10230 | 87300 | 900 |
| 98.6 | 67.1 | 1.7 | 9860 | 67100 | 1700 |
| 79.89 | 48.9 | 1.9 | 7989 | 48900 | 1900 |

The regression model reports as that shown in Minitab Output 1. Take note of the size of the coefficients and the other statistics as displayed. As you can see, a one-unit increase in income ($1,000) will increase Consumption on the average by 0.878 units, or $87.80. A one-unit increase in population (1 million people) will cause Consumption, on the average, to increase by 5.33 hundred dollars, or $533.

## Minitab Output 1

The regression equation is

Consumption = 26.2 + 0.878 Income + 5.33 Population

| Predictor | Coef | SE Coef | T | P |
|---|---|---|---|---|
| Constant | 26.214 | 8.118 | 3.23 | 0.014 |
| Income | 0.8784 | 0.1160 | 7.58 | 0.000 |
| Population | 5.330 | 2.162 | 2.47 | 0.043 |

$S_e$ = 5.02870  $R^2$ = 89.7%  Adjusted $R^2$ = 86.8%

Analysis of Variance

| Source | DF | SS | MS | F | P |
|---|---|---|---|---|---|
| Regression | 2 | 1547.80 | 773.90 | 30.60 | 0.000 |
| Residual Error | 7 | 177.01 | 25.29 | | |
| Total | 9 | 1724.81 | | | |

## ● Rescaling the Dependent Variable

Now let's rescale the dependent variable, consumption, and express it in units of one dollar by multiplying the values in column 1 of Table 5.2 by 100 (since they were originally expressed in hundreds). Minitab Output 2 provides the results.

## Minitab Output 2

```
The regression equation is

Consumption(100) = 2621 + 87.8 Income + 533 Population

Predictor        Coef      SE Coef      T        P
Constant        2621.4      811.8     3.23     0.014
Income           87.84      11.60     7.58     0.000
Population       533.0      216.2     2.47     0.043

S_e = 502.870   R² = 89.7%   Adjusted R² = 86.8%

Analysis of Variance

Source            DF       SS        MS        F      P
Regression         2    15477988   7738994   30.60  0.000
Residual Error     7     1770149    252878
Total              9    17248136
```

All of the coefficients as well as their standard error have changed. However, their interpretation has not. The model now shows that for every one-unit increase in Income ($1,000), Consumption will rise by 87.8 of its units, or $87.80. This is the same result as before.

The same analysis is applied to Population. After the rescaling, a one-unit increase (1 million people) will be followed by a rise in Consumption of 533 of its units—that is, $533. That too is the same as before.

Notice too that the standard error of the estimate, $S_e$, is now 502.87. That's 100 times what it was in the first model. Remember, $S_e$ is measured in the same units as the dependent variable. Consumption is now expressed in values 100 times larger than what they were in the first model. For example, the first observation is now $5,887, 100 times what it was earlier as $58.87 (hundred).

Rescaling the dependent variable by a given factor (100 in this case) causes the coefficients, their standard errors, $S_b$, and the standard error of the estimate, $S_e$, to increase by the same factor. However, notice that the $t$-values, the $F$-value, and the $p$-values did not change. These statistics are ratios and the scaling effect of the numerator and the denominator cancel out. After all, they measure the degree of significance and that must remain constant regardless of how the variables are measured.

## ● Rescaling an Independent Variable

Now let's examine the impact of changing one of the RHS variables. Let's return to Consumption measured in hundreds of dollars as before and use income measured in single dollars instead of thousands. This is shown as Income(1000) in Table 5.2. Population will again be treated in millions. The model becomes that seen in Minitab Output 3.

## Minitab Output 3

```
The regression equation is

Consumption = 26.2 + 0.000878 Income(1000) + 5.33 Population

Predictor              Coef        SE Coef          T           P
Constant             26.214          8.118       3.23       0.014
Income(1000)      0.0008784      0.0001160       7.58       0.000
Population            5.330          2.162       2.47       0.043

S_e = 5.02870  R² = 89.7%   Adjusted R² = 86.8%

Analysis of Variance

Source            DF           SS           MS           F           P
Regression         2      1547.80       773.90       30.60       0.000
Residual Error     7       177.01        25.29
Total              9      1724.81
```

Here we see that the coefficient for Income has changed. Now a one-unit change in income ($1) is associated with a mean change of 0.000878 units ($1,000) in Consumption. This is the same ratio as in both of the other models. If income goes up by $1,000, consumption rises by 0.878 units, or $87.80, which is the same change as displayed in the first model.

If you rescale the dependent variable, the coefficients and standard errors of the RHS variables all change in accord with the rescaling. So does the standard error of the estimate, $S_e$.

If you rescale an RHS variable, only its coefficient and standard error are altered.

In both cases, the measures of significance and measures of correlation remain constant.

## 5.5 THE LAGRANGE MULTIPLIER TEST FOR SIGNIFICANT VARIABLES

Chapter 4 demonstrated how the partial $F$-test could be used to determine if a particular subset of RHS variables could contribute to a model's explanatory nature. A distinction was made between restricted and unrestricted forms and an $F$-test was performed based on the sums of the squared errors.

A complement to that procedure is the Lagrange Multiplier test. It too recognizes a distinction between restricted and unrestricted models. Presume we wish to estimate the unrestricted form of the model

$$Y = \beta_0 + \beta_1 X_1 + \beta_2 X_2 + \beta_3 X_3 + \beta_4 X_4 + \varepsilon_U$$

but wish to evaluate the wisdom of including $X_3$ and $X_4$ in the model. The restricted form of the model becomes

$$Y = \beta_0 + \beta_1 X_1 + \beta_2 X_2 + \varepsilon_R$$

This is referred to as the restricted form of the model because it restricts the values of $\beta_3$ and $\beta_4$ to zero, thereby justifying their exclusion from the model.

The hypothesis to test is

$$H_0: \beta_3 = \beta_4 = 0$$

$$H_a: \text{At least one is not zero}$$

If the unrestricted version is the true and proper form, then $\beta_3$ and $\beta_4$ should be included in the estimation. In their absence their effect is captured by $\varepsilon_R$ in the restricted form. Thus, there will be some correlation between $\varepsilon_R$ and $\beta_3$ and $\beta_4$.

To execute the Lagrange Multiplier test, you must first run the restricted form of the model, taking care to save the residuals, $e_R$. Next, you will regress these residuals on all RHS variables in the unrestricted model. This model is termed the *auxiliary equation*. It has been shown by Engle[2] that given a large sample, $nR^2$ approximates a chi-square distribution with $m$ degrees of freedom, where $n$ is the sample size, $R^2$ is the coefficient of determination from the *auxiliary* equation, and $m$ is the number of variables omitted from the restricted model—two in this case, $X_3$ and $X_4$. If $nR^2 > \chi^2_{a,m}$, the null is rejected. The logic should be clear. If the excluded variables do carry explanatory power, $R^2$ for the auxiliary equation should be high. Thus, $nR^2$ would be elevated and likely would exceed the critical chi-square value.

Similarity with the partial $F$-test should also be obvious. The $F$-test often proves more practical in that, unlike the Lagrange test, it can be requested by much of the available software. However, the

Lagrangian is used in many cases and an awareness of its ease of use can be an asset. It offers an advantage over the $F$-test in that only the restricted form of the model need be estimated, while the $F$-test requires that both the restricted and the unrestricted forms be computed.

---

**EXAMPLE 5.1: Viability of Homeownership**

**Problem Statement**: As economic conditions worsen across the nation the likelihood that a family can afford their own home is called into question. A model designed to estimate the proportion of residents living in their own house ($P$) is estimated using personal income ($I$), the employment level ($E$), property taxes ($T$), average family size ($F$), and average educational level. A sample of 150 localities is sampled. Data were taken from http://www.census.gov/hhes/www/housing.html. Concern arises as to the advisability that the last two variables be included in the model. A Lagrangian Multiplier test is to be conducted to determine the proper form of the model.

**Solution**: The restricted form of the model, $P = (I, E)$, produced an $R^2$ of 0.588. The hypothesis that $\beta_3 = \beta_4 = 0$ is to be tested at the 1% level. $nR^2 = (150)(0.588) = 88.2$. Using the Excel command for an alpha of 1% and $m = 2$ degrees of freedom for $X_3$ and $X_4$ we find = chiinv(.01,2) produces a critical value for chi-square of 9.21.

**Interpretation**: Since 88.2 > 9.2, the null is rejected. Either family size or education levels or both have a significant impact on the ability of a family to own their own home.

---

## CHAPTER PROBLEMS

**CHAPTER PROBLEMS 5**

### Conceptual Problems

1. Discuss the characteristics residuals must exhibit to ensure that the regression model obey all the Gauss–Markov assumptions. Use graphical work in each case.

2. What is meant by the statement that error terms must display a constant variance? Use a graph in your answer.

3. Distinguish between homoscedasticity and heteroscedasticity. Use a graph.

4. What conditions are most likely to precipitate heteroscedasticity?

5. What is meant by a standardized regression coefficient? How is it used in regression analysis?

6. A model is reported to be $\hat{Y} = 5 + 7.2A + 5.8B - 2.4C$. The standard deviation of each is $S_Y = 2.7$, $S_A = 3.8$, $S_B = 0.58$, and $S_C = 6.5$. Which variable, $A$, $B$, or $C$, is most influential in determining $Y$?

7. Describe how backward elimination, forward selection, and stepwise regression operate to produce a model. What caution should be exercised in their use?

8. A model with $n = 65$ observations is reported as seen below with $t$-values in parentheses. $Y$ is expressed in thousands, $X_1$ in hundreds, $X_2$ in thousands, and $X_3$ in single units.

$$\hat{Y} = 52 + 23.5X_1 - 41.8X_2 + 56.7X_3$$

(2.35)   (3.65)   (−5.68)   (3.54)

$R^2 = 0.65$; $S_e = 5.69$

A. What are the standard errors for each variable?
B. What are the $p$-values for all variables?
C. What is the adjusted coefficient of determination?
D. Rescale $Y$ into single units. What are the model coefficients and standard errors now? What happened to the $R^2$ value? Why?
E. Rescale $X_1$ into single units. What are the coefficients and standard errors of the model now?

# COMPUTER PROBLEMS

COMPUTER PROBLEMS

5

1. Access the file PUBLIC TRADING. It contains data for the rate of return (ROR) measured in percentages, a risk level, the amount of the original investment (OIV), whether the stock is traded publically (entered as a "1" if it is), and the number of years the investor has held the stock. The intent is to develop a model to explain the rate of return to the investor. There is some doubt as to the need to include PUBLIC and YEARS in the model. Offer your suggestion based on the Lagrangian Multiplier.

2. King Soda, a nation-wide bottling company, notices that their best-selling product does not conform to the mean weight of 30 ounces in each container. Management suspects that the temperature in their three plants in Kansas City, Chicago, and Denver may explain the malfunction. A study of 40 bottles, some taken from each location, produces the data contained in the data set KING SODA. Fills are measured in ounces, temperature in Fahrenheit, and the cities in which the bottles were filled is specified.

Access the data file. Using your preferred software regress Fills on the other variables and determine the residuals. Notice that data for all three cities (dummy variables) is given. You need only two cities in the model as discussed in Chapter 4 in our examination of dummy variables. Eliminate Denver from the model in your estimation process.

A. Plot the residuals and comment on the relevant features.
B. Does it appear the residuals are random?
C. What observations might you make about the potential for heteroscedasticity?
D. What other comments and remarks can you offer for the violations of all the basic assumptions of the OLS model?
E. Which variable, temperature or Chicago, has the greater impact on Fills?

*Chapter 6*

# USING QUALITATIVE AND LIMITED DEPENDENT VARIABLES

## INTRODUCTION

In Chapter 4 we examined the use of indicator or dummy variables as independent, RHS variables. The dependent variable was always seen as a continuous variable. It is also possible, however, to include a dummy variable in a regression model as a dependent variable. There are many cases in business and economic analysis when we wish to know whether an observation might fall in one category or another. Will a borrower pay back a loan? Is a product defective or not defective? Based on certain demographic and financial characteristics we may want to estimate the probability a family will buy a car or not buy one. An investor may wish to evaluate the potential benefits from three or more possible portfolios in order to choose among them. In each of these illustrations the dependent variables are no longer treated as continuous variables but are qualitative (non-quantitative) measures and can be treated as dummy variables. In each of these instances the dependent variable falls into one category or another.

Closely related to models with categorical dependent variables are those characterized by *limited dependent variables* (LimDep models). For example, instead of estimating the likelihood a family might buy a car (a binary model—either the car was purchased or it was not), we may be interested in determining how much money was spent on a car. Here the model is *not* binary. Instead, in these models the dependent variables are restricted to only certain values. It is said that the data are *truncated*. For example, the values are never negative. Further, we have no data for the dependent variable for those families who did not make the purchase. We can only record a zero for such observations. There is then a large discrete jump at zero for those who did not make a purchase to some purchase price of several thousand dollars for those who did. A sample in which data are available for only some observations is referred to as a *censored sample*.

Both kinds of models are examined in this chapter. Let's begin with those that include a categorical dependent variable.

## 6.1 LOGIT ANALYSIS

*Logit* (or *logistic*) analysis is well suited to model relationships in which the dependent variable is categorical. A logit model estimates the probability a given observation will fall into a particular category.

> Logit analysis is an estimation technique to model equations with dummy dependent variables. It is intended to estimate the likelihood a given observation will fall into a pre-identified category.

If $P_i$ is the probability an observation will appear in category $i$, $1 - P_i$ is the probability it will not do so. Then, $P_i/(1 - P_i)$ is the odds ratio that the observation will appear in category $i$. If the probability of $i$ is 0.8, then the odds are $0.8/(1 - 0.8) = 4$ to 1 (written 4:1) the observation will report category $i$.

The probability of $i$ as expressed by Equation (6.1.1) is the *cumulative logistic distribution function*:

$$P_i = \frac{e^{Z_i}}{1 + e^{Z_i}} \tag{6.1.1}$$

where $e$ is the base of the natural logarithm system, 2.718, and

$$Z_i = \beta_0 + \beta_1 X_1 + \beta_2 X_2 + \cdots + \beta_k X_k \tag{6.1.2}$$

However, Equation (6.1.1) is not linear in the parameters (or the $X_i$ for that matter) and therefore cannot be estimated with standard OLS techniques. We must form a linear expression by taking the log of Equation (6.1.1). The model can be linearized as

$$\ln\left[\frac{P_i}{1 - P_i}\right] = Z_i = \beta_0 + \beta_1 X_1 + \beta_2 X_2 + \cdots + \beta_k X_k \tag{6.1.3}$$

where $\ln[P_i/(1 - P_i)]$ is the *log of the odds ratio* that the observation will fall into category $i$. It is said that the model is "linear in the logs." Expressed in this manner, Equation (6.1.3) is linear in both the $X_i$ and the coefficients.

The coefficients measure the change in the log of the odds ratio given a one-unit change in $X_i$. If $Z = 1.2 + 0.2X_1 - 1.5X_2$, a one-unit change in $X_1$ will increase the log of the odds ratio by 0.2, holding $X_2$ constant. A one-unit change in $X_2$ will decrease the log of the odds ratio by 1.5, holding $X_1$ constant.

The coefficients measure the change in the *log* of the odds ratio as shown in Equation (6.1.3), not the change in the odds ratio as is commonly misconceived.

$Z$ is a measure of the total contribution of all the independent variables used in the model and is known as the logit. The logit function is bounded by 0 and 1 and therefore serves well in determining probabilities.

Given the rules of logarithms, from Equation (6.1.1) we can derive

$$0 \leq P = \frac{e^{Z_i}}{1 + e^{Z_i}} \leq 1 \tag{6.1.4}$$

As $Z_i$ ranges from $-\infty$ to $+\infty$, $P$ ranges between 0 and 1. The function graphs as an S-curve as seen in Figure 6.1. It forms the *cumulative density function* with some category, $C_i$ (will repay loan, will buy a car, etc.), on the vertical axis and the value of an RHS variable on the horizontal axis.

This is called a *threshold model*. The probability of $C_i$ increases dramatically as $X_i$ approaches a threshold, $X^*$, holding all other RHS variables constant, and then slows in its ascent as it nears unity.

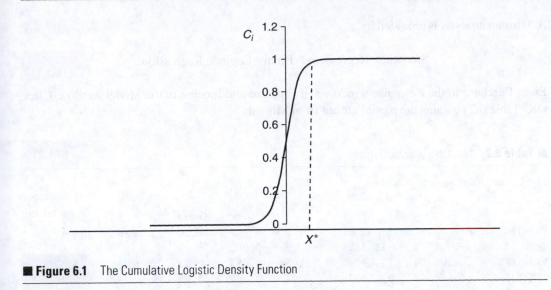

■ **Figure 6.1**  The Cumulative Logistic Density Function

## ● An Example of a Logit Model

To demonstrate, the Excel file AUTO PURCHASE contains data for $n = 43$ families in a certain socio-economic group in the Chicago, Illinois area. The data are encoded with a "1" if the family purchased an automobile in the past year and a "0" if they did not. FAMSIZE is the number of family members and income is measured in thousands of dollars annually. Although the data are held in an Excel file for convenience, Excel will not perform logit regression and it is necessary to copy and paste the data into your preferred statistical package such as Minitab, SPSS, SAS, or some other software that is capable of performing logit analysis. Table 6.1 contains the first eight observations for illustration purposes. In all eight cases a purchase was made and therefore the column for "Purchase" contains a "1" for all observations. In the entire Excel data set the last 20 observations record data for those families that did not acquire a new vehicle and the column records all "0s."

■ **Table 6.1**  Auto Purchases

|  | A | B | C |
|---|---|---|---|
| 1 | PURCHASE | FAMSIZE | INCOME |
| 2 | 1 | 3 | 76.8 |
| 3 | 1 | 3 | 76.8 |
| 4 | 1 | 3 | 72.8 |
| 5 | 1 | 2 | 76 |
| 6 | 1 | 3 | 73.6 |
| 7 | 1 | 3 | 74.4 |
| 8 | 1 | 3 | 78.4 |

Extracted from http://www.illinoistollway.com, October 2011

A Minitab analysis is provided by

Statistic > Regression > Binary Logistic Regression

Enter Purchase in the Response window and FamSize and Income in the Model window. Click OK. Table 6.2 contains the partial output from Minitab.

■ **Table 6.2** Minitab's Logistic Output

```
Logistic Regression Table
```

|           |         |         |       |       | Odds  | 95%   | CI    |
|-----------|---------|---------|-------|-------|-------|-------|-------|
| Predictor | Coef    | SE Coef | Z     | P     | Ratio | Lower | Upper |
| Constant  | -52.6764| 16.3124 | -3.23 | 0.001 |       |       |       |
| FAMSIZE   | 2.08304 | 1.07043 | 1.95  | 0.052 | 8.03  | 0.99  | 65.43 |
| INCOME    | 0.666503| 0.212025| 3.14  | 0.002 | 1.95  | 1.29  | 2.95  |

```
Log-Likelihood = -13.368
Test that all slopes are zero: G = 32.665, DF = 2, P-Value = 0.000
```

Based on Equation (6.1.2), the model is

$$Z_i = -52.6764 + 2.08304\text{FAMSIZE} + 0.666503\text{INCOME}$$

To determine the probability the "average" family in the Chicago land area will purchase new transportation, the mean values for family size and income for this particular cohort of consumers are inserted into Equation (6.1.1). Given these mean values are 2.65 and 71.0, we have

$$Z_i = -52.6765 + 2.08304(2.65) + 0.666503(71.0) = 0.165$$

Equation (6.1.4) then yields

$$P = \frac{e^{0.165}}{1 + e^{0.165}} = 0.541$$

There is a 54.1% chance the average family will purchase a new automobile. To find the probability any given family will make such a purchase merely plug its size and income into Equation (6.1.2) and then apply the resulting $Z_i$ to Equation (6.1.4).

The partial slope coefficients are interpreted somewhat differently than was the case with our standard OLS models. The coefficient for Family Size suggests that a one-unit change in the number of family members will change the average *logit* value for that observation by 2.08. By taking the antilog of 2.08 as $e^{2.08} = 2.718^{2.08} = 8.004$ we find that a family with one more member is more than eight times as likely to buy a new car.

## ● The Log-Likelihood Statistic

In the logit model $R^2$ and $\bar{R}^2$ are not suitable as measures of goodness of fit. Given the binary nature of the dependent variable such a statistic is meaningless at best. Instead the logit model relies on the *log-likelihood statistic* seen in the Minitab output (Table 6.2) as −13.368. This allows a comparison of two models to test whether the model with only the intercept (the restricted model[1]) explains the value of $Z$ better than the fitted model with the RHS variables (the unrestricted model). It functions much as did the partial $F$-test we studied in Chapter 4 that permitted us to test the significance of a subset of RHS variables.

Some computer programs multiply the log-likelihood value by −2 to make it positive. As seen in Table 6.3, SPSS is one of those programs. In this case, −13.368(−2) = 26.736. The SPSS output for a logit model is obtained as:

Analyze > Regression > Binary Logit Regression

■ **Table 6.3**   SPSS Measure of the Log-Likelihood

**Model Summary**

| Step | -2 Log-likelihood | Cox & Snell R Square | Nagelkerke R Square |
|------|-------------------|----------------------|---------------------|
| 1    | 26.736[a]         | .532                 | .711                |

a. Estimation terminated at iteration number 7 because parameter estimates changed by less than .001.

**Omnibus Tests of Model Coefficients**

|        |       | Chi-square | df | Sig. |
|--------|-------|------------|----|------|
| Step 1 | Step  | 32.665     | 2  | .000 |
|        | Block | 32.665     | 2  | .000 |
|        | Model | **32.665** | 2  | .000 |

A −2 log-likelihood *ratio* (−2LLR) is then formed using the two −2 log-likelihood values from the two models. The −2 log-likelihood ratio, indicated by Greek $\varLambda$ (lambda), is found as

$$\varLambda \equiv -2LLR = -2\ln\left(\frac{LL_R}{LL_U}\right) = -2\left(\ln LL_R - \ln LL_U\right) = -2\ln LL_R + 2\ln LL_U \qquad (6.1.5)$$

where $LL_R$ is the $-2$ log-likelihood value from the restricted model (the one with only the intercept) and $LL_U$ is the $-2$ log-likelihood from the unrestricted model (the one that includes the explanatory variables).

Remember, the object of this exercise is to determine if the model with only the intercept (the restricted model) explains the value of $Z$ better than the fitted model containing the RHS variables (the unrestricted model). It tests the hypothesis that the betas of all the RHS variables are all equal to zero: $H_0: \beta_1 = \beta_2 = \cdots = \beta_K = 0$. The test follows a chi-square distribution ($\chi^2$) with $k$ degrees of freedom, where $k$ is the number of RHS variables.

From Table 6.2 we find the $-2$ log-likelihood for the unrestricted model is $-2(13.368) = 26.736$. The *lower* this value the *better* the model fits the data. A good model that fits the data well will exhibit a high probability or likelihood (not *log*-likelihood) of fit. This means the $-2$ log-likelihood would be a small number. If a perfect fit means a likelihood of 1 (100%), then, since $\ln(1) = 0$, the $-2$ log-likelihood is $-2(\ln 1) = -2(0) = 0$. That is, as opposed to the $R^2$ in an OLS model, a low $-2$ log-likelihood (close to 0) indicates a strong model.

In its last row Table 6.3 also shows the $\chi^2$ for the model to be 32.665. This allows us to compare the restricted model with the unrestricted model as promised above. The $-2$ log-likelihood for the restricted model is

$$\chi^2 \text{ plus the } -2 \text{ log-likelihood for the unrestricted model}$$
$$= 32.665 + 26.736 = 59.401$$

This reveals that incorporating family size and income into the model decreases the $-2$ log-likelihood from 59.401 to 26.736, the amount of the $\chi^2$! Since, as noted above, a lower $-2$ log-likelihood is preferred, this testifies to the model's improvement in using the unrestricted form through the insertion of family size and income.

This can be verified by estimating the restricted model in which the dependent variable is regressed on only the constant and noting its $-2$ log-likelihood. However, SPSS will not allow a regression without at least one RHS variable. Therefore, the restricted model can be estimated only through a bit of trickery. This sleight-of-hand involves creating a new "variable" consisting only of "1s" and regressing $Y$ on that new variable after instructing SPSS to exclude the constant from the equation. This model yields a $-2$ log-likelihood of 59.401. The $\chi^2$-value for the unrestricted model is then verified to be $59.401 - 26.736 = 32.665$.

The critical value for $\chi^2$ against which our 32.665 is tested can be obtained from Excel by entering in any cell $=\text{CHIINV}(\alpha, \text{d.f.})$ where $\alpha$ is a chosen alpha-value and d.f. is the number of degrees of freedom, that is, the number of RHS variables in the unrestricted model. If we choose an alpha value of 0.05, $=\text{CHIINV}(.05, 2)$ yields 5.991. Since 32.665 exceeds 5.991 we will reject the null and conclude that the unrestricted model containing the RHS variables predicts the category into which an observation falls better than does the restricted model. The $p$-value associated with the test can be found using Excel as $=\text{CHIINV}(32.665, 2)$. Excel reports a value of $8.07022\text{E-}08 \approx 0.000$.

The −2 log-likelihood for the restricted model is analogous to the SST in the OLS model. The −2 log-likelihood for the unrestricted model is equivalent to the SSE in the OLS model. The model's $\chi^2$ is the difference between the −2 log-likelihood for the restricted model and the unrestricted model and corresponds to the SSR inherent in OLS.

Notice from the Minitab output in Table 6.2 that Minitab reports the $\chi^2$ as a *G*-value of 32.665 along with the *p*-value. In statistics, *G*-tests are likelihood-ratios or maximum likelihood statistical significance tests that are used increasingly in situations where chi-square tests were previously recommended.

● **Classification Tables**

SPSS also provides a Classification Table such as that seen in Table 6.4 that summarizes the success of the model. Of the 20 families that did not purchase a car (an entry of 0), the model predicted 16 of them correctly. Twenty of 23 families who bought a new auto were correctly identified as having done so. Of the 44 observations in the data set, 36 were placed in the correct category for an overall percentage of 83.7%. This value is often cited in place of the $R^2$ or $\overline{R}^2$ used in the OLS model to measure explanatory power.

■ **Table 6.4**    SPSS Classification Table

**Classification Table[a]**

| Observed | | | Predicted | | |
|---|---|---|---|---|---|
| | | | PURCHASE | | Percentage Correct |
| | | | .00 | 1.00 | |
| Step 1 | PURCHASE | .00 | 16 | 4 | 80.0 |
| | | 1.00 | 3 | 20 | 87.0 |
| | Overall Percentage | | | | 83.7 |

a. The cut value is .500

To classify an observation in one category or the other a *cut-value* is identified. If the *Z*-value for that observation as per Equation (6.1.2) is below the cut-value, it is placed in one category. If the *Z*-value exceeds that cut-value, it is placed in the other category. A cut-value of 0.50 is common (more on cut-values in our discussion of discriminant analysis later in this chapter).

Table 6.5 is obtained from the SPSS Logistic Regression window with Save > Probabilities > Group Membership. PRE_1 is the probability the observation will fall in category *i* and PGR_1 is the group into which the model will place the observation. Using the first observation in Table 6.5 as an illustration,

$$Z = -52.6764 + 2.083(3) + 0.6665(76.8) = 4.826$$

Then,

$$P = \frac{e^{4.826}}{1 + e^{4.826}} = 0.9916$$

Since 0.9916 > 0.50, the observation is placed in Group 1 (family purchased car). The seven misclassified observations are 19, 20, and 24 through 28. For example, observation 19 was a family that purchased a new car but was classified as having not purchased one since its PRE_1 was so low—due likely to the lower income level.

■ **Table 6.5** Classification Record

| OBS | PUR-CHASE | FAM-SIZE | INCOME | PRE_1 | PGR_1 | OBS | PUR-CHASE | FAM-SIZE | INCOME | PRE_1 | PGR_1 |
|---|---|---|---|---|---|---|---|---|---|---|---|
| 1 | 1 | 3 | 76.8 | 0.99151 | 1 | 23 | 1 | 3 | 70.4 | 0.62118 | 1 |
| 2 | 1 | 3 | 76.8 | 0.99151 | 1 | **24** | **1** | **3** | **69.6** | **0.49034** | **0** |
| 3 | 1 | 3 | 72.8 | 0.89033 | 1 | **25** | **0** | **2** | **74.4** | **0.74602** | **1** |
| 4 | 1 | 2 | 76 | 0.8951 | 1 | **26** | **0** | **3** | **72** | **0.82649** | **1** |
| 5 | 1 | 3 | 73.6 | 0.9326 | 1 | **27** | **0** | **3** | **72.8** | **0.89033** | **1** |
| 6 | 1 | 3 | 74.4 | 0.95932 | 1 | **28** | **0** | **2** | **72.8** | **0.50278** | **1** |
| 7 | 1 | 3 | 78.4 | 0.99706 | 1 | 29 | 0 | 2 | 70.4 | 0.1696 | 0 |
| 8 | 1 | 3 | 73.6 | 0.9326 | 1 | 30 | 0 | 3 | 68.8 | 0.36081 | 0 |
| 9 | 1 | 3 | 77.6 | 0.995 | 1 | 31 | 0 | 3 | 63.2 | 0.01333 | 0 |
| 10 | 1 | 3 | 76 | 0.98561 | 1 | 32 | 0 | 3 | 66.4 | 0.10234 | 0 |
| 11 | 1 | 3 | 79.2 | 0.99827 | 1 | 33 | 0 | 2 | 63.2 | 0.00168 | 0 |
| 12 | 1 | 3 | 71.2 | 0.73648 | 1 | 34 | 0 | 2 | 70.4 | 0.1696 | 0 |
| 13 | 1 | 3 | 75.2 | 0.97573 | 1 | 35 | 0 | 3 | 64.8 | 0.03777 | 0 |
| 14 | 1 | 3 | 73.6 | 0.9326 | 1 | 36 | 0 | 3 | 68 | 0.24879 | 0 |
| 15 | 1 | 3 | 75.2 | 0.97573 | 1 | 37 | 0 | 2 | 65.6 | 0.00826 | 0 |
| 16 | 1 | 3 | 72 | 0.82649 | 1 | 38 | 0 | 3 | 65.6 | 0.0627 | 0 |
| 17 | 1 | 2 | 72.8 | 0.50278 | 1 | 39 | 0 | 2 | 64.8 | 0.00486 | 0 |
| 18 | 1 | 3 | 72 | 0.82649 | 1 | 40 | 0 | 2 | 68.8 | 0.06569 | 0 |
| **19** | **1** | **3** | **68.8** | **0.36081** | **0** | 41 | 0 | 3 | 64.8 | 0.03777 | 0 |
| **20** | **1** | **2** | **72** | **0.37237** | **0** | 42 | 0 | 2 | 68 | 0.03962 | 0 |
| 21 | 1 | 2 | 72.8 | 0.50278 | 1 | 43 | 0 | 2 | 66.4 | 0.014 | 0 |
| 22 | 1 | 3 | 70.4 | 0.62118 | 1 | 44 | 0 | 2 | 64.8 | 0.00486 | 0 |

## EXAMPLE 6.1: Finding Employment I

**Problem Statement:** As economic conditions worsen, a "headhunters" firm that specializes in finding qualified applicants for executive positions wishes to develop a model to aid in determining the probability a seasoned administrator can find acceptable employment, based on years of experience and salary constraints. A total of 43 candidates were included in the study. They were recorded as a "1" if they secured a position and a "0" if they were still in the job market. A logit model produced the results seen here. What can be learned from this study?

**Solution:** A Minitab printout reveals these results:

```
Logistic Regression Table

Predictor        Coef     SE Coef       Z       P    Ratio    Lower    Upper
Constant      3.64847     2.32708    1.57   0.117
EXP         -0.0500001   0.0425723   -1.17   0.240     0.95     0.88     1.03
SALARY      -0.0485213   0.0353579   -1.37   0.170     0.95     0.89     1.02

Log-Likelihood = -22.569
Test that all slopes are zero: G = 3.125, DF = 2, P-Value = 0.210
```

**Interpretation:** Given that an applicant has 12 years of experience and demands a salary of 60 ($60,000), $Z = 3.65 - 0.05(12) - 0.049(60) = 0.11$. Then, the probability of finding a job is found as

$$P = \frac{e^{0.11}}{1 + e^{0.11}} = 0.527$$

Furthermore, the –2 log-likelihood value is –2(–22.569) = 45.138 and $\chi^2 = G = 3.125$. This means that including the RHS variables of experience and salary decreases the –2 log-likelihood value of the unrestricted model from that of the restricted model that does not use the RHS variables by only 3.125—not a large decrease! The –2 log-likelihood value of the restricted model is only 45.138 + 3.125 = 48.263. It doesn't appear that the model offers much explanatory help. This is further borne out by the insignificant p-value of 0.210. It seems salary requirements and years of experience do little to predict the possibility of employment. The employment firm should search for an alternative model.

● **Maximum Likelihood and the Use of Iterations**

Logit is based on a maximum likelihood (ML) principle. The logit command estimates the parameters so as to maximize the probability the data set used in the estimation process could occur. That is, it seeks out the parameters most likely to occur given the sample data.

> The maximum likelihood principle produces those parametric estimates that maximize the probability (likelihood) of obtaining the data that are found in the sample.

The computer will first choose initial estimates of the parameters. Then, given these preliminary estimates, is it likely these sample data could occur? If not, changes in the parametric estimates will be made. This continues through several iterations until the likelihood that the sample data could be obtained is maximized. Usually, when the changes in the estimates become smaller than 0.001, the computer reports the final model.

## SECTION 6.1 PROBLEMS

1. A logit model estimating the probability a borrower will repay a loan is $Z = 1.3 + 0.03I + 0.004A + 0.01M$, where $I$ is monthly income in thousands, $A$ is age, and $M$ is a dummy variable encoded as "1" if the subject is married. The bank established a policy in which the loan will be granted if the probability of repayment is more than 90%, additional information will be required if the probability is between 89% and 70%, and the loan will be refused otherwise. A potential borrower who is married, is 47 years old, and has monthly income of $5,000 applies for a loan. Will he receive it?

2. Explain what is meant by the maximum likelihood principle and the role iterations play in logit analysis.

3. A logit model intended to measure the probability a new medication will prevent the reoccurrence of a disease reports a –2LL of 14.3 using $k = 4$ RHS variables. The restricted version of the model records a –2LL of 27.3. Does the unrestricted model offer significantly more predictive power than the restricted model at the 5% level?

4. Access the file BANKRUPTCY. The data are entered as a "1" if the subject declared bankruptcy and a "0" if not based on income and debt levels, both measured in thousands of dollars. Estimate a logit regression model. Interpret the results. What is the probability someone with an income of $82,000 and debt of $78,000 will declare bankruptcy?

5. A partial classification table for a logit model designed to predict whether a product meets all production specifications appears as:

**Classification Table**

| Observed | | Predicted | | |
|---|---|---|---|---|
| | | MEETS | | Percentage |
| | | .00 | 1.00 | Correct |
| MEETS | .00 | 52 | 12 | |
| | 1.00 | 13 | 120 | |
| Overall Percentage | | | | |

Compute the three missing percentages and comment.

6. The $-2LL$ for an unrestricted model with 4 RHS variables is 42.7, while the $-2LL$ for the restricted model is 49.3. Calculate the $\chi^2$ value and determine if the betas are all zero at the 1% level.

7. Given $Z = -5 + .07X_1 + 1.4X_2$, what is the probability an observation with $X_1 = 12$ and $X_2 = 4.3$ will be placed in category 1?

## 6.2 THE LINEAR PROBABILITY MODEL AND WEIGHTED LEAST SQUARES

Two other popular approaches to dealing with dichotomous models are the linear probability model and weighted least squares. Each is considered in this section.

### ● The Linear Probability Model

The linear probability model (LPM) can be structured in standard OLS form such as Equation (6.2.1). It is so-called because the RHS is a linear expression and the dependent variable is a statement of probability that an observation falls in a given category.

$$Y_i = \beta_0 + \beta_1 X_i + \varepsilon_i \tag{6.2.1}$$

However, applied in this manner, the model suffers serious shortcomings. To begin with it can be shown that the residuals are not normally distributed. Given the binary nature of the dependent variable, let $P_i$ be the probability $Y_i = 1$. Then, given Equation (6.2.1), $\varepsilon_i = 1 - \beta_0 - \beta_1 X_i$. Further, $(1 - P_i)$ must be the probability $Y = 0$ and we have $\varepsilon_i = -\beta_0 - \beta_1 X_i$. From this we can see that the residuals are indeed not normally distributed, but are binomial instead.

Since the hypothesis tests for the parameters depend so heavily on normality, such tests are unreliable. This is particularly true when working with small samples. If large samples are in use the Central Limit Theorem can be applied to assume normality. Despite the absence of normality the OLS estimates will remain unbiased and consistent as defined in Chapter 1.

> The Central Limit Theorem states that as the sample size increases, the sampling distribution asymptotically approaches normality even if the population from which the sample was taken is non-normal.

Another problem associated with the LPM is the presence of heteroscedasticity in the residuals. It can be shown that the variance of the residuals, var($e_i$), is equal to $(\beta_0 + \beta X_i)(1 - \beta_0 X_i)$. Since the $X_i$ will vary among observations, so will the variance of the residuals—the very definition of heteroscedasticity.

In the past we have been able to rely on the coefficient of determination, $R^2$, as a measure of our model's explanatory power. Such is not the case with the LPM. The actual values for the dependent variable must be recorded as only 0 or 1. However, the predicted values based on the model, $\hat{Y}$, can take on continuous measures as they move from one extreme to the other. Table 6.6 shows the Minitab worksheet with the first few observations for our auto purchase example. The FITS1 column contains the predicted values based on the OLS model regressing PURCHASE on FAMSIZE and INCOME. As you can see, none of these predicted values is 0 or 1.

■ **Table 6.6** Predicted Values

| ↓ | C1 | C2 | C3 | C4 |
|---|---|---|---|---|
| | PURCHASE | FAMSIZE | INCOME | FITS1 |
| 1 | 1 | 3 | 76.8 | 1.05075 |
| 2 | 1 | 3 | 76.8 | 1.05075 |
| 3 | 1 | 3 | 72.8 | 0.74604 |
| 4 | 1 | 2 | 76.0 | 0.75826 |
| 5 | 1 | 3 | 73.6 | 0.80698 |
| 6 | 1 | 3 | 74.4 | 0.86792 |
| 7 | 1 | 3 | 78.4 | 1.17263 |

Figure 6.2 illustrates why the $R^2$ value does not provide a measure of goodness of fit. The linear regression line can approximate only a few of the observations. There results large error measures. That portion of the change in $Y$ explained by the model will be quite small compared to the unexplained portion and $R^2$ will drastically understate the power of the model.

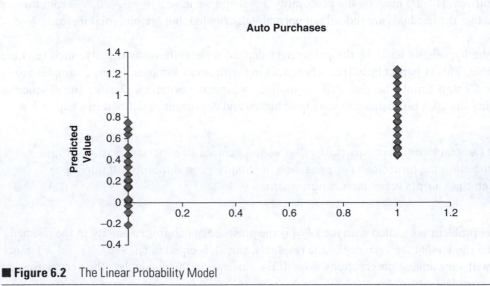

■ **Figure 6.2** The Linear Probability Model

From Figure 6.2 you can also note still another vexing problem presented by LPM. Some of the predicted values for the probabilities are less than zero and some are greater than one. Not all the probability measures fall between zero and 1 as probabilities must. Some of the probabilities of purchase/not purchase are less than zero on the left side of the graph and some are greater than one on the right side of the graph.

## ● Weighted Least Squares

Given these drawbacks of the LPM model it should come as no surprise that the logit model discussed earlier is a more popular approach to binary dependent models. However, remedies for these shortcomings are easily attained. The problem of lack of normality in the residuals might be addressed by collecting large samples and allowing the Central Limit Theorem to work in your favor. The heteroscedasticity issue can be approached by the use of Weighted Least Squares. WLS involves transforming the data in such a manner that will rid the residuals of their heteroscedastic character.

A few simple steps provide the transformations and then the standard OLS method can be used to estimate the model. The steps are as follows:

■ Run the standard OLS model ignoring the presence of multicollinearity. Capture the predicted (fitted) values for $\hat{Y}$. As you were warned above, not all of the predicted values fall between 0 and 1 as probabilities should. You must then assign new values to the stray predictions. Simply encode a value of 0.001 for estimates less than zero and 0.999 for values greater than 1.

■ Construct the 'weight' that will be used to transform the variables as

$$W_i = \sqrt{\hat{Y}_i(1 - \hat{Y}_i)} \qquad (6.2.2)$$

where $\hat{Y}_i$ is the fitted values after assigning the values of 0.001 and 0.999 for the values that fell out of the allowed range of 0 to 1.

■ Transform the variables using the weights as

$$Y_i^* = \frac{Y_i}{W_i}; \quad X_i^* = \frac{X_i}{W_i}; \quad W_i^* = \frac{1}{W_i} \qquad (6.2.3)$$

where $Y_i^*, X_i^*$, and $W_i^*$ are the transformed values and $Y_i, X_i$, and $W_i$ are the original values.

■ Finally, use OLS to regress $Y_i^*$ on all the $X_i^*$ and $W_i^*$. It is important that you suppress the intercept (the constant). Most computer packages will do this upon request.

Table 6.7 shows the transformations for the first few observations of our example dealing with the families' purchases of an automobile. "YHat" is the initial predicted values and "CORRYHat" are the values after correcting for values less than zero or more than 1.

■ **Table 6.7**   Transformed Values for the LPM

| ↓ | C1 | C2 | C3 | C4 | C5 | C6 | C7 | C8 | C9 | C10 |
|---|----|----|----|----|----|----|----|----|----|-----|
|   | PURCHASE | FAMSIZE | INCOME | YHat | CORRYHat | WEIGHTS | 1/WEIGHT | TransYi | TrnsFam | TrnsInc |
| 1 | 1 | 3 | 76.8 | 1.05075 | 0.999000 | 0.031607 | 31.6386 | 31.6386 | 94.9158 | 2429.84 |
| 2 | 1 | 3 | 76.8 | 1.05075 | 0.999000 | 0.031607 | 31.6386 | 31.6386 | 94.9158 | 2429.84 |
| 3 | 1 | 3 | 72.8 | 0.74604 | 0.746042 | 0.435274 | 2.2974 | 2.2974 | 6.8922 | 167.25 |
| 4 | 1 | 2 | 76.0 | 0.75826 | 0.758258 | 0.428139 | 2.3357 | 2.3357 | 4.6714 | 177.51 |
| 5 | 1 | 3 | 73.6 | 0.80698 | 0.806983 | 0.394666 | 2.5338 | 2.5338 | 7.6014 | 186.49 |
| 6 | 1 | 3 | 74.4 | 0.86792 | 0.867924 | 0.338573 | 2.9536 | 2.9536 | 8.8607 | 219.75 |

Table 6.8 displays the Minitab output from the LPM regression.

■ **Table 6.8**   Regression Analysis: TransYi Versus 1/WEIGHT, TrnsFam, TrnsInc

```
The regression equation is
TransYi = -3.93 1/WEIGHT + 0.336 TrnsFam + 0.0504 TrnsInc

Predictor       Coef     SE Coef        T        P
Noconstant
1/WEIGHT      -3.9252      0.2539   -15.46    0.000
TrnsFam       0.33581     0.08273     4.06    0.000
TrnsInc      0.050354    0.006265     8.04    0.000
```

It now remains to interpret the results. The intercept of –3.93 has no logical interpretation in this model. Normally it would suggest that a family with zero family members and no income (that is, family size and income both set equal to zero) would have a "probability" of –3.9 of buying a car. This is meaningless in that a family must have at least one member.

In a model in which the RHS variables can take on meaningful zero values, the –3.9252 would carry an interpretation. For example, presume a model in which we are trying to predict the probability a person would find employment based on the number of dependent children and years of work experience. In this model both RHS variables can logically take on zero values. The regression model would then estimate the probability of finding work as –3.9252. However, since probabilities cannot be negative, this value would be adjusted to a probability of zero.

More realistically for our present model, the probability a family with three family members and an income of 60 ($60,000) buys a new car would be

$$-3.925 + 0.335(3) + 0.05(60) = 0.105$$

That is, the probability a family of three with an income of $60,000 will purchase a new automobile is estimated to be 10.5%.

The individual coefficients can be interpreted as follows: Holding family size constant, an increase of $1,000 in income (one more unit) will increase the probability of purchasing a car by 5%. A similar interpretation can be applied to the coefficient of family size.

The need to suppress the intercept when estimating the model arises because the transformation process results in using the reciprocal of the weight as the intercept. The coefficient of that term serves as the intercept.

> In an LPM the coefficient of a RHS variable measures the change in *probability* an observation will fall in category *i* holding all other RHS variables constant.

Under the logit model earlier we found that the "average" family with 2.65 members and an income of 71 reported a 54.1% probability of buying a new car. Using our LPM model the results are $-3.9252 + 0.33581(2.65) + 0.050354(71) = 0.54 = 54\%$.

## SECTION 6.2 PROBLEMS

1. Access the file BANKRUPTCY and estimate a linear probability model. Compare it with the logit model you estimated in Section 6.1.

2. Describe the steps necessary to carry out a linear probability model based on weighted least squares.

3. Explain why a standard OLS model will not yield an adequate estimate with a model with binary dependent variables.

4. Using the file BANKRUPTCY estimate the weighted least squares model. Provide your comments as to a comparison with the linear probability model and the logit model.

## 6.3 DISCRIMINANT ANALYSIS

Like the logit model, discriminant analysis is used if the dependent variable is categorical (non-numeric). It is most useful if the dependent variable can naturally be divided into two or more parts and we wish to "discriminate" between or among these groups. As with logit models, discriminant analysis will produce a functional relationship and the probability that a given observation will fall into one group or another.

However, the discriminant model requires certain limiting assumptions not incumbent upon the logit form. Discriminant models dictate that the distinct groups fit a normal distribution with respect to the characteristic under study. Further, it must be assumed that the variances between or among the groups are all equal. Finally, while logit will provide probability measures directly, discriminant analysis requires some further manipulation.

For these reasons, logit is often considered a superior method of analysis. Nevertheless, discriminant has its uses. It is quite adept at classifying observations into predetermined groups. For example, discriminant models are often used to distinguish between "bad" and "good" credit risks. Distinguishing which type of training program produces more productive employees or what advertising forms are more likely to promote sales can also be effectively accomplished via discriminant analysis.

> Given two (or more) populations of interest it is possible to discriminate between (or among) them on the basis of variables chosen specifically for that purpose. Discriminant analysis determines which (linear) combination of those variables does the best job of predicting in which group an observation will fall.

Each observation is assigned a discriminant score on the basis of Equation (6.3.1):

$$Z = \beta_0 + \sum_{i=1}^{k} \beta_i X_i \qquad (6.3.1)$$

where $\beta_0$ is the constant term and $\beta_i X_i$ is the parameterized vector of predictor variables 1 through $k$. The betas are discriminant coefficients which maximize the distance between the means of the criterion (dependent) variable.

Using Bayesian principles, discriminant analysis maximizes the between-group variance relative to the within-group variance. It classifies each case based on its discriminant score into that group in which it has the higher probability of belonging according to the standard conditional probability expression as shown by Equation (6.3.2):

$$P(G_i|D) = \frac{[P(D|G_i)*P(G_i)]}{\sum [P(D|G_i)*P(G_i)]} \qquad (6.3.2)$$

where:

$P(G_i|D)$ is the posterior probability a case is in group $i$, given it has a specific discriminant score;

$P(D|G_i)$ is the conditional probability a case has a discriminant score of $D$, given it's in group $G_i$; and

$P(G_i)$ is the prior probability the case is in $G_i$, which is defined as $n_i/N$, where $n_i$ is the number of cases in group $i$ and $N$ is the total number of observations.

After each observation is given a discriminant score using Equation (6.3.1), these scores are averaged for each group. This mean discriminant score for a group is called its *centroid*. The average of the two centroids is the *cutoff score* used to classify each case into one of the groups. If both groups are of the same size, $n_1 = n_2$, and the variance/covariance matrices are equal, the cutoff score will be zero because both groups will have the same mean centroid except for sign. That is, $\bar{Z}_2 = -\bar{Z}_1$ where $\bar{Z}_i$ is the mean discriminant score, the centroid, for group $i$. Those observations with lower $Z$-scores will take on a negative value and be classified into one group, while those with high scores will carry a positive sign and be classified into the other group.

However, if $n_1$ and $n_2$ are not equal the cutoff is the simple *unweighted* mean of the centroids. The mean absolute values of the centroids will not be equal. The cutoff score is found as

$$(\bar{Z}_1 + \bar{Z}_2)/2$$

and it is not equal to zero. SPSS provides the results through

Analyze > Classify > Discriminant

Then enter the variable names and select

Statistics > Fisher's > Unstandardized

Finally, choose

Classify > Compute From Group Size > Casewise Results > Summary Table

A full report is produced.

The process relies on canonical analysis designed to identify the relationships between groups of variables in a data set. The data set is split into two or more groups. Then a search is conducted to find the linear combination of variables.

Using the data for the auto purchases, SPSS provides the canonical discriminant function coefficients for both the unstandardized and standardized models seen in Table 6.9.

■ **Table 6.9**  Canonical Discriminant Function Coefficients

| Variables | Unstandardized Coefficients | Standardized Coefficients |
|---|---|---|
| Income | 0.300 | 0.924 |
| Family Size | 0.912 | 0.409 |
| Constant | −23.753 | |

The unstandardized coefficients are used to estimate the discriminant scores ($Z$-scores) yielding

$$Z = -23.753 + 0.300(\text{INC}) + 0.912(\text{FAMSIZE})$$

As Table 6.7 shows, the family size and income for the first observation in the data set are 3 and 76.8, respectively. The $Z$-score is therefore 2.023. The standardized coefficients serve in much the same capacity as standardized coefficient values in a multiple regression model. Sometimes referred to as "weights," they measure the relative importance in terms of their contributions to the power of the model to properly discriminate among or between groups. Those predictor variables with the higher absolute values provide greater discriminatory power.

■ **Table 6.10** Mean Discriminant Scores for Both Groups

**Functions at Group Centroids**

| PURCHASE | Function |
|---|---|
| | 1 |
| .00 | −1.170 |
| 1.00 | 1.018 |

Unstandardized canonical discriminant functions evaluated at group means

The centroids as noted above are now calculated based on the mean discriminant scores for all observations in each group. Table 6.10 shows the SPSS output.

The cutoff score is $(−1.17 + 1.018)/2 = −0.076$. We can now estimate the probability a new observation will fall in one group or the other. Given the family size and income, a $Z$-value is calculated using the data from Table 6.9. If that family's score is less than $−0.076$ it is concluded that it will not buy a new automobile. If it is more than $−0.076$, it is predicted such a purchase will be made.

To estimate the success of our model we can examine the classification results of the 43 observations used in the data set to estimate the model. Table 6.11 reports the results of the SPSS printout.

■ **Table 6.11** SPSS Classification Results

**Classification Results[a]**

| | | PURCHASE | Predicted Group Membership | | Total |
|---|---|---|---|---|---|
| | | | .00 | 1.00 | |
| Original | Count | .00 | 16 | 4 | 20 |
| | | 1.00 | 2 | 21 | 23 |
| | % | .00 | 80.0 | 20.0 | 100.0 |
| | | 1.00 | 8.7 | 91.3 | 100.0 |

a. 86.0% of original grouped cases correctly classified.

Sixteen of the 20 families that did not make the purchase (in group 0) were properly classified. Further, 21 of the 23 families who bought a new vehicle were classified as having done so. Percentages in each group are shown in the bottom portion of the table. An overall "hit rate" of 86% is reported.

● **Evaluation**

Comparing the hit ratio with chance models is done to determine if the model carries any discriminatory power. Chance models contrast the function's hit ratio with what could be obtained just by mere chance. That is, does the model perform any better than pure happenstance? The Maximum Chance Criterion is one method of comparison open to models with unequal group sizes. It is most often used when the objective of discriminate analysis is to maximize the percentage of cases that are properly classified. It is applied by merely assigning all observations to the larger group. Since 23 out of the 43 cases fell in the Purchased group the Maximum Chance Criterion is 53.5%. The hit rate of the present model of 86% is well above chance and strongly suggests that it carries useful discriminatory power.

The Proportional Chance Criterion is also a revealing method of evaluating a model. It is found as $C_p = P^2 + (1 - P)^2$, where $P$ is the proportion of cases in either group. Given the proportion of new car buyers is 23/43 = 53.5%, $C_p = 50.2\%$. Again, this chance occurrence is significantly less than the hit rate of 86% provided by the model.

This significance of the model can be tested using PRESS'S $Q$-statistic. An acronym for prediction sum of squares, PRESS'S $Q$-statistic is

$$Q = \frac{[N - (n)(g)]^2}{N - (g - 1)} \tag{6.3.3}$$

where:

   $N$ is the size of the entire sample;

   $n$ is the number of correct classifications;

   $g$ is the number of groups.

In the present case $Q = 20.02$. The test is based on a $\chi^2$-statistic with one degree of freedom. Thus, =CHIINV(0.01,1) = 6.635 < 20.02. The null hypothesis that the model is no better than chance is rejected with a $p$-value of =CHIDIST(20.02,1) = 0.00.

## ● Cross-Validation

Complete confirmation of the model requires a process of cross-validation. Only in this manner can it be determined how accurate the model is in classifying the cases. Cross-validation involves using a different data set to test the classification accuracy. This can be done by dividing the data set into two parts. One part, referred to as the analysis sample, is used to estimate the model. The second part, called the hold-out sample, is used to test the accuracy of the model. This approach is suggested if the initial data set is quite large and dividing it in half still provides ample data to derive the discriminant function.

However, using the same data to form the model and then using that model to classify those data, a process referred to as *post hoc* prediction, will result in an upward bias. That action is analogous to shooting the arrow into a wall and then drawing the target around the arrow. The archer is certain to hit the bull's eye every time.

An equally popular method of cross-validation made easier by advancements in computer technology is the Mahalanobis procedure, which relies on the generalized Euclidian distance, which adjusts for unequal variances. Mahalanobis distance is the statistical distance between two points that takes into account the covariance and correlation among variables. For a $k$-variable case, the Mahalanobis distance between two points is

$$M_{ip} = (X_i - X_p)' S^{-1} (X_i - X_p)$$

where:

    $i$ and $p$ are two observations;

    $X$ is a $k \times 1$ vector and $S$ is a $k \times k$ covariance matrix.

For uncorrelated variables, that is, if $r \approx 0$, $S$ is a matrix with variances on the main diagonal, and for uncorrelated standardized variables, $S$ is an identity matrix. The large variance/covariance matrices that result are not presented here in the interest of brevity.

In order to use the Mahalanobis distance to classify a test point as belonging to one of $i$ classes, it is necessary to first estimate the covariance matrix of each class, based on samples known to belong to each class. Then, given a test sample of one or more observations, it remains to compute the Mahalanobis distance to the average or center mass of each class for that set of observations. The test point is then identified as belonging to that class for which the Mahalanobis distance is least. This is equivalent to selecting the class with the maximum likelihood.

Still another approach to estimate the misclassification rate is the *leave-one-out* method. SPSS offers a convenient method, which is demonstrated here. The discriminant function is estimated using all but one of the observations. That function is then used to classify the observation that was excluded. This is done once for each observation in the sample. All observations are classified using a discriminant model unaffected by the observation being classified, thus avoiding the "archer's conundrum" mentioned above. In addition, it offers the advantage of using virtually all of the data that have been collected except for the single case left out and doesn't require dividing the data set into smaller, less efficient units.

The results are shown in Table 6.12. Of the 20 families who did not purchase a vehicle, 16, or 80.0%, were correctly classified. Further, 18 of the 23, or 78.3% of new car owners, were placed in the proper group. Overall, 79.1% of the cross-validated cases were correctly classified. This is just under the 81.4% hit rate reported by the original model (see footnotes a, b, and c to Table 6.12). This minimal upward bias between the original and the cross-validated groups testifies to the model's ability to reliably classify cases into their proper groups. Notice also that the 81.4% of the original group's proper classification is slightly less than the 86.0% from Table 6.11. This is because Table 6.12 was formed on the basis of the leave-one-out method which eliminated the archer's advantage described above.

■ **Table 6.12**   Cross-Validation Analysis

**Classification Results[b,c]**

| | | PURCHASE | Predicted Group Membership | | Total |
|---|---|---|---|---|---|
| | | | .00 | 1.00 | |
| Original | Count | .00 | 17 | 3 | 20 |
| | | 1.00 | 5 | 18 | 23 |
| | % | .00 | 85.0 | 15.0 | 100.0 |
| | | 1.00 | 21.7 | 78.3 | 100.0 |
| Cross-validated[a] | Count | .00 | 16 | 4 | 20 |
| | | 1.00 | 5 | 18 | 23 |
| | % | .00 | 80.0 | 20.0 | 100.0 |
| | | 1.00 | 21.7 | 78.3 | 100.0 |

a. Cross-validation is done only for those cases in the analysis. In cross-validation, each case is classified by the functions derived from all cases other than that case.

b. 81.4% of original grouped cases correctly classified.

c. 79.1% of cross-validated grouped cases correctly classified.

## ● The Eigenvalue and Wilks' Lambda

In matrix algebra, an eigenvalue ($\lambda$) is a constant which, if subtracted from the diagonal elements of a matrix, results in a new matrix with a determinant equal to zero. If $\lambda = 0.00$, the model has no discriminatory power. The larger the value of $\lambda$, the greater the discriminatory power of the model.

By using the eigenvalue, it is possible to calculate the canonical correlation coefficient, $R_c$, for the model. The canonical correlation is a multivariate statistical tool that examines the relationship among sets of multiple dependent variables and multiple independent variables. That is, while a multiple regression model predicts a single dependent variable given RHS variables, canonical correlation *simultaneously* estimates multiple dependent variables based on several RHS variables. This is exactly what we are trying to do with discriminant analysis. We wish to predict the structure of two or more dependent variables.

The square of this coefficient, $R_c^2$, also called the canonical root, measures the percentage of the variation in the dependent variable that is accounted for by the predictor variables. It measures the correlation of the discriminant function with the discriminant scores. As it approaches one, that is, unity, it can be reasoned that most of the variance in the discriminant scores can be attributed to group differences. The closer to one, the more discriminant power the model displays and the better the model's performance in classifying observations between or among groups.

It is calculated as

$$R_c = \sqrt{\frac{\lambda}{1+\lambda}} \qquad\qquad (6.3.4)$$

Wilks' lambda ($\lambda$) is defined as the proportion of the categories' difference in means that is not explained by the model. It is therefore a number between 0 and 1 and the closer it is to 0 the more well defined is the difference between the two groups. If only a small fraction of the total difference is not explained, then these groups are well separated, and their means are significantly different. Because lambda is an *inverse* measure, values of lambda which are near zero denote high discrimination between groups. Thus, a small (close to 0) value of Wilks' lambda means that the groups are well separated by the model.

These values are reported by most computers as shown by the SPSS printout in Table 6.13. The eigenvalue of 1.249 for the model resulted in a correlation of 0.745 and a canonical root of 55.5%. Thus, 55.5% of the variation between the two groups is accounted for by the discriminator variables.

■ **Table 6.13**   The Eigenvalue and Wilks' Lambda

**Eigenvalues**

| Function | Eigenvalue | % of Variance | Cumulative % | Canonical Correlation |
|---|---|---|---|---|
| 1 | 1.249[a] | 100.0 | 100.0 | .745 |

a. First 1 canonical discriminant functions were used in the analysis.

**Wilks' Lambda**

| Test of Function(s) | Wilks' Lambda | Chi-square | df | Sig. |
|---|---|---|---|---|
| 1 | .445 | 32.423 | 2 | .000 |

The Wilks' lambda of 0.445 is compared with a $\chi^2$-value of 32.423 to determine its statistical significance. As seen in Table 6.13, the *p*-value of 0.000 indicates the model is highly significant.

**EXAMPLE 6.2: Finding Employment II**

**Problem Statement:** The executive employment agency (headhunters) we have been following in this chapter now wants to estimate a discriminate model to explain the employment trends of its clients.

**Solution:** With the aid of Minitab and/or SPSS the data are subjected to the proper statistical tests. The SPSS output reveals the discriminate function to be

$$-6.062 + 0.078(\text{EXP}) + 0.077(\text{SALARY})$$

### Canonical Discriminant Function Coefficients

| | Function |
| --- | --- |
| | 1 |
| EXP | .078 |
| SALARY | .077 |
| (Constant) | −6.062 |

Unstandardized coefficients

### Functions at Group Centroids

| EMPT | Function |
| --- | --- |
| | 1 |
| .00 | .272 |
| 1.00 | −.323 |

Unstandardized canonical discriminate functions evaluated at group means

### Classification Results[a]

| | | EMPT | Predicted Group Membership | | Total |
| --- | --- | --- | --- | --- | --- |
| | | | .00 | 1.00 | |
| Original | Count | .00 | 14 | 5 | 19 |
| | | 1.00 | 7 | 9 | 16 |
| | % | .00 | 73.7 | 26.3 | 100.0 |
| | | 1.00 | 43.8 | 56.3 | 100.0 |

a. 65.7% of original grouped cases correctly classified.

### Classification Results[b,c]

| | | EMPT | Predicted Group Membership | | Total |
| --- | --- | --- | --- | --- | --- |
| | | | .00 | 1.00 | |
| Original | Count | .00 | 14 | 5 | 19 |
| | | 1.00 | 7 | 9 | 16 |
| | % | .00 | 73.7 | 26.3 | 100.0 |
| | | 1.00 | 43.8 | 56.3 | 100.0 |
| Cross-validated[a] | Count | .00 | 13 | 6 | 19 |
| | | 1.00 | 8 | 8 | 16 |
| | % | .00 | 68.4 | 31.6 | 100.0 |
| | | 1.00 | 50.0 | 50.0 | 100.0 |

a. Cross-validation is done only for those cases in the analysis. In cross-validation, each case is classified by the functions derived from all cases other than that case.

b. 65.7% of original grouped cases correctly classified.

c. 60.0% of cross-validated grouped cases correctly classified.

**Interpretation:** Since the data were encoded with a "1" if the applicant had found employment and a "0" if he or she was still in the search phase, the model is better at predicting failure to locate employment (73.7%) as opposed to securing placement (56.3%). The model was correct in 65.7% of the cases.

## CHAPTER PROBLEMS

### Conceptual Problems

1. Discuss the destructive nature of the problems that beset the linear probability model.

2. Distinguish between a logit model and a limited dependent variable model. Give an example of each.

3. Write out and explain the equation for the cumulative distribution function.

4. Your colleague at work argues that the cumulative logistic distribution function is linear in the parameters but not in the variables. Is she correct? Explain your response.

5. Explain the statement, "the cumulative logistic distribution function is linear in the logs." Use an equation in your answer.

6. Why is Equation (6.1.3) called the "log of the odds ratio"?

7. What exactly does the coefficient of Equation (6.1.3) measure?

8. Why is $R^2$ not a good measure of fit in a logit model?

9. Explain the nature of the log-likelihood ratio. What does it measure?

10. Explain why a low log-likelihood ratio indicates a better fit.

11. Discuss the limitations imposed by the restrictive assumption placed on the discriminant model.

12. What is the role of the centroid and how is it formed?

13. How is the cutoff score computed and what role does it play in modeling?

14. What is meant by cross-validation in a discriminant model? Why is it done and how does it work?

15. What role does the Maximum Chance Criterion play in discriminant analysis?

16. How is PRESS'S $Q$-statistic used in discriminant analysis?

### Computational Problems

1. Over the last few years Standard and Poor's, a financial services company and credit-rating agency, has downgraded, or threatened to downgrade, the credit rating for several nations around the globe. "It's always possible the rating will come back for many of these countries, but we don't think it's coming back anytime soon," said David Beers, head of S&P's government debt rating unit. To identify nations likely to suffer this re-evaluation, data on 45 countries are collected and a logit function seen here results:

$$Z_i = -3.56 + 1.25D + 0.65DR$$
$$(3.25) \quad (2.55) \quad (5.66)$$

where $D$ is the nation's public debt measured in trillions of dollars and $DR$ is the debt ratio to GNP. $t$-values are in parentheses.

A. Interpret the coefficients.
B. If a nation has debt of 3.7 and a debt-to-GNP ratio of 0.85 how likely is it to suffer re-evaluation?

2. Investment analysts for a large international consulting firm in Paris estimate a logit model to predict the likelihood their major clients will withdraw their account and move to a competing firm. The predictor variables are the monetary value ($MV$) of the present account and the rate of return ($ROR$) the client has enjoyed over the past 12 months. Twenty clients are included in the study. The resulting logit model proves to be

$$Z_i = 0.69 - 1.33MV - 0.68ROR$$

If the probability of losing the client is greater than 30%, the consulting firm will personally visit the client's headquarters to provide reassurance. If a client has an account with a monetary value of 56 and a rate of return of 12.5%, should they schedule a visit?

3. Thirty shipments by TransAtlantic Express designed to predict the likelihood a shipment would reach its port of destination on time yields the following information:

```
Logistic Regression Table

Predictor        Coef      SE Coef       Z        P
Constant      -5.32145     3.47658    -1.53    0.126
MILES       -0.0001820   0.0006630    -0.27    0.784
WEIGHT       0.0114764   0.0053601     2.14    0.032


Log-Likelihood = -16.538
Test that all slopes are zero: G = 7.304, DF = 2, P-Value = 0.026
```

A. What is the likelihood a 500-ton shipment destined for a port 2,000 miles away will reach port on time?
B. Given the results seen here, calculate and interpret the −2 log-likelihood for the restricted model.

### Omnibus Tests of Model Coefficients

|        |       | Chi-square | df | Sig. |
|--------|-------|------------|----|------|
| Step 1 | Step  | 7.304      | 2  | .026 |
|        | Block | 7.304      | 2  | .026 |
|        | Model | 7.304      | 2  | .026 |

**Model Summary**

| Step | −2 Log-likelihood | Cox & Snell R Square | Nagelkerke R Square |
|------|-------------------|----------------------|---------------------|
| 1 | 33.077[a] | .216 | .292 |

a. Estimation terminated at iteration number 5 because parameter estimates changed by less than .001.

C.  Complete the classification table. Twelve of the 30 shipments did not arrive in a timely manner (were encoded as a "0"). Comment on its findings.

**Classification Table[a]**

| Observed | | | Predicted | | |
|----------|--|--|-----------|--|--|
| | | | D | | Percentage Correct |
| | | | .00 | 1.00 | |
| Step 1 | D | .00 | 5 | 7 | 41.7 |
| | | 1.00 | | 14 | 77.8 |
| | Overall Percentage | | | | |

a. The cut value is .500.

4.  A logit model with 50 observations and three RHS variables reports a $\chi^2$ of 13.7, a −2 log-likelihood for the restricted model of 42.7, and a −2 log-likelihood for the unrestricted model of 29. If =CHIINV(.01,3) = 11.344, is the model significant at the 1% level? That is, does including the three RHS explanatory variables add to the explanatory power of the model?

5.  The dean of a business school wants to identify students most likely to successfully complete a master's degree in economics on the basis of a test score and their rank in undergraduate school. The data in the accompanying table produced the discriminant function seen here. Each observation that proved less than successful was encoded with a "0." A "1" was used if the student achieved success in the program.

$$Z = -2.873 - 0.011TEST + 0.472RANK$$

The centroids are

**Functions at Group Centroids**

| VAR00010 | Function |
|----------|----------|
| | 1 |
| .00 | .242 |
| 1.00 | −.212 |

Unstandardized canonical discriminant functions evaluated at group means

A.  Calculate and interpret the cutoff score.
B.  Complete the Summary Table by calculating the discriminate scores (Z-scores) for each observation and identify into which group each observation should be placed. Which ones are misclassified?

## SUMMARY TABLE

| Actual Group | Score | Rank | Z-Score | Predicted Group |
|:---:|:---:|:---:|:---:|:---:|
| 1 | 42 | 5 | | |
| 1 | 33 | 6 | | |
| 0 | 25 | 9 | | |
| 0 | 2 | 8 | | |
| 0 | 54 | 4 | | |
| 1 | 25 | 3 | | |
| 0 | 26 | 6 | | |
| 1 | 35 | 8 | | |
| 1 | 35 | 9 | | |
| 0 | 39 | 10 | | |
| 1 | 32 | 5 | | |
| 0 | 25 | 6 | | |
| 1 | 20 | 7 | | |
| 1 | 19 | 8 | | |
| 0 | 25 | 8 | | |

C.  Complete and comment on the classification results. What percent of all cases were correctly classified?

### Classification Results[a]

| | | GROUP | Predicted Group Membership | | Total |
|:---|:---|:---:|:---:|:---:|:---:|
| | | | .00 | 1.00 | |
| Original | Count | 0 | | 3 | 7 |
| | | 1.00 | 4 | | 8 |
| | % | 0 | 57.1 | | 100.0 |
| | | 1.00 | 50.0 | | 100.0 |

a. ????? of original grouped cases correctly classified.

Cross-validation results based on the leave-one-out method are seen here. Complete the table and provide an insight into its meaning.

**Classification Results[b,c]**

| | | VAR00010 | Predicted Group Membership | | Total |
|---|---|---|---|---|---|
| | | | .00 | 1.00 | |
| Original | Count | .00 | 4 | | 7 |
| | | 1.00 | | 4 | 8 |
| | % | .00 | | 42.9 | 100.0 |
| | | 1.00 | | 50.0 | 100.0 |
| Cross-validated[a] | Count | .00 | 2 | | 7 |
| | | 1.00 | | 4 | |
| | % | .00 | | 71.4 | 100.0 |
| | | 1.00 | 50.0 | 50.0 | 100.0 |

a. Cross-validation is done only for those cases in the analysis. In cross-validation, each case is classified by the functions derived from all cases other than that case.
b. 53.3% of original grouped cases correctly classified.
c. 40.0% of cross-validated grouped cases correctly classified.

## COMPUTER PROBLEM

COMPUTER PROBLEM 6

Bissey Ltd. produces metal products used to manufacture luxurious dinnerware and other costly household furnishings. Lately, the frequency with which defective units have resulted from the production process has become a troublesome matter. The final product is subjected to two curative procedures involving a closely regulated exposure to heat and a final immersion in a chemical bath. It is suspected that an improper period of time for both treatments is the cause for the unacceptable rate of defects.

Data have been collected and saved in the file BISSEY LTD. The data are encoded with a "1" if the finished metal plate was defective and a "0" if not. The duration for the treatments is recorded in minutes.

Access the file and apply both logit analysis and discriminant analysis to the data to determine if time of exposure can explain the number of flawed units. Use all possible statistical tests associated with both forms of analysis. Interpret the results and prepare a formal statement of your conclusions.

*Chapter 7*

# HETEROSCEDASTICITY

## INTRODUCTION

One of the basic assumptions of the standard OLS model is that the error terms are homoscedastic in that they have a constant variance for all values of $X$. The assumption can be expressed as

$$\sigma^2_{X_i} = \sigma^2_{X_j}$$

where $X_i$ and $X_j$ are two different values for the independent variable.

To the extent that this assumption is violated, it is said that the model suffers from *heteroscedasticity*; that is, the variations in the error terms around the regression line are not all the same for all values of $X$. This problem is most likely to arise in the use of cross-sectional data as opposed, for example, to time series data. The reason for this phenomenon is that heteroscedasticity is likely to be caused by disparity in sizes. With time series data pertaining to, for example, annual sales for a single enterprise, the data will not exhibit wide fluctuations from year to year. However, if we are using cross-sectional data we would likely find that sales varied considerably from smaller to larger firms in our data set.

The classic illustration of heteroscedasticity can be expressed with the Keynesian consumption function in which John Maynard Keynes, the noted British economist, expressed the relationship between personal consumption and personal income. He demonstrated how consumption was a function of income.[1] Those of us on the lower end of the income spectrum can spend our hard-earned gains on a few of the basic necessities of life. Hence, there is little variation in consumption expenditures. The more fortunate at the upper end can express much more individuality in their consumption pattern and enjoy considerably more latitude in spending practices. Thus, the variation in expenditures among consumers at higher income levels is much more pronounced. Figure 7.1 illustrates. Notice that the variation (the variance) in consumption is markedly different across income levels. Individuals with smaller incomes such as $I_1$ have a much more consistent spending pattern. There is less variation in their consumption levels. Those consumers with larger incomes such as $I_4$ demonstrate considerable diversity in their spending practices. There is much greater variation in consumption among those in the latter group. This is classic heteroscedasticity.

We might also distinguish between *pure* and *impure* heteroscedasticity. Pure heteroscedasticity occurs when the model is properly specified, that is, it contains the correct explanatory variables, yet the variances in the error terms are still unequal due to the inherent characteristics of the relationship between the variables. Impure heteroscedasticity results from a misspecification of the model. Heteroscedasticity occurs in this instance because the impact of the omitted variable must now be

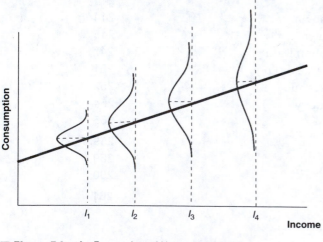

■ **Figure 7.1**    An Expression of Heteroscedasticity

registered by the error term. As we shall see, the latter is more easily remedied by reforming the model to its proper specification.

After a brief introduction to the matters surrounding the concept of heteroscedasticity, this chapter:

■ examines techniques to test for the presence of heteroscedasticity;

■ discusses the remedial measures that can be taken to mitigate the disorder it can cause.

We begin by noting its unfortunate consequences.

> Heteroscedasticity occurs when the variance of the Y-values around (above and below) their mean is not the same for all values of X. As Figure 7.1 shows, this also means that the error variances are not the same at all values of income. Errors above and below the regression line are larger at higher income levels.

## 7.1 CONSEQUENCES OF HETEROSCEDASTICITY

In the presence of heteroscedasticity the model will no longer be BLUE. Specifically, the model will not possess minimum variance as required by the Gauss–Markov Theorem and will therefore not be "efficient" as described in Chapter 1. This is true, unfortunately, even in the presence of large samples.

Perhaps most disturbing is the impact of heteroscedasticity on the standard errors of the coefficients, something we have been calling $S_{b_i}$. Heteroscedasticity will produce biased and inconsistent estimates of the standard errors. This has the effect of invalidating $t$-values associated with any hypothesis test and confidence intervals based upon those $t$-values. That is, since the hypothesis test is based on a $t$-value expressed as

$$t = \frac{b_i - \beta_i}{S_{b_i}}$$

any decrease, for example in the $S_{b_i}$, will inflate the $t$-value, pushing the test results into the rejection region. If the null hypothesis is true, rejecting it will produce a Type I error. As a consequence, hypothesis tests and confidence intervals formed on the basis of models suffering from heteroscedasticity are unreliable.

This means, as noted above, that heteroscedasticity will result in inefficient estimators. The coefficient estimators, the $b_i$, produced by OLS will suffer a greater variance than would estimators derived by other means. These "other means" often involve *weighted least squares* (see Chapter 6) discussed later in this chapter.

*Pure* heteroscedasticity will *not* cause bias in the estimates—it is the standard errors of the estimates that become biased. There will be undue variance in the estimates; large positive errors are just as likely as large negative errors. Therefore, they will average out and the OLS estimates themselves remain unbiased.

Despite the presence of heteroscedasticity, the coefficient estimators will remain consistent as defined in Chapter 1. Thus, by definition, as the sample size increases, the value of the estimator approaches that of the true coefficient, $\beta_i$.

> Heteroscedasticity will bias the standard errors of the estimated regression coefficients and thereby invalidate hypothesis tests and confidence intervals. The estimates of the coefficients themselves, the $b_i$, will not be biased, but their standard errors will be.

## SECTION 7.1 PROBLEMS

1. Why is heteroscedasticity more likely to occur with the use of cross-sectional data? Give an example to illustrate.

2. As a research analyst for a large chemical firm in Western Europe, you are assigned the task of determining the length of time required to complete a chemical reaction. Your model is hindered by heteroscedasticity. You decide to combat the presence of heteroscedasticity by increasing your sample size. Comment on your chances for success.

3. Your co-worker at the chemical plant mentioned in question 2 conducts a hypothesis test and concludes that the RHS variable is significant. What response do you offer? How does your reply relate to the $t$-value associated with test on models impaired by heteroscedasticity?

4. Distinguish between pure and impure heteroscedasticity. Why is the latter more easily corrected?

5. Define heteroscedasticity. Propose an original model of your own creation that might likely suffer from heteroscedasticity. Illustrate by means of a graph.

6. Discuss the effects heteroscedasticity has on the coefficient estimates and the standard errors of the coefficients.

## 7.2 DETECTING HETEROSCEDASTICITY

Given the destructive nature of heteroscedasticity it is advisable to carefully examine each model to determine if it might have infected your model. This is especially true if you are using cross-sectional data. This section discusses a few of the more popular methods of testing for heteroscedasticity.

### ● Using Plots of Residuals

One quick-and-dirty method of detecting heteroscedasticity is to run the model using standard OLS procedures and then plot the residuals. If any pattern is revealed that suggests the variances in the residuals are correlated with the values of the RHS variable(s) such as that seen in Figure 7.1, we may reasonably suspect heteroscedasticity has distorted your analysis.

Consider the Income/Consumption data for 46 consumers in thousands of dollars in Table 7.1. They depict a typical consumption function like that referenced above. As the dependent variable, Consumption was regressed on Income and the residuals were collected. The model proved to be $\hat{C} = -0.758 + 0.958285I$. The coefficient of Income is, by definition, the increase in Consumption given a one unit increase in Income. As such, it is referred to as the "marginal propensity to consume" in the standard Keynesian lexicon. The estimated consumption for the first observation is $\hat{C} = -0.75765 + 0.958285(25.5) = 23.6786$. Recall the residual is found as $(Y_i - \hat{Y})$. That is, it's the difference between the actual value of the dependent variable and that value estimated by the model. For the first observation in our Income/Consumption data, that's $26.5 - 23.6786 = 2.821379$ as seen in the table. The remaining residuals are found in like fashion and shown in Table 7.1.

An easy, yet admittedly crude, method of detecting heteroscedasticity is to plot the residuals as well as residuals-squared. If any pattern emerges, heteroscedasticity might be the cause. As emphasized many times in the past, OLS assumes that the residuals are random and exhibit no discernible arrangement.

Plots as seen in Figure 7.2, however, suggest the presence of heteroscedasticity. The residuals are plotted on the vertical axis and income on the horizontal in 7.2A. Notice that the spread (variance) in the residuals becomes larger as we move from lower to higher income levels. Hence,

$$\sigma^2_{X_i} \neq \sigma^2_{X_j}$$

where $X_i$ and $X_j$ are income levels such that $X_i < X_j$.

Figure 7.2B plots residuals-squared against income. Again, it can be seen that the squared values of the residuals increase as income increases. In both cases the variance in the residuals is not constant.

However, an examination of residual plots can be very subjective. While one researcher might view a plot as evidencing heteroscedasticity, another may deny any such pattern. In most cases the graphical plots of residuals are far less obvious than those shown here. Thankfully there are more analytical methods of testing for heteroscedasticity. We examine a few of the popular ones below.

## ● The Park Test[2]

If heteroscedasticity is present, we may find that the differing variances, $\sigma^2_i$, may be systematically associated with one of the RHS variables.[3] The Park test is performed by identifying a suspect variable thought to be the source of the problem. The approach used to do so is discussed shortly.

■ **Table 7.1** Income/Consumption Data that Exhibit Heteroscedasticity

| Income | Cons | Resid | Income | Cons | Resid |
|--------|------|-------|--------|------|-------|
| 25.5 | 26.5 | 2.821379 | 100 | 98.5 | 3.429129 |
| 35.7 | 36.2 | 2.74687 | 100 | 93.5 | −1.57087 |
| 35.7 | 35.0 | 1.53387 | 100 | 93.5 | −1.57087 |
| 35.7 | 35.0 | 1.53387 | 104 | 105.9 | 6.995988 |
| 35.7 | 35.0 | 1.53387 | 104 | 97.1 | −1.76401 |
| 49 | 45.2 | −0.99832 | 104 | 97.1 | −1.76401 |
| 49 | 47.1 | 0.891676 | 104 | 97.1 | −1.76401 |
| 49 | 52.4 | 6.201676 | 111.2 | 103.7 | −2.11167 |
| 58.2 | 53.2 | −1.81455 | 112.2 | 110.2 | 3.43805 |
| 59.2 | 56.4 | 0.399167 | 149.9 | 138.9 | −3.9803 |
| 66.3 | 62.8 | 0.056342 | 149.9 | 138.9 | −3.9803 |
| 66.3 | 62.8 | 0.056342 | 151 | 148.3 | 4.356582 |
| 68.3 | 65.3 | 0.606771 | 160.1 | 148.2 | −4.47281 |
| 69.4 | 71.9 | 6.152658 | 171.4 | 169.3 | 5.807564 |
| 69.4 | 65.7 | −0.09334 | 171.4 | 158.5 | −5.01844 |
| 79.6 | 74.9 | −0.58585 | 171.4 | 158.5 | −5.01844 |
| 79.6 | 74.9 | −0.58585 | 181.6 | 174.3 | 1.033054 |
| 87.3 | 81.9 | −0.95765 | 181.6 | 167.8 | −5.51095 |
| 88.7 | 83.2 | −1.02525 | 188.7 | 174.2 | −5.85377 |
| 88.7 | 83.2 | −1.02525 | 251.9 | 231.7 | −8.9054 |
| 96.9 | 90.7 | −1.42119 | 251.9 | 247.9 | 7.265602 |
| 96.9 | 90.7 | −1.42119 | 256 | 247.3 | 2.736633 |
| 100 | 89.5 | −5.57087 | 372.3 | 365.2 | 9.18806 |

Then you must regress the log of the squared error terms from the OLS model on the log of that variable. The method is expressed as Equation (7.2.1):

$$\ln e^2 = \beta_0 + \beta_1 \ln X_i + v_i \qquad (7.2.1)$$

where $e^2$ is the squared errors from the original OLS regression model and $X_i$ is the RHS variable identified as the suspect. There are four steps to completing the Park test for heteroscedasticity.

7.2A Residuals Plotted Against Income      7.2B Residuals Squared

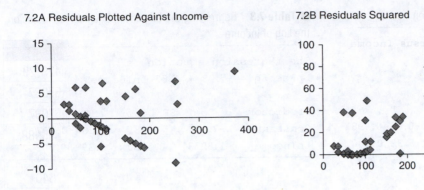

■ **Figure 7.2**   Evidence of Heteroscedasticity

1. Run the initial OLS model as if there were no concern over heteroscedasticity and collect the residuals.

2. Square those residuals.

3. Regress the log of those squared residuals on the suspect variable according to Equation (7.2.1).

4. Test the significance of the resulting coefficient of the suspect variable. The null hypothesis states that no heteroscedasticity exists. If the null is rejected, you may conclude that the model suffers from heteroscedasticity and the attendant problems it fosters.

This procedure is applied to the consumption function data in Table 7.1. The results of the initial OLS model are seen in Table 7.2.

The residuals were saved and the logs of the squared values were obtained. In accord with Equation (7.2.1), the regression yielded the results shown in Table 7.3.

Clearly, the coefficient for LnIncome is highly significant. It reports a *p*-value of 0.2%. The presence of heteroscedasticity has been confirmed, thereby substantiating our suspicions raised by the earlier residual plots.

The Park test provides a rather simple and unequivocal test for heteroscedasticity. However, it does suffer from two deficiencies. The first stumbling block involves identifying which variable is associated with the error variances. If there is only one RHS variable as in this case, the decision is obvious.

But if the original model contains two or more RHS variables, a decision has to be made. How does the researcher determine which variable might be the source of the heteroscedasticity?

**■ Table 7.2** Regressing Consumption on Income

**Regression Analysis: Cons versus Income**

The regression equation is
Cons = −0.76 + 0.958 Income

| Predictor | Coef | SE Coef | T | P |
|-----------|------|---------|---|---|
| Constant | −0.758 | 1.110 | −0.68 | 0.498 |
| Income | 0.958285 | 0.008310 | 115.32 | 0.000 |

**■ Table 7.3** Regressing the Log of the Squared Residuals on the Log of Income

The regression equation is
LnResdSq = −7.08 + 1.83 LnIncome

| Predictor | Coef | SE Coef | T | P |
|-----------|------|---------|---|---|
| Constant | −7.084 | 2.481 | −2.86 | 0.007 |
| LnIncome | 1.8253 | 0.5390 | 3.39 | 0.002 |

Recall that heteroscedasticity in cross-sectional data is often caused by disparities in the magnitude. Therefore, any variable that might reflect size is a reasonable candidate. For example, suppose you are trying to model sales tax revenues across states. Variables such as population and disposable income would prove likely candidates for the suspect variable. They reflect scale and overall levels of economic activity. On the other hand, states' birth rates or the proportion of forested land would likely not serve well in that capacity. They have less capacity to gage retail sales or general levels of consumption.

In addition, the Park test also faces the threat that the error term in Equation (7.2.1) may itself suffer from heteroscedasticity. Any hypothesis test based on its results is therefore suspect. Nevertheless, if the Park test suggests that heteroscedasticity may prevail, it is wise to take the remedial actions described shortly.

### ● The Glejser Test[4]

The Glejser test is similar to that proposed by Park in that it begins with an estimation of the model based on the original data with no deliberation given to the potential for heteroscedasticity. But instead of using the squared values of the residuals, Glejser suggested using the absolute values of the residuals as the regressand. He offered several functional forms that might be used in this regard, some of which are shown in Equations (7.2.2A, B, and C):

$$|e| = \beta_0 + \beta_1 X_i + v_i \tag{7.2.2A}$$

$$|e| = \beta_0 + \beta_1 \sqrt{X_i} + v_i \tag{7.2.2B}$$

$$|e| = \beta_0 + \beta_1 \frac{1}{X_i} + v_i \tag{7.2.2C}$$

All three functional forms were applied to the consumption function data. All three resulted in the conclusion that heteroscedasticity characterized the data set.

To summarize the Glejser test:

1. Run the initial regression OLS model with no concern over heteroscedasticity and collect the residuals.

2. Find the absolute values for the residuals.

3. Regress these absolute values on the suspect variable according to Equations (7.2.2A, B, and C).

4. Test the significance of the resulting coefficient of the suspect variable. The null hypothesis states that no heteroscedasticity exists. If the null is rejected, you may conclude that the model suffers from heteroscedasticity and the attendant problems it fosters.

As you can see, the Glejser test parallels the Park test in many respects. It also suffers the same downsides presented by the Park test and must be dealt with in similar fashion. Further, it is argued that the squared values of the residuals more appropriately reflect the nature of residuals than do the absolute values. Therefore, the Park test is often preferred.

### ● White's Test[5]

Both tests discussed above require that we must identify that variable proportionally associated with the heteroscedastic variances. White avoids that problem by using all RHS variables—and several of their modified forms—in his detection method. As with the Park method, the squared residuals of the original OLS model are computed. These values are used as the regressand in a model containing all independent variables, their squared values, and all interaction terms from the initial data set. If the original model was expressed as

$$Y = \beta_0 + \beta_1 X_1 + \beta_2 X_2 + \varepsilon$$

White's formulation would be

$$e^2 = \beta_0 + \beta_1 X_1 + \beta_2 X_2 + \beta_3 X_1^2 + \beta_4 X_2^2 + \beta_5 X_1 X_2 \qquad (7.2.3)$$

The only exception occurs if one of the RHS variables is a dummy variable encoded as a "1" or a "0." Then the squared values are omitted from Equation (7.2.3) because $0^2 = 0$ and $1^2 = 1$ and so there would result perfect multicollinearity between the dummy variables and their squared values.

Testing for heteroscedasticity requires computing $nR^2$, where $n$ is the number of observations and $R^2$ is the coefficient of determination from Equation (7.2.3) (not the coefficient of determination of the original equation that produced the $\varepsilon$ terms in the first place). This statistic is compared with a critical chi-square ($\chi^2$) value to test the hypothesis that all $\beta_i = 0$ in Equation (7.2.3). The chi-square carries $k$ degrees of freedom, where $k$ is the number of regressors in Equation (7.2.3).

Our consumption function data produced the following results:

```
The regression equation is
RESI1 = 4.96 - 0.0829 Income + 0.000251 IncomeSq
```

There are no interaction terms since there was only one regressor in the original model. There were $n = 43$ observations and the coefficient of determination reported as 24.2%. Thus, $nR^2 = (42)(0.242) = 11.132$. Setting alpha at 1% with two degrees of freedom, we find Excel yields =CHIINV(0.01,2) = 9.21034 < 11.132. The null hypothesis is rejected and the presence of heteroscedasticity is supported.

## ● The Goldfeld–Quandt Test[6]

The Goldfeld–Quandt method of detecting heteroscedasticity is often considered the most popular and effective approach. It faces the least "snags" and requires fewer assumptions about the nature of the data set and the form heteroscedasticity might take. The idea behind this test is that if heteroscedasticity results from size differences, then the variances for observations with low values of $X_i$ should be different from the variances associated with high values for $X_i$ where $X_i$ is the suspect variable. This process involves sorting the data from low to high based on the suspect variable. Let's take it step-by-step.

**Step 1:** Sort the entire data set by that variable suspected to be associated with the error variances. Remember, a likely candidate for this procedure would be an RHS variable that reflects some measure of size.

**Step 2:** Remove some of the observations in the middle of the sorted data set to exaggerate the difference between "low" and "high" values. There is no hard and fast rule as to how many observations should be eliminated, but most researchers have found that at least 20% should be deleted. If $m$ observations are removed that leaves $[(n - m)/2]$ observations in each data set.

**Step 3:** Run a standard regression for both sets of data.

**Step 4:** Collect the sums of the squared errors (SSE) from both models. Compute an $F$-ratio such that

$$F = \frac{SSE_L/\text{d.f.}}{SSE_S/\text{d.f.}}$$

where $SSE_L$ is the sum of the squared errors from the regression model using the larger values of $X$ and $SSE_S$ is the sum of the squared errors from the regression using the smaller values of $X$. The d.f. is the degrees of freedom which is equal for both the numerator and the denominator and is found as

$$\frac{n-m}{2} - 2$$

**Step 5:** Compare the result in Step 4 with an $F$-statistic at a chosen alpha-value and the degrees of freedom found in Step 4.

If the $F$-ratio from Step 4 exceeds the critical value from Step 5, it may be concluded that heteroscedasticity exists.

To apply the Goldfeld–Quandt method to our Income/Consumption data, 10 of the 46 observations (about 22%) were eliminated from the data set. That left 36/2 = 18 observations in each data set. $SSE_L = 392$ and $SSE_S = 72.8$. There are

$$\frac{46-10}{2} - 2 = 16 - \text{d.f.}$$

Step 4 yields

$$F = \frac{392/16}{72.8/16} = 5.38$$

As the critical $F$-value, Excel produces =FINV(0.01,16,16) = 3.372046 < 5.38. The conclusion that heteroscedasticity is present is upheld. Using Excel, =FDIST(5.38,16,16) reveals a $p$-value of 0.000826.

---

**EXAMPLE 7.1: Crime and Statistics I**

**Problem Statement:** In 2011 a national law enforcement agency in the United States collected data on the weekly number of crimes in all 50 states along with the population and unemployment rates in each state. The intent was to study the impact of population and joblessness on the crime levels. Given the cross-sectional nature of the data set and the disparity in the sizes of the states' population it was deemed prudent to test for heteroscedasticity.

*(Continued)*

**EXAMPLE 7.1: (Continued)**

**Solution:** The first action is to plot the residuals in a search for any patterned results. The graph shown here clearly raises suspicion. More definitive, analytical tests must be conducted.

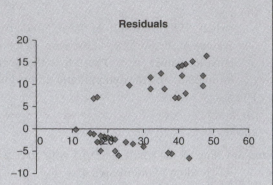

Certainly, population is a clear measure of size and is chosen as the suspect variable upon which to base the tests.

*Park Test:* Following the four steps outlined above to complete the Park test produces the model seen here:

$$\ln(e^2) = -2.1 + 2.3\ln(POP)$$

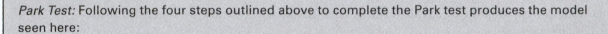

After running the regression in accord with the Park test, the significance of the log of population is examined using a standard hypothesis test based on the *t*-value and the *p*-value. The *t*-value for population proved to be 5.36. If testing the hypothesis $H_0: \beta_{pop} = 0$ is carried out at the 1% level of significance with 48 degrees of freedom, the *p*-value is reported as =TDIST(5.36,48,2) = 0.000 < 0.01. The null is rejected. The coefficient for population of 2.3 is found to be significant and the suspicion of heteroscedasticity is confirmed.

It is no longer necessary to use the states' unemployment rates to test for heteroscedasticity. Population has served effectively in this effort. Also, unemployment rates are not a measure of size. If the *number* of unemployed workers was used as the explanatory variable, perhaps it too could have served in this capacity. The disparity in the number of jobless workers among the states meets the criterion of size, but the *rate* of unemployment does not reflect magnitude or dimension.

*Glejser Test:* The Glejser test relies on the logs of the absolute values of the residuals as the dependent variable which are regressed on the nominal values of the suspect variable. The regression proves to be

$$|e| = -5.7 + 3.11POP$$

The subsequent hypothesis for the significance of population reports another *p*-value of 0.000. Again, the conclusion that heteroscedasticity is a concern is founded. Regressions based on the square root of population as well as its reciprocal in accord with Equations (7.2.2A, B, and C) produced similar results.

*White Test:* The White test requires that the squared residuals be regressed on all RHS variables, the squares of all RHS variables, and all interaction terms. The outcome is

$$e^2 = 166.6 - 1.53POP - 24.32UNEMPT - 0.015POPSQED$$
$$+ 1.29UNEMPTSQED + 0.427POPUNEMPT$$

The test is based on a chi-square value. First, we must find $nR^2$, where $n$ is the number of observations (50 in this case) and $R^2$ is the coefficient of determination of the White formulation above, which reported as 0.377. This proves to be 50(0.377) = 18.85. The critical chi-square in this case has five degrees of freedom—one for each of the regressors in White's formula. At a 1% level of significance we find =CHIINV(.01,5) = 15.08 < 18.85. The null is rejected and heteroscedasticity remains problematic.

*Goldfeld–Quandt Test:* To complete the Goldfeld–Quandt test, the data are ordered from lowest to highest based on population. Ten of the states in the middle of the array (20% of the 50 observations) are withdrawn from the data set. Standard OLS models for each subset are estimated and the sum of the squared errors, SSEs, are captured for each model. The model based on the observations with the lower observations for population produced $SSE_L = 84.3$, while the larger states reported $SSE_S = 1256$. Since there are

$$\frac{n-m}{2} - 2$$

degrees of freedom, where $n$ is the original number of observations (50 in this case) and $m$ is the number of observations removed from the data set to exaggerate the difference between "small" and "large" sub-populations (10 in this case), the number of degrees of freedom is 18.

Then, using the requisite *F*-test

$$F = \frac{SSE_{L4}/\text{d.f.}}{SSE_S/\text{d.f.}} = \frac{1256/18}{84.3/18} = 14.89$$

Comparing this *F*-value to a critical *F*-value, we find =FINV(.01,18,18) = 3.12 < 14.89. Again, the same conclusion is forthcoming: heteroscedasticity is present.

**Interpretation**: Conclusively, reliance on standard OLS models to estimate the impact of population and joblessness on crime rates will produce questionable results. The attendant heteroscedasticity will bias any results and place outcomes in a fragile position at best.

Some corrective action must be taken before a reliable model designed to explain the number of crimes can be estimated. Such remedial efforts are the subject of the next section.

## SECTION 7.2 PROBLEMS

Consider the data for the year 2011 given in the following table and work the problems listed below. The data can also be found as the Excel file LifeExp. These and many more variables can be obtained for most of the world's nations at the source cited below the table.

Life expectance (LifeExp) is in years, birth rate (BR) is per 1,000 population, population (Pop) is in millions, and the infant mortality rate (InfMor) is per 1,000 births. Use population as the measure of size (the suspect variable).

| Country | LifeExp | BR | Pop | InfMor |
|---|---|---|---|---|
| Australia | 82 | 12 | 21.767 | 5 |
| Hong Kong | 82 | 7 | 7.123 | 3 |
| Canada | 81 | 10 | 34.031 | 5 |
| China | 75 | 12 | 1330.1 | 17 |
| United States | 78 | 14 | 311.051 | 6 |
| United Kingdom | 80 | 12 | 62.698 | 5 |
| Brazil | 73 | 18 | 203.43 | 21 |
| Afghanistan | 49 | 40 | 29.758 | 124 |
| Egypt | 73 | 25 | 82.08 | 25 |
| Finland | 79 | 10 | 5.259 | 3 |
| Germany | 80 | 8 | 81.472 | 4 |
| Ireland | 80 | 16 | 4.671 | 4 |
| Mexico | 79 | 19 | 113.724 | 17 |
| Puerto Rico | 79 | 11 | 3.989 | 8 |
| Spain | 81 | 11 | 46.755 | 3 |

Source: http://www.census.gov/population/international/data/idb/country.php

1. With life expectancy as the regressand, plot the residuals using the other three variables as regressors. Comment on any suggestion of heteroscedasticity.

2. Based on your results from problem 1, use the Park test to test for heteroscedasticity. Use population as the size (suspect) variable.

3. Using the data from problem 1, perform and comment on the Glejser test.

4. Perform White's test and comment.

5. Sort the data by population. Remove the middle four observations. Perform the Goldfeld–Quandt test and comment.

Work problems 6 through 9 using the data presented below for the European Union:

| Country | Bank Transfer | Foreign Investment | Bank Balances |
|---|---|---|---|
| Austria | 31.2 | 24.99 | 17 |
| Belgium | 39.24 | 34.986 | 15 |
| Bulgaria | 39.5 | 34.986 | 23 |
| Cyprus | 39.24 | 34.986 | 21 |
| Czech Republic | 36.8 | 34.986 | 20 |
| Denmark | 108.1 | 98.3 | 80.55 |
| Estonia | 110.5 | 92.3 | 88.65 |
| Finland | 103.54 | 89.6 | 84.15 |
| France | 103.54 | 98 | 84.15 |
| Germany | 52.54 | 48.02 | 21.2 |
| Greece | 52.54 | 48.02 | 25.3 |
| Hungary | 52.54 | 48.02 | 15.6 |
| Ireland | 71.84 | 66.934 | 25.6 |
| Italy | 90.84 | 85.554 | 73.7487 |
| Latvia | 92.24 | 86.926 | 74.8953 |
| Lithuania | 61.74 | 57.036 | 15 |
| Luxembourg | 62.74 | 58.016 | 14.7 |
| Malta | 69.84 | 64.974 | 14.9 |
| Netherlands | 83.14 | 78.008 | 67.4424 |
| Poland | 72.94 | 68.012 | 64.71 |
| Portugal | 83.14 | 78.008 | 67.4424 |
| Romania | 69.84 | 64.974 | 21.3 |
| Slovakia | 100.44 | 94.962 | 81.6111 |
| Spain | 72.94 | 68.012 | 59.0886 |
| Sweden | 100.44 | 94.962 | 81.6111 |
| United Kingdom | 92.24 | 86.926 | 74.8953 |

The Council of the European Union[7] has raised concern regarding the international trading practices of its member nations. Data have been collected for three important variables for each of the members with the intent of examining their economic behavior. Respond to the questions below on the basis of these data. These data can also be found in the Excel data file EU. Slovenia is left out of this analysis due to incomplete data. There are $n = 26$ observations.

6. Using *bank transfers* as the dependent variable and *bank balances* as the variable suspected of creating heteroscedasticity, use the Park test to test for heteroscedasticity.

7. Perform the Glejser test using the data for bank transfers.

8. Perform White's test using the data for bank transfers.

9. Perform the Goldfeld–Quandt test by removing the middle six observations using the data for bank transfers.

## 7.3 REMEDIAL MEASURES

Although heteroscedasticity does not bias the OLS coefficients, it does cause the estimates to become quite inefficient even in the presence of large samples. Standard regression tactics are therefore speculative at best and will likely prove misleading. Therefore, if heteroscedasticity is suspected some remedial measure must be pursued to mitigate its ill-effects.

The tests for detecting heteroscedasticity discussed above suggested that our income/consumption model suffered from some form and degree of heteroscedasticity. This section examines what can be done to combat the destructive nature of the beast.

### ● If the Population Error Variances Are Known

In the unlikely event the population variance is known it can be used to alleviate the problems associated with heteroscedasticity. Assume the population regression function of Equation (7.3.1):

$$Y = \beta_0 + \beta_1 X + \varepsilon_i \tag{7.3.1}$$

We can transform the model by dividing through by $\sigma_i$, the square root of the variance in each case. This produces Equation (7.3.2).

$$\frac{Y_i}{\sigma_i} = \beta_0 \frac{1}{\sigma_i} + \beta_1 \frac{X_i}{\sigma_i} + \frac{\varepsilon_i}{\sigma_i} \tag{7.3.2}$$

The result will be a model that no longer suffers from heteroscedasticity and produces estimates that are BLUE in every sense.

This is a form of *weighted least squares* much like that we considered in Chapter 6. The standard deviations of the errors are used as the weights.

If we let $v_i = \varepsilon_i/\sigma_i$, we can show that the error term in Equation (7.3.2) is indeed homoscedastic. It follows that

$$v_i^2 = \frac{\varepsilon_i^2}{\sigma_i^2}$$

$$E\left(v_i^2\right) = E\left(\frac{\varepsilon_i^2}{\sigma_i^2}\right)$$

$$= \left(\frac{1}{\sigma_i^2}\right)E\left(\varepsilon_i^2\right)$$

$$= \frac{1}{\sigma_i^2}\left(\sigma_i^2\right) = 1$$

which is a constant. Therefore, we have homoscedasticity. It is then permissible to run Equation (7.3.2) with confidence that the resulting coefficients are free of heteroscedasticity.

However, the foregoing approach is rather improbable given that $\sigma_i^2$ is seldom if ever known. It is tendered here only to set the backdrop for other, more feasible, forms of weighted least squares that follow, and frankly, because most other sources offer such a scenario. Let's take a look at a more reasonable form of weighted least squares that presents a potential solution to the problem of heteroscedasticity.

## ● Weighted Least Squares with $\sigma_i^2$ Unknown

In the likely event $\sigma_i^2$ is unknown we must identify an RHS variable that may be related to the error variance. A practical point of departure would be to plot the residuals from an initial run against each *individual* RHS variable and search for any emerging pattern such as that seen in Figure 7.2. If such a discovery is made with more than one of the independent variables, any one of the offending variables can be chosen as the weighting factor. Since our income/consumption data set has only one RHS variable, the choice is obvious.

Once the proper variable has been chosen, we must make some assumption about its relationship with the error variances (i.e., the variances in the errors at different values of $X$) and the form the weight must take to suitably transform the model. For the sake of simplified discussion, presume the model can be expressed as Equation (7.3.3). Extension to a multiple regression model can easily be made.

$$Y_i = \beta_0 + \beta_1 X_i + \varepsilon_i \qquad (7.3.3)$$

We may find that the error variances, $\sigma_i^2$, at different values for $X$ are related in some manner to $X_i$ ($X$ may or may not be one of the RHS variables). As noted earlier, $X$ is likely a measure of size among the observations. For example, if you are modeling agricultural output among nations, $X$ may be the acres of arable land. If unemployment levels is your dependent variable, absolute changes in GDP or the number of individuals in the work force may serve well as a measure for $X$.

Presume that the variances of the errors at different $X$-values, $\sigma_i^2$, are related to the RHS variable $X_i$ in some proportion such that

$$\text{Var}(\varepsilon_i) = \sigma_i^2 = \sigma^2 X_i^2 \qquad (7.3.4)$$

where $\sigma^2$ is a constant term and is called the *constant of proportionality*; $X_i^2$ is the squared values of the suspect variable. Equation (7.3.4) simply says that the different error variances at different values of $X$ are all proportional to their $X$-values. That is, each error term has some *constant* proportional relationship with its $X$-value.

The constant of proportionality states that given some value of $X$, call it $X_i$, the variance in the error terms will have the *same* proportional relationship with that $X$-value that the error terms do at all $X$-values. The proportional relationship between the variance of the error terms at $X_i$ will be the same as the proportional relationship between the variance of the error terms at the $X$-value $X_j$ where $i \neq j$.

This is NOT to say that the error variances are the same at all values of $X$. Then we would not have the problem of heteroscedasticity. This says that the proportional relationship between the errors at $X_i$ is the same as the proportional relationship between the errors at $X_j$.

If Equation (7.3.4) prevails, the appropriate transformation to avoid heteroscedasticity is accomplished by dividing both sides of Equation (7.3.3) by $X_i$, producing Equation (7.3.5):

$$\frac{Y_i}{X_i} = \beta_0 \frac{1}{X_i} + \beta_1 \frac{X_i}{X_i} + \frac{\varepsilon_i}{X_i} \qquad (7.3.5)$$

If we let $\varepsilon_i/X_i = v_i$, and recognize that in the second term of Equation (7.3.5) $X_i/X_i = 1$, we have

$$\text{Var}(v_i) = \text{Var}\left(\frac{\varepsilon_i}{X_i}\right) \qquad (7.3.6)$$

It can be seen from Equation (7.3.6) that the slope of Equation (7.3.3) before transformation becomes the constant term (the intercept) in the transformed version, Equation (7.3.6). Further, the constant in the pre-transformed equation becomes the slope after transformation.

Perhaps more importantly, $v_i$ is now homoscedastic! This is shown in the following manner. Since we let

$$v_i = \frac{\varepsilon_i}{X_i}$$

then,

$$\text{Var}(v_i) = \text{Var}\left(\frac{\varepsilon_i}{X_i}\right)$$

Since $X_i$ is a constant at any given value along the horizontal axis, it is squared when removed from the parentheses and we have

$$Var(v_i) = \frac{Var(\varepsilon_i)}{X_i^2}$$

Given Equation (7.3.4) we can substitute in the numerator and find

$$Var(v_i) = \frac{\sigma^2 X_i^2}{X_i^2}$$

Both $X_i^2$ cancel out leaving $Var(v_i) = \sigma^2$, which is the *constant* of proportionality.

By dividing through by $X_i$, we reduce each $\varepsilon_i$ in proportion to its standard deviation (since we are assuming the error term is proportional to $X_i$). The resulting error terms, $v_i$, therefore all have the same standard deviation and variance and are by definition homoscedastic.

This process works because the variance in the error terms at each value for $X$ is different (heteroscedasticity). However, each variance is proportional to some variable, $X$. That is, the error terms have some *constant* proportional relationship to the $X$-values. Thus, by dividing through by that $X$ and "deflating" or "adjusting" the data, you remove that proportionality and produce equal variances for all $X$-values (homoscedasticity).

Now standard OLS methods can be applied to Equation (7.3.6). But it must be remembered to force the regression through the origin since the data have been transformed.

Force the transformed regression through the origin using the option provided by your chosen computer software.

## ● Applying WLS to Our Income/Consumption Data

Since our consumption function data have only one RHS variable, Income, we will use it as the suspect variable. It is necessary to determine the nature of the proportional relationship between the error variance and the suspect variable. It is often the case that the error variance is proportional to the square of $X$ as noted[8] by Equation (7.3.4), $\sigma_i^2 = \sigma^2 X^2$. That is, the error variance is not linearly related to $X$, but increases proportionately to the *square* of $X$. This can be detected by plotting OLS residuals. If Equation (7.3.4) holds and the proportionality of the error variance relates to the square of $X$, the residuals will plot as seen in Figure 7.3. Notice that the residuals "flare" out as $X$ increases. If this proves to be the case, the proper model is as

■ **Table 7.4**   Transformed Data I

```
The regression equation is
cons/inc = 0.929 inc/inc + 2.13 1/inc

Predictor          Coef  SE Coef      T       P
Noconstant
inc/inc       0.929101 0.009133 101.73   0.000
1/inc           2.1317   0.6241   3.42   0.001
```

presented in Equation (7.3.5). All values are divided through by $X_i$. Applying this model to our consumption function data yields the results seen in Table 7.4.

The model is reported to be

$$\frac{Cons}{Inc} = 0.929\frac{Inc}{Inc} + 2.1317\frac{1}{Inc}$$

However, since we divided all variables by Income, we must now multiply by income to return to the original model. The final form of the consumption function reports as

$$Cons = 2.1317 + 0.929\,Inc$$

On the other hand, if the error variance appears to be proportional to $X$ such that $\sigma_i^2 = \sigma^2 X$, the functional form becomes

$$\frac{Y_i}{\sqrt{X_i}} = \beta_0\frac{1}{\sqrt{X_i}} + \beta_1\sqrt{X_i} + \frac{\varepsilon_i}{\sqrt{X_i}} \tag{7.3.7}$$

That is, all division is by the square root of $X$, where $\varepsilon_i/\sqrt{X_i} = v_i$ and is homoscedastic for the same reason stated above. This proportional relationship can be detected by graphing the OLS residuals and finding them to appear as in Figure 7.5. Notice that the residuals expand *evenly* as $X$ increases.

The results appear in Table 7.5.

The model is reported as

$$\frac{Cons}{SqrtInc} = 0.942\frac{Inc}{SqrtInc} + 1.0875\frac{1}{SqrtInc}$$

But again, since we divided by the square root of income, we must multiply by it to return to the original model. Thus,

$$Cons = 1.0875 + 0.942\,Inc$$

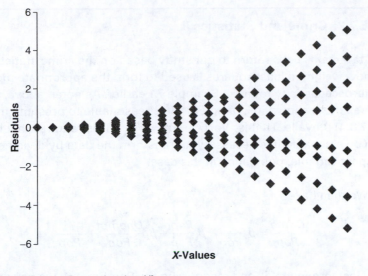

■ **Figure 7.3**   Error Variance Proportional to $X^2$

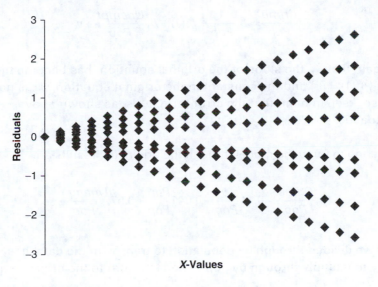

■ **Figure 7.4**   The Relationship Between Elasticity and Sales Revenues

■ **Table 7.5**   Transformed Data II

```
The regression equation is
cons/SqrtInc = 1.09 1/SqrtInc + 0.942 Inc/SqrtInc

Predictor       Coef   SE Coef       T      P
Noconstant
1/SqrtInc      1.0875    0.8207    1.33  0.192
Inc/SqrtInc  0.942060  0.008567  109.96  0.000
```

### EXAMPLE 7.2: Crime and Statistics II

**Problem Statement**: Let's return to our study based on the crime statistics to illustrate how weighted least squares is used to form the appropriate model in the face of heteroscedasticity found in Example 7.1 earlier. As noted above, given the pattern of residuals shown in Example 7.1, it is reasonable to presume that Equation (7.3.4) prevails. That is, $\text{Var}(\varepsilon_i) = \sigma_i^2 = \sigma^2 X_i^2$. This requires that before the model can be estimated it is necessary to transform the data by dividing through by the suspect variable, population in this case.

**Solution**: We then have

$$\frac{Crime}{Pop} = \beta_0 \frac{1}{Pop} + \beta_1 \frac{Pop}{Pop} + \beta_2 \frac{Unempt}{Pop} + \frac{\varepsilon_i}{Pop}$$

Letting the last term equal $v_i$ and recognizing the Pop/Pop = 1, we have

$$\frac{Crime}{Pop} = \beta_0 \frac{1}{Pop} + \beta_1 (1) + \beta_2 \frac{Unempt}{Pop} + v_i$$

Notice again that $\beta_1$, the slope of the original equation, has become the intercept $(\beta_1(1) = \beta_1)$ and the constant in the original equation, $\beta_0$, is now the slope. Also, keep in mind that the error term, $v_i$, is, as shown above, homoscedastic.

Remembering to force the model through the origin, the results are

$$\frac{Crime}{Pop} = 0.14 \frac{1}{Pop} + 0.041 \frac{Pop}{Pop} + 0.57 \frac{Unempt}{Pop}$$

Now that we divided through by population to transform the data, it is necessary to multiply through by population to return to the original equation. Thus,

$$Crime = 0.14 + 0.041 Pop + 0.57 Unempt$$

We now have a model free of heteroscedasticity!

**Interpretation**: It is now possible to test the significance of the RHS variables and perform all tests and interval estimates normally associated with regression and correlation procedures. This can be done with the confidence that bias and inefficiency due to heteroscedasticity have been eliminated.

## ● Heteroscedasticity, Elasticities, and the Use of Logs

The coefficient of elasticity, $\eta$ (Greek letter eta), reflects the degree of responsiveness of the dependent variable to a change in the independent variable. It measures the percentage change in $Y$ relative to a percentage change in $X$.

Elasticity measures the percentage change in $Y$ relative to a percentage change in $X$.

Elasticity is expressed as

$$\eta = \frac{\frac{\Delta Y}{Y}}{\frac{\Delta X}{X}} \qquad (7.3.8)$$

where $\Delta Y$ and $\Delta X$ are the changes in $Y$ and $X$. With a bit of algebraic manipulation Equation (7.3.8) becomes

$$\eta = \frac{\Delta Y}{\Delta X} * \frac{X}{Y} \qquad (7.3.9)$$

But $\Delta Y / \Delta X$ is the very definition of the regression coefficient, $\beta$. It is the change in $Y$ given a one-unit change in $X$. Elasticity is, therefore,

$$\eta = \beta \left[ \frac{X}{Y} \right] \qquad (7.3.10)$$

Elasticity is generally divided into two broad categories: *elastic* and *inelastic*. In an elastic function, $Y$ is very responsive to a change in $X$. A small change in $X$ is associated with a large change in $Y$. An inelastic relationship is one in which $Y$ does not readily respond to a change in $X$. A large change in $X$ is associated with only a small change in $Y$. Expressed in its absolute form (ignoring the algebraic sign) if $\eta > 1$ it is said the relationship is elastic. If the coefficient of elasticity is less than 1, $\eta < 1$, the relationship is characterized as inelastic. In the unlikely event $\eta$ equals 1, elasticity is termed *unitary*.

Actually, although a linear function has a constant slope, its elasticity will vary along its entire length. Therefore, any measurement of elasticity must be done at given values for $X$ and $Y$. It is customary to measure the elasticity of a linear function at the mean values for $X$ and $Y$ (i.e., $\bar{X}$ and $\bar{Y}$). Therefore, elasticity is generally calculated as

$$\eta = \beta_i \left[ \frac{\bar{X}}{\bar{Y}} \right] \qquad (7.3.11)$$

In Table 7.2 we found that by regressing consumption on income the coefficient reported as 0.958291. The mean values of income and consumption were 113.9 and 108.4, respectively. Thus, the income elasticity of consumption is $(0.958291)(113.9/108.4) = 1.0069$. This reveals that elasticity is near unitary. A 1% change in income leads to a 1.0069% change in consumption. This should come as no surprise since the coefficient is so close to 1.

## ● Elasticity of Demand and Total Sales Revenue

Perhaps the most common application of elasticity is measuring the responsiveness of quantity demanded to a change in price in the study of consumer demand, using the Hicksian[9] form of the demand function in which quantity is expressed as a function of price.

Generally stated, the relationship between elasticity of demand and sales revenue holds that if demand is inelastic, then, by definition, quantity purchased in the market will not respond very much to a change in price. If price is increased, consumers purchase about the same amount and thus sales revenues will actually go up due to the higher price. On the other hand, if price is lowered, consumers do not respond to this price change and still purchase about the same amount. With sales holding relatively constant at this lower price, sales revenues drop. Thus, with an inelastic demand, price and total sales revenues move in the same direction.

To the contrary, if demand is elastic, then, by definition, quantity purchased proves to be quite responsive to a change in price. As price goes up, consumer purchases drop off dramatically and sales revenues fall despite the higher price. If price is lowered, many more consumers enter the market and the dramatic rise in sales more than offsets the lower price and sales revenues increase in the face of the lower price. If demand is elastic, price and revenues move in opposite directions.

> With an inelastic demand curve, quantity is less responsive to a change in price. Therefore, price and sales revenue vary directly. As price goes up, sales will not fall proportionately and revenues will rise. If demand is elastic, a rise (fall) in price will provoke a fall (rise) in revenues due to the highly responsive nature of quantity. Thus, price and revenues vary inversely.

As noted above, even in the case of a linear demand function, while the slope of the demand curve remains constant along the entire curve, elasticity varies. As Figure 7.5 shows, at higher prices, demand elasticity proves to be elastic: $\eta > 1$. This results because elasticity measures the *percentage* change in quantity with respect to the *percentage* change in price. At higher prices, a given change is a smaller percentage, while at the jointly occurring lower quantities a given change represents a larger percentage change. The percentage

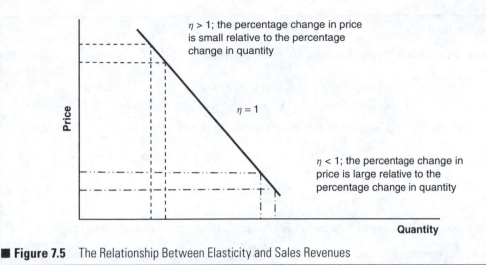

■ **Figure 7.5**   The Relationship Between Elasticity and Sales Revenues

change in quantity is large relative to the percentage change in price. This is the case for elastic demand.

At lower prices demand is inelastic. With low prices, any change in price is a large percentage change, while the attendant higher quantities report a smaller percentage change. This is the very definition of an inelastic demand. Unitary elasticity in which $\eta = 1$ takes up residence in between the two extremes.

Example 7.3 further illustrates.

**EXAMPLE 7.3:  Elasticity and Sales Revenues**

**Problem Statement:** A retailer of men's fashion in the St James area of London, England, finds the demand curve for its Milanese Italian-style suits to be $Q = 7 - 0.4P$, where $Q$ is quantity and $P$ is price. This linear function will have the same slope along its entire length, but its elasticity will vary in accordance with Figure 7.5. In order to establish pricing policy, the retailer wants to measure this elasticity and its connection with sales revenue at different price levels.

**Solution:** Elasticity is determined to be

$$\eta = \frac{\Delta Q}{\Delta P} * \frac{P}{Q}$$

*(Continued)*

**EXAMPLE 7.3: (Continued)**

Ignoring the algebraic sign and at a "high" price of 10, this becomes

$$\eta = 0.4 * \frac{10}{3} = 1.33$$

Demand is clearly elastic. Any change in price will cause revenue to move in the opposite direction.

At a "low" price of 2, we find

$$\eta = 0.4 * \frac{2}{6.2} = 0.129$$

Demand reports to be inelastic. If price is increased (decreased), total revenue will rise (fall).

**Interpretation:** Since total revenue is price times quantity, at a price of 10, quantity is 3 and total revenue is 30. If price is raised to 12, quantity is 2.2 and revenue is 26.40 < 30. As price went up, total revenue decreased. This is characteristic of an elastic demand curve.

At the price of 2, quantity is 6.2 and total revenue is 12.4. If price is lowered to 1.5, quantity is 6.4 and total revenue becomes 9.6 < 12.4. As price went down, revenue fell. This is the case with inelastic demand.

Experiment on your own by setting price at 10 and lowering price. Note what happens to total revenue. Then set price at 2 and raise it. What happens to revenue?

## ● How Elasticity Relates to Heteroscedasticity

A model based on *logarithms* can also mitigate the effects of heteroscedasticity. This occurs because the use of logs dampens the variances by compressing the values used in the regression model. A double-log model such as that expressed in Equation (7.3.12) illustrates.

$$\ln Y_i = \beta_0 + \beta_1 \ln X_i + \varepsilon_i \tag{7.3.12}$$

Applying the double-log model to our income/consumption data produces the results seen in Table 7.6.

■ **Table 7.6**   A Measure of Elasticity Using Logs

```
The regression equation is
lnCons = 0.0510 + 0.979 lnIncome

Predictor     Coef   SE Coef        T      P
Constant   0.05099   0.04087     1.25  0.219
lnIncome   0.978714  0.008880  110.21  0.000
```

The coefficient of 0.978714 is interpreted differently than that of other models. In a double-log model of this nature the coefficient measures the *percentage* change in $Y$ given a 1% change in $X$. For every 1% change in income, consumption changes by 0.9787%.

Not incidentally, this is the very definition of elasticity. It is the measure of the percentage change in consumption relative to the percentage change in income. In this manner, the double-log model has the added advantage of providing a *direct* measure of elasticity. Specifically, it is a direct measure in that the coefficient itself serves as the estimate of elasticity. There is no need to calculate elasticity using, for example, Equation (7.3.10). Notice that the coefficient is very close to the estimate provided by the linear model above. The next segment examines how log models estimate elasticities.

It is possible to test the hypothesis for the coefficient from the log function using a standard $t$-test as to the value of $\eta$. The null hypothesis is generally stated as $H_0$: $\eta = 1$; that is, that the elasticity is unitary. In our present case, this becomes

$$t = \frac{b_i - \eta}{S_{b_i}} = \frac{0.978714 - 1}{0.00888} = -2.397$$

Since the critical $t$-value for an alpha of 1% and 44 degrees of freedom is $\pm 2.69$, and $-2.397 > -2.69$, we do not reject the null that elasticity is unitary.

### ● How Logs Estimate Elasticities

As noted above, elasticity measures the degree of responsiveness of the dependent variable to changes in the independent variable and is defined as

$$\eta = \frac{\frac{\Delta Y}{Y}}{\frac{\Delta X}{X}} = \frac{\Delta Y}{Y} * \frac{X}{\Delta X} = \frac{\Delta Y}{\Delta X} * \frac{X}{Y} \qquad (7.3.13)$$

Then, a model such as that seen in Equation (7.3.14)

$$Y = AX^b \qquad (7.3.14)$$

can be linearized with the double-log transformation in the form of

$$\ln Y = \ln A + b \ln X \qquad (7.3.15)$$

We will find that the measure (coefficient) of elasticity is $b$, the coefficient of the log of the independent variable.

We wish to find the change in $Y$ with respect to a change in $X$. This involves the use of derivatives. But to avoid any complexities, we will refer to the derivative as simply a "change in," indicated by the lower-case "d," keeping in mind that in the spirit of a derivative, the change is infinitesimally small. A more complete discussion of logs and elasticity is offered in the appendix to this chapter.

Based on Equation (7.3.14), we then write the derivative of $Y$ with respect to $X$ as

$$\frac{dY}{dX} = bAX^{b-1} \tag{7.3.16}$$

Elasticity is then

$$\eta = \frac{dY}{dX} * \frac{X}{Y} \tag{7.3.17}$$

Substituting Equation (7.3.16) and Equation (7.3.14), we have

$$\eta = bAX^{b-1} * \frac{X}{AX^b} \tag{7.3.18}$$

Then,

$$\eta = \frac{bAX^{b-1}X}{AX^b} = b \tag{7.3.19}$$

where $b$ is indeed the coefficient of the log value of the independent variable just as promised.

Perhaps this can best be demonstrated with a non-linear demand curve such as

$$Q = 500P^{-2} \tag{7.3.20}$$

The expression graphs as Figure 7.6.

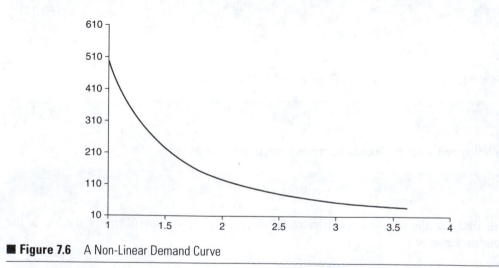

■ **Figure 7.6**　A Non-Linear Demand Curve

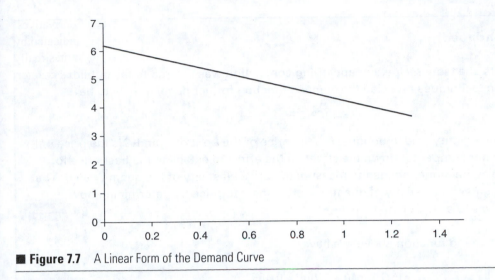

**■ Figure 7.7** A Linear Form of the Demand Curve

We can linearize Equation (7.3.20) with logs as seen in Figure 7.7.

$$\ln Q = \ln 500 - 2\ln P \qquad (7.3.21)$$

The demand function then graphs in linear fashion as Figure 7.8.

Then, taking the derivative as demonstrated in Equation (7.3.16) and using Equation (7.3.18) to solve for elasticity, we have

$$\eta = \frac{-2(500)P^{-3} * P}{500P^{-2}} = -2 \qquad (7.3.22)$$

and

$$\eta = -2(500)P^{-3} * \frac{P}{500P^{-2}} \qquad (7.3.23)$$

where $-2$ is the coefficient of $\ln P$ in (7.3.21). As mentioned above, it is customary to ignore the algebraic sign and report $\eta = 2$.

---

### EXAMPLE 7.4: Elasticity and Logs

**Problem Statement**: In December of 2011 the *Wall Street Journal* reported that a pastry chef in New York City attended a Yankees baseball game and ordered her usual soft pretzel and lite beer. It struck her that beer-flavored bonbons might make a popular splash on the commercial market.

*(Continued)*

## EXAMPLE 7.4: (Continued)

After several attempts at a tasty recipe, her appetizing concoction was offered to the public. Non-linear regression techniques revealed the demand function for her novel morsel to be

$$Q = 10P^{0.7}C^{0.4}$$

where $Q$ is the weekly quantity sold in pounds, $P$ is the price of the bonbons, and $C$ is the price of similar treats sold by her competitor down the street. In the effort to establish the best price for the unusual item, the confectioner needed to measure the price elasticity of the quantity sold. That is, she wished to evaluate the elasticity of quantity with respect to price by determining how responsive quantity was to a change in price.

**Solution:** Given the demand function above, we have

$$\ln Q = \ln 10 + 0.7\ln P + 0.4\ln C$$

Then,

$$\eta = \frac{1}{Q} * \frac{\Delta Q}{\Delta P}$$

$$= 0.7\frac{1}{P} * \frac{\Delta P}{\Delta P}$$

$$= \frac{\Delta Q}{Q\Delta P} = \frac{0.7}{P}$$

$$= \frac{P\Delta Q}{Q\Delta P} = \frac{0.7P}{P}$$

$$= \frac{\Delta Q}{\Delta P} * \frac{P}{Q} = 0.7$$

**Interpretation:** Apparently, the demand for the new treat is inelastic. Quantity demanded will not respond very much to a change in price. An increase in price will not cause a large drop in quantity, and therefore total sales revenue can be increased with a rise in price—at least up to some point covered by the data for price used to form the demand function in the first place. A drop in price will not result in an increase in sales sufficient to offset the lower price, and revenues will fall.

## SECTION 7.3 PROBLEMS

1. Write and explain the formula you would use to correct for heteroscedasticity if the population variances were known. Why and how does this process correct for heteroscedasticity?

2. Prove that after transforming the data as explained in the question above, homoscedasticity prevails.

3. Why is the solution to heteroscedasticity as proposed in the first two questions unlikely to occur?

4. Explain the meaning behind Equation (7.3.4). What is it telling you to do?

5. Explain how the transformation described in this section turns the pre-transformed slope into the intercept and vice versa.

6. Using your preferred computer software and the data from problem 6 in Section 7.2, correct for heteroscedasticity. Assume $\text{Var}\left(\varepsilon_i\right) = \sigma_i^2 = \sigma^2 X_i^2$, where $X_i$ is bank balances.

7. Define elasticity. How is it measured?

8. Explain how the use of logs produces a measure of elasticity.

## CHAPTER PROBLEMS

### Conceptual Problems

1. Your research assistant has discovered that the model you have been working with to explain changes in shipping costs suffers from heteroscedasticity. She bemoans the loss of time and the increased expense required to collect a larger data set in order to correct the problem. How do you respond?

2. As a city planner for the National Health Service in London, England, your duties include reconciling differences with the provisions for healthcare elsewhere in the United Kingdom. Would you expect to encounter any problems with heteroscedasticity among the numerous metropolitan areas? Explain and illustrate with an example.

3. Why are cross-sectional studies less likely to be afflicted with autocorrelation but highly subject to heteroscedasticity?

4. Clearly describe the steps that must be taken to test for heteroscedasticity using the tests described in this chapter. What advantages and disadvantages does each offer?

5. Explain how the slope coefficient and the intercept become interchanged when correcting for heteroscedasticity.

6. Define and give examples of elasticity. Clearly explain how the use of logs results in measures of elasticity.

7. Prove that weighted least squares result in homoscedastic models. Use all necessary equations in your response.

8. Distinguish between pure and impure heteroscedasticity.

9. Discuss the relationship between elasticity and the manner in which price changes affect total revenue. If a firm's goal is to raise revenues, should it increase or decrease price if demand is elastic? Inelastic? Explain your answers.

10. Demonstrate using the proper formulas discussed in this chapter how a double-log model gives the measure of elasticity for a function.

## Computational Problems

1. The International Textile and Apparel Association is a professional, educational association composed of scholars, educators, and students in the textile, apparel, and merchandising disciplines in higher education. Ecological disasters worldwide threaten the textile industry through rising costs from agricultural failures in the cotton sector as well as other fabric materials. Cotton production is currently the focus of a study carried out by the ITAA in an effort to alleviate financial burdens on populations, especially in less developed countries. Access the data file COTTON. The data were taken primarily from http://www.ina.gr/cotton_producing_countries. htm, http://www.icac.org/cotton_info/speeches/Chaudhry/rcbremen96.PDF, and http://en.wikipedia.org/wiki/List_of_countries_by_population

Population is in millions, cost is in U.S. dollars per hectare, and amount is in thousands of bales.

Regress Amount on Cost and Population. Using Population as the suspect variable, test for heteroscedasticity using the Park test, the Glejser test assuming Equation (7.2.2A), White's test, and the Goldfeld–Quandt method. Remove the middle five observations for the Goldfeld–Quandt method. Comment on the results in each case.

Given the results of these tests, assume Equation (7.3.4) and correct for the heteroscedasticity.

2. Using the data file COTTON find the degree of elasticity of Amt with respect to both Pop and Cost. Interpret the model.

3. A firm kept weekly records of different prices set for its product and the quantities sold at those prices over a period of 10 weeks. The data are seen here. Prices are per pound and quantities are in pounds sold that week. The Quantitative Analysis department for the firm wanted to estimate a demand curve for the product and compute the elasticity of demand—the degree of responsiveness of quantity to a change in price. Based on standard OLS procedures, the demand curve proved to be as follows:

```
The regression equation is
Q = 25.3 - 1.25 P

Predictor     Coef     SE Coef        T        P
Constant    25.3109     0.1495    169.29    0.000
P          -1.24559     0.02299    -54.17    0.000
```

If price is currently set at $5.00, should price be increased or decreased to raise total revenue? Base your answer on the role elasticity plays. State your conclusion. Then "prove" your answer by example by computing revenue at $5.00. Then either raise or lower price and re-calculate revenue. What happened to revenue? Does it agree with your answer to the first part of this question?

4.  A production function is found to be $Q = TK^\alpha L^\beta$, where $T$ is time, and $K$ and $L$ are the amounts of capital and labor used in the production process. Express the function as a double-log model and prove algebraically that a 1% increase in $K$ leads to a $\alpha$% increase in $Q$.

5.  Given the production function in problem 4, set $T = 5$, $K = 10$, $L = 12$, $\alpha = 0.6$, and $\beta = 0.2$. Calculate $Q$. Show that a 1% increase in $K$ leads to a 0.006 or $\alpha = 0.6\%$ increase in $Q$.

# APPENDIX: LOGS AND ELASTICITY

■  Elasticity measures the degree of responsiveness of one variable to changes in another.

■  Elasticity of demand is often used as an example.

■  It measures the reaction of quantity to a change in price. More precisely, it measures the percentage change in quantity with respect to the percentage change in price:

$$\eta = \frac{\%\Delta Q}{\%\Delta P} = \frac{\dfrac{\Delta Q}{\dfrac{Q_1 + Q_2}{2}}}{\dfrac{\Delta P}{\dfrac{P_1 + P_2}{2}}} \qquad (1)$$

where:

$\eta$ is the elasticity coefficient;

$Q_1$ and $P_1$ are the beginning price and quantity;

$Q_2$ and $P_2$ are the ending price and quantity.

Equation (1) can be rewritten as

$$\eta = \frac{\Delta Q}{\dfrac{Q_1 + Q_2}{2}} * \frac{\dfrac{P_1 + P_2}{2}}{\Delta P} \qquad (2)$$

Then, by interchanging denominators we have

$$\eta = \frac{\Delta Q}{\Delta P} * \frac{\dfrac{P_1 + P_2}{2}}{\dfrac{Q_1 + Q_2}{2}} \qquad (3)$$

It can be seen that by dividing by 2 finds the *average* change in both $P$ and $Q$.

This expresses *arc* elasticity.

However, let $\Delta P$ be *infinitesimally* small. We are then dealing with derivatives and we find:

$$\eta = \frac{dQ}{dP} * \frac{P}{Q} \qquad (4)$$

We are finding elasticity at a particular *point*, $P$—thus point elasticity!

Note: It is the case that $\eta < 0$ since $P$ and $Q$ vary inversely. It is customary to multiply $\eta$ by $-1$ or, more commonly, to simply ignore the negative sign.

In terms of logs and elasticities:

■ Given a demand curve of the nature

$$Q = \beta_0 P^{\beta_1} \qquad (5)$$

■ Based on the rules of logarithms, the log transformation becomes

$$\ln Q = \ln \beta_0 + \beta_1 \ln P \qquad (6)$$

■ It remains then to show that $\beta_1$ *is not merely a slope coefficient but is a measure of elasticity.*

■ Differentiating (5) with respect to $P$ gives

$$\frac{dQ}{dP} = \beta_1 \beta_0 P^{\beta_1 - 1} \qquad (7)$$

■ Given Equation (4) above and substituting (7) for $dQ/dP$ and substituting (5) for $Q$ into (4), we have

$$\eta = \beta_1 \beta_0 P^{\beta_1 - 1} \left( \frac{P}{\beta_0 P^{\beta_1}} \right) \qquad (8)$$

■ Clearing parentheses, we have

$$\eta = \frac{\beta_1 \beta_0 P^{\beta_1}}{\beta_0 P^{\beta_1}} = \beta_1 \qquad (9)$$

That is: $\eta = \beta_1$.

Thus, if you were to derive a regression model of the form

$$\ln Y = 5.2 + 0.25 \ln X$$

this would be interpreted as a 1% increase in $X$ and associated with a 0.25% increase in $Y$.

Another way to view elasticity is shown here.[10] This one is based on a Cobb–Douglas production function which holds that output is a function of the amount of capital ($K$) and labor ($L$) used in the production process.

1.  Keep in mind $\eta = \%\Delta Y / \%\Delta X$.

2.  Given a standard Cobb–Douglas production function

$$Q = AK^{\alpha}L^{\beta} \tag{1}$$

    where all terms are positive values.

3.  Linearize it with logs:

$$\ln Q = \ln A + \alpha \ln K + \beta \ln L \tag{2}$$

4.  Now we can show $\alpha$ is not merely a slope coefficient but is a measure of elasticity. It will measure the responsiveness—the elasticity—of a $\Delta Q$ with respect to $\Delta K$.

5.  We will change $K$ but hold $L$ constant.

6.  The first and third terms of (2) drop out since they do not contain $K$. Then we can simplify (2) as

$$\ln Q = \alpha \ln K \tag{3}$$

    Technically, the "equality" in Equation (3) is *not* true—$\ln Q$ equals Equation (2)—but expressing it as Equation (3) draws attention to proper focal points: $Q$, $K$, and $\alpha$.

7.  Given Equation (3) we have

$$\alpha = \frac{\ln Q}{\ln K}$$

8.  Since the derivative of the ln of any value equals the reciprocal of that value, the derivative $\ln X = 1/X$.

9.  Then

$$\alpha = \frac{d\ln Q}{d\ln K} = \frac{\frac{1}{Q} * dQ}{\frac{1}{K} * dK} = \frac{K * dQ}{Q * dK} = \frac{dQ}{dK} * \frac{K}{Q} = \varepsilon$$

We recognize the last term as elasticity and it's equal to alpha.

# Chapter 8

# AUTOCORRELATION

# INTRODUCTION

In Chapter 2 we briefly examined the problem of autocorrelation and the disruptive effects it can have on our regression model. Autocorrelation is a violation of one of the basic assumptions of the OLS regression model, which requires that the error terms are independent of each other. To the extent that this condition is breached, the model suffers in its reliability and accuracy.

Autocorrelation is the most common problem to haunt econometric models, especially those that rely on time series data. It is likely to produce parametric estimates that are not BLUE (Best Linear Unbiased Estimates) and, just as damaging, autocorrelation will result in the failure of those models to properly predict turning points in economic activity over time. If an economic system is in decline, it may have started to right itself long before the model recognizes and reports the adjustment. Or, conversely, autocorrelation may cause the model to prematurely foresee an improvement long before it will actually occur.

Similar problems arise if a healthy economy begins to sour. Any model beset by autocorrelation will likely miss the downturn. It will foretell the plunge long after it becomes painfully obvious.

Not only will autocorrelation cause the parametric estimates to be inefficient, but it will also result in inflated $R^2$-values and $t$-values that are biased upward. Higher than warranted coefficients of determination suggest more explanatory power to the model than is rightfully justified. This leaves the researcher with an unjustifiable sense of confidence in the model. Any undue emphasis placed upon such a distorted model will likely result in misdirected decisions that will ultimately prove quite costly. Exaggerated $t$-values will increase the probability of a Type I error, thereby further promoting unwarranted assurance in a faulty model.

## 8.1 THE NATURE OF AUTOCORRELATION

Recall that one of the basic assumptions of the OLS model is that the error terms, $\varepsilon_i$, are random and uncorrelated with each other with a mean of zero and a constant variance, call it $\sigma^2$. When using cross-sectional data these assumptions usually hold true. Cross-sectional data are derived from a random sample of unrelated observations such as different individual business firms. This random nature of the data set often generates error terms for these isolated observations that are indeed uncorrelated.

However, with the use of time series data this assumption may be violated because, by their very nature, time series data follow a natural ordering across time. The observations consist of time-sequential data for a single variable that form a patterned progression through time. Due to this time relationship there often occurs a correlation in error terms. The error in one time period, $\varepsilon_t$, may be related to the error in the previous time period, $\varepsilon_{t-1}$. Thus, corr($\varepsilon_t, \varepsilon_{t-1}) \neq 0$. This is referred to as *first-order autocorrelation*, or, more simply, AR(1). This is shown as Equation (8.1.1):

$$\varepsilon_t = \rho\varepsilon_{t-1} + v_t \qquad (8.1.1)$$

where $\rho$ (Greek letter rho) is the first-order autocorrelation coefficient. If $\rho \neq 0$ it may be concluded that autocorrelation exists. As with all correlation coefficients, $-1 < \rho < +1$. As the absolute value of $\rho$ approaches 1 the value of $\varepsilon_{t-1}$ has greater and greater influence on $\varepsilon_t$.

If $\text{corr}(\varepsilon_t, \varepsilon_{t-2}) \neq 0$, *second-order autocorrelation*, AR(2), is said to be present. Although rare, higher orders of autocorrelation can also be identified.

This correlation in successive error terms results from the fact that much business and economic data are cyclical in nature. To illustrate, assume the economy is currently in a bit of a slump. The unemployment rate for this month, $Y_i$, is higher than it might typically be on the average over the long run. Since our regression model estimates that long-run mean using $\hat{Y}$ it is likely that the currently elevated level of unemployment will produce a situation in which $Y_i > \hat{Y}$. That is, due to the fact the economy is suffering from a decline, current unemployment, $Y_i$, is above the long-run average as measured by the model, $\hat{Y}$. The error term, measured as $(Y_i - \hat{Y})$, would therefore be positive. If the unemployment rate is particularly high this month it is probably still above normal the next month, and for several months thereafter. Economic conditions don't correct themselves that quickly. Instead, they tend to exhibit a "stickiness" that persists over a period of several months or even several years. Therefore, in each of those successive months the error term reported by our model will continue to be positive.

Eventually, the level of economic activity may pick up and the current unemployment rate will drop below its long-run average, in which case $Y_i < \hat{Y}$. The measured error term, $(Y_i - \hat{Y})$, therefore becomes negative. Due to that same stickiness this condition too will reoccur for several consecutive months.

We have, then, several months in a row in which the error terms are positive followed by several consecutive months reporting negative errors. This is hardly a case of randomness. The errors are inarguably correlated from month to month resulting in autocorrelation.

> Autocorrelation results when error terms are correlated with each other and thereby violate the OLS assumption of independency of errors.

Table 8.1 contains data for national unemployment rates ($U$) and U.S. imports ($M$) in millions of dollars from January 2008 to November 2010. By regressing monthly unemployment rates in the United States on U.S. imports we obtain a model estimating the impact of imports on the domestic unemployment level. The model is seen here with $t$-values in parentheses and $p$-values shown in the brackets:

$$\hat{U} = 17.676 - 0.00005011M$$
$$(8.865) \quad (-4.784)$$
$$[0.000] \quad [0.000]$$

We may well expect in an *a priori* sense to find a positive correlation between imports and the unemployment rate. This presumption might be based on the contention that as imports rise there is less need for domestic labor. The inverse relationship shown by the negative coefficient reported here contradicts this position.

On the other hand, the negative sign on the coefficient for imports might be explained by the fact that as the economy prospers the consumption of both foreign and domestically produced goods increases. Thus, as imports increase, consumers also add to their purchases of U.S. commodities, causing a drop in unemployment figures. Which assertion better describes reality is the question. Evidence seems to favor the argument that prosperous economic conditions foster both an increase in imports and a reduction of the joblessness.

In any event, the model clearly suggests significant explanatory power. The high absolute value of the *t*-statistic for imports reveals that it is statistically significant at better than the 1% level. However, the residuals seen in the table appear somewhat suspicious. The first 19 residuals are negative while the remaining residuals are all positive. These hardly appear to be random.

■ **Table 8.1**   Unemployment and Imports for the United States from January 2008 to November 2010

| DATE | IMPORTS | UNEMPT | RESID | DATE | IMPORTS | UNEMPT | RESID |
|------|---------|--------|-------|------|---------|--------|-------|
| Jan-08 | 210028 | 5 | −2.15039 | Jul-09 | 162702 | 9.4 | −0.12211 |
| Feb-08 | 215354 | 4.8 | −2.08348 | Aug-09 | 161421 | 9.7 | 0.1137 |
| Mar-08 | 211348 | 5.1 | −1.98423 | Sep-09 | 169343 | 9.8 | 0.6107 |
| Apr-08 | 219757 | 5 | −1.66282 | Oct-09 | 170396 | 10.1 | 0.96347 |
| May-08 | 219947 | 5.4 | −1.2533 | Nov-09 | 174270 | 10 | 1.05762 |
| Jun-08 | 224845 | 5.5 | −0.90784 | Dec-09 | 180485 | 10 | 1.36908 |
| Jul-08 | 232079 | 5.8 | −0.24531 | Jan-10 | 179352 | 9.7 | 1.0123 |
| Aug-08 | 224342 | 6.1 | −0.33305 | Feb-10 | 184279 | 9.7 | 1.25921 |
| Sep-08 | 212662 | 6.2 | −0.81838 | Mar-10 | 189734 | 9.7 | 1.53259 |
| Oct-08 | 209603 | 6.6 | −0.57168 | Apr-10 | 188536 | 9.9 | 1.67255 |
| Nov-08 | 184924 | 6.9 | −1.50846 | May-10 | 194202 | 9.7 | 1.7565 |
| Dec-08 | 172925 | 7.4 | −1.60979 | Jun-10 | 200199 | 9.5 | 1.85704 |
| Jan-09 | 161528 | 7.7 | −1.88094 | Jul-10 | 195977 | 9.5 | 1.64545 |
| Feb-09 | 153286 | 8.2 | −1.79399 | Aug-10 | 199864 | 9.6 | 1.94025 |
| Mar-09 | 154002 | 8.6 | −1.3581 | Sep-10 | 198374 | 9.6 | 1.86558 |
| Apr-09 | 152565 | 8.9 | −1.13012 | Oct-10 | 197957 | 9.6 | 1.84468 |
| May-09 | 150696 | 9.4 | −0.72378 | Nov-10 | 197957 | 9.8 | 2.04468 |
| Jun-09 | 155009 | 9.5 | −0.40764 | | | | |

Source: St Louis Federal Reserve Bank

Extracted from: http://research.stlouisfed.org/fred2/data/PCE.t; accessed January 2012

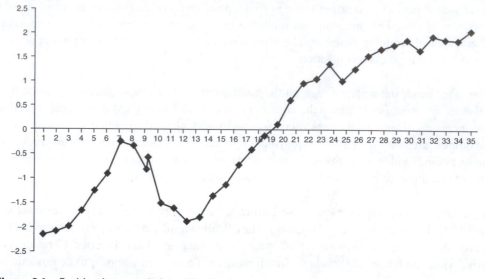

**▪ Figure 8.1**  Positive Autocorrelation of Residuals

A plot of these residuals seen in Figure 8.1 confirms our suspicions. A definite pattern is clearly displayed evidencing the presence of *positive* autocorrelation. A series of negative errors is followed by numerous positive errors. Any given error is more likely to be followed by an error of the *same* sign. Algebraically, like signs imply a positive association. Hence, the term positive autocorrelation. In this case, $\rho$, the autoregressive correlation coefficient, is greater than zero; $\rho > 0$.

Although less common, *negative* autocorrelation may occur in some models. This results when a negative error is more likely to be followed by a positive error which is then followed by another negative error. The errors tend to alternate to some degree by reporting opposite signs. Since different signs algebraically signal a negative relationship the term negative autocorrelation is applied. A hypothetical example is shown in Figure 8.2.

Notice that the first four errors alternate in sign starting with a positive error. In most, but not all, cases this tendency to change sign continues from one error to the next. This inclination to fluctuate in sign is a clear signal that negative autocorrelation is likely a problem. In this case $\rho < 0$.

> Positive autocorrelation results when errors of a given sign (positive or negative) are more likely to be followed by errors of the same sign, in which case $\rho > 0$. If an error of some given sign is more likely to be followed by an error of the opposite sign, negative autocorrelation exists and $\rho < 0$.

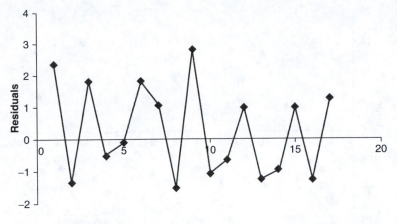

■ **Figure 8.2** A Negative Autocorrelation of Residuals

## SECTION 8.1 PROBLEMS

1.  Define autocorrelation. Why is it more likely to occur with the use of time series data than with cross-sectional data?

2.  Distinguish between first-order and higher-order autocorrelation. Give examples of each.

3.  Why does the cyclical nature of economic and business activity tend to result in autocorrelation? What does the issue of "stickiness" have to do with this matter?

4.  Distinguish between positive and negative autocorrelation. Define and give examples. How might a graph of each appear?

5.  Examine the graphs below and comment on your perception of whether autocorrelation might be an issue and if so, is it positive or negative autocorrelation?

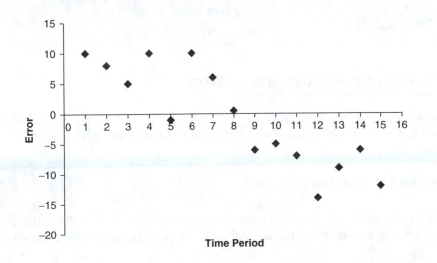

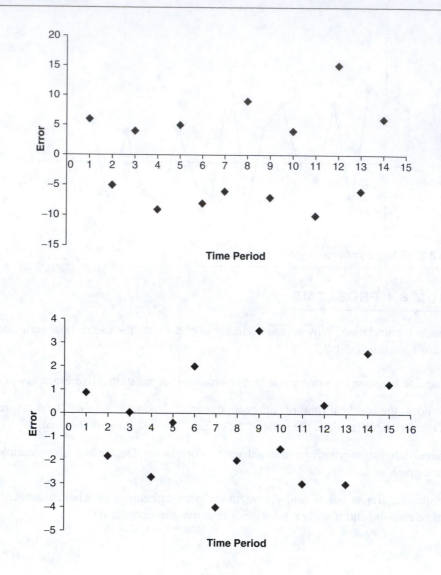

## 8.2 CAUSES OF AUTOCORRELATION

Two primary causes of autocorrelation can be cited: model misspecification and the stickiness noted above. The most common, and the most serious, is model misspecification.

### ● Model Misspecification

A model is properly specified only if two necessary conditions prevail. First, the model must contain the correct predictor variables. All relevant variables that offer explanatory power must be included in the model. The omission of any germane explanatory variables will distort the model and often result in autocorrelation. Second, these variables must be of the proper functional form. With respect to the first condition, consider a model that is correctly stated as

$$Y_t = \beta_0 + \beta_1 X_{1t} + \beta_2 X_{2t} + \varepsilon_t \qquad (8.2.1)$$

If, however, $X_{2t}$ is mistakenly omitted the model becomes

$$Y_t = \beta_0 + \beta_1 X_{1t} + \varepsilon_t^* \qquad (8.2.2)$$

In this case $\varepsilon_t^*$ would capture the impact of the missing predictor variable $X_{2t}$ and be expressed as

$$\varepsilon_t^* = \alpha_2 X_{2t} + v_t \qquad (8.2.3)$$

$\varepsilon_t^*$ would then reflect a systematic pattern evidencing autocorrelation.

Not only must the model contain all essential predictor variables but they must be of the correct functional form as well. That is, autocorrelation may occur if the model includes the proper variables, but they are of an improper form. Perhaps one or more of the variables should be incorporated in log form. The correct specification for Equation (8.2.1) may be

$$Y_t = \beta_0 + \beta_1 \ln X_{1t} + \beta_2 \ln X_{2t} + \varepsilon_t \qquad (8.2.4)$$

If the predictor variables were incorporated without the logarithmic transformations, autocorrelation may be introduced into the model. Alternatively, perhaps a power function is required in which the squared values of one or more of the variables should be incorporated. In more complex models, a cubic function might be optimal. There are obviously many ways to err in specifying your model.

## ● The Issue of Stickiness

There is little or nothing the researcher can do about the problem of stickiness as described above. This would require control over the relevant economic pressures and conditions that mere mortals do not possess. He or she can only manipulate the model in order to mitigate the ill-effects of autocorrelation. The efforts to do so are the subject of the rest of this chapter.

## SECTION 8.2 PROBLEMS

1.  What are the primary causes of autocorrelation? Which is more difficult for the researchers to correct for?

2.  How does an omitted variable affect the error term in a model and what implications does that have for autocorrelation?

3.  Why does "stickiness" occur more often in time series data?

4.  Why is autocorrelation more likely to occur with time series data than with cross-sectional data? Distinguish between the two types of data, giving examples of each, in your response.

5.  What two conditions must exist to ensure a model is properly specified? Give examples in both cases.

## 8.3 THE CONSEQUENCES OF AUTOCORRELATION

Damage to the model brought on by autocorrelation can take many forms. In general, the estimators can no longer be considered BLUE. More specifically, consider these grave consequences of autocorrelation.

1.  Even in the presence of autocorrelation, if the model is specified correctly the $b$-coefficients (the sample estimates of the parametric regression coefficients, $\beta_i$) are still unbiased. This means that the expected value of the regression coefficient estimates, $E(b_j)$, is still the true value of $\beta$. Further, the estimates will also prove to be consistent as described in Chapter 1. Again, this is true only *if* the model is properly specified. Recall that a properly specified model must contain all the relevant explanatory variables in their appropriate functional form. Finally, autocorrelation becomes a hazard if the model contains any lagged values for the dependent variable (see Figure 1.1 in Chapter 1).

    However, if a relevant explanatory variable is missing, the coefficient estimates of the remaining variable may be biased. That is, while autocorrelation itself may not cause bias in the coefficient estimates, if the autocorrelation is the result of a missing variable the regression results may indeed be biased due to that omission.

2.  Caution: Just because an estimate is not biased does not mean it is dependable. As explained in Chapter 1 an estimate is biased if it tends to report a value that is *consistently* too high or *consistently* too low. Models with autocorrelated errors are *equally* likely to provide inflated estimates as well as estimates that are understated. In that sense, they are unbiased. However, that does not mean that any particular estimate affords a reasonable degree of accuracy because autocorrelation *will increase the variance of the coefficient estimators, $b_i$*.

The sampling distribution of the estimators is wider and more dispersed. In that sense, the estimators are not efficient as defined in Chapter 1 (see Figure 1.2). As a result of this inflated variance in the coefficient estimators any one estimate is likely to differ from the true value of the coefficient more than if autocorrelation was not a problem.

3. While the coefficient estimates are not biased, autocorrelation will cause the standard errors of the coefficients, $S_b$, to be biased. Specifically, the standard errors are biased downward. This is a serious problem in testing hypotheses regarding the significance of the reported regression coefficient, $H_0: \beta_i = 0$. Since hypothesis tests are based on

$$t = \frac{b_i - \beta_i}{S_{b_i}}$$

if the standard error is smaller, the resulting $t$-value is inflated and is more likely to fall in the rejection region. This predisposition may result in the suggestion that the variable carries significant explanatory power when in actuality it does not. If the variable is in fact not significant a Type I error has occurred. You must therefore be quite careful in placing any faith in hypothesis tests or confidence intervals resulting from the use of models suffering from autocorrelation.

The standard errors are biased downward because the pattern that prevails in the model's errors suggests a better fit than is warranted. This tighter fit results because, by the definition of autocorrelation, the error terms correspond more closely to each other. By "model's errors" we mean the error in the estimate, $e$, as in $Y = b_0 + b_1 X + e$. We do not mean "model's error" as in the standard error of the coefficient, $S_b$.

4. Just because the estimates are unbiased doesn't mean they will be "good" (as in close) estimates of the true parametric values. Due to the large variance an estimate is as likely to be above the true parametric value as it is to be below that value. Its expected value is zero— hence, by definition, it is unbiased as noted in Chapter 1.

## SECTION 8.3 PROBLEMS

1. How might autocorrelation bias the coefficient estimates, $b_i$?

2. How does autocorrelation impact the standard error of the coefficient estimate?

3. What is meant by bias in an estimator? What is meant by consistency of an estimator? What is the difference between an estimate and an estimator? Give examples (you may have to return to Chapter 1 for a brief review).

4. Does autocorrelation promote inefficiency in estimators? Explain.

## 8.4 DETECTING AUTOCORRELATION

Since autocorrelation is so commonly associated with time series data it is essential that we check for its presence anytime we are using a time-oriented data set. Although plotting the residuals as shown above is one method of exposing autocorrelation, it can be quite unreliable. The plots are often difficult to read with any degree of clarity and any prevailing pattern is unlikely to be as obvious as the two figures illustrated above. A more definitive method of testing for autocorrelation is required. This section examines six of the more popular methods of testing for autocorrelation. They include:

■ the Durbin–Watson statistic;

■ the Durbin–Watson *h*-statistic;

■ a simple hypothesis test;

■ the runs test;

■ the Lagrangian multiplier;

■ the Breusch–Godfrey test.

### ● The Durbin–Watson Statistic

Fortunately, in 1950 and 1951 James Durbin and Geoffrey Watson published the results of their work detailing the manner in which such a test can be conducted.[1] The *Durbin–Watson statistic* tests for first-order autocorrelation using Equation (8.4.1). Notice that a lagged value ($e_{t-1}$) is required in the *numerator*. We must start with the second time period because there is no time period prior to the first one. Thus, $t = 2$, to allow a previous time period—that is, time period $t - 1$. If we are using monthly time periods beginning in January, *t in the numerator* must be February to allow $t - 1$ to be January. In the *denominator*, $t = 1$ and is set back to January.

$$d = \frac{\sum_{t=2}^{n} (e_t - e_{t-1})^2}{\sum_{t=1}^{n} (e_t)^2}$$

(8.4.1)

where

$e_t$ is the error in the given time period

$e_{t-1}$ is the error in the previous time period

$n$ is the number of observations

In English, the numerator of this equation tells you to find the squared difference between consecutive residuals and to then sum up those squared differences. The denominator says to divide by the sum of *all* the squared residuals, including January. Using the first three observations and the last two observations of Table 8.1 to demonstrate, we have

$$d = \frac{(-2.15039 - -2.08348)^2 + (-2.08348 - -1.98423)^2 + \ldots + (1.84468 - 2.04468)^2}{(-2.15039)^2 + (-2.08348)^2 + \ldots + (2.04468)^2} \quad (8.4.2)$$

Of course, such work is done with the aid of computer statistical packages. Based on the data in Table 8.1, SPSS reports a Durbin–Watson of $d = 0.052$.

The Durbin–Watson test is simply a test for correlation between successive error terms, $\text{Corr}(e_t, e_{t-1})$. It tests the hypothesis

$$H_0: \rho_{e_t, e_{t-1}} = 0$$

$$H_a: \rho_{e_t, e_{t-1}} \neq 0 \quad (8.4.3)$$

where $\rho$ is the correlation at the population level between the error in time period $t$ and time period $t-1$.

If the null is *not* rejected it is concluded that the correlation is zero and no autocorrelation exists.

Values for the Durbin–Watson range from zero to four. If it is close to zero, positive autocorrelation is likely. If it is close to four, negative autocorrelation probably prevails. We will discuss what is meant by "close" in a moment. First, let's examine why the bounds are zero and four.

Differences in the residuals would be small only if positive residuals were clustered with other positive residuals followed then by a group of negative residuals. This can be visualized from Figure 8.1. Notice that, since several of the residuals are positive, there isn't much difference between one residual and the next. If the differences between successive residuals are small, the numerator of Equation (8.4.1) is small and the Durbin–Watson approaches zero.

On the other hand, if they alternated in sign, as is characteristic of negative autocorrelation, the *absolute* difference between one residual and the next would be much larger.

This too can be seen from Figure 8.2. In such a case, the numerator of Equation (8.4.1) would be much larger and the Durbin–Watson would increase, approaching four, where it will terminate.

This circumstance is borne out by Equation (8.4.4), which can be used as a facile approximation of the Durbin–Watson statistic:

$$d \approx 2(1 - r) \tag{8.4.4}$$

is an estimate of the Durbin–Watson statistic in which $r$ is the correlation coefficient between successive error values.

where $r$ is the simple correlation coefficient between successive error terms. If the error terms display a perfect negative correlation such that $r = -1$, then $d = 4$. Thus, as noted above, if the statistic approaches four, negative autocorrelation may be present in the model. If perfect positive autocorrelation prevails $r = 1$ and then $d = 0$.

The correlation between the error terms in the unemployment model we have been following is $\text{Corr}(e_t, e_{t-1}) = 0.976$. Then, $d \approx 2(1 - 0.976) = 0.048$, which closely approximates the Durbin–Watson reported by SPSS of 0.052.

After calculating your Durbin–Watson you must compare it with critical values found in the table located in Appendix B. Both an upper value, $d_U$, and a lower value, $d_L$, are identified. These Durbin–Watson values depend on (1) the sample size, (2) the number of right-hand-side variables, and (3) the level of significance chosen for the test. Using our present unemployment illustration with a sample size of $n = 35$, with only one RHS value ($k = 1$), and choosing a level of significance for the hypothesis test of $\alpha = 0.05$, we find from the table that $d_L = 1.40$ and $d_U = 1.52$. Figure 8.3 demonstrates how the test proceeds. Regions are established based on the lower value of 1.40 and the upper value of 1.52. Then the other two values are found as $4 - d_U = 2.48$ and $4 - d_L = 2.60$; these delineate the remaining regions. The results of the test are shown in each region. If the Durbin–Watson is less than 1.40 we can conclude with 5% level of significance that positive autocorrelation is present in our model. If our Durbin–Watson reports in excess of 2.60, we experience negative autocorrelation.

In general, if the Durbin–Watson is close to 2, it can be concluded that no autocorrelation exists. This is based on the fact that if there is no autocorrelation then $r = 0$ and $d \approx 2(1 - r) = 2$. In our present case, if it is between 1.52 and 2.48 we can conclude with 5% significance that autocorrelation does not threaten our model. Our unemployment model registered a Durbin–Watson of 0.052, confirming our fears of positive autocorrelation.

It is also possible to estimate the Durbin–Watson statistic using Equation (8.4.5) in which the error terms are regressed on past values of themselves. Thus, $e_t$ is set as a function of $e_{t-1}$. Simply obtain the residuals in the usual manner from the OLS model, $Y_t = b_0 + b_1 X_t + e_t$. Then, estimate the model $e_t = f(e_{t-1})$ as seen in Equation (8.4.5):

$$e_t = \hat{\rho} e_{t-1} + v_t \tag{8.4.5}$$

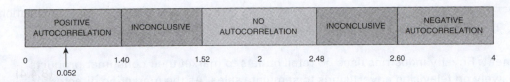

| POSITIVE AUTOCORRELATION | INCONCLUSIVE | NO AUTOCORRELATION | INCONCLUSIVE | NEGATIVE AUTOCORRELATION |

0          1.40          1.52          2          2.48          2.60          4
  0.052

■ **Figure 8.3**  The Durbin–Watson Scale for $n = 35$, $K = 1$, $\alpha = 0.05$

where $\hat{\rho}$ is the *autocorrelation coefficient* between $e_t$ and $e_{t-1}$ and is substituted into Equation (8.4.6):

$$d \approx 2(1 - \hat{\rho}) \qquad\qquad (8.4.6)$$

**is an estimate of the Durbin–Watson statistic in which the autocorrelation coefficient is used.**

Our present data set yields a value for $\hat{\rho}$ of 0.969, producing $d \approx 2(1 - 0.969) = 0.062$, which provides a close approximation of the Durbin–Watson value of 0.052 reported by our model. In practice, the simple correlation coefficient between successive error terms shown above as $r = 0.976$ will prove to be quite close to $\hat{\rho}$, as was our case here, and either can be used to estimate the Durbin–Watson using Equation (8.4.6).

Equation (8.4.5) is a *first-order autoregressive model*, often denoted AR(1). It's an autoregressive model because it involves regressing a variable on past values of itself—anything that is automatic is self-starting. It's first-order, since the error term is lagged only one time period.

It is stipulated that $|\hat{\rho}| < 1$. If it were not, then over time Equation (8.4.2) would require that $e_t$ expand to infinity, and the regression model is said to become *unstable*. Further, $v_t$ is uncorrelated over time and carries a mean of zero and a constant variance. It therefore exhibits the statistical properties associated with the standard OLS model.

Notice that Equation (8.4.5) does not contain a constant term. The model must be forced through the origin using some statistical package that allows this procedure. The expression is called first-order autocorrelation in that $e_t$ is purely a function of $e_{t-1}$. This is done because we want a measure of the relationship between successive error terms uncontaminated by a constant term.

The logic behind Equation (8.4.5) rests on the recognition that $\hat{\rho}$ measures the degree of "stickiness" inherent in economic phenomena. It reflects the tendency for corrections and adjustments in the economy to require time before becoming complete. The larger the value of $\hat{\rho}$, the greater the influence of past errors and the longer it will likely take for the adjustment to complete its cycle.

## EXAMPLE 8.1: Testing the Effectiveness of Advertising

**Problem Statement**: Royalty Industries uses no retail outlets to market their consumer products and relies exclusively on television advertisings to stimulate sales. As the marketing director for Royalty, you have been charged with the task of measuring the effectiveness of advertisements. Your first task was to collect quarterly data for the number of calls from TV viewers interested in purchasing your product received by your offices, the number of hours of TV commercials, and the number of telephone operators on staff to handle incoming calls.

After estimating the model using the data for $n = 17$ quarters seen in the Minitab screen shot shown here, you develop reservations regarding the presence of autocorrelation and the damage it can do to your calculations. You decide to analyze the residuals and compute the Durbin–Watson statistic to determine if your fears are justified.

| ↓ | C1<br>CALLS | C2<br>ADVERTISEMENTS | C3<br>OPERATORS | C4<br>RESI1 |
|---|---|---|---|---|
| 1 | 125 | 78 | 32 | 6.05793 |
| 2 | 136 | 85 | 36 | 9.38922 |
| 3 | 109 | 68 | 35 | 2.26831 |
| 4 | 99 | 59 | 25 | 1.42852 |
| 5 | 152 | 102 | 27 | 4.06987 |
| 6 | 151 | 105 | 29 | -0.17557 |
| 7 | 103 | 65 | 35 | -0.19820 |
| 8 | 163 | 115 | 29 | 0.04613 |
| 9 | 175 | 125 | 20 | -1.02841 |
| 10 | 126 | 87 | 24 | -4.69475 |
| 11 | 130 | 95 | 48 | -6.66077 |
| 12 | 99 | 64 | 45 | -1.58011 |
| 13 | 155 | 109 | 30 | -0.74286 |
| 14 | 94 | 58 | 20 | -3.11378 |
| 15 | 107 | 69 | 25 | -2.34978 |
| 16 | 118 | 78 | 26 | -1.80623 |
| 17 | 107 | 69 | 35 | -0.90952 |

**Solution**: The results of the estimation produce the following:

```
The regression equation is
CALLS = 31.7 + 1.18 ADVERTISEMENTS - 0.144 OPERATORS

Predictor           Coef     SE Coef           T        P
Constant          31.680       6.406        4.95    0.000
ADVERTISEMENTS    1.17783     0.04995       23.58    0.000
OPERATORS         -0.1440      0.1342       -1.07    0.301

Durbin-Watson statistic = 0.586385
```

A plot of the residuals appears as:

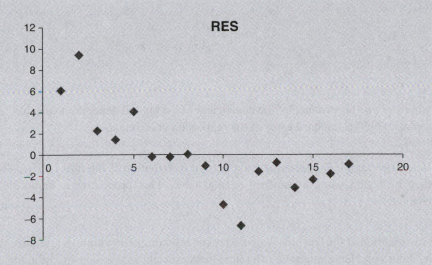

**Interpretation**: While residual plots are difficult to read and are as much an art as a science, the plot generated in this case does appear to show positive autocorrelation. Five positive residuals lead off the pattern, followed by several negative residuals.

More importantly, the Durbin–Watson statistic of 0.586 is quite revealing. The upper and lower critical values at the 5% level with $n = 17$ and $k = 2$ are 1.54 and 1.02. The Durbin–Watson of 0.586 is below the lower critical value and falls in the area warning of positive autocorrelation. It would appear that autocorrelation is indeed an issue with which you must contend in your analysis.

### ● The Durbin–Watson $h$-Statistic

Unfortunately, the Durbin–Watson statistic is not wholly reliable. For instance, if the error distribution is not normal, if there is higher-order autocorrelation [$e_t = f(e_{t-i})$ where $i > 1$], or if the dependent variable is used in a lagged form as an independent variable [$Y_t = f(X_{1t}, X_{2t}, Y_{t-1})$], the Durbin–Watson is not an appropriate test for autocorrelation. Instead, it is strongly suggested that the Breusch–Godfrey (serial correlation LM) test be used in that it does not suffer from these limitations.[2]

In the event the model contains a lagged value of the dependent variable, $Y_{t-1}$, the Durbin–Watson is biased toward 2 and a Type II error is likely. In such a case, it is suggested that the $h$-statistic be employed.[3] It is expressed as

$$h = \left(1 - \frac{d}{2}\right)\sqrt{\frac{n}{1 - n * (\widehat{\sigma^2 \beta})^2}} \qquad (8.4.7)$$

where $\widehat{\sigma^2}$, is the variance of the coefficient of the lagged dependent variable, $\hat{\beta}$. In practice it is replaced by the standard error of the regression coefficient, $s_{b_i}$.

In a large sample $h$ approximates a normal distribution if the null is true. The hypothesis can then be tested using a standard normal table. This procedure is demonstrated later in this chapter.

Any mention of the Durbin–Watson statistic is incomplete without a reference to the contribution by John von Neumann, who offered valuable insight into a measure of autocorrelation *prior* to that developed by Durbin and Watson. In 1941 von Neumann published a path-breaking approach to the small-sample distribution of this ratio.[4]

### ● A Simple Hypothesis Test

Since autocorrelation is merely a correlation between error terms it is possible to expose its presence by a simple hypothesis test much like that performed in Chapter 2. We simply test the hypothesis

$$H_0: \rho_{et, et-1} = 0$$

$$H_a: \rho_{et, et-1} \neq 0$$

where $\rho$ is the *autocorrelation coefficient* between $e_t$ and $e_{t-1}$. If the null is rejected, we can conclude that autocorrelation is present. You should recall from Chapter 2 this test is accomplished using a *t*-test based on Equation (8.4.8):

$$t = \frac{r - \rho}{\sqrt{\dfrac{1 - r^2}{n - 2}}} \qquad (8.4.8)$$

is a *t*-test for the significance of the correlation between successive error terms in which *r* is the Corr($e_t$, $e_{t-1}$) and the hypothesized value of the population correlation, $\rho$, is set equal to zero.

As noted above, the correlation coefficient for successive error terms in our unemployment model was reported to be 0.976. This yields

$$t = \frac{0.976 - 0}{\sqrt{\dfrac{1 - 0.976^2}{33}}} = 25.75$$

A *t*-value that high will result in a rejection of the null at any acceptable alpha level. Regardless of the chosen alpha-value, the null is rejected and evidence of autocorrelation is established. Further, since $r > 0$ we can again conclude that positive autocorrelation exists.

## ● A Nonparametric Runs Test

A run is a series of consecutive residuals of the same sign. We might find, for example, that our residuals report several positive values followed by several negative values only to be followed again by several positive values. Each series represents a run.

If we were to observe too many runs or too few runs we might conclude the residuals were not independent. As an analogy, consider a series of 20 coin flips. While the results of flipping a coin are considered purely random events, if there occurred 10 heads followed by 10 tails, producing only two runs, we would have to question whether this was a "fair" coin producing random results. We would expect more than only two runs. On the other hand, if the results alternated between heads and tails, producing 20 runs, we would likely presume that was too many runs. There is some reasonable range within which the number of runs should fall.

The same is true for residuals. If the number of runs of positive and negative values is exceedingly small or excessively large we must question the OLS assumption of randomness. It might seem that some form of association or correlation among the residuals prevailed.

A nonparametric test for the "proper" number of runs can be conducted to determine if the null hypothesis of $H_0$: $\rho_{e_t,e_{t-1}} = 0$ should be rejected. It is called a nonparametric test because no assumption is made regarding the distribution of the population parameters.

Suppose we have a model that generated 19 positive residuals followed by 16 negative residuals. Obviously, this is too few runs—only two. But we can perform a runs test to provide verification.

Minitab offers a very simple procedure to perform this test. The residuals are entered in any column in a Minitab worksheet. We then select the Minitab procedure as

$$\text{STAT} > \text{NONPARAMETRICS} > \text{RUNS TEST}$$

The column containing the data is entered into the "Variables" window and "Above and Below" is selected to identify a baseline value separating the runs. A value of "0" should be entered, since we want to test for positive versus negative errors. Select OK. Minitab responds with

**Minitab Output 1** _____

**Runs Test: C3**

Runs test for C3

Runs above and below K = 0

The observed number of runs = 2
The expected number of runs = 18.3714
19 observations above K, 16 below
P-value = 0.000

_____

It shows that there were only two runs when about 18 would have been expected if the errors were truly random. The $p$-value of 0.000 leads to an unequivocal rejection of the null that the correlation between successive error terms is zero. There is correlation among the error terms. Autocorrelation is unfortunately confirmed! Of course, we already knew that given that there were only two runs. But generally it's not nearly that obvious and a test of this nature needs to be conducted.

If you don't want to enter all the residual values you can encode only the signs of the residuals using a "1" to indicate negative residuals and a "0" to record a positive residual. We have then 19 "1"s followed by 16 "0"s in a column in a Minitab worksheet. Actually, any values can be entered, rather than "1" or "0," such as "5" and "6."

---

**EXAMPLE 8.2: Further Tests for Autocorrelation**

**Problem Statement**: In support of your test for autocorrelation as marketing director of Royalty Industries, you choose to perform the standard hypothesis test for residual correlation as well as a runs test. The correlation between successive residuals proves to be $r = 0.69$. A $t$-test at the 5% level is to be conducted.

**Solution**: The set of hypotheses is

$$H_0: \rho = 0 \text{ (no autocorrelation)}$$

$$H_a: \rho \neq 0 \text{ (autocorrelation exists)}$$

$$t = \frac{r - \rho}{\sqrt{\dfrac{1 - r^2}{n - 2}}} = 3.69$$

Using the feature in Minitab to perform the runs test yields

```
The observed number of runs = 4
The expected number of runs = 8.76471
6 observations above K, 11 below
* N is small, so the following approximation may be invalid.
P-value = 0.009
```

**Interpretation**: The critical $t$-value is $t_{.05, 15} = 2.1513 < 3.69$ indicating that the null should be rejected in favor of the conclusion that autocorrelation exists at the 5% level of significance. While the sample size in this example is restricted for instructional purposes and Minitab issues the warning regarding the question of validity of the test, the $p$-value of 0.009 suggests a problem with autocorrelation.

● **The Lagrangian Multiplier Test**

The Lagrangian multiplier test we used in Chapter 5 to test for significant variables is also a practical method of testing for first-order autocorrelation. The first step is to run the regression with no concern for autocorrelation. Be certain to save the residuals. With, for example, three RHS variables, the model would appear as

$$Y_t = b_0 + b_1 X_{t1} + b_2 X_{t2} + b_3 X_{t3} + e_t$$

Next, run the auxiliary model by regressing the residuals on all three RHS variables and on the lagged residual as

$$e_t = b_0 + b_1 X_{t1} + b_2 X_{t2} + b_3 X_{t3} + b_4 e_{t-1} + v_t$$

Due to the lagged residual on the RHS you will lose one observation and the auxiliary model is based on $n - 1$ observations.

A simple test of the significance of $b_4$ will then reveal whether there is any correlation between $e_t$ and $e_{t-1}$. The test is based on a chi-square statistic with one degree of freedom. The Lagrangian multiplier is found as $LM = (n - 1)R^2$, where $R^2$ is the coefficient of determination from the auxiliary equation. $n - 1$ is used because one observation was lost due to the single lagged value. $LM$ is then compared with a critical $\chi^2$.

---

**EXAMPLE 8.3: The Lagrangian Multiplier Test Applied to Royalty Industries**

**Problem Statement**: Concern remains as to the presence of autocorrelation at Royalty. It is decided that the Lagrangian test should be performed.

**Solution**: The initial model is estimated by regressing Calls on Advertising and Operators, and the residuals are saved. These residuals are then regressed on the two RHS variables and the lagged residuals. This produces an $R^2 = 0.49$. Then, $LM = (16)(0.49) = 7.84$. One observation is lost due to the lag. Testing for autocorrelation at the 1% level yields $\chi^2_{.01, 1} = 6.63$.

**Interpretation**: Since 6.63 < 7.84, the null that the correlation between successive error terms is zero is rejected. Instead, it is concluded that autocorrelation exists.

---

● **The Breusch–Godfrey Test**

While the Lagrangian test above can test for first-order autocorrelation, AR(1), higher orders of the problem may exist. In separate studies Breusch[5] and Godfrey[6] provided a straight-forward approach to this matter. It simply involves adding additional lagged residuals to the auxiliary equation. The number of lags is chosen by the researcher based on concern as to how far in the past residuals might carry some correlation.

Although there is no generally accepted method to determine the proper number of lagged residuals to include in the auxiliary equation, the periodicity of the data can serve as a guide. Generally, the number of lags should be sufficient to encompass an entire year to capture seasonal trends. If quarterly data are in use, a four-period lag should be considered. However, even this rule of thumb is worthy of some skepticism. If monthly data are used, 12 lags become a bit excessive. That would require 12 additional coefficients which would constitute a very large model and sacrifice perhaps too many observations. If $k$ lags are used in the analysis, then $k$ observations are lost.

The hypothesis being tested is that all coefficients for the lagged residuals are equal to zero tested against the alternative that at least one is not. A chi-square with $k$ degrees of freedom is used as the test statistic, compared with a test value of $(n-k)R^2$, where $R^2$ is taken from the auxiliary equation.

## SECTION 8.4 PROBLEMS

1. Explain how the Durbin–Watson statistic tests for autocorrelation.

2. Explain why Durbin–Watson values can distinguish between positive and negative autocorrelation.

3. Why does the Durbin–Watson fall between 0 and 4?

4. Why does a Durbin–Watson close to 2 indicate the absence of autocorrelation?

5. How does the Durbin–Watson $h$ adjust in the test for autocorrelation? Under what condition(s) should it be used?

6. Under what conditions is the Durbin–Watson test unreliable in its search for autocorrelation?

7. How can a simple hypothesis test be used to test for autocorrelation?

8. How can a runs test for randomness be used to test for autocorrelation?

9. Given the residuals 4, –5, 6, –7, –2, 6, and –7, with $k=1$, does autocorrelation exist at the 5% level? At the 1% level?

## 8.5 CORRECTING FOR AUTOCORRELATION

Given that one or more of the tests above reveal that autocorrelation is present we must take steps to mitigate its ill-effects. This generally requires some type of transformation of the data. Standard OLS models can then be applied to estimate the transformed regression model. The ensuing model will then behave in accordance with the Gauss–Markov conditions yielding residuals that are no longer correlated across time. The methods to correct for autocorrelation discussed here are:

■ generalized least squares—the Cochrane–Orcutt method;

■ Prais–Winsten adjustment;

■ use of a lagged dependent variable;

■ practice of first-differencing.

## ● Generalized Least Squares—The Cochrane–Orcutt Method

A common method of transforming the data is called *generalized least squares* (GLS). It may also be called the *quasi-differencing procedure* or *generalized differencing* because, as we will see, it involves subtracting one derived equation from another. Several specific steps are required to perform this transformation. We begin by estimating the standard OLS model:

$$Y_t = \beta_0 + \beta_1 X_t + e_t \tag{8.5.1}$$

The intent is to remove the $e_t$ from Equation (8.5.1), since it has been found to suffer from autocorrelation, and replace it with a term that obeys the rules set forth by the Gauss–Markov conditions.

> The objective in correcting for autocorrelation is to substitute a different error term that does not display correlation. The focus is on *replacing* the corrupted error term with one that is not autocorrelated. This is done by *transforming* the data as described below.

This requires that we return to our AR(1) model displayed above as Equation (8.4.5) and repeated here for convenience as Equation (8.5.2). All error terms, $e_t$, from (8.5.1) for $t = 1, ..., n$ are collected and regressed on their lagged values as per (8.5.2):

$$e_t = \hat{\rho}\, e_{t-1} + v_t \tag{8.5.2}$$

> The autoregressive model in which error terms are regressed on their own previous values.

The autocorrelation $\hat{\rho}$ coefficient in Equation (8.5.2) measures the degree to which past error terms influence current errors. For example, if $\hat{\rho}$ is 0.5 then *on average* each error tends to be one-half of the previous error. This is not to say that any given error will be one-half of the previous error. $v_t$ is itself a random error term for the model displayed in Equation (8.5.2) and as such it too influences $e_t$. Of importance, $v_t$ is an uncorrelated error term that satisfies the assumptions of the standard OLS estimation model in that $E(v_t) = 0$, $var(v_t) = \sigma_v^2$ and $cov(v_i, v_j) = 0$; $i \neq j$.

The value of $\hat{\rho}$ from Equation (8.5.2) is then used to transform the variables. The new transformed variables, $Y_t^*$ and $X_t^*$, and the transformed constant term, $\beta_0^*$, are shown in Equations (8.5.3)–(8.5.5):

$$Y_t^* = Y_t - \hat{\rho} Y_{t-1} \tag{8.5.3}$$

$$X_t^* = X_t - \hat{\rho} X_{t-1} \tag{8.5.4}$$

and

$$\beta_0^* = \beta_0 (1 - \hat{\rho}) \tag{8.5.5}$$

The new transformed dependent variable, $Y_t^*$, is found by subtracting from each value of $Y$ the product derived by multiplying $\hat{\rho}$ by the previous value of $Y$. The same treatment is applied to the $X$-values to gain the transformed values for the explanatory variable. The actual algebraic transformation that produces these results is found in the Appendix to this chapter for those who are interested. The new model to be estimated then becomes

$$Y_t^* = \beta_0^* + X_t^* + v_t \tag{8.5.6}$$

in which $v_t$ is an uncorrelated error term. This results in a transformation of the data for both $X$ and $Y$ that produces a model in which the correlated error term, $e_t$, is replaced by $v_t$, which does not exhibit autocorrelation.

To promote precision within your model it is suggested that you repeat the process until the value of $\hat{\rho}$ stabilizes. To do so, obtain the residuals from (8.5.6) and re-estimate $\hat{\rho}$ via Equation (8.5.2). This new value for the autocorrelation coefficient is used to obtain values for a second version of Equation (8.5.6). Practice has shown that no more than three iterations are required to produce the desired results. Oftentimes there is very little change between the first and second iterations.

Treating our Unemployment–Imports data above in this manner, after one iteration we derive the model

$$\hat{U} = 0.476 - 0.00001489M$$
$$(11.84) \quad (-3.291)$$
$$[0.000] \quad [0.002]$$

With *t*-values in parentheses and *p*-values shown in brackets we find the model, as before, to be highly significant. More importantly, this model reports a Durbin–Watson statistic of $d = 1.88$. According to Figure 8.3 this is well within the range denoting the absence of autocorrelation.

As proof of further improvement, the standard error of the estimate displayed by the earlier autocorrelated model was 1.46, while the corrected model reveals a standard error of only 0.184. It appears the reduction in error correlation has substantially strengthened the model.

Unfortunately, one problem remains. Equation (8.5.2) requires that we regress the error terms on their lagged values. However, there is no error term prior to the first one. Therefore, one of the observations is lost. The total number of observations in the model becomes $n - 1$. This problem is occasionally dealt with by simply ignoring the omission as we did here. This form of GLS is often identified as the Cochrane–Orcutt Method.[7]

---

### EXAMPLE 8.4: Royalty's Use of Cochrane–Orcutt to Adjust for Autocorrelation

**Problem Statement**: Having found autocorrelation in your model for Royalty Industries you feel it necessary to correct the model through the use of GLS via the Cochrane–Orcutt method. All the adjustments in the variables must be made. These adjustments can be seen in the data file ROYALTY and are also shown here.

| CALLS | ADV | OPER | RES | LAGRES | LAGCALLS | LAGADV | LAGOPER | ADJCALLS | ADJADV | ADJOPER |
|---|---|---|---|---|---|---|---|---|---|---|
| 125 | 78 | 32 | 6.06 | | | | | | | |
| 136 | 85 | 36 | 9.39 | 6.06 | 125 | 78 | 32 | 49.75 | 31.18 | 13.92 |
| 109 | 68 | 35 | 2.27 | 9.39 | 136 | 85 | 36 | 15.16 | 9.35 | 10.16 |
| 99 | 59 | 25 | 1.43 | 2.27 | 109 | 68 | 35 | 23.79 | 12.08 | 0.85 |
| 152 | 102 | 27 | 4.07 | 1.43 | 99 | 59 | 25 | 83.69 | 61.29 | 9.75 |
| 151 | 105 | 29 | −0.18 | 4.07 | 152 | 102 | 27 | 46.12 | 34.62 | 10.37 |
| 103 | 65 | 35 | −0.2 | −0.18 | 151 | 105 | 29 | −1.19 | −7.45 | 14.99 |
| 163 | 115 | 29 | 0.05 | −0.2 | 103 | 65 | 35 | 91.93 | 70.15 | 4.85 |
| 175 | 125 | 20 | −1.03 | 0.05 | 163 | 115 | 29 | 62.53 | 45.65 | −0.01 |
| 126 | 87 | 24 | −4.69 | −1.03 | 175 | 125 | 20 | 5.25 | 0.75 | 10.2 |
| 130 | 95 | 48 | −6.66 | −4.69 | 126 | 87 | 24 | 43.06 | 34.97 | 31.44 |
| 99 | 64 | 45 | −1.58 | −6.66 | 130 | 95 | 48 | 9.3 | −1.55 | 11.88 |
| 155 | 109 | 30 | −0.74 | −1.58 | 99 | 64 | 45 | 86.69 | 64.84 | −1.05 |
| 94 | 58 | 20 | −3.11 | −0.74 | 155 | 109 | 30 | −12.95 | −17.21 | −0.7 |
| 107 | 69 | 25 | −2.35 | −3.11 | 94 | 58 | 20 | 42.14 | 28.98 | 11.2 |
| 118 | 78 | 26 | −1.81 | −2.35 | 107 | 69 | 25 | 44.17 | 30.39 | 8.75 |
| 107 | 69 | 35 | −0.91 | −1.81 | 118 | 78 | 26 | 25.58 | 15.18 | 17.06 |

**Solution:** The initial regression run produced the residuals seen in the fourth column. These residuals are then lagged as shown in the next column. The correlation between the residuals and their lagged values is 0.69, which is used to adjust all the variables as required by Cochrane–Orcutt.

Regressing the adjusted variables produces the following results:

```
The regression equation is
ADJCALLS = 8.77 + 1.20 ADJADV - 0.151 ADJOPER


16 cases used, 1 case contains missing values


Predictor        Coef     SE Coef        T        P
Constant        8.772       1.342     6.54    0.000
ADJADV        1.20471     0.02725    44.22    0.000
ADJOPER      -0.15064     0.08726    -1.73    0.108


Durbin-Watson statistic = 2.31483
```

**Interpretation:** It can now be seen that the Durbin–Watson of 2.31483, as opposed to the 0.586 for the unadjusted model, alleviates the fear of autocorrelation. The model as estimated here is less likely to suffer from the complications brought on by autocorrelation.

## ● Modification of the Cochrane–Orcutt Method

Some sources suggest that the issue of the lost observation be treated by reconstructing the first observations for the dependent and independent variables as

$$Y_1^* = \sqrt{1 - \rho^2} Y_1 \tag{8.5.7}$$

and

$$X_1^* = \sqrt{1 - \rho^2} X_1 \tag{8.5.8}$$

This procedure is known as the Prais–Winsten transformation.[8]

Frankly, in practice this correction will make little difference, especially with larger samples. Treating our current model in this manner produced a higher standard error of 0.252 and a Durbin–Watson of 1.71, as opposed to 0.184 and 1.88 for the Cochrane–Orcutt model. The Prais–Winsten "correction" actually detracted from the model. However, without this adjustment the error terms may no longer be homoscedastic, thus violating another of the basic assumptions upon which the OLS model is based.

### ● Incorporating a Lagged Value of the Dependent Variable

Including a lagged value of the dependent variable can often mitigate the ill-effects of autocorrelation. However, as we noted above, doing so can bias the Durbin–Watson value toward 2 and thereby increase the probability of a Type II error. This danger evokes the need to apply the Durbin $h$-statistic using Equation (8.4.7). Applying this technique to our current data we find

$$\hat{U}_t = 1.97 - 0.00000599 M_t + 0.914 U_{t-1}$$

with $d = 1.967$ and a standard error of the lagged dependent variable, $s_{U_{t-1}}$, of 0.02. Then, using Equation (8.4.7), we find $h = 0.0969$. Based on this value we can now test the hypothesis for no error correlation, $H_0$: $\rho_{e_t, e_{t-1}} = 0$, by comparing our $h$-value with the appropriate $Z$-value.

If a level of significance of $\alpha = 0.01$ is selected, the decision rule directs us to *not* reject the null if $h$ falls between the critical $Z$-values of $\pm 2.58$, thereby ruling out the potential for autocorrelation. Given $h = 0.0969$, our results unambiguously argue that autocorrelation is no longer a problem as it was in the original model. Further, the $R^2$ value for this model is 0.991 and the standard error of the estimate is only 0.1786. The coefficients for both imports and the lagged values for unemployment are significant at the 0.000 level. It seems unequivocal that incorporating the lagged value for the dependent variable corrected for autocorrelation and, at the same time, provided a highly significant model with extreme explanatory power.

### ● First-Differencing

We know that the coefficient of autocorrelation, $\rho$, falls somewhere between $\pm 1.00$. If $\rho = 1.00$, GLS can be performed through *first-differencing*. While it's unlikely that $\rho = 1.00$, first-differencing can also be applied if the Durbin–Watson, $d$, is "low" and the $\rho$ is "high." A generally accepted practice holds that if $d < \rho^2$, first-differencing can be used to transform the data.[9]

The transformation from the original model of Equation (8.2.1), $Y_t = \beta_0 + \beta_1 X_{1t} + \varepsilon_t$, is completed by simply finding the differences between successive values of the variables. The transformed dependent and independent variables are expressed as

$$Y_t^* = (Y_t - Y_{t-1}) \tag{8.5.9}$$

and

$$X_t^* = (X_t - X_{t-1}) \tag{8.5.10}$$

In the transformation process the intercept $\beta_0^* = \beta_0(1-\rho)$. If $\rho = 1$ the intercept disappears and the regression model does not contain an intercept term. The fully transformed model becomes

$$Y_t^* = \beta_1 X_t^* + \varepsilon_t \qquad (8.5.11)$$

Equation (8.5.11) is then estimated using standard OLS procedures by forcing the model through the origin.

Transformation back to the original form is accomplished as

$$\hat{Y}_t = b_0 + b_1 X_t \qquad (8.5.12)$$

where $b_0 = \bar{Y} - \hat{\beta}_1 \bar{X}$.

Based on our Unemployment–Imports data, Equation (8.5.11) yields $U_t = -0.00001692M_t$. Conversion back to Equation (8.5.12) produces the final model of $\hat{U}_t = 2.54 - 0.00001692M_t$.

## ● Summary

Table 8.2 displays some of the pertinent results of the transformed models along with the standard OLS treatment of the data. An examination of the table reveals several vital observations. All the transformations produced improved results with respect to damping autocorrelation. The Durbin–Watson statistics ranged from 1.18 for the first-differencing model to a high of 1.967 for the lagged model. With the exception of the slope coefficient for the Prais–Winsten adjustment all regression coefficients proved significant at highly acceptable levels. All the models also resulted in reductions in the standard error.

Clearly, the lagged transformation outperformed all the other models. It not only provided the highest $R^2$, but it also reported the lowest standard error of the estimate of only 0.179. The standard errors of the coefficients are not reported here, but they too appeared superior to those found in the other models.

Obviously, not all transformation models work with equal efficiency. While the lagged model proved optimal in the present applications this is not always the case. Modern computer software programs make comparisons feasible and in some cases even easy. Some offer GLS results with merely the click of a button. The same can be said for the other transformations. If you are not fortunate enough to have access to such facilitating software you can force solutions through the steps outlined above for each model.

■ **Table 8.2** A Comparison of the Regression Results

| Model | Durbin–Watson | $R^2$ | $b_0$ (p-value) | $b_1$ (p-value) | $U_{t-1}$ (p-value) | $S_e$ |
|---|---|---|---|---|---|---|
| OLS | 0.052 | 0.409 | 17.7 (0.000) | −0.00005 (0.000) | | 1.465 |
| GLS | 1.88 | 0.253 | 0.476 (0.000) | −0.00001489 (0.002) | | 0.184 |
| Prais–Winsten | 1.71 | 0.022 | 0.394 (0.000) | 0.00000357 (0.393) | | 0.252 |
| Lagged | 1.967 | 0.991 | 1.97 (0.000) | 0.00000599 (0.001) | 0.914 (0.000) | 0.179 |
| First-difference | 1.18 | 0.187* | 2.54 | −0.0000169 (0.005) | | 0.236 |

*$R^2$ for the first-differencing model is not comparable to the others, since the intercept has been altered.

You should always keep in mind that corrections for autocorrelation are not the optimal solution to the problem. The best approach is to avoid autocorrelation in the first place. This requires that your model be properly specified to begin with. The proper specification means that all relevant explanatory variables be included in the model and that they be included in their proper form. Decisions must be made as to whether the variables should be included in log form and whether quadratics or other non-linear forms should be investigated.

## SECTION 8.5 PROBLEMS

1. What is meant by generalized least squares (GLS)? How does it work to correct for autocorrelation?

2. What is "transformed" in the application of GLS? Describe how that transformation takes place.

3. How does the Prais–Winsten technique modify the GLS?

4. How can a lagged variable be used to mitigate the ill-effects of autocorrelation? Devise your own original model to illustrate.

5. What is first-differencing and how does it reduce the harm imposed on a model by the presence of autocorrelation? Devise your own original model to illustrate.

# CHAPTER PROBLEMS

## Conceptual Problems

1. What happens to the standard errors of the regression coefficients in the presence of autocorrelation? Why is this likely to increase the probability of a Type II error?

2. Fully discuss the consequences of autocorrelation.

3. Discuss the advantages and disadvantages of each of the methods discussed in this chapter to transform data to deal with the problems of autocorrelation. Under what conditions would one method prove superior to the others?

4. What problems are caused by the presence of autocorrelation and how might they affect your model?

5. Explain clearly why the Durbin–Watson statistic ranges between 0 and 4.

6. How does autocorrelation increase the probability of a Type I error? Use a graph to fully explain.

7. Discuss in detail the steps that must be carried out to transform the data for the Cochrane–Orcutt method of correcting for autocorrelation.

8. Discuss the merits and drawbacks of each of the methods presented in the chapter to correct for autocorrelation.

## Computational Problems

1. A large manufacturing company relies heavily on its exports to foreign customers. Management is concerned about its sales to one of its largest buyers in the European market. Quarterly data taken from the U.S. Department of Commerce/ Bureau of Economic Analysis for the period 2006-I to 2010-IV (http://www.bea.gov/national/nipaweb/TableView.asp) produced the model $PercX = 6.75 + 0.217 PercCons$ with a Durbin–Watson of 0.322 and a standard error of the estimate of $S_e = 0.85$. $PercX$ is U.S. exports as a percentage of gross national product and $PercCons$ is personal consumption of consumer durable and non-durable goods as a percentage of GNP. Test the model for first-order autocorrelation using the Durbin–Watson. What corrective actions might you suggest?

2. Given the information in the preceding problem explain step by step how you would apply the Cochrane–Orcutt procedure to reduce the impact of autocorrelation.

3. Access the data file SALARYLEVELS. The file contains data for the salaries in thousands of dollars and the years of experience for 13 executives employed by an international marketing firm. Test for first-order autocorrelation using Salary as the dependent variable. What conclusion do you reach at the 5% level of significance? At the 1% level of significance?

4. Given the data in SALARYLEVELS what improvements are provided by the Cochrane–Orcutt method? How does the result of that transformation compare to first-differencing? Does a lagged variable offer further improvements? Compute each transformed model and provide a comparative evaluation.

5. Given the quarterly data in the accompanying table in trillions of current dollars, use standard OLS procedures to estimate the regression model. Calculate the error terms. Compute by hand the Durbin–Watson statistics and comment on the likelihood of autocorrelation.

| Observation | Savings ($Y$) | Income ($X$) |
|---|---|---|
| 2008I | 1.54 | 12.30 |
| 2008II | 1.33 | 12.46 |
| 2008III | 1.44 | 12.45 |
| 2008IV | 1.44 | 12.36 |
| 2009I | 1.21 | 12.09 |
| 2009II | 1.11 | 12.20 |
| 2009III | 1.12 | 12.16 |
| 2009IV | 1.12 | 12.24 |
| 2010I | 1.13 | 12.35 |
| 2010II | 1.15 | 12.52 |
| 2010III | 1.18 | 12.59 |
| 2010IV | 1.21 | 12.72 |

Source: U.S. Department of Commerce; Bureau of Economic Analysis. Extracted January 30, 2011: http://www.bea.gov/national/nipaweb/TableView.asp?SelectedTable=58&Freq=Qtr&FirstYear=2008&LastYear=2010

6. A model with $n = 32$ observations reported as $Y_t = 0.73 + 1.4X_t$ with a Durbin of 2.73. After a transformation it is found to be $Y_t = 0.13 + 2.7X_t - 0.58Y_{t-1}$ and has a Durbin of 2.47.

   A. Does it appear that the model originally suffers from autocorrelation at the 1%?
   B. Did the transformation including the lagged term seem to correct the problem?

7. Use the data in Table 8.1 for unemployment and imports and test for autocorrelation at the 1% level using the Lagrangian multiplier.

# APPENDIX: TRANSFORMING DATA TO ELIMINATE AUTOCORRELATION

We start with the standard OLS model:

$$Y_t = \beta_0 + \beta_1 X_t + e_t \qquad (8.A.1)$$

If testing for autocorrelation reveals that the errors, $e_t$, are correlated across time, we collect all error terms from Equation (8.A.1) for $t = 1, ..., n$. Using these error terms we estimate the autocorrelation coefficient, $\hat{\rho}$, by regressing each error term on its previous value using

$$e_t = \rho e_{t-1} + v_t \qquad (8.A.2)$$

where $v_t$ is an uncorrelated error term that satisfies the assumptions of the standard OLS estimation model in that $E(v_t) = 0$, $\text{var}(v_t) = \sigma_v^2$, and $\text{cov}(v_i, v_j)$ $i \neq j$.

Given Equation (8.A.1), we can express the lagged version as

$$Y_{t-1} = \beta_0 + \beta_1 X_{t-1} + e_{t-1} \qquad (8.A.3)$$

Multiplying Equation (8.A.3) by $\hat{\rho}$ we find

$$\hat{\rho} Y_{t-1} = \hat{\rho} \beta_0 + \hat{\rho} \beta_1 X_{t-1} + \hat{\rho} e_{t-1} \qquad (8.A.4)$$

Now we subtract (8.A.4) from (8.A.1):

$$Y_t - \hat{\rho} Y_{t-1} = \beta_0 - \hat{\rho} \beta_0 + \beta_1 X_t - \hat{\rho} \beta_1 X_{t-1} + e_t - \hat{\rho} e_{t-1} \qquad (8.A.5)$$

Given (8.A.2) we have

$$v_t = e_t - \hat{\rho} e_{t-1} \qquad (8.A.6)$$

Substituting (8.A.6) into the last term of (8.A.5) finds

$$Y_t - \hat{\rho}Y_{t-1} = \beta_0 - \hat{\rho}\beta_0 + \beta_1 X_t - \hat{\rho}\beta_1 X_{t-1} + v_t \tag{8.A.7}$$

By substituting (8.A.6) into (8.A.5) we *eliminate* the e term that was causing the problem in the first place!

Then, we can set the equalities shown below:

$$Y_t^* = Y_t - \hat{\rho}Y_{t-1} \tag{8.A.8}$$

$$X_t^* = X_t - \hat{\rho}X_{t-1} \tag{8.A.9}$$

and

$$\beta_0^* = \beta_0(1 - \hat{\rho}) \tag{8.A.10}$$

We have the transformed values for the dependent and independent variables and perform the regression shown above as Equation (8.5.6), which contains the error term $v_t$, which behaves in accordance with Gauss–Markov conditions.

Chapter 9

# NON-LINEAR REGRESSION AND THE SELECTION OF THE PROPER FUNCTIONAL FORM

## INTRODUCTION

Until now we have assumed that the relationship between the dependent and independent variables could be explained on the basis of a linear model. However, the real world is not linear. There are many business and economic relationships that are non-linear (or curvilinear). In fact, most economic functions do not fit a linear model. Cost curves, production functions, earnings functions, measures of profitability, revenues, sales, and most other business-related measures are all best explained with non-linear models.

In Chapter 2 we distinguished between models that were linear in the parameters and those that were linear in the variables. To apply OLS methodology, the model must be linear in the parameters (coefficients) but it is not necessary that it be linear in the variables. An equation is linear in the parameters only if the values for the parameters (the $\beta_i$) are expressed in their simplest form. $\hat{Y} = \beta_0 + \beta_1^2 X$ was cited as an example of a model that is not linear in the parameters because $\beta_1$ is squared.

On the other hand, $\hat{Y} = \beta_0 + \beta_1 X$ is linear in both the parameters and the variable $X$, since they are raised only to the first power. The expression $\hat{Y} = \beta_0 + \beta_1 X^2$ is linear in only the parameters. It is not linear in the variables, since $X$ takes on a squared value. Both of the last two models can be estimated using OLS, since both are linear in the parameters. The model $\hat{Y} = \beta_0 + \beta_1 X^2$, however, will require the non-linear methods described in this chapter.

Curvilinear models are generally formed through some transformation of the variables used in the model. There are many possible transformations that might result in a suitable non-linear fit. Unfortunately, the appropriate transformation to generate the best model is seldom obvious. It is only with practice and keen insight that the skillful analyst can identify the transformations that must be undertaken in order to produce the optimum model. This chapter examines some of the most common non-linear models frequently encountered in business and economic applications.

## 9.1 THE NATURE OF CURVILINEAR MODELS

Perhaps one of the most common non-linear models is the quadratic model[1] expressed as $Y = \beta_0 + \beta_1 X + \beta_2 X^2$ where the non-linear term is the squared values of the independent variable. Typically, it graphs as a *parabola* as seen in Figure 9.1. If the coefficient of the squared term $\beta_2$ is positive, the parabola is "concave up"—from above it appears as if you are looking into a cave. If $\beta_2$ is negative the parabola is "concave down." Figure 9.1 shows six common non-linear models and the shapes of the curves they produce.

A quadratic is a polynomial (defined more fully below) in which the highest power of the variable is two. In the expression $Y = \beta_0 + \beta_1 X + \beta_2 X^2 + \varepsilon$, $\beta_2 \neq 0$. If it is, the expression becomes linear like those we have studied in all previous chapters. All quadratics are polynomials. Not all polynomials are quadratics. For example, $Y = \beta_0 + \beta_1 X + \beta_2 X^3$ is a polynomial but not a quadratic. Why?

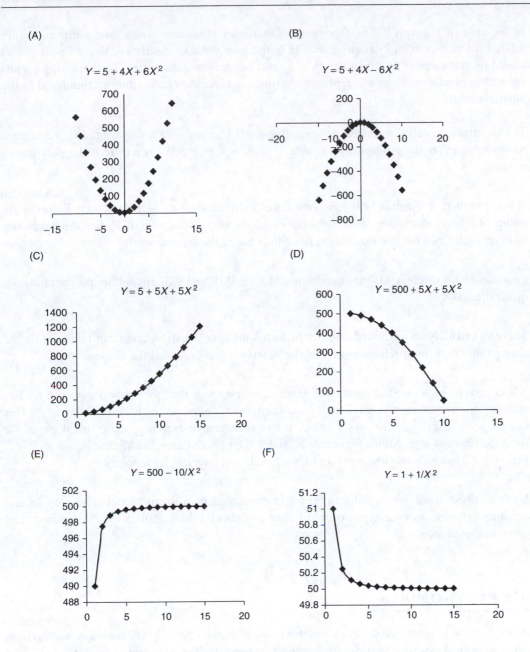

■ **Figure 9.1** Non-Linear Functions: (A) $\beta_2 > 0$; (B) $\beta_2 < 0$; (C) $Y$ Increases at an Increasing Rate; (D) $Y$ Decreases at an Increasing Rate; (E) $Y$ Increases at a Decreasing Rate; (F) $Y$ Decreases at a Decreasing Rate

In business and economic matters we are often concerned with only positive values for our variables. You cannot produce a negative number of units, experience negative costs of production, or invest in a negative number of projects. All these variables must take on positive values. These measures involve only Quadrant I—the upper right quadrant—of the Cartesian coordinates.[2] Our concern with non-linear functions can therefore be better expressed by referencing only positive values for $X$ and $Y$ as shown in Figures 9.1C through 9.1F.

In the case of Figure 9.1C, as $X$ goes up, $Y$ increases at an *increasing* rate, while in Figure 9.1D, $Y$ *decreases* at an increasing rate. In both cases you can clearly see that a linear model would produce a poor fit with a very low $R^2$ and a large standard error. The remaining graphs are self-explanatory. Each one represents a functional relation commonly encountered in the business world.

The quadratic is called a *second-order polynomial*. The *order* of a polynomial is the highest power assigned to the explanatory variable. $Y = \beta_0 + \beta_1 X^2 + \beta_2 X^3$ is a third-order polynomial or *cubic*.

When graphed, a function will have one fewer extrema than its highest power. Extrema are points of relative minimum or maximum at which the slope changes sign. Notice the quadratics in Figure 9.1. Each has one extremum, since they are of the second order.

Functions 9.1A through 9.1D are quadratics. Figures 9.1E and 9.1F are neither polynomials nor quadratics. Why?

There is virtually an unlimited number of forms the non-linear function can take. Figure 9.2 shows other non-linear relationships and the functions that produced the shapes.

Notice that in each case the number of extrema is one fewer than the highest power. Each has one low point (extremum) or one high point (extremum) less than the highest power of $X$. This is best seen in Figure 9.2A. As a cubic, it has two relative extrema where the slope of the function changes sign. Notice Figures 9.2C and 9.2D. In both cases, the highest power of $X$ is 2. Figure 9.2C has only one low point and Figure 9.2D has only one high point.

None of these functions is going to be well represented by a linear model. The next several sections examine specific types of non-linear models and their applications to business and economic matters.

## 9.2 POLYNOMIALS

A polynomial is constructed from variables using only the operations of addition, subtraction, and multiplication, with non-negative integer exponents. For example, $2X^2 - 5X + 17$ is a polynomial. However,

$$5X^2 - \frac{74}{X} + 7X^{4/5}$$

is not because its second term involves division by the variable $X$ and the third term contains an exponent that is not a whole number (4/5).

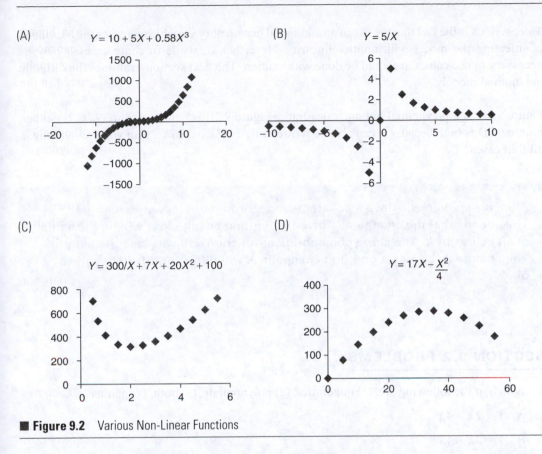

(A) $Y = 10 + 5X + 0.58X^3$

(B) $Y = 5/X$

(C) $Y = 300/X + 7X + 20X^2 + 100$

(D) $Y = 17X - \dfrac{X^2}{4}$

■ **Figure 9.2** Various Non-Linear Functions

> A polynomial is an expression of finite length constructed from variables (also known as indeterminants) and constants using only the operations of addition, subtraction, and multiplication. Exponents must be positive whole integers.

Now do you know why Figures 9.1E and 9.1F are not polynomials or quadratics? Because polynomials must have positive integers for exponents. Figure 9.1E can be written as $Y = 500 - 10X^{-2}$. The exponent is not positive. The same is true for Figure 9.1F.

Polynomial relationships are extremely common in many business and economic relationships. The quadratic is a useful way to explore parabolic ∪-shaped average cost curves, while the total revenue curves and total product curves are graphed as ∩-shaped parabolas. The cubic function is illustrative of total cost curves and the logit models we studied in Chapter 6.

However, it is suggested that polynomials of an order greater than two be avoided if possible. The introduction of another RHS variable such as $X^3$ leads to a loss of a degree of freedom.

More serious is the fact that the use of an additional explanatory variable increases the likelihood of infecting the model with multicollinearity. Nevertheless, while in some cases it may be necessary to use cubics, it should be done with caution. The next section examines the different polynomial models.

Figure 9.2A is a polynomial but not a quadratic. Figure 9.2B is neither. Figure 9.2C is neither. Figure 9.2D is both because it can also be written as $Y = 17X - 0.25X^2$. Can you answer why in all four cases?

> A linear function will have a constant slope throughout its entire length. This means that the change in $Y$ given a one-unit change in $X$ will be the same at all values of $X$. The slope of a non-linear function will vary over its length. The change in $Y$ given a one-unit change in $X$ will differ for different values of $X$.

## SECTION 9.2 PROBLEMS

1. Which of the following are: (1) quadratics, (2) polynomials, (3) both, (4) neither?

   A. $Y = 2X - 4X^2$

   B. $Y = 2X - 4X^3$

   C. $Y = 23X + 0.59X^3$

   D. $Y = \dfrac{-5x}{2}$

   E. $Y = X - \dfrac{4}{X}$

   F. $Y = 5 - \dfrac{X}{X^2}$

   G. $Y = \dfrac{20}{X} + 5$

   H. $Y = 5 + \dfrac{10}{X^{-5}}$

2. Can a cubic be a polynomial? Explain and give an example.

3. Are all quadratics polynomials? Give examples and explain your answer.

4. Are all polynomials quadratics? Give examples to support your answer.

## 9.3 QUADRATICS AND CUBICS

As noted, a quadratic is a polynomial of degree two. It carries a universal application throughout many business and economic concerns. This section illustrates some of the wide-spread uses of quadratics to explain these relationships. A comparison of quadratics and cubics is also presented. Remember, a cubic can be a polynomial but a cubic cannot be a quadratic.

### ● The Average Cost Curve

The ∪-shaped average cost curve is characteristic of many cost analysis studies and can be readily applied in any effort to examine the relationship between cost and output. To illustrate, Farm Assurance has been a significant element of British livestock production since the early 1990s.[3] However, in recent years farmers have begun to question the value of farm assurance schemes because they result in added costs to the farmers that are not reflected in the prices they receive for livestock. This is a pronounced drawback to British farmers, especially since livestock producers overseas are not subject to the same assurance standards and thus may enjoy a competitive advantage. A study was conducted to measure the benefits of farm assurance schemes to livestock producers in England.

Data are displayed in Table 9.1 for $n = 40$ farms detailing the average cost in British sterling pounds added to each farm as a result of farm assurance plans and the output of each farm measured in units of 1,000 pounds of marketable livestock. These data can also be found in the data sets as FARM ASSURANCE.

The National Farmers Union of Great Britain wishes to determine if there is any relationship between the added average costs brought on by farm assurance plans and the size of the farm. The intent is to use output (or size) as a predictor of average costs.

As a logical first step it is always wise to graph the variables to determine if a linear or non-linear relationship might exist. Although plots are extremely subjective and don't always offer clear perceptions, they are a handy way to gain an initial impression of the prevailing correspondence that might exist between the two variables. The graph for the data in Table 9.1 is shown in Figure 9.3. It can clearly be seen that a non-linear relationship does indeed exist. The dotted curve representing the data is unmistakably visible.

Excel permits the creation of trendlines that track the data plot. A trendline is formed by first right-clicking directly on the data plot, choosing Format Trendline, and selecting your preference. Figure 9.3 displays the results of a *linear* trend as the broken straight line. Unequivocally, a linear model will produce a poor fit. The unbroken line represents a polynomial of order two. A more promising fit is suggested.

Three models are fitted to the data and the results are shown in Table 9.2. Model 1 is a simple *linear* regression model based on standard OLS procedures. At first glance, the results do not

■ **Table 9.1** Costs and Output Associated with Farm Assurance Plans in Great Britain

| Farm | AC | OUTPUT | Farm | AC | OUTPUT |
|------|-----|--------|------|------|--------|
| 1 | 400 | 14.1 | 21 | 589 | 17.1 |
| 2 | 350 | 13.2 | 22 | 579 | 17 |
| 3 | 347 | 13.1 | 23 | 625 | 17.6 |
| 4 | 320 | 12.6 | 24 | 600 | 17.3 |
| 5 | 298 | 12.1 | 25 | 800 | 20 |
| 6 | 280 | 11.8 | 26 | 823 | 20.2 |
| 7 | 270 | 11.6 | 27 | 830 | 20.3 |
| 8 | 260 | 11.3 | 28 | 962 | 21.9 |
| 9 | 154 | 8.7 | 29 | 1157 | 24 |
| 10 | 124 | 7.8 | 30 | 1113 | 23.6 |
| 11 | 200 | 9.9 | 31 | 1145 | 23.9 |
| 12 | 171 | 9.2 | 32 | 1275 | 25.2 |
| 13 | 201 | 9.9 | 33 | 1200 | 24.5 |
| 14 | 300 | 12.2 | 34 | 1449 | 26.9 |
| 15 | 263 | 11.4 | 35 | 200 | 8 |
| 16 | 300 | 12.2 | 36 | 210 | 7.6 |
| 17 | 214 | 10.3 | 37 | 227 | 7 |
| 18 | 381 | 13.7 | 38 | 311 | 5 |
| 19 | 514 | 16 | 39 | 357 | 4.2 |
| 20 | 457 | 15.1 | 40 | 401 | 3.5 |

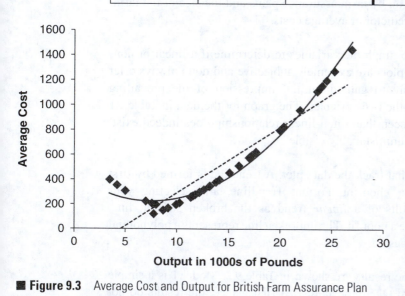

■ **Figure 9.3** Average Cost and Output for British Farm Assurance Plan

seem particularly alarming. The measures of correlation ($R$, $R^2$, and the adjusted $R^2$) are acceptable. Further, the coefficient for Output is reasonable and proves statistically significant based on the $t$-value and the $p$-value. However, as expected, the standard error of the estimate is quite high.

Model 2 is estimated as Cost as a function of Output Squared in order to capture the non-linear effect suggested in Figure 9.3. All statistics report improvements. The measures of correlation are higher and the standard error has been reduced. Again, the $t$-value and the $p$-value indicate the model is highly significant.

■ **Table 9.2**  Regression Models for Farm Assurance

|  | Model 1 | Model 2 | Model 3 |
|---|---|---|---|
| $R$ | 0.917 | 0.975 | 0.99 |
| $R^2$ | 0.841 | 0.951 | 0.985 |
| Adjusted $R^2$ | 0.837 | 0.950 | 0.984 |
| Output | 53.7<br>($t = 14.2$)<br>[$p = 0.00$] |  | −52.4<br>($t = -9.02$)<br>[$p = 0.00$] |
| Output Squared |  | 1.82<br>($t = 7.2$)<br>[$p = 0.00$] | 3.45<br>($t = 18.7$)<br>[$p = 0.00$] |
| Intercept | −250.1 | 77 | 430 |
| Standard Error | 146.5 | 81.2 | 46 |

Finally, Model 3 incorporates both Output and Output Squared as explanatory variables. Here we find the best results. All measures of correlation are further improved and the standard error is the lowest of all three models. Both RHS variables carry significant $p$-values of zero. Our firm conclusion is that the linear model is unacceptable.

The non-linear models unquestionably provide a better fit. A question may arise whether to keep the lower-order variable (Output in this model) if the higher-order variable (Output Squared) is significant. Arguments support the practice of including the lower-order variable in a polynomial model even if it reports as insignificant. It is used in such a case as a control variable and maintains the integrity of the other coefficients. Recall that changing the RHS variables by adding one or removing one will cause the coefficients of the other variables to vary. In this model, retaining the lower-order term is further supported by its highly significant status.

● **The Revenue Function**

Firms are always concerned about their total sales revenue. Traditionally, the total revenue function graphs as concave from below. Consider the data in Table 9.3 for Reynolds Industry, a large retailer in the center of Chicago, Illinois.

■ **Table 9.3**  Reynolds Sales Figures

| UNITS SOLD ($X$) | SALES REVENUE ($Y$) |
|---|---|
| 0 | 0 |
| 5 | 93 |
| 10 | 200 |
| 15 | 321 |
| 20 | 300 |
| 25 | 350 |
| 30 | 400 |
| 35 | 390 |
| 40 | 368 |
| 45 | 394 |
| 50 | 375 |
| 55 | 350 |
| 60 | 300 |
| 65 | 240 |
| 70 | 175 |
| 75 | 125 |

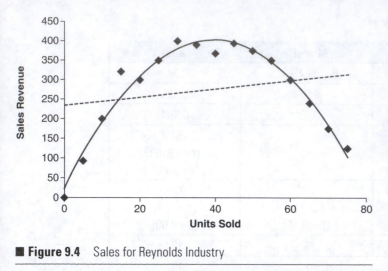

■ **Figure 9.4** Sales for Reynolds Industry

Management wishes to develop a model using units sold to explain changes in sales revenues. Again, as a first step a graph of the relevant data is prepared as shown in Figure 9.4. The anticipated ∩-shape appears. The linear model represented by the dashed line fails to adequately explain sales patterns. The quadratic trend line does so in a much more precise manner. Table 9.4 reports the results of the three models estimated on the basis of Reynolds' data. The conclusion is unequivocal. The quadratic model incorporating both Sales and Sales Squared (Model 3) is far superior. The other two models even report negative adjusted coefficients of determination, their coefficients are not significant, and the standard errors are higher.

■ **Table 9.4** Regression Models for Reynolds Industry

|                       | Model 1                             | Model 2                                   | Model 3                              |
|-----------------------|-------------------------------------|-------------------------------------------|--------------------------------------|
| **R**                 | 0.208                               | 0.053                                     | 0.983                                |
| **$R^2$**             | 0.043                               | 0.0028                                    | 0.966                                |
| **Adjusted $R^2$**    | −0.025                              | −0.07                                     | 0.961                                |
| **Sales**             | 1.067<br>($t = 0.794$)<br>[$p = 0.443$] |                                       | 19.13<br>($t = 19.14$)<br>[$p = 0.00$] |
| **Sales Squared**     |                                     | −0.0035<br>($t = −0.19$)<br>[$p = 0.843$] | −0.241<br>($t = −18.73$)<br>[$p = 0.00$] |
| **Intercept**         | 233.8                               | 280.6                                     | 23.1                                 |
| **Standard Error**    | 123.8                               | 126.0                                     | 24.3                                 |

● **Solving Quadratic Equations and the Vertex**

Given the universal applications of quadratics to so many business and economic concerns, it's often useful to find solutions to quadratic equations. There are three common ways of solving quadratic equations. Each is discussed here.

## The Quadratic Equation

To generalize, if $Y = aX^2 + bX + c$ the quadratic equation is

$$\frac{-b \pm \sqrt{b^2 - 4ac}}{2a} \tag{9.3.1}$$

Solving Equation (9.3.1) yields those values where $Y = 0$. Our revenue function above for Reynolds Industry solved as $Rev = 23.1 + 19.13U - 0.241U^2$, where $U$ is units sold, $a = -0.241$, $b = 19.13$, and $c = 23.1$. Using Equation (9.3.1), the solution values are $-1.19$ and $80.56$. That means that if the number of units sold is $-1.19$ or $80.56$, revenue will be zero. Of course, you cannot sell a negative number of units so, as is the case with many economic examples, if a negative answer results it is generally ignored. The expanded revenue function is displayed in the accompanying graph. It can be seen that when units sold is either $-1.19$ or $80.56$, the revenue curve passes through the horizontal axis and is zero. To sell 80 units would require a price of zero.

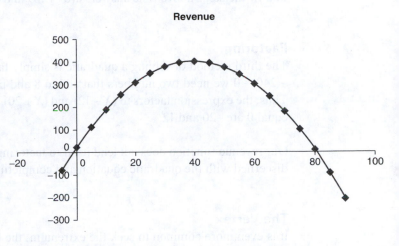

**Revenue**

Generally, quadratics have two solutions. As a standard rule, however, if the *discriminant* (that's the value under the radical—the square root sign) is negative, there is no solution in real terms. If the discriminant equals zero there is only one solution. But if the discriminant is greater than zero there are two solutions as is the case here.

You may also note from the regression model that if units sold is zero, sales revenues are still 23.1. How can that occur? If there are no sales, there can be no revenues! Remember, the model is an estimate based on sample data. This anomaly also explains why the intercept in an econometric model is often ignored.

## Completing the Square

A second method of solving quadratics is "completing the square." Specific steps must be followed. Assume an equation of the form $X^2 + 8X - 240 = 0$. The first step is to place the constant on the RHS.

$$X^2 + 8X = 240$$

Then, add $(b/2)^2$ to both sides. That's $(8/2)^2 = 16$.

$$X^2 + 8X + 16 = 256$$

Next, factor the LHS. This is easily done by recognizing that the factoring value is $b/2$ (or the square root of $c$). In this case, this is $8/2 = 4$ or $\sqrt{16} = 4$. Thus, we have $(X + 4)^2 = 256$. Then, $X + 4 = \pm \sqrt{256}$, and $X = -4 \pm 16$. So the solutions are $-20$ and $12$.

This process works only if $a = 1$. If the above expression were $2X^2 + 8X - 240 = 0$, you would have to divide all values by 2 so that $a = 1$, and perform the steps above. The answers are $-13.136$ and $9.136$. Try it for practice.

Let's use our revenue function for Reynolds Industry of $Rev = 23.1 + 19.13U - 0.241U^2$ again to illustrate. Rewrite it as $-0.241U^2 + 19.13U + 23.1 = 0$. Divide all values by $-0.241$ (that's a *negative* 0.241).

Follow the steps above. The answers are $-1.189$ and $80.57$ just as before.

## Factoring

The third method of solving a quadratic is simply factoring the expression. If we have $X^2 + 8X - 240 = 0$ we need two numbers that add to 8 and multiply to give $-240$. They are $-12$ and 20. Thus, the expression factors to $(X - 12)$ and $(X + 20)$. The solution values to make the expression equal 0 are $-20$ and 12.

Our revenue function does not lend itself to factoring in this case, but the solution values can be discerned with the quadratic equation and completing the square.

## The Vertex

It is even more common to seek the extremum, the high point or low point, of a quadratic. We often want to determine where revenues, profits, and sales, for example, are maximized or where costs can be minimized. This is accomplished by finding the *vertex* of the function as $\frac{-b}{2a}$. Reynolds' revenue function above yields

$$\frac{-19.13}{2(-0.241)} = 39.68$$

Revenue is maximized when sales total 39.68. By examining Figure 9.4 you can see that this is indeed the case. Remember, if $a$, the coefficient of $X^2$, is less than zero, the graph of the function is concave down and the vertex represents a maximum.

In contrast, the average cost function for the Farm Assurance data was found to be $AC = 3.45Q^2 - 52.4Q + 430$ and thus reports a vertex of

$$\frac{-(-52.4)}{2(3.45)} = 7.59$$

Since the coefficient for $Q^2$ is $3.45 > 0$, the graph is concave from above and the vertex identifies a *minimum*. This too can be verified with a quick glance at Figure 9.4.

The average cost function was obtained using Minitab as explained in Example 9.1 below.

## EXAMPLE 9.1: Analyzing The Angry Shrimp

**Problem Statement**: The Angry Shrimp is a fresh seafood restaurant on the Gulf shores in Mobile, Alabama. They offer a wide selection of the local catch including varieties of shellfish. The Certified Public Accountant who finalizes all accounting forms for the establishment recorded a total revenue curve of $R(Q) = -15Q^2 + 250Q$, where $Q$ is the number of tons of seafood sold to hungry patrons. The manager of this fine bistro wanted to know what level of $Q$ would maximize total revenue. A portion of the data used to estimate the revenue function is shown here. Revenue is measured in dollars.

| Q | R |
|---|---|
| 0 | 0 |
| 5 | 875 |
| 12 | 840 |
| 10 | 1000 |
| 9 | 1035 |
| 11 | 935 |
| 10 | 1000 |
| 15 | 375 |
| 7 | 1015 |
| 2 | 440 |
| 3 | 615 |
| 13 | 715 |

**Solution**: A plot of the data will provide a general idea as to the nature of the relationship between the dependent and independent variables. Based on the partial data set above, the graph appears as seen below. Clearly, a non-linear, quadratic relationship is evidenced of the form $R = aQ^2 + bQ + 0$. Since the curve is concave from below, it may be surmised that $a < 0$.

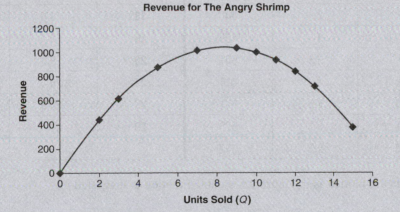

**Revenue for The Angry Shrimp**

Minitab's non-linear regression module is used by choosing

Stat > Regression > Fitted Line Plot > Quadratic

Regressing all the data (not just the partial set shown above) yields

$$Rev = -15.1Q^2 + 250Q$$

The vertex is found as

$$\frac{-b}{2a} = \frac{-250}{2(-15.1)} = 8.33$$

which can be verified in the graph.

**Interpretation**: Revenue will be maximized at $R = -15.1(8.33)^2 + 250(8.33) = 1034.72$. If a different $Q$ is sold, revenue will be less. As an illustration, presume seven units are sold. Revenue is $-15.1(7)^2 + 250(7) = 1010.1 < 1034.72$. If more than 8.33 units are sold, such as nine units, revenue is $1026.9 < 1034.72$.

## ● Cubic Functions

Although, as mentioned above, functions higher than order two must be used with caution, many cost functions are best fitted with a cubic. Presume we have the Cost–Output data for 23 months for a manufacturing plant in Berlin, Germany shown in Table 9.5. Notice fixed costs must be 250 because in the first observation output is zero but there is still a cost of 250.

■ **Table 9.5**   Cost–Output Data for a Manufacturer

| Month | Output | Cost | Month | Output | Cost |
|-------|--------|------|-------|--------|------|
| 1 | 0 | 250 | 13 | 6 | 539 |
| 2 | 0.5 | 257 | 14 | 6.5 | 547 |
| 3 | 1 | 285 | 15 | 7 | 556 |
| 4 | 1.5 | 375 | 16 | 7.5 | 568 |
| 5 | 2 | 439 | 17 | 8 | 570 |
| 6 | 2.5 | 440 | 18 | 8.5 | 618 |
| 7 | 3 | 489 | 19 | 9 | 648 |
| 8 | 3.5 | 501 | 20 | 9.5 | 658 |
| 9 | 4 | 514 | 21 | 10 | 758 |
| 10 | 4.5 | 521 | 22 | 10.5 | 778 |
| 11 | 5 | 528 | 23 | 11 | 789 |
| 12 | 5.5 | 532 | | | |

If the data are plotted as in Figure 9.5, a cubic function is suggested.

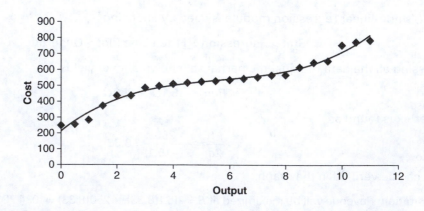

■ **Figure 9.5**   A Cubic Cost Function

Regressing Cost on Output, Output Squared, and Output Cubed yielded the model

$$\widehat{Cost} = 213.82 + 139.77Q - 21.88Q^2 + 1.289Q^3$$
$$(10.94) \quad (-8.00) \quad (7.899)$$

The $t$-values shown in parentheses reveal that all three RHS variables are significant. $\overline{R}^2 = 0.977$ and the standard error is 22.2. Regressing Cost on just Output produced an inferior model with $\overline{R}^2 = 0.91$ and a standard error in excess of 44.

## SECTION 9.3 PROBLEMS

1. Solve the following quadratic equations using all three methods demonstrated in this section.

   A. $12X^2 - 52X + 50$
   B. $10 + 18X^2 - 50X$
   C. $10X - 14X^2 - 45$
   D. $2X^2 - 10X + 2$

2. A revenue curve proves to be $R = -X^2 + 58X + 52$, where $X$ is output. Use the vertex to determine how many units of output the producer should sell to maximize revenue. Roughly graph the revenue function. Does it confirm your answer?

3. An average cost curve reports to be $AC = 214 + 5X^2 - 10X$. At what level of output is average cost minimized?

4. Access the file PRODUCTION FUNCTION in which output is expressed as a function of the number of labor hours used in the production process. Graph the relationship with output on the vertical axis. What do you presume is the relationship between the two variables? Estimate the model using your computer software of choice. Evaluate and discuss the model.

5. Access the file PRODUCTION FUNCTION 2 in which Input is used as an independent variable to explain changes in Output.

   A. Graph the relationship with Output on the vertical axis. What do you observe?
   B. Estimate the proper model using your chosen computer software. Collect the residuals.
   C. Plot the residuals and comment.
   D. Based on the vertex, at what level of input is output maximized?

6. Access the file COST FUNCTION. It is a model in which the total cost of production is a function of factor inputs used in the production process.

   A. Graph the function. Comment on its likely functional form.
   B. Create the additional variables needed to correspond to the form you have chosen in part A.
   C. Estimate the model and comment on its significance and fit.

## 9.4 THE USE OF LOGARITHMIC TRANSFORMATIONS: THE DOUBLE-LOG MODEL

In Chapter 7 we examined the manner in which logarithms could be used to linearize a non-linear model. We found that a non-linear model could be estimated with OLS procedures if the variables were expressed as logarithms. It was said that the models were *linear in the logs*. This section expands on that discussion and examines the several forms the logarithmic transformations might take.

One of the more applicable logarithmic forms is the double-log model.[4] The expression in Equation (9.4.1) is non-linear:

$$Y = AX^B \tag{9.4.1}$$

However, it can be linearized as a double-log model such as Equation (9.4.2):

$$\ln Y = \ln A + B \ln X \tag{9.4.2}$$

Figure 9.6 illustrates the differences that result when $B > 0$ and when $B < 0$. But notice in both cases, the double-log forms result in a linear function that can be estimated using the standard OLS procedures. Given a function in which $B < 0$ such that $Y = 100X^{-2}$ we have the graphs shown in Figure 9.6A. Take note of the shapes of the graphs. Specifically, they are negatively sloped. On the other hand, if $B > 0$ as in Figure 9.6B such that $Y = 100X^2$, the functions are positively sloped.

In Chapter 7 we saw how the use of double-log models can be used to measure elasticity. You are encouraged to return to that material for a quick review of its fundamentals.

A useful principle behind the double-log model that makes it so popular in applied studies is the fact that the slope coefficient of Equation (9.4.2), $B$, provides a direct estimate of the elasticity of $Y$, which, as you recall from your reading in Chapter 7, reflects the degree of responsiveness of $Y$ to a change in $X$. That is, elasticity measures the percentage change in $Y$ with respect to a percentage change in $X$.

If $B < 0$ as in Figure 9.6B, the function could represent a demand curve for a given commodity. The elasticity of demand is then measured by the slope coefficient, $B$. Furthermore, that elasticity coefficient remains constant across its domain for all values along the horizontal axis when *expressed in logarithmic form*. For this reason the function is often referred to as a *constant elasticity model*.

However, it's important to keep in mind that slope and elasticity are not the same thing. Given a linear function, the slope is always constant, but generally the elasticity will change along its length. It is only with this double-log model that the two are equivalent. Again, return to Chapter 7 for a review of the all-important concept of elasticity.

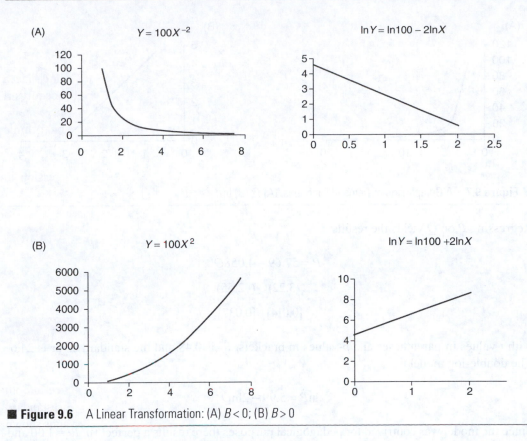

**Figure 9.6**  A Linear Transformation: (A) $B < 0$; (B) $B > 0$

## ● The Demand Curve as an Example

A demand function such that $P = 400Q^{-2}$ is derived from data for $P$ and $Q$ such as that shown in Table 9.6. The next two columns contain the natural log values for $P$ and $Q$.

**Table 9.6**  A Non-Linear Demand Function

| Q | P | ln Q | ln P |
|---|---|---|---|
| 2 | 100 | 0.693147 | 4.60517 |
| 4 | 25 | 1.386294 | 3.218876 |
| 6 | 11.11111 | 1.791759 | 2.407946 |
| 8 | 6.25 | 2.079442 | 1.832581 |
| 10 | 4 | 2.302585 | 1.386294 |
| 12 | 2.777778 | 2.484907 | 1.021651 |
| 14 | 2.040816 | 2.639057 | 0.71335 |
| 16 | 1.5625 | 2.772589 | 0.446287 |
| 18 | 1.234568 | 2.890372 | 0.210721 |

Figure 9.7A shows the graph for the Price–Quantity data, which are clearly non-linear. Figure 9.7B graphs the log values for the two variables, thereby producing a linear function.

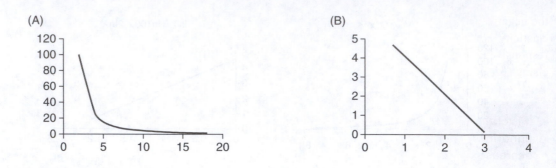

(A)

(B)

■ **Figure 9.7**  A Comparison of Demand Functions: (A) $P$; (B) $\ln P$

Regressing $P$ on $Q$ yields the results

$$\hat{P} = 57.69 - 4.058Q$$

$$(3.22) \quad (-2.55)$$

$$[0.014] \quad [0.037]$$

with $t$-values in parentheses and $p$-values in brackets. $R^2$ is 0.48 and the standard error is 24.6. The double-log model is

$$\ln\hat{P} = 5.99 - 2\ln Q$$

Since the model was contrived for pedagogical purposes there results a perfect fit. $R^2 = 1.00$ and the standard error and $p$-values are zero. But the point is, the double-log model is linear and can be more effectively estimated with linear regression techniques.

The fifth observation shows that when $Q = 10$, $P = 4$. The linear model predicts a value of $P = 17$ when $Q = 10$. But the double-log model reveals

$$\ln P = 5.99 - 2(\ln Q)$$

$$\ln P = 5.99 - 2[\ln(10)]$$

$$\ln P = 5.99 - 2(2.3026) = 1.3848$$

Taking the anti-log of 1.3848 we get the value of $P = 3.99 \approx 4.00$.

> You must always remember to take the anti-log of the outcome of the regression model to get the actual value of $Y$.

Moreover, the coefficient of $-2$ is a measure of the elasticity of $P$ with respect to $Q$. It measures the percentage change in $P$ relative to a percentage change in $Q$. It is common practice to ignore the negative sign in the estimate of price elasticity in a demand curve. Since the coefficient of elasticity is greater than 1 ($\eta > 1$), the function is said to be *elastic*. That is, price is highly responsive to a change in quantity. The percentage change in price is greater than the percentage change in quantity.

> It is critical to recall that since the model is double-log, the coefficient of 2 (ignoring the sign) is a measure of elasticity. It states that if Q increases 1%, P will decrease on the average by 2%.

> Furthermore, when formed as a double-log model the coefficient of ln X is not only a measure of elasticity, but as a coefficient of the linear function it is the slope, and since the slope of a linear function is constant, the elasticity is constant. Hence the term *constant elasticity model.*

## ● The Cobb–Douglas Production Function

In 1928 Charles Cobb and Paul Douglas formulated the oft-cited Cobb–Douglas production function which displays the relationship between output and the factor inputs used to produce that product.[5] The general function form is

$$Q = AK^{\alpha}L^{\beta} \qquad (9.4.3)$$

where $Q$ is output, $L$ and $K$ are the amounts of labor and capital used in the production process, and $A$ is "factor productivity." $\alpha$ and $\beta$ are the *output elasticities* of labor and capital, respectively, and represent the parameters to be estimated. They are constants and are determined by the prevailing level of technology.

It can be shown that if:

■ $\alpha + \beta = 1$, the production process exhibits *constant returns to scale*. That is, if all inputs (labor and capital) are doubled, output will double.

■ $\alpha + \beta > 1$, the production process will enjoy *increasing returns to scale*. If all inputs are doubled, output will more than double.

■ $\alpha + \beta < 1$, *decreasing returns to scale* are present. Then, with a doubling of all inputs, output will less than double.

Expressed as $Q = AK^{\alpha}L^{\beta}$, the Cobb–Douglas production function can be used to measure returns to the production process referred to as the degree of *homogeneity*.

> The production process is said to be homogeneous of degree $M$ if, when all inputs are increased by some constant called $\lambda$ (Greek letter lambda), output increases by $\lambda^M$.

For the sake of simplicity assume $A$ is 1 in the standard expression. Then, $Q_1 = K^\alpha L^\beta$. Increase $K$ and $L$ by $\lambda$. We have $Q_2 = \lambda^\alpha K^\alpha \lambda^\beta L^\beta$. Factoring out, we find $Q_2 = \lambda^{\alpha+\beta}(K^\alpha L^\beta)$ or $Q_2 = \lambda^{\alpha+\beta}(Q_1)$. Thus, $Q$ has increased by a factor of $\lambda^{\alpha+\beta}$. Let $\alpha + \beta = M$ and we see the function is homogeneous of degree $M$.

A firm finds that its production function is $Q_1 = 20K^{0.5}L^{0.5}$. The firm decides to double all inputs; that is, let $\lambda = 2$. Then,

$$\begin{aligned}
Q_2 &= 20\lambda^{0.5}K^{0.5}\lambda^{0.5}L^{0.5} \\
&= 20(2^{0.5})K^{0.5}2^{0.5}L^{0.5} \\
&= 2^1(20K^{0.5}L^{0.5}) \\
&= 2Q_1
\end{aligned}$$

The degree of homogeneity is found as the power of $\lambda$ that can be factored out of the expression. In this case, we found $\lambda^1$. The function is homogeneous of degree 1.

By doubling all inputs, output doubled. $Q_2$ is now twice $Q_1$. Let $K = 5$ units and $L = 10$ units. Then $Q_1 = 20K^{0.5}L^{0.5} = 141.421$. If both $K$ and $L$ are doubled, $Q_2 = 282.843$, or $(2)(141.421)$.

It is said that the production function exhibits *constant returns to scale*. That is, as all inputs doubled, output doubled. If $K$ and $L$ had been tripled, $Q_2$ would have been three times as much as $Q_1$.

If the power of $\lambda$ that can be factored out is less than 1, the function will be homogeneous of something less than 1 and is said to exhibit *decreasing returns to scale*. Presume $Q_1 = 30K^{0.3}L^{0.6}$. If all inputs are doubled ($\lambda = 2$) then

$$\begin{aligned}
Q_2 &= 30\lambda^{0.3}K^{0.3}\lambda^{0.6}L^{0.6} \\
&= 30(2^{0.3})K^{0.3}2^{0.6}L^{0.6} \\
&= 2^{0.9}(30K^{0.3}L^{0.6}) \\
&= 2^{0.9}Q_1
\end{aligned}$$

The exponent (power) of $\lambda$ is $0.9 < 1.00$. Decreasing returns to scale prevail. If all inputs are doubled, output will less than double. If $K = 5$ and $L = 10$, $Q_1 = 194$. If both $K$ and $L$ are doubled, $Q_2 = 361$ which is less than twice $Q_1$.

As you might imagine, if the exponent (power) of $\lambda$ that can be factored out is greater than 1, the function boasts *increasing returns to scale* and a doubling of all inputs will more than double output.

---

**EXAMPLE 9.2: The Sound of Three Hands Clapping**

**Problem Statement:** Using non-linear techniques, Three Brothers Manufacturing estimated their production function as $Q = K^3 + 2KL^2$. Interest arose as to how profits might be increased through higher levels of production. Could output be effectively expanded by an inflow of additional resources without causing an undue rise in costs? To answer this critical question, the three brothers recognized the need to examine the production function they faced.

**Solution:** Increasing all inputs by $\lambda$ results in

$$Q_2 = \lambda^3 K^3 + 2(\lambda K)(\lambda^2 L^2)$$
$$= \lambda^3(K^3 + 2KL^2)$$

The function is homogeneous of degree 3 and promises increasing returns to scale. Currently, the firm employs three units of capital and four units of labor. $Q_1$ is therefore 123 units of output. If both $K$ and $L$ are doubled, $Q_2 = 984$ units. This represents an eight-fold increase in output. This is found as $2^3 = 8$, since $K$ and $L$ were doubled and the degree of homogeneity is 3.

**Interpretation:** However, this information alone is insufficient to determine if the three brothers should indeed expand operations. The impact on profits depends on the costs of $K$ and $L$ and on the price of the product the firm markets. This question is addressed in the section problems.

---

Expressed as Equation (9.4.3), the Cobb–Douglas function cannot be estimated using standard OLS procedures. However, the function proves to be "linear in the logs" and submits to a log transformation of the form

$$\ln Q = \ln A + \alpha \ln L + \beta \ln K + \ln \varepsilon \qquad (9.4.4)$$

This form has the advantage of providing direct estimates of elasticities as well as mitigating any ill effects of heteroscedasticity that might otherwise prevail as revealed in Chapter 7.

An application of the Cobb–Douglas to the national economy of Great Britain was based on data collected from 1995 to 2009 for GDP used as a measure of total output ($Q$), the size of the labor force, and the stock of capital measured in British sterling pounds.[6] The data were expressed in their logarithms and the model was estimated. The results were

$$\widehat{\ln Q} = 1.73 + 0.679 \ln L + 0.273 \ln K$$
$$(4.98) \qquad (5.973)$$
$$[0.00] \qquad [0.00]$$

$$\bar{R}^2 = 0.743 \quad S_e = 0.202$$

Output (Q)

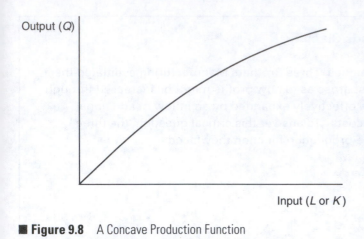

Input (L or K)

◼ **Figure 9.8**   A Concave Production Function

A 1% increase in the size of the labor force is associated with an average increase in output of 0.679%. The coefficient for capital is interpreted similarly. While much discord surrounds the interpretation of empirical production functions, this suggests that labor is more productive than capital in augmenting a nation's output. It might be conjectured that the reason for this outcome is due to the fact that the acquired capital is used by labor to increase the latter's productivity. Some researchers argue that some of the increase in output assigned to labor should therefore rightfully be accredited to the growth of capital. But no reliable method has been devised to accurately apportion the increased output between the two factor inputs.

Further, since $\alpha + \beta = 0.679 + 0.273 = 0.952 < 1.00$, these findings suggest the presence of decreasing returns to scale. This should come as no surprise. Traditionally, production functions are characterized as concave from below as seen in Figure 9.8.

This effect results from the fact that the most productive resources are used first. As output is increased the need to rely on less effective inputs causes output to expand more slowly. This is referred to as the *law of diminishing returns*.

## SECTION 9.4 PROBLEMS

1.  Access the file QUANTITY OF TEA. It contains data for the amount of tea purchased in 50 different cities during a selected month of the year 2009 in Ireland and the prices of both tea and coffee. Estimate and discuss a model to explain the quantity of tea based on the prices of tea and coffee. Determine the price elasticities associated with each commodity. Explain the signs of the coefficients for both prices.

2.  Economic theory is often concerned with utility functions that measure the satisfaction (utility) economic agents derive from participating in the market. A "risk-taker" is one who gains such utility from economic gambles, whether they are found at the gaming tables in casinos or involved with perilous business ventures that may or may not pay off. Paula Peril is such an adventurer, for whom the higher the risk, the greater the thrill. The data in the accompanying table reflects the

| Wager | Utility | Wager | Utility |
|---|---|---|---|
| 1 | 50 | 25 | 79 |
| 3 | 60 | 27 | 80 |
| 5 | 64 | 29 | 80 |
| 7 | 68 | 31 | 81 |
| 9 | 70 | 33 | 81 |
| 11 | 72 | 35 | 82 |
| 13 | 73 | 37 | 82 |
| 15 | 74 | 39 | 83 |
| 17 | 75 | 41 | 83 |
| 19 | 76 | 43 | 84 |
| 21 | 77 | 45 | 84 |
| 23 | 78 | 52 | 88 |

Wager in thousands of euros, and the Utility is measured in units of satisfaction called "utils."

Encode the data in your selected computer software and graph the relationship. What do you find? Does there appear to be a positive association? Selecting Utility as a function of the size of the Wager, estimate the linear model. Comment on its results. Form a double-log model and discuss the results including the elasticity measure that the model reports. Graph the double-log model. Compare the linear nature of the two graphs.

3. Economists use utility functions to assess the degree of utility or satisfaction consumers receive from consuming goods and services. The functions are derived using regression techniques and measure satisfaction in hypothetical units called "utils." A consumer's utility function is estimated to be $U = 5X^2Y^{0.2}$, where $X$ and $Y$ are two consumer goods.

A. Based on returns to scale, by how much will utility rise if the consumption of $X$ and $Y$ is doubled?
B. If the consumer is consuming eight units of $X$ and four of $Y$, what is his total utility? Calculate utility if 16 units of $X$ and eight units of $Y$ are consumed. Does this agree with your answer in part A?
C. What are the elasticities for both $X$ and $Y$? Calculate and interpret.

4. Express the utility function in the previous problem in double-log terms. Does the expression confirm your answer to part C of the previous problem?

## 9.5 OTHER LOGARITHMIC TRANSFORMATIONS

There are many forms logarithmic transformations can take in addition to the double-log model discussed above. We may find, for example, that a model such as $\ln Y = f(X)$ may prove useful. Here, only the values of the dependent variable are stated in their log forms. It is therefore often referred to as a *log-linear* model. Conversely, $Y = f(\ln X)$, a *lin-log* model, may provide improved results. Both models are *semi-log* models, since only one of the variables is in log form.

### ● The Log-Linear Model[7]

A typical application of the log-linear model is found in the study of human capital designed to develop *earnings functions* that explain and estimate incomes. Traditionally, they focus on the manner in which income depends on investments in human capital such as education, training, and work experience. Standard economic theory dictates that the *log* of income be used as the dependent variable. Thus, the model becomes $\ln Income = f(Experience, Education, Training)$. Other variables that strengthen labor productivity and add to one's earnings may of course also be considered.

Since people usually exhibit lower earnings early in their careers, enjoy rising wages over time, and then experience reduced incomes after retirement, the concave shape of their earnings function suggests a quadratic model. Many designs for earnings functions have been offered in the past.[8] A quadratic form might call for squared values and perhaps interaction terms as well. It might appear, for one of many possible examples, as

$$\ln Income = f(EX, ED, TR, EX^2, ED^2, TR^2, EXED)$$

The analyst must be careful to test for multicollinearity, as some of these variables could be correlated. Think about it!

Suppose because of insignificant $p$-values and the presence of multicollinearity, the model falls out to be

$$\widehat{\ln Income} = 12.2 + 0.073ED^2 + 0.013EX$$

The coefficient of 0.013 for $EX$ tells us that for each additional year of experience income will, on the average, increase by 1.3%. If $ED = 10$ and $EX = 5$, $\ln Income = 13.955$ and $Income = 1,149,686.70$. If $EX$ increases to 11, $\ln Income = 13.968$ and $Income = 1,164,730.16$. The percentage change is $(1,164,730.16 - 1,149,686.70)/1,149,686.70 = 0.013$, or 1.3%.

> The coefficient of the RHS variable measures the percentage change in $Y$.

This represents the instantaneous rate of change at a specific point in time and does not reflect the compound growth rate over time. It is usually calculated by taking the derivative of the function.

To obtain the compound rate you must subtract 1 from the anti-log of 0.013 and multiply by 100. Thus, since the anti-log of 0.013 is 1.0131, the compounded rate is 1.31%. This may seem to be a small difference, but in this case that's only because the coefficient of 0.013 is so small. Try this experiment with a coefficient of 0.985 or even 2.54 and see what you get. With 0.985 we would conclude that the instantaneous rate of change is 98.5%, but the compounded rate is 168%.

The model also tells us that if $ED^2$ increases by one unit, Income will rise by 7.3%. However, that's not a very insightful statement, since a year of education *squared* is rather meaningless. What is a "year-squared"? Nevertheless, the model is still quite useful for prediction given a person's level of education and experience.

If we were to use the same data to estimate a linear model we might find

$$\widehat{Income} = 1225 + 45ED^2 + 65EX$$

This states that income will increase by 65 units (in whatever units we have been measuring income) for each additional year of experience. Which model you might choose depends on whether you want a measure of the relative change (the log-linear model) or the actual, absolute change (the linear model).

> Whether you use a linear model or a semi-log model depends on what it is you wish to measure. If you want to know the absolute change in income given a one unit change in education, you must choose the linear model. If you seek to determine the relative change in income, the log-linear model is necessary.

However, as noted above, standard economic theory prefers the log-linear model. In which case the coefficients measure the marginal impact on the log of income, not on income itself.

---

### EXAMPLE 9.3: Keeping Pace at the Horse Track

**Problem Statement:** Employees at the Churchill Downs race track in Louisville, Kentucky threatened a work stoppage unless wages were standardized based on the workers' qualifications. It was determined that the level of education and years of work experience should be used to establish employee remuneration. Weekly wages were collected for several employees along with data on the two explanatory variables. Preliminary work indicated that a non-linear relationship prevails between wages and education. It was therefore decided that education should enter the model as a squared value. To provide you with a clear perception of the nature of the data, a portion of the complete data set is shown here. Does it appear that education and experience serve to explain wage levels for all employees?

| WAGES | EDUCATION | EDUCATION SQUARED | EXPERIENCE | LnWAGES |
|-------|-----------|-------------------|------------|---------|
| 2251 | 12 | 144 | 10 | 7.71913 |
| 1365 | 12 | 144 | 9 | 7.21891 |
| 728 | 11 | 121 | 8 | 6.590301 |
| 448 | 15 | 225 | 6 | 6.104793 |
| 1236 | 18 | 324 | 7 | 7.119636 |
| 915 | 8 | 64 | 9 | 6.818924 |
| 2978 | 10 | 100 | 11 | 7.999007 |
| 185 | 12 | 144 | 5 | 5.220356 |

*(Continued)*

*(Continued)*

**Solution:** Given the non-linear nature of earnings functions mentioned above it was decided to regress the log of earnings on the explanatory variables. With *t*-values in parentheses, the first model attempted was

$$\ln Wages = 2.01 + 0.0052ED^2 - 0.0053ED + 0.501EX$$
$$(14.77) \qquad (-0.56) \qquad (240.83)$$

Education is clearly not significant. The model was estimated without Education and reported to be

$$\ln Wages = 1.98 + 0.0050ED^2 + 0.501EX$$
$$(106.0) \qquad (265.6)$$

**Interpretation:** Inarguably, the high *t*-values for both variables testify to the fact that both Education and Experience are highly significant in determining wages. The employees' qualifications already receive the highest consideration in terms of setting wage levels. Should Education have been retained in the model as a control variable to preserve the integrity of the coefficients of the remaining variables? This practice was mentioned earlier in the chapter. That decision must be made by the researcher based on previous research and the theoretical precepts held by the researcher.

Learning curves measure the progress in a person's skills as he or she gains additional training and study. Past research has shown that log-linear models are useful in describing such relationships. The data in Table 9.7 were collected for 20 employees who have received training on a new computerized device installed into the work space at a local factory in Toronto, Canada. Their productivity after training is also shown.

■ **Table 9.7**   A Learning Function

| Training (hours) | Output | Training (hours) | Output |
|---|---|---|---|
| 2 | 16.4 | 4 | 49.4 |
| 6 | 44.7 | 12 | 200.3 |
| 10 | 121.5 | 15 | 424.1 |
| 15 | 445.9 | 18 | 897.9 |
| 14 | 492.8 | 20 | 1480.4 |
| 10 | 36.6 | 24 | 4024.1 |
| 9 | 94.6 | 23 | 3134 |
| 8 | 73.7 | 15 | 424.1 |
| 5 | 34.8 | 8 | 73.7 |
| 9 | 94.6 | 12 | 200.3 |

A data plot showed the relationship to be non-linear (try it and see) so a log-linear model is estimated. The results are

$$\widehat{\ln Output} = 2.31649 + 0.247976TR$$

The $p$-value is 0.000 and the $R^2$ is 95.67%. Thus, for a one-unit (one hour) increase in training, output will, on the *average*, increase by 24.8%. With 10 hours of training, the model predicts the log of output to be 4.796. Taking the anti-log, we find output to be 121.056 units. At a training level of 9 hours, the log of output is 4.548 and output is the anti-log of 4.548 = 94.469. The percentage increase is (121.056 – 94.469)/94.469 = 28.1% ≈ 24.8%.

## ● The Linear-Log Model

The linear-log model, $Y = \beta_0 + \beta_1 \ln X + \varepsilon$, is used to estimate the *absolute* change in $Y$ given a *percentage* change in $X$. The coefficient, $\beta_1$, measures the absolute change in $Y$ based on a one-unit change in the *log* of $X$. If the *log* of $X$ changes by one unit, the *absolute* change in $Y$ equals $\beta_1$.

The change in the log of a number is a relative change; that is, it is the change in the number relative to its current value. In our present case, it's the change in $X$ relative to $X$, or $\Delta X/X$. $\beta_1$ is therefore the absolute change in $Y$ compared with the relative change in $X$ and is designated as

$$\beta_1 = \frac{\Delta Y}{\frac{\Delta X}{X}}$$

This allows us then to get a measure of the absolute change in $Y$ which is the purpose of the model. Specifically,

$$\Delta Y = \beta_1 \frac{\Delta X}{X}$$

> The absolute change in $Y$ is equal to the coefficient, $\beta_1$, times the relative change in $X$.

If the relative change in $X$ is 1%, the absolute change in $Y$ is $\beta_1(0.01)$.

If our model reports to be

$$\hat{Y} = 1.25 + 5.6\ln X$$

then, if the relative change in $X$ is 1%, the absolute change in $Y$ is 0.056. If the relative change in $X$ is 5%, the absolute change in $Y$ is 5.6(0.05) = 0.28.

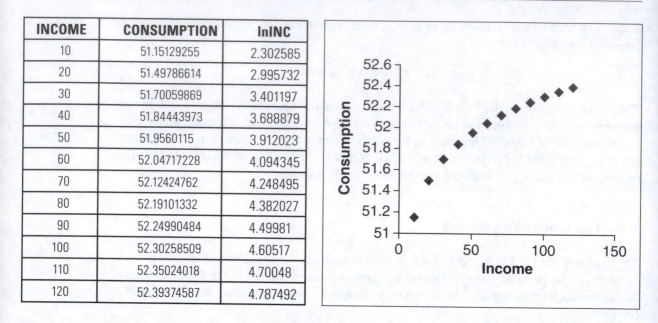

| INCOME | CONSUMPTION | lnINC |
|--------|-------------|---------|
| 10 | 51.15129255 | 2.302585 |
| 20 | 51.49786614 | 2.995732 |
| 30 | 51.70059869 | 3.401197 |
| 40 | 51.84443973 | 3.688879 |
| 50 | 51.9560115 | 3.912023 |
| 60 | 52.04717228 | 4.094345 |
| 70 | 52.12424762 | 4.248495 |
| 80 | 52.19101332 | 4.382027 |
| 90 | 52.24990484 | 4.49981 |
| 100 | 52.30258509 | 4.60517 |
| 110 | 52.35024018 | 4.70048 |
| 120 | 52.39374587 | 4.787492 |

■ **Figure 9.9** The Lin-Log Model: $Y = \beta_0 + \beta_1 \ln X + \varepsilon$, where $\beta_1 > 0$

In a linear-log (semi-log) model the general expression is $Y = \beta_0 + \beta_1 \ln X + \varepsilon$. If $\beta_1 > 0$, $Y$ increases at a decreasing rate as $X$ increases. Thus, if theory suggests such a relationship, this model should be applied. Figure 9.9 is typical of a non-linear consumption function. As income goes up, consumption will continue to rise. However, at higher income levels a smaller percentage of income is spent for consumption purposes and the rise in consumption tends to dampen.

Given the data shown in Figure 9.9 we find the regression model is

$$\widehat{CONS} = b_1 + b_2 \ln INC = 50 + 0.5 \ln INC$$

That is, consumption is regressed on the *log values* of income. For example, in the first case we find $CONS = 50 + 0.5\ln(10) = 50 + 0.5(2.3026) = 51.15$.

If $\beta_1 < 0$, $Y$ decreases at a decreasing rate as $X$ increases. This is typical of many non-linear demand curves. This is seen in Figure 9.10. The data yields

$$\hat{Q} = 50 - 2\ln P$$

The relationship prevails because as price goes up, quantity will fall in accordance with the law of demand which denotes the inverse relationship between price and quantity. However, given the utility the consumer derives from the commodity, consumption will persist, just at a lower level.

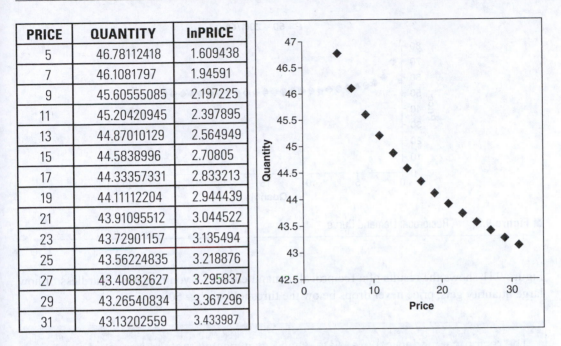

| PRICE | QUANTITY | lnPRICE |
|-------|----------|---------|
| 5 | 46.78112418 | 1.609438 |
| 7 | 46.1081797 | 1.94591 |
| 9 | 45.60555085 | 2.197225 |
| 11 | 45.20420945 | 2.397895 |
| 13 | 44.87010129 | 2.564949 |
| 15 | 44.5838996 | 2.70805 |
| 17 | 44.33357331 | 2.833213 |
| 19 | 44.11112204 | 2.944439 |
| 21 | 43.91095512 | 3.044522 |
| 23 | 43.72901157 | 3.135494 |
| 25 | 43.56224835 | 3.218876 |
| 27 | 43.40832627 | 3.295837 |
| 29 | 43.26540834 | 3.367296 |
| 31 | 43.13202559 | 3.433987 |

■ **Figure 9.10**   The Lin-Log Model: $Y = \beta_0 + \beta_1 \ln X + \varepsilon$, where $\beta_1 < 0$

## ● The Reciprocal Model

The reciprocal model is

$$\hat{Y} = \beta_0 + \beta_1 \frac{1}{X} \qquad (9.5.1)$$

It is especially useful in the application of *threshold models* in which the dependent variable should not breach a certain ceiling or fall below a minimum floor. For example, with a demand function, price cannot fall below zero. If a linear demand curve is specified, such as $P = \beta_0 - \beta_1 Q$ (ignoring the error term for simplicity), $P$ is less than 0 if $Q > \beta_0/\beta_1$. Given $P = 50 - 10Q$, for values of $Q$ greater than $50/10 = 5$, the model reports a negative price.

However, with the reciprocal model of

$$P = \beta_0 + \beta_1 \frac{1}{Q}$$

this anomaly would not occur. Notice that in the linear function $Q$ enters with a negative coefficient ($\beta_1 < 0$) in accordance with the *law of demand*, which states there is an inverse relationship between price and quantity. In the reciprocal form, $\beta_1 > 0$, but the inverse relationship between $P$ and $Q$ is maintained, since $Q$ is found in the denominator. Experiment with a few different values for $\beta_1$.

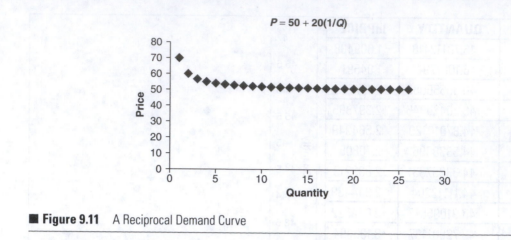

$$P = 50 + 20(1/Q)$$

**■ Figure 9.11** A Reciprocal Demand Curve

Figure 9.11 shows the results of a reciprocal demand curve. As you can see, regardless of how large quantity gets, price never drops below the threshold of $\beta_0 = 50$.

> The reciprocal model is appropriate when it is expected that the impact of an independent variable will approach zero.

## ● An Exponential Model

In general form, the exponential model is

$$Y = f(X) = b^X \tag{9.5.2}$$

where $b$ is the base and $X$ is the exponent. Unlike a quadratic such as $Y = X^2$ or a cubic like $Y = X^3$ in which the variable is the base, in an exponential model, $b$ is the base and it is a constant while the exponent is the variable. The base, $b$, must be greater than 0, but not equal to 1. If $b = 1$ then $Y = b^X = 1$, regardless of the value of $X$. That is, $X$ can change and $Y$ does not. $Y$ doesn't depend on $X$; it is not a function of $X$. $b$ must be greater than 0 to avoid imaginary numbers when $X < 1$. If $Y = (-5)^{0.3}$ we have $Y = 0.953 + 1.311i$, where $i$ indicates an imaginary number.

The range (all the $Y$-values on the vertical axis) of an exponential function is all real positive numbers and the domain (all $X$-values on the horizontal axis) is all real numbers, both positive and negative. When written in the form of Equation (9.5.2) all exponential functions pass through the point $(0, 1)$. If $X = 0$, $Y$ must be 1 regardless of $b$. Figure 9.12 shows this to be the case. The positively sloped function is $Y = 3^X$ and the negatively sloped function is $Y = 0.5^X$. If $b < 1$ a negative relationship exists, but a positive relationship is witnessed when $b > 1$.

An exponential model, often referred to as a *growth model*, serves as a popular method of finding values in the future for some specific variable. A common application is found in

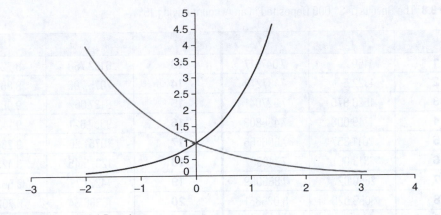

▪ **Figure 9.12** Exponential Functions

financial analysis to determine the *time value of money*. Given a certain sum of money that is expected to grow at a specified rate, analysts seek to ascertain its value at some future point in time. To find the *future value* of a sum of money, they use Equation (9.5.3):

$$FV_t = PV_0(1 + r)^t \qquad (9.5.3)$$

in which $FV_t$ is the value of the account in time period $t$, $PV_0$ is the present value at the beginning of the time period, and $r$ is the interest rate being earned.

As an example, your rich uncle just gave you \$1,000, which you deposit in an account paying an interest rate of 15% annually. You want to know the value in that account 24 years from now. Equation (9.5.3) reports

$$Y_{24} = 1,000(1.15)^{24} = 28,625.18$$

Table 9.8 records all the transactions, along with the log values we will need shortly.

As Figure 9.13 reveals, Equation (9.5.3) is clearly not linear. However, a linearized form is established that can be estimated using standard OLS methods by stating the exponential model in log-linear form. This too is shown in Figure 9.13. Notice it is indeed linear.

Regressing $\ln Y_t$ on $t$ (not on the log of $t$) we obtain the results

$$\widehat{\ln Y_t} = 6.91 + 0.1465t$$

The slope coefficient estimates that, on average, the value of the *log* of $Y$ increased at the rate of 14.65% per time period. Of course, we know the rate of increase was 15%, since this was specified at the outset. But in the absence of such a pre-determined progression we would not have been aware of the rate of increase and the regression model would have been necessary as

■ **Table 9.8**  The Results of $1,000 Deposited in an Account Paying 15%

| t | $Y_t$ | $\ln Y_t$ | t | $Y_t$ | $\ln Y_t$ |
|---|---|---|---|---|---|
| 1 | 1150 | 7.047517 | 13 | 6152.788 | 8.724661 |
| 2 | 1322.5 | 7.187279 | 14 | 7075.706 | 8.864422 |
| 3 | 1520.875 | 7.327041 | 15 | 8137.062 | 9.004184 |
| 4 | 1749.006 | 7.466803 | 16 | 9357.621 | 9.143946 |
| 5 | 2011.357 | 7.606565 | 17 | 10761.26 | 9.283708 |
| 6 | 2313.061 | 7.746327 | 18 | 12375.45 | 9.42347 |
| 7 | 2660.02 | 7.886089 | 19 | 14231.77 | 9.563232 |
| 8 | 3059.023 | 8.025851 | 20 | 16366.54 | 9.702994 |
| 9 | 3517.876 | 8.165613 | 21 | 18821.52 | 9.842756 |
| 10 | 4045.558 | 8.305375 | 22 | 21644.75 | 9.982518 |
| 11 | 4652.391 | 8.445137 | 23 | 24891.46 | 10.12228 |
| 12 | 5350.25 | 8.584899 | 24 | 28625.18 | 10.26204 |

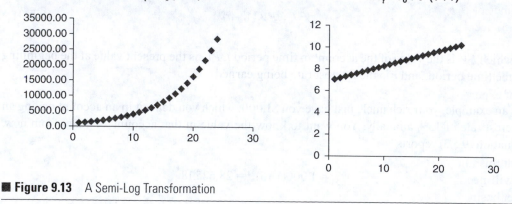

$$Y_t = Y_0 (1 + r)^t$$      $$\ln Y_t = Y_0 + t^* (1 + r)$$

■ **Figure 9.13**  A Semi-Log Transformation

our next example demonstrates. The intercept is the estimate of the *log* of Y when $t = 0$. To determine the actual value of Y at $t = 0$ we would have to find the anti-log of 6.91.

Under this strictly controlled process in which the growth rate is kept constant at 15% each time period, it is possible to use the formula for the *future value* of money. This was done above using Equation (9.5.3), which yielded a value of $28,625.18.

Perhaps an even more convenient method to determine average growth rate is to calculate the *geometric mean* using Equation (9.5.4):

$$GM = \sqrt[n-1]{\frac{Last\ Value}{First\ Value}} - 1 \qquad (9.5.4)$$

In our present case this becomes

$$GM = \sqrt[23]{\frac{28,625.18}{1,150}} - 1 = 1.15 - 1 = 15\%$$

We must find the twenty-third root of the ratio under the radical, since there were $n = 24$ data points.

## ● Continuous Growth Models

In many growth models the growth process is *continuous*, thereby requiring the use of Equation (9.5.5):

$$N_t = N_0 e^{kt} \qquad (9.5.5)$$

$N_t$ and $N_0$ are the values in time period $t$ and at the start of the growth process, respectively; $e$ is the base of the natural logarithm system, 2.17828; $k$ is the continuous rate of growth; and $t$ is the number of time periods involved. If $k < 0$ the balance will diminish over time and Equation (9.5.5) becomes a *decaying process*.

This year, exports for a textile firm in Great Britain are £32 million. They have been increasing at a rate of 0.6 per year for the past several years. The factory manager wishes to determine what exports will be in five years. Based on Equation (9.5.5) he figures

$$N_5 = (32)(2.17828)^{(0.6)(5)} = £642$$

With this knowledge, he now knows what to plan for in terms of shipping costs, raw materials he will need, packaging requirements, employment levels, inventories, and an entire host of other business-related issues. If a business manager knows what is going to happen in the future, it means decision-making is much easier today. It's like a crystal ball you can use to look into the future!

Due to increased mechanization and declining demand, employment in the auto industry has been decreasing at the rate of 0.218 per year ($k = -0.218$). Currently, there are 89 thousand workers in an industrial area in Stuttgart, Germany. Concern on the part of the government prompts the need to determine how many people will still be employed three years from now. Using Equation (9.5.5), and recognizing this is a decaying function as mentioned above since $k < 0$, we find

$$N_5 = (89)(2.17828)^{(0.218)(3)} = 46.28 \text{ thousand}$$

When discussing the time value of money if compounding is not continuous, the proper formula is Equation (9.5.3), $FV = PV(1 + r)^n$. That is, if continuous growth is not the case, the base of the natural logarithm system, $e$, is not involved. Equation (9.5.3) must be used. As an example, you have deposited \$1,000 in an account paying 5% annually (i.e., *not* continuous compounding, but annual compounding). In four years, it will be worth

$$FV = \$1,000(1 + .05)^4 = \$1,215.06$$

| Time Period | Value |
|---|---|
| 0 | 1,000 |
| 1 | $(1,000)(1.05) = 1,050$ |
| 2 | $(1,050)(1.05) = 1,102.50$ |
| 3 | $(1,102.5)(1.05) = 1,157.63$ |
| 4 | $(1,157.63)(1.05) = 1,215.06$ |

If the compounding is continuous the proper formula is Equation (9.5.5), or its equivalent,

$$FV = PV(e)^{i*n}$$

where:

$e$ is the base of the natural logarithm system, 2.71828;

$n$ is the number of time periods;

$i$ is the interest (growth) rate.

Thus, if the case above involved continuous compounding, the value in four years would be

$$FV = 1,000(e)^{.05*4} = 1,221.40$$

Equation (9.5.5), $N_t = N_0 e^{kt}$, is automatically used if the exponential function applies to anything other than money growth. In any growth process (if $k > 0$) or decay process (if $k < 0$) the process is generally continuous.

> A clear distinction is made between continuous growth models and those that do not involve continuous growth (and therefore rely on Equation (9.5.3) or its equivalent) in the appendix to this chapter.

## ● Mixed Models

The term "mixed model" is usually reserved for a multiple regression model in which only some of the RHS variables are expressed in log form. The model $Y = \beta_0 + \beta_1 X_1 + \beta_2 X_2 + \beta_3 \ln X_3 + \beta_4 X_4 + \varepsilon$ is an example. The logged value for $X_3$ means that the impact on $Y$ of a change in $X_3$ is less at higher values for $X_3$.

If $\hat{Y} = 5 + 6X + 7\ln Z$, let $X = 5$ and $Z = 12$, then $\hat{Y} = 52.394$. If $Z = 13$, an increase of 1 unit, $\hat{Y} = 52.955$; an increase of 0.5603. Now let $Z = 20$, $\hat{Y} = 55.970$. But if $Z$ increases by one unit to 21, $\hat{Y} = 56.312$. The change in $\hat{Y}$ is then only $0.340 < 0.5603$.

Many economic functions posit such a condition. The demand for certain food products may be stated as $D = f(N, P*, I, T)$, where $N$ is the number of consumers, $P*$ is the price of related goods (*not* the price of the good in question), $I$ is consumer income, and $T$ is the tastes and preferences of consumers. It has been empirically shown that as income goes up it has less and less impact on the demand for "inferior" foods that are purchased only because the consumer cannot afford to buy better quality products. A classic example is hamburger versus steak. As his income goes up, the consumer tends to switch to steak and slow his consumption of hamburger.

## CHAPTER PROBLEMS

### Conceptual Problems

1.  Identify and give examples of the following terms:

    A.  Polynomial.
    B.  Quadratic.
    C.  Second-order polynomial.
    D.  Degrees of homogeneity.
    E.  Increasing, decreasing, and constant returns to scale.
    F.  Elasticity of $Y$ with respect to $X$.
    G.  Utility function.
    H.  Time value of money.
    I.  Future of money.
    J.  Geometric mean.
    K.  Earnings function.
    L.  Continuous growth.

2.  Describe the functions listed here. Under what conditions would each be appropriate? What are the characteristics of each?

    A.  Double-log.
    B.  Log-linear.
    C.  Linear-log.
    D.  Reciprocal.
    E.  Exponential.
    F.  Mixed models.

### Computational Problems

1.  Solve the following quadratic equations using all three methods described in the chapter.

    A.  $4X^2 - 6X - 8$.
    B.  $4X^2 + 5X - 8$.
    C.  $0.8X^2 - 8X$.
    D.  $0.8X^2 + 4X + 12$.

2.  A firm's total revenue curve is estimated to be $TR = -2.5Q^2 + 15Q + 56$. At what level of output should the firm operate to maximize revenue? What is $TR$ at that point? What are the measures of $TR$ for levels of $Q$ one unit below and one unit above that point, where $TR$ is maximized? Graph the function.

3.  An average cost curve is found to be $AC = 89.96 + 0.0179Q^2 - 2.294Q$. At what level of output is average cost minimized?

4.  Given the $AC$ curve in the previous problem, what is the total cost function?

5.  Corell Transport hauls heavy cargo between several major cities across the country. Rising fuel costs have caused a concern within upper management over future profit levels. Access the file CORELL TRANSPORT containing data for miles driven in thousands and average costs in hundreds of dollars. Using your preferred software, estimate the average cost curve for Corell's operations. Keep in mind that the average cost curve is a $\cup$-shaped quadratic of the general form $AC = f(Q, Q^2)$.

    A.  Create the required squared term for $Q$ (Miles$^2$ in this case) and regress $AC$ on Miles and Miles$^2$. Discuss and evaluate the results.
    B.  At what level of output (Miles) is average cost minimized?
    C.  Plot the average cost curve.

6.  Given the data for Corell Transport in the previous problem, estimate the linear model and compare it with the non-linear, quadratic model.

7.  Residents of Lonesome, Arizona operate a co-operative agricultural center on the outskirts of town. Data for the quantity of kumquats sold in hundreds of pounds along with the total revenues and total costs associated with the operations are found in the data file LONESOME. Using your preferred software:

    A.  Estimate the Total Revenue function, $TR$. Remember:

        (1)  If $Q$ equals zero, $TR$ will equal zero. You must therefore force the function through the origin.
        (2)  $TR$ is a quadratic requiring the values for $Q^2$. You must therefore create a second variable for the $TR$ function. Regress $TR$ on $Q$ and $Q^2$.

    B.  Estimate the Total Cost function, $TC$. Recall that $TC$ is a cubic and requires $Q$, $Q^2$, and $Q^3$. Create the $Q^3$ variable and estimate the model.
    C.  Calculate the Profit function as $TR - TC$.
    D.  Plot all three functions on the same graph. Comment on the results.

8.  The demand function for lumber products is thought to take the form $P = AQ^{-b}$. Data were collected and displayed in the table below.

One of your co-workers suggests a linear model regressing $P$ on $Q$. Based on the anticipated function shown above, you suggest a double-log model.

| Q | P | ln Q | ln P |
|---|---|---|---|
| 2 | 45.23 | 0.693147 | 3.811761 |
| 4 | 15.6 | 1.386294 | 2.747271 |
| 6 | 8.51 | 1.791759 | 2.141242 |
| 8 | 5.52 | 2.079442 | 1.708378 |
| 10 | 3.95 | 2.302585 | 1.373716 |
| 12 | 3 | 2.484907 | 1.098612 |
| 14 | 2.39 | 2.639057 | 0.871293 |
| 16 | 1.95 | 2.772589 | 0.667829 |
| 18 | 1.64 | 2.890372 | 0.494696 |

A. Using your preferred software estimate both models. Save the residuals.
B. Compare and contrast the results. What can you say about the elasticity of demand?
C. Plot the residuals. What can you conclude?
D. Can you compare the $R^2$ values? Explain why or why not.

9. Utility functions measure the satisfaction consumers derive from the consumption of goods and services. They are often expressed as $U = AQ_1^a Q_2^b$, where $Q_1$ and $Q_2$ are two commodities and $A$ is a parameter. What are the measures of elasticity of $U$ with respect to the two goods? Under what conditions would $U$ prove to be inelastic in response to changes in $Q_1$ and $Q_2$?

10. Based on data compiled from the American Farmers Association, a non-profit organization established in 1983, demand for Idaho potatoes is estimated as $\hat{P} = 3.558 - 0.8879Q$, while demand for imported agricultural crops is $\hat{P} = 2.3Q^{-3.5}$. What are the relevant coefficients in each model? Interpret the coefficients.

11. A Cobb–Douglas production function is $Q = 12L^{.6}K^{.5}$. What happens to $Q$ if $L$ increases by 1%? If $K$ increases by 1%? What can you say about returns to scale?

12. With the Cobb–Douglas production function in problem 11, if $L = 10$ and $K = 15$, what is $Q$? If $L$ increases by 1% what is the level of output, $Q$? What percentage increase is that? How does that compare with the exponent of the function?

13. A semi-log (log-lin) consumption function states $\ln C = 2 + 0.058I$ in which $\ln C$ is the log of consumption for a small national economy measured in billions of monetary units and $I$ is the income (measured as GDP) in trillions of units. If $I$ increases by one unit:

A. What happens to $C$?
B. Calculate $C$.

14. Based on the information in problem 13, if $I$ is currently 10 what is $C$? If $I$ increases by one unit to 11, what is $C$? What percentage increase is that?

15. Given the data shown here for profits in 1,000s and tons sold:

| Profits (Y) | Tons (X) | In Profits |
|---|---|---|
| 25 | 7.07 | 3.218876 |
| 35 | 9.66 | 3.555348 |
| 48 | 12.09 | 3.871201 |
| 29 | 8.07 | 3.367296 |
| 39 | 12.65 | 3.663562 |
| 37 | 11.25 | 3.610918 |
| 58 | 12.58 | 4.060443 |
| 47 | 11.93 | 3.850148 |

   A. Compute the linear model and the log-linear model. What happens to $Y$ as $X$ changes by one ton according to both models?
   B. According to the linear model, what is $Y$ if $X = 7.07$? What does the semi-log model predict if $X = 7.07$? How do these values compare to the actual value of $X$ when $X = 7.07$ (the first observation)?
   C. Find the values of $Y$ for both models if $X = 8.07$—a change of one unit.
   D. What is the change in $Y$ when $X$ changes from 7.08 to 8.07?
   E. How do these changes compare with the changes predicted by both models?

16. Access the file UTILITY, which contains data for the utility or satisfaction ($Y$) a consumer derives from the consumption of a certain good as a function of the number of units consumed ($X$). Graph the function. Based on the graph, what form of the function do you feel would best estimate the relationship? Try (1) a quadratic, (2) a reciprocal model, and (3) a lin-log model. Comment on the differences.

17. A catastrophic plague has infected the citizens of Ephinacious, a small country somewhere in an obscure part of the world. Currently, 4,000 poor souls are infected and the disease is growing at the rate of 23.5% per day. The locals want to know how many will be contaminated in 10 days. What is your diagnosis?

18. Employees at Harvard Trust and Insurance number 1,258. Hard economic times have caused HTI to dismiss some workers at the rate of 3.5%. If less than 1,000 employees remain after three years, a bond rating agency will downgrade HTI's debt issue. Will this happen?

19. You currently have $43,000 at your ready disposal. An investment you plan to pursue in six years requires $60,000. If you place the $43,000 in an account paying 5.5% annually, will you have the required amount to make the investment?

20. If the interest in problem 19 is paid continuously, will you have the $60,000?

21. Monthly sales at Freeman International have been, in thousands, 45.2, 56.3, 54.8, 62.5, 74.5, 69.3, and 71.2. If the growth rate in sales exceeds 8%, the Chief Financial Officer will give himself a 30% raise. Does he get it?

22. The Three Brothers from Example 9.2 face per unit costs of $100 for capital and $50 for labor. They sell the product for $3.75 per unit. If they double all inputs it is felt that they will have no effect on the market price of the inputs, but to sell the additional output they will have to lower the price to $3.20. Should they expand operations?

23. A societal utility function for an entire nation is found to be $\ln U = 3.2 - 0.52 \ln G + 0.47 \ln B$, where $G$ and $B$ are guns and butter. Interpret the coefficients. What happens to utility for the nation if 1% more guns are produced? 1% more butter?

24. Travel expenses for Remi Electronics have been increasing at an alarming rate. In an effort to control this unfortunate trend, management has declared that if costs reach or exceed $70 thousand by 2014 drastic measures must be taken. Given the costs in thousands shown here, calculate the geometric mean rate of increase and determine if corrective measures are in order.

| Year | Expenses |
|------|----------|
| 2007 | 42 |
| 2008 | 53 |
| 2009 | 49 |
| 2010 | 57 |
| 2011 | 63 |
| 2012 | 62 |

25. Inventory levels for Remi are currently held at $400,000 and have been increasing at a rate of 6% over the past 10 years. In order to hold down inventory costs, Remi has decided that if they exceed $530,000 in five years alternative methods must be used to satisfy customer demand in a timely manner. What is your conclusion?

26. If the growth rate was continuous for Remi in the previous problem, what is your conclusion?

## APPENDIX: WITH RESPECT TO EXPONENTIAL FUNCTIONS

CHAPTER
APPENDIX

9

1. When discussing the time value of money the proper formula is, for example,

$$FV = PV(1 + r)^n \tag{1}$$

2. That is, it does *not* involve continuous growth and the base of the natural logarithm system, $e$, is *not* involved. For example:

$$FV = \$1,000(1 + .05)^4 = \$1,215.06$$

| Time Period | Value |
|-------------|-------|
| 0 | 1,000 |
| 1 | $(1,000)(1.05) = 1,050$ |
| 2 | $(1,050)(1.05) = 1,102.50$ |
| 3 | $(1,102.5)(1.05) = 1,157.63$ |
| 4 | $(1,157.63)(1.05) = 1,215.06$ |

If the compounding *is* "continuous" the proper formula is

$$FV = PV(e)^{i*n} \qquad (2)$$

where:

e is the base of the natural logarithm system, 2.71828;

n is the number of time periods;

i is the interest (growth) rate.

With respect *only* to money growth if compounding is continuous, *this has to be stated in the problem*. The proper equation is then Equation (2).

If no declaration of continuous compounding is made, it is assumed compounding is *not* continuous, and Equation (1) is appropriate.

3.  If the exponential function applies to germs, insects, or, more appropriately for a business-oriented course, customers, net exports, *continuous* compound interest (as noted above), radioactive decay, population growth, plant growth, etc. (basically, anything other than money growth that is *not* continuous), it is recognized that growth or decay occurs in a continuous manner. Thus, we find that Equation (3) is always appropriate *whether or not* the declaration of continuous growth is made:

$$N_t = N_0 e^{k*t} \qquad (3)$$

Equation (3) is the same as Equation (2) except that customarily the symbols in (2) apply when the matter involves the *continuous* compounding of *money* and (3) applies if the matter focuses on the growth ($k > 0$) or decay ($k < 0$) of something *other* than money.

4.  This is because germs, sales, population, etc. are *always* changing at a constant rate. That is, the growth or decay process is continuous. While quarterly compounding of money is *halted* and then started every quarter (that is, not continuously), the growth of population, customers, germs, etc. is continuous. Population grows at a certain constant rate. Population does not hold constant at a certain amount (as would money in an account) and then jump to a new level instantaneously as would an addition of interest to the account. The growth is continuous—not discrete. Thus, e is the proper tool to use in computations.

# Chapter 10

# SIMULTANEOUS EQUATIONS

## Two-Stage Least Squares

## INTRODUCTION

Until now we have been using only one equation to display the relationship between and among our variables. However, there are many instances in which economic phenomena can be adequately explained only by two or more equations. A system of *simultaneous equations* is needed to examine many common and crucial issues essential to a full comprehension of how the world works. The classical example of such a case is a market in which the equilibrium price, $P^*$, and the equilibrium quantity, $Q^*$, are determined simultaneously in the market by the intersection of the supply curve and the demand curve. Here *two* equations are needed to solve for the prevailing market conditions because two values need to be determined: equilibrium price and equilibrium quantity.

Simultaneity occurs under many business and economic conditions due to the interconnection between two (or more) dependent variables that must be jointly determined. Presume a system of two equations such that $Y_1 = f(Y_2, X_1, X_2, X_3)$ and $Y_2 = f(Y_1, X_2, X_4)$. Each of the $Y$-variables is, in part, a function of the other. Any change in one affects the other and neither can be determined without the other. They must be jointly determined.

A classic depiction of the simultaneous nature of equation systems is offered by the standard Keynesian macro-economic model of income determination.[1] In its simplest form, the model is expressed as

$$C_t = \beta_0 + \beta_1 Y_t + \varepsilon_t \tag{1}$$

$$Y_t = C_t + I_t \tag{2}$$

where $C_t$ is personal consumption expenditures at time $t$, $Y_t$ is personal income at time period $t$, and $I_t$ is business investment expenditures at time period $t$. In this basic model the economy is presumed to be closed in that no foreign trade takes place. Further, there is no government involvement.

Here we can clearly see the *feedback* or simultaneous nature of the model. Income affects consumption through Equation (1), but consumption is a component of income in Equation (2). Thus, $C$ and $Y$ are interdependent, or jointly determined, and must be determined simultaneously.

Equation (1) is a *behavioral* or *structural* equation in that it describes the structure of a segment of the economy: specifically, the consumption sector. It describes the behavior of consumers. Equation (2) is actually an *identity* in that it is true by definition. Income is equal to consumption plus business investment.

There are many more instances in which simultaneity occurs in business and economic modeling. This chapter examines the nature of these simultaneous systems and how they can be solved to avoid bias in estimation efforts. This chapter also demonstrates how to *identify* the system of equations so that they may be estimated using the process of two-stage least squares

(2SLS) that results in solution values. Let's begin with a simple two-equation model based on supply and demand functions.

## 10.1 THE TWO-EQUATION MODEL

Presume we wish to estimate the demand and supply functions (curves) for bread as seen in Equations (10.1.1) and (10.1.2), respectively. The objective is to determine equilibrium price and quantity in the market. This model offers a different perspective to the problem of simultaneity from that presented in the Keynesian model above. In the case of the Keynesian system, each equation contained on its right-hand side the dependent variable from the other equation. Here the same dependent variable appears on the RHS of both equations. In this case the troublesome dependent variable is price. In order to establish market equilibrium conditions, both price and quantity must be determined. However, as shown in the system presented here, price falls on the RHS of both equations:

$$Q_d = \beta_0 + \beta_1 P + \beta_2 I + \varepsilon_d \qquad (10.1.1)$$

$$Q_s = \alpha_0 + \alpha_1 P + \alpha_2 F + \alpha_3 Y + \varepsilon_s \qquad (10.1.2)$$

where:

$P$ is the market price of the bread;

$I$ is consumer income;

$F$ is the cost of flour;

$Y$ is the cost of yeast.

Notice that the price of bread is on the RHS in both equations even though it is a dependent variable. Even though it is seen as a dependent variable because it must be determined by the system of equations to identify equilibrium, it appears on the RHS. Therein "lies the rub" as we shall see. Equations (10.1.1) and (10.1.2) are both *structural* (or *behavior*) equations. They show how economic agents behave in the market and define its internal theoretical structure.

Some of the variables are *endogenous* in that they are determined *within* (i.e., *by*) the system. Specifically, the price and quantity of bread are resolved simultaneously by the interaction of the supply and demand functions. These are the variables the system is designed to determine. As with any system of equations, there must be at least as many equations as there are endogenous variables if the system is to be solved.

A third equation, $Q_d = Q_s$ (actually, it's an *identity*), is often added to the system. Given this equality we can express quantity as a single variable: $Q_d = Q_s = Q$. We then have two equations and only two unknowns, $Q$ and $P$.

The other variables are determined outside the market-model for bread and are considered *exogenous*. Prices for flour and yeast are set in their own markets, not within this market for bread. The same is true for income. It is set in the labor market separate from our market for bread. These variables are introduced into our model as "givens" and are seen as exogenous.

The model may contain *predetermined variables* in the form of past, or lagged, values of endogenous variables. If either of the two equations above contained previous prices for bread in earlier time periods, they would be treated as exogenous even though at one time they were established by our model for bread. We thus have endogenous variables and exogenous variables, including predetermined endogenous variables.

> Endogenous variables are determined by and within the system in the current time period. Exogenous variables are determined outside the current system and are taken as givens to be introduced into the system. Exogenous variables may include predetermined values of lagged endogenous variables from previous time periods.

## 10.2 SIMULTANEITY BIAS

Unfortunately, we cannot use standard OLS methods to estimate the structural equations due to *simultaneity bias*. This bias occurs because in the simultaneous system we find that two RHS variables are correlated. This is a violation of one of the basic assumptions of the OLS model. As a result, OLS estimates would produce bias and inconsistent results. The expected value of a coefficient is not equal to the actual coefficient: $E(\hat{\beta}_1) \neq \beta_i$.

Any change in $Y$, the dependent variable, not explained by a change in $X$ must be attributed to the error term, $\varepsilon$. If the error term for any given observation is elevated, this means that $Y$ will increase. Therefore, $Y$ and $\varepsilon$ are correlated. This is not a problem. It occurs in every regression model.

However, applying this to Equation (10.1.1) tells us that $Q$ and $\varepsilon$ are correlated. Since the system of equations determines $P$ and $Q$ simultaneously, that means that $P$ and $Q$ are related. Thus, in Equation (10.1.1) $P$ and $\varepsilon$ must be correlated. That is, if $Q$ and $\varepsilon$ are correlated via Equation (10.1.1) and $Q$ and $P$ are correlated because they are determined jointly, then $P$ and $\varepsilon$ must be correlated. Thus, the two RHS values in Equation (10.1.1), $P$ and $\varepsilon$, are related. The same reasoning is applied to Equation (10.1.2). This is in violation of the basic assumptions upon which OLS is based.

The correlation between $Q$ and $\varepsilon$ in Equation (10.1.1) is no problem. $Q$ is on the LHS, as are all well-behaved dependent variables. We always expect a relationship between the dependent variable and the error term. But $P$ is on the RHS of both equations. Thus, the correlation between $P$ and $\varepsilon$ is problematic.

Simultaneity bias occurs in a system of equations when the error term, $\varepsilon$, is correlated with an endogenous variable appearing on the RHS of the equation.

## 10.3 THE REDUCED-FORM EQUATIONS

Since Equations (10.1.1) and (10.1.2) cannot be estimated due to the presence of endogenous variables on the RHS, we must rewrite them into a form that can be estimated. This requires that we remove all endogenous variables from the RHS. Only exogenous variables can appear on the RHS. These are called the *reduced-form equations*.

After considerable algebraic manipulation (not shown here) we can express the reduced-form equations as

$$Q = \Pi_0 + \Pi_1 I + \Pi_2 F + \Pi_3 Y + \varepsilon \tag{10.3.1}$$

$$P = \Omega_0 + \Omega_1 I + \Omega_2 F + \Omega_3 Y + \varepsilon \tag{10.3.2}$$

Equations (10.3.1) and (10.3.2) have *only* exogenous variables on the RHS and can now be estimated with OLS standard methods. Take note that the parameters have changed. They are now symbolized by $\Pi$ (Greek letter pi) and $\Omega$ (Greek letter omega). They are parameters, but not parameters of the all-important structural equations defined above as Equations (10.1.1) and (10.1.2). They are *not* estimates of the slopes of the supply and demand curves.

The reduced-form equations are *not* the supply and demand equations. They tell us very little about the way consumers and suppliers respond to changes in price, income, and other determinants of supply and demand. The structural equations, Equations (10.1.1) and (10.1.2), do that. But Equations (10.3.1) and (10.3.2) do allow us now to estimate their parameters without interference from simultaneous bias because there are no endogenous variables on the RHS. They do show us how changes in the exogenous variables affect price and quantity.

## 10.4 THE IDENTIFICATION PROBLEM

We can now estimate the reduced-form equations without the simultaneous bias that plagues Equations (10.1.1) and (10.1.2). But we can do so only if the equations are properly *identified*. Under usual conditions neither the supply curve nor the demand curve can be fully observed. This is because we generally do not have data points that prescribe the curves. In the market place we can detect only those points where they cross at equilibrium. Figure 10.1 demonstrates this problem.

For example, we may have only certain points of equilibrium such as points $A$, $B$, and $C$. However, these do not provide any information about the supply and demand curves other than the fact

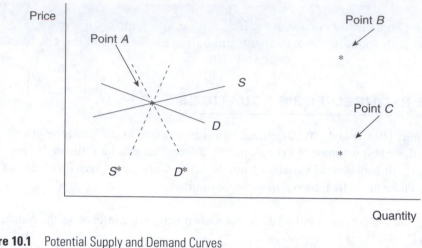

**■ Figure 10.1**   Potential Supply and Demand Curves

that the curves crossed at those points producing conditions of equilibrium. It's unknown whether point $A$, for example, was created by the intersection of the solid supply and demand curves ($S$ and $D$) or the broken lines representing the supply and demand curves ($S^*$ and $D^*$)—or by $D$ and $S^*$ for that matter. The shape, slope, and positioning of the actual curves are unknown.

We must find a variable that causes one of the curves to shift along the other curve which in turn remains stationary. Such a variable is often referred to as a *shift parameter*. Let's use the variable Income in that capacity. As Income rises, the demand curve will shift up and to the right. This is depicted in Figure 10.2. As Income goes up, the demand curve will shift up from $D_1$ to $D_2$ and on to $D_3$ but the supply curve will remain stable. This occurs because demand is a function (in part) of Income but supply is not. Any change in Income will impact demand but leave supply unchanged. The result is to trace out the supply curve along those equilibrium points, thereby identifying its shape, slope, and position.

Income becomes an *instrumental variable* (IV) in this process. An instrumental variable is an *exogenous* variable within the model that is excluded from at least one of the equations in the system.

> An instrumental variable (IV) for one equation is an exogenous variable that does *not* appear in that equation but does appear in at least one other equation in the system.

To be properly identified an equation must have one IV for each RHS endogenous variable. To illustrate, presume this structural system:

$$Y_1 = \alpha_0 + \alpha_1 Y_2 + \alpha_2 Y_3 + \alpha_3 X_1 + \alpha_4 X_2 + \varepsilon_1 \tag{1}$$

$$Y_2 = \beta_0 + \beta_1 Y_1 + \beta_2 Y_3 + \beta_3 X_2 + \beta_4 X_3 + \beta_5 X_4 + \varepsilon_2 \tag{2}$$

$$Y_3 = \Omega_0 + \Omega_1 Y_1 + \Omega_2 Y_2 + \Omega_3 X_3 + \varepsilon_3 \tag{3}$$

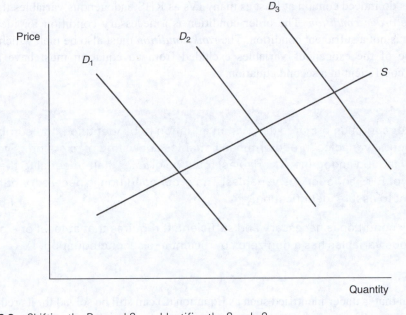

where the $Y$s are endogenous variables and the $X$s are exogenous variables. The system has three endogenous variables and four exogenous variables.

Equation (1) has two RHS endogenous variables, $Y_2$ and $Y_3$. It therefore needs two IVs. That is, the system must have two $X$-variables that are *not* in Equation (1). These variables would be $X_3$ and $X_4$, both of which are in the system, but not in Equation (1). Therefore, Equation (1) is said to be *just identified*; it has the same number of RHS endogenous variables as IVs and can therefore be solved.

Equation (2) has two RHS endogenous variables, $Y_1$ and $Y_3$. But it has only one IV. That would be $X_1$ in that it is an exogenous variable that is in the system, but not in Equation (2). It is said to be *under-identified* because it has fewer IVs than it does RHS endogenous variables. It therefore cannot be solved.

Finally, Equation (3) has two RHS endogenous variables, $Y_1$ and $Y_2$. But there are three exogenous variables in the system that are not in Equation (3). It has three IVs. They are $X_1$, $X_2$, and $X_4$. Equation (3) is *over-identified* because it has more IVs than it does RHS endogenous variables. This equation can be solved but it may lead to more than one solution.

For an equation to be properly identified it must have one IV for each RHS endogenous variable.

If equations do indeed contain at least as many IVs as RHS endogenous variables they are said to meet the *order condition*. The order condition is a necessary condition for identification. However, it is not a sufficient condition. The *rank condition* must also be met, which states that at least one of the exogenous variables excluded from an equation must have a non-zero population coefficient in a second equation.

> The order condition requires that, for an equation to be identified, the number of instrumental variables (predetermined variables consisting of exogenous variables plus any lagged endogenous variables) must be greater than or equal to the number of RHS endogenous variables. The order condition is necessary but not sufficient to assure identification.
>
> The rank condition is necessary and sufficient. It requires that at least one of the exogenous variables has a non-zero coefficient in a second equation.

An equation that is under-identified such as Equation (2) can still be solved for its reduced form. This allows us to determine how changes in the exogenous variables affect the equilibrium position in the market. However, we cannot solve for the parameters in the structural form of the equation using standard OLS techniques. Instead, *two-stage least squares* (2SLS) must be applied as demonstrated below.

### ● Finding the Proxy

This correlation between any one of the RHS variables and the error term is the cause of the bias and inconsistent estimates provided by OLS. To rid the estimates of such bias requires finding a proxy (IV) for the offending RHS variable. This is done by regressing the troublesome variable on all exogenous variables (including predetermined, lagged variables).

Consider the system

$$Y_1 = \alpha_0 + \alpha_1 X_1 + \alpha_2 X_2 + \alpha_3 Y_2 + \mu_1 \tag{1}$$

$$Y_2 = \beta_0 + \beta_1 Y_1 + \mu_2 \tag{2}$$

The likely correlation between $Y_1$ and $\mu_2$ in (2) requires that we find some proxy, or IV, for $Y_1$ that is similar to $Y_1$ but not correlated with $\mu_2$.

We begin by regressing $Y_1$ on all exogenous variables. In this case there are only two exogenous variables, $X_1$ and $X_2$:

$$Y_1 = \Pi_0 + \Pi_1 X_1 + \Pi_2 X_2 + v \tag{3}$$

The parameters can be expressed as $\Pi$, since they will differ from those in Equations (1) and (2) above. Estimating (3) yields

$$\hat{Y}_1 = \hat{\pi}_0 + \hat{\pi}_1 X_1 + \hat{\pi}_2 X_2 \tag{4}$$

thereby providing estimates of the $\Pi$ in (3) symbolized as $\hat{\pi}$ as evidenced by the presence of "hats" (carets), which customarily characterize estimates.

Substituting (4) into (3) yields

$$Y_1 = \hat{Y}_1 + v \tag{5}$$

which shows that $Y_1$ consists of the exogenous variables, $X_1$ and $X_2$, plus the random variable $v$. Following standard OLS principles, this means that $\hat{Y}_1$ and $v$ are uncorrelated. Therefore we can safely use $\hat{Y}$ as a proxy in place of $Y_1$. Equation (2) is then estimated as

$$Y_2 = \beta_0' + \beta_1' \hat{Y}_1 + \Omega \tag{6}$$

Now we can estimate (1). Or can we? Why or why not?

> A proxy is an IV that replaces the offending RHS dependent variable that is correlated with the error term but itself is *not* correlated with the error term.

## 10.5 AN ILLUSTRATION OF 2SLS

Now that we have a basic conceptual understanding of the conditions prompting the use of 2SLS, let's take a look at a hypothetical case before returning to our supply and demand functions for bread (Equations (10.1.1) and (10.1.2)). Presume this new system of structural equations:

$$Y_1 = \beta_0 + \beta_1 Y_2 + \beta_2 X_1 + \beta_3 X_2 + \varepsilon_1 \tag{1}$$

$$Y_2 = \Omega_0 + \Omega_1 Y_1 + \Omega_2 X_1 + \Omega_3 X_3 + \varepsilon_2 \tag{2}$$

where the $Y$s are endogenous variables and the $X$s are exogenous variables.

Equation (1) has one RHS endogenous variable, $Y_2$. It must therefore have one IV. $X_3$ serves in that capacity; it is in the system (in Equation (2) to be specific) but not in Equation (1). Equation (2) has one RHS endogenous variable, $Y_1$. It also has one IV, $X_2$, which is in the system (in Equation (1)) but not in Equation (2).

Both equations suffer from simultaneity bias as discussed above in Section 10.2. Each equation violates Gauss–Markov principles by the fact that in both equations correlations appear on the RHS. In Equation (1), $Y_2$ and $\varepsilon_1$ are correlated. In Equation (2), $Y_1$ and $\varepsilon_2$ are correlated. OLS cannot be used to solve the system. 2SLS is required.

■ **Stage 1:** We must first create the reduced forms of the equations by placing all exogenous variables on the RHS of each equation:

$$Y_1 = \lambda_0 + \lambda_1 X_1 + \lambda_2 X_2 + \lambda_3 X_3 + \mu_1 \tag{3}$$

$$Y_2 = \Pi_0 + \Pi_1 X_1 + \Pi_2 X_2 + \Pi_3 X_3 + \mu_2 \tag{4}$$

Next, we simply regress $Y_1$ and $Y_2$ on all exogenous variables as per Equations (3) and (4), being careful to save the estimated values, $\hat{Y}_1$ and $\hat{Y}_2$.

The exogenous variables in (3) and (4) are uncorrelated with the error terms, $\mu_i$. Therefore, the estimators, $\lambda$ and $\Pi$, are unbiased. They can then be used to provide unbiased estimates of the endogenous variables. These estimates of $Y_1$ and $Y_2$ are saved as $\hat{Y}_1$ and $\hat{Y}_2$. These estimates are then used as replacements in the structural equations in Stage 2.

■ **Stage 2:** Now return to the structural equations (1) and (2). Replace the $Y_1$ values with the $\hat{Y}_1$ values from Stage 1 and the $Y_2$ values with the $\hat{Y}_2$ values from Stage 1 as shown in Equations (5) and (6):

$$Y_1 = \beta_0 + \beta_1 \hat{Y}_2 + \beta_2 X_1 + \beta_3 X_2 + \varepsilon_1 \tag{5}$$

$$Y_2 = \Omega_0 + \Omega_1 \hat{Y}_1 + \Omega_2 X_1 + \Omega_3 X_3 + \varepsilon_2 \tag{6}$$

Equations (5) and (6) can now be estimated with OLS procedures. They contain no endogenous RHS variables. That is, $Y_1$ and $Y_2$, the endogenous variables, have been replaced. In (5), $\hat{Y}_2$ has replaced $Y_2$ and in (6), $\hat{Y}_1$ has replaced $Y_1$.

In this manner we are capturing all the information provided by all the exogenous variables. Nothing is lost. This benefit is attained since the reduced-form equations contain all exogenous variables as explanatory factors. The entire wealth of all explanatory power is encapsulated by the reduced-form equations in Stage 1 and inserted into the structural equations in Stage 2.

## 10.6 APPLYING 2SLS TO OUR MARKET FOR BREAD

Returning to our model for the supply and demand for bread, recall that the system of structural equations consisted of

$$Q_d = \beta_0 + \beta_1 P + \beta_2 I + \varepsilon_d \tag{10.1.1}$$

$$Q_s = \alpha_0 + \alpha_1 P + \alpha_2 F + \alpha_3 Y + \varepsilon_s \tag{10.1.2}$$

We must first determine if the equations are identified. Equation (10.1.1) has one RHS endogenous variable (price) and two IVs ($F$ and $Y$). This means we can use 2SLS to estimate it. Equation (10.1.2) has one RHS endogenous variable (price) and one IV ($I$). It has at least as many IVs as it does RHS endogenous variables. Therefore, it too can be estimated.

In the illustration in Section 10.5, Equation (1) had one RHS endogenous variable, $Y_2$, and Equation (2) had one endogenous variable, $Y_1$. Therefore we had to estimate two reduced-form equations, (5) and (6). Equation (5) was necessary to obtain $\hat{Y}_2$, and Equation (6) had to be estimated to derive $\hat{Y}_1$.

In our present model there is only one RHS endogenous variable in the entire system, $P$. Thus, we have only to estimate one reduced-form equation in which price is regressed on all exogenous variables in the system, $I$, $F$, and $Y_e$. Therefore, the only reduced-form equation necessary is $P = f(I,F,Y_e)$. Thus, we have

$$P = \lambda_0 + \lambda_1 I + \lambda_2 F + \lambda_3 Y + \varepsilon$$

This will provide $\hat{P}$, which can be used to replace $P$ in both of the structural equations, (10.1.1) and (10.1.2).

Data pertaining to the market for bread were collected and are shown in Table 10.1. $Q$ is the number of units (tons, truck loads, loaves—however it might be measured) of bread. $P$, $F$, and $Y$ are the unit prices of the bread, flour, and yeast, respectively. $INC$ is the average income in thousands of dollars in the cities in which the data were collected. $FITS1$ is the estimate of the dependent variable generated by Minitab when a regression model is estimated. It will soon serve as $\hat{P}$.

If we were to estimate Equation (10.1.1) for the demand for bread we would suffer simultaneity bias due to the presence of an endogenous variable, $P$, on the RHS. Therefore, we must regress

■ **Table 10.1**   Data for the Bread Market

| Q | P | INC | F | Y | FITS1 |
|---|---|-----|---|---|-------|
| 115.25 | 1.25 | 32 | 2.3 | 6.9 | 2.717754 |
| 121.54 | 3.25 | 36 | 2.5 | 9.5 | 2.476553 |
| 211.3 | 2.56 | 58 | 3.5 | 3.5 | 2.688086 |
| 168.3 | 3.58 | 47 | 1.5 | 4.5 | 2.614593 |
| 251.86 | 2.47 | 69 | 3.8 | 5.2 | 2.419872 |
| 321.97 | 1.69 | 87 | 4.6 | 5.9 | 2.164276 |
| 133.34 | 2.78 | 39 | 3.8 | 3.8 | 2.970354 |
| 196.77 | 3.54 | 57 | 5.9 | 4.3 | 2.834039 |
| 212.44 | 2.48 | 59 | 4.3 | 3.8 | 2.714472 |

$P$ on all exogenous variables in the model as per Equation (10.3.2), being careful to save the estimated values for $P$. These values, $\hat{P}$, are then used in the structural equations.

SPSS performs the analysis in one step. To estimate the demand curve you need only to choose

$$\text{Analyze} > \text{Regression} > \text{2SLS}$$

Then enter $Q$ in the Dependent window, $P$ and $I$ in the Explanatory window, and $I$, $F$, and $Y$ in the Instrumental window.

> To apply SPSS to the solution, you must enter the dependent variable in the Dependent window, the explanatory variables for that equation in the Explanatory window, and *all* of the IVs for the entire system (not just the IVs for that equation) in the Instrumental window.

The results are shown in Table 10.2. Similarly, the supply curve requires that $Q$ be entered in the Dependent window, $P$, $F$, and $Y$ in the Explanatory window, and $I$, $F$, and $Y$ in the Instrumental window. The supply curve is also displayed in Table 10.2.

■ **Table 10.2**    The Demand and Supply Curves for Bread Using SPSS

Demand Curve:

**Coefficients**

| | | Unstandardized Coefficients | | | | |
| | | B | Std. Error | Beta | t | Sig. |
|---|---|---|---|---|---|---|
| Equation 1 | (Constant) | 14.818 | 34.845 | | .425 | .685 |
| | P | −9.260 | 11.062 | −.109 | −.837 | .435 |
| | INC | 3.756 | .152 | .977 | 24.759 | .000 |

Supply Curve:

**Coefficients**

| | | Unstandardized Coefficients | | | | |
| | | B | Std. Error | Beta | t | Sig. |
|---|---|---|---|---|---|---|
| Equation 1 | (Constant) | 935.302 | 1346.999 | | .694 | .518 |
| | P | −267.156 | 419.291 | −3.135 | −.637 | .552 |
| | Flour | 18.525 | 72.741 | .367 | .255 | .809 |
| | Yeast | −20.603 | 56.170 | −.593 | −.367 | .729 |

With some other software packages the procedure must be performed in two steps. Minitab requires that you regress $P$ on $INC$, $F$, and $Y$. To save the estimated values for $P$, from the Regression menu you must click on Storage > Fits. This is seen in the last column in Table 10.1.

Next estimate the structural equations, (10.1.1) and (10.1.2), using the estimated values for $P$ you have saved from the first step. The demand and supply curves estimated in this way are shown in Table 10.3. In both cases, $FITS1$ is the estimated values for $P$ produced by Minitab in Stage 1. A similar two-step process is used with Excel.

The beta-estimates are identical under both approaches. Whether the final estimates are provided in one step using SPSS or two steps with Minitab, the coefficients are the same. However, quite different results are reported in terms of the $t$-statistics and the $p$-values (remember, SPSS calls the $p$-values "Sig"). It is generally agreed that the application of the one-step method permitted by SPSS is preferred. If the steps are completed separately as required by Excel and Minitab the $t$-statistics and standard errors will not be correct. This happens because the software doesn't realize that the second phase is part of a 2SLS estimation.

Using the output from Table 10.2, we can see in the demand curve that while price carries the expected sign, it does not report as a significant explanatory variable. Speculation might lead us to believe that the price of bread is so low relative to other food products that it is given little consideration by shoppers in determining their buying habits. More research is called for to make a final determination in that regard. Income reveals a positive and significant relationship to demand. That's why, as Figure 10.2 illustrates, income served as an instrumental variable by generating different demand curves that traced out the supply curve.

Just as an analytical exercise, what might we conclude if income had reported in with a negative sign? That would suggest that as income falls, the consumption of bread increases. This might be explained by the fact that lower-income families substitute more bread in their diets as an alternative for more expensive food products. Again, additional research is in order to explain that potential outcome.

■ **Table 10.3**　2SLS With Minitab

**Demand Curve:**

| Predictor | Coef | SE Coef | T | P |
|---|---|---|---|---|
| Constant | 14.82 | 25.92 | 0.57 | 0.588 |
| INC | 3.7561 | 0.1128 | 33.29 | 0.000 |
| FITS1 | -9.260 | 8.227 | -1.13 | 0.303 |

S = 4.29581 R-Sq = 99.7% R-Sq(adj) = 99.6%

**Supply Curve:**

| Predictor | Coef | SE Coef | T | P |
|---|---|---|---|---|
| Constant | 935.30 | 18.66 | 50.12 | 0.000 |
| F | 18.525 | 1.008 | 18.38 | 0.000 |
| YE | -20.6031 | 0.7782 | -26.48 | 0.000 |
| FITS1 | -267.156 | 5.809 | -45.99 | 0.000 |

S = 3.47135 R-Sq = 99.8% R-Sq(adj) = 99.7%

Surprisingly, all the variables in the supply curve generated by SPSS are insignificant. In contrast, Minitab reports highly significant results for all variables. However, their signs require some consideration. The negative coefficient for the price of bread ($FITS1$) and the positive coefficient for the price of flour are difficult to explain. We would anticipate just the opposite signs in both cases. As the price of bread increases we would expect the quantity of supply to rise, not fall. Further, how can we explain the positive relationship between the supply of bread and the price of flour? Flour serves as a cost of production for the baker. As production costs rise the market would dictate a decline in supply. Only further efforts at market analysis might provide answers to these perplexing problems. However, it's quite likely that these abnormalities occurred because, as Table 10.2 reveals, the variables are not significant in the first place. The most likely explanation is, as mentioned above, Minitab produces mistaken $t$-values and standard errors in the second-stage analysis.

Some small-sample bias may still remain even in the 2SLS estimates. But the extent of the bias diminishes rapidly as the sample size increases. Thus, the larger the sample size the greater the improvement in the 2SLS estimates over those provided by OLS. The 2SLS fit also improves if the IV is closely correlated with the endogenous variable you are trying to replace. Finally, the fit is also better if the first stage has a high adjusted coefficient of determination.

## 10.7 A COMPARISON OF 2SLS AND OLS

A brief comparison of the two methods of estimation is in order. If an OLS estimate of the demand curve is attempted the results may seem quite impressive, as displayed in Table 10.4. The standard error of the estimate, $S_e$, is 3.2 and the $R^2$ is an inspiring 0.998. The coefficients take on the expected signs but differ considerably from those obtained using 2SLS. All looks quite well in the world. However, therein lies the trap. Despite the seemingly favorable results you as the researcher must recognize that simultaneity most likely plagues the system. These impressive results must therefore be called into question!

It's also borne out in this comparison that OLS estimates are generally greater than those provided by 2SLS. For Price, the OLS estimate of $-3.887$ exceeds the 2SLS estimate of $-9.26$. The same is true for Income. The OLS estimate for Income is 3.803, which is greater than the 3.756 reported by 2SLS.

> If OLS is used to estimate a simultaneous model suffering correlation between RHS variables the estimates will be biased and inconsistent. This results because the OLS procedure will attribute changes in the dependent variable to one or more of the independent variables that should actually be associated with the error term.

■ **Table 10.4** An OLS Estimate of the Demand Curve

**Coefficients[a]**

| Model | | Unstandardized Coefficients | | Standardized Coefficients | t | Sig. |
|---|---|---|---|---|---|---|
| | | B | Std. Error | Beta | | |
| 1 | (Constant) | −1.805 | 5.807 | | −.311 | .766 |
| | p | −3.887 | 1.462 | −.046 | −2.658 | .038 |
| | i | 3.803 | .066 | .989 | 57.642 | .000 |

a. Dependent Variable: q

## EXAMPLE 10.1:  A 2SLS Look at Liverpool

**Problem Statement**: Financial analysts for Liverpool Industries have informed management that profit levels are beginning to drop to alarmingly low levels. To combat this trend, profit estimates must be devised. The necessary system of equations recognizes that profit depends on costs of production, product price, and the quantity of production. The cost function also depends on quantity as well as the wage rate. It is further understood that profits affect the ability to produce and incur costs. The system can be summed up as

$$Profit = f(Cost, Price, Quantity)$$

$$Cost = f(Quantity, Wages, Profits)$$

The feedback between profits and costs necessitates two-stage least squares. The data for this illustration are contained in the file LIVERPOOL.

**Solution**: We must first determine if the equations are identified. Is there an exogenous variable in one equation that is not in the other? That is, can we identify an instrumental variable for both equations? The endogenous variables are Profit and Cost. The exogenous variables are Quantity, Wages, and Price. The profit function does *not* contain Wages. It serves as the IV for the Profit function. The Cost function does *not* contain Price which serves as the IV for that function.

Now it is necessary to create the reduced-form equations. Remember, there will be one reduced-form equation for each endogenous variable and each expression will contain all exogenous variables. They are

$$Profit = f(Quantity, Wages, Price)$$

and

$$Cost = f(Quantity, Wages, Price)$$

Using Minitab, these functions are then estimated and the values for estimated Profits (PROFITSHAT) and Costs (COSTSHAT) are retained. They are used to estimate the structural equations. The Profits function becomes *Profits* = f(*CostHat, Price, Quantity*) and the Cost function is *Cost* = f(*Quantity, Wages, ProfitsHat*). The results of the regression runs are shown here.

```
The regression equation is
PROFIT = 2800 - 1.44 COSTHAT + 22.0 PRICE + 0.525 QUANTITY

Predictor    Coef    SE Coef      T       P
Constant    2799.6     163.3    17.14   0.000
```

*(Continued)*

**EXAMPLE 10.1: (Continued)**

```
COSTHAT      -1.4446       0.3162      -4.57      0.000
PRICE        22.009        5.500        4.00      0.000
QUANTITY      0.5251       0.2629       2.00      0.056
```

S = 84.4308 R-Sq = 71.3% R-Sq(adj) = 68.0%

The regression equation is
COST = -2986 + 1.84 QUANTITY + 67.0 WAGE + 0.421 PROFITHAT

```
Predictor      Coef      SE Coef        T         P
Constant      -2986       1575       -1.90      0.069
QUANTITY      1.8367      0.4878      3.76      0.001
WAGE          66.99       24.38       2.75      0.011
PROFITHAT     0.4213      0.3072      1.37      0.182
```

S = 56.7928 R-Sq = 77.2% R-Sq(adj) = 74.5%

SPSS produces these results in one step.

For the Profit function, we find

**Coefficients**

| | | Unstandardized Coefficients | | Beta | t | Sig. |
|---|---|---|---|---|---|---|
| | | B | Std. Error | | | |
| Equation 1 | (Constant) | 2799.555 | 304.439 | | 9.196 | .000 |
| | Cost | −1.445 | .589 | −1.089 | −2.451 | .021 |
| | Price | 22.009 | 10.252 | .437 | 2.147 | .041 |
| | Quantity | .525 | .490 | .415 | 1.072 | .294 |

Notice the similarities in the coefficients and the differences in the *t*-values and *p*-values.

The Cost function is

**Coefficients**

| | | Unstandardized Coefficients | | Beta | t | Sig. |
|---|---|---|---|---|---|---|
| | | B | Std. Error | | | |
| Equation 1 | (Constant) | −2985.626 | 1003.831 | | −2.974 | .006 |
| | Quantity | 1.837 | .311 | 1.925 | 5.908 | .000 |
| | Wage | 66.989 | 15.533 | 1.271 | 4.313 | .000 |
| | Profit | .421 | .196 | .559 | 2.152 | .041 |

**Interpretation:** The interpretation is the same as for all regression models. The coefficients and their levels of significance can clearly be discerned. Access the file LIVERPOOL, repeat the steps above, and check to see if you get the results reported in the example. Compare the results of OLS.

# 10.8 THE DURBIN–WU–HAUSMAN TEST FOR SIMULTANEITY

In the examples cited above, the presence of an RHS endogenous variable and the simultaneity it can cause were fairly obvious. There was little need to question whether the problem existed.

In many other cases we may find this is not the case. It is possible for simultaneity to creep into a model unnoticed due to the use of an exogenous RHS variable. If the researcher has some question as to whether an RHS variable may indeed be correlated with the error term it is possible to conduct a simple test.[2]

First, using OLS techniques regress the suspect RHS variable on all exogenous variables, just as you would with a reduced-form equation, being careful to save the error terms. Then estimate the structural form of the equation in which the suspect variable is found *including* the error terms you saved from the previous model as an independent variable. A simple *t*-test for the significance of the coefficient for the error variable is conducted to determine if simultaneity exists. If the error term is significant, it is providing some explanatory value for the dependent variable in the structural equation. This should not happen. As we know, the error terms should be wholly random, offering no contribution to the explanation of changes in the dependent variable. If this is not the case, if the error term's coefficient displays significance, simultaneity is presumed, necessitating the use of 2SLS.

---

**EXAMPLE 10.2: Does Liverpool Need 2SLS?**

**Problem Statement**: Applying Durbin–Wu–Hausman to our Liverpool Industries example to test Cost for simultaneity, we must first estimate the reduced-form equation *Cost* = f(*Quantity, Price, Wages*), ensuring that we save the error terms. The structural form of the Profits function including the errors is then estimated. A *t*-test is then imposed on the coefficient of the error terms to determine if it is significant.

**Solution**: The results of the transformed structural form are shown here where RESI1 is the error term.

```
The regression equation is
PROFIT = 2800 - 1.44 COST + 22.0 PRICE + 0.525 QUANTITY + 2.62 RESI1

Predictor    Coef    SE Coef      T       P
Constant    2799.6    102.7     27.26   0.000
```

*(Continued)*

---

**EXAMPLE 10.2: (Continued)**

| | | | | |
|---|---|---|---|---|
| COST | -1.4446 | 0.1988 | -7.27 | 0.000 |
| PRICE | 22.009 | 3.458 | 6.36 | 0.000 |
| QUANTITY | 0.5251 | 0.1653 | 3.18 | 0.004 |
| RESI1 | 2.6150 | 0.2704 | 9.67 | 0.000 |

S = 53.0857 R-Sq = 89.1% R-Sq(adj) = 87.4%

**Interpretation:** The error terms report as highly significant with a *p*-value of 0.000, evidencing simultaneity bias and justifying the need for 2SLS. The error terms should offer no significant explanatory value. Based on the assumptions of standard OLS models, the error terms should be totally random and independent. Their unequivocal significance testifies to the contrary. A like test for Profits produced surprising results. Try it and see.

---

## 10.9 A MACROECONOMIC MODEL

Basic macroeconomic theory leans heavily on the Keynesian model offered by the noted British economist John Maynard Keynes (1883–1946). In a highly simplistic form we can state the following set of simultaneous equations based loosely on his model:

$$GNP = C + I + G \tag{1}$$

$$C = f(Y, W) \tag{2}$$

$$I_v = f(GNP, r) \tag{3}$$

$$Y = GNP - T \tag{4}$$

where *GNP* is a nation's gross national product, *C* is personal consumption, *Y* is private disposable income, $I_v$ is private business investment, *r* is the interest rate, and *T* is personal taxes. These are the structural equations that represent the economic system. Only Equations (2) and (3) are behavior equations that portray the conduct of economic participants and only they have to be estimated. Equations (1) and (4) are identities and can be determined by summation.

The endogenous variables are *GNP*, *C*, $I_v$, and *Y*. The remaining variables are exogenous. Satisfy yourself that the two structural equations are identified. Can you state the reduced form of the system? A problem at the end of this chapter deals directly with this model.

# CHAPTER PROBLEMS

## Conceptual Problems

1. Define and give examples of each of the following:
   A. Endogenous variables.
   B. Exogenous variables.
   C. Pre-determined variables.
   D. Structural equations.
   E. Reduced-form equations.
   F. Order and rank conditions.
   G. Shift parameter.

2. Given these structural systems in which the $Y$-variables are endogenous and the $X$-variables are exogenous, place them in reduced form:

   A. $Y_1 = \alpha_0 + \alpha_1 Y_2 + \alpha_2 Y_3 + \alpha_3 X_1 + \alpha_4 X_2 + \varepsilon_1$
      $Y_2 = \beta_0 + \beta_1 Y_1 + \beta_2 Y_3 + \beta_3 X_2 + \beta_4 X_3 + \beta_5 X_4 + \varepsilon_2$
      $Y_3 = \Omega_0 + \Omega_1 Y_1 + \Omega_2 Y_2 + \Omega_3 X_3 + \varepsilon_3$

   B. $Y_1 = \alpha_0 + \alpha_1 X_5 + \alpha_2 X_3 + \alpha_3 X_1 + \alpha_4 Y_2 + \varepsilon_1$
      $Y_2 = \beta_0 + \beta_1 Y_1 + \beta_2 Y_3 + \beta_4 X_3 + \beta_5 X_4 + \varepsilon_2$
      $Y_3 = \Omega_0 + \Omega_1 Y_2 + \Omega_2 Y_1 + \Omega_3 X_4 + \varepsilon_3$

   C. $Y_1 = \alpha_0 + \alpha_1 Y_2 + \alpha_2 X_3 + \alpha_3 X_1 + \varepsilon_1$
      $Y_2 = \beta_0 + \beta_1 Y_1 + \beta_2 Y_3 + \beta_3 X_2 + \beta_4 X_3 + \beta_5 X_4 + \varepsilon_2$
      $Y_3 = \Omega_0 + \Omega_1 Y_1 + \Omega_2 X_2 + \Omega_3 X_3 + \varepsilon_3$

   D. $Y_1 = \alpha_0 + \alpha_1 X_2 + \alpha_2 Y_3 + \alpha_3 X_1 + \alpha_4 X_3 + \varepsilon_1$
      $Y_2 = \beta_0 + \beta_1 Y_1 + \beta_2 Y_3 + \beta_3 X_2 + \beta_4 X_3 + \beta_5 X_4 + \varepsilon_2$
      $Y_3 = \Omega_0 + \Omega_1 Y_1 + \Omega_2 Y_2 + \Omega_3 X_3 + X_4 + \varepsilon_3$

3. Which equations are identified in each of the systems in question 2 and which are not? Explain.

4. Clearly explain under what conditions a 2SLS model is required. Construct a system of your own making that illustrates.

5. Clearly explain why bias occurs in a simultaneous system. What does your response have to do with the error terms?

6. How do the coefficients of OLS models and those obtained from 2SLS models differ? What does this say about the bias that exists in the estimations?

7. In your own words thoroughly explain the identification problem and give an example.

## Computational Problems

1. Most business offices throughout the world use photocopiers in their daily operations. The device creates copies of documents and other visual images quickly and cheaply. Most current photocopiers use a technology called xerography, which is a process relying on heat and a photoconductive drum. The drum is one of the more expensive components of the copier. Data were collected on the market activities for office copiers and saved in the file COPIERS. The demand and supply functions are to be estimated as $Q_d = f(P, Profits)$ and $Q_s = f(P, Drum, Wage)$ where $P$ is the price of the copier, $Profits$ is the quarterly profits in thousands of firms using copiers, $Drum$ is the cost of the photoconductive drum, and $Wage$ is the cost of labor. Clearly, a 2SLS model is suggested. Access the file COPIERS and perform the necessary analysis. Interpret your results.

2. Perform the Durbin–Wu–Hausman test for Price and discuss the results.

3. In a college town in the Midwest a study was conducted to examine the crime pattern prevailing over the past several academic years. Data were collected for (1) the number of crimes each year, (2) the number of students enrolled in the local college, (3) the tax collection by the city government, (4) the number of police officers on the city payroll, and (5) the number of citizens living below the poverty level. The number of crimes was thought to be a function of the number of students, the poverty measure, and the number of police officers. It was also felt that the city would establish the level of crime control in terms of the required number of police officers on the basis of the number of students, the crimes being committed, and the tax revenues on hand to hire police. Access the data stored in the file CRIMES and estimate the models for Crimes and Police as dependent variables. You must determine what variables are included in each equation, based on the information given above, and perform 2SLS regression.

4. If you have specified your models correctly in the preceding question, the equation for Crimes is a function of Students, Poverty, and Police, while that for Police is Students, Taxes, and Crimes. Police is an RHS endogenous variable for the first equation. Use the Durbin–Wu–Hausman test to determine if it is a source of simultaneity.

5. The data file KEYNES contains the data for the macro model described above in Section 10.9.

   A. Identify the endogenous variables and the exogenous variables.
   B. Write the reduced-form equations.
   C. Using 2SLS estimate the two structural equations.

*Chapter 11*

# FORECASTING WITH TIME SERIES DATA AND DISTRIBUTED LAG MODELS

## INTRODUCTION

In Chapter 1 a distinction was made between cross-sectional data and time series data. The latter is the focus of this chapter. Recall that time series data are data that have been collected for some series (variable) for each of several successive time periods. A nation's annual GNP for the years 1999 through 2012 is an example. So are the data for a factory's output for each of the past several years, months, or weeks.

Oftentimes we find that there is a lag between the change in the independent variable and the corresponding response from the dependent variable. *Time series models* are designed to recognize that fact and capture the delayed impact of a change in the RHS variable. They involve the incorporation of lagged values for both the dependent and independent variables.

For example, do you think your consumption expenditures this month (or any given time period) depend only on your disposable income this month? Probably not. The money you spend for consumption in any given time period most likely depends on income earned from previous time periods as well. The model might appear as

$$C_t = \alpha_0 + \beta_0 I_t + \beta_1 I_{t-1} + \beta_2 I_{t-2} + \cdots + \beta_p I_{t-p} + \varepsilon_t$$

This expression suggests that current consumption ($C_t$) is a function of current income ($I_t$) plus income lagged $p$-time periods. It is common to use $\alpha_0$ for the constant term rather than the standard $\beta_0$. In this manner each $\beta$ is linked with a corresponding lag in the independent variable. Notice for example that the $\beta$ characterized with the subscript 2 is associated with the Income measure lagged two time periods ago.

An *autoregressive* time series model regresses current values of a variable on past values of the same variable. It can appear as

$$Y_t = \beta_0 + \beta_1 Y_{t-1} + \beta_2 Y_{t-2} + \cdots + \beta_p Y_{t-p} + \varepsilon_t$$

This type of model recognizes that the best predictor of current and future values for a variable are past values of the same variable. Notice that in an autoregressive model we return to $\beta_0$ as the constant to preserve the coordination between the $\beta_s$ and the lagged values of the variable under study.

Time series data allows us to forecast and predict future values. It's like building a virtual crystal ball that permits us to gaze into the future and forecast pending events. This chapter examines many of the applications of time series models to common business and economic conditions. We begin with a simple time series model in which the dependent variable is set as a function of time itself.

## 11.1 A SIMPLE TIME SERIES MODEL

A simple regression model in which the variable under analysis is regressed on time is a common and quite useful method of forecasting future values. In 2011 many of the world's news agencies reported that the world's population would reach nearly 7 billion souls by the end of the year. Such projections are usually the result of a time series model that traces trends in the variable in question based on past growth patterns. Table 11.1 contains data on world-wide population levels at the end of each year for the years 1990 to 2010.

The projection can be derived using either Year or Time Period as the independent variable. Table 11.2 shows the results of both models based on standard OLS procedures. The values for Population were expressed in billions before the models were estimated to simplify computations and interpretation.

To predict population levels using the first model for the year 2016, you simply insert that year into the model as $Pop = -151.5810 + 0.078848(2016) = 7.376$ billion people. If you forecast with the model using Time Period as the independent variable, insert 27, which is the time period for 2016, and find $Pop = 5.24713 + 0.078848(27) = 7.376$ billion.

Notice that the coefficient of 0.078847748 is the same for both models. It must be. It tells us that for each year (time period) population increases by 0.078847748 billion (or almost 79 million). Only the intercept is different to adjust for the use of 2016 in the first model and 27 in the second.

In this example the data are expressed annually and years can be used in the calculations. Years are numbers and can be mathematically manipulated. However, if the data are not annual, but

■ **Table 11.1** World Population Levels

| Year | Time Period | Population | Year | Time Period | Population |
|------|-------------|------------|------|-------------|------------|
| 1990 | 1 | 5,306,425,154 | 2001 | 12 | 6,200,002,758 |
| 1991 | 2 | 5,392,938,741 | 2002 | 13 | 6,276,721,836 |
| 1992 | 3 | 5,478,009,489 | 2003 | 14 | 6,353,195,588 |
| 1993 | 4 | 5,561,743,942 | 2004 | 15 | 6,429,757,631 |
| 1994 | 5 | 5,644,416,076 | 2005 | 16 | 6,506,649,175 |
| 1995 | 6 | 5,726,239,315 | 2006 | 17 | 6,583,958,568 |
| 1996 | 7 | 5,807,211,831 | 2007 | 18 | 6,661,637,460 |
| 1997 | 8 | 5,887,259,665 | 2008 | 19 | 6,739,610,289 |
| 1998 | 9 | 5,966,464,736 | 2009 | 20 | 6,817,737,123 |
| 1999 | 10 | 6,044,931,358 | 2010 | 21 | 6,895,889,018 |
| 2000 | 11 | 6,122,770,220 | | | |

Source: http://www.geohive.com/earth/his_history3.aspx; extracted November 23, 2011

■ **Table 11.2** Regression Results

Model Using Year as the Independent Variable

|  | Coefficients | Standard Error | t Stat | p-Value |
|---|---|---|---|---|
| Intercept | −151.5810402 | 0.58171407 | −260.57654 | 3.1706E-35 |
| Year | 0.078847748 | 0.000290856 | 271.088885 | 1.4958E-35 |

$R^2 = 0.999727921$  $S_e = 0.008070918$

Model Using Time Period as the Independent Variable

|  | Coefficients | Standard Error | t Stat | p-Value |
|---|---|---|---|---|
| Intercept | 5.247130486 | 0.003652141 | 1436.727283 | 2.59933E-49 |
| Time Period | 0.078847748 | 0.000290856 | 271.0888849 | 1.4958E-35 |

$R^2 = 0.999727921$  $S_e = 0.008070918$

are instead, say, monthly data, it is necessary to create time periods that must be used to estimate the model. After all, months, such as January, February, March, and so on, are not numeric and do not lend themselves to calculation. Each month must be assigned a time period starting at "1." These numbers are then used in the computations. Example 11.1 demonstrates.

---

## EXAMPLE 11.1: Forecasting Monthly Unemployment Rates

**Problem Statement:** Economists closely follow the unemployment rate as an indicator of economic health. Government policy decisions often depend on its trend over the course of several months. The table shown here provides the U.S. unemployment rates for the year 2011. The data were extracted from a website provided by the Bureau of Labor Statistics, a division of the Department of Labor.

| Jan | Feb | Mar | Apr | May | Jun | Jul | Aug | Sep | Oct | Nov | Dec |
|---|---|---|---|---|---|---|---|---|---|---|---|
| 9.1 | 9 | 8.9 | 9 | 9 | 9.1 | 9.1 | 9.1 | 9 | 8.9 | 8.7 | 8.5 |

Data from http://data.bls.gov/timeseries/LNS14000000

As an economist for the U.S. Department of Labor, you wish to estimate a model that can be used to predict future unemployment rates based on the inherent time trend present in the data.

**Solution:** Since the units of time are expressed in months, time periods must be artificially created to serve as the RHS variable. The data might then appear as opposite.

You are also required to forecast unemployment for August 2012 based on an OLS model of the form

$$U_t = \alpha_0 + \beta_1 TP_t + \varepsilon_t$$

where $U_t$ is the unemployment rate for time period $t$ and $TP_t$ is the time period (month) for $t$. With $t$-values in parentheses and $p$-values in brackets, the model reports as

$$U_t = 9.15 - 0.0315 TP_t$$
$$(98.43) \quad (-2.49)$$
$$[0.00] \quad [0.032]$$

$$R^2 = 0.383; \ S_e = 0.151$$

| Month | Time Period | Unemployment |
|-------|-------------|--------------|
| Jan | 1 | 9.1 |
| Feb | 2 | 9 |
| Mar | 3 | 8.9 |
| Apr | 4 | 9 |
| May | 5 | 9 |
| Jun | 6 | 9.1 |
| Jul | 7 | 9.1 |
| Aug | 8 | 9.1 |
| Sep | 9 | 9 |
| Oct | 10 | 8.9 |
| Nov | 11 | 8.7 |
| Dec | 12 | 8.5 |

August is the twentieth time period in the sequence. Your forecast is therefore

$$U_{Aug} = 9.15 - 0.032(20) = 8.51$$

**Interpretation:** You can report a projected unemployment rate of 8.51%. A graph of unemployment over the time period in question is shown here. Does it appear your forecast is headed in the correct direction and might be somewhat accurate?

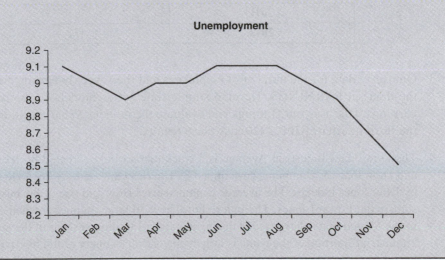

## SECTION 11.1 PROBLEMS

1. As sales decline at Duddly Dufus Enterprises, inventories tend to reach an abnormally high level. The accompanying monthly data in hundreds of dollars record these trends. Develop and interpret the simple time series model for each variable shown here. What is your forecast for April of the next year for each variable? You can perform the calculations by hand, since each model is a simple regression model, just as we did back in Chapter 2, or transfer the data to a computer file.

| Month | Sales ($00) | Inventories ($) |
|---|---|---|
| January 1 | 6.3 | 2.1 |
| February 1 | 6.4 | 2.6 |
| March 1 | 6.2 | 3.1 |
| April 1 | 5.6 | 3.5 |
| May 1 | 5.5 | 3.4 |
| June 1 | 5 | 3.6 |
| July 1 | 4.9 | 4.6 |
| August 1 | 4.2 | 5.2 |
| September 1 | 3.5 | 5.9 |
| October 1 | 3.2 | 6.2 |
| November 1 | 3.5 | 6.5 |

2. Annual measures of output measured in thousands of tons produced for LLW Industries are shown in the accompanying table. If productivity exceeds 19 tons by 2016 the CEO of the firm will give all employees an additional increase in pay of $10,000. Will they receive the bonus?

| Year | Tons |
|---|---|
| 2004 | 12.3 |
| 2005 | 13.5 |
| 2006 | 13.9 |
| 2007 | 14.5 |
| 2008 | 15.2 |
| 2009 | 15.6 |
| 2010 | 15.1 |
| 2011 | 16.8 |
| 2012 | 17.2 |

3. Quarterly data for the number of employees and their weekly earnings are contained in the data set EARNINGS. Develop simple time series models for both employees and earnings. Discuss your findings and evaluate the models. What are your predictions for the third quarter of 2012? Discuss these results.

4. The Dow Jones Industrial Average is a stock market index created by *Wall Street Journal* and Dow Jones & Company, co-founded by Charles Dow on May 26, 1896, and now owned by Dow Jones Indexes. The average is named after Dow and one of his business associates, statistician Edward Jones. The index shows how 30 large, publicly owned companies based in the United States have traded during a standard trading session in the stock market. The "Industrial" portion of the name is largely historical, as many of the modern 30 components have little or nothing to do with traditional heavy industry. The 30 stocks that are included in the index and additional information about the DJIA can be found at http://www.google.com/finance/historical?q=INDEXDJX:.DJI#.

Data from September 21, 2011 to November 1, 2011 can be found in the data set DOW-JONES INDUSTRIALS. Access the data and develop a time series model for volume. What is your estimate for November 16, 2011? How do you explain the $R^2$ value and the estimated trading volume?

## 11.2 AUTOREGRESSIVE MODELS

Oftentimes the best predictor of future values for a variable is past values of the same variable. We may find, for example, that the most accurate predictor of personal consumption levels are consumption patterns from past time periods. The model can be expressed as

$$C_t = \alpha_0 + \beta_1 C_{t-1} + \varepsilon_t$$

where $C_t$ is consumption for the current time period and $C_{t-1}$ is consumption in the most recent previous time period. A model such as this is referred to as an *autoregressive* (AR) model because we are regressing a variable on past values of itself. This is a *first-order* AR model because only the most recent time period is used as a regressor. A *second-order* AR model is one in which current values are regressed on the two most recent time periods: $C_t = \alpha_0 + \beta_1 C_{t-1} + \beta_2 C_{t-2} + \varepsilon_t$. In general, a *pth-order* AR model is expressed as $C_t = \alpha_0 + \beta_1 C_{t-1} + \beta_2 C_{t-2} + \cdots + \beta_p C_{t-p} + \varepsilon_t$. As noted in the Introduction, it is common to symbolize the constant term as $\alpha_0$ rather than $\beta_0$ as was done with previous models so that the subscripts on the coefficients match the number of lags of the independent variables.

> "Auto" implies self, as in automatic or self-starting. Thus, regressing a variable on past values of itself is termed autoregression.

In the effort to forecast revenue, Investors' Assurance, a small privately owned financial consulting firm, collected quarterly data in thousands of dollars from the second quarter of 2007 (7/2) to the third quarter of 2011 (11/3) as shown in Table 11.3. Lagged values for the previous three time periods are also given. The Minitab results of a third-order autoregressive model are reported as

```
Revenue(t) = 38.4 + 1.06 Revenue(t-1) - 0.166 Revenue(t-2) + 0.126 Revenue(t-3)
             (1.25) (2.34)                (-0.24)               (0.30)
             [0.239] [0.039]              [0.815]               [0.773]
```

The *p*-values in brackets reveal that only the first lag is statistically significant. The model is estimated a second time after removing the 2-period and 3-period lags. The results are

```
Revenue(t) = 26.3 +  1.03 Revenue(t-1)
             (1.54)     (35.36)
             [0.143]    [0.000]
```

The $R^2$ is 98.8% and the standard error of the estimate, $S_e$, of 25.5 reveals that a short-term forecast could be off typically by $25,500.

It should be kept in mind that you will lose $p$ observations in the estimation process, where $p$ is the highest-order lagged value: 3 in our first example and only 1 in the final example using only one lagged term. That's because in regressing the variable on its lagged values the number of usable observations is equal to the number of observations minus the number of lags incorporated into your model; $p$ observations must be sacrificed (see Table 11.3). For the first model we ran using three lagged values for revenue, the viable data set runs only from 8/1 to 11/3. Only those time periods that contain data for all four variables in the model can be used to develop the model.

The number of degrees of freedom is therefore equal to

$$n - 2p - 1$$

You forfeit: (1) one degree of freedom for each of the lagged terms (that's $p$), (2) one degree of freedom for each RHS variable as is always the case in all regression models (that's $p$ again), and (3) one for the constant term.

> The number of degrees of freedom in an autoregressive model equals $n - 2p - 1$.

Returning to our model using only the most recent lag that proved significant, the forecast for the next quarter, 11/4 (fourth quarter of 2011), is found by using the actual value of 972 from 11/3. Thus,

$$\widehat{Rev}_{11/4} = 26.3 + 1.03(972) = 1027.5 \text{ thousand}$$

The first quarter forecast for 2012 uses the 11/4 forecast in similar fashion. Then,

$$\widehat{Rev}_{12/1} = 26.3 + 1.03(1027.5) = 1084.6 \text{ thousand}$$

For the second quarter of 2012, the forecast is found by using the 12/1 forecast:

$$\widehat{Rev}_{12/2} = 26.3 + 1.03(108.4) = 1143.44 \text{ thousand}$$

■ **Table 11.3**  Quarterly Revenues for Investors' Assurance

| Year/Quarter | Revenue($t$) | Revenue ($t-1$) | Revenue ($t-2$) | Revenue ($t-3$) |
|:---:|:---:|:---:|:---:|:---:|
| 7/2 | 236.4 | * | * | * |
| 7/3 | 248 | 236.4 | * | * |
| 7/4 | 279.6 | 248 | 236.4 | * |
| 8/1 | 312.4 | 279.6 | 248 | 236.4 |
| 8/2 | 356.4 | 312.4 | 279.6 | 248 |
| 8/3 | 397.2 | 356.4 | 312.4 | 279.6 |
| 8/4 | 444.4 | 397.2 | 356.4 | 312.4 |
| 9/1 | 459.6 | 444.4 | 397.2 | 356.4 |
| 9/2 | 520.4 | 459.6 | 444.4 | 397.2 |
| 9/3 | 576 | 520.4 | 459.6 | 444.4 |
| 9/4 | 664.4 | 576 | 520.4 | 459.6 |
| 10/1 | 708 | 664.4 | 576 | 520.4 |
| 10/2 | 740.4 | 708 | 664.4 | 576 |
| 10/3 | 781.6 | 740.4 | 708 | 664.4 |
| 10/4 | 809.2 | 781.6 | 740.4 | 708 |
| 11/1 | 831.6 | 809.2 | 781.6 | 740.4 |
| 11/2 | 858.4 | 831.6 | 809.2 | 781.6 |
| 11/3 | 972 | 858.4 | 831.6 | 809.2 |
|  | * | 972 | 858.4 | 831.6 |
|  | * | * | 972 | 858.4 |
|  | * | * | * | 972 |

This continues through successive time periods to the point in which the analyst is interested. It should be emphasized that the farther into the future the analyst tries to predict, the larger the error is likely to be.

It is always of interest to *post-predict* by forecasting past values. Given the value for 7/2, it is possible to determine what your model would predict 7/3 to be and compare it with the known value for 7/3 of 248. Thus,

$$\widehat{Rev}_{7/3} = 26.3 + 1.03(236.4) = 269.792$$

The error is 248 − 269.792 = −21.792 and the absolute value of the error is 21.792. The model would overestimate the value by $21,792. These computations along with the sums and averages of the errors and the absolute values of the errors are seen in Table 11.4.

■ **Table 11.4** Post Predictions

| Year/Quarter | Revenue ($t$) | Forecast1 | Error | Abs Error |
|:---:|:---:|:---:|:---:|:---:|
| 7/2 | 236.4 | | | |
| 7/3 | 248 | 269.792 | −21.792 | 21.792 |
| 7/4 | 279.6 | 281.74 | −2.14 | 2.14 |
| 8/1 | 312.4 | 314.288 | −1.888 | 1.888 |
| 8/2 | 356.4 | 348.072 | 8.328 | 8.328 |
| 8/3 | 397.2 | 393.392 | 3.808 | 3.808 |
| 8/4 | 444.4 | 435.416 | 8.984 | 8.984 |
| 9/1 | 459.6 | 484.032 | −24.432 | 24.432 |
| 9/2 | 520.4 | 499.688 | 20.712 | 20.712 |
| 9/3 | 576 | 562.312 | 13.688 | 13.688 |
| 9/4 | 664.4 | 619.58 | 44.82 | 44.82 |
| 10/1 | 708 | 710.632 | −2.632 | 2.632 |
| 10/2 | 740.4 | 755.54 | −15.14 | 15.14 |
| 10/3 | 781.6 | 788.912 | −7.312 | 7.312 |
| 10/4 | 809.2 | 831.348 | −22.148 | 22.148 |
| 11/1 | 831.6 | 859.776 | −28.176 | 28.176 |
| 11/2 | 858.4 | 882.848 | −24.448 | 24.448 |
| 11/3 | 972 | 910.452 | 61.548 | 61.548 |
| **Sum** | | | 11.78 | 311.996 |
| **Average** | | | 0.6929 | 18.35 |

## SECTION 11.2 PROBLEMS

1. Using the data from the first problem in Section 11.1 for Duddly Dufus Enterprises, estimate an autoregressive model. Experiment with different values for *p-order* models until you have what you think is the most justifiable model. Explain your final model. Compare it with the time series model you estimated in Section 11.1.

2. Using the data from the second problem in Section 11.1 for LLW Industries, estimate an autoregressive model. Experiment with different values for *p-order* models until you have what you think is the most justifiable model. Explain your final model. Compare it with the time series model you estimated in Section 11.1.

3. Using the data from the third problem in Section 11.1 for the data set EARNINGS, estimate an autoregressive model. Experiment with different values for *p-order* models until you

have what you think is the most justifiable model. Explain your final model. Compare it with the time series model you estimated in Section 11.1.

4. Using the data from the fourth problem in Section 11.1 for DOW-JONES INDUSTRIALS, estimate an autoregressive model. Experiment with different values for *p-order* models until you have what you think is the most justifiable model. Explain your final model. Compare it with the time series model you estimated in Section 11.1.

## 11.3 DISTRIBUTED LAG MODELS

The models we have examined so far (simple time series and AR models) rely on only lagged values of the dependent variable as regressors. Under many economic circumstances we often find that lagged values of an independent variable may influence current values of the dependent variable. Such a model is expressed as

$$Y_t = \alpha_0 + \beta_0 X_t + \beta_1 X_{t-1} + \beta_2 X_{t-2} + \cdots + \beta_p X_{t-p} + \varepsilon_t \qquad (11.3.1)$$

This is called a *distributed lag model* because the impact of the X-variable is distributed or spread out over several earlier time periods. It is expected that the impact of X decreases as the length of the lag increases. The influence of a more distant value for X is of a lesser effect than more recent values. It is likely that $\beta_1 > \beta_2 > \cdots \beta_p$.

Clearly, a model such as (11.3.1) can suffer certain problems, most evident of which is the potential for multicollinearity. The lagged X-values are likely to be highly correlated. Of further concern is the loss of degrees of freedom. Remember, for every additional RHS variable that is added to a model, a degree of freedom must be sacrificed. If there are several lagged values, that is, if $p$ is large, the cost can be a bit excessive. Finally, the expected decline in the impact of the more distant values of X noted above is not assured. The estimated model may therefore experience certain inexplicable characteristics that call into question its veracity and forecasting prowess. Each of these problems can be dealt with by means of a single adjustment generally referred to as the Koyck transformation.[1]

### ● The Koyck Transformation (Geometric Lag)

This correction simply requires replacing all the lagged X-variables seen in Equation (11.3.1) with only one lagged value of the dependent variable as Equation (11.3.2) displays. After all, if $Y_t = f(X_{t-p})$ then $Y_{t-p}$ can be used as a proxy for all the X-values. The Koyck model is stated as

$$Y_t = \alpha_0 + \beta_0 X_t + \lambda Y_{t-1} + v_t \qquad (11.3.2)$$

where $\lambda$ (Greek lambda) is between 0 and 1. Each $\beta_i$ in Equation (11.3.1) becomes $\beta_i = \beta_0 \lambda^i$. That is,

$$\beta_i = \beta_0 \lambda^i \qquad (11.3.3)$$

For example, $\beta_2 = \beta_0 \lambda^2$.

With Equation (11.3.1) we have to estimate $p$-lagged coefficients, plus the slope coefficient for the current time period, $t$, plus the constant term. Several degrees of freedom are lost and the fear of multicollinearity arises. But in the case of Equation (11.3.2) we must estimate only three values: the constant, the slope coefficient for the $X$-variable, and the slope coefficient for the lagged dependent variable.

In this manner, all three problems associated with a distributed lag model cited above are eliminated. Using Equation (11.3.2) removes multicollinearity in that there is no longer a multitude of terms that might prove to be correlated. Nor does the model "eat up" a lot of degrees of freedom, since there are not as many coefficients to estimate.

Finally, given that $0 < \lambda < 1$ assures us that the $\beta_i$ will decline as the length of the lag increases. If $\beta_0$ is 10 and $\lambda = 0.5$, $\beta_2 = (10)(0.5)^2 = 2.5$, while the coefficient for an earlier term that is lagged, say, three time periods ago, would be $\beta_3 = (10)(0.05)^3 = 1.25 < 2.5$. The algebra demonstrating the transformation is shown in the appendix to this chapter for those who are interested.

As noted above, a common application of distributed lag models focuses on typical consumption functions in which personal consumption levels are regressed on income levels. Annual data in current dollars from 1970 to 2010 are taken from the U.S. Department of Commerce, Bureau of Economic Analysis, and used to illustrate.[2] Applying Equation (11.3.2) yields the following results:

```
Personal Cons = -134 + 0.581 Income + 0.319 Ct-1

   Predictor      Coef    SE Coef      T       P
   Constant     -133.6      101.9   -1.31   0.207
   Ct-1         0.3191     0.1221    2.61   0.018
   Income       0.5814     0.1026    5.67   0.000

S = 96.2937 R-Sq = 99.8% R-Sq(adj) = 99.8%
```

We find $\beta_0 = 0.581$ and the slope coefficient for the lagged term is $\lambda = 0.319$. Slope coefficients for the lagged values of income are then determined using Equation (11.3.3) as shown in Table 11.5.

Additional lags can be determined as well if desired. If three lagged values for income are used in the model, it becomes

$$C_t = -133.6 + 0.581I_t + 0.185I_{t-1} + 0.059I_{t-2} + 0.019I_{t-3}$$

The Koyck transformation also allows us to determine the full effect of a change in the independent variable in both the short run and the long run that is associated with a one-unit change in the independent variable. These impacts are often termed *multiplier effects*. Specifically, the slope coefficient of the X-variable, $\beta_0$, measures the short-run effect of a one-unit change in $X_t$ on the mean value of $Y_t$. It gives the change in the mean value of $Y_t$ following a one-unit change in $X_t$ in the same time period. In our present case, a one-unit change in income will lead to a $0.58 increase in consumption during the same time period.

■ **Table 11.5**  Slope Coefficients

| Using Equation (11.3.3): $\beta_i = \beta_0 \lambda^i$ |
| --- |
| $\beta_0 = \beta_0\lambda^0 = (0.581)(0.319^0) = 0.581$ |
| $\beta_1 = \beta_0\lambda^1 = (0.581)(0.319^1) = 0.185$ |
| $\beta_2 = \beta_0\lambda^2 = (0.581)(0.319^2) = 0.059$ |
| $\beta_3 = \beta_0\lambda^3 = (0.581)(0.319^3) = 0.019$ |
| Etc. |

The long-run effect is measured as Equation (11.3.4):

$$\frac{\widehat{\beta_0}}{1 - \widehat{\lambda}} \qquad (11.3.4)$$

It measures the total impact of a change in $X$ on $Y$ after all lagged effects have played out. It can also be found by summing all the $\beta_i$ in Equation (11.3.1). Our current consumption function yields a long-run multiplier of $0.581/(1 - 0.319) = 0.853$. Thus, a $1 increase in income will generate a $0.85 increase in consumption in the long run. This is the total change in consumption over time from a $1 rise in disposable income. This long-run impact identifies the *marginal propensity to consume* in economic studies of consumer behavior.

> The Koyck transformation permits a determination of both the short-run and long-run multiplier effects associated with a change in the independent variable.

## ● The Problem of Autocorrelation

Models that employ lagged values of the dependent variable as explanatory variables often suffer from autocorrelation. The appendix to this chapter reveals how $v_t$ is correlated with both $\varepsilon_t$ and $\varepsilon_{t-1}$ as $v_t = \varepsilon_t - \lambda\varepsilon_{t-1}$. Therefore, it follows that $v_t$ and $v_{t-1}$ must be related, thereby causing autocorrelation.

Unfortunately, the standard Durbin–Watson statistic we examined in earlier chapters is not suited to testing for autocorrelation when a lagged value for the dependent variable is found on the RHS. In such a case the Durbin–Watson is biased toward 2, thereby denying the presence of autocorrelation even if it exists (a Type II error).[3] Durbin suggests the use of an alternative, the *Durbin h* test,[4] as follows:

1.  Estimate the Koyck model as Equation (11.3.2), saving the error terms, $\hat{v}_t$.

2.  Calculate the correlation coefficient of these error terms as

$$\hat{\rho} = \frac{\sum \hat{v}_t \hat{v}_{t-1}}{\sum \hat{v}_t^2} \tag{11.3.5}$$

3.  Calculate the Durbin *h* as

$$h = \hat{\rho} \sqrt{\frac{n-1}{1-(n-1)(S_\beta^2)}}$$

where $S_\beta^2$ is the variance of the slope coefficient for $Y_{t-1}$.

4.  The *h*-statistic approaches a normal distribution for large samples. Therefore, the simple decision rule is established in the usual fashion. If, for example, you wish to test the hypothesis for autocorrelation at the 5% level, the critical value for *h* is ±1.96. The hypotheses are

$$H_0: \text{No autocorrelation}$$

$$H_a: \text{Autocorrelation exists}$$

Given the variance from the regression above of $(0.1221)^2$, $h = 3.77 > 1.96$. This is a clear indication that autocorrelation exists in the model.

A problem arises if $(n-1)(S_\beta^2)$ is greater than 1. Then the value under the radical is negative and further computations are halted, since you can't take the square of a negative number. The problem is dealt with by using the error term from Equation (11.3.2) as a dependent variable and regressing it on $X_t$, $Y_{y-1}$ with the error terms lagged one time period:

$$e_t = \alpha + \beta_1 X_t + \beta_2 Y_{t-1} + e_{t-1}$$

If the slope coefficient of the lagged error is statistically significant based on a standard *t*-test, it is concluded that autocorrelation exists.

If autocorrelation is detected, the question then becomes what to do about it. The best solution is to identify the explanatory variable that is likely missing from the model. Missing explanatory variables are a common cause of autocorrelation. Potential candidates might include consumer wealth, price expectations, levels of consumer savings, the level of household debt, or the unemployment rate. All of these have been found to correlate with consumer expenditures.

Barring a successful effort to reduce autocorrelation via the inclusion of additional explanatory variables, the application of two-stage least squares might be a solution. This involves the substitution of instrumental variables that are highly correlated with $Y_{t-1}$ but *not* correlated with $v_t$. This will eliminate the correlation between $Y_{t-1}$ and $v_t$. Identifying such variables, however, is often quite difficult. The remaining corrective action involves the use of more complex least squares models such as maximum likelihood techniques.

## ● Stationarity and the Dickey–Fuller Test

A variable is said to be *stationary* over time if it exhibits no upward or downward trend. This requires that its long-run mean and variance remain relatively constant over time. Time series models often report individual variables as being more significant than they actually are. This occurs if the dependent and independent variables exhibit the same trend pattern. This can likely result if these variables are influenced by the same economic forces. Commonly, inflationary forces tend to drive up many economic measures. During periods of rapid expansion wages, prices, interest rates, and many other economic measures all tend to rise. These corresponding movements are often due to *spurious correlation* which is simply a strong association between two or more variables that is not the result of any true relationship. These variables just have a common impetus (inflation) but are not necessarily related.

This tends to inflate the $R^2$ and $t$-values, giving rise to the conclusion that models offer more explanatory value than they actually do. It happens because the spurious regression model assigns to $X_t$ much of the change in $Y_t$ that is actually caused by the common trend that economic variables possess and actually has little to do with $X_t$.

Much of the ill-effects expressed here can be mitigated by including a trend factor in the model by the regression $Y_t = f(T, X_t)$, where $T$ is a time variable set equal to 1, 2, 3, ..., $n$. Even after accounting for the time trend in this manner, there often still remains troublesome *non-stationarity* in the form of a *random walk*. This random-walk effect is evidenced by the fact that the value of the variable in question in the next time period equals the value of the variable in this time period plus some random error term. This can be demonstrated with a simple autoregressive model such as

$$Y_t = \lambda Y_{t-1} + \varepsilon_t \tag{11.3.6}$$

where $\varepsilon_t$ meets the assumptions of the OLS process in that it is random with a mean of zero and some variance, $\sigma^2$.

It can then be concluded that if $|\lambda| < 1$, the lagged values for $Y$ will continue to decrease and the expected value (mean) of $Y$ will approach the constant zero, which means by definition that it is stationary. If $|\lambda| > 1$, the expected value of $Y$ will not approach any constant but will continue to rise. By definition, this means it is non-stationary.

Finally, if $|\lambda| = 1$, a pure random-walk effect is produced. This is true because $Y_t = (1)Y_{t-1} + \varepsilon_t$. Since $\varepsilon_t$ is a random error, $Y_t$ equals $Y_{t-1}$ plus some random *shock*. As the value of $Y$ randomly moves about it fails to approach any specific value and is non-stationary. If $|\lambda| = 1$, it is said to possess a *unit-root* and be non-stationary.

> We can conclude that the variable is stationary if and only if $|\lambda| < 1$. In the presence of non-stationarity any attempt at modeling will result in only a spurious regression model with falsely elevated $R^2$ and $t$-values.

To avoid these drawbacks we must ensure that the variables are stationary. This requires that we test the hypothesis that $\lambda$ in Equation (11.3.6) is equal to or greater than 1. If the null is not rejected, we can conclude that stationarity exists. Perhaps the most common assessment of stationarity is the Dickey–Fuller (DF) test.[5] Starting with Equation (11.3.6), we must find *first-differences* by subtracting $Y_{t-1}$ from both sides.

To eliminate the trend factor and any spurious correlation it might cause, a trend variable is also included along with a constant term, $\alpha_0$. After incorporating the explanatory variable, $X_t$, the expression is seen as Equation (11.3.7).

$$Y_t = \alpha_0 + \beta_0 T + \beta_1 X_t + \lambda Y_{t-1} + \varepsilon_t \tag{11.3.7}$$

Then, the first-differences are found, producing

$$Y_t - Y_{t-1} = \alpha_0 + \beta_0 T + \beta_1 X_t + (\lambda - 1)Y_{t-1} + \varepsilon_t \tag{11.3.8}$$

Let $\beta_2 = (\lambda - 1)$, the coefficient of the lagged term. Then, if $\lambda = 1$, meaning $Y_{t-1}$ has a unit-root and non-stationarity exists, $\beta_2$ will equal zero. The test becomes

$$H_0: \beta_2 \geq 0$$

$$H_a: \beta_2 < 0$$

If the null is not rejected, a unit-root exists and the equation suffers from non-stationarity.

Let's now apply this process to our income–consumption data from 1970 to 2010. In doing so, the trend component is reported as insignificant (the $p$-value is 0.119). In such a case the test should be conducted without the trend. Equation (11.3.7) is estimated to the exclusion of $T$, and the model is reported as $C_t = \alpha_0 + \beta_1 I_t + \beta_2 C_{t-1}$. The $t$-value for the lagged term necessary to perform the DF test is $t = 5.10$. However, the standard $t$-table cannot be used to find the critical $t$-value. Those $t$-values are valid only if the variable under question is stationary in the first place.

As implied above, there are three main versions of the DF test. The first is a simple test for $F$ performed as $Y_t - Y_{t-1} = (\lambda - 1)Y_{t-1} + \varepsilon_t$. The second is a test for a unit-root with "drift." This is accomplished by including a constant term and estimating $Y_t - Y_{t-1} = \alpha_0 + (\lambda - 1)Y_{t-1} + \varepsilon_t$. Finally, including a trend factor yields $Y_t - Y_{t-1} = \alpha_0 + \beta_0 T + (\lambda - 1)Y_{t-1} + \varepsilon_t$. Of course there is the model specified as Equation (11.3.8) that includes the $X$-variable on the RHS.

Each version of the test has its own critical $t$-value which depends on the size of the sample. Which of the three main versions of the test should be used is not a minor issue. It has a direct bearing on whether the null is rejected. Inappropriate exclusion of the intercept or deterministic time trend term tends to bias the results. If the trend component is inappropriately excluded when $\alpha_0$ is estimated, then the power of the unit-root test can be substantially reduced as a trend may be captured through the random-walk-with-drift model. Similarly, inclusion of the intercept *or* time trend term when it is not called for also reduces the power of the unit-root test.

Various tests have been proposed to make these critical determinations.[6] In any event, different critical $t$-values are required for the DF test. Derivation of these $t$-values can also be found in the original 1979 work by Dickey and Fuller (see note 5). Given the $t$-value of 5.10 for our income–consumption data the null hypothesis is surprisingly rejected. We can conclude that $\beta_2 < 0$ (i.e., $\lambda < 1$) and no unit-root exists. The model is stationary.

However, suppose non-stationarity had been discovered. The question becomes what to do about it. The most common response is to perform first-differencing on not only the dependent variable as described above in the DF test, but to first-difference the $X$-variable as well: $Y_t - Y_{t-1} = f(X_t - X_{t-1})$. But before doing that you should check for *cointegration*.

## ● Cointegration

Cointegration occurs in a model when the variables are nonstationary but the trends in the variables over time are related in such a manner that the error term is stationary. While the variables in the model may not be stationary, it is possible that the linear combination of these variables is cointegrated, making them stationary. This may result because if $Y_t$ and $X_t$ are related in some equilibrium manner any departure from that equilibrium will be small and temporary. Therefore, the error term will be stationary.

> Cointegration may result when there prevails a long-run stable equilibrium relationship between (or among) nonstationary variables in the model, in which case the model as a whole is said to be stationary in that the error term will exhibit conditions of stationarity.

To determine if this might be the case, you must first estimate the model as $Y_t = f(X_t)$ and save the residuals, $e_t$. Next, perform the DF test on the residuals *without* any intercept or trend factor as

$e_t - e_{t-1} = \lambda e_{t-1}$. If the null is rejected we can conclude that $X_t$ and $Y_t$ are cointegrated. Then, regardless of whether $X_t$ or $Y_t$ are nonstationary, OLS procedures will produce results that are *not* spurious.

## ● The Almon (Polynomial) Lag

An alternative to the Koyck model is the Almon polynomial lag.[7] Rather than offer a continuously declining impact as does the Koyck method, this procedure recognizes that, as the title of Almon's article suggests, there is often a delay between the time a decision is made and when action is subsequently taken. Or a lapse of time may occur between when an action is taken and when the effect is felt. If a company invests in its productive capacity, several time periods may pass before the increase in output reaches the market.

To apply the Almon lag it is first necessary to make two decisions. The analyst must choose a degree for the polynomial and the number of lags to incorporate into the model. To demonstrate, let's presume a polynomial of degree 2 (a quadratic) and $K = 4$ lag periods are chosen. Since $K = 4$, we will have five RHS variables: $X_t$, $X_{t-1}$, $X_{t-2}$, $X_{t-3}$, and $X_{t-4}$. The model appears as

$$Y_t = \alpha_0 + \beta_0 X_t + \beta_1 X_{t-1} + \beta_2 X_{t-2} + \beta_3 X_{t-3} + \beta_4 X_{t-4} \tag{11.3.9}$$

All five $\beta_i$ coefficients are estimated as

$$\beta_i = \lambda_0 + \lambda_1 i + \lambda_2 i^2 \tag{11.3.10}$$

That is, since we are assuming a quadratic (polynomial of degree 2), the highest power for $\beta_i$ is 2. Thus,

the coefficient of $X_t$ is $\beta_0 = \lambda_0$;
the coefficient of $X_{t-1}$ is $\beta_1 = \lambda_0 + \lambda_1 1 + \lambda_2 1^2$;
the coefficient of $X_{t-2}$ is $\beta_2 = \lambda_0 + \lambda_1 2 + \lambda_2 2^2$;
the coefficient of $X_{t-3}$ is $\beta_3 = \lambda_0 + \lambda_1 3 + \lambda_2 3^2$;
the coefficient of $X_{t-4}$ is $\beta_4 = \lambda_0 + \lambda_1 4 + \lambda_2 4^2$.

Substituting these values in Equation (11.3.9), we get

$$Y_t = \alpha_0 + \lambda_0(X_t) + (\lambda_0 + \lambda_1 1 + \lambda_2 1^2)X_{t-1} + (\lambda_0 + \lambda_1 2 + \lambda_2 2^2)X_{t-2}$$
$$+ (\lambda_0 + \lambda_1 3 + \lambda_2 3^2)X_{t-3} + (\lambda_0 + \lambda_1 4 + \lambda_2 4^2)X_{t-4} + \varepsilon_t \tag{11.3.11}$$

Collecting terms yields

$$Y_t = \alpha_0 + \lambda_0(X_t + X_{t-1} + X_{t-2} + X_{t-3} + X_{t-4}) + \lambda_1(X_{t-1} + 2X_{t-2} + 3X_{t-3} + 4X_{t-4})$$
$$+ \lambda_2(X_{t-1} + 4X_{t-2} + 9X_{t-3} + 16X_{t-4}) + \varepsilon_t \tag{11.3.12}$$

Now, for simplicity in notation, let the three regressors (the $X_i$ in the three sets of parentheses) equal $W_0$, $W_1$, and $W_2$. We then find

$$Y_t = \alpha_0 + \lambda_0 W_0 + \lambda_1 W_1 + \lambda_2 W_2 + \varepsilon_t \qquad (11.3.13)$$

After estimating $\lambda_0$, $\lambda_1$, and $\lambda_2$ we can estimate the $\beta_i$ using the expressions given above for each of them. Equation (11.3.9) is then derived.

Table 11.6 contains data for Income Before Taxes, Income After Taxes, and Consumer Expenditures in billions of dollars over several years. The data were taken from the U.S. Bureau of Economic Analysis and placed in a Minitab worksheet.

■ **Table 11.6** BEA Data

| ↓ | C1 | C2 | C3 | C4 | C5 | C6 | C7 | C8 | C9 | C10 | C11 |
|---|------|-------|-------|-------|---------|---------|---------|---------|--------|--------|---------|
| | Year | IBT | IAT | EXP | LagInc1 | LagInc2 | LagInc3 | LagInc4 | W0 | W1 | W2 |
| 1 | 1984 | 23464 | 21237 | 22546 | * | * | * | * | * | * | * |
| 2 | 1985 | 25127 | 22887 | 23976 | 23464 | * | * | * | * | * | * |
| 3 | 1986 | 25460 | 23172 | 24439 | 25127 | 23464 | | * | * | * | * |
| 4 | 1987 | 27326 | 24871 | 24776 | 25460 | 25127 | 23464 | * | * | * | * |
| 5 | 1988 | 28540 | 26149 | 26389 | 27326 | 25460 | 25127 | 23464 | 129917 | 247483 | 730733 |
| 6 | 1989 | 31308 | 28496 | 27810 | 28540 | 27326 | 25460 | 25127 | 137761 | 260080 | 769016 |
| 7 | 1990 | 31889 | 28937 | 29062 | 31308 | 28540 | 27326 | 25460 | 144523 | 272206 | 798762 |
| 8 | 1991 | 33901 | 30729 | 30487 | 31889 | 31308 | 28540 | 27326 | 152964 | 289429 | 851197 |
| 9 | 1992 | 33854 | 30786 | 30527 | 33901 | 31889 | 31308 | 28540 | 159492 | 305763 | 899869 |
| 10 | 1993 | 34868 | 31890 | 31436 | 33854 | 33901 | 31889 | 31308 | 165820 | 322555 | 957387 |
| 11 | 1994 | 36181 | 33098 | 32740 | 34868 | 33854 | 33901 | 31889 | 170693 | 331835 | 985617 |
| 12 | 1995 | 36918 | 33864 | 33597 | 36181 | 34868 | 33854 | 33901 | 175722 | 343083 | 1022755 |
| 13 | 1996 | 38014 | 34864 | 35591 | 36918 | 36181 | 34868 | 33854 | 179835 | 349300 | 1037118 |
| 14 | 1997 | 39926 | 36684 | 36146 | 38014 | 36918 | 36181 | 34868 | 185907 | 359865 | 1069203 |
| 15 | 1998 | 41622 | 38358 | 37260 | 39926 | 38014 | 36918 | 36181 | 192661 | 371432 | 1103140 |
| 16 | 1999 | 43951 | 40652 | 39143 | 41622 | 39926 | 38014 | 36918 | 200431 | 383188 | 1134140 |
| 17 | 2000 | 44649 | 41532 | 40238 | 43951 | 41622 | 39926 | 38014 | 208162 | 399029 | 1177997 |
| 18 | 2001 | 47507 | 44587 | 41395 | 44649 | 43951 | 41622 | 39926 | 217655 | 417121 | 1233867 |
| 19 | 2002 | 49430 | 46934 | 42557 | 47507 | 44649 | 43951 | 41622 | 227159 | 435146 | 1287614 |
| 20 | 2003 | 51128 | 48596 | 40817 | 49430 | 47507 | 44649 | 43951 | 236665 | 454195 | 1344515 |
| 21 | 2004 | 54453 | 52287 | 43395 | 51128 | 49430 | 47507 | 44649 | 247167 | 471105 | 1390795 |
| 22 | 2005 | 58712 | 56304 | 46409 | 54453 | 51128 | 49430 | 47507 | 261230 | 495027 | 1463947 |
| 23 | 2006 | 60533 | 58101 | 48398 | 58712 | 54453 | 51128 | 49430 | 274256 | 518722 | 1527556 |
| 24 | 2007 | 63091 | 60858 | 49638 | 60533 | 58712 | 54453 | 51128 | 287917 | 545828 | 1603506 |
| 25 | 2008 | 63563 | 61774 | 50486 | 63091 | 60533 | 58712 | 54453 | 300352 | 578105 | 1704879 |
| 26 | 2009 | 62857 | 60753 | 49067 | 63563 | 63091 | 60533 | 58712 | 308756 | 606192 | 1800116 |
| 27 | 2010 | 62481 | 60712 | 48109 | 62857 | 63563 | 63091 | 60533 | 312525 | 621388 | 1853456 |

The data are used to perform an Almon lag like the one described above in Equation (11.3.9) with $K = 4$ for a quadratic. The values for $W_0$, $W_1$, and $W_2$ are computed in the last three columns in accordance with Equations (11.3.12) and (11.3.13). Current consumption is estimated, yielding Table 11.7.

■ **Table 11.7**  Minitab Results

Average Annual Expenditures = 9318 + 0.670 W0 - 0.742 W1 + 0.158 W2
23 cases used, 4 cases contain missing values

| Predictor | Coef | SE Coef | T | P |
|-----------|------|---------|---|---|
| Constant | 9318 | 1105 | 8.44 | 0.000 |
| W0 | 0.6701 | 0.1719 | 3.90 | 0.001 |
| W1 | -0.7425 | 0.3684 | -2.02 | 0.058 |
| W2 | 0.15752 | 0.09737 | 1.62 | 0.122 |

S = 1226.57  R-Sq = 97.8%  R-Sq(adj) = 97.4%

Notice the *p*-values reveal that when greater emphasis is placed on longer lags, the level of significance decreases, which seems logical. This may *not* always occur, however. It may be that, unlike the Koyck lag model, the most recent time period(s) is (are) of less impact. The most influential impact may not occur until after the passage of one or two time periods. This is one of the strengths of the Almon lag. The strongest stimulus does not have to be the most recent time period as is assumed by the Koyck method.

Returning to our interpretation of the regression results, $\lambda_0 = 0.6701$, $\lambda_1 = -0.7425$, and $\lambda_2 = 0.1575$. Therefore, $\beta_0 = 0.6701$, $\beta_1 = 0.0851$, $\beta_2 = -0.1849$, $\beta_3 = -0.1399$, and $\beta_4 = 0.2201$. The final model is

$$C_t = 9318 + 0.6701(IBT_t) + 0.0851(IBT_{t-1}) - 0.1849(IBT_{t-2}) - 0.1399(IBT_{t-3}) + 0.2201(IBT_{t-4})$$

The usual interpretations apply to the model as a whole.

## SECTION 11.3 PROBLEMS

1. In what way does the Koyck transformation resolve problems often associated with distributed lag models?

2. Given $Y_t = \beta_0 X_t + \lambda Y_{t-1}$, what is the short-run effect of a one-unit change in $X$? What is the long-run impact (multiplier) for the model?

3. Presume $Y_t = 4 + 0.73X_t + 0.291Y_{t-1}$ in a model with two lagged values. Find the coefficients for the lagged $X$-values.

4. Access the file KOYCK. Test for autocorrelation based on a Koyck model.

5. Discuss the differences between the Koyck and Almon lag procedures. Which do you feel is more applicable to real-world data? Why? What are the advantages and disadvantages of each?

## 11.4 GRANGER CAUSALITY

While regression cannot establish a cause-and-effect relationship, it is possible to identify Granger causality.[8] If there is a pattern of a change in $X$ followed by a change in $Y$ it might be argued that a change in $X$ Granger-causes a change in $Y$. The test for Granger causality is based on distributed lag models. Actually, two such models are estimated and compared. The *restricted model* is an autoregressive model in which $Y_t$ is regressed on past values of itself. It can be specified as

$$Y_t = \alpha_0 + \beta_1 Y_{t-1} + \beta_2 Y_{t-2} + \cdots + \beta_p Y_{t-p} + \varepsilon_t \qquad (11.4.1)$$

It's referred to as the restricted form because the $\beta$-values of $X$ are restricted to zero. That's why they are not included in the model. It is assumed that $\beta_{X1} = \beta_{X2} = \cdots = \beta_{XP} = 0$. Therefore, there is no need to measure their impact on $Y_t$.

The *unrestricted model* does not make this limiting assumption. It is based on the premise that $X_t \cdots X_{t-i}$ may have a bearing on the current value of $Y$. Past values of the $X$-variable are therefore encompassed in the model, which is seen as Equation (11.4.2):

$$Y_t = \alpha_0 + \alpha_1 Y_{t-1} + \alpha_2 Y_{t-2} + \cdots + \alpha_p Y_{t-p} + \beta_0 X_t + \beta_1 X_{t-1} + \beta_2 X_{t-2} + \cdots + \beta_m X_{t-m} + \varepsilon_t \qquad (11.4.2)$$

where $p$ and $m$ may or may not be equal.

Of course, when you estimate each model you will get a sum of the squared errors, $SSE$. You will have an $SSE_R$ for the restricted model and an $SSE_U$ for the unrestricted model. The null hypothesis to be tested states that $\beta_{Xt} = \beta_{Xt-1} = \cdots = \beta_{Xt-m} = 0$. Failure to reject the null leads to the conclusion that Granger causality does not exist. The impact of lagged $X$-variables on $Y_t$ is zero.

The test is based on an $F$-test shown in Equation (11.4.3):

$$F_{test} = \frac{\dfrac{SSE_R - SSE_U}{m}}{\dfrac{SSE_U}{n-k}} \qquad (11.4.3)$$

where $n$ is the number of observations in the unrestricted model (which may or may not be equal to the number of observations in the restricted model because of the potential for missing data), $m$ is the number of lagged terms for the $X$-variable, and $k$ is the number of parameters to be estimated in the unrestricted model. Thus, $m$ is the degrees of freedom for the numerator and $n - k$ is the degrees of freedom for the denominator. The critical $F$-value is $F_{\alpha, m, n-k}$.

Given two variables that are being tested, $X$ and $Y$, there are four possible outcomes. Causation may be unilateral from $X$ to $Y$, it may be unilateral from $Y$ to $X$, it may be bilateral, or there may be no causality in either direction.

For eons, economists have debated the effectiveness of traditional monetary policy and its ability to manage the economy by controlling the money supply. The debate rages as to whether there is any causal effect of changes in the nation's money stock on GNP. Table 11.8 is taken from the Economic Report of the President 2010 and is displayed in a Minitab worksheet.

A Granger test with $m = 3$ lagged terms is conducted to isolate causality if it exists. Unilateral causality from the money supply to GNP is first tested by treating GNP as the dependent variable. The restricted model, $GNP_t = f(GNP_{t-1}, GNP_{t-2}, GNP_{t-3})$ produces $SSE_R = 233{,}890$. The unrestricted model, which also includes the current value for MS as well as the three lagged terms, has an $SSE_U$ of 166,910. Given $m = 3$ and $n - k = 12 - 8 = 4$, the $F$-value is only 0.535. Tested at 0.10, the critical $F$-value is $F_{0.10,3,4} = 4.19$. The null is not rejected. It appears that changes in the money supply do not Granger-cause changes in GNP. This bodes poorly for those who argue that monetary policy should be used to control economic conditions through the manipulation of the money supply.

A test for causality from GNP to the money supply can be used to draw conclusions whether changes in the GNP affect the money stock in the economy. The restricted model, $MS_t = f(MS_{t-1}, MS_{t-2}, MS_{t-3})$, produces $SSE_R = 44{,}583$, and the unrestricted model, which also includes the current measure of GNP as well as its three lagged values, has $SSE_U = 11{,}108$. Since $m$ and $n - k$ remain the same, $F = 4.018$. Given the critical $F$-value of 4.19, the null is

■ **Table 11.8**  Data on the Money Supply and GNP (Both in Billions of Dollars)

| → | C1 | C2 | C3 | C4 | C5 | C6 | C7 | C8 | C9 |
|---|---|---|---|---|---|---|---|---|---|
| | Year | GNP | MS | LAGGNP1 | LAGGNP2 | LAGGNP3 | LAGMS1 | LAGMS2 | LAGMS3 |
| 1 | 1995 | 7414.7 | 1127.5 | * | * | * | * | * | * |
| 2 | 1996 | 7838.5 | 1081.6 | 7414.7 | * | * | 1127.5 | * | * |
| 3 | 1997 | 8332.4 | 1072.8 | 7838.5 | 7414.7 | * | 1081.6 | 1127.5 | * |
| 4 | 1998 | 8793.5 | 1095.8 | 8332.4 | 7838.5 | 7414.7 | 1072.8 | 1081.6 | 1127.5 |
| 5 | 1999 | 9353.5 | 1122.7 | 8793.5 | 8332.4 | 7838.5 | 1095.8 | 1072.8 | 1081.6 |
| 6 | 2000 | 9951.5 | 1087.7 | 9353.5 | 8793.5 | 8332.4 | 1122.7 | 1095.8 | 1072.8 |
| 7 | 2001 | 10286.2 | 1182.2 | 9951.5 | 9353.5 | 8793.5 | 1087.7 | 1122.7 | 1095.8 |
| 8 | 2002 | 10642.3 | 1220.4 | 10286.2 | 9951.5 | 9353.5 | 1182.2 | 1087.7 | 1122.7 |
| 9 | 2003 | 11142.1 | 1306.9 | 10642.3 | 10286.2 | 9951.5 | 1220.4 | 1182.2 | 1087.7 |
| 10 | 2004 | 11867.8 | 1377.1 | 11142.1 | 10642.3 | 10286.2 | 1306.9 | 1220.4 | 1182.2 |
| 11 | 2005 | 12638.4 | 1375.3 | 11867.8 | 11142.1 | 10642.3 | 1377.1 | 1306.9 | 1220.4 |
| 12 | 2006 | 13398.9 | 1367.9 | 12638.4 | 11867.8 | 11142.1 | 1375.3 | 1377.1 | 1306.9 |
| 13 | 2007 | 14077.6 | 1375.8 | 13398.9 | 12638.4 | 11867.8 | 1367.9 | 1375.3 | 1377.1 |
| 14 | 2008 | 14441.4 | 1594.7 | 14077.6 | 13398.9 | 12638.4 | 1375.8 | 1367.9 | 1375.3 |
| 15 | 2009 | 14258.7 | 1693.3 | 14441.4 | 14077.6 | 13398.9 | 1594.7 | 1375.8 | 1367.9 |

again not rejected. There appears to be no causality running from GNP to the money supply either.

Take note that these findings run contrary to many studies conducted in the past that find causality. This anomaly is likely due to the small sample size used here for pedagogical purposes. The first problem at the end of this section is a bit more realistic.

## SECTION 11.4 PROBLEMS

1. Access the file GRANGER. The data set contains more extensive data for GNP and the money supply. Perform Granger causality tests with $m = 3$. Test for causality at 10% in both directions.

2. Under what conditions can the Granger causality be applied? What is its purpose?

3. In what way is the Granger test a distributed lag model?

## 11.5 METHODS OF FORECASTING: MOVING AVERAGES AND EXPONENTIAL SMOOTHING

Time series data typically exhibit four components. The *secular trend*, or simply trend, is the long-run behavior of the series over many time periods. Nonstationary data tend to trend up or trend down over time. Figure 11.1 shows the upper trend in GNP taken from the data set GRANGER.

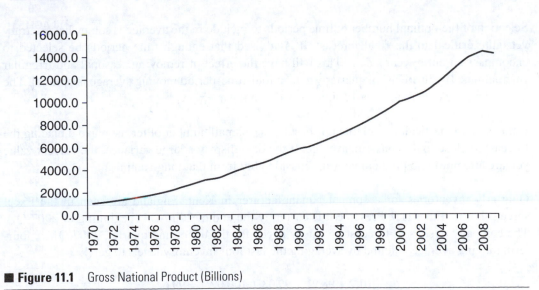

■ **Figure 11.1**   Gross National Product (Billions)

Time series will also often exhibit a *seasonal component* in which repeated patterns at specific points throughout the year are evident. Obviously, retail sales will show a "bump" near the end of each calendar year as holiday shoppers prepare for Christmas. Seasonal sales of winter items such as coats, snow skis, and other commodities associated with winter weather become evident each autumn. Seasonal components generally last less than one year.

*Cyclical variations*, or business cycles, fluctuate above and below the long-term trend. They cover longer time periods than do seasonal components, often encompassing three or more years in duration.

Finally, *irregular fluctuations* are the result of some unique shock to the economy that is unlikely to reoccur in the same fashion on a regular basis. A far-reaching financial crisis, widespread international hostilities, or a world energy shortage are examples.

All of these components pose a challenge to forecasting future values of the time series under study. Two simple and commonly used methods of forecasting time series values are the moving average and exponential smoothing. Both have the effect of smoothing out wild fluctuations in the data, thereby making forecasting a less daunting task. Each is examined in turn in this section.

## ● Moving Average

A moving average is computed by averaging out a fixed number of values in the time series. As time passes, the oldest value is replaced with the most recent, maintaining the set number of values chosen for the process. The moving average is most useful for short-term forecasts and enjoys its greatest success when the data fluctuate in a stationary manner around a stable, long-run average. It may be necessary to apply first-differencing to the original data to produce some degree of stationarity and then perform a moving average on the first-differences.

Selection of the optimal number of time periods to include in the average is somewhat arbitrary yet quite critical to the final forecast. It is advised that enough time periods be selected to encompass an entire year's data. This will have the effect of removing seasonal and irregular fluctuations. If you are using quarterly data, a four-time-period moving average is optimal. The use of monthly data requires a 12-time-period moving average.

If the data are particularly volatile it is best to use a small number of terms to avoid placing the forecast to close to the long-run average. If the data display a large variance, the current value you are attempting to predict may vary considerably from that long-run mean.

Quarterly inventories for a computer manufacturer in Kent, England are seen in the Excel screen shot in Table 11.9. Presume it is currently the end of 2006-Q4 (beginning of 2007-Q1). The company desires to forecast inventory needs for the upcoming quarter, 2007-Q1. A four-term moving average is found by averaging the last four inventory levels to get

$$101.2 + 98.21 + 99.03 + 100.02/4 = 99.62$$

as seen in column C of the screen shot. At the end of 2007-Q1 the company realizes it needed 100.67 during that quarter. These actual inventory needs are recorded in column B. The error in column D is found as the actual inventory level minus the forecast. In the first case it's 100.67 − 99.615 = 1.055.

The prediction for inventory needs in the next time period of 2007-Q2 is found by dropping the oldest value of 101.2 in 2006-Q1 and picking up the newest level of 100.67 now that it is known. The moving average for 2007-Q2 is then estimated to be

$$98.21 + 99.03 + 100.02 + 100.67/4 = 99.48$$

At the end of 2007-Q2, or subsequently thereafter, the company will learn that it actually needed 99.6 in 2007-Q2. The error of 0.1175 can be figured.

This process continues for the indefinite duration. The mean of the most recent four values is taken as the forecast for the ensuing time period.

■ **Table 11.9**  Forecasts of Inventory Levels

| | A | B | C | D |
|---|---|---|---|---|
| 1 | Time Period | Required Inventories | Forecast | Errors |
| 2 | 2006-Q1 | 101.2 | | |
| 3 | 2006 - Q2 | 98.21 | #N/A | |
| 4 | 2006 -Q3 | 99.03 | #N/A | |
| 5 | 2006-Q4 | 100.02 | #N/A | |
| 6 | 2007 -Q1 | 100.67 | 99.615 | 1.055 |
| 7 | 2007 - Q2 | 99.6 | 99.4825 | 0.1175 |
| 8 | 2007 -Q3 | 100.69 | 99.83 | 0.86 |
| 9 | 2007-Q4 | 98.37 | 100.245 | -1.875 |
| 10 | 2008 -Q1 | 100.55 | 99.8325 | 0.7175 |
| 11 | 2008-Q2 | 99.05 | 99.8025 | -0.7525 |
| 12 | 2008-Q3 | 100.6 | 99.665 | 0.935 |
| 13 | 2008-Q4 | 102.41 | 99.6425 | 2.7675 |
| 14 | 2009-Q1 | 100.25 | 100.6525 | -0.4025 |
| 15 | 2009-Q2 | 100.01 | 100.5775 | -0.5675 |
| 16 | 2009-Q3 | 99.62 | 100.8175 | -1.1975 |
| 17 | 2009-Q4 | 99.74 | 100.5725 | -0.8325 |
| 18 | 2010-Q1 | 98.8 | 99.905 | -1.105 |
| 19 | 2010-Q2 | 98.14 | 99.5425 | -1.4025 |
| 20 | 2010-Q3 | 100.46 | 99.075 | 1.385 |
| 21 | 2010-Q4 | 99.29 | 99.285 | 0.005 |
| 22 | 2011-Q1 | | 99.1725 | |

The Excel worksheet pictured in Table 11.9 is generated by selecting

Data > Data Analysis > Moving Average > OK

Then enter B1:B21 in the "Input Range" window, check Labels in First Row, and enter a 4 in the "Interval" window. Enter C3 for the output range. *Note:* The output range should start one row below the first value of the target variable which is 101.2 found in B2.

Notice that if four time periods are used to form the moving average, then four values are lost at the beginning of the process. That results because four time periods must pass before the average can be computed.

A forecast can be obtained from Minitab with

Statistic > Time Series > Moving Average > Results > Summary and Results Table

However, the first forecast will be in the fourth row adjacent to the value of 100.02. This is *incorrect*. The column must be copied and moved one row to appear as it does in the Excel printout above.

As seen in Figure 11.2, Minitab also gives the

$$\textit{Mean Absolute Percentage Error (MAPE)} = \frac{\sum\left[\frac{|e_t|}{A_t} * 100\right]}{no.\,of\,errors} \qquad (11.5.1)$$

where $|e_t|$ is the absolute value of the errors and $A_t$ is the actual value of the variable.

Further,

$$\textit{Mean Absolute Deviation (MAD)} = \frac{\sum|e_t|}{no.\,of\,errors} \qquad (11.5.2)$$

Finally,

$$\textit{Mean Square Deviation (MSD)} = \frac{\sum e_t^2}{no.\,of\,errors} \qquad (11.5.3)$$

Each of these error measurements can be used to compare alternative forecasting schemes. A four-period moving average can be compared with a five- or six-term moving average as to which offers the smallest error. The results can also be compared with the forecasts derived from a smoothing technique discussed next. That method disclosing the least error should be considered as the preferred approach.

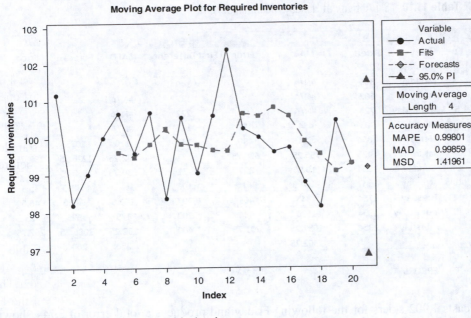

**Figure 11.2** Minitab's Output for a Moving Average

The smoothing effect that averaging has is seen in Figure 11.2. The actual values for inventories are more erratic and display greater unpredictability, while the "fits," or averages, are dampened and less volatile.

## ● First-Differencing

The moving average does not correct well for trends and cyclical fluctuations. If we were to forecast prices for home heating oil for the month of October, using a four-month moving average for the four previous months of June, July, August, and September, we would likely produce a poor approximation for the more chilly month of October. Perhaps using the past four Octobers of previous years might prove more effective. But changes in technology over such a long time period, as well as structural modifications in housing, or perhaps even climate changes over the years, might taint the forecast.

If the data trend up or down, a simple moving average will always lag behind the actual values. To offset these deficiencies it is often wise to perform a moving average on the *first-differences* of the raw data. The forecast is then based on the subsequent adjustment.

Consider the data in Table 11.10 for the number of "snow bunnies" who have graced the slopes over the past several days at Holiday Mountain Ski Lift somewhere in the Alps.

Clearly the number of skiers is mounting throughout the time period. There is an unmistakable upward movement in the traffic on the slopes. The four-period (day) moving average in column

■ **Table 11.10** Ski Activity at Holiday Mountain Ski Lift

| | A | B | C | D | E | F | G | H |
|---|---|---|---|---|---|---|---|---|
| 1 | Day | Skiers | MA4 | Error | First Difference | MAFD4 | Forecast | Error |
| 2 | Sunday | 225 | | | | | | |
| 3 | Monday | 365 | #N/A | | 140 | | | |
| 4 | Tuesday | 502 | #N/A | | 137 | #N/A | | |
| 5 | Wednesday | 724 | #N/A | | 222 | #N/A | | |
| 6 | Thursday | 905 | 454 | 451 | 181 | #N/A | | |
| 7 | Friday | 1054 | 624 | 430 | 149 | 170 | 1075 | -21 |
| 8 | Saturday | 1425 | 796.25 | 628.75 | 371 | 172.25 | 1226.25 | 198.75 |
| 9 | Sunday | 1354 | 1027 | 327 | -71 | 230.75 | 1655.75 | -301.75 |
| 10 | Monday | 1547 | 1184.5 | 362.5 | 193 | 157.5 | 1511.5 | 35.5 |
| 11 | Tuesday | 1754 | 1345 | 409 | 207 | 160.5 | 1707.5 | 46.5 |
| 12 | Wednesday | 1954 | 1520 | 434 | 200 | 175 | 1929 | 25 |
| 13 | Thursday | 2354 | 1652.25 | 701.75 | 400 | 132.25 | 2086.25 | 267.75 |
| 14 | | | 1902.25 | | | 250 | 2604 | |
| 15 | | | | | | | | |
| 16 | ERRORS | | | 3744 | | | | 250.75 |

C forecasts 1,902 skiers for the following Friday and produces a total error of 3,744 shown in column D. First-differences are taken in column E by subtracting one day's traffic from the following day. In the first instance it's found as 365 – 225 = 140. Column F displays the four-period moving average of the first-differences.

The actual forecast is then determined by adding the moving average of the first-difference to the actual value of the previous day. The forecast for the second Monday is 157.5 + 1,354 = 1,511.5. At the end of Monday we can see that the actual count was 1,547 and the error was only 35 people. It was 362 without the first differencing. The errors sum to only 250.75, much less than the 3,744 suffered without first differencing.

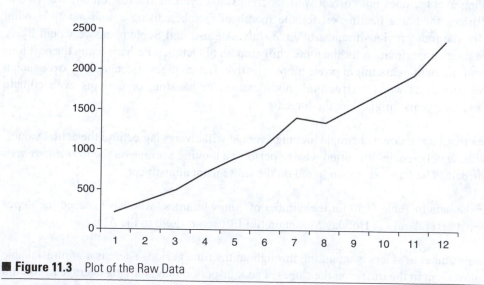

■ **Figure 11.3** Plot of the Raw Data

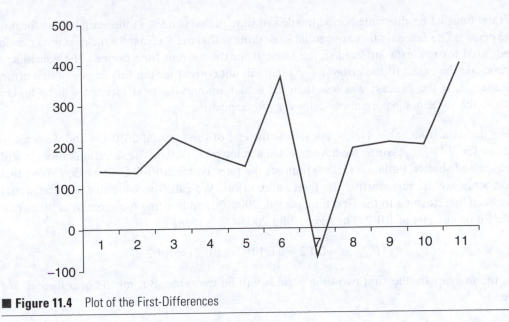

**■ Figure 11.4** Plot of the First-Differences

While the original raw data in column A show the troublesome upward trend in Figure 11.3, this is not the case with the first-differences.

Figure 11.4 reveals that the differenced values are much more stationary.

## ● Single Exponential Smoothing

While a moving average is a very useful form of forecasting, it suffers from the disadvantage of assigning the same weight of importance to older data that it does to more recent values.[9] As a forecasting method, exponential smoothing can be used to avoid this dilemma by conferring more significance to more recent data. The logic in this procedure seems evident. Last month's data are likely more important in determining next month's value than are data from several time periods in the past. Exponential smoothing can capture that advantage.

Single exponential smoothing is used if the data exhibit no upward or downward trend. A simple plot of the data will allow you to make this determination. If a trend is detected, double exponential smoothing discussed below is the desired method of forecasting.

The process involves a *smoothing constant*, $\alpha$, such that $0 < \alpha < 1$. Equation (11.5.4) produces the desired forecast, $F_{t+1}$, for the next time period:

$$F_{t+1} = F_t + \alpha(A_t - F_t) \qquad (11.5.4)$$

$F_t$ is the forecast for this time period (made last time period) and $A_t$ is the actual value for this time period. The rationale for exponential smoothing is that the forecast for the next time period is adjusted for the error suffered in the forecast for the current time period. The adjustment depends on the extent of the error $(Y_t - F_t)$ but will not correct for the full degree of that error, since $\alpha < 1$. If the forecast was less than the actual amount the next forecast will be higher because the value in the parentheses, $A_t - F_t$, will be positive.

Using the data from Table 11.9, suppose it is the end of time period 2010-Q4 and we want to forecast for 2011-Q1. Assume we have selected a value for $\alpha$ of 0.6. The selection rationale will be discussed shortly. Equation (11.5.4) requires the forecast for 2010-Q4 but we don't have that value, since we are just starting the forecasting effort. We can find what that forecast would have been by returning to the first time period, 2006-Q1, and setting the forecast at the actual value for inventories of 101.2. The forecast for 2006-Q2 is then

$$F_{2006\text{-}Q2} = 101.2 + 0.6(101.2 - 101.2) = 101.2$$

Yes, the forecast for the first two time periods will be the same. But for the next forecast we have

$$F_{2006\text{-}Q3} = 101.2 + 0.6(98.21 - 101.2) = 99.406$$

Furthermore,

$$F_{2006\text{-}Q4} = 99.406 + 0.6(99.03 - 99.406) = 99.1804$$

This continues down the line until we arrive at the current date of 2010-Q4. The forecast then for 2011-Q1 is

$$F_{2011\text{-}Q1} = 99.70171 + 0.6(99.29 - 99.70171) = 99.4547$$

Of course, the work can be done using Excel by choosing Data > Data Analysis > Exponential Smoothing. You *must* enter $1 - \alpha$ (not $\alpha$) in the "Damping Factor" window. Specify cell C2 for the output range. Table 11.11 displays the results. The 99.29 and 99.70171 are taken from the table and used to get $F_{2011\text{-}Q1}$.

Minitab requires Stat > Time Series > Single Exponential Smoothing. Enter $\alpha$ (*not* $1 - \alpha$ as with Excel) in the USE window. Minitab will produce the error measures and the forecast along with a 95% confidence interval for the forecast.

```
Accuracy Measures

MAPE 1.12066
MAD  1.11970
MSD  1.63759

Forecasts

Period  Forecast  Lower    Upper
21       99.4547   96.7115  102.198
```

■ **Table 11.11**  Excel's Exponential Smoothing

| | A | B | C |
|---|---|---|---|
| | Time Period | Required Inventories | Forecast |
| 1 | | | |
| 2 | 2006-Q1 | 101.2 | 101.2 |
| 3 | 2006 - Q2 | 98.21 | 101.2 |
| 4 | 2006 -Q3 | 99.03 | 99.406 |
| 5 | 2006-Q4 | 100.02 | 99.1804 |
| 6 | 2007 -Q1 | 100.67 | 99.68416 |
| 7 | 2007 - Q2 | 99.6 | 100.2757 |
| 8 | 2007 -Q3 | 100.69 | 99.87027 |
| 9 | 2007-Q4 | 98.37 | 100.3621 |
| 10 | 2008 -Q1 | 100.55 | 99.16684 |
| 11 | 2008-Q2 | 99.05 | 99.99674 |
| 12 | 2008-Q3 | 100.6 | 99.42869 |
| 13 | 2008-Q4 | 102.41 | 100.1315 |
| 14 | 2009-Q1 | 100.25 | 101.4986 |
| 15 | 2009-Q2 | 100.01 | 100.7494 |
| 16 | 2009-Q3 | 99.62 | 100.3058 |
| 17 | 2009-Q4 | 99.74 | 99.89431 |
| 18 | 2010-Q1 | 98.8 | 99.80172 |
| 19 | 2010-Q2 | 98.14 | 99.20069 |
| 20 | 2010-Q3 | 100.46 | 98.56428 |
| 21 | 2010-Q4 | 99.29 | 99.70171 |
| 22 | 2011-Q1 | | 99.45468 |

The damping effect that exponential smoothing has can be seen in Figure 11.5. The smaller the $\alpha$-value, the greater will be the damping effect, and the less influence the current actual value will have on the forecast. So if the data are less volatile, it is best to use a smaller $\alpha$. If the data show a pronounced variation the current actual value may be quite different from the mean the data may exhibit, and its use in forecasting should be minimized with a smaller $\alpha$. There is no hard and fast rule as to what is "less volatile." You should experiment with different values for $\alpha$ and use the one that produces the smaller error measurements.

## ● Double Exponential Smoothing

If the data show a trend up or down over time, the Holt method of double exponential smoothing should be used.[10] A second smoothing constant, $\beta$, is identified to adjust for the trend as shown in Equations (11.5.5A), (11.5.5B), and (11.5.5C).

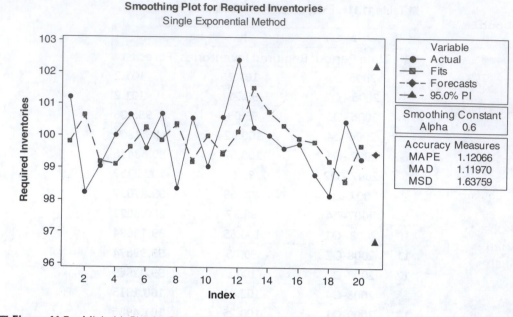

**Figure 11.5**  Minitab's Plot for Single Exponential Smoothing

$$L_t = \alpha A_t + (1 - \alpha)(L_{t-1} + T_{t-1}) \qquad (11.5.5A)$$

$$T_t = \beta(L_t - L_{t-1}) - (1 - \beta)T_{t-1} \qquad (11.5.5B)$$

$$F_{t+k} = L_t + kT_t \qquad (11.5.5C)$$

where $L_t$ is the *level* of the series at time period $t$, $T$ is the trend factor inherent in the series, and $k$ is the number of time periods into the future you wish to forecast. Selection of values for $\alpha$ and $\beta$ is done similarly to that applied in single exponential smoothing.

The initial forecast for $L_0$ and $T_0$ can be attained by a simple regression model in which the time series is regressed on the time period using standard OLS techniques. The intercept, $b_0$, is taken as the value for $L_0$, and the slope coefficient, $b_1$, serves as $T_0$. However, due to the arithmetic complexity of the calculations we will perform the analysis using Minitab. Any statistical package that provides double exponential smoothing can be used.

The data in Table 11.12 provide the exchange rate between the U.S. dollar and the South Korean won from 1988 to 2009. The graph in Figure 11.6 shows a clear upward trend in the number of won needed to purchase one U.S. dollar.

Minitab produces the desired results with Statistic > Time Series > Double Exponential Smoothing. Using the default values of 0.20 just for illustration purposes for $\alpha$ and $\beta$ (Minitab calls it Gamma), the Minitab output is

```
Double Exponential Smoothing for Won

Data  Won
Length 22

Smoothing Constants

Alpha (level)    0.2
Gamma (trend)    0.2

Accuracy Measures

MAPE       11.5
MAD        121.5
MSD        32033.1

Forecasts

Period   Forecast   Lower     Upper
23       1192.20    894.616   1489.79
```

**Table 11.12** The U.S. Dollar and the South Korean Won

| Year | Won |
|------|---------|
| 1988 | 734.52 |
| 1989 | 674.13 |
| 1990 | 710.64 |
| 1991 | 736.73 |
| 1992 | 784.66 |
| 1993 | 805.75 |
| 1994 | 806.93 |
| 1995 | 772.69 |
| 1996 | 805 |
| 1997 | 953.19 |
| 1998 | 1400.4 |
| 1999 | 1189.84 |
| 2000 | 1130.9 |
| 2001 | 1292.02 |
| 2002 | 1250.31 |
| 2003 | 1192.08 |
| 2004 | 1145.24 |
| 2005 | 1023.75 |
| 2006 | 954.32 |
| 2007 | 928.97 |
| 2008 | 1098.71 |
| 2009 | 1274.63 |

Again, experimentation with different values for $\alpha$ and $\beta$ can be attempted to determine optimality based on error measurements. Holt's method for trended data is considered superior in most instances because, given a trend, single exponential smoothing will always trail behind the trend. If the trend is upward, single exponential smoothing will likely underestimate the actual value, while a downward trend will produce an overestimate.

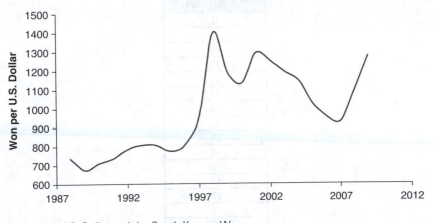

■ **Figure 11.6** The U.S. Dollar and the South Korean Won

## SECTION 11.5 PROBLEMS

### Conceptual Problems

1. Define and give examples of:

   A. Secular trend.
   B. Seasonal component.
   C. Cyclical variation.
   D. Irregular fluctuations.

2. What is the purpose of moving average and exponential smoothing?

3. Describe, define, and give examples of the following—detail the advantages and disadvantages of each:

   A. Mean Absolute Percentage Error.
   B. Mean Absolute Deviation.
   C. Mean Square Deviation.

4. When does a moving average fail to best perform its purpose as well as it should?

5. Why and when might first-differencing be necessary? What function does it perform?

### Computational Problems

1. Plot the data for the output in tons of steel for a plant in Asia based on the data seen below. Do they appear to be trended up or down? If not, you can use a moving average of the original data to forecast. Compute the three-period moving average by hand or using your preferred software. Plot the moving average on the same graph as the original data. Comment on the outcome. How does the moving average facilitate your ability to forecast? Forecast the value for two time periods in the future.

| Output (Tons) |
|:---:|
| 12 |
| 6 |
| 15 |
| 20 |
| 25 |
| 17 |
| 5 |
| 12 |
| 25 |
| 15 |
| 9 |
| 14 |
| 18 |
| 8 |
| 8 |

2. Plot the data seen here. Does a trend appear to prevail? If so, you must apply first-differencing to forecast with a four-period moving average. What is your forecast for two time periods in the future?

| Data |
|------|
| 5 |
| 6 |
| 8 |
| 7 |
| 9 |
| 10 |
| 11 |
| 10 |
| 12 |
| 15 |
| 14 |

3. Given the data in problem 1, compute and interpret the MAPE, MAD, and MSD.

4. Using the data from problem 3, set a smoothing constant of $\alpha = 0.3$ and use exponential smoothing to forecast the next value.

## 11.6 AUTOREGRESSIVE MOVING AVERAGES

An application of a "moving average" that is totally different from the one just discussed above uses a finite number of unrelated lagged error terms as independent variables. An example is shown in Equation (11.6.1) in which $e_{t-i}$ represent the error terms.

$$Y_t = \beta_0 + \beta_1 e_{t-1} + \beta_2 e_{t-2} + \cdots + \beta_q e_{t-q} + e_t \qquad (11.6.1)$$

This is a model of order $q$ and is written as MA($q$), since $q$ lagged error terms are incorporated. It's called moving average because it describes the moving average of past error terms and should not be confused with the moving average discussed in Section 11.5.

Of course, the pressing question concerns the level of $q$. That is, how many lagged error terms should be integrated into the model. The order of the MA process can be decided with an *autocorrelation function* (ACF). The ACF measures the correlation between $Y_t$ and $Y_{t-i}$ in which the actual impact of intermediate lags is retained and not assumed to be constant. Thus, the correlation between $Y_t$ and $Y_{t-2}$ *includes* the effects of the correlation between $Y_t$ and $Y_{t-1}$ and $Y_{t-1}$ and $Y_{t-2}$, and so on. This distinction will become important in a moment.

The equations and actual computations to construct an ACF are complex and esoteric. We will not consider them here, since this work will thankfully be performed on a computer. It is only essential that you comprehend the *concept* behind these statistical tools, that is, understand *what* they measure or reflect and not the actual mathematical calculation. Minitab can produce the ACF with Statistic > Time Series > Autocorrelation. Use the default number of lags or specify a desired number and click "Store ACF," "Store t-statistics," and "Store Ljung-Box Statistics" (LBQ).

Returning to our data for the Korean won produces the Minitab output:

```
Autocorrelation Function: Won

Lag   ACF        T       LBQ
1     0.742757   3.48    13.87
2     0.501033   1.62    20.50
3     0.400390   1.16    24.95
4     0.279489   0.77    27.24
5     0.165987   0.44    28.10
6     0.043426   0.11    28.16
```

We are essentially testing for significant correlation between error terms. The null is that no significant correlation exists. A *correlogram* that graphs these correlations shown in Figure 11.7 reveals that only the first lag carries significance. This is revealed by the "spike" that extends outside the slightly curved lines that indicate the range for a 5% hypothesis test. This is further borne out by the *t*-values. One commonly used rule is that a *t*-statistic with an absolute value greater than 1.65 for lags 1 through 3, or greater than 2 for lags 4 and beyond, indicates a correlation not equal to zero. $q$ is then identified optimally as a model of order 1 MA(1).

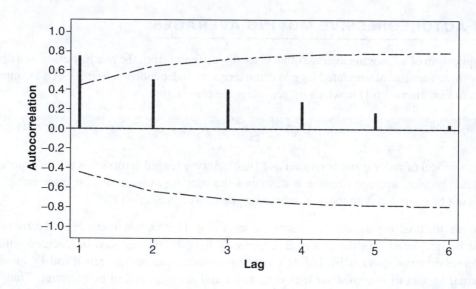

■ **Figure 11.7**  Autocorrelation Function for the South Korean Won (With 5% Significance Limits for the Autocorrelations)

● **The ARMA Model**

If we were to combine this MA model with the AR model presented in Section 11.2 we have an *autoregressive moving average model* (ARMA). This approach expresses the current value of $Y_t$ as a linear function of past values of $Y$ *and* of the error terms. The order of the model is written as ARMA($p$, $q$), where $p$ is the number of lags of the dependent variable and $q$ is the number of lagged error terms. ARMA(2, 3) is

$$Y_t = \beta_0 + \beta_1 Y_{t-1} + \beta_2 Y_{t-2} + \alpha_1 e_{t-1} + \alpha_2 e_{t-2} + \alpha_3 e_{t-3} + e_t$$

The proper order for the AR portion of the model is determined using a *partial* ACF, which measures the correlations between $Y_t$ and $Y_{t-i}$ in which intermediate correlations *are* held constant. The correlation between $Y_t$ and $Y_{t-3}$ is not impacted by that between $Y_t$ and $Y_{t-2}$, which is effectively removed. Use of the data for the Korean won yields these results by Minitab:

```
Partial Autocorrelation Function: Won

Lag    PACF         T
1       0.742757    3.48
2      -0.112989   -0.53
3       0.158429    0.74
4      -0.125417   -0.59
5      -0.011735   -0.06
6      -0.146083   -0.69
```

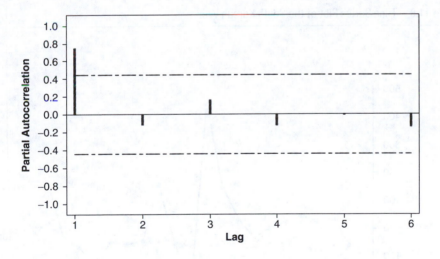

■ **Figure 11.8** Partial Autocorrelation Function for the South Korean Won (With 5% Significance Limits for the Partial Autocorrelations)

The partial ACF is shown in Figure 11.8. Again, only the first lag appears to exhibit any statistical significance. It would seem the ARMA(1, 1) is appropriate.

### ● Integration—ARIMA

Before any further work can be done the data must be stationary as defined above in Section 11.3. This is done, you recall, by differencing the data one or more times. First, let's graph the original data in Figure 11.9. Clearly the data are not stationary.

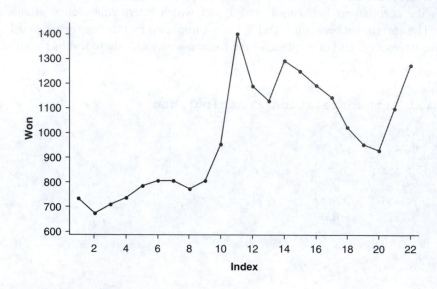

**■ Figure 11.9** Time Series Plot of the South Korean Won

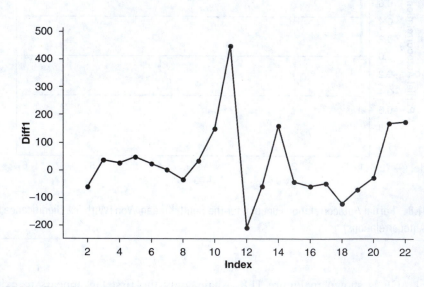

**■ Figure 11.10** Time Series Plot of $Y_t - Y_{t-1}$ (Diff1)

The data are first-differenced as $(Y_t - Y_{t-1})$ using Minitab by selecting Statistic > Time Series > Differences and entering a lag of 1. Table 11.13 contains the differenced values as well as the original data for the won.

The differenced data are said to be *integrated* to the order of *d* producing an *autoregressive integrated moving average* model. The order of the model is ARIMA(*p, d, q*), where *d* is the number of times the series was differenced to produce stationarity. Setting *d* = 1, the differenced data appear as in Figure 11.10.

Despite the two "spikes" in the data the mean seems to be stable over time which is required for stationarity. Stationarity can be also detected using the unit-root test described in Section 11.3. In performing that test, Equation (11.3.6) produced a *p*-value of 0.921.

After the data have been first-differenced, an ARMA(1,1) model is estimated using the Minitab commands Statistic > Time Series > ARIMA. Enter 1,0,1 in the three windows for Autoregressive, Differencing, and Moving Average. Minitab provides

■ **Table 11.13**   First-Differences for the South Korean Won

| ↓ | C1 | C2 | C3 |
|---|------|--------|-----------|
|   | date | won | First Diff |
| 1 | 1988 | 734.52 | * |
| 2 | 1989 | 674.13 | -60.39 |
| 3 | 1990 | 710.64 | 36.51 |
| 4 | 1991 | 736.73 | 26.09 |
| 5 | 1992 | 784.66 | 47.93 |
| 6 | 1993 | 805.75 | 21.09 |
| 7 | 1994 | 806.93 | 1.18 |
| 8 | 1995 | 772.69 | -34.24 |
| 9 | 1996 | 805.00 | 32.31 |
| 10 | 1997 | 953.19 | 148.19 |
| 11 | 1998 | 1400.40 | 447.21 |
| 12 | 1999 | 1189.84 | -210.56 |
| 13 | 2000 | 1130.90 | -58.94 |
| 14 | 2001 | 1292.02 | 161.12 |
| 15 | 2002 | 1250.31 | -41.71 |
| 16 | 2003 | 1192.08 | -58.23 |
| 17 | 2004 | 1145.24 | -46.84 |
| 18 | 2005 | 1023.75 | -121.49 |
| 19 | 2006 | 954.32 | -69.43 |
| 20 | 2007 | 928.97 | -25.35 |
| 21 | 2008 | 1098.71 | 169.74 |
| 22 | 2009 | 1274.63 | 175.92 |

```
Final Estimates of Parameters

Type          Coef         SE Coef            T              P
AR 1          0.6316        0.3240          1.95          0.067
MA 1          0.9204        0.2782          3.31          0.004
Constant      9.005         3.809           2.36          0.029
Mean          24.44         10.34

Number of observations: 21

Forecasts from period 22

                    95% Limits
Period   Forecast   Lower     Upper     Actual
23       8.359     -259.270   275.988
```

The forecast of 8.359 is then added to the last entry for the won (see Table 11.13) to generate a value of 1,274.63 + 8.359 = 1,282.989. The same results are accomplished with an ARIMA (1, 1, 1) model on the values of the won (not on the first-differences as done above). The results are

```
Final Estimates of Parameters

Type          Coef       SE Coef       T         P
AR 1          0.6316      0.3240      1.95      0.067
MA 1          0.9204      0.2782      3.31      0.004
Constant      9.005       3.809       2.36      0.029
```

```
Differencing: 1 regular difference
Number of observations: Original series 22, after differencing 21
Residuals: SS = 335469 (backforecasts excluded)
          MS = 18637 DF = 18

Forecasts from period 22

                    95% Limits
Period  Forecast  Lower    Upper      Actual
23      1282.99   1015.36  1550.62
```

Notice that the forecast is 1,282.99, which is exactly the same as obtained with the ARIMA (1,0,1) model performed on the differenced data.

## ● Box–Jenkins Methodology

Actually, the material presented above in this section is based on the Box–Jenkins process.[11] The methodology is often broken down into four stages or steps.

The first step is *identification*. This involves determination of the values for $p$, $d$, and $q$ with the use of correlograms, the ACF, and the PACF as described earlier.

The second step is the estimation procedure accomplished with the use of modern computer software such as Minitab. This too was demonstrated above.

The third stage is *diagnostic checking* by comparing several different models. Alternatives can be used to create different forecasts like that done with the moving average and exponential smoothing models cited earlier. Comparison of the subsequent errors can be completed to isolate the model that generated the least error. An examination of the errors that result from a single model can be undertaken to determine if they behave in the random manner we normally associate with regression models.

The fourth and final step of the Box–Jenkins process is the art of actually forecasting the variable. The entire procedure is complex in its methodological application. The reader is advised to consult other sources that focus on the Box–Jenkins method of forecasting.

**CHAPTER PROBLEMS 11**

## CHAPTER PROBLEMS

### Conceptual Problems

1. Define and describe the autoregressive model. Give an example.

2. How many observations will you lose in the example you gave above?

3. An autoregressive model has 55 observations and four lagged variables. How many degrees of freedom will it have?

4. Define a distributed lagged model. Why is it called a distributed lagged model? Give an example.

5. Discuss and describe a Koyck transformation. Why is it also called a geometric lagged model? Give an example.

6. A variable is said to be stationary over time if it exhibits what characteristic? What restrictions does this impose on the variable's long-run mean and variance?

7. Define cointegration.

8. Discuss and describe the Almon polynomial lag. Discuss in detail how it differs from the Koyck lag.

9. Under what conditions can Granger causality be applied? What is its purpose? Create a complete example of your own devising, choosing carefully what variables you include in your model. Explain just how you would apply Granger causality to this model.

10. Explain how moving averages work. If the data are not stationed, what adjustments should be made?

11. How does single exponential smoothing work? What are its advantages compared with the moving average?

12. When should a double exponential smoothing technique be used?

13. Describe a correlogram. What is its purpose?

14. Briefly describe the four steps to the Box–Jenkins methodology.

## Computational Problems

1. An autoregressive model is reported to be as seen below with $t$-values in parentheses. How many lagged terms should be included in the model's final form?

$$Y_t = 47.3 + 0.47Y_{t-1} - 4.2Y_{t-2} + 1.72Y_{t-3}$$
$$(2.5) \quad (-3.7) \quad (1.02)$$

2. A model is formed as $Y_t = f(X_t, X_{t-1}, X_{t-2}, X_{t-3}, X_{t-4})$ such that $Y_t = 73.2 + 1.4X_t + 0.471Y_{t-1}$. Create the Koyck transformation.

3. Riley Supplies, Ltd. ships computer software throughout the Midwest. The daily number of late shipments in the past two weeks are shown in the table to the right. Use a 3-period moving average to forecast the number of late shipments for the next day.

| Late Shipments |
| --- |
| 5 |
| 9 |
| 10 |
| 15 |
| 14 |
| 16 |
| 18 |
| 21 |
| 23 |
| 20 |
| 24 |
| 18 |
| 28 |
| 35 |

4. Given the data in problem 3, is a moving average a suitable method of forecasting? Compute the Mean Absolute Percentage Error, the Mean Absolute Deviation, and the Mean Square Deviation.

5. Use a smoothing factor of 0.7 on the data for problem 3 and provide the forecast.

## APPENDIX: THE KOYCK TRANSFORMATION

To transform Equation (11.3.1),

$$Y_t = \alpha_0 + \beta_0 X_t + \beta_1 X_{t-1} + \beta_2 X_{t-2} + \cdots + \beta_p X_{t-p} + \varepsilon_t \qquad (11.3.1)$$

into Equation (11.3.2),

$$Y_t = \alpha_0 + \beta_0 X_t + \lambda Y_{t-1} + \upsilon_t \qquad (11.3.2)$$

first substitute $\beta_0 \lambda^i$ for all $\beta_i$ slope coefficients in Equation (11.3.1) as stated in Equation (11.3.3). Equation (11.3.1) becomes

$$Y_t = \alpha_0 + \beta_0 X_t + \beta_0 \lambda X_{t-1} + \beta_0 \lambda^2 X_{t-2} + \cdots + \beta_0 \lambda^p X_{t-p} + \varepsilon_t \qquad (11.A.1)$$

This is simplified by removing $\beta_0$ from each term on the RHS, yielding

$$Y_t = \alpha_0 + \beta_0 (X_t + \lambda z X_{t-1} + \lambda^2 X_{t-2} + \cdots + \lambda^p X_{t-p}) + \varepsilon_t \qquad (11.A.2)$$

Next, lag all terms in (11.A.2):

$$Y_{t-1} = \alpha_0 + \beta_0 (X_{t-1} + \lambda X_{t-2} + \lambda^2 X_{t-3} + \cdots + \lambda^{p-1} X_{t-p} + \lambda^p X_{t-p-1}) + \varepsilon_{t-1} \qquad (11.A.3)$$

Multiply both sides of (11.A.3) by $\lambda$:

$$\lambda Y_{t-1} = \lambda \alpha_0 + \beta_0 (\lambda X_{t-1} + \lambda^2 X_{t-2} + \lambda^3 X_{t-3} + \cdots + \lambda^p X_{t-p} + \lambda^{p+1} X_{t-p-1}) + \lambda \varepsilon_{t-1} \qquad (11.A.4)$$

Next, subtract (11.A.4) from (11.A.2) and add $\lambda Y_{t-1}$ to both sides of the equation. With some substitution, the final expression is Equation (11.3.2).

# APPENDICES

# ANSWERS TO SELECTED EVEN PROBLEMS

## CHAPTER 2

### Section 2.1

2.

| X | Y | Predicted Y | Residuals |
|---|---|---|---|
| 5 | 10 | 7.91598023 | 2.08402 |
| 9 | 12 | 12.8121911 | −0.812191 |
| 1 | 3 | 3.01976936 | −0.019769 |
| 8 | 11 | 11.5881384 | −0.588138 |
| 0 | 1 | 1.79571664 | −0.795717 |
| 6 | 11 | 9.14003295 | 1.859967 |
| 8 | 12 | 11.5881384 | 0.411862 |
| 6 | 7 | 9.14003295 | −2.140033 |
|   |   |   |   |
| Sum |   |   | 0 |

### Section 2.2

2.

|  | X | Y | $(X - \bar{X})^2$ | $(Y - \bar{Y})^2$ | $(X - \bar{X})(Y - \bar{Y})$ |
|---|---|---|---|---|---|
| Sums | 133.60 | 436.84 | 331.02 | 375.75 | 313.99 |
| n = | 9 |  | $SS_X$ | $SS_Y$ | $SS_{XY}$ |
| Means | 14.844 | 48.538 |  |  |  |
|  |  |  |  |  |  |
| $b_1$ = | 0.949 |  |  |  |  |
| $b_0$ = | 34.45 |  |  |  |  |

$\hat{Y} = 48.54$

4.

|  | Coefficients |
|---|---|
| Intercept | 3.04 |
| Expenditures | 1.18 |

| Expenditures | Patents | Predicted Patents | Residuals |
|:---:|:---:|:---:|:---:|
| 5 | 8 | 8.94 | −0.94 |
| 6 | 9 | 10.12 | −1.12 |
| 9 | 12 | 13.66 | −1.66 |
| 3 | 7 | 6.58 | 0.42 |
| 7 | 15 | 11.3 | 3.7 |
| 2 | 5 | 5.4 | −0.4 |

## Section 2.6
**6.**

| | Coefficients | Standard Error | t Stat | p-Value |
|:---|:---:|:---:|:---:|:---:|
| Intercept | −170.8001942 | 123.872687 | −1.378836597 | 0.210392 |
| NI | 0.095522952 | 0.011484578 | 8.317497956 | 7.1E-05 |

## Chapter Problems
*Computational Problems*
**2.**

| | $X$ | $Y$ | $(X-\bar{X})^2$ | $(Y-\bar{Y})^2$ | $(X-\bar{X})(Y-\bar{Y})$ |
|:---|:---:|:---:|:---:|:---:|:---:|
| **Sums** | 146.00 | 1105.00 | 60.18 | 4890.73 | 382.64 |
| $n =$ | 11 | | $SS_X$ | $SS_Y$ | $SS_{XY}$ |
| **Means** | 13.273 | 100.455 | | | |
| | | | | | |
| $b_1 =$ | 6.358 | | | | |
| $b_0 =$ | 16.067 | | | | |

B.  (i) $\hat{Y} = 73.289$ ; (ii) $\hat{Y} = 16.067 + 6.358(18) = 130.85$.

C.  Income increases by \$6,358.

**4.** It makes no difference which variable you identify as $X$ and which as $Y$ if you want only to calculate the $r^2$ using Equation (2.6.3). $r^2 = 0.0012$ indicates a very weak relationship.

**6.**

| Debt | GDP | Population | Debt/GDP | Debt/Pop |
|:---:|:---:|:---:|:---:|:---:|
| 1 | 1.56 | 34 | 0.641026 | 0.029412 |
| 8.9 | 2.26 | 62 | 3.938053 | 0.143548 |
| 4.7 | 3.31 | 82 | 1.41994 | 0.057317 |
| 0.48 | 1.48 | 143 | 0.324324 | 0.003357 |
| 2.2 | 5.39 | 128 | 0.408163 | 0.017188 |
| 14.4 | 14.62 | 310 | 0.984952 | 0.046452 |
| 4.7 | 2.56 | 66 | 1.835938 | 0.071212 |
| 2.2 | 2.04 | 61 | 1.078431 | 0.036066 |
| 0.129 | 0.35 | 40 | 0.368571 | 0.003225 |
| 0.0058 | 0.0056 | 13 | 1.035714 | 0.000446 |

|            | Debt     | GDP      | Population   | Debt/GDP   | Debt/Pop |
|------------|----------|----------|--------------|------------|----------|
| Debt       | 1        |          |              |            |          |
| GDP        | 0.834475 | 1        |              |            |          |
| Population | 0.728883 | 0.932547 | 1            |            |          |
| Debt/GDP   | 0.493142 | −0.04125 | −0.154556271 | 1          |          |
| Debt/Pop   | 0.620687 | 0.134869 | 0.011419264  | 0.94994812 | 1        |

|       | $X$         | $Y$    | $(X-\bar{X})^2$ | $(Y-\bar{Y})^2$ | $(X-\bar{X})(Y-\bar{Y})$ |
|-------|-------------|--------|------------------|------------------|---------------------------|
| Sums  | 939.00      | 38.71  | 66330.90         | 191.79           | 2599.76                   |
| $n=$  | 10          |        | $SS_X$           | $SS_Y$           | $SS_{XY}$                 |
| Means | 93.900      | 3.871  |                  |                  |                           |
|       |             |        |                  |                  |                           |
| $b_1=$ | 0.0392     |        |                  |                  |                           |
| $b_0=$ | 0.1906     |        |                  |                  |                           |
| $S_e=$ | 3.351922547 |        |                  |                  |                           |
| $r^2=$ | 0.531270003 |        |                  |                  |                           |
| $r=$   | 0.728882709 |        |                  |                  |                           |

**8.**

|       | $X$         | $Y$    | $(X-\bar{X})^2$ | $(Y-\bar{Y})^2$ | $(X-\bar{X})(Y-\bar{Y})$ |
|-------|-------------|--------|------------------|------------------|---------------------------|
| Sums  | 12.08       | 12.60  | 2.99             | 8.17             | −2.24                     |
| $n=$  | 8           |        | $SS_X$           | $SS_Y$           | $SS_{XY}$                 |
| Means | 1.510       | 1.575  |                  |                  |                           |
|       |             |        |                  |                  |                           |
| $b_1=$ | −0.7495    |        |                  |                  |                           |
| $b_0=$ | 2.7067     |        |                  |                  |                           |
| $S_e=$ | 1.040163821 |        |                  |                  |                           |

*Computer Problems*
**2.**

|       | $X$         | $Y$     | $(X-\bar{X})^2$ | $(Y-\bar{Y})^2$ | $(X-\bar{X})(Y-\bar{Y})$ |
|-------|-------------|---------|------------------|------------------|---------------------------|
| Sums  | 437.00      | 438.30  | 1826.78          | 1250.88          | −1011.33                  |
| $n=$  | 40          |         | $SS_X$           | $SS_Y$           | $SS_{XY}$                 |
| Means | 10.925      | 10.958  |                  |                  |                           |
|       |             |         |                  |                  |                           |
| $b_1=$ | −0.5536    |         |                  |                  |                           |
| $b_0=$ | 17.0056    |         |                  |                  |                           |
| $S_e=$ | 4.264315969 |         |                  |                  |                           |

# CHAPTER 3

## Section 3.1

**2.**

| Pred Int | | | | Radical = | 1.048884637 |
|---|---|---|---|---|---|
| | | | | $S_{yi}=$ | 3.861522568 |
| | 23.9976 | − | 7.180686697 | = | 16.8169133 |
| | 23.9976 | + | 7.180686697 | = | 31.1782867 |

**4.**

| C.I. for $\beta_1$ | | | | | | |
|---|---|---|---|---|---|---|
| | 2.124 | − | 2.306 | 0.464145367 | = | 1.0536808 |
| | 2.124 | + | 2.306 | 0.464145367 | = | 3.1943192 |
| | | | | | | |
| | | | | | | |
| C.I. for $\beta$ | | | | | | |
| | 0.850594397 | − | 2.306 | 0.185906284 | = | 0.4218945 |
| | 0.850594397 | + | 2.306 | 0.185906284 | = | 1.2792943 |

**6.**

A.

| $SS_X$ | $SS_Y$ | $SS_{XY}$ | $b_1$ | $b_0$ | $n$ | $S_e$ |
|---|---|---|---|---|---|---|
| 174.24 | 1888.3 | −448.4 | −2.573 | 55.9 | 13 | 8.17183 |

There is a negative relationship—the more training the lower the increase in the score. Training should be altered or discontinued!

B.

| C.I. Mean | | | | | |
|---|---|---|---|---|---|
| | 37.8574 | − | 6.4827 | = | 31.3747 |
| | 37.8574 | + | 6.4827 | = | 44.3401 |
| | | | | | |
| Pred Int | | | | | |
| | | | | | |
| | | | | Radical = | 1.0417 |
| | | | | $S_{yi}=$ | 8.5113 |
| | 37.8574 | − | 23.1346 | = | 14.7228 |
| | 37.8574 | + | 23.1346 | = | 60.992 |

C.

| C.I. for $\beta_1$ | | | | | | |
|---|---|---|---|---|---|---|
| | −2.5735 | − | 2.201 | 0.619 | = | −3.935919 |
| | −2.5735 | + | 2.201 | 0.619 | = | −1.211081 |
| | | | | | | |
| C.I. for $\rho$ | | | | | | |
| | −0.78173 | − | 2.201 | 0.18803 | = | −1.195584 |
| | −0.78173 | + | 2.201 | 0.18803 | = | −0.367876 |
| | | | | | | |

**Section 3.2**

**2.**

A.

**Output**

B.

| $H_0$: $b_1 = 0$ | | |
|---|---|---|
| | $S_b =$ | 0.656588682 |
| | | |
| | Critical $t$ or $Z =$ | 3.249835541 |
| | $t$ or $Z =$ | 7.666138841 |
| | | |
| | REJ | |
| | | |
| | $p$-value for $Z =$ | 1.77636E-14 |
| | $p$-value for $t =$ | 3.10548E-05 |

| $H_0: \rho = 0$ | | | |
|---|---|---|---|
| | | | |
| | $S_r =$ | 0.12652721 | |
| | | | |
| | Critical $t$ or $Z =$ | 2.776445105 | |
| | $t$ or $Z =$ | −7.64619756 | |
| | | | |
| | REJ | | |
| | | | |
| | | | |
| | | $p$-value for $Z =$ | 2.06501E-14 |
| | | $p$-value for $t =$ | 0.001571814 |

4.

| $H_0: \rho = 0$ | | | |
|---|---|---|---|
| | | | |
| | $S_r =$ | 0.12652721 | |
| | | | |
| | Critical $t$ or $Z =$ | 2.776445105 | |
| | $t$ or $Z =$ | −7.64619756 | |
| | | | |
| | REJ | | |
| | | | |
| | | | |
| | | $p$-value for $Z =$ | 2.06501E-14 |
| | | $p$-value for $t =$ | 0.001571814 |

6.

Children:

| $H_0: \rho = 0$ | | | |
|---|---|---|---|
| | | | |
| | $S_r =$ | 0.075608464 | |
| | | | |
| | Critical $t$ or $Z =$ | 2.262157158 | |
| | $t$ or $Z =$ | 12.88130181 | |
| | | | |
| | REJ | | |
| | | | |
| | | | |
| | | $p$-value for $Z =$ | 0 |
| | | $p$-value for $t =$ | 4.20101E-07 |

Age:

| $H_0$: $\rho = 0$ | | | |
|---|---|---|---|
| | | | |
| | $S_r =$ | 0.294078608 | |
| | | | |
| | Critical $t$ or $Z =$ | 2.262157158 | |
| | $t$ or $Z =$ | 1.600958896 | |
| | | | |
| | DNR | | |
| | | | |
| | | | |
| | $p$-value for $Z =$ | 0.109386023 | |
| | $p$-value for $t =$ | 0.143850077 | |

## Section 3.4

4.

A.

| | $X$ | $Y$ | $(X - \bar{X})^2$ | $(Y - \bar{Y})^2$ | $(X - \bar{X})(Y - \bar{Y})$ |
|---|---|---|---|---|---|
| Sums | 10201.00 | 1955.60 | 642067.71 | 23639.66 | 111070.93 |
| $n =$ | 55 | | $SS_X$ | $SS_Y$ | $SS_{XY}$ |
| Means | 185.473 | 35.556 | | | |
| | | | | | |
| $b_1 =$ | 0.173 | | | | |
| $b_0 =$ | 3.4696 | | | | |
| $S_e =$ | 9.136680786 | | | | |

| $\hat{Y}$ | 24.2296 | $X_i =$ | 120 |
|---|---|---|---|

B. and C.

| $H_0$: $b_1 = 0$ | | |
|---|---|---|
| | $S_b =$ | 0.011402446 |
| | | |
| | Critical $t$ or $Z =$ | 1.959963985 |
| | $t$ or $Z =$ | 15.17218277 |
| | | |
| | REJ | |
| | | |
| | $p$-value for $Z =$ | 0 |
| | $p$-value for $t =$ | 6.27512E-21 |

**6.**

A.

| | X | Y | $(X-\bar{X})^2$ | $(Y-\bar{Y})^2$ | $(X-\bar{X})(Y-\bar{Y})$ |
|---|---|---|---|---|---|
| Sums | 386.00 | 481.60 | 216.91 | 407.56 | 286.62 |
| n = | 11 | | $SS_X$ | $SS_Y$ | $SS_{XY}$ |
| Means | 35.091 | 43.782 | | | |
| | | | | | |
| $b_1$ = | 1.3214 | | | | |
| $b_0$ = | −2.5873 | | | | |
| $S_e$ = | 1.789447406 | | | | |

B.

| $H_0: b_1 = 0$ | | |
|---|---|---|
| | $S_b$ = | 0.121501059 |
| | | |
| | Critical $t$ or $Z$ = | 2.262157158 |
| | $t$ or $Z$ = | 10.87562542 |
| | | |
| | REJ | |
| | | |
| | $p$-value for $Z$ = | 0 |
| | $p$-value for $t$ = | 1.774E-06 |

## Chapter Problems
*Computational Problems*

**2.**

| | X | Y | $(X-\bar{X})^2$ | $(Y-\bar{Y})^2$ | $(X-\bar{X})(Y-\bar{Y})$ |
|---|---|---|---|---|---|
| Sums | 139.6 | 94.74 | 53.03 | 58.93 | 19.17 |
| n = | 43 | | $SS_X$ | $SS_Y$ | $SS_{XY}$ |
| Means | 3.246511628 | 2.203255814 | | | |
| | | | | | |
| $b_1$ = | 0.361 | | | | |
| $b_0$ = | 1.031 | | | | |
| $S_e$ = | 1.126289288 | | | | |

| $H_0: b_1 = 0$ | | | | | | |
|---|---|---|---|---|---|---|
| $S_b$ = | 0.1547 | $t$ or $Z$ = | 2.3341 | DNR | $p$ = | 0.0196 |

**4.**

|  | $X$ | $Y$ | $(X - \bar{X})^2$ | $(Y - \bar{Y})^2$ | $(X - \bar{X})(Y - \bar{Y})$ |
|---|---|---|---|---|---|
| Sums | 71.6 | 135.64 | 39.4 | 155.23 | 48.19 |
| $n =$ | 14 |  | $SS_X$ | $SS_Y$ | $SS_{XY}$ |
| Means | 5.114285714 | 9.688571429 |  |  |  |
|  |  |  |  |  |  |
| $b_1 =$ | 1.223 |  |  |  |  |
| $b_0 =$ | 3.434 |  |  |  |  |
| $S_e =$ | 2.832749401 |  |  |  |  |

A.

| $H_0: b_1 = 0$ |  |  |  |  |  |  |
|---|---|---|---|---|---|---|
| $S_b =$ | 0.4513 | $t$ or $Z =$ | 2.71 | DNR | $p =$ | 0.0189 |

B.

| $H_0: b_1 = 0$ |  |  |  |  |  |  |
|---|---|---|---|---|---|---|
| $S_b =$ | 0.4513 | $t$ or $Z =$ | 2.71 | REJ | $p =$ | 0.0189 |

C. $p = 0.0189$.

**6.**

|  | CD ($X$) | Smog ($Y$) | $(X - \bar{X})^2$ | $(Y - \bar{Y})^2$ | $(X - \bar{X})(Y - \bar{Y})$ |
|---|---|---|---|---|---|
| Sums | 155 | 465 | 520.92 | 4904.31 | 1052.77 |
| $n =$ | 13 |  | $SS_X$ | $SS_Y$ | $SS_{XY}$ |
| Means | 11.92307692 | 35.76923077 |  |  |  |
|  |  |  |  |  |  |
| $b_1 =$ | 2.021 |  |  |  |  |
| $b_0 =$ | 11.673 |  |  |  |  |
| $S_e =$ | 15.88785079 |  |  |  |  |

A. and B.

| $H_0: \rho = 0$ |  |
|---|---|
| $S_r =$ | 0.10581124 |
| Critical $t$ or $Z =$ | 2.30600413 |
| $t$ or $Z_{test} =$ | 9.01761974 |
| REJ |  |
| $p$-value for $Z =$ | 0 |
| $p$-value for $t =$ | 1.8267E-05 |

C.

| **p-value for t =** | 1.8267E-05 |
|---|---|

D.

| **H$_0$: b$_1$ = 0** | |
|---|---|
| **S$_b$ =** | 0.529798 |
| **Critical t or Z =** | 3.35538733 |
| **t or Z$_{test}$ =** | 9.01475652 |
| **REJ** | |

**8.**

A.

| **Ŷ =** | 15.132 |
|---|---|

| **C.I. Mean** | | | | | |
|---|---|---|---|---|---|
| | 15.132 | – | 6.105123005 | = | 9.026876995 |
| | 15.132 | + | 6.105123005 | = | 21.23712301 |

B. 73.6% of any increase in income will go toward consumption.

C. You will increase consumption by $736.

D. $r^2 = 0.0599$; apparently, many other economic forces contribute to changes in consumption patterns.

E.

| **H$_0$: ρ = 0** | |
|---|---|
| **S$_r$ =** | 0.10978336 |
| **Critical t or Z =** | 1.95996398 |
| **t or Z$_{test}$ =** | 2.22959981 |
| **REJ** | |
| **p-value for Z =** | 0.02577402 |
| **p-value for t =** | 0.02865043 |

| **H$_0$: b$_1$ = 0** | |
|---|---|
| **S$_b$ =** | 0.32992006 |
| **Critical t or Z =** | 1.95996398 |
| **t or Z$_{test}$ =** | 2.23084344 |
| **REJ** | |
| **p-value for Z =** | 0.0256915 |
| **p-value for t =** | 0.02865043 |

## CHAPTER 4

### Section 4.1

2. Even at the highest level of significance of 0.01, we find $t_{.01,19} = 2.861 <$ either of the variables' $t$-values. Thus, reject the nulls. Both are statistically significant at any common alpha-value.

=TDIST(3.66,19,2) = 0.0017. If you use the $t$-table the alpha-value is less than 1%.
=TDIST(5.26,19,2) = 0.00.

**4.**

|  | Coefficients | Standard Error | t Stat | p-Value |
|---|---|---|---|---|
| Intercept | 5.382573 | 6.975536 | 0.771636 | 0.458176 |
| X1 | 19.08475 | 0.907834 | 21.02229 | 1.32E-09 |
| X2 | −4.7808 | 0.96402 | −4.95924 | 0.000571 |

| | |
|---|---|
| Multiple R | 0.988919 |
| R Square | 0.977962 |
| Adjusted R Square | 0.973554 |
| Standard Error | 7.495381 |
| Observations | 13 |

### Section 4.2

2. Because it increases the standard error of the regression coefficient, thereby decreasing the absolute value of the $t$-statistic used in the hypothesis test and moving it into the do not reject region.

4. $t_{test} = 3.997$; $t_{.05,10} = 2.2281$; reject null.

### Section 4.3

**4.**

**ANOVA**

|  | d.f. | SS | MS | F | Significance F |
|---|---|---|---|---|---|
| Regression | 2 | 1740.887461 | 870.4437307 | 1.807010043 | 0.188749501 |
| Residual | 21 | 10115.78127 | 481.70387 |  |  |
| Total | 23 | 11856.66873 |  |  |  |

## Section 4.4

**2.**

|  | Coefficients | Standard Error | t Stat | p-Value |
| --- | --- | --- | --- | --- |
| Intercept | 0.25 | 0.096899225 | 2.58 | 0.0131 |
| A | 0.45 | 0.181451613 | 2.48 | 0.0168 |
| C | 0.55 | 0.327380952 | 1.68 | 0.0996 |
| SC | 0.87 | 0.416267943 | 2.09 | 0.0421 |
| COA | 0.988 | 0.278309859 | 3.55 | 0.0009 |

A. $\hat{Y} = 34.738$ thousand.

**4.**

|  | Coefficients | Standard Error | t Stat | p-Value |
| --- | --- | --- | --- | --- |
| Intercept | 3.55 | 1.375968992 | 2.58 | 0.0105 |
| Edu | 2.58 | 1.040322581 | 2.48 | 0.0138 |
| Experience | 1.54 | 0.916666667 | 1.68 | 0.0942 |
| Gender | 3.65 | 6.403508772 | 0.57 | 0.5692 |
| East | 1.25 | 0.352112676 | 3.55 | 0.0005 |
| South | 3.2 | 0.987654321 | 3.24 | 0.0014 |
| MidWest | 2.47 | 0.957364341 | 2.58 | 0.0105 |

B. 78.6.

## Section 4.5

**2.**

|  | Coefficients | Standard Error | t Stat | p-Value |
| --- | --- | --- | --- | --- |
| Intercept | 5.71 | 2.213178295 | 2.58 | 0.0175 |
| P | 3.24 | 1.306451613 | 2.48 | 0.0217 |
| B | 6.54 | 3.892857143 | 1.68 | 0.1078 |
| I | 6.25 | 0.992063492 | 6.3 | 0 |
| P*B | 3.55 | 1 | 3.55 | 0.0019 |

## Section 4.8

**2.** $F = 24.99 > F_{.01,3,18} = 5.09$.

## Chapter Problems

*Computational Problems*

**2.**

|  | Coefficients | Standard Error | t Stat | p-Value |
|---|---|---|---|---|
| Intercept | 1.05 | 0.333810205 | 3.1455 | 0.002 |
| TEMP | 2.5 | 1.287266361 | 1.9421 | 0.054 |
| DURATION | 0.354 | 0.217058066 | 1.6309 | 0.105 |
| SOURCE | 1.2 | 0.526246547 | 2.2803 | 0.024 |

**4.**

|  | Coefficients | Standard Error | t Stat | p-Value |
|---|---|---|---|---|
| Intercept | 3.2 | 0.927482465 | 3.4502 | 0.002 |
| X1 | 6.55 | 3.239366963 | 2.022 | 0.054 |
| X2 | 2.58 | 1.533797039 | 1.6821 | 0.105 |
| X3 | 7.66 | 3.187549415 | 2.4031 | 0.024 |
| X4 | 12.33 | 19.89351404 | 0.6198 | 0.541 |

**6.**

A. and B.

### SUMMARY OUTPUT

| Regression Statistics | |
|---|---|
| Multiple R | 0.942142683 |
| R Square | 0.887632834 |
| Adjusted R Square | 0.863976589 |
| Standard Error | 3.860174877 |
| Observations | 24 |

### ANOVA

|  | df | SS | MS | F | Significance F |
|---|---|---|---|---|---|
| Regression | 4 | 2236.461844 | 559.1154611 | 37.52213504 | 9.03029E-09 |
| Residual | 19 | 283.1180515 | 14.90095008 |  |  |
| Total | 23 | 2519.579896 |  |  |  |

|  | Coefficients | Standard Error | t Stat | p-Value |
|---|---|---|---|---|
| Intercept | 15.15059944 | 4.343729415 | 3.487924314 | 0.002461883 |
| X1 | 1.244327021 | 0.147703422 | 8.424496896 | 7.71095E-08 |
| X2 | −0.317456297 | 0.037305292 | −8.509685332 | 6.61713E-08 |
| X3 | 7.152891064 | 1.699767447 | 4.208158636 | 0.000476368 |
| X4 | −0.029179594 | 0.35761513 | −0.081594964 | 0.935822223 |

C. For inclement weather $= 22.3 + 1.24X_1 - 0.317X + 2 - 0.29X_4$.
For good weather $= 15.15 + 1.24X_1 - 0.317X_2 - 0.029X_4$.

D. 1.23 late.

E. 2.64 minutes early.

**8.**

**ANOVA**

|  | df | SS | MS | F | Significance F |
|---|---|---|---|---|---|
| Regression | 4 | 6585328 | 1646332 | 0.449914574 | 0.771200319 |
| Residual | 19 | 69524993 | 3659210 |  |  |
| Total | 23 | 76110321 |  |  |  |

**10.**

| FINV(0.05,4,19) | 2.895107 |
|---|---|
| FINV(0.01,4,19) | 4.500258 |

**12.**

|  | Coefficients | Standard Error | t Stat | p-Value |
|---|---|---|---|---|
| Intercept | 0.65 | 1.153300213 | 0.5636 | 0.58 |
| Price | 0.95 | 0.2880621 | 3.2979 | 0.004 |
| EPS | 1.2 | 0.592709671 | 2.0246 | 0.058 |
| Public | −0.58 | 0.268792288 | −2.1578 | 0.0447 |

## CHAPTER 5

### Section 5.2
2.

**Descriptive Statistics**

|  | N | Minimum | Maximum | Mean | Std. Deviation |
|---|---|---|---|---|---|
| X1 | 13 | 125.00 | 985.00 | 539.3077 | 242.92673 |
| X2 | 13 | 2.00 | 9.00 | 5.4615 | 1.89804 |
| Y | 13 | 873.30 | 2317.30 | 1468.5385 | 453.47526 |
| Valid N (listwise) | 13 |  |  |  |  |

**Coefficients[a]**

| Model | | Unstandardized Coefficients | | Standardized Coefficients | | |
|---|---|---|---|---|---|---|
|  |  | B | Std. Error | Beta | t | Sig. |
| 1 | (Constant) | 37.709 | 40.752 |  | .925 | .377 |
|  | X1 | 1.972 | .039 | 1.056 | 50.280 | .000 |
|  | X2 | 67.282 | 5.019 | .282 | 13.405 | .000 |

a. Dependent Variable: Y

### Computer Problems
2.

| Regression Statistics | |
|---|---|
| Multiple R | 0.793394224 |
| R Square | 0.629474395 |
| Adjusted R Square | 0.598597261 |
| Standard Error | 1.879712799 |
| Observations | 40 |

**ANOVA**

|  | df | SS | MS | F | Significance F |
|---|---|---|---|---|---|
| Regression | 3 | 216.0953098 | 72.03177 | 20.38642573 | 6.81984E-08 |
| Residual | 36 | 127.1995274 | 3.53332 |  |  |
| Total | 39 | 343.2948372 |  |  |  |

|  | Coefficients | Standard Error | t Stat | p-Value |
|---|---|---|---|---|
| Intercept | −2.224475192 | 6.155752718 | −0.36137 | 0.71993867 |
| TEMPERATURE | 0.427337249 | 0.078528794 | 5.441791 | 3.87409E-06 |
| KC | −2.897785932 | 0.836088219 | −3.46589 | 0.001384508 |
| CHICAGO | −2.96855398 | 0.702321909 | −4.22677 | 0.000154734 |

**Residuals**

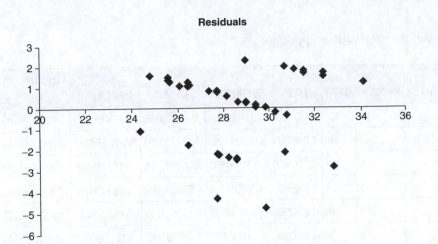

# CHAPTER 6

## Section 6.1

**4.**

```
Response Information

Variable      Value   Count
BANKRUPTCY    1           24   (Event)
              0           18
              Total       42


Logistic Regression Table

                                              Odds      95% CI
Predictor       Coef      SE Coef     Z     P  Ratio  Lower Upper
Constant     -29.1676    11.2547   -2.59  0.010
INCOME         0.353613   0.161580  2.19  0.029  1.42   1.04  1.95
DEBT           0.0275068  0.0155788 1.77  0.077  1.03   1.00  1.06


Log-Likelihood = -14.748
Test that all slopes are zero: G = 27.869, DF = 2, P-Value = 0.000
```

**6.** $\chi^2 = 49.3 - 42.7 = 6.6$; using Excel =chiinv(.01,4) yields critical $\chi^2$ of $13.2767 > 6.6$; Do Not Reject. The *p*-value is =chidist(6.6,4), which yields 0.158598.

## Section 6.2

**4.** A few of the observations appear as:

| BANKRUPTCY | INCOME | DEBT | FITS | WEIGHTS | YSTAR | DEBTSTAR | INCOME-STAR | 1/W |
|---|---|---|---|---|---|---|---|---|
| 1 | 85 | 162 | 0.999 | 0.031606961 | 31.63859986 | 5125.453177 | 2689.280988 | 31.6386 |
| 1 | 76.8 | 196 | 0.999951 | 0.006972963 | 143.4110497 | 28108.56575 | 11013.96862 | 143.41105 |
| 1 | 72.8 | 184 | 0.776567 | 0.41654592 | 2.400695705 | 441.7280096 | 174.7706473 | 2.4006957 |
| 1 | 76 | 194 | 0.956947 | 0.202975705 | 4.926698004 | 955.7794128 | 374.4290483 | 4.926698 |
| 1 | 73.6 | 190 | 0.836299 | 0.370004026 | 2.702673292 | 513.5079254 | 198.9167543 | 2.7026733 |
| 1 | 74.4 | 198 | 0.904394 | 0.294049507 | 3.400787882 | 673.3560006 | 253.0186184 | 3.4007879 |
| 0 | 64.8 | 102 | 0.087249 | 0.282199425 | 0 | 361.44652 | 229.624848 | 3.5435933 |
| 0 | 68.8 | 98 | 0.243722 | 0.429327172 | 0 | 228.2641455 | 160.250747 | 2.329226 |
| 0 | 64.8 | 108 | 0.11234 | 0.315784674 | 0 | 342.0051986 | 205.2031191 | 3.1667148 |
| 0 | 68 | 95 | 0.196537 | 0.397378798 | 0 | 239.0666047 | 171.1213592 | 2.5164906 |

The model is:

|  | Coefficients | Standard Error | t Stat | P-value |
|---|---|---|---|---|
| Intercept | 0 | #N/A | #N/A | #N/A |
| DEBTSTAR | 0.005049121 | 0.000250888 | 20.12499 | 3.34E-22 |
| INCOMESTAR | 0.023044983 | 0.002605306 | 8.845403 | 7.33E-11 |
| 1/W | −1.76508745 | 0.160853562 | −10.9733 | 1.73E-13 |

## Chapter Problems

*Computational Problems*

**2.**

$MV = 56$

$ROR = 12.5$

$z = 0.69 + 0.23MV − 0.68ROR$

$z = 5.07$

$$\frac{e^z}{1+e^z} = 0.994$$

Yes, they should visit this firm.

**4.** $42.7 = 13.7 + 29$. $13.7 > 11.344$. Yes, adding the RHS variables improves the model.

# CHAPTER 7

## Section 7.1

2. Increasing the sample size will do nothing to mitigate the ill-effects of heteroscedasticity.

## Section 7.2

2.

```
The regression equation is
LnResSq = -1.64 + 0.107 LnPop


Predictor      Coef    SE Coef       T      P
Constant     -1.638      1.862   -0.88  0.395
LnPop        0.1069     0.4558    0.23  0.818
```

The coefficient of log population is not significant. No evidence of heteroscedasticity.

4.

```
The regression equation is
ResSq = -7.4 + 1.76 BR - 0.0541 Pop - 0.34 InfMor - 0.085 BRSQ +
0.000005 PopSq -0.0069 InfMorSq + 0.00352 BRPop + 0.044 BRInfMor +
0.00022 PopInfMor


Predictor          Coef      SE Coef        T      P
Constant          -7.43        12.09    -0.61  0.566
BR                1.758        2.490     0.71  0.512
Pop            -0.05408      0.08948    -0.60  0.572
InfMor           -0.339        1.574    -0.22  0.838
BRSQ            -0.0846       0.1244    -0.68  0.527
PopSq        0.00000464   0.00002991     0.16  0.883
InfMorSq       -0.00691      0.02127    -0.33  0.758
BRPop          0.003519     0.006504     0.54  0.612
```

$nR^2 = (15)(0.548) = 8.22$; $=chidist(.01,7) = 18.4753 > 8.22$. Do Not Reject null of no heteroscedasticity.

6.

```
Predictor      Coef    SE Coef       T       P
Constant     -9.258      2.210   -4.19   0.000
LnBB         2.5228     0.5981    4.22   0.000
```

The p-value for Ln*BB* is significant. Heteroscedasticity can be assumed to exist.

**8.**

```
The regression equation is
RedSq = 23.0 + 0.82 Foreign Investment - 2.21 Bank Balances + 0.0000
ForInvSq + 0.0755 BBSQ - 0.0529 FIBB
```

$nR^2 = (26)(0.71) = 18.46$; $\chi^2$ with alpha of .01 and d.f. = 5 is $15.08 < 18.46$. Reject null of no heteroscedasticity; conclude heteroscedasticity exists.

## Section 7.3

**2.**

$$v_i^2 = \frac{\varepsilon_i^2}{\sigma_i^2}$$

$$E\left(v_i^2\right) = E\left(\frac{\varepsilon_i^2}{\sigma_i^2}\right)$$

$$= \left(\frac{1}{\sigma_i^2}\right) E\left(\varepsilon_i^2\right)$$

$$= \frac{1}{\sigma_i^2}\left(\sigma_i^2\right) = 1$$

**4.** It says that the population variances at the different $X$-values have a constant proportionality with the $X$-values squared.

**6.**

```
The regression equation is
BT/BB = 3.49 1/BB + 0.0324 BB/BB + 1.01 FI/BB
```

Multiply through by $BB$ and we get $BT = 3.49 + 0.0324BB + 1.01FI$.

## Chapter Problems
### Computational Problems

**2.**

```
The regression equation is
lnAmt = 1.97 + 0.476 lnCost + 0.600 lnPop
```

| Predictor | Coef | SE Coef | T | P |
|-----------|--------|---------|------|-------|
| Constant | 1.969 | 2.816 | 0.70 | 0.492 |
| lnCost | 0.4759 | 0.4843 | 0.98 | 0.336 |
| lnPop | 0.6000 | 0.1285 | 4.67 | 0.000 |

**4.** Follow Example 7.4.

# CHAPTER 8

## Chapter Problems
*Computational Problems*
4.

Cochrane–Orcutt

| QUARTER | SALARY | EXPERIENCE | RES | RESLAG | LAGSAL | LAGEXP | ADJSAL | ADJEXP |
|---|---|---|---|---|---|---|---|---|
| 2009-I | 137.5 | 31 | 6.37638604 | | | | | |
| 2009-II | 149.6 | 34 | 8.94173511 | 6.37638604 | 137.5 | 31 | 68.6125 | 15.741 |
| 2009-III | 119.9 | 27 | 1.48925394 | 8.94173511 | 149.6 | 34 | 31.7856 | 6.974 |
| 2009-IV | 108.9 | 24 | 0.02390486 | 1.48925394 | 119.9 | 27 | 38.2789 | 8.097 |
| 2010-I | 167.2 | 41 | 4.29421629 | 0.02390486 | 108.9 | 24 | 103.0579 | 26.864 |
| 2010-II | 166.1 | 42 | 0.01599932 | 4.29421629 | 167.2 | 41 | 67.6192 | 17.851 |
| 2010-III | 113.3 | 26 | −1.9325291 | 0.01599932 | 166.1 | 42 | 15.4671 | 1.262 |
| 2010-IV | 179.3 | 46 | 0.50313142 | −1.9325291 | 113.3 | 26 | 112.5663 | 30.686 |
| 2011-I | 192.5 | 50 | 0.99026352 | 0.50313142 | 179.3 | 46 | 86.8923 | 22.906 |
| 2011-II | 138.6 | 35 | −5.2364819 | 0.99026352 | 192.5 | 50 | 25.2175 | 5.55 |
| 2011-III | 143 | 38 | −10.371133 | −5.2364819 | 138.6 | 35 | 61.3646 | 17.385 |
| 2011-IV | 108.9 | 25 | −3.1543121 | −10.371133 | 143 | 38 | 24.673 | 2.618 |
| 2012-I | 170.5 | 44 | −1.9404346 | −3.1543121 | 108.9 | 25 | 106.3579 | 29.275 |

```
The regression equation is
ADJSAL = 10.9 + 3.30 ADJEXP


12 cases used, 1 case contains missing values


Predictor    Coef    SE Coef      T       P
Constant    10.924    2.031     5.38    0.000
ADJEXP      3.2979    0.1103   29.89    0.000


Durbin-Watson statistic = 2.23557
```

First-differencing:

```
The regression equation is
SALt-SALt-1 = -0.83 + 3.31 EXPt-EXP-t-1
```

```
12 cases used, 1 case contains missing values


Predictor        Coef   SE Coef        T       P
Constant        -0.834    1.276    -0.65   0.528
EXPt-EXP-t-1    3.3079    0.1044    31.69   0.000


Durbin-Watson statistic = 2.62751
```

Use of lagged term for Salary:

```
The regression equation is
SALARY = 36.7 + 3.21 EXPERIENCE - 0.0399 LAGSAL


12 cases used, 1 case contains missing values


Predictor        Coef    SE Coef        T        P
Constant        36.74      10.42     3.52    0.006
EXPERIENCE     3.2079     0.1732    18.52    0.000
LAGSAL       -0.03992    0.05492    -0.73    0.486


Durbin-Watson statistic = 0.939823
```

# CHAPTER 9

## Section 9.3

2.

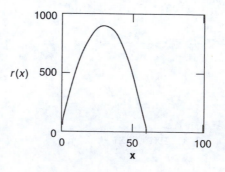

vertex = −58/−2 = 29 units

**4.**

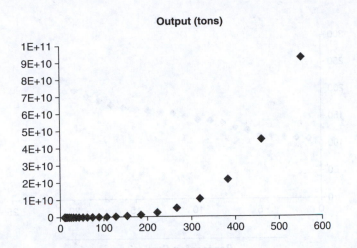

**Output (tons)**

Model in which Output = f(Labor)

| Regression Statistics | |
|---|---|
| Multiple R | 0.83106946 |
| R Square | 0.690676448 |
| Adjusted R Square | 0.675946755 |
| Standard Error | 12034174128 |
| Observations | 23 |

| | Coefficients | Standard Error | t Stat | p-Value |
|---|---|---|---|---|
| Intercept | −8198023685 | 3427586285 | −2.39178 | 0.026203 |
| Labor Units | 112768076.9 | 16468183.52 | 6.847633 | 9.06E-07 |

Model in which Output = f(Labor, Labor Sqed)

| Regression Statistics | |
|---|---|
| Multiple R | 0.986011001 |
| R Square | 0.972217694 |
| Adjusted R Square | 0.969439464 |
| Standard Error | 3695630901 |
| Observations | 23 |

| | Coefficients | Standard Error | t Stat | p-Value |
|---|---|---|---|---|
| Intercept | 4006045785 | 1357503156 | 2.951039757 | 0.007898605 |
| Labor Units | −121919250.7 | 17243257.99 | −7.070546112 | 7.43452E-07 |
| Lb Sqed | 486395.6627 | 34165.50346 | 14.2364553 | 6.28143E-12 |

**6.**

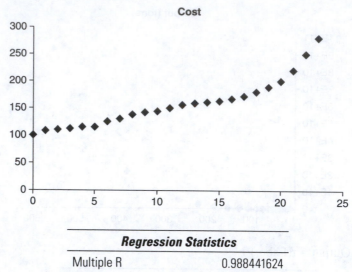

| Regression Statistics | |
| --- | --- |
| Multiple R | 0.988441624 |
| R Square | 0.977016845 |
| Adjusted R Square | 0.973569372 |
| Standard Error | 7.387115786 |
| Observations | 24 |

| | Coefficients | Standard Error | t Stat | p-Value |
| --- | --- | --- | --- | --- |
| Intercept | 93.16296296 | 5.199614414 | 17.91728 | 8.71538E-14 |
| InputCubed | 0.033136643 | 0.005842851 | 5.671314 | 1.4998E-05 |
| InputSqed | −0.880109906 | 0.204641645 | −4.30074 | 0.000348264 |
| Input | 10.25893907 | 2.000325556 | 5.128635 | 5.11726E-05 |

## Section 9.4

**2.**

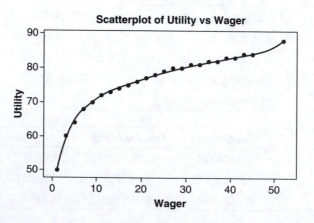

```
The regression equation is
Utility = 62.9 + 0.542 Wager

Predictor        Coef    SE Coef        T        P
Constant       62.873     1.529     41.11    0.000
Wager         0.54224   0.05447      9.95    0.000

S = 3.79491   R-Sq = 81.8%    R-Sq(adj) = 81.0%

The regression equation is
lnUtility = 3.94 + 0.131 lnWager

Predictor        Coef    SE Coef        T        P
Constant      3.94398    0.00780    505.76   0.000
lnWager      0.131357   0.002566     51.18   0.000

S = 0.0118087   R-Sq = 99.2%    R-Sq(adj) = 99.1%
```

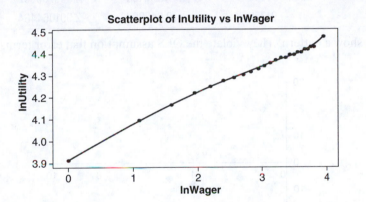

**Scatterplot of lnUtility vs lnWager**

## Chapter Problems

*Computational Problems*

**2.** Vertex $= -b/(2a) = -15/-5 = 3$ units of $Q$. At $Q = 3$, $TR = 22.5$. At both $Q = 2$ and $Q = 4$, $TR = 20$.

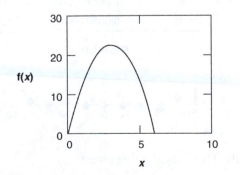

**4.** $TC = 89.96Q + 0.0179Q^3 - 2.294Q^2$.

**6.**

| Regression Statistics | |
|---|---|
| Multiple R | 0.121449 |
| R Square | 0.01475 |
| Adjusted R Square | −0.02466 |
| Standard Error | 18.4823 |
| Observations | 27 |

| | Coefficients | Standard Error | t Stat | p-Value |
|---|---|---|---|---|
| Intercept | 28.244442 | 6.999174998 | 4.035395888 | 0.000452369 |
| MILES | 0.055875458 | 0.091333306 | 0.611775271 | 0.546210348 |

**8.**

For the linear model $R^2 = 0.56$ and $S_e = 9.9$:

| | Coefficients | Standard Error | t Stat | p-Value |
|---|---|---|---|---|
| Intercept | 28.92694444 | 7.214133 | 4.009760352 | 0.005125869 |
| Q | −1.91725 | 0.640993 | −2.991064464 | 0.020195889 |

The residuals show a pattern. They violate the OLS assumption that error terms are random.

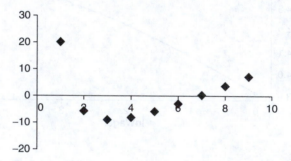

For the log-log model:

$R^2 = 0.99; S_e = 0.006$

| | Coefficients | Standard Error | t Stat | p-Value |
|---|---|---|---|---|
| Intercept | 4.846747686 | 0.006748076 | 718.2413987 | 2.67833E-18 |
| lnQ | −1.5076524 | 0.003037486 | −496.3487602 | 3.55818E-17 |

**Residuals**

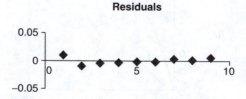

Not sure about the residuals. They may show a pattern!

Can't compare $R^2$ values.

$\varepsilon = 1.5$: an elastic demand curve.

**10.** The $-0.8879$ says for every one unit $Q$ goes up, $P$ must go down by 0.8879 of its units. The coefficient for $\ln P = \ln 2.3 - 3.5 \ln Q$ says for every 1% $Q$ goes up, $P$ must go down by 3.5%.

**12.** At $L = 10.1$ (a 1% increase), $Q = 186.131$: a 0.6% increase.

**14.** At $I = 10$, $\ln C = 2.58$ and $C = 13.2$. At $I = 11$, $\ln C = 2.638$ and $C = 13.98$. This is a 5.9% increase. (Difference is due to rounding.)

**16.**

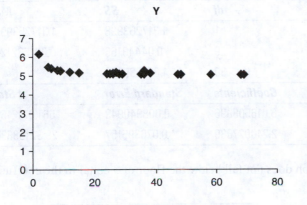

| Regression Statistics | |
| --- | --- |
| Multiple R | 0.756417455 |
| R Square | 0.572167366 |
| Adjusted R Square | 0.541607892 |
| Standard Error | 0.144243539 |
| Observations | 31 |

**ANOVA**

| | df | SS | MS | F |
| --- | --- | --- | --- | --- |
| Regression | 2 | 0.779112095 | 0.389556048 | 18.72307644 |
| Residual | 28 | 0.582573562 | 0.020806199 | |
| Total | 30 | 1.361685658 | | |

| | Coefficients | Standard Error | t Stat | p-Value |
| --- | --- | --- | --- | --- |
| Intercept | 5.574357529 | 0.072903184 | 76.46247062 | 4.67802E-34 |
| XSqed | 0.000257942 | 7.08301E-05 | 3.641700681 | 0.001088413 |
| X | −0.024425108 | 0.005048145 | −4.838432512 | 4.31379E-05 |

| Regression Statistics | |
|---|---|
| Multiple R | 0.983549747 |
| R Square | 0.967370105 |
| Adjusted R Square | 0.966244936 |
| Standard Error | 0.039142384 |
| Observations | 31 |

**ANOVA**

| | df | SS | MS | F |
|---|---|---|---|---|
| Regression | 1 | 1.317253998 | 1.317253998 | 859.7555437 |
| Residual | 29 | 0.04443166 | 0.001532126 | |
| Total | 30 | 1.361685658 | | |

| | Coefficients | Standard Error | t Stat | p-Value |
|---|---|---|---|---|
| Intercept | 5.016508896 | 0.008940949 | 561.0712156 | 4.46361E-60 |
| 1/X | 2.240027339 | 0.076395157 | 29.32158836 | 4.17982E-23 |

Notice how the graph does not fall below the floor of 5 equal to the coefficient of the reciprocal model of 5.0165.

| Regression Statistics | |
|---|---|
| Multiple R | 0.839634736 |
| R Square | 0.70498649 |
| Adjusted R Square | 0.694813611 |
| Standard Error | 0.117695643 |
| Observations | 31 |

**ANOVA**

| | df | SS | MS | F |
|---|---|---|---|---|
| Regression | 1 | 0.959969993 | 0.959969993 | 69.300583 |
| Residual | 29 | 0.401715665 | 0.013852264 | |
| Total | 30 | 1.361685658 | | |

| | Coefficients | Standard Error | t Stat | p-Value |
|---|---|---|---|---|
| Intercept | 5.810332486 | 0.078788667 | 73.74578973 | 1.49616E-34 |
| lnx | −0.206027353 | 0.024748931 | −8.324697172 | 3.54753E-09 |

**18.** $(1258)(2.718^{-0.105}) = 1133 > 1000$. No downgrade.

**20.** $FV = 43,000e^{0.055*6} = \$59,811$. Closer!

**22.** Currently, costs are $100(3) + 50(4) = 500$. Revenues are $123(3.75) = 461$ for a loss of 39. If more inputs are added to the business, costs are $100(6) + 50(8) = 1000$ and revenues are $984(3.2) = 3149$ for a profit of 2149.

**24.** $GM = \sqrt[5]{\frac{62}{42}} - 1 = 8\%$. In 2013 costs will be $62(1.08) = 66.96$. In 2014 they will be $66.96(1.08)$

$$= 72.32 > 70.$$

**26.** $N_5 = 400(e^{0.06*5}) = 539$.

# CHAPTER 10

## Chapter Problems
### Computational Problems

**2.** Durbin–Wu–Hausman Test:

**Coefficients[a]**

| Model | | Unstandardized Coefficients | | Standardized Coefficients | | |
|---|---|---|---|---|---|---|
| | | B | Std. Error | Beta | t | Sig. |
| 1 | (Constant) | 427.041 | 18.306 | | 23.328 | .000 |
| | PROFITS | 15.679 | 2.472 | .491 | 6.343 | .000 |
| | P | −35.315 | 4.582 | −.679 | −7.706 | .000 |
| | Unstandardized Residual | 81.170 | 9.524 | .746 | 8.522 | .000 |

a. Dependent Variable: Q

**4.** *Durbin–Wu–Hausman test for Police in the equation for Crimes:* Obtain the errors for Police as a function of all exogenous variables Students, Poverty, and Taxes. Regress the structural equation for Crimes on the explanatory variables and the error values from the first regression run. The errors are significant. They are offering explanatory power to Crimes which means they are *not* random and are a source of bias.

**Coefficients[a]**

| Model | | Unstandardized Coefficients | | Standardized Coefficients | | |
|---|---|---|---|---|---|---|
| | | B | Std. Error | Beta | t | Sig. |
| 1 | (Constant) | 111.394 | 4.818 | | 23.122 | .000 |
| | STUDENTS | −.004 | .001 | −.411 | −3.559 | .002 |
| | POLICE | .067 | .063 | .129 | 1.069 | .295 |
| | Unstandardized Residual | −1.226 | .134 | −.717 | −9.141 | .000 |
| | POVRT | .052 | .007 | .516 | 7.279 | .000 |

a. Dependent Variable: CRIMES

*Durbin–Wu–Hausman test for Police in the equation for Police:* Regress Crimes on all exogenous variables and use the errors to estimate the structural equation for Police. The error terms are not significant.

**Coefficients**[a]

| Model | | Unstandardized Coefficients | | Standardized Coefficients | | |
|---|---|---|---|---|---|---|
| | | B | Std. Error | Beta | t | Sig. |
| 1 | (Constant) | 205.901 | 19.163 | | 10.745 | .000 |
| | STUDENTS | .009 | .001 | .447 | 11.163 | .000 |
| | TAXES | −.019 | .001 | −.684 | −20.058 | .000 |
| | CRIMES | −.610 | .119 | −.317 | −5.139 | .000 |
| | Unstandardized Residual | −.074 | .138 | −.029 | −.537 | .596 |

a. Dependent Variable: POLICE

# CHAPTER 11

## Section 11.1

**2.** Using Year:

```
The regression equation is
TONS = -1089 + 0.550 YEAR


Predictor     Coef    SE Coef      T       P
Constant    -1089.5     109.5   -9.95   0.000
YEAR        0.55000   0.05455   10.08   0.000


S = 0.422577   R-Sq = 93.6%   R-Sq(adj) = 92.6%
```

Using Time Periods 1 through 9:

```
The regression equation is
TONS = 12.2 + 0.550 TIME


Predictor     Coef    SE Coef      T       P
Constant    12.1500    0.3070   39.58   0.000
TIME        0.55000   0.05455   10.08   0.000
```

Forecast for 2016 = 19.3.

**4.** After creating a column for Time Periods 1 through 30, regress Time on Volume:

|  | Regression Statistics |
|---|---|
| Multiple R | 0.348673126 |
| R Square | 0.121572949 |
| Adjusted R Square | 0.090200554 |
| Standard Error | 41064951.11 |
| Observations | 30 |

**ANOVA**

|  | df | SS | MS | F | Significance F |
|---|---|---|---|---|---|
| Regression | 1 | 6.53E+15 | 6.53479E+15 | 3.875157 | 0.058977601 |
| Residual | 28 | 4.72E+16 | 1.68633E+15 |  |  |
| Total | 29 | 5.38E+16 |  |  |  |

|  | Coefficients | Standard Error | t Stat | p-Value | Lower 95% |
|---|---|---|---|---|---|
| Intercept | 222845739.6 | 15377708 | 14.49147982 | 1.54E-14 | 191345933.9 |
| Time Period | −1705163.784 | 866206.5 | −1.968541796 | 0.058978 | −3479507.429 |

For Nov 16: $222845739.6 − 1705163.784(45) = −54447762$.*

*The data were collected during a period of world-wide economic instability and turmoil. Forecasts based on time trends were extremely tenuous. Reliance on them and the use of $R^2$ values and standard errors was quite hazardous at best. Obviously, a negative value for Volume is impossible. Furthermore the "45" used in the forecast included weekends when the market did not trade. Perhaps only 11 trading days should be added on to the 30 already found in the data set, making it 41 instead of 45.

**Section 11.2**

2. Regression analysis: TONS versus LagTons1:

```
The regression equation is
TONS = 3.09 + 0.830 LagTons1


8 cases used, 1 case contains missing values



Predictor    Coef   SE Coef     T      P
Constant    3.091     2.593   1.19   0.278
LagTons1    0.8304    0.1768  4.70   0.003



S = 0.648304   R-Sq = 78.6%   R-Sq(adj) = 75.1%
```

```
Analysis of Variance

Source             DF        SS        MS        F        P
Regression          1     9.2732    9.2732    22.06    0.003
Residual Error      6     2.5218    0.4203
Total               7    11.7950
```

**4.** Regression analysis: Volume versus VolLag1:

```
The regression equation is
Volume = 1.24E+08 + 0.365 VolLag1


29 cases used, 1 case contains missing values


Predictor          Coef      SE Coef      T        P
Constant       124083240    35817145    3.46    0.002
VolLag1           0.3652      0.1788    2.04    0.051


S = 41266719    R-Sq = 13.4%    R-Sq(adj) = 10.2%


Analysis of Variance

Source             DF           SS              MS          F       P
Regression          1    7.10285E+15    7.10285E+15      4.17    0.051
Residual Error     27    4.59794E+16    1.70294E+15
Total              28    5.30823E+16
```

## Section 11.3

**4.** Since the value of the radical is negative the alternative test must be used. The results are shown here:

```
Predictor      Coef    SE Coef       T        P
Constant      -8.64     52.12     -0.17    0.869
X           -0.0039    0.2004     -0.02    0.985
LagY         0.0497    0.2517      0.20    0.844
LagRes1     -0.0686    0.2957     -0.23    0.818
```

The lagged residual is *not* significant so no autocorrelation is suspected.

**Section 11.5**
*Computational Problems*

**2.**

| Data | First-Difference | 4MAFD |
|------|------------------|-------|
| **5** | | |
| **6** | 1 | |
| **8** | 2 | #N/A |
| **7** | −1 | #N/A |
| **9** | 2 | #N/A |
| **10** | 1 | 1 |
| **11** | 1 | 1 |
| **10** | −1 | 0.75 |
| **12** | 2 | 0.75 |
| **15** | 3 | 0.75 |
| **14** | −1 | 1.25 |
| **14.75\*** | 0.75\* | 0.75 |
| | | 1.875[a] |

[a] Forecast.

Forecast for next day is 14.75. For second day, 1.875 is MA4, which is added to 14.75 for forecast of 16.63.

**4.**

| Data | Forecast |
|------|----------|
| **5** | #N/A |
| **6** | 5 |
| **8** | 5.3 |
| **7** | 6.11 |
| **9** | 6.377 |
| **10** | 7.1639 |
| **11** | 8.01473 |
| **10** | 8.910311 |
| **12** | 9.237218 |
| **15** | 10.06605 |
| **14** | 11.54624 |

## Chapter Problems
*Computational Problems*

2.  $\beta_0 = \beta_0(\lambda)^0 = 1.4(0.471)^0 = 1.4.$
    $\beta_1 = \beta_0(\lambda)^1 = 1.4(0.471)^1 = 0.659.$
    $\beta_2 = \beta_0(\lambda)^2 = 1.4(0.471)^2 = 0.311.$
    $\beta_3 = \beta_0(\lambda)^3 = 1.4(0.471)^3 = 0.146.$
    $\beta_4 = \beta_0(\lambda)^4 = 1.4(0.471)^4 = 0.0689.$

4.

| Late Shipments | Forecast | Error | Absolute Error | Error Squared | Abs Error/At | *100 |
|---|---|---|---|---|---|---|
| 5 | | | | | | |
| 9 | #N/A | | | | | |
| 10 | #N/A | | | | | |
| 15 | 8 | 7 | 7 | 49 | 0.466666667 | 46.66667 |
| 14 | 11.33333 | 2.666667 | 2.666666667 | 7.111111111 | 0.19047619 | 19.04762 |
| 16 | 13 | 3 | 3 | 9 | 0.1875 | 18.75 |
| 18 | 15 | 3 | 3 | 9 | 0.166666667 | 16.66667 |
| 21 | 16 | 5 | 5 | 25 | 0.238095238 | 23.80952 |
| 23 | 18.33333 | 4.666667 | 4.666666667 | 21.77777778 | 0.202898551 | 20.28986 |
| 20 | 20.66667 | −0.66667 | 0.666666667 | 0.444444444 | 0.033333333 | 3.333333 |
| 24 | 21.33333 | 2.666667 | 2.666666667 | 7.111111111 | 0.111111111 | 11.11111 |
| 18 | 22.33333 | −4.33333 | 4.333333333 | 18.77777778 | 0.240740741 | 24.07407 |
| 28 | 20.66667 | 7.333333 | 7.333333333 | 53.77777778 | 0.261904762 | 26.19048 |
| 35 | 23.33333 | 11.66667 | 11.66666667 | 136.1111111 | 0.333333333 | 33.33333 |
| | 27 | | | | | |
| | | | | | | |
| SUMS | | | 52 | 337.1111111 | 2.432726593 | 243.2727 |

Moving average is probably not a suitable method because the data are trended upward.

MAPE = 243.27/11 = 22.115.

MAD = 52/11 = 4.72.

MSD = 337.11/11 = 30.65.

# Appendix B

# STATISTICAL TABLES

## B.1 CHI-SQUARE TABLE

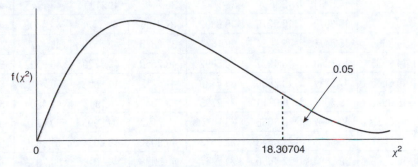

Given 10 degrees of freedom, there is only a 5% chance your data will yield a chi-square value above 18.30704.

| Alpha Value d.f. | 0.995 | 0.99 | 0.975 | 0.95 | 0.9 | 0.1 | 0.05 | 0.025 | 0.01 | 0.005 |
|---|---|---|---|---|---|---|---|---|---|---|
| 1 | 0.0000 | 0.0002 | 0.0010 | 0.0039 | 0.0158 | 2.7055 | 3.8415 | 5.0239 | 6.6349 | 7.8794 |
| 2 | 0.0100 | 0.0201 | 0.0506 | 0.1026 | 0.2107 | 4.6052 | 5.9915 | 7.3778 | 9.2103 | 10.5966 |
| 3 | 0.07 17 | 0.1148 | 0.2158 | 0.3518 | 0.5844 | 6.2514 | 7.8147 | 9.3484 | 11.3449 | 12.8382 |
| 4 | 0.2070 | 0.2971 | 0.4844 | 0.7107 | 1.0636 | 7.7794 | 9.4877 | 11.1433 | 13.2767 | 14.8603 |
| 5 | 0.4117 | 0.5543 | 0.8312 | 1.1455 | 1.6103 | 9.2364 | 11.0705 | 12.8325 | 15.0863 | 16.7496 |
| 6 | 0.6757 | 0.8721 | 1.2373 | 1.6354 | 2.2041 | 10.6446 | 12.5916 | 14.4494 | 16.8119 | 18.5476 |
| 7 | 0.9893 | 1.2390 | 1.6899 | 2.1673 | 2.8331 | 12.0170 | 14.0671 | 16.0128 | 18.4753 | 20.2777 |
| 8 | 1.3444 | 1.6465 | 2.1797 | 2.7326 | 3.4895 | 13.3616 | 15.5073 | 17.5345 | 20.0902 | 21.9550 |
| 9 | 1.7349 | 2.0879 | 2.7004 | 3.3251 | 4.1682 | 14.6837 | 16.9190 | 19.0228 | 21.6660 | 23.5894 |
| 10 | 2.1559 | 2.5582 | 3.2470 | 3.9403 | 4.8652 | 15.9872 | **18.3070** | 20.4832 | 23.2093 | 25.1882 |
| 11 | 2.6032 | 3.0535 | 3.8157 | 4.5748 | 5.5778 | 17.2750 | 19.6751 | 21.9200 | 24.7250 | 26.7568 |
| 12 | 3.0738 | 3.5706 | 4.4038 | 5.2260 | 6.3038 | 18.5493 | 21.0261 | 23.3367 | 26.2170 | 28.2995 |
| 13 | 3.5650 | 4.1069 | 5.0088 | 5.8919 | 7.0415 | 19.8119 | 22.3620 | 24.7356 | 27.6882 | 29.8195 |
| 14 | 4.0747 | 4.6604 | 5.6287 | 6.5706 | 7.7895 | 21.0641 | 23.6848 | 26.1189 | 29.1412 | 31.3193 |

| | | | | | | | | | |
|---|---|---|---|---|---|---|---|---|---|
| **15** | 4.6009 | 5.2293 | 6.2621 | 7.2609 | 8.5468 | 22.3071 | 24.9958 | 27.4884 | 30.5779 | 32.8013 |
| **16** | 5.1422 | 5.8122 | 6.9077 | 7.9616 | 9.3122 | 23.5418 | 26.2962 | 28.8454 | 31.9999 | 34.2672 |
| **17** | 5.6972 | 6.4078 | 7.5642 | 8.6718 | 10.0852 | 24.7690 | 27.5871 | 30.1910 | 33.4087 | 35.7185 |
| **18** | 6.2648 | 7.0149 | 8.2307 | 9.3905 | 10.8649 | 25.9894 | 28.8693 | 31.5264 | 34.8053 | 37.1565 |
| **19** | 6.8440 | 7.6327 | 8.9065 | 10.1170 | 11.6509 | 27.2036 | 30.1435 | 32.8523 | 36.1909 | 38.5823 |
| **20** | 7.4338 | 8.2604 | 9.5908 | 10.8508 | 12.4426 | 28.4120 | 31.4104 | 34.1696 | 37.5662 | 39.9968 |
| **21** | 8.0337 | 8.8972 | 10.2829 | 11.5913 | 13.2396 | 29.6151 | 32.6706 | 35.4789 | 38.9322 | 41.4011 |
| **22** | 8.6427 | 9.5425 | 10.9823 | 12.3380 | 14.0415 | 30.8133 | 33.9244 | 36.7807 | 40.2894 | 42.7957 |
| **23** | 9.2604 | 10.1957 | 11.6886 | 13.0905 | 14.8480 | 32.0069 | 35.1725 | 38.0756 | 41.6384 | 44.1813 |
| **24** | 9.8862 | 10.8564 | 12.4012 | 13.8484 | 15.6587 | 33.1962 | 36.4150 | 39.3641 | 42.9798 | 45.5585 |
| **25** | 10.5197 | 11.5240 | 13.1197 | 14.6114 | 16.4734 | 34.3816 | 37.6525 | 40.6465 | 44.3141 | 46.9279 |
| **26** | 11.1602 | 12.1981 | 13.8439 | 15.3792 | 17.2919 | 35.5632 | 38.8851 | 41.9232 | 45.6417 | 48.2899 |
| **27** | 11.8076 | 12.8785 | 14.5734 | 16.1514 | 18.1139 | 36.7412 | 40.1133 | 43.1945 | 46.9629 | 49.6449 |
| **28** | 12.4613 | 13.5647 | 15.3079 | 16.9279 | 18.9392 | 37.9159 | 41.3371 | 44.4608 | 48.2782 | 50.9934 |
| **29** | 13.1211 | 14.2565 | 16.0471 | 17.7084 | 19.7677 | 39.0875 | 42.5570 | 45.7223 | 49.5879 | 52.3356 |
| **30** | 13.7867 | 14.9535 | 16.7908 | 18.4927 | 20.5992 | 40.2560 | 43.7730 | 46.9792 | 50.8922 | 53.6720 |
| **31** | 14.4578 | 15.6555 | 17.5387 | 19.2806 | 21.4336 | 41.4217 | 44.9853 | 48.2319 | 52.1914 | 55.0027 |
| **32** | 15.1340 | 16.3622 | 18.2908 | 20.0719 | 22.2706 | 42.5847 | 46.1943 | 49.4804 | 53.4858 | 56.3281 |
| **33** | 15.8153 | 17.0735 | 19.0467 | 20.8665 | 23.1102 | 43.7452 | 47.3999 | 50.7251 | 54.7755 | 57.6484 |
| **34** | 16.5013 | 17.7891 | 19.8063 | 21.6643 | 23.9523 | 44.9032 | 48.6024 | 51.9660 | 56.0609 | 58.9639 |
| **35** | 17.1918 | 18.5089 | 20.5694 | 22.4650 | 24.7967 | 46.0588 | 49.8018 | 53.2033 | 57.3421 | 60.2748 |
| **36** | 17.8867 | 19.2327 | 21.3359 | 23.2686 | 25.6433 | 47.2122 | 50.9985 | 54.4373 | 58.6192 | 61.5812 |
| **37** | 18.5858 | 19.9602 | 22.1056 | 24.0749 | 26.4921 | 48.3634 | 52.1923 | 55.6680 | 59.8925 | 62.8833 |
| **38** | 19.2889 | 20.6914 | 22.8785 | 24.8839 | 27.3430 | 49.5126 | 53.3835 | 56.8955 | 61.1621 | 64.1814 |
| **39** | 19.9959 | 21.4262 | 23.6543 | 25.6954 | 28.1958 | 50.6598 | 54.5722 | 58.1201 | 62.4281 | 65.4756 |
| **40** | 20.7065 | 22.1643 | 24.4330 | 26.5093 | 29.0505 | 51.8051 | 55.7585 | 59.3417 | 63.6907 | 66.7660 |
| **45** | 24.3110 | 25.9013 | 28.3662 | 30.6123 | 33.3504 | 57.5053 | 61.6562 | 65.4102 | 69.9568 | 73.1661 |
| **50** | 27.9907 | 29.7067 | 32.3574 | 34.7643 | 37.6886 | 63.1671 | 67.5048 | 71.4202 | 76.1539 | 79.4900 |
| **55** | 31.7348 | 33.5705 | 36.3981 | 38.9580 | 42.0596 | 68.7962 | 73.3115 | 77.3805 | 82.2921 | 85.7490 |
| **60** | 35.5345 | 37.4849 | 40.4817 | 43.1880 | 46.4589 | 74.3970 | 79.0819 | 83.2977 | 88.3794 | 91.9517 |
| **65** | 39.3831 | 41.4436 | 44.6030 | 47.4496 | 50.8829 | 79.9730 | 84.8206 | 89.1771 | 94.4221 | 98.1051 |
| **70** | 43.2752 | 45.4417 | 48.7576 | 51.7393 | 55.3289 | 85.5270 | 90.5312 | 95.0232 | 100.4252 | 104.2149 |
| **75** | 47.2060 | 49.4750 | 52.9419 | 56.0541 | 59.7946 | 91.0615 | 96.2167 | 100.8393 | 106.3929 | 110.2856 |
| **80** | 51.1719 | 53.5401 | 57.1532 | 60.3915 | 64.2778 | 96.5782 | 101.8795 | 106.6286 | 112.3288 | 116.3211 |
| **85** | 55.1696 | 57.6339 | 61.3888 | 64.7494 | 68.7772 | 102.0789 | 107.5217 | 112.3934 | 118.2357 | 122.3246 |
| **90** | 59.1963 | 61.7541 | 65.6466 | 69.1260 | 73.2911 | 107.5650 | 113.1453 | 118.1359 | 124.1163 | 128.2989 |
| **95** | 63.2496 | 65.8984 | 69.9249 | 73.5198 | 77.8184 | 113.0377 | 118.7516 | 123.8580 | 129.9727 | 134.2465 |
| **100** | 67.3276 | 70.0649 | 74.2219 | 77.9295 | 82.3581 | 118.4980 | 124.3421 | 129.5612 | 135.8067 | 140.1695 |

## B.2 DURBIN–WATSON VALUES

$k$ is the number of explanatory variables (constant term not included).

**1% Values**

| n | k = 1 dL | dU | k = 2 dL | dU | k = 3 dL | dU | k = 4 dL | dU | k = 5 dL | dU | k = 6 dL | dU |
|---|---|---|---|---|---|---|---|---|---|---|---|---|
| 6 | 0.390 | 1.142 | | | | | | | | | | |
| 7 | 0.435 | 1.036 | 0.294 | 1.676 | | | | | | | | |
| 8 | 0.497 | 1.003 | 0.345 | 1.489 | 0.229 | 2.102 | | | | | | |
| 9 | 0.554 | 0.998 | 0.408 | 1.389 | 0.279 | 1.875 | 0.183 | 2.433 | | | | |
| 10 | 0.604 | 1.001 | 0.466 | 1.333 | 0.340 | 1.733 | 0.230 | 2.193 | 0.150 | 2.690 | | |
| 11 | 0.653 | 1.010 | 0.519 | 1.297 | 0.396 | 1.640 | 0.286 | 2.030 | 0.193 | 2.453 | 0.124 | 2.892 |
| 12 | 0.697 | 1.023 | 0.569 | 1.274 | 0.449 | 1.575 | 0.339 | 1.913 | 0.244 | 2.280 | 0.164 | 2.665 |
| 13 | 0.738 | 1.038 | 0.616 | 1.261 | 0.499 | 1.526 | 0.391 | 1.826 | 0.294 | 2.150 | 0.211 | 2.490 |
| 14 | 0.776 | 1.054 | 0.660 | 1.254 | 0.547 | 1.490 | 0.441 | 1.757 | 0.343 | 2.049 | 0.257 | 2.354 |
| 15 | 0.811 | 1.070 | 0.700 | 1.252 | 0.591 | 1.465 | 0.487 | 1.705 | 0.390 | 1.967 | 0.303 | 2.244 |
| 16 | 0.844 | 1.086 | 0.738 | 1.253 | 0.633 | 1.447 | 0.532 | 1.664 | 0.437 | 1.901 | 0.349 | 2.153 |
| 17 | 0.873 | 1.102 | 0.773 | 1.255 | 0.672 | 1.432 | 0.574 | 1.631 | 0.481 | 1.847 | 0.393 | 2.078 |
| 18 | 0.902 | 1.118 | 0.805 | 1.259 | 0.708 | 1.422 | 0.614 | 1.604 | 0.522 | 1.803 | 0.435 | 2.015 |
| 19 | 0.928 | 1.133 | 0.835 | 1.264 | 0.742 | 1.416 | 0.650 | 1.583 | 0.561 | 1.767 | 0.476 | 1.963 |
| 20 | 0.952 | 1.147 | 0.862 | 1.270 | 0.774 | 1.410 | 0.684 | 1.567 | 0.598 | 1.736 | 0.515 | 1.918 |
| 21 | 0.975 | 1.161 | 0.889 | 1.276 | 0.803 | 1.408 | 0.718 | 1.554 | 0.634 | 1.712 | 0.552 | 1.881 |
| 22 | 0.997 | 1.174 | 0.915 | 1.284 | 0.832 | 1.407 | 0.748 | 1.543 | 0.666 | 1.691 | 0.587 | 1.849 |
| 23 | 1.017 | 1.186 | 0.938 | 1.290 | 0.858 | 1.407 | 0.777 | 1.535 | 0.699 | 1.674 | 0.620 | 1.821 |
| 24 | 1.037 | 1.199 | 0.959 | 1.298 | 0.881 | 1.407 | 0.805 | 1.527 | 0.728 | 1.659 | 0.652 | 1.797 |
| 25 | 1.055 | 1.210 | 0.981 | 1.305 | 0.906 | 1.408 | 0.832 | 1.521 | 0.756 | 1.645 | 0.682 | 1.776 |
| 26 | 1.072 | 1.222 | 1.000 | 1.311 | 0.928 | 1.410 | 0.855 | 1.517 | 0.782 | 1.635 | 0.711 | 1.759 |
| 27 | 1.088 | 1.232 | 1.019 | 1.318 | 0.948 | 1.413 | 0.878 | 1.514 | 0.808 | 1.625 | 0.738 | 1.743 |
| 28 | 1.104 | 1.244 | 1.036 | 1.325 | 0.969 | 1.414 | 0.901 | 1.512 | 0.832 | 1.618 | 0.764 | 1.729 |
| 29 | 1.119 | 1.254 | 1.053 | 1.332 | 0.988 | 1.418 | 0.921 | 1.511 | 0.855 | 1.611 | 0.788 | 1.718 |
| 30 | 1.134 | 1.264 | 1.070 | 1.339 | 1.006 | 1.421 | 0.941 | 1.510 | 0.877 | 1.606 | 0.812 | 1.707 |
| 31 | 1.147 | 1.274 | 1.085 | 1.345 | 1.022 | 1.425 | 0.960 | 1.509 | 0.897 | 1.601 | 0.834 | 1.698 |
| 32 | 1.160 | 1.283 | 1.100 | 1.351 | 1.039 | 1.428 | 0.978 | 1.509 | 0.917 | 1.597 | 0.856 | 1.690 |
| 33 | 1.171 | 1.291 | 1.114 | 1.358 | 1.055 | 1.432 | 0.995 | 1.510 | 0.935 | 1.594 | 0.876 | 1.683 |
| 34 | 1.184 | 1.298 | 1.128 | 1.364 | 1.070 | 1.436 | 1.012 | 1.511 | 0.954 | 1.591 | 0.896 | 1.677 |
| 35 | 1.195 | 1.307 | 1.141 | 1.370 | 1.085 | 1.439 | 1.028 | 1.512 | 0.971 | 1.589 | 0.914 | 1.671 |

## B.2 DURBIN–WATSON VALUES (CONTINUED)

**5% Values**

| n | k=1 dL | k=1 dU | k=2 dL | k=2 dU | k=3 dL | k=3 dU | k=4 dL | k=4 dU | k=5 dL | k=5 dU | k=6 dL | k=6 dU |
|---|---|---|---|---|---|---|---|---|---|---|---|---|
| 6 | 0.610 | 1.400 | | | | | | | | | | |
| 7 | 0.700 | 1.356 | 0.467 | 1.896 | | | | | | | | |
| 8 | 0.763 | 1.332 | 0.559 | 1.777 | 0.367 | 2.287 | | | | | | |
| 9 | 0.824 | 1.320 | 0.629 | 1.699 | 0.455 | 2.128 | 0.296 | 2.588 | | | | |
| 10 | 0.879 | 1.320 | 0.697 | 1.641 | 0.525 | 2.016 | 0.376 | 2.414 | 0.243 | 2.822 | | |
| 11 | 0.927 | 1.324 | 0.758 | 1.604 | 0.595 | 1.928 | 0.444 | 2.283 | 0.315 | 2.645 | 0.203 | 3.004 |
| 12 | 0.971 | 1.331 | 0.812 | 1.579 | 0.658 | 1.864 | 0.512 | 2.177 | 0.380 | 2.506 | 0.268 | 2.832 |
| 13 | 1.010 | 1.340 | 0.861 | 1.562 | 0.715 | 1.816 | 0.574 | 2.094 | 0.444 | 2.390 | 0.328 | 2.692 |
| 14 | 1.045 | 1.350 | 0.905 | 1.551 | 0.767 | 1.779 | 0.632 | 2.030 | 0.505 | 2.296 | 0.389 | 2.572 |
| 15 | 1.077 | 1.361 | 0.946 | 1.543 | 0.814 | 1.750 | 0.685 | 1.977 | 0.562 | 2.220 | 0.447 | 2.471 |
| 16 | 1.106 | 1.371 | 0.982 | 1.539 | 0.857 | 1.728 | 0.734 | 1.935 | 0.615 | 2.157 | 0.502 | 2.388 |
| 17 | 1.133 | 1.381 | 1.015 | 1.536 | 0.897 | 1.710 | 0.779 | 1.900 | 0.664 | 2.104 | 0.554 | 2.318 |
| 18 | 1.158 | 1.391 | 1.046 | 1.535 | 0.933 | 1.696 | 0.820 | 1.872 | 0.710 | 2.060 | 0.603 | 2.258 |
| 19 | 1.180 | 1.401 | 1.074 | 1.536 | 0.967 | 1.685 | 0.859 | 1.848 | 0.752 | 2.023 | 0.649 | 2.206 |
| 20 | 1.201 | 1.411 | 1.100 | 1.537 | 0.998 | 1.676 | 0.894 | 1.828 | 0.792 | 1.991 | 0.691 | 2.162 |
| 21 | 1.221 | 1.420 | 1.125 | 1.538 | 1.026 | 1.669 | 0.927 | 1.812 | 0.829 | 1.964 | 0.731 | 2.124 |
| 22 | 1.239 | 1.429 | 1.147 | 1.541 | 1.053 | 1.664 | 0.958 | 1.797 | 0.863 | 1.940 | 0.769 | 2.090 |
| 23 | 1.257 | 1.437 | 1.168 | 1.543 | 1.078 | 1.660 | 0.986 | 1.785 | 0.895 | 1.920 | 0.804 | 2.061 |
| 24 | 1.273 | 1.446 | 1.188 | 1.546 | 1.101 | 1.656 | 1.013 | 1.775 | 0.925 | 1.902 | 0.837 | 2.035 |
| 25 | 1.288 | 1.454 | 1.206 | 1.550 | 1.123 | 1.654 | 1.038 | 1.767 | 0.953 | 1.886 | 0.868 | 2.013 |
| 26 | 1.302 | 1.461 | 1.224 | 1.553 | 1.143 | 1.652 | 1.062 | 1.759 | 0.979 | 1.873 | 0.897 | 1.992 |
| 27 | 1.316 | 1.469 | 1.240 | 1.556 | 1.162 | 1.651 | 1.084 | 1.753 | 1.004 | 1.861 | 0.925 | 1.974 |
| 28 | 1.328 | 1.476 | 1.255 | 1.560 | 1.181 | 1.650 | 1.104 | 1.747 | 1.028 | 1.850 | 0.951 | 1.959 |
| 29 | 1.341 | 1.483 | 1.270 | 1.563 | 1.198 | 1.650 | 1.124 | 1.743 | 1.050 | 1.841 | 0.975 | 1.944 |
| 30 | 1.352 | 1.489 | 1.284 | 1.567 | 1.214 | 1.650 | 1.143 | 1.739 | 1.071 | 1.833 | 0.998 | 1.931 |
| 31 | 1.363 | 1.496 | 1.297 | 1.570 | 1.229 | 1.650 | 1.160 | 1.735 | 1.090 | 1.825 | 1.020 | 1.920 |
| 32 | 1.373 | 1.502 | 1.309 | 1.574 | 1.244 | 1.650 | 1.177 | 1.732 | 1.109 | 1.819 | 1.041 | 1.909 |
| 33 | 1.383 | 1.508 | 1.321 | 1.577 | 1.258 | 1.651 | 1.193 | 1.730 | 1.127 | 1.813 | 1.061 | 1.900 |
| 34 | 1.393 | 1.514 | 1.333 | 1.580 | 1.271 | 1.652 | 1.208 | 1.728 | 1.144 | 1.808 | 1.079 | 1.891 |
| 35 | 1.402 | 1.519 | 1.343 | 1.584 | 1.283 | 1.653 | 1.222 | 1.726 | 1.160 | 1.803 | 1.097 | 1.884 |

## B.3 F-DISTRIBUTION TABLE

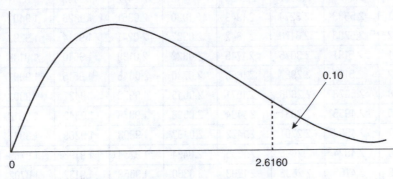

With 5 and 9 degrees of freedom $P(F > 2.616) = 0.10$.

| | Alpha-Value = 0.10 | | | | | | | | | |
|---|---|---|---|---|---|---|---|---|---|---|
| | **Degrees of Freedom for the Numerator** | | | | | | | | | |
| | 1 | 2 | 3 | 4 | 5 | 6 | 7 | 8 | 9 | 10 |
| **Degrees of Freedom for the Denominator** | | | | | | | | | | |
| 1 | 39.8635 | 49.5000 | 53.5932 | 55.8330 | 57.2401 | 58.2044 | 58.9060 | 59.4390 | 59.8576 | 60.1950 |
| 2 | 8.5263 | 9.0000 | 9.1618 | 9.2434 | 9.2926 | 9.3255 | 9.3491 | 9.3668 | 9.3805 | 9.3916 |
| 3 | 5.5383 | 5.4624 | 5.3908 | 5.3426 | 5.3092 | 5.2847 | 5.2662 | 5.2517 | 5.2400 | 5.2304 |
| 4 | 4.5448 | 4.3246 | 4.1909 | 4.1072 | 4.0506 | 4.0097 | 3.9790 | 3.9549 | 3.9357 | 3.9199 |
| 5 | 4.0604 | 3.7797 | 3.6195 | 3.5202 | 3.4530 | 3.4045 | 3.3679 | 3.3393 | 3.3163 | 3.2974 |
| 6 | 3.7759 | 3.4633 | 3.2888 | 3.1808 | 3.1075 | 3.0546 | 3.0145 | 2.9830 | 2.9577 | 2.9369 |
| 7 | 3.5894 | 3.2574 | 3.0741 | 2.9605 | 2.8833 | 2.8274 | 2.7849 | 2.7516 | 2.7247 | 2.7025 |
| 8 | 3.4579 | 3.1131 | 2.9238 | 2.8064 | 2.7264 | 2.6683 | 2.6241 | 2.5893 | 2.5612 | 2.5380 |
| 9 | 3.3603 | 3.0065 | 2.8129 | 2.6927 | **2.6106** | 2.5509 | 2.5053 | 2.4694 | 2.4403 | 2.4163 |
| 10 | 3.2850 | 2.9245 | 2.7277 | 2.6053 | 2.5216 | 2.4606 | 2.4140 | 2.3772 | 2.3473 | 2.3226 |
| 11 | 3.2252 | 2.8595 | 2.6602 | 2.5362 | 2.4512 | 2.3891 | 2.3416 | 2.3040 | 2.2735 | 2.2482 |
| 12 | 3.1765 | 2.8068 | 2.6055 | 2.4801 | 2.3940 | 2.3310 | 2.2828 | 2.2446 | 2.2135 | 2.1878 |
| 13 | 3.1362 | 2.7632 | 2.5603 | 2.4337 | 2.3467 | 2.2830 | 2.2341 | 2.1953 | 2.1638 | 2.1376 |
| 14 | 3.1022 | 2.7265 | 2.5222 | 2.3947 | 2.3069 | 2.2426 | 2.1931 | 2.1539 | 2.1220 | 2.0954 |
| 15 | 3.0732 | 2.6952 | 2.4898 | 2.3614 | 2.2730 | 2.2081 | 2.1582 | 2.1185 | 2.0862 | 2.0593 |
| 16 | 3.0481 | 2.6682 | 2.4618 | 2.3327 | 2.2438 | 2.1783 | 2.1280 | 2.0880 | 2.0553 | 2.0281 |
| 17 | 3.0262 | 2.6446 | 2.4374 | 2.3077 | 2.2183 | 2.1524 | 2.1017 | 2.0613 | 2.0284 | 2.0009 |
| 18 | 3.0070 | 2.6239 | 2.4160 | 2.2858 | 2.1958 | 2.1296 | 2.0785 | 2.0379 | 2.0047 | 1.9770 |
| 19 | 2.9899 | 2.6056 | 2.3970 | 2.2663 | 2.1760 | 2.1094 | 2.0580 | 2.0171 | 1.9836 | 1.9557 |
| 20 | 2.9747 | 2.5893 | 2.3801 | 2.2489 | 2.1582 | 2.0913 | 2.0397 | 1.9985 | 1.9649 | 1.9367 |
| 21 | 2.9610 | 2.5746 | 2.3649 | 2.2333 | 2.1423 | 2.0751 | 2.0233 | 1.9819 | 1.9480 | 1.9197 |

| 22 | 2.9486 | 2.5613 | 2.3512 | 2.2193 | 2.1279 | 2.0605 | 2.0084 | 1.9668 | 1.9327 | 1.9043 |
|---|---|---|---|---|---|---|---|---|---|---|
| 23 | 2.9374 | 2.5493 | 2.3387 | 2.2065 | 2.1149 | 2.0472 | 1.9949 | 1.9531 | 1.9189 | 1.8903 |
| 24 | 2.9271 | 2.5383 | 2.3274 | 2.1949 | 2.1030 | 2.0351 | 1.9826 | 1.9407 | 1.9063 | 1.8775 |
| 25 | 2.9177 | 2.5283 | 2.3170 | 2.1842 | 2.0922 | 2.0241 | 1.9714 | 1.9292 | 1.8947 | 1.8658 |
| 26 | 2.9091 | 2.5191 | 2.3075 | 2.1745 | 2.0822 | 2.0139 | 1.9610 | 1.9188 | 1.8841 | 1.8550 |
| 27 | 2.9012 | 2.5106 | 2.2987 | 2.1655 | 2.0730 | 2.0045 | 1.9515 | 1.9091 | 1.8743 | 1.8451 |
| 28 | 2.8938 | 2.5028 | 2.2906 | 2.1571 | 2.0645 | 1.9959 | 1.9427 | 1.9001 | 1.8652 | 1.8359 |
| 29 | 2.8870 | 2.4955 | 2.2831 | 2.1494 | 2.0566 | 1.9878 | 1.9345 | 1.8918 | 1.8568 | 1.8274 |
| 30 | 2.8807 | 2.4887 | 2.2761 | 2.1422 | 2.0492 | 1.9803 | 1.9269 | 1.8841 | 1.8490 | 1.8195 |
| 31 | 2.8748 | 2.4824 | 2.2695 | 2.1355 | 2.0424 | 1.9734 | 1.9198 | 1.8769 | 1.8417 | 1.8121 |
| 32 | 2.8693 | 2.4765 | 2.2635 | 2.1293 | 2.0360 | 1.9668 | 1.9132 | 1.8702 | 1.8348 | 1.8052 |
| 33 | 2.8641 | 2.4710 | 2.2577 | 2.1234 | 2.0300 | 1.9607 | 1.9070 | 1.8639 | 1.8284 | 1.7987 |
| 34 | 2.8592 | 2.4658 | 2.2524 | 2.1179 | 2.0244 | 1.9550 | 1.9012 | 1.8580 | 1.8224 | 1.7926 |
| 35 | 2.8547 | 2.4609 | 2.2474 | 2.1128 | 2.0191 | 1.9496 | 1.8957 | 1.8524 | 1.8168 | 1.7869 |
| 36 | 2.8503 | 2.4563 | 2.2426 | 2.1079 | 2.0141 | 1.9446 | 1.8905 | 1.8471 | 1.8115 | 1.7815 |
| 37 | 2.8463 | 2.4520 | 2.2381 | 2.1033 | 2.0094 | 1.9398 | 1.8856 | 1.8422 | 1.8064 | 1.7764 |
| 38 | 2.8424 | 2.4479 | 2.2339 | 2.0990 | 2.0050 | 1.9352 | 1.8810 | 1.8375 | 1.8017 | 1.7716 |
| 39 | 2.8388 | 2.4440 | 2.2299 | 2.0948 | 2.0008 | 1.9309 | 1.8767 | 1.8331 | 1.7972 | 1.7670 |
| 40 | 2.8354 | 2.4404 | 2.2261 | 2.0909 | 1.9968 | 1.9269 | 1.8725 | 1.8289 | 1.7929 | 1.7627 |
| 41 | 2.8321 | 2.4369 | 2.2225 | 2.0872 | 1.9930 | 1.9230 | 1.8686 | 1.8249 | 1.7888 | 1.7586 |
| 42 | 2.8290 | 2.4336 | 2.2191 | 2.0837 | 1.9894 | 1.9193 | 1.8649 | 1.8211 | 1.7850 | 1.7547 |
| 43 | 2.8260 | 2.4304 | 2.2158 | 2.0804 | 1.9860 | 1.9159 | 1.8613 | 1.8175 | 1.7813 | 1.7509 |
| 44 | 2.8232 | 2.4274 | 2.2127 | 2.0772 | 1.9828 | 1.9125 | 1.8579 | 1.8140 | 1.7778 | 1.7474 |
| 45 | 2.8205 | 2.4245 | 2.2097 | 2.0742 | 1.9796 | 1.9094 | 1.8547 | 1.8107 | 1.7745 | 1.7440 |
| 46 | 2.8179 | 2.4218 | 2.2069 | 2.0712 | 1.9767 | 1.9063 | 1.8516 | 1.8076 | 1.7713 | 1.7408 |
| 47 | 2.8154 | 2.4192 | 2.2042 | 2.0685 | 1.9738 | 1.9034 | 1.8486 | 1.8046 | 1.7682 | 1.7377 |
| 48 | 2.8131 | 2.4167 | 2.2016 | 2.0658 | 1.9711 | 1.9006 | 1.8458 | 1.8017 | 1.7653 | 1.7347 |
| 49 | 2.8108 | 2.4143 | 2.1991 | 2.0633 | 1.9685 | 1.8980 | 1.8431 | 1.7989 | 1.7625 | 1.7319 |
| 50 | 2.8087 | 2.4120 | 2.1967 | 2.0608 | 1.9660 | 1.8954 | 1.8405 | 1.7963 | 1.7598 | 1.7291 |
| 55 | 2.7990 | 2.4017 | 2.1862 | 2.0500 | 1.9549 | 1.8841 | 1.8290 | 1.7846 | 1.7479 | 1.7171 |
| 60 | 2.7911 | 2.3933 | 2.1774 | 2.0410 | 1.9457 | 1.8747 | 1.8194 | 1.7748 | 1.7380 | 1.7070 |
| 65 | 2.7843 | 2.3861 | 2.1700 | 2.0334 | 1.9380 | 1.8668 | 1.8113 | 1.7666 | 1.7297 | 1.6985 |
| 70 | 2.7786 | 2.3800 | 2.1637 | 2.0269 | 1.9313 | 1.8600 | 1.8044 | 1.7596 | 1.7225 | 1.6913 |
| 75 | 2.7736 | 2.3747 | 2.1583 | 2.0214 | 1.9256 | 1.8542 | 1.7985 | 1.7535 | 1.7164 | 1.6850 |
| 80 | 2.7693 | 2.3701 | 2.1535 | 2.0165 | 1.9206 | 1.8491 | 1.7933 | 1.7483 | 1.7110 | 1.6796 |
| 85 | 2.7655 | 2.3661 | 2.1494 | 2.0122 | 1.9162 | 1.8446 | 1.7887 | 1.7436 | 1.7063 | 1.6748 |
| 90 | 2.7621 | 2.3625 | 2.1457 | 2.0084 | 1.9123 | 1.8406 | 1.7846 | 1.7395 | 1.7021 | 1.6705 |
| 95 | 2.7591 | 2.3593 | 2.1424 | 2.0050 | 1.9089 | 1.8371 | 1.7810 | 1.7358 | 1.6983 | 1.6667 |
| 100 | 2.7564 | 2.3564 | 2.1394 | 2.0019 | 1.9057 | 1.8339 | 1.7778 | 1.7324 | 1.6949 | 1.6632 |

| | | | | Alpha-Value = 0.10 | | | | | | |
|---|---|---|---|---|---|---|---|---|---|---|
| | | | | **Degrees of Freedom for the Numerator** | | | | | | |
| | 11 | 12 | 13 | 14 | 15 | 16 | 17 | 18 | 19 | 20 |
| **Degrees of Freedom for the Denominator** | | | | | | | | | | |
| 1 | 60.4727 | 60.7052 | 60.9028 | 61.0727 | 61.2203 | 61.3499 | 61.4644 | 61.5664 | 61.6579 | 61.7403 |
| 2 | 9.4006 | 9.4081 | 9.4145 | 9.4200 | 9.4247 | 9.4289 | 9.4325 | 9.4358 | 9.4387 | 9.4413 |
| 3 | 5.2224 | 5.2156 | 5.2098 | 5.2047 | 5.2003 | 5.1964 | 5.1929 | 5.1898 | 5.1870 | 5.1845 |
| 4 | 3.9067 | 3.8955 | 3.8859 | 3.8776 | 3.8704 | 3.8639 | 3.8582 | 3.8531 | 3.8485 | 3.8443 |
| 5 | 3.2816 | 3.2682 | 3.2567 | 3.2468 | 3.2380 | 3.2303 | 3.2234 | 3.2172 | 3.2117 | 3.2067 |
| 6 | 2.9195 | 2.9047 | 2.8920 | 2.8809 | 2.8712 | 2.8626 | 2.8550 | 2.8481 | 2.8419 | 2.8363 |
| 7 | 2.6839 | 2.6681 | 2.6545 | 2.6426 | 2.6322 | 2.6230 | 2.6148 | 2.6074 | 2.6008 | 2.5947 |
| 8 | 2.5186 | 2.5020 | 2.4876 | 2.4752 | 2.4642 | 2.4545 | 2.4458 | 2.4380 | 2.4310 | 2.4246 |
| 9 | 2.3961 | 2.3789 | 2.3640 | 2.3510 | 2.3396 | 2.3295 | 2.3205 | 2.3123 | 2.3050 | 2.2983 |
| 10 | 2.3018 | 2.2841 | 2.2687 | 2.2553 | 2.2435 | 2.2330 | 2.2237 | 2.2153 | 2.2077 | 2.2007 |
| 11 | 2.2269 | 2.2087 | 2.1930 | 2.1792 | 2.1671 | 2.1563 | 2.1467 | 2.1380 | 2.1302 | 2.1230 |
| 12 | 2.1660 | 2.1474 | 2.1313 | 2.1173 | 2.1049 | 2.0938 | 2.0839 | 2.0750 | 2.0670 | 2.0597 |
| 13 | 2.1155 | 2.0966 | 2.0802 | 2.0658 | 2.0532 | 2.0419 | 2.0318 | 2.0227 | 2.0145 | 2.0070 |
| 14 | 2.0729 | 2.0537 | 2.0370 | 2.0224 | 2.0095 | 1.9981 | 1.9878 | 1.9785 | 1.9701 | 1.9625 |
| 15 | 2.0366 | 2.0171 | 2.0001 | 1.9853 | 1.9722 | 1.9605 | 1.9501 | 1.9407 | 1.9321 | 1.9243 |
| 16 | 2.0051 | 1.9854 | 1.9682 | 1.9532 | 1.9399 | 1.9281 | 1.9175 | 1.9079 | 1.8992 | 1.8913 |
| 17 | 1.9777 | 1.9577 | 1.9404 | 1.9252 | 1.9117 | 1.8997 | 1.8889 | 1.8792 | 1.8704 | 1.8624 |
| 18 | 1.9535 | 1.9333 | 1.9158 | 1.9004 | 1.8868 | 1.8747 | 1.8638 | 1.8539 | 1.8450 | 1.8368 |
| 19 | 1.9321 | 1.9117 | 1.8940 | 1.8785 | 1.8647 | 1.8524 | 1.8414 | 1.8314 | 1.8224 | 1.8142 |
| 20 | 1.9129 | 1.8924 | 1.8745 | 1.8588 | 1.8449 | 1.8325 | 1.8214 | 1.8113 | 1.8022 | 1.7938 |
| 21 | 1.8956 | 1.8750 | 1.8570 | 1.8412 | 1.8271 | 1.8146 | 1.8034 | 1.7932 | 1.7840 | 1.7756 |
| 22 | 1.8801 | 1.8593 | 1.8411 | 1.8252 | 1.8111 | 1.7984 | 1.7871 | 1.7768 | 1.7675 | 1.7590 |
| 23 | 1.8659 | 1.8450 | 1.8267 | 1.8107 | 1.7964 | 1.7837 | 1.7723 | 1.7619 | 1.7525 | 1.7439 |
| 24 | 1.8530 | 1.8319 | 1.8136 | 1.7974 | 1.7831 | 1.7703 | 1.7587 | 1.7483 | 1.7388 | 1.7302 |
| 25 | 1.8412 | 1.8200 | 1.8015 | 1.7853 | 1.7708 | 1.7579 | 1.7463 | 1.7358 | 1.7263 | 1.7175 |
| 26 | 1.8303 | 1.8090 | 1.7904 | 1.7741 | 1.7596 | 1.7466 | 1.7349 | 1.7243 | 1.7147 | 1.7059 |
| 27 | 1.8203 | 1.7989 | 1.7802 | 1.7638 | 1.7492 | 1.7361 | 1.7243 | 1.7137 | 1.7040 | 1.6951 |

| 28 | 1.8110 | 1.7895 | 1.7708 | 1.7542 | 1.7395 | 1.7264 | 1.7146 | 1.7039 | 1.6941 | 1.6852 |
|-----|--------|--------|--------|--------|--------|--------|--------|--------|--------|--------|
| 29 | 1.8024 | 1.7808 | 1.7620 | 1.7454 | 1.7306 | 1.7174 | 1.7055 | 1.6947 | 1.6849 | 1.6759 |
| 30 | 1.7944 | 1.7727 | 1.7538 | 1.7371 | 1.7223 | 1.7090 | 1.6970 | 1.6862 | 1.6763 | 1.6673 |
| 31 | 1.7869 | 1.7651 | 1.7461 | 1.7294 | 1.7145 | 1.7012 | 1.6891 | 1.6783 | 1.6683 | 1.6593 |
| 32 | 1.7799 | 1.7581 | 1.7390 | 1.7222 | 1.7072 | 1.6938 | 1.6818 | 1.6708 | 1.6608 | 1.6517 |
| 33 | 1.7733 | 1.7514 | 1.7323 | 1.7154 | 1.7004 | 1.6869 | 1.6748 | 1.6638 | 1.6538 | 1.6446 |
| 34 | 1.7672 | 1.7452 | 1.7260 | 1.7091 | 1.6940 | 1.6805 | 1.6683 | 1.6573 | 1.6472 | 1.6380 |
| 35 | 1.7614 | 1.7394 | 1.7201 | 1.7031 | 1.6880 | 1.6744 | 1.6622 | 1.6511 | 1.6410 | 1.6317 |
| 36 | 1.7559 | 1.7338 | 1.7145 | 1.6974 | 1.6823 | 1.6687 | 1.6564 | 1.6453 | 1.6351 | 1.6258 |
| 37 | 1.7508 | 1.7286 | 1.7092 | 1.6921 | 1.6769 | 1.6632 | 1.6509 | 1.6397 | 1.6296 | 1.6202 |
| 38 | 1.7459 | 1.7237 | 1.7042 | 1.6871 | 1.6718 | 1.6581 | 1.6457 | 1.6345 | 1.6243 | 1.6149 |
| 39 | 1.7413 | 1.7190 | 1.6995 | 1.6823 | 1.6670 | 1.6532 | 1.6408 | 1.6296 | 1.6193 | 1.6099 |
| 40 | 1.7369 | 1.7146 | 1.6950 | 1.6778 | 1.6624 | 1.6486 | 1.6362 | 1.6249 | 1.6146 | 1.6052 |
| 41 | 1.7327 | 1.7103 | 1.6908 | 1.6735 | 1.6581 | 1.6442 | 1.6318 | 1.6204 | 1.6101 | 1.6006 |
| 42 | 1.7288 | 1.7063 | 1.6867 | 1.6694 | 1.6539 | 1.6401 | 1.6276 | 1.6162 | 1.6058 | 1.5963 |
| 43 | 1.7250 | 1.7025 | 1.6829 | 1.6655 | 1.6500 | 1.6361 | 1.6235 | 1.6121 | 1.6017 | 1.5922 |
| 44 | 1.7214 | 1.6989 | 1.6792 | 1.6618 | 1.6462 | 1.6323 | 1.6197 | 1.6083 | 1.5979 | 1.5883 |
| 45 | 1.7180 | 1.6954 | 1.6757 | 1.6582 | 1.6426 | 1.6287 | 1.6161 | 1.6046 | 1.5941 | 1.5846 |
| 46 | 1.7147 | 1.6921 | 1.6723 | 1.6548 | 1.6392 | 1.6252 | 1.6126 | 1.6011 | 1.5906 | 1.5810 |
| 47 | 1.7115 | 1.6889 | 1.6691 | 1.6516 | 1.6359 | 1.6219 | 1.6092 | 1.5977 | 1.5872 | 1.5776 |
| 48 | 1.7085 | 1.6859 | 1.6660 | 1.6485 | 1.6328 | 1.6187 | 1.6060 | 1.5945 | 1.5839 | 1.5743 |
| 49 | 1.7057 | 1.6830 | 1.6631 | 1.6455 | 1.6298 | 1.6157 | 1.6030 | 1.5914 | 1.5808 | 1.5711 |
| 50 | 1.7029 | 1.6802 | 1.6602 | 1.6426 | 1.6269 | 1.6128 | 1.6000 | 1.5884 | 1.5778 | 1.5681 |
| 55 | 1.6906 | 1.6677 | 1.6477 | 1.6299 | 1.6140 | 1.5998 | 1.5869 | 1.5752 | 1.5645 | 1.5547 |
| 60 | 1.6805 | 1.6574 | 1.6372 | 1.6193 | 1.6034 | 1.5890 | 1.5760 | 1.5642 | 1.5534 | 1.5435 |
| 65 | 1.6719 | 1.6487 | 1.6284 | 1.6104 | 1.5943 | 1.5799 | 1.5668 | 1.5549 | 1.5440 | 1.5340 |
| 70 | 1.6645 | 1.6413 | 1.6209 | 1.6028 | 1.5866 | 1.5721 | 1.5589 | 1.5470 | 1.5360 | 1.5259 |
| 75 | 1.6582 | 1.6348 | 1.6143 | 1.5962 | 1.5799 | 1.5653 | 1.5521 | 1.5401 | 1.5290 | 1.5189 |
| 80 | 1.6526 | 1.6292 | 1.6086 | 1.5904 | 1.5741 | 1.5594 | 1.5461 | 1.5340 | 1.5230 | 1.5128 |
| 85 | 1.6477 | 1.6243 | 1.6036 | 1.5853 | 1.5690 | 1.5542 | 1.5409 | 1.5287 | 1.5176 | 1.5073 |
| 90 | 1.6434 | 1.6199 | 1.5992 | 1.5808 | 1.5644 | 1.5496 | 1.5362 | 1.5240 | 1.5128 | 1.5025 |
| 95 | 1.6395 | 1.6159 | 1.5952 | 1.5768 | 1.5603 | 1.5455 | 1.5320 | 1.5198 | 1.5085 | 1.4982 |
| 100 | 1.6360 | 1.6124 | 1.5916 | 1.5731 | 1.5566 | 1.5418 | 1.5283 | 1.5160 | 1.5047 | 1.4943 |

| | | | | | Alpha-Value = 0.10 | | | | |
|---|---|---|---|---|---|---|---|---|---|
| | | | | **Degrees of Freedom for the Numerator** | | | | | |
| | 21 | 22 | 23 | 24 | 25 | 26 | 27 | 28 | 29 | 30 |
| **Degrees of Freedom for the Denominator** | | | | | | | | | | |
| 1 | 61.8150 | 61.8829 | 61.9450 | 62.0020 | 62.0545 | 62.1030 | 62.1480 | 62.1897 | 62.2286 | 62.2650 |
| 2 | 9.4437 | 9.4458 | 9.4478 | 9.4496 | 9.4513 | 9.4528 | 9.4542 | 9.4556 | 9.4568 | 9.4579 |
| 3 | 5.1822 | 5.1801 | 5.1781 | 5.1764 | 5.1747 | 5.1732 | 5.1718 | 5.1705 | 5.1693 | 5.1681 |
| 4 | 3.8405 | 3.8371 | 3.8339 | 3.8310 | 3.8283 | 3.8258 | 3.8235 | 3.8213 | 3.8193 | 3.8174 |
| 5 | 3.2021 | 3.1979 | 3.1941 | 3.1905 | 3.1873 | 3.1842 | 3.1814 | 3.1788 | 3.1764 | 3.1741 |
| 6 | 2.8312 | 2.8266 | 2.8223 | 2.8183 | 2.8147 | 2.8113 | 2.8082 | 2.8053 | 2.8025 | 2.8000 |
| 7 | 2.5892 | 2.5842 | 2.5796 | 2.5753 | 2.5714 | 2.5677 | 2.5643 | 2.5612 | 2.5582 | 2.5555 |
| 8 | 2.4188 | 2.4135 | 2.4086 | 2.4041 | 2.3999 | 2.3961 | 2.3925 | 2.3891 | 2.3860 | 2.3830 |
| 9 | 2.2922 | 2.2867 | 2.2816 | 2.2768 | 2.2725 | 2.2684 | 2.2646 | 2.2611 | 2.2578 | 2.2547 |
| 10 | 2.1944 | 2.1887 | 2.1833 | 2.1784 | 2.1739 | 2.1697 | 2.1657 | 2.1621 | 2.1586 | 2.1554 |
| 11 | 2.1165 | 2.1106 | 2.1051 | 2.1000 | 2.0953 | 2.0909 | 2.0869 | 2.0831 | 2.0795 | 2.0762 |
| 12 | 2.0530 | 2.0469 | 2.0412 | 2.0360 | 2.0312 | 2.0267 | 2.0225 | 2.0186 | 2.0149 | 2.0115 |
| 13 | 2.0001 | 1.9939 | 1.9881 | 1.9827 | 1.9778 | 1.9732 | 1.9689 | 1.9649 | 1.9611 | 1.9576 |
| 14 | 1.9555 | 1.9490 | 1.9431 | 1.9377 | 1.9326 | 1.9279 | 1.9235 | 1.9194 | 1.9155 | 1.9119 |
| 15 | 1.9172 | 1.9106 | 1.9046 | 1.8990 | 1.8939 | 1.8891 | 1.8846 | 1.8804 | 1.8765 | 1.8728 |
| 16 | 1.8840 | 1.8774 | 1.8712 | 1.8656 | 1.8603 | 1.8554 | 1.8508 | 1.8466 | 1.8426 | 1.8388 |
| 17 | 1.8550 | 1.8482 | 1.8420 | 1.8362 | 1.8309 | 1.8259 | 1.8213 | 1.8169 | 1.8128 | 1.8090 |
| 18 | 1.8294 | 1.8225 | 1.8162 | 1.8103 | 1.8049 | 1.7999 | 1.7951 | 1.7907 | 1.7866 | 1.7827 |
| 19 | 1.8066 | 1.7997 | 1.7932 | 1.7873 | 1.7818 | 1.7767 | 1.7719 | 1.7674 | 1.7632 | 1.7592 |
| 20 | 1.7862 | 1.7792 | 1.7727 | 1.7667 | 1.7611 | 1.7559 | 1.7510 | 1.7465 | 1.7422 | 1.7382 |
| 21 | 1.7678 | 1.7607 | 1.7541 | 1.7481 | 1.7424 | 1.7372 | 1.7322 | 1.7276 | 1.7233 | 1.7193 |
| 22 | 1.7512 | 1.7440 | 1.7374 | 1.7312 | 1.7255 | 1.7202 | 1.7152 | 1.7106 | 1.7062 | 1.7021 |
| 23 | 1.7360 | 1.7288 | 1.7221 | 1.7159 | 1.7101 | 1.7047 | 1.6997 | 1.6950 | 1.6906 | 1.6864 |
| 24 | 1.7222 | 1.7149 | 1.7081 | 1.7019 | 1.6960 | 1.6906 | 1.6855 | 1.6808 | 1.6763 | 1.6721 |
| 25 | 1.7095 | 1.7021 | 1.6953 | 1.6890 | 1.6831 | 1.6776 | 1.6725 | 1.6677 | 1.6632 | 1.6589 |
| 26 | 1.6978 | 1.6904 | 1.6835 | 1.6771 | 1.6712 | 1.6657 | 1.6605 | 1.6556 | 1.6511 | 1.6468 |
| 27 | 1.6870 | 1.6795 | 1.6726 | 1.6662 | 1.6602 | 1.6546 | 1.6494 | 1.6445 | 1.6399 | 1.6356 |

| | | | | | | | | | |
|---|---|---|---|---|---|---|---|---|---|
| 28 | 1.6770 | 1.6695 | 1.6625 | 1.6560 | 1.6500 | 1.6444 | 1.6391 | 1.6342 | 1.6295 | 1.6252 |
| 29 | 1.6677 | 1.6601 | 1.6531 | 1.6465 | 1.6405 | 1.6348 | 1.6295 | 1.6246 | 1.6199 | 1.6155 |
| 30 | 1.6590 | 1.6514 | 1.6443 | 1.6377 | 1.6316 | 1.6259 | 1.6206 | 1.6156 | 1.6109 | 1.6065 |
| 31 | 1.6509 | 1.6432 | 1.6361 | 1.6295 | 1.6234 | 1.6176 | 1.6123 | 1.6072 | 1.6025 | 1.5980 |
| 32 | 1.6433 | 1.6356 | 1.6284 | 1.6218 | 1.6156 | 1.6098 | 1.6044 | 1.5994 | 1.5946 | 1.5901 |
| 33 | 1.6362 | 1.6284 | 1.6212 | 1.6146 | 1.6083 | 1.6025 | 1.5971 | 1.5920 | 1.5872 | 1.5827 |
| 34 | 1.6295 | 1.6217 | 1.6145 | 1.6077 | 1.6015 | 1.5957 | 1.5902 | 1.5851 | 1.5802 | 1.5757 |
| 35 | 1.6232 | 1.6154 | 1.6081 | 1.6013 | 1.5950 | 1.5892 | 1.5837 | 1.5785 | 1.5737 | 1.5691 |
| 36 | 1.6173 | 1.6094 | 1.6021 | 1.5953 | 1.5890 | 1.5831 | 1.5775 | 1.5723 | 1.5675 | 1.5629 |
| 37 | 1.6116 | 1.6037 | 1.5964 | 1.5896 | 1.5832 | 1.5773 | 1.5717 | 1.5665 | 1.5616 | 1.5570 |
| 38 | 1.6063 | 1.5984 | 1.5910 | 1.5841 | 1.5778 | 1.5718 | 1.5662 | 1.5610 | 1.5560 | 1.5514 |
| 39 | 1.6013 | 1.5933 | 1.5859 | 1.5790 | 1.5726 | 1.5666 | 1.5610 | 1.5557 | 1.5508 | 1.5461 |
| 40 | 1.5965 | 1.5884 | 1.5810 | 1.5741 | 1.5677 | 1.5617 | 1.5560 | 1.5507 | 1.5458 | 1.5411 |
| 41 | 1.5919 | 1.5839 | 1.5764 | 1.5695 | 1.5630 | 1.5570 | 1.5513 | 1.5460 | 1.5410 | 1.5363 |
| 42 | 1.5876 | 1.5795 | 1.5720 | 1.5650 | 1.5586 | 1.5525 | 1.5468 | 1.5415 | 1.5365 | 1.5317 |
| 43 | 1.5834 | 1.5753 | 1.5678 | 1.5608 | 1.5543 | 1.5482 | 1.5425 | 1.5372 | 1.5321 | 1.5274 |
| 44 | 1.5795 | 1.5714 | 1.5638 | 1.5568 | 1.5503 | 1.5442 | 1.5384 | 1.5331 | 1.5280 | 1.5232 |
| 45 | 1.5757 | 1.5676 | 1.5600 | 1.5530 | 1.5464 | 1.5403 | 1.5345 | 1.5291 | 1.5241 | 1.5193 |
| 46 | 1.5721 | 1.5639 | 1.5563 | 1.5493 | 1.5427 | 1.5366 | 1.5308 | 1.5254 | 1.5203 | 1.5155 |
| 47 | 1.5687 | 1.5605 | 1.5529 | 1.5458 | 1.5392 | 1.5330 | 1.5272 | 1.5218 | 1.5167 | 1.5118 |
| 48 | 1.5654 | 1.5571 | 1.5495 | 1.5424 | 1.5358 | 1.5296 | 1.5238 | 1.5183 | 1.5132 | 1.5084 |
| 49 | 1.5622 | 1.5539 | 1.5463 | 1.5392 | 1.5325 | 1.5263 | 1.5205 | 1.5150 | 1.5099 | 1.5050 |
| 50 | 1.5592 | 1.5509 | 1.5432 | 1.5361 | 1.5294 | 1.5232 | 1.5173 | 1.5118 | 1.5067 | 1.5018 |
| 55 | 1.5456 | 1.5372 | 1.5295 | 1.5222 | 1.5155 | 1.5092 | 1.5033 | 1.4977 | 1.4924 | 1.4875 |
| 60 | 1.5343 | 1.5259 | 1.5180 | 1.5107 | 1.5039 | 1.4975 | 1.4915 | 1.4859 | 1.4806 | 1.4755 |
| 65 | 1.5248 | 1.5163 | 1.5083 | 1.5010 | 1.4941 | 1.4876 | 1.4816 | 1.4759 | 1.4705 | 1.4654 |
| 70 | 1.5166 | 1.5080 | 1.5000 | 1.4926 | 1.4857 | 1.4791 | 1.4730 | 1.4673 | 1.4618 | 1.4567 |
| 75 | 1.5096 | 1.5009 | 1.4929 | 1.4854 | 1.4783 | 1.4718 | 1.4656 | 1.4598 | 1.4544 | 1.4492 |
| 80 | 1.5034 | 1.4947 | 1.4866 | 1.4790 | 1.4720 | 1.4653 | 1.4591 | 1.4533 | 1.4478 | 1.4426 |
| 85 | 1.4979 | 1.4891 | 1.4810 | 1.4734 | 1.4663 | 1.4597 | 1.4534 | 1.4475 | 1.4420 | 1.4367 |
| 90 | 1.4930 | 1.4842 | 1.4761 | 1.4684 | 1.4613 | 1.4546 | 1.4483 | 1.4424 | 1.4368 | 1.4315 |
| 95 | 1.4887 | 1.4799 | 1.4716 | 1.4640 | 1.4568 | 1.4501 | 1.4438 | 1.4378 | 1.4322 | 1.4269 |
| 100 | 1.4848 | 1.4759 | 1.4677 | 1.4600 | 1.4528 | 1.4460 | 1.4397 | 1.4337 | 1.4280 | 1.4227 |

| | Alpha-Value = 0.10 | | | | | | | | |
|---|---|---|---|---|---|---|---|---|---|
| | **Degrees of Freedom for the Numerator** | | | | | | | | |
| | 31 | 32 | 33 | 34 | 35 | 36 | 37 | 38 | 39 | 40 |
| **Degrees of Freedom for the Denominator** | | | | | | | | | | |
| 1 | 62.2990 | 62.3309 | 62.3609 | 62.3891 | 62.4157 | 62.4409 | 62.4647 | 62.4873 | 62.5087 | 62.5291 |
| 2 | 9.4590 | 9.4600 | 9.4610 | 9.4618 | 9.4627 | 9.4635 | 9.4642 | 9.4649 | 9.4656 | 9.4662 |
| 3 | 5.1670 | 5.1660 | 5.1651 | 5.1642 | 5.1633 | 5.1625 | 5.1618 | 5.1611 | 5.1604 | 5.1597 |
| 4 | 3.8157 | 3.8140 | 3.8124 | 3.8110 | 3.8096 | 3.8082 | 3.8070 | 3.8058 | 3.8047 | 3.8036 |
| 5 | 3.1719 | 3.1699 | 3.1680 | 3.1662 | 3.1645 | 3.1629 | 3.1614 | 3.1600 | 3.1586 | 3.1573 |
| 6 | 2.7976 | 2.7953 | 2.7932 | 2.7912 | 2.7893 | 2.7875 | 2.7858 | 2.7842 | 2.7826 | 2.7812 |
| 7 | 2.5529 | 2.5504 | 2.5481 | 2.5459 | 2.5439 | 2.5419 | 2.5401 | 2.5383 | 2.5367 | 2.5351 |
| 8 | 2.3803 | 2.3777 | 2.3752 | 2.3729 | 2.3707 | 2.3686 | 2.3667 | 2.3648 | 2.3630 | 2.3614 |
| 9 | 2.2518 | 2.2491 | 2.2465 | 2.2441 | 2.2418 | 2.2396 | 2.2376 | 2.2356 | 2.2337 | 2.2320 |
| 10 | 2.1524 | 2.1496 | 2.1469 | 2.1444 | 2.1420 | 2.1397 | 2.1375 | 2.1355 | 2.1335 | 2.1317 |
| 11 | 2.0731 | 2.0701 | 2.0674 | 2.0647 | 2.0623 | 2.0599 | 2.0577 | 2.0556 | 2.0535 | 2.0516 |
| 12 | 2.0083 | 2.0052 | 2.0024 | 1.9997 | 1.9971 | 1.9947 | 1.9924 | 1.9902 | 1.9881 | 1.9861 |
| 13 | 1.9543 | 1.9511 | 1.9482 | 1.9454 | 1.9428 | 1.9403 | 1.9379 | 1.9357 | 1.9335 | 1.9315 |
| 14 | 1.9085 | 1.9053 | 1.9023 | 1.8995 | 1.8968 | 1.8942 | 1.8918 | 1.8895 | 1.8873 | 1.8852 |
| 15 | 1.8693 | 1.8660 | 1.8630 | 1.8600 | 1.8573 | 1.8547 | 1.8522 | 1.8498 | 1.8475 | 1.8454 |
| 16 | 1.8353 | 1.8319 | 1.8288 | 1.8258 | 1.8230 | 1.8203 | 1.8178 | 1.8153 | 1.8130 | 1.8108 |
| 17 | 1.8054 | 1.8020 | 1.7988 | 1.7958 | 1.7929 | 1.7902 | 1.7876 | 1.7851 | 1.7828 | 1.7805 |
| 18 | 1.7790 | 1.7756 | 1.7723 | 1.7692 | 1.7663 | 1.7635 | 1.7609 | 1.7584 | 1.7560 | 1.7537 |
| 19 | 1.7555 | 1.7520 | 1.7487 | 1.7456 | 1.7426 | 1.7398 | 1.7371 | 1.7345 | 1.7321 | 1.7298 |
| 20 | 1.7345 | 1.7309 | 1.7275 | 1.7243 | 1.7213 | 1.7185 | 1.7157 | 1.7132 | 1.7107 | 1.7083 |
| 21 | 1.7154 | 1.7118 | 1.7084 | 1.7052 | 1.7021 | 1.6992 | 1.6965 | 1.6939 | 1.6914 | 1.6890 |
| 22 | 1.6982 | 1.6946 | 1.6911 | 1.6878 | 1.6847 | 1.6818 | 1.6790 | 1.6763 | 1.6738 | 1.6714 |
| 23 | 1.6825 | 1.6788 | 1.6753 | 1.6720 | 1.6689 | 1.6659 | 1.6631 | 1.6604 | 1.6578 | 1.6554 |
| 24 | 1.6681 | 1.6644 | 1.6609 | 1.6575 | 1.6544 | 1.6514 | 1.6485 | 1.6458 | 1.6432 | 1.6407 |
| 25 | 1.6550 | 1.6512 | 1.6476 | 1.6442 | 1.6410 | 1.6380 | 1.6351 | 1.6323 | 1.6297 | 1.6272 |
| 26 | 1.6428 | 1.6390 | 1.6354 | 1.6320 | 1.6287 | 1.6256 | 1.6227 | 1.6199 | 1.6173 | 1.6147 |
| 27 | 1.6315 | 1.6277 | 1.6240 | 1.6206 | 1.6173 | 1.6142 | 1.6113 | 1.6085 | 1.6058 | 1.6032 |

| 28 | 1.6211 | 1.6172 | 1.6135 | 1.6101 | 1.6068 | 1.6036 | 1.6006 | 1.5978 | 1.5951 | 1.5925 |
| 29 | 1.6114 | 1.6075 | 1.6038 | 1.6003 | 1.5969 | 1.5938 | 1.5908 | 1.5879 | 1.5851 | 1.5825 |
| 30 | 1.6023 | 1.5984 | 1.5946 | 1.5911 | 1.5877 | 1.5846 | 1.5815 | 1.5786 | 1.5759 | 1.5732 |
| 31 | 1.5938 | 1.5899 | 1.5861 | 1.5825 | 1.5792 | 1.5759 | 1.5729 | 1.5700 | 1.5672 | 1.5645 |
| 32 | 1.5859 | 1.5819 | 1.5781 | 1.5745 | 1.5711 | 1.5679 | 1.5648 | 1.5618 | 1.5590 | 1.5564 |
| 33 | 1.5784 | 1.5744 | 1.5706 | 1.5670 | 1.5635 | 1.5603 | 1.5572 | 1.5542 | 1.5514 | 1.5487 |
| 34 | 1.5714 | 1.5674 | 1.5635 | 1.5599 | 1.5564 | 1.5531 | 1.5500 | 1.5470 | 1.5442 | 1.5415 |
| 35 | 1.5648 | 1.5607 | 1.5569 | 1.5532 | 1.5497 | 1.5464 | 1.5433 | 1.5403 | 1.5374 | 1.5346 |
| 36 | 1.5585 | 1.5544 | 1.5506 | 1.5469 | 1.5434 | 1.5400 | 1.5369 | 1.5338 | 1.5310 | 1.5282 |
| 37 | 1.5526 | 1.5485 | 1.5446 | 1.5409 | 1.5374 | 1.5340 | 1.5308 | 1.5278 | 1.5249 | 1.5221 |
| 38 | 1.5470 | 1.5429 | 1.5389 | 1.5352 | 1.5317 | 1.5283 | 1.5251 | 1.5220 | 1.5191 | 1.5163 |
| 39 | 1.5417 | 1.5375 | 1.5336 | 1.5298 | 1.5263 | 1.5229 | 1.5197 | 1.5166 | 1.5137 | 1.5108 |
| 40 | 1.5366 | 1.5325 | 1.5285 | 1.5247 | 1.5211 | 1.5177 | 1.5145 | 1.5114 | 1.5084 | 1.5056 |
| 41 | 1.5318 | 1.5276 | 1.5236 | 1.5199 | 1.5163 | 1.5128 | 1.5096 | 1.5065 | 1.5035 | 1.5007 |
| 42 | 1.5273 | 1.5230 | 1.5190 | 1.5152 | 1.5116 | 1.5082 | 1.5049 | 1.5018 | 1.4988 | 1.4959 |
| 43 | 1.5229 | 1.5186 | 1.5146 | 1.5108 | 1.5072 | 1.5037 | 1.5004 | 1.4973 | 1.4943 | 1.4914 |
| 44 | 1.5187 | 1.5145 | 1.5104 | 1.5066 | 1.5029 | 1.4995 | 1.4962 | 1.4930 | 1.4900 | 1.4871 |
| 45 | 1.5147 | 1.5105 | 1.5064 | 1.5025 | 1.4989 | 1.4954 | 1.4921 | 1.4889 | 1.4859 | 1.4830 |
| 46 | 1.5109 | 1.5066 | 1.5026 | 1.4987 | 1.4950 | 1.4915 | 1.4882 | 1.4850 | 1.4819 | 1.4790 |
| 47 | 1.5073 | 1.5030 | 1.4989 | 1.4950 | 1.4913 | 1.4878 | 1.4844 | 1.4812 | 1.4782 | 1.4752 |
| 48 | 1.5038 | 1.4994 | 1.4953 | 1.4914 | 1.4877 | 1.4842 | 1.4808 | 1.4776 | 1.4745 | 1.4716 |
| 49 | 1.5004 | 1.4961 | 1.4919 | 1.4880 | 1.4843 | 1.4808 | 1.4774 | 1.4742 | 1.4711 | 1.4681 |
| 50 | 1.4972 | 1.4928 | 1.4887 | 1.4848 | 1.4810 | 1.4775 | 1.4741 | 1.4708 | 1.4677 | 1.4648 |
| 55 | 1.4828 | 1.4784 | 1.4742 | 1.4702 | 1.4664 | 1.4628 | 1.4593 | 1.4560 | 1.4529 | 1.4498 |
| 60 | 1.4708 | 1.4663 | 1.4620 | 1.4580 | 1.4541 | 1.4505 | 1.4470 | 1.4436 | 1.4404 | 1.4373 |
| 65 | 1.4606 | 1.4561 | 1.4518 | 1.4477 | 1.4437 | 1.4400 | 1.4365 | 1.4331 | 1.4298 | 1.4267 |
| 70 | 1.4519 | 1.4473 | 1.4429 | 1.4388 | 1.4348 | 1.4311 | 1.4275 | 1.4240 | 1.4208 | 1.4176 |
| 75 | 1.4443 | 1.4397 | 1.4353 | 1.4311 | 1.4271 | 1.4233 | 1.4196 | 1.4162 | 1.4129 | 1.4097 |
| 80 | 1.4376 | 1.4330 | 1.4285 | 1.4243 | 1.4203 | 1.4164 | 1.4128 | 1.4093 | 1.4059 | 1.4027 |
| 85 | 1.4318 | 1.4271 | 1.4226 | 1.4183 | 1.4143 | 1.4104 | 1.4067 | 1.4032 | 1.3998 | 1.3966 |
| 90 | 1.4265 | 1.4218 | 1.4173 | 1.4130 | 1.4089 | 1.4050 | 1.4013 | 1.3977 | 1.3943 | 1.3911 |
| 95 | 1.4219 | 1.4171 | 1.4126 | 1.4082 | 1.4041 | 1.4002 | 1.3965 | 1.3929 | 1.3894 | 1.3862 |
| 100 | 1.4176 | 1.4128 | 1.4083 | 1.4039 | 1.3998 | 1.3959 | 1.3921 | 1.3885 | 1.3850 | 1.3817 |

| | | | | | Alpha-Value = 0.05 | | | | |
|---|---|---|---|---|---|---|---|---|---|---|
| | | | | **Degrees of Freedom for the Numerator** | | | | | | |
| | 1 | 2 | 3 | 4 | 5 | 6 | 7 | 8 | 9 | 10 |
| **Degrees of Freedom for the Denominator** | | | | | | | | | | |
| 1 | 161.4476 | 199.5000 | 215.7073 | 224.5832 | 230.1619 | 233.9860 | 236.7684 | 238.8827 | 240.5433 | 241.8817 |
| 2 | 18.5128 | 19.0000 | 19.1643 | 19.2468 | 19.2964 | 19.3295 | 19.3532 | 19.3710 | 19.3848 | 19.3959 |
| 3 | 10.1280 | 9.5521 | 9.2766 | 9.1172 | 9.0135 | 8.9406 | 8.8867 | 8.8452 | 8.8123 | 8.7855 |
| 4 | 7.7086 | 6.9443 | 6.5914 | 6.3882 | 6.2561 | 6.1631 | 6.0942 | 6.0410 | 5.9988 | 5.9644 |
| 5 | 6.6079 | 5.7861 | 5.4095 | 5.1922 | 5.0503 | 4.9503 | 4.8759 | 4.8183 | 4.7725 | 4.7351 |
| 6 | 5.9874 | 5.1433 | 4.7571 | 4.5337 | 4.3874 | 4.2839 | 4.2067 | 4.1468 | 4.0990 | 4.0600 |
| 7 | 5.5914 | 4.7374 | 4.3468 | 4.1203 | 3.9715 | 3.8660 | 3.7870 | 3.7257 | 3.6767 | 3.6365 |
| 8 | 5.3177 | 4.4590 | 4.0662 | 3.8379 | 3.6875 | 3.5806 | 3.5005 | 3.4381 | 3.3881 | 3.3472 |
| 9 | 5.1174 | 4.2565 | 3.8625 | 3.6331 | 3.4817 | 3.3738 | 3.2927 | 3.2296 | 3.1789 | 3.1373 |
| 10 | 4.9646 | 4.1028 | 3.7083 | 3.4780 | 3.3258 | 3.2172 | 3.1355 | 3.0717 | 3.0204 | 2.9782 |
| 11 | 4.8443 | 3.9823 | 3.5874 | 3.3567 | 3.2039 | 3.0946 | 3.0123 | 2.9480 | 2.8962 | 2.8536 |
| 12 | 4.7472 | 3.8853 | 3.4903 | 3.2592 | 3.1059 | 2.9961 | 2.9134 | 2.8486 | 2.7964 | 2.7534 |
| 13 | 4.6672 | 3.8056 | 3.4105 | 3.1791 | 3.0254 | 2.9153 | 2.8321 | 2.7669 | 2.7144 | 2.6710 |
| 14 | 4.6001 | 3.7389 | 3.3439 | 3.1122 | 2.9582 | 2.8477 | 2.7642 | 2.6987 | 2.6458 | 2.6022 |
| 15 | 4.5431 | 3.6823 | 3.2874 | 3.0556 | 2.9013 | 2.7905 | 2.7066 | 2.6408 | 2.5876 | 2.5437 |
| 16 | 4.4940 | 3.6337 | 3.2389 | 3.0069 | 2.8524 | 2.7413 | 2.6572 | 2.5911 | 2.5377 | 2.4935 |
| 17 | 4.4513 | 3.5915 | 3.1968 | 2.9647 | 2.8100 | 2.6987 | 2.6143 | 2.5480 | 2.4943 | 2.4499 |
| 18 | 4.4139 | 3.5546 | 3.1599 | 2.9277 | 2.7729 | 2.6613 | 2.5767 | 2.5102 | 2.4563 | 2.4117 |
| 19 | 4.3807 | 3.5219 | 3.1274 | 2.8951 | 2.7401 | 2.6283 | 2.5435 | 2.4768 | 2.4227 | 2.3779 |
| 20 | 4.3512 | 3.4928 | 3.0984 | 2.8661 | 2.7109 | 2.5990 | 2.5140 | 2.4471 | 2.3928 | 2.3479 |
| 21 | 4.3248 | 3.4668 | 3.0725 | 2.8401 | 2.6848 | 2.5727 | 2.4876 | 2.4205 | 2.3660 | 2.3210 |
| 22 | 4.3009 | 3.4434 | 3.0491 | 2.8167 | 2.6613 | 2.5491 | 2.4638 | 2.3965 | 2.3419 | 2.2967 |
| 23 | 4.2793 | 3.4221 | 3.0280 | 2.7955 | 2.6400 | 2.5277 | 2.4422 | 2.3748 | 2.3201 | 2.2747 |
| 24 | 4.2597 | 3.4028 | 3.0088 | 2.7763 | 2.6207 | 2.5082 | 2.4226 | 2.3551 | 2.3002 | 2.2547 |
| 25 | 4.2417 | 3.3852 | 2.9912 | 2.7587 | 2.6030 | 2.4904 | 2.4047 | 2.3371 | 2.2821 | 2.2365 |
| 26 | 4.2252 | 3.3690 | 2.9752 | 2.7426 | 2.5868 | 2.4741 | 2.3883 | 2.3205 | 2.2655 | 2.2197 |
| 27 | 4.2100 | 3.3541 | 2.9604 | 2.7278 | 2.5719 | 2.4591 | 2.3732 | 2.3053 | 2.2501 | 2.2043 |

| 28 | 4.1960 | 3.3404 | 2.9467 | 2.7141 | 2.5581 | 2.4453 | 2.3593 | 2.2913 | 2.2360 | 2.1900 |
|-----|--------|--------|--------|--------|--------|--------|--------|--------|--------|--------|
| 29 | 4.1830 | 3.3277 | 2.9340 | 2.7014 | 2.5454 | 2.4324 | 2.3463 | 2.2783 | 2.2229 | 2.1768 |
| 30 | 4.1709 | 3.3158 | 2.9223 | 2.6896 | 2.5336 | 2.4205 | 2.3343 | 2.2662 | 2.2107 | 2.1646 |
| 31 | 4.1596 | 3.3048 | 2.9113 | 2.6787 | 2.5225 | 2.4094 | 2.3232 | 2.2549 | 2.1994 | 2.1532 |
| 32 | 4.1491 | 3.2945 | 2.9011 | 2.6684 | 2.5123 | 2.3991 | 2.3127 | 2.2444 | 2.1888 | 2.1425 |
| 33 | 4.1393 | 3.2849 | 2.8916 | 2.6589 | 2.5026 | 2.3894 | 2.3030 | 2.2346 | 2.1789 | 2.1325 |
| 34 | 4.1300 | 3.2759 | 2.8826 | 2.6499 | 2.4936 | 2.3803 | 2.2938 | 2.2253 | 2.1696 | 2.1231 |
| 35 | 4.1213 | 3.2674 | 2.8742 | 2.6415 | 2.4851 | 2.3718 | 2.2852 | 2.2167 | 2.1608 | 2.1143 |
| 36 | 4.1132 | 3.2594 | 2.8663 | 2.6335 | 2.4772 | 2.3638 | 2.2771 | 2.2085 | 2.1526 | 2.1061 |
| 37 | 4.1055 | 3.2519 | 2.8588 | 2.6261 | 2.4696 | 2.3562 | 2.2695 | 2.2008 | 2.1449 | 2.0982 |
| 38 | 4.0982 | 3.2448 | 2.8517 | 2.6190 | 2.4625 | 2.3490 | 2.2623 | 2.1936 | 2.1375 | 2.0909 |
| 39 | 4.0913 | 3.2381 | 2.8451 | 2.6123 | 2.4558 | 2.3423 | 2.2555 | 2.1867 | 2.1306 | 2.0839 |
| 40 | 4.0847 | 3.2317 | 2.8387 | 2.6060 | 2.4495 | 2.3359 | 2.2490 | 2.1802 | 2.1240 | 2.0772 |
| 41 | 4.0785 | 3.2257 | 2.8327 | 2.6000 | 2.4434 | 2.3298 | 2.2429 | 2.1740 | 2.1178 | 2.0710 |
| 42 | 4.0727 | 3.2199 | 2.8270 | 2.5943 | 2.4377 | 2.3240 | 2.2371 | 2.1681 | 2.1119 | 2.0650 |
| 43 | 4.0670 | 3.2145 | 2.8216 | 2.5888 | 2.4322 | 2.3185 | 2.2315 | 2.1625 | 2.1062 | 2.0593 |
| 44 | 4.0617 | 3.2093 | 2.8165 | 2.5837 | 2.4270 | 2.3133 | 2.2263 | 2.1572 | 2.1009 | 2.0539 |
| 45 | 4.0566 | 3.2043 | 2.8115 | 2.5787 | 2.4221 | 2.3083 | 2.2212 | 2.1521 | 2.0958 | 2.0487 |
| 46 | 4.0517 | 3.1996 | 2.8068 | 2.5740 | 2.4174 | 2.3035 | 2.2164 | 2.1473 | 2.0909 | 2.0438 |
| 47 | 4.0471 | 3.1951 | 2.8024 | 2.5695 | 2.4128 | 2.2990 | 2.2118 | 2.1427 | 2.0862 | 2.0391 |
| 48 | 4.0427 | 3.1907 | 2.7981 | 2.5652 | 2.4085 | 2.2946 | 2.2074 | 2.1382 | 2.0817 | 2.0346 |
| 49 | 4.0384 | 3.1866 | 2.7939 | 2.5611 | 2.4044 | 2.2904 | 2.2032 | 2.1340 | 2.0775 | 2.0303 |
| 50 | 4.0343 | 3.1826 | 2.7900 | 2.5572 | 2.4004 | 2.2864 | 2.1992 | 2.1299 | 2.0734 | 2.0261 |
| 55 | 4.0162 | 3.1650 | 2.7725 | 2.5397 | 2.3828 | 2.2687 | 2.1813 | 2.1119 | 2.0552 | 2.0078 |
| 60 | 4.0012 | 3.1504 | 2.7581 | 2.5252 | 2.3683 | 2.2541 | 2.1665 | 2.0970 | 2.0401 | 1.9926 |
| 65 | 3.9886 | 3.1381 | 2.7459 | 2.5130 | 2.3560 | 2.2417 | 2.1541 | 2.0844 | 2.0274 | 1.9798 |
| 70 | 3.9778 | 3.1277 | 2.7355 | 2.5027 | 2.3456 | 2.2312 | 2.1435 | 2.0737 | 2.0166 | 1.9689 |
| 75 | 3.9685 | 3.1186 | 2.7266 | 2.4937 | 2.3366 | 2.2221 | 2.1343 | 2.0644 | 2.0073 | 1.9594 |
| 80 | 3.9604 | 3.1108 | 2.7188 | 2.4859 | 2.3287 | 2.2142 | 2.1263 | 2.0564 | 1.9991 | 1.9512 |
| 85 | 3.9532 | 3.1038 | 2.7119 | 2.4790 | 2.3218 | 2.2072 | 2.1193 | 2.0493 | 1.9919 | 1.9440 |
| 90 | 3.9469 | 3.0977 | 2.7058 | 2.4729 | 2.3157 | 2.2011 | 2.1131 | 2.0430 | 1.9856 | 1.9376 |
| 95 | 3.9412 | 3.0922 | 2.7004 | 2.4675 | 2.3102 | 2.1955 | 2.1075 | 2.0374 | 1.9799 | 1.9318 |
| 100 | 3.9361 | 3.0873 | 2.6955 | 2.4626 | 2.3053 | 2.1906 | 2.1025 | 2.0323 | 1.9748 | 1.9267 |

| | | | | | Alpha-Value = 0.05 | | | | | |
|---|---|---|---|---|---|---|---|---|---|---|
| | | | | **Degrees of Freedom for the Numerator** | | | | | | |
| | 11 | 12 | 13 | 14 | 15 | 16 | 17 | 18 | 19 | 20 |
| **Degrees of Freedom for the Denominator** | | | | | | | | | | |
| 1 | 242.9835 | 243.9060 | 244.6898 | 245.3640 | 245.9499 | 246.4639 | 246.9184 | 247.3232 | 247.6861 | 248.0131 |
| 2 | 19.4050 | 19.4125 | 19.4189 | 19.4244 | 19.4291 | 19.4333 | 19.4370 | 19.4402 | 19.4431 | 19.4458 |
| 3 | 8.7633 | 8.7446 | 8.7287 | 8.7149 | 8.7029 | 8.6923 | 8.6829 | 8.6745 | 8.6670 | 8.6602 |
| 4 | 5.9358 | 5.9117 | 5.8911 | 5.8733 | 5.8578 | 5.8441 | 5.8320 | 5.8211 | 5.8114 | 5.8025 |
| 5 | 4.7040 | 4.6777 | 4.6552 | 4.6358 | 4.6188 | 4.6038 | 4.5904 | 4.5785 | 4.5678 | 4.5581 |
| 6 | 4.0274 | 3.9999 | 3.9764 | 3.9559 | 3.9381 | 3.9223 | 3.9083 | 3.8957 | 3.8844 | 3.8742 |
| 7 | 3.6030 | 3.5747 | 3.5503 | 3.5292 | 3.5107 | 3.4944 | 3.4799 | 3.4669 | 3.4551 | 3.4445 |
| 8 | 3.3130 | 3.2839 | 3.2590 | 3.2374 | 3.2184 | 3.2016 | 3.1867 | 3.1733 | 3.1613 | 3.1503 |
| 9 | 3.1025 | 3.0729 | 3.0475 | 3.0255 | 3.0061 | 2.9890 | 2.9737 | 2.9600 | 2.9477 | 2.9365 |
| 10 | 2.9430 | 2.9130 | 2.8872 | 2.8647 | 2.8450 | 2.8276 | 2.8120 | 2.7980 | 2.7854 | 2.7740 |
| 11 | 2.8179 | 2.7876 | 2.7614 | 2.7386 | 2.7186 | 2.7009 | 2.6851 | 2.6709 | 2.6581 | 2.6464 |
| 12 | 2.7173 | 2.6866 | 2.6602 | 2.6371 | 2.6169 | 2.5989 | 2.5828 | 2.5684 | 2.5554 | 2.5436 |
| 13 | 2.6347 | 2.6037 | 2.5769 | 2.5536 | 2.5331 | 2.5149 | 2.4987 | 2.4841 | 2.4709 | 2.4589 |
| 14 | 2.5655 | 2.5342 | 2.5073 | 2.4837 | 2.4630 | 2.4446 | 2.4282 | 2.4134 | 2.4000 | 2.3879 |
| 15 | 2.5068 | 2.4753 | 2.4481 | 2.4244 | 2.4034 | 2.3849 | 2.3683 | 2.3533 | 2.3398 | 2.3275 |
| 16 | 2.4564 | 2.4247 | 2.3973 | 2.3733 | 2.3522 | 2.3335 | 2.3167 | 2.3016 | 2.2880 | 2.2756 |
| 17 | 2.4126 | 2.3807 | 2.3531 | 2.3290 | 2.3077 | 2.2888 | 2.2719 | 2.2567 | 2.2429 | 2.2304 |
| 18 | 2.3742 | 2.3421 | 2.3143 | 2.2900 | 2.2686 | 2.2496 | 2.2325 | 2.2172 | 2.2033 | 2.1906 |
| 19 | 2.3402 | 2.3080 | 2.2800 | 2.2556 | 2.2341 | 2.2149 | 2.1977 | 2.1823 | 2.1683 | 2.1555 |
| 20 | 2.3100 | 2.2776 | 2.2495 | 2.2250 | 2.2033 | 2.1840 | 2.1667 | 2.1511 | 2.1370 | 2.1242 |
| 21 | 2.2829 | 2.2504 | 2.2222 | 2.1975 | 2.1757 | 2.1563 | 2.1389 | 2.1232 | 2.1090 | 2.0960 |
| 22 | 2.2585 | 2.2258 | 2.1975 | 2.1727 | 2.1508 | 2.1313 | 2.1138 | 2.0980 | 2.0837 | 2.0707 |
| 23 | 2.2364 | 2.2036 | 2.1752 | 2.1502 | 2.1282 | 2.1086 | 2.0910 | 2.0751 | 2.0608 | 2.0476 |
| 24 | 2.2163 | 2.1834 | 2.1548 | 2.1298 | 2.1077 | 2.0880 | 2.0703 | 2.0543 | 2.0399 | 2.0267 |
| 25 | 2.1979 | 2.1649 | 2.1362 | 2.1111 | 2.0889 | 2.0691 | 2.0513 | 2.0353 | 2.0207 | 2.0075 |
| 26 | 2.1811 | 2.1479 | 2.1192 | 2.0939 | 2.0716 | 2.0518 | 2.0339 | 2.0178 | 2.0032 | 1.9898 |
| 27 | 2.1655 | 2.1323 | 2.1035 | 2.0781 | 2.0558 | 2.0358 | 2.0179 | 2.0017 | 1.9870 | 1.9736 |

| | | | | | | | | | |
|------|--------|--------|--------|--------|--------|--------|--------|--------|--------|--------|
| 28 | 2.1512 | 2.1179 | 2.0889 | 2.0635 | 2.0411 | 2.0210 | 2.0030 | 1.9868 | 1.9720 | 1.9586 |
| 29 | 2.1379 | 2.1045 | 2.0755 | 2.0500 | 2.0275 | 2.0073 | 1.9893 | 1.9730 | 1.9581 | 1.9446 |
| 30 | 2.1256 | 2.0921 | 2.0630 | 2.0374 | 2.0148 | 1.9946 | 1.9765 | 1.9601 | 1.9452 | 1.9317 |
| 31 | 2.1141 | 2.0805 | 2.0513 | 2.0257 | 2.0030 | 1.9828 | 1.9646 | 1.9481 | 1.9332 | 1.9196 |
| 32 | 2.1033 | 2.0697 | 2.0404 | 2.0147 | 1.9920 | 1.9717 | 1.9534 | 1.9369 | 1.9219 | 1.9083 |
| 33 | 2.0933 | 2.0595 | 2.0302 | 2.0045 | 1.9817 | 1.9613 | 1.9430 | 1.9264 | 1.9114 | 1.8977 |
| 34 | 2.0838 | 2.0500 | 2.0207 | 1.9949 | 1.9720 | 1.9516 | 1.9332 | 1.9166 | 1.9015 | 1.8877 |
| 35 | 2.0750 | 2.0411 | 2.0117 | 1.9858 | 1.9629 | 1.9424 | 1.9240 | 1.9073 | 1.8922 | 1.8784 |
| 36 | 2.0666 | 2.0327 | 2.0032 | 1.9773 | 1.9543 | 1.9338 | 1.9153 | 1.8986 | 1.8834 | 1.8696 |
| 37 | 2.0587 | 2.0248 | 1.9952 | 1.9692 | 1.9462 | 1.9256 | 1.9071 | 1.8904 | 1.8752 | 1.8612 |
| 38 | 2.0513 | 2.0173 | 1.9877 | 1.9616 | 1.9386 | 1.9179 | 1.8994 | 1.8826 | 1.8673 | 1.8534 |
| 39 | 2.0443 | 2.0102 | 1.9805 | 1.9545 | 1.9313 | 1.9107 | 1.8921 | 1.8752 | 1.8599 | 1.8459 |
| 40 | 2.0376 | 2.0035 | 1.9738 | 1.9476 | 1.9245 | 1.9037 | 1.8851 | 1.8682 | 1.8529 | 1.8389 |
| 41 | 2.0312 | 1.9971 | 1.9673 | 1.9412 | 1.9179 | 1.8972 | 1.8785. | 1.8616 | 1.8462 | 1.8321 |
| 42 | 2.0252 | 1.9910 | 1.9612 | 1.9350 | 1.9118 | 1.8910 | 1.8722 | 1.8553 | 1.8399 | 1.8258 |
| 43 | 2.0195 | 1.9852 | 1.9554 | 1.9292 | 1.9059 | 1.8850 | 1.8663 | 1.8493 | 1.8338 | 1.8197 |
| 44 | 2.0140 | 1.9797 | 1.9499 | 1.9236 | 1.9002 | 1.8794 | 1.8606 | 1.8436 | 1.8281 | 1.8139 |
| 45 | 2.0088 | 1.9745 | 1.9446 | 1.9182 | 1.8949 | 1.8740 | 1.8551 | 1.8381 | 1.8226 | 1.8084 |
| 46 | 2.0039 | 1.9695 | 1.9395 | 1.9132 | 1.8898 | 1.8688 | 1.8500 | 1.8329 | 1.8173 | 1.8031 |
| 47 | 1.9991 | 1.9647 | 1.9347 | 1.9083 | 1.8849 | 1.8639 | 1.8450 | 1.8279 | 1.8123 | 1.7980 |
| 48 | 1.9946 | 1.9601 | 1.9301 | 1.9037 | 1.8802 | 1.8592 | 1.8402 | 1.8231 | 1.8075 | 1.7932 |
| 49 | 1.9902 | 1.9557 | 1.9257 | 1.8992 | 1.8757 | 1.8546 | 1.8357 | 1.8185 | 1.8029 | 1.7886 |
| 50 | 1.9861 | 1.9515 | 1.9214 | 1.8949 | 1.8714 | 1.8503 | 1.8313 | 1.8141 | 1.7985 | 1.7841 |
| 55 | 1.9675 | 1.9329 | 1.9026 | 1.8760 | 1.8523 | 1.8311 | 1.8120 | 1.7946 | 1.7788 | 1.7644 |
| 60 | 1.9522 | 1.9174 | 1.8870 | 1.8602 | 1.8364 | 1.8151 | 1.7959 | 1.7784 | 1.7625 | 1.7480 |
| 65 | 1.9393 | 1.9044 | 1.8739 | 1.8470 | 1.8231 | 1.8017 | 1.7823 | 1.7648 | 1.7488 | 1.7342 |
| 70 | 1.9283 | 1.8932 | 1.8627 | 1.8357 | 1.8117 | 1.7902 | 1.7708 | 1.7531 | 1.7371 | 1.7223 |
| 75 | 1.9188 | 1.8836 | 1.8530 | 1.8259 | 1.8018 | 1.7802 | 1.7607 | 1.7430 | 1.7269 | 1.7121 |
| 80 | 1.9105 | 1.8753 | 1.8445 | 1.8174 | 1.7932 | 1.7716 | 1.7520 | 1.7342 | 1.7180 | 1.7032 |
| 85 | 1.9031 | 1.8679 | 1.8371 | 1.8099 | 1.7856 | 1.7639 | 1.7443 | 1.7265 | 1.7102 | 1.6953 |
| 90 | 1.8967 | 1.8613 | 1.8305 | 1.8032 | 1.7789 | 1.7571 | 1.7375 | 1.7196 | 1.7033 | 1.6883 |
| 95 | 1.8909 | 1.8555 | 1.8246 | 1.7973 | 1.7729 | 1.7511 | 1.7314 | 1.7134 | 1.6971 | 1.6821 |
| 100 | 1.8857 | 1.8503 | 1.8193 | 1.7919 | 1.7675 | 1.7456 | 1.7259 | 1.7079 | 1.6915 | 1.6764 |

| | Alpha-Value = 0.05 | | | | | | | | |
|---|---|---|---|---|---|---|---|---|---|
| | **Degrees of Freedom for the Numerator** | | | | | | | | |
| | 21 | 22 | 23 | 24 | 25 | 26 | 27 | 28 | 29 | 30 |
| **Degrees of Freedom for the Denominator** | | | | | | | | | | |
| 1 | 248.3094 | 248.5791 | 248.8256 | 249.0518 | 249.2601 | 249.4525 | 249.6309 | 249.7966 | 249.9510 | 250.0951 |
| 2 | 19.4481 | 19.4503 | 19.4523 | 19.4541 | 19.4558 | 19.4573 | 19.4587 | 19.4600 | 19.4613 | 19.4624 |
| 3 | 8.6540 | 8.6484 | 8.6432 | 8.6385 | 8.6341 | 8.6301 | 8.6263 | 8.6229 | 8.6196 | 8.6166 |
| 4 | 5.7945 | 5.7872 | 5.7805 | 5.7744 | 5.7687 | 5.7635 | 5.7586 | 5.7541 | 5.7498 | 5.7459 |
| 5 | 4.5493 | 4.5413 | 4.5339 | 4.5272 | 4.5209 | 4.5151 | 4.5097 | 4.5047 | 4.5001 | 4.4957 |
| 6 | 3.8649 | 3.8564 | 3.8486 | 3.8415 | 3.8348 | 3.8287 | 3.8230 | 3.8177 | 3.8128 | 3.8082 |
| 7 | 3.4349 | 3.4260 | 3.4179 | 3.4105 | 3.4036 | 3.3972 | 3.3913 | 3.3858 | 3.3806 | 3.3758 |
| 8 | 3.1404 | 3.1313 | 3.1229 | 3.1152 | 3.1081 | 3.1015 | 3.0954 | 3.0897 | 3.0844 | 3.0794 |
| 9 | 2.9263 | 2.9169 | 2.9084 | 2.9005 | 2.8932 | 2.8864 | 2.8801 | 2.8743 | 2.8688 | 2.8637 |
| 10 | 2.7636 | 2.7541 | 2.7453 | 2.7372 | 2.7298 | 2.7229 | 2.7164 | 2.7104 | 2.7048 | 2.6996 |
| 11 | 2.6358 | 2.6261 | 2.6172 | 2.6090 | 2.6014 | 2.5943 | 2.5877 | 2.5816 | 2.5759 | 2.5705 |
| 12 | 2.5328 | 2.5229 | 2.5139 | 2.5055 | 2.4977 | 2.4905 | 2.4838 | 2.4776 | 2.4718 | 2.4663 |
| 13 | 2.4479 | 2.4379 | 2.4287 | 2.4202 | 2.4123 | 2.4050 | 2.3982 | 2.3918 | 2.3859 | 2.3803 |
| 14 | 2.3768 | 2.3667 | 2.3573 | 2.3487 | 2.3407 | 2.3333 | 2.3264 | 2.3199 | 2.3139 | 2.3082 |
| 15 | 2.3163 | 2.3060 | 2.2966 | 2.2878 | 2.2797 | 2.2722 | 2.2652 | 2.2587 | 2.2525 | 2.2468 |
| 16 | 2.2642 | 2.2538 | 2.2443 | 2.2354 | 2.2272 | 2.2196 | 2.2125 | 2.2059 | 2.1997 | 2.1938 |
| 17 | 2.2189 | 2.2084 | 2.1987 | 2.1898 | 2.1815 | 2.1738 | 2.1666 | 2.1599 | 2.1536 | 2.1477 |
| 18 | 2.1791 | 2.1685 | 2.1587 | 2.1497 | 2.1413 | 2.1335 | 2.1262 | 2.1195 | 2.1131 | 2.1071 |
| 19 | 2.1438 | 2.1331 | 2.1233 | 2.1141 | 2.1057 | 2.0978 | 2.0905 | 2.0836 | 2.0772 | 2.0712 |
| 20 | 2.1124 | 2.1016 | 2.0917 | 2.0825 | 2.0739 | 2.0660 | 2.0586 | 2.0517 | 2.0452 | 2.0391 |
| 21 | 2.0842 | 2.0733 | 2.0633 | 2.0540 | 2.0454 | 2.0374 | 2.0299 | 2.0229 | 2.0164 | 2.0102 |
| 22 | 2.0587 | 2.0478 | 2.0377 | 2.0283 | 2.0196 | 2.0116 | 2.0040 | 1.9970 | 1.9904 | 1.9842 |
| 23 | 2.0356 | 2.0246 | 2.0144 | 2.0050 | 1.9963 | 1.9881 | 1.9805 | 1.9734 | 1.9668 | 1.9605 |
| 24 | 2.0146 | 2.0035 | 1.9932 | 1.9838 | 1.9750 | 1.9668 | 1.9591 | 1.9520 | 1.9453 | 1.9390 |
| 25 | 1.9953 | 1.9842 | 1.9738 | 1.9643 | 1.9554 | 1.9472 | 1.9395 | 1.9323 | 1.9255 | 1.9192 |
| 26 | 1.9776 | 1.9664 | 1.9560 | 1.9464 | 1.9375 | 1.9292 | 1.9215 | 1.9142 | 1.9074 | 1.9010 |
| 27 | 1.9613 | 1.9500 | 1.9396 | 1.9299 | 1.9210 | 1.9126 | 1.9048 | 1.8975 | 1.8907 | 1.8842 |

| 28 | 1.9462 | 1.9349 | 1.9244 | 1.9147 | 1.9057 | 1.8973 | 1.8894 | 1.8821 | 1.8752 | 1.8687 |
| 29 | 1.9322 | 1.9208 | 1.9103 | 1.9005 | 1.8915 | 1.8830 | 1.8751 | 1.8677 | 1.8608 | 1.8543 |
| 30 | 1.9192 | 1.9077 | 1.8972 | 1.8874 | 1.8782 | 1.8698 | 1.8618 | 1.8544 | 1.8474 | 1.8409 |
| 31 | 1.9071 | 1.8956 | 1.8849 | 1.8751 | 1.8659 | 1.8574 | 1.8494 | 1.8419 | 1.8349 | 1.8283 |
| 32 | 1.8957 | 1.8842 | 1.8735 | 1.8636 | 1.8544 | 1.8458 | 1.8378 | 1.8303 | 1.8233 | 1.8166 |
| 33 | 1.8851 | 1.8735 | 1.8627 | 1.8528 | 1.8436 | 1.8350 | 1.8269 | 1.8194 | 1.8123 | 1.8056 |
| 34 | 1.8751 | 1.8634 | 1.8527 | 1.8427 | 1.8334 | 1.8248 | 1.8167 | 1.8091 | 1.8020 | 1.7953 |
| 35 | 1.8657 | 1.8540 | 1.8432 | 1.8332 | 1.8239 | 1.8152 | 1.8071 | 1.7995 | 1.7923 | 1.7856 |
| 36 | 1.8568 | 1.8451 | 1.8343 | 1.8242 | 1.8149 | 1.8061 | 1.7980 | 1.7904 | 1.7832 | 1.7764 |
| 37 | 1.8485 | 1.8367 | 1.8258 | 1.8157 | 1.8064 | 1.7976 | 1.7894 | 1.7818 | 1.7745 | 1.7678 |
| 38 | 1.8406 | 1.8288 | 1.8179 | 1.8077 | 1.7983 | 1.7895 | 1.7813 | 1.7736 | 1.7664 | 1.7596 |
| 39 | 1.8331 | 1.8212 | 1.8103 | 1.8001 | 1.7907 | 1.7819 | 1.7736 | 1.7659 | 1.7586 | 1.7518 |
| 40 | 1.8260 | 1.8141 | 1.8031 | 1.7929 | 1.7835 | 1.7746 | 1.7663 | 1.7586 | 1.7513 | 1.7444 |
| 41 | 1.8192 | 1.8073 | 1.7963 | 1.7861 | 1.7766 | 1.7677 | 1.7594 | 1.7516 | 1.7443 | 1.7374 |
| 42 | 1.8128 | 1.8009 | 1.7898 | 1.7796 | 1.7701 | 1.7611 | 1.7528 | 1.7450 | 1.7377 | 1.7308 |
| 43 | 1.8067 | 1.7947 | 1.7837 | 1.7734 | 1.7638 | 1.7549 | 1.7465 | 1.7387 | 1.7313 | 1.7244 |
| 44 | 1.8009 | 1.7889 | 1.7778 | 1.7675 | 1.7579 | 1.7489 | 1.7406 | 1.7327 | 1.7253 | 1.7184 |
| 45 | 1.7953 | 1.7833 | 1.7722 | 1.7618 | 1.7522 | 1.7432 | 1.7348 | 1.7270 | 1.7195 | 1.7126 |
| 46 | 1.7900 | 1.7780 | 1.7668 | 1.7564 | 1.7468 | 1.7378 | 1.7294 | 1.7215 | 1.7140 | 1.7070 |
| 47 | 1.7849 | 1.7729 | 1.7617 | 1.7513 | 1.7416 | 1.7326 | 1.7241 | 1.7162 | 1.7088 | 1.7017 |
| 48 | 1.7801 | 1.7680 | 1.7568 | 1.7464 | 1.7367 | 1.7276 | 1.7191 | 1.7112 | 1.7037 | 1.6967 |
| 49 | 1.7754 | 1.7633 | 1.7521 | 1.7416 | 1.7319 | 1.7228 | 1.7143 | 1.7064 | 1.6989 | 1.6918 |
| 50 | 1.7709 | 1.7588 | 1.7475 | 1.7371 | 1.7273 | 1.7183 | 1.7097 | 1.7017 | 1.6942 | 1.6872 |
| 55 | 1.7511 | 1.7388 | 1.7275 | 1.7169 | 1.7071 | 1.6979 | 1.6893 | 1.6812 | 1.6736 | 1.6664 |
| 60 | 1.7346 | 1.7222 | 1.7108 | 1.7001 | 1.6902 | 1.6809 | 1.6722 | 1.6641 | 1.6564 | 1.6491 |
| 65 | 1.7207 | 1.7082 | 1.6967 | 1.6860 | 1.6759 | 1.6666 | 1.6578 | 1.6496 | 1.6419 | 1.6345 |
| 70 | 1.7088 | 1.6962 | 1.6846 | 1.6738 | 1.6638 | 1.6543 | 1.6455 | 1.6372 | 1.6294 | 1.6220 |
| 75 | 1.6985 | 1.6859 | 1.6742 | 1.6633 | 1.6532 | 1.6437 | 1.6348 | 1.6265 | 1.6186 | 1.6112 |
| 80 | 1.6895 | 1.6768 | 1.6651 | 1.6542 | 1.6440 | 1.6345 | 1.6255 | 1.6171 | 1.6092 | 1.6017 |
| 85 | 1.6815 | 1.6688 | 1.6571 | 1.6461 | 1.6358 | 1.6263 | 1.6173 | 1.6088 | 1.6009 | 1.5934 |
| 90 | 1.6745 | 1.6618 | 1.6499 | 1.6389 | 1.6286 | 1.6190 | 1.6100 | 1.6015 | 1.5935 | 1.5859 |
| 95 | 1.6682 | 1.6554 | 1.6435 | 1.6325 | 1.6222 | 1.6125 | 1.6034 | 1.5949 | 1.5869 | 1.5793 |
| 100 | 1.6626 | 1.6497 | 1.6378 | 1.6267 | 1.6163 | 1.6067 | 1.5976 | 1.5890 | 1.5809 | 1.5733 |

| | | | | Alpha-Value = 0.05 | | | | | | |
|---|---|---|---|---|---|---|---|---|---|---|
| | **Degrees of Freedom for the Numerator** | | | | | | | | | |
| | 31 | 32 | 33 | 34 | 35 | 36 | 37 | 38 | 39 | 40 |
| **Degrees of Freedom for the Denominator** | | | | | | | | | | |
| 1 | 250.2301 | 250.3567 | 250.4757 | 250.5878 | 250.6934 | 250.7933 | 250.8878 | 250.9774 | 251.0624 | 251.1432 |
| 2 | 19.4635 | 19.4645 | 19.4654 | 19.4663 | 19.4672 | 19.4680 | 19.4687 | 19.4694 | 19.4701 | 19.4707 |
| 3 | 8.6137 | 8.6111 | 8.6085 | 8.6062 | 8.6039 | 8.6018 | 8.5998 | 8.5979 | 8.5961 | 8.5944 |
| 4 | 5.7422 | 5.7387 | 5.7354 | 5.7323 | 5.7294 | 5.7267 | 5.7241 | 5.7216 | 5.7192 | 5.7170 |
| 5 | 4.4916 | 4.4878 | 4.4842 | 4.4808 | 4.4775 | 4.4745 | 4.4716 | 4.4689 | 4.4663 | 4.4638 |
| 6 | 3.8038 | 3.7998 | 3.7959 | 3.7923 | 3.7889 | 3.7856 | 3.7826 | 3.7797 | 3.7769 | 3.7743 |
| 7 | 3.3713 | 3.3670 | 3.3630 | 3.3592 | 3.3557 | 3.3523 | 3.3491 | 3.3461 | 3.3432 | 3.3404 |
| 8 | 3.0747 | 3.0703 | 3.0662 | 3.0623 | 3.0586 | 3.0551 | 3.0518 | 3.0486 | 3.0456 | 3.0428 |
| 9 | 2.8588 | 2.8543 | 2.8500 | 2.8460 | 2.8422 | 2.8386 | 2.8352 | 2.8320 | 2.8289 | 2.8259 |
| 10 | 2.6946 | 2.6900 | 2.6856 | 2.6815 | 2.6776 | 2.6739 | 2.6704 | 2.6670 | 2.6639 | 2.6609 |
| 11 | 2.5654 | 2.5607 | 2.5562 | 2.5520 | 2.5480 | 2.5442 | 2.5406 | 2.5372 | 2.5340 | 2.5309 |
| 12 | 2.4611 | 2.4563 | 2.4517 | 2.4474 | 2.4433 | 2.4395 | 2.4358 | 2.4323 | 2.4290 | 2.4259 |
| 13 | 2.3751 | 2.3702 | 2.3655 | 2.3611 | 2.3570 | 2.3530 | 2.3493 | 2.3458 | 2.3424 | 2.3392 |
| 14 | 2.3029 | 2.2979 | 2.2932 | 2.2887 | 2.2845 | 2.2805 | 2.2767 | 2.2731 | 2.2696 | 2.2664 |
| 15 | 2.2414 | 2.2363 | 2.2315 | 2.2270 | 2.2227 | 2.2186 | 2.2148 | 2.2111 | 2.2076 | 2.2043 |
| 16 | 2.1884 | 2.1832 | 2.1783 | 2.1738 | 2.1694 | 2.1653 | 2.1614 | 2.1576 | 2.1541 | 2.1507 |
| 17 | 2.1422 | 2.1369 | 2.1320 | 2.1274 | 2.1229 | 2.1188 | 2.1148 | 2.1110 | 2.1074 | 2.1040 |
| 18 | 2.1015 | 2.0963 | 2.0913 | 2.0865 | 2.0821 | 2.0778 | 2.0738 | 2.0700 | 2.0664 | 2.0629 |
| 19 | 2.0655 | 2.0602 | 2.0551 | 2.0504 | 2.0458 | 2.0416 | 2.0375 | 2.0336 | 2.0299 | 2.0264 |
| 20 | 2.0334 | 2.0280 | 2.0229 | 2.0180 | 2.0135 | 2.0091 | 2.0050 | 2.0011 | 1.9974 | 1.9938 |
| 21 | 2.0045 | 1.9990 | 1.9939 | 1.9890 | 1.9844 | 1.9800 | 1.9758 | 1.9719 | 1.9681 | 1.9645 |
| 22 | 1.9784 | 1.9729 | 1.9677 | 1.9627 | 1.9581 | 1.9537 | 1.9495 | 1.9455 | 1.9417 | 1.9380 |
| 23 | 1.9547 | 1.9491 | 1.9439 | 1.9389 | 1.9342 | 1.9297 | 1.9255 | 1.9215 | 1.9176 | 1.9139 |
| 24 | 1.9330 | 1.9274 | 1.9221 | 1.9171 | 1.9124 | 1.9079 | 1.9036 | 1.8995 | 1.8957 | 1.8920 |
| 25 | 1.9132 | 1.9076 | 1.9022 | 1.8972 | 1.8924 | 1.8879 | 1.8836 | 1.8794 | 1.8755 | 1.8718 |
| 26 | 1.8950 | 1.8893 | 1.8839 | 1.8789 | 1.8740 | 1.8695 | 1.8651 | 1.8610 | 1.8570 | 1.8533 |
| 27 | 1.8782 | 1.8725 | 1.8670 | 1.8619 | 1.8571 | 1.8525 | 1.8481 | 1.8439 | 1.8399 | 1.8361 |

| 28 | 1.8626 | 1.8568 | 1.8514 | 1.8462 | 1.8414 | 1.8367 | 1.8323 | 1.8281 | 1.8241 | 1.8203 |
|-----|--------|--------|--------|--------|--------|--------|--------|--------|--------|--------|
| 29 | 1.8482 | 1.8424 | 1.8369 | 1.8317 | 1.8268 | 1.8221 | 1.8176 | 1.8134 | 1.8094 | 1.8055 |
| 30 | 1.8347 | 1.8289 | 1.8233 | 1.8181 | 1.8132 | 1.8085 | 1.8040 | 1.7997 | 1.7957 | 1.7918 |
| 31 | 1.8221 | 1.8163 | 1.8107 | 1.8055 | 1.8005 | 1.7957 | 1.7912 | 1.7870 | 1.7829 | 1.7790 |
| 32 | 1.8104 | 1.8045 | 1.7989 | 1.7936 | 1.7886 | 1.7838 | 1.7793 | 1.7750 | 1.7709 | 1.7670 |
| 33 | 1.7994 | 1.7934 | 1.7878 | 1.7825 | 1.7775 | 1.7727 | 1.7681 | 1.7638 | 1.7596 | 1.7557 |
| 34 | 1.7890 | 1.7830 | 1.7774 | 1.7721 | 1.7670 | 1.7622 | 1.7576 | 1.7532 | 1.7491 | 1.7451 |
| 35 | 1.7793 | 1.7733 | 1.7676 | 1.7622 | 1.7571 | 1.7523 | 1.7477 | 1.7433 | 1.7391 | 1.7351 |
| 36 | 1.7701 | 1.7640 | 1.7584 | 1.7530 | 1.7478 | 1.7430 | 1.7383 | 1.7339 | 1.7297 | 1.7257 |
| 37 | 1.7614 | 1.7553 | 1.7496 | 1.7442 | 1.7390 | 1.7342 | 1.7295 | 1.7251 | 1.7208 | 1.7168 |
| 38 | 1.7531 | 1.7471 | 1.7413 | 1.7359 | 1.7307 | 1.7258 | 1.7211 | 1.7167 | 1.7124 | 1.7084 |
| 39 | 1.7454 | 1.7393 | 1.7335 | 1.7280 | 1.7228 | 1.7179 | 1.7132 | 1.7087 | 1.7045 | 1.7004 |
| 40 | 1.7380 | 1.7318 | 1.7261 | 1.7206 | 1.7154 | 1.7104 | 1.7057 | 1.7012 | 1.6969 | 1.6928 |
| 41 | 1.7309 | 1.7248 | 1.7190 | 1.7135 | 1.7082 | 1.7033 | 1.6985 | 1.6940 | 1.6897 | 1.6856 |
| 42 | 1.7242 | 1.7181 | 1.7122 | 1.7067 | 1.7015 | 1.6965 | 1.6917 | 1.6872 | 1.6828 | 1.6787 |
| 43 | 1.7179 | 1.7117 | 1.7058 | 1.7003 | 1.6950 | 1.6900 | 1.6852 | 1.6807 | 1.6763 | 1.6722 |
| 44 | 1.7118 | 1.7056 | 1.6997 | 1.6941 | 1.6888 | 1.6838 | 1.6790 | 1.6744 | 1.6701 | 1.6659 |
| 45 | 1.7060 | 1.6998 | 1.6939 | 1.6883 | 1.6830 | 1.6779 | 1.6731 | 1.6685 | 1.6641 | 1.6599 |
| 46 | 1.7004 | 1.6942 | 1.6883 | 1.6827 | 1.6773 | 1.6723 | 1.6674 | 1.6628 | 1.6584 | 1.6542 |
| 47 | 1.6951 | 1.6889 | 1.6829 | 1.6773 | 1.6719 | 1.6669 | 1.6620 | 1.6574 | 1.6530 | 1.6488 |
| 48 | 1.6900 | 1.6837 | 1.6778 | 1.6722 | 1.6668 | 1.6617 | 1.6568 | 1.6522 | 1.6478 | 1.6435 |
| 49 | 1.6852 | 1.6789 | 1.6729 | 1.6672 | 1.6618 | 1.6567 | 1.6518 | 1.6472 | 1.6428 | 1.6385 |
| 50 | 1.6805 | 1.6742 | 1.6682 | 1.6625 | 1.6571 | 1.6520 | 1.6471 | 1.6424 | 1.6379 | 1.6337 |
| 55 | 1.6596 | 1.6532 | 1.6472 | 1.6414 | 1.6359 | 1.6307 | 1.6258 | 1.6210 | 1.6165 | 1.6122 |
| 60 | 1.6423 | 1.6358 | 1.6297 | 1.6239 | 1.6183 | 1.6131 | 1.6080 | 1.6032 | 1.5987 | 1.5943 |
| 65 | 1.6276 | 1.6211 | 1.6149 | 1.6090 | 1.6034 | 1.5981 | 1.5930 | 1.5882 | 1.5835 | 1.5791 |
| 70 | 1.6151 | 1.6085 | 1.6022 | 1.5963 | 1.5906 | 1.5853 | 1.5801 | 1.5752 | 1.5706 | 1.5661 |
| 75 | 1.6042 | 1.5975 | 1.5912 | 1.5853 | 1.5796 | 1.5741 | 1.5690 | 1.5640 | 1.5593 | 1.5548 |
| 80 | 1.5947 | 1.5880 | 1.5816 | 1.5756 | 1.5699 | 1.5644 | 1.5592 | 1.5542 | 1.5494 | 1.5449 |
| 85 | 1.5863 | 1.5795 | 1.5731 | 1.5671 | 1.5613 | 1.5558 | 1.5506 | 1.5455 | 1.5407 | 1.5361 |
| 90 | 1.5788 | 1.5720 | 1.5656 | 1.5595 | 1.5537 | 1.5482 | 1.5429 | 1.5378 | 1.5330 | 1.5284 |
| 95 | 1.5721 | 1.5653 | 1.5589 | 1.5527 | 1.5469 | 1.5413 | 1.5360 | 1.5309 | 1.5261 | 1.5214 |
| 100 | 1.5661 | 1.5593 | 1.5528 | 1.5466 | 1.5407 | 1.5351 | 1.5298 | 1.5247 | 1.5198 | 1.5151 |

| | Alpha-Value = 0.01 | | | | | | | | | |
|---|---|---|---|---|---|---|---|---|---|---|
| | **Degrees of Freedom for the Numerator** | | | | | | | | | |
| | 1 | 2 | 3 | 4 | 5 | 6 | 7 | 8 | 9 | 10 |
| **Degrees of Freedom for the Denominator** | | | | | | | | | | |
| 1 | 4052.18 | 4999.50 | 5403.35 | 5624.58 | 5763.65 | 5858.99 | 5928.35 | 5981.07 | 6022.47 | 6055.84 |
| 2 | 98.5025 | 99.0000 | 99.1662 | 99.2494 | 99.2993 | 99.3326 | 99.3564 | 99.3742 | 99.3881 | 99.3992 |
| 3 | 34.1162 | 30.8165 | 29.4567 | 28.7099 | 28.2371 | 27.9107 | 27.6717 | 27.4892 | 27.3452 | 27.2287 |
| 4 | 21.1977 | 18.0000 | 16.6944 | 15.9770 | 15.5219 | 15.2069 | 14.9758 | 14.7989 | 14.6591 | 14.5459 |
| 5 | 16.2582 | 13.2739 | 12.0600 | 11.3919 | 10.9670 | 10.6723 | 10.4555 | 10.2893 | 10.1578 | 10.0510 |
| 6 | 13.7450 | 10.9248 | 9.7795 | 9.1483 | 8.7459 | 8.4661 | 8.2600 | 8.1017 | 7.9761 | 7.8741 |
| 7 | 12.2464 | 9.5466 | 8.4513 | 7.8466 | 7.4604 | 7.1914 | 6.9928 | 6.8400 | 6.7188 | 6.6201 |
| 8 | 11.2586 | 8.6491 | 7.5910 | 7.0061 | 6.6318 | 6.3707 | 6.1776 | 6.0289 | 5.9106 | 5.8143 |
| 9 | 10.5614 | 8.0215 | 6.9919 | 6.4221 | 6.0569 | 5.8018 | 5.6129 | 5.4671 | 5.3511 | 5.2565 |
| 10 | 10.0443 | 7.5594 | 6.5523 | 5.9943 | 5.6363 | 5.3858 | 5.2001 | 5.0567 | 4.9424 | 4.8491 |
| 11 | 9.6460 | 7.2057 | 6.2167 | 5.6683 | 5.3160 | 5.0692 | 4.8861 | 4.7445 | 4.6315 | 4.5393 |
| 12 | 9.3302 | 6.9266 | 5.9525 | 5.4120 | 5.0643 | 4.8206 | 4.6395 | 4.4994 | 4.3875 | 4.2961 |
| 13 | 9.0738 | 6.7010 | 5.7394 | 5.2053 | 4.8616 | 4.6204 | 4.4410 | 4.3021 | 4.1911 | 4.1003 |
| 14 | 8.8616 | 6.5149 | 5.5639 | 5.0354 | 4.6950 | 4.4558 | 4.2779 | 4.1399 | 4.0297 | 3.9394 |
| 15 | 8.6831 | 6.3589 | 5.4170 | 4.8932 | 4.5556 | 4.3183 | 4.1415 | 4.0045 | 3.8948 | 3.8049 |
| 16 | 8.5310 | 6.2262 | 5.2922 | 4.7726 | 4.4374 | 4.2016 | 4.0259 | 3.8896 | 3.7804 | 3.6909 |
| 17 | 8.3997 | 6.1121 | 5.1850 | 4.6690 | 4.3359 | 4.1015 | 3.9267 | 3.7910 | 3.6822 | 3.5931 |
| 18 | 8.2854 | 6.0129 | 5.0919 | 4.5790 | 4.2479 | 4.0146 | 3.8406 | 3.7054 | 3.5971 | 3.5082 |
| 19 | 8.1849 | 5.9259 | 5.0103 | 4.5003 | 4.1708 | 3.9386 | 3.7653 | 3.6305 | 3.5225 | 3.4338 |
| 20 | 8.0960 | 5.8489 | 4.9382 | 4.4307 | 4.1027 | 3.8714 | 3.6987 | 3.5644 | 3.4567 | 3.3682 |
| 21 | 8.0166 | 5.7804 | 4.8740 | 4.3688 | 4.0421 | 3.8117 | 3.6396 | 3.5056 | 3.3981 | 3.3098 |
| 22 | 7.9454 | 5.7190 | 4.8166 | 4.3134 | 3.9880 | 3.7583 | 3.5867 | 3.4530 | 3.3458 | 3.2576 |
| 23 | 7.8811 | 5.6637 | 4.7649 | 4.2636 | 3.9392 | 3.7102 | 3.5390 | 3.4057 | 3.2986 | 3.2106 |
| 24 | 7.8229 | 5.6136 | 4.7181 | 4.2184 | 3.8951 | 3.6667 | 3.4959 | 3.3629 | 3.2560 | 3.1681 |
| 25 | 7.7698 | 5.5680 | 4.6755 | 4.1774 | 3.8550 | 3.6272 | 3.4568 | 3.3239 | 3.2172 | 3.1294 |
| 26 | 7.7213 | 5.5263 | 4.6366 | 4.1400 | 3.8183 | 3.5911 | 3.4210 | 3.2884 | 3.1818 | 3.0941 |
| 27 | 7.6767 | 5.4881 | 4.6009 | 4.1056 | 3.7848 | 3.5580 | 3.3882 | 3.2558 | 3.1494 | 3.0618 |

| 28 | 7.6356 | 5.4529 | 4.5681 | 4.0740 | 3.7539 | 3.5276 | 3.3581 | 3.2259 | 3.1195 | 3.0320 |
|-----|--------|--------|--------|--------|--------|--------|--------|--------|--------|--------|
| 29 | 7.5977 | 5.4204 | 4.5378 | 4.0449 | 3.7254 | 3.4995 | 3.3303 | 3.1982 | 3.0920 | 3.0045 |
| 30 | 7.5625 | 5.3903 | 4.5097 | 4.0179 | 3.6990 | 3.4735 | 3.3045 | 3.1726 | 3.0665 | 2.9791 |
| 31 | 7.5298 | 5.3624 | 4.4837 | 3.9928 | 3.6745 | 3.4493 | 3.2806 | 3.1489 | 3.0428 | 2.9555 |
| 32 | 7.4993 | 5.3363 | 4.4594 | 3.9695 | 3.6517 | 3.4269 | 3.2583 | 3.1267 | 3.0208 | 2.9335 |
| 33 | 7.4708 | 5.3120 | 4.4368 | 3.9477 | 3.6305 | 3.4059 | 3.2376 | 3.1061 | 3.0003 | 2.9130 |
| 34 | 7.4441 | 5.2893 | 4.4156 | 3.9273 | 3.6106 | 3.3863 | 3.2182 | 3.0868 | 2.9810 | 2.8938 |
| 35 | 7.4191 | 5.2679 | 4.3957 | 3.9082 | 3.5919 | 3.3679 | 3.2000 | 3.0687 | 2.9630 | 2.8758 |
| 36 | 7.3956 | 5.2479 | 4.3771 | 3.8903 | 3.5744 | 3.3507 | 3.1829 | 3.0517 | 2.9461 | 2.8589 |
| 37 | 7.3734 | 5.2290 | 4.3595 | 3.8734 | 3.5579 | 3.3344 | 3.1668 | 3.0357 | 2.9302 | 2.8431 |
| 38 | 7.3525 | 5.2112 | 4.3430 | 3.8575 | 3.5424 | 3.3191 | 3.1516 | 3.0207 | 2.9151 | 2.8281 |
| 39 | 7.3328 | 5.1944 | 4.3274 | 3.8425 | 3.5277 | 3.3047 | 3.1373 | 3.0064 | 2.9010 | 2.8139 |
| 40 | 7.3141 | 5.1785 | 4.3126 | 3.8283 | 3.5138 | 3.2910 | 3.1238 | 2.9930 | 2.8876 | 2.8005 |
| 41 | 7.2964 | 5.1634 | 4.2986 | 3.8148 | 3.5007 | 3.2781 | 3.1109 | 2.9802 | 2.8749 | 2.7879 |
| 42 | 7.2796 | 5.1491 | 4.2853 | 3.8021 | 3.4882 | 3.2658 | 3.0988 | 2.9681 | 2.8628 | 2.7758 |
| 43 | 7.2636 | 5.1356 | 4.2726 | 3.7899 | 3.4764 | 3.2541 | 3.0872 | 2.9567 | 2.8514 | 2.7644 |
| 44 | 7.2484 | 5.1226 | 4.2606 | 3.7784 | 3.4651 | 3.2430 | 3.0762 | 2.9457 | 2.8405 | 2.7536 |
| 45 | 7.2339 | 5.1103 | 4.2492 | 3.7674 | 3.4544 | 3.2325 | 3.0658 | 2.9353 | 2.8301 | 2.7432 |
| 46 | 7.2200 | 5.0986 | 4.2383 | 3.7570 | 3.4442 | 3.2224 | 3.0558 | 2.9254 | 2.8203 | 2.7334 |
| 47 | 7.2068 | 5.0874 | 4.2279 | 3.7470 | 3.4344 | 3.2128 | 3.0463 | 2.9160 | 2.8108 | 2.7240 |
| 48 | 7.1942 | 5.0767 | 4.2180 | 3.7374 | 3.4251 | 3.2036 | 3.0372 | 2.9069 | 2.8018 | 2.7150 |
| 49 | 7.1821 | 5.0664 | 4.2084 | 3.7283 | 3.4162 | 3.1948 | 3.0285 | 2.8983 | 2.7932 | 2.7064 |
| 50 | 7.1706 | 5.0566 | 4.1993 | 3.7195 | 3.4077 | 3.1864 | 3.0202 | 2.8900 | 2.7850 | 2.6981 |
| 55 | 7.1194 | 5.0132 | 4.1591 | 3.6809 | 3.3700 | 3.1493 | 2.9834 | 2.8534 | 2.7485 | 2.6617 |
| 60 | 7.0771 | 4.9774 | 4.1259 | 3.6490 | 3.3389 | 3.1187 | 2.9530 | 2.8233 | 2.7185 | 2.6318 |
| 65 | 7.0416 | 4.9474 | 4.0981 | 3.6223 | 3.3128 | 3.0930 | 2.9276 | 2.7980 | 2.6933 | 2.6066 |
| 70 | 7.0114 | 4.9219 | 4.0744 | 3.5996 | 3.2907 | 3.0712 | 2.9060 | 2.7765 | 2.6719 | 2.5852 |
| 75 | 6.9854 | 4.8999 | 4.0540 | 3.5801 | 3.2716 | 3.0524 | 2.8874 | 2.7580 | 2.6534 | 2.5668 |
| 80 | 6.9627 | 4.8807 | 4.0363 | 3.5631 | 3.2550 | 3.0361 | 2.8713 | 2.7420 | 2.6374 | 2.5508 |
| 85 | 6.9428 | 4.8639 | 4.0207 | 3.5482 | 3.2405 | 3.0218 | 2.8571 | 2.7279 | 2.6233 | 2.5368 |
| 90 | 6.9251 | 4.8491 | 4.0070 | 3.5350 | 3.2276 | 3.0091 | 2.8445 | 2.7154 | 2.6109 | 2.5243 |
| 95 | 6.9094 | 4.8358 | 3.9947 | 3.5232 | 3.2162 | 2.9978 | 2.8333 | 2.7042 | 2.5998 | 2.5132 |
| 100 | 6.8953 | 4.8239 | 3.9837 | 3.5127 | 3.2059 | 2.9877 | 2.8233 | 2.6943 | 2.5898 | 2.5033 |

| | | | | | Alpha-Value = 0.01 | | | | | |
|---|---|---|---|---|---|---|---|---|---|---|
| | | | | | **Degrees of Freedom for the Numerator** | | | | | |
| | 11 | 12 | 13 | 14 | 15 | 16 | 17 | 18 | 19 | 20 |
| **Degrees of Freedom for the Denominator** | | | | | | | | | | |
| 1 | 6083.31 | 6106.32 | 6125.86 | 6142.67 | 6157.28 | 6170.10 | 6181.43 | 6191.52 | 6200.57 | 6208.7302 |
| 2 | 99.4083 | 99.4159 | 99.4223 | 99.4278 | 99.4325 | 99.4367 | 99.4404 | 99.4436 | 99.4465 | 99.4492 |
| 3 | 27.1326 | 27.0518 | 26.9831 | 26.9238 | 26.8722 | 26.8269 | 26.7867 | 26.7509 | 26.7188 | 26.6898 |
| 4 | 14.4523 | 14.3736 | 14.3065 | 14.2486 | 14.1982 | 14.1539 | 14.1146 | 14.0795 | 14.0480 | 14.0196 |
| 5 | 9.9626 | 9.8883 | 9.8248 | 9.7700 | 9.7222 | 9.6802 | 9.6429 | 9.6096 | 9.5797 | 9.5526 |
| 6 | 7.7896 | 7.7183 | 7.6575 | 7.6049 | 7.5590 | 7.5186 | 7.4827 | 7.4507 | 7.4219 | 7.3958 |
| 7 | 6.5382 | 6.4691 | 6.4100 | 6.3590 | 6.3143 | 6.2750 | 6.2401 | 6.2089 | 6.1808 | 6.1554 |
| 8 | 5.7343 | 5.6667 | 5.6089 | 5.5589 | 5.5151 | 5.4766 | 5.4423 | 5.4116 | 5.3840 | 5.3591 |
| 9 | 5.1779 | 5.1114 | 5.0545 | 5.0052 | 4.9621 | 4.9240 | 4.8902 | 4.8599 | 4.8327 | 4.8080 |
| 10 | 4.7715 | 4.7059 | 4.6496 | 4.6008 | 4.5581 | 4.5204 | 4.4869 | 4.4569 | 4.4299 | 4.4054 |
| 11 | 4.4624 | 4.3974 | 4.3416 | 4.2932 | 4.2509 | 4.2134 | 4.1801 | 4.1503 | 4.1234 | 4.0990 |
| 12 | 4.2198 | 4.1553 | 4.0999 | 4.0518 | 4.0096 | 3.9724 | 3.9392 | 3.9095 | 3.8827 | 3.8584 |
| 13 | 4.0245 | 3.9603 | 3.9052 | 3.8573 | 3.8154 | 3.7783 | 3.7452 | 3.7156 | 3.6888 | 3.6646 |
| 14 | 3.8640 | 3.8001 | 3.7452 | 3.6975 | 3.6557 | 3.6187 | 3.5857 | 3.5561 | 3.5294 | 3.5052 |
| 15 | 3.7299 | 3.6662 | 3.6115 | 3.5639 | 3.5222 | 3.4852 | 3.4523 | 3.4228 | 3.3961 | 3.3719 |
| 16 | 3.6162 | 3.5527 | 3.4981 | 3.4506 | 3.4089 | 3.3720 | 3.3391 | 3.3096 | 3.2829 | 3.2587 |
| 17 | 3.5185 | 3.4552 | 3.4007 | 3.3533 | 3.3117 | 3.2748 | 3.2419 | 3.2124 | 3.1857 | 3.1615 |
| 18 | 3.4338 | 3.3706 | 3.3162 | 3.2689 | 3.2273 | 3.1904 | 3.1575 | 3.1280 | 3.1013 | 3.0771 |
| 19 | 3.3596 | 3.2965 | 3.2422 | 3.1949 | 3.1533 | 3.1165 | 3.0836 | 3.0541 | 3.0274 | 3.0031 |
| 20 | 3.2941 | 3.2311 | 3.1769 | 3.1296 | 3.0880 | 3.0512 | 3.0183 | 2.9887 | 2.9620 | 2.9377 |
| 21 | 3.2359 | 3.1730 | 3.1187 | 3.0715 | 3.0300 | 2.9931 | 2.9602 | 2.9306 | 2.9039 | 2.8796 |
| 22 | 3.1837 | 3.1209 | 3.0667 | 3.0195 | 2.9779 | 2.9411 | 2.9082 | 2.8786 | 2.8518 | 2.8274 |
| 23 | 3.1368 | 3.0740 | 3.0199 | 2.9727 | 2.9311 | 2.8943 | 2.8613 | 2.8317 | 2.8049 | 2.7805 |
| 24 | 3.0944 | 3.0316 | 2.9775 | 2.9303 | 2.8887 | 2.8519 | 2.8189 | 2.7892 | 2.7624 | 2.7380 |
| 25 | 3.0558 | 2.9931 | 2.9389 | 2.8917 | 2.8502 | 2.8133 | 2.7803 | 2.7506 | 2.7238 | 2.6993 |
| 26 | 3.0205 | 2.9578 | 2.9038 | 2.8566 | 2.8150 | 2.7781 | 2.7451 | 2.7153 | 2.6885 | 2.6640 |
| 27 | 2.9882 | 2.9256 | 2.8715 | 2.8243 | 2.7827 | 2.7458 | 2.7127 | 2.6830 | 2.6561 | 2.6316 |

| 28 | 2.9585 | 2.8959 | 2.8418 | 2.7946 | 2.7530 | 2.7160 | 2.6830 | 2.6532 | 2.6263 | 2.6017 |
| 29 | 2.9311 | 2.8685 | 2.8144 | 2.7672 | 2.7256 | 2.6886 | 2.6555 | 2.6257 | 2.5987 | 2.5742 |
| 30 | 2.9057 | 2.8431 | 2.7890 | 2.7418 | 2.7002 | 2.6632 | 2.6301 | 2.6003 | 2.5732 | 2.5487 |
| 31 | 2.8821 | 2.8195 | 2.7655 | 2.7182 | 2.6766 | 2.6396 | 2.6064 | 2.5766 | 2.5496 | 2.5249 |
| 32 | 2.8602 | 2.7976 | 2.7435 | 2.6963 | 2.6546 | 2.6176 | 2.5844 | 2.5546 | 2.5275 | 2.5029 |
| 33 | 2.8397 | 2.7771 | 2.7231 | 2.6758 | 2.6341 | 2.5971 | 2.5639 | 2.5340 | 2.5069 | 2.4822 |
| 34 | 2.8205 | 2.7580 | 2.7039 | 2.6566 | 2.6150 | 2.5779 | 2.5447 | 2.5147 | 2.4876 | 2.4629 |
| 35 | 2.8026 | 2.7400 | 2.6859 | 2.6387 | 2.5970 | 2.5599 | 2.5266 | 2.4967 | 2.4695 | 2.4448 |
| 36 | 2.7857 | 2.7232 | 2.6691 | 2.6218 | 2.5801 | 2.5430 | 2.5097 | 2.4797 | 2.4526 | 2.4278 |
| 37 | 2.7698 | 2.7073 | 2.6532 | 2.6059 | 2.5642 | 2.5270 | 2.4938 | 2.4638 | 2.4366 | 2.4118 |
| 38 | 2.7549 | 2.6923 | 2.6382 | 2.5909 | 2.5492 | 2.5120 | 2.4787 | 2.4487 | 2.4215 | 2.3967 |
| 39 | 2.7407 | 2.6782 | 2.6241 | 2.5768 | 2.5350 | 2.4978 | 2.4645 | 2.4345 | 2.4072 | 2.3824 |
| 40 | 2.7274 | 2.6648 | 2.6107 | 2.5634 | 2.5216 | 2.4844 | 2.4511 | 2.4210 | 2.3937 | 2.3689 |
| 41 | 2.7147 | 2.6522 | 2.5981 | 2.5507 | 2.5089 | 2.4717 | 2.4384 | 2.4083 | 2.3810 | 2.3561 |
| 42 | 2.7027 | 2.6402 | 2.5860 | 2.5387 | 2.4969 | 2.4596 | 2.4263 | 2.3962 | 2.3688 | 2.3439 |
| 43 | 2.6913 | 2.6287 | 2.5746 | 2.5273 | 2.4854 | 2.4482 | 2.4148 | 2.3847 | 2.3573 | 2.3324 |
| 44 | 2.6804 | 2.6179 | 2.5638 | 2.5164 | 2.4746 | 2.4373 | 2.4039 | 2.3737 | 2.3463 | 2.3214 |
| 45 | 2.6701 | 2.6076 | 2.5534 | 2.5060 | 2.4642 | 2.4269 | 2.3935 | 2.3633 | 2.3359 | 2.3109 |
| 46 | 2.6602 | 2.5977 | 2.5436 | 2.4962 | 2.4543 | 2.4170 | 2.3835 | 2.3533 | 2.3259 | 2.3009 |
| 47 | 2.6508 | 2.5883 | 2.5342 | 2.4868 | 2.4449 | 2.4075 | 2.3741 | 2.3439 | 2.3164 | 2.2914 |
| 48 | 2.6418 | 2.5793 | 2.5252 | 2.4777 | 2.4358 | 2.3985 | 2.3650 | 2.3348 | 2.3073 | 2.2823 |
| 49 | 2.6333 | 2.5707 | 2.5166 | 2.4691 | 2.4272 | 2.3899 | 2.3564 | 2.3261 | 2.2986 | 2.2736 |
| 50 | 2.6250 | 2.5625 | 2.5083 | 2.4609 | 2.4190 | 2.3816 | 2.3481 | 2.3178 | 2.2903 | 2.2652 |
| 55 | 2.5887 | 2.5261 | 2.4719 | 2.4244 | 2.3824 | 2.3450 | 2.3114 | 2.2810 | 2.2535 | 2.2283 |
| 60 | 2.5587 | 2.4961 | 2.4419 | 2.3943 | 2.3523 | 2.3148 | 2.2811 | 2.2507 | 2.2230 | 2.1978 |
| 65 | 2.5335 | 2.4710 | 2.4167 | 2.3691 | 2.3270 | 2.2895 | 2.2557 | 2.2252 | 2.1975 | 2.1722 |
| 70 | 2.5122 | 2.4496 | 2.3953 | 2.3477 | 2.3055 | 2.2679 | 2.2341 | 2.2036 | 2.1758 | 2.1504 |
| 75 | 2.4938 | 2.4312 | 2.3768 | 2.3292 | 2.2870 | 2.2493 | 2.2155 | 2.1849 | 2.1571 | 2.1316 |
| 80 | 2.4777 | 2.4151 | 2.3608 | 2.3131 | 2.2709 | 2.2332 | 2.1993 | 2.1686 | 2.1408 | 2.1153 |
| 85 | 2.4637 | 2.4011 | 2.3467 | 2.2990 | 2.2567 | 2.2190 | 2.1851 | 2.1544 | 2.1264 | 2.1009 |
| 90 | 2.4513 | 2.3886 | 2.3342 | 2.2865 | 2.2442 | 2.2064 | 2.1725 | 2.1417 | 2.1137 | 2.0882 |
| 95 | 2.4402 | 2.3775 | 2.3231 | 2.2754 | 2.2330 | 2.1952 | 2.1612 | 2.1304 | 2.1024 | 2.0768 |
| 100 | 2.4302 | 2.3676 | 2.3132 | 2.2654 | 2.2230 | 2.1852 | 2.1511 | 2.1203 | 2.0923 | 2.0666 |

| | Alpha-Value = 0.01 | | | | | | | | | |
|---|---|---|---|---|---|---|---|---|---|---|
| | **Degrees of Freedom for the Numerator** | | | | | | | | | |
| | 21 | 22 | 23 | 24 | 25 | 26 | 27 | 28 | 29 | 30 |
| **Degrees of Freedom for the Denominator** | | | | | | | | | | |
| 1 | 6216.11 | 6222.84 | 6228.99 | 6234.63 | 6239.82 | 6244.62 | 6249.07 | 6253.20 | 6257.05 | 6260.64 |
| 2 | 99.4516 | 99.4537 | 99.4557 | 99.4575 | 99.4592 | 99.4607 | 99.4621 | 99.4635 | 99.4647 | 99.4658 |
| 3 | 26.6635 | 26.6396 | 26.6176 | 26.5975 | 26.5790 | 26.5618 | 26.5460 | 26.5312 | 26.5174 | 26.5045 |
| 4 | 13.9938 | 13.9703 | 13.9488 | 13.9291 | 13.9109 | 13.8940 | 13.8784 | 13.8639 | 13.8503 | 13.8377 |
| 5 | 9.5281 | 9.5058 | 9.4853 | 9.4665 | 9.4491 | 9.4331 | 9.4182 | 9.4043 | 9.3914 | 9.3793 |
| 6 | 7.3722 | 7.3506 | 7.3309 | 7.3127 | 7.2960 | 7.2805 | 7.2661 | 7.2527 | 7.2402 | 7.2285 |
| 7 | 6.1324 | 6.1113 | 6.0921 | 6.0743 | 6.0580 | 6.0428 | 6.0287 | 6.0157 | 6.0034 | 5.9920 |
| 8 | 5.3364 | 5.3157 | 5.2967 | 5.2793 | 5.2631 | 5.2482 | 5.2344 | 5.2214 | 5.2094 | 5.1981 |
| 9 | 4.7856 | 4.7651 | 4.7463 | 4.7290 | 4.7130 | 4.6982 | 4.6845 | 4.6717 | 4.6598 | 4.6486 |
| 10 | 4.3831 | 4.3628 | 4.3441 | 4.3269 | 4.3111 | 4.2963 | 4.2827 | 4.2700 | 4.2581 | 4.2469 |
| 11 | 4.0769 | 4.0566 | 4.0380 | 4.0209 | 4.0051 | 3.9904 | 3.9768 | 3.9641 | 3.9522 | 3.9411 |
| 12 | 3.8363 | 3.8161 | 3.7976 | 3.7805 | 3.7647 | 3.7500 | 3.7364 | 3.7237 | 3.7119 | 3.7008 |
| 13 | 3.6425 | 3.6224 | 3.6038 | 3.5868 | 3.5710 | 3.5563 | 3.5427 | 3.5300 | 3.5182 | 3.5070 |
| 14 | 3.4832 | 3.4630 | 3.4445 | 3.4274 | 3.4116 | 3.3969 | 3.3833 | 3.3706 | 3.3587 | 3.3476 |
| 15 | 3.3498 | 3.3297 | 3.3111 | 3.2940 | 3.2782 | 3.2635 | 3.2499 | 3.2372 | 3.2253 | 3.2141 |
| 16 | 3.2367 | 3.2165 | 3.1979 | 3.1808 | 3.1650 | 3.1503 | 3.1366 | 3.1238 | 3.1119 | 3.1007 |
| 17 | 3.1394 | 3.1192 | 3.1006 | 3.0835 | 3.0676 | 3.0529 | 3.0392 | 3.0264 | 3.0145 | 3.0032 |
| 18 | 3.0550 | 3.0348 | 3.0161 | 2.9990 | 2.9831 | 2.9683 | 2.9546 | 2.9418 | 2.9298 | 2.9185 |
| 19 | 2.9810 | 2.9607 | 2.9421 | 2.9249 | 2.9089 | 2.8941 | 2.8804 | 2.8675 | 2.8555 | 2.8442 |
| 20 | 2.9156 | 2.8953 | 2.8766 | 2.8594 | 2.8434 | 2.8286 | 2.8148 | 2.8019 | 2.7898 | 2.7785 |
| 21 | 2.8574 | 2.8370 | 2.8183 | 2.8010 | 2.7850 | 2.7702 | 2.7563 | 2.7434 | 2.7313 | 2.7200 |
| 22 | 2.8052 | 2.7849 | 2.7661 | 2.7488 | 2.7328 | 2.7179 | 2.7040 | 2.6910 | 2.6789 | 2.6675 |
| 23 | 2.7583 | 2.7378 | 2.7191 | 2.7017 | 2.6856 | 2.6707 | 2.6568 | 2.6438 | 2.6316 | 2.6202 |
| 24 | 2.7157 | 2.6953 | 2.6765 | 2.6591 | 2.6430 | 2.6280 | 2.6140 | 2.6010 | 2.5888 | 2.5773 |
| 25 | 2.6770 | 2.6565 | 2.6377 | 2.6203 | 2.6041 | 2.5891 | 2.5751 | 2.5620 | 2.5498 | 2.5383 |
| 26 | 2.6416 | 2.6211 | 2.6022 | 2.5848 | 2.5686 | 2.5536 | 2.5395 | 2.5264 | 2.5141 | 2.5026 |
| 27 | 2.6092 | 2.5887 | 2.5697 | 2.5522 | 2.5360 | 2.5209 | 2.5069 | 2.4937 | 2.4814 | 2.4699 |

| 28 | 2.5793 | 2.5587 | 2.5398 | 2.5223 | 2.5060 | 2.4909 | 2.4768 | 2.4636 | 2.4513 | 2.4397 |
|-----|--------|--------|--------|--------|--------|--------|--------|--------|--------|--------|
| 29 | 2.5517 | 2.5311 | 2.5121 | 2.4946 | 2.4783 | 2.4631 | 2.4490 | 2.4358 | 2.4234 | 2.4118 |
| 30 | 2.5262 | 2.5055 | 2.4865 | 2.4689 | 2.4526 | 2.4374 | 2.4233 | 2.4100 | 2.3976 | 2.3860 |
| 31 | 2.5024 | 2.4818 | 2.4627 | 2.4451 | 2.4287 | 2.4135 | 2.3993 | 2.3861 | 2.3736 | 2.3619 |
| 32 | 2.4803 | 2.4596 | 2.4405 | 2.4229 | 2.4065 | 2.3912 | 2.3770 | 2.3637 | 2.3513 | 2.3395 |
| 33 | 2.4596 | 2.4389 | 2.4198 | 2.4021 | 2.3857 | 2.3704 | 2.3562 | 2.3428 | 2.3304 | 2.3186 |
| 34 | 2.4403 | 2.4195 | 2.4004 | 2.3827 | 2.3662 | 2.3509 | 2.3367 | 2.3233 | 2.3108 | 2.2990 |
| 35 | 2.4222 | 2.4014 | 2.3822 | 2.3645 | 2.3480 | 2.3327 | 2.3184 | 2.3050 | 2.2924 | 2.2806 |
| 36 | 2.4051 | 2.3843 | 2.3651 | 2.3473 | 2.3308 | 2.3155 | 2.3011 | 2.2877 | 2.2752 | 2.2633 |
| 37 | 2.3891 | 2.3682 | 2.3490 | 2.3312 | 2.3147 | 2.2993 | 2.2849 | 2.2715 | 2.2589 | 2.2470 |
| 38 | 2.3739 | 2.3531 | 2.3338 | 2.3160 | 2.2994 | 2.2840 | 2.2696 | 2.2562 | 2.2435 | 2.2317 |
| 39 | 2.3596 | 2.3387 | 2.3195 | 2.3016 | 2.2850 | 2.2696 | 2.2552 | 2.2417 | 2.2290 | 2.2171 |
| 40 | 2.3461 | 2.3252 | 2.3059 | 2.2880 | 2.2714 | 2.2559 | 2.2415 | 2.2280 | 2.2153 | 2.2034 |
| 41 | 2.3333 | 2.3123 | 2.2930 | 2.2751 | 2.2585 | 2.2430 | 2.2285 | 2.2150 | 2.2023 | 2.1903 |
| 42 | 2.3211 | 2.3001 | 2.2808 | 2.2629 | 2.2462 | 2.2307 | 2.2162 | 2.2026 | 2.1899 | 2.1780 |
| 43 | 2.3095 | 2.2885 | 2.2692 | 2.2512 | 2.2345 | 2.2190 | 2.2045 | 2.1909 | 2.1782 | 2.1662 |
| 44 | 2.2985 | 2.2775 | 2.2581 | 2.2401 | 2.2234 | 2.2079 | 2.1934 | 2.1797 | 2.1670 | 2.1550 |
| 45 | 2.2880 | 2.2670 | 2.2476 | 2.2296 | 2.2129 | 2.1973 | 2.1827 | 2.1691 | 2.1563 | 2.1443 |
| 46 | 2.2780 | 2.2570 | 2.2375 | 2.2195 | 2.2028 | 2.1872 | 2.1726 | 2.1590 | 2.1461 | 2.1341 |
| 47 | 2.2685 | 2.2474 | 2.2279 | 2.2099 | 2.1931 | 2.1775 | 2.1629 | 2.1493 | 2.1364 | 2.1244 |
| 48 | 2.2594 | 2.2383 | 2.2188 | 2.2007 | 2.1839 | 2.1683 | 2.1537 | 2.1400 | 2.1271 | 2.1150 |
| 49 | 2.2506 | 2.2295 | 2.2100 | 2.1919 | 2.1751 | 2.1594 | 2.1448 | 2.1311 | 2.1182 | 2.1061 |
| 50 | 2.2423 | 2.2211 | 2.2016 | 2.1835 | 2.1667 | 2.1510 | 2.1363 | 2.1226 | 2.1097 | 2.0976 |
| 55 | 2.2052 | 2.1840 | 2.1644 | 2.1462 | 2.1293 | 2.1135 | 2.0988 | 2.0849 | 2.0720 | 2.0598 |
| 60 | 2.1747 | 2.1533 | 2.1336 | 2.1154 | 2.0984 | 2.0825 | 2.0677 | 2.0538 | 2.0408 | 2.0285 |
| 65 | 2.1490 | 2.1276 | 2.1078 | 2.0895 | 2.0724 | 2.0565 | 2.0416 | 2.0276 | 2.0145 | 2.0022 |
| 70 | 2.1271 | 2.1057 | 2.0858 | 2.0674 | 2.0503 | 2.0343 | 2.0194 | 2.0053 | 1.9922 | 1.9797 |
| 75 | 2.1083 | 2.0868 | 2.0669 | 2.0484 | 2.0312 | 2.0152 | 2.0002 | 1.9861 | 1.9729 | 1.9604 |
| 80 | 2.0919 | 2.0703 | 2.0504 | 2.0318 | 2.0146 | 1.9985 | 1.9835 | 1.9693 | 1.9560 | 1.9435 |
| 85 | 2.0775 | 2.0558 | 2.0359 | 2.0173 | 2.0000 | 1.9839 | 1.9688 | 1.9546 | 1.9413 | 1.9287 |
| 90 | 2.0647 | 2.0430 | 2.0230 | 2.0044 | 1.9871 | 1.9709 | 1.9557 | 1.9415 | 1.9281 | 1.9155 |
| 95 | 2.0533 | 2.0316 | 2.0115 | 1.9929 | 1.9755 | 1.9593 | 1.9441 | 1.9299 | 1.9164 | 1.9038 |
| 100 | 2.0431 | 2.0214 | 2.0012 | 1.9826 | 1.9652 | 1.9489 | 1.9337 | 1.9194 | 1.9059 | 1.8933 |

| | | | | | Alpha-Value = 0.01 | | | | |
|---|---|---|---|---|---|---|---|---|---|
| | | | | **Degrees of Freedom for the Numerator** | | | | | |
| | 31 | 32 | 33 | 34 | 35 | 36 | 37 | 38 | 39 | 40 |
| **Degrees of Freedom for the Denominator** | | | | | | | | | | |
| 1 | 6264. 01 | 6267.17 | 6270.13 | 6272.93 | 6275.56 | 6278.05 | 6280.41 | 6282.64 | 6284.76 | 6286.7821 |
| 2 | 99.4669 | 99.4679 | 99.4689 | 99.4698 | 99.4706 | 99.4714 | 99.4721 | 99.4728 | 99.4735 | 99.4742 |
| 3 | 26.4925 | 26.4812 | 26.4705 | 26.4605 | 26.4511 | 26.4421 | 26.4337 | 26.4257 | 26.4180 | 26.4108 |
| 4 | 13.8258 | 13.8147 | 13.8042 | 13.7943 | 13.7850 | 13.7762 | 13.7679 | 13.7600 | 13.7525 | 13.7454 |
| 5 | 9.3680 | 9.3574 | 9.3474 | 9.3380 | 9.3291 | 9.3207 | 9.3127 | 9.3052 | 9.2980 | 9.2912 |
| 6 | 7.2176 | 7.2073 | 7.1976 | 7.1885 | 7.1799 | 7.1718 | 7.1641 | 7.1568 | 7.1498 | 7.1432 |
| 7 | 5.9813 | 5.9712 | 5.9618 | 5.9528 | 5.9444 | 5.9364 | 5.9289 | 5.9217 | 5.9149 | 5.9084 |
| 8 | 5.1876 | 5.1776 | 5.1683 | 5.1595 | 5.1512 | 5.1433 | 5.1358 | 5.1287 | 5.1220 | 5.1156 |
| 9 | 4.6381 | 4.6282 | 4.6190 | 4.6102 | 4.6020 | 4.5941 | 4.5867 | 4.5797 | 4.5730 | 4.5666 |
| 10 | 4.2365 | 4.2267 | 4.2174 | 4.2087 | 4.2005 | 4.1927 | 4.1853 | 4.1783 | 4.1716 | 4.1653 |
| 11 | 3.9307 | 3.9209 | 3.9117 | 3.9030 | 3.8948 | 3.8870 | 3.8796 | 3.8726 | 3.8659 | 3.8596 |
| 12 | 3.6904 | 3.6806 | 3.6713 | 3.6626 | 3.6544 | 3.6466 | 3.6392 | 3.6322 | 3.6255 | 3.6192 |
| 13 | 3.4966 | 3.4868 | 3.4776 | 3.4688 | 3.4606 | 3.4528 | 3.4454 | 3.4383 | 3.4317 | 3.4253 |
| 14 | 3.3371 | 3.3273 | 3.3181 | 3.3093 | 3.3010 | 3.2932 | 3.2858 | 3.2787 | 3.2720 | 3.2656 |
| 15 | 3.2036 | 3.1938 | 3.1845 | 3.1757 | 3.1674 | 3.1596 | 3.1521 | 3.1450 | 3.1383 | 3.1319 |
| 16 | 3.0902 | 3.0803 | 3.0710 | 3.0622 | 3.0539 | 3.0460 | 3.0385 | 3.0314 | 3.0247 | 3.0182 |
| 17 | 2.9927 | 2.9828 | 2.9734 | 2.9646 | 2.9563 | 2.9484 | 2.9408 | 2.9337 | 2.9269 | 2.9205 |
| 18 | 2.9079 | 2.8980 | 2.8886 | 2.8798 | 2.8714 | 2.8634 | 2.8559 | 2.8487 | 2.8419 | 2.8354 |
| 19 | 2.8336 | 2.8236 | 2.8142 | 2.8053 | 2.7969 | 2.7889 | 2.7813 | 2.7742 | 2.7673 | 2.7608 |
| 20 | 2.7678 | 2.7578 | 2.7484 | 2.7395 | 2.7310 | 2.7230 | 2.7154 | 2.7082 | 2.7013 | 2.6947 |
| 21 | 2.7093 | 2.6992 | 2.6898 | 2.6808 | 2.6723 | 2.6643 | 2.6566 | 2.6494 | 2.6425 | 2.6359 |
| 22 | 2.6568 | 2.6467 | 2.6372 | 2.6282 | 2.6197 | 2.6116 | 2.6039 | 2.5967 | 2.5897 | 2.5831 |
| 23 | 2.6095 | 2.5993 | 2.5898 | 2.5808 | 2.5722 | 2.5641 | 2.5564 | 2.5491 | 2.5421 | 2.5355 |
| 24 | 2.5666 | 2.5564 | 2.5468 | 2.5378 | 2.5292 | 2.5211 | 2.5133 | 2.5060 | 2.4990 | 2.4923 |
| 25 | 2.5275 | 2.5173 | 2.5077 | 2.4986 | 2.4900 | 2.4818 | 2.4741 | 2.4667 | 2.4597 | 2.4530 |
| 26 | 2.4918 | 2.4816 | 2.4719 | 2.4628 | 2.4542 | 2.4460 | 2.4382 | 2.4308 | 2.4237 | 2.4170 |
| 27 | 2.4590 | 2.4487 | 2.4391 | 2.4299 | 2.4213 | 2.4130 | 2.4052 | 2.3978 | 2.3907 | 2.3840 |

| | | | | | | | | | | |
|---|---|---|---|---|---|---|---|---|---|---|
| 28 | 2.4288 | 2.4185 | 2.4088 | 2.3996 | 2.3909 | 2.3827 | 2.3748 | 2.3674 | 2.3603 | 2.3535 |
| 29 | 2.4009 | 2.3906 | 2.3808 | 2.3716 | 2.3629 | 2.3546 | 2.3468 | 2.3393 | 2.3321 | 2.3253 |
| 30 | 2.3750 | 2.3647 | 2.3549 | 2.3457 | 2.3369 | 2.3286 | 2.3207 | 2.3132 | 2.3060 | 2.2992 |
| 31 | 2.3509 | 2.3406 | 2.3308 | 2.3215 | 2.3127 | 2.3044 | 2.2965 | 2.2889 | 2.2818 | 2.2749 |
| 32 | 2.3285 | 2.3181 | 2.3083 | 2.2990 | 2.2902 | 2.2818 | 2.2739 | 2.2663 | 2.2591 | 2.2523 |
| 33 | 2.3076 | 2.2971 | 2.2873 | 2.2780 | 2.2691 | 2.2608 | 2.2528 | 2.2452 | 2.2380 | 2.2311 |
| 34 | 2.2879 | 2.2775 | 2.2676 | 2.2583 | 2.2494 | 2.2410 | 2.2330 | 2.2254 | 2.2181 | 2.2112 |
| 35 | 2.2695 | 2.2590 | 2.2491 | 2.2398 | 2.2309 | 2.2225 | 2.2144 | 2.2068 | 2.1995 | 2.1926 |
| 36 | 2.2522 | 2.2417 | 2.2318 | 2.2224 | 2.2135 | 2.2050 | 2.1970 | 2.1893 | 2.1820 | 2.1751 |
| 37 | 2.2359 | 2.2254 | 2.2154 | 2.2060 | 2.1971 | 2.1886 | 2.1805 | 2.1728 | 2.1655 | 2.1585 |
| 38 | 2.2205 | 2.2099 | 2.2000 | 2.1905 | 2.1816 | 2.1731 | 2.1650 | 2.1573 | 2.1500 | 2.1430 |
| 39 | 2.2059 | 2.1954 | 2.1854 | 2.1759 | 2.1669 | 2.1584 | 2.1503 | 2.1426 | 2.1352 | 2.1282 |
| 40 | 2.1922 | 2.1816 | 2.1715 | 2.1621 | 2.1531 | 2.1445 | 2.1364 | 2.1287 | 2.1213 | 2.1142 |
| 41 | 2.1791 | 2.1685 | 2.1584 | 2.1489 | 2.1399 | 2.1313 | 2.1232 | 2.1154 | 2.1080 | 2.1010 |
| 42 | 2.1667 | 2.1560 | 2.1460 | 2.1365 | 2.1274 | 2.1188 | 2.1107 | 2.1029 | 2.0955 | 2.0884 |
| 43 | 2.1549 | 2.1442 | 2.1341 | 2.1246 | 2.1155 | 2.1069 | 2.0987 | 2.0910 | 2.0835 | 2.0764 |
| 44 | 2.1437 | 2.1330 | 2.1229 | 2.1133 | 2.1042 | 2.0956 | 2.0874 | 2.0796 | 2.0721 | 2.0650 |
| 45 | 2.1329 | 2.1222 | 2.1121 | 2.1025 | 2.0934 | 2.0848 | 2.0766 | 2.0688 | 2.0613 | 2.0542 |
| 46 | 2.1227 | 2.1120 | 2.1019 | 2.0923 | 2.0832 | 2.0745 | 2.0663 | 2.0584 | 2.0509 | 2.0438 |
| 47 | 2.1130 | 2.1022 | 2.0921 | 2.0825 | 2.0733 | 2.0646 | 2.0564 | 2.0485 | 2.0410 | 2.0339 |
| 48 | 2.1036 | 2.0929 | 2.0827 | 2.0731 | 2.0639 | 2.0552 | 2.0470 | 2.0391 | 2.0316 | 2.0244 |
| 49 | 2.0947 | 2.0839 | 2.0737 | 2.0641 | 2.0549 | 2.0462 | 2.0379 | 2.0300 | 2.0225 | 2.0153 |
| 50 | 2.0862 | 2.0754 | 2.0652 | 2.0555 | 2.0463 | 2.0376 | 2.0293 | 2.0214 | 2.0138 | 2.0066 |
| 55 | 2.0482 | 2.0374 | 2.0271 | 2.0173 | 2.0081 | 1.9993 | 1.9909 | 1.9829 | 1.9753 | 1.9680 |
| 60 | 2.0169 | 2.0059 | 1.9956 | 1.9857 | 1.9764 | 1.9675 | 1.9591 | 1.9510 | 1.9434 | 1.9360 |
| 65 | 1.9905 | 1.9795 | 1.9691 | 1.9592 | 1.9498 | 1.9409 | 1.9324 | 1.9242 | 1.9165 | 1.9091 |
| 70 | 1.9680 | 1.9570 | 1.9465 | 1.9365 | 1.9271 | 1.9181 | 1.9095 | 1.9014 | 1.8936 | 1.8861 |
| 75 | 1.9486 | 1.9375 | 1.9270 | 1.9170 | 1.9075 | 1.8984 | 1.8898 | 1.8816 | 1.8738 | 1.8663 |
| 80 | 1.9317 | 1.9205 | 1.9099 | 1.8999 | 1.8904 | 1.8813 | 1.8726 | 1.8644 | 1.8565 | 1.8489 |
| 85 | 1.9168 | 1.9056 | 1.8950 | 1.8849 | 1.8753 | 1.8662 | 1.8575 | 1.8492 | 1.8413 | 1.8337 |
| 90 | 1.9036 | 1.8924 | 1.8817 | 1.8716 | 1.8619 | 1.8528 | 1.8441 | 1.8357 | 1.8278 | 1.8201 |
| 95 | 1.8919 | 1.8806 | 1.8699 | 1.8597 | 1.8500 | 1.8408 | 1.8321 | 1.8237 | 1.8157 | 1.8080 |
| 100 | 1.8813 | 1.8699 | 1.8592 | 1.8490 | 1.8393 | 1.8301 | 1.8213 | 1.8129 | 1.8049 | 1.7972 |

## B.4 *t*-VALUES FOR A TWO-TAILED TEST—EXAMPLE: $t_{.05,19} = \pm 2.0930$

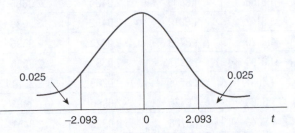

| Alpha | 0.1 | 0.08 | 0.07 | 0.05 | 0.025 | 0.02 | 0.01 |
|---|---|---|---|---|---|---|---|
| **d.f.** | | | | | | | |
| 1 | 6.3138 | 7.9158 | 9.0579 | 12.7062 | 25.4517 | 31.8205 | 63.6567 |
| 2 | 2.9200 | 3.3198 | 3.5782 | 4.3027 | 6.2053 | 6.9646 | 9.9248 |
| 3 | 2.3534 | 2.6054 | 2.7626 | 3.1824 | 4.1765 | 4.5407 | 5.8409 |
| 4 | 2.1318 | 2.3329 | 2.4559 | 2.7764 | 3.4954 | 3.7469 | 4.6041 |
| 5 | 2.0150 | 2.1910 | 2.2974 | 2.5706 | 3.1634 | 3.3649 | 4.0321 |
| 6 | 1.9432 | 2.1043 | 2.2011 | 2.4469 | 2.9687 | 3.1427 | 3.7074 |
| 7 | 1.8946 | 2.0460 | 2.1365 | 2.3646 | 2.8412 | 2.9980 | 3.4995 |
| 8 | 1.8595 | 2.0042 | 2.0902 | 2.3060 | 2.7515 | 2.8965 | 3.3554 |
| 9 | 1.8331 | 1.9727 | 2.0554 | 2.2622 | 2.6850 | 2.8214 | 3.2498 |
| 10 | 1.8125 | 1.9481 | 2.0283 | 2.2281 | 2.6338 | 2.7638 | 3.1693 |
| 11 | 1.7959 | 1.9284 | 2.0067 | 2.2010 | 2.5931 | 2.7181 | 3.1058 |
| 12 | 1.7823 | 1.9123 | 1.9889 | 2.1788 | 2.5600 | 2.6810 | 3.0545 |
| 13 | 1.7709 | 1.8989 | 1.9742 | 2.1604 | 2.5326 | 2.6503 | 3.0123 |
| 14 | 1.7613 | 1.8875 | 1.9617 | 2.1448 | 2.5096 | 2.6245 | 2.9768 |
| 15 | 1.7531 | 1.8777 | 1.9509 | 2.1314 | 2.4899 | 2.6025 | 2.9467 |
| 16 | 1.7459 | 1.8693 | 1.9417 | 2.1199 | 2.4729 | 2.5835 | 2.9208 |
| 17 | 1.7396 | 1.8619 | 1.9335 | 2.1098 | 2.4581 | 2.5669 | 2.8982 |
| 18 | 1.7341 | 1.8553 | 1.9264 | 2.1009 | 2.4450 | 2.5524 | 2.8784 |
| 19 | 1.7291 | 1.8495 | 1.9200 | 2.0930 | 2.4334 | 2.5395 | 2.8609 |
| 20 | 1.7247 | 1.8443 | 1.9143 | 2.0860 | 2.4231 | 2.5280 | 2.8453 |
| 21 | 1.7207 | 1.8397 | 1.9092 | 2.0796 | 2.4138 | 2.5176 | 2.8314 |
| 22 | 1.7171 | 1.8354 | 1.9045 | 2.0739 | 2.4055 | 2.5083 | 2.8188 |
| 23 | 1.7139 | 1.8316 | 1.9003 | 2.0687 | 2.3979 | 2.4999 | 2.8073 |
| 24 | 1.7109 | 1.8281 | 1.8965 | 2.0639 | 2.3909 | 2.4922 | 2.7969 |
| 25 | 1.7081 | 1.8248 | 1.8929 | 2.0595 | 2.3846 | 2.4851 | 2.7874 |
| 26 | 1.7056 | 1.8219 | 1.8897 | 2.0555 | 2.3788 | 2.4786 | 2.7787 |

| 27 | 1.7033 | 1.8191 | 1.8867 | 2.0518 | 2.3734 | 2.4727 | 2.7707 |
|----|--------|--------|--------|--------|--------|--------|--------|
| 28 | 1.7011 | 1.8166 | 1.8839 | 2.0484 | 2.3685 | 2.4671 | 2.7633 |
| 29 | 1.6991 | 1.8142 | 1.8813 | 2.0452 | 2.3638 | 2.4620 | 2.7564 |
| 30 | 1.6973 | 1.8120 | 1.8789 | 2.0423 | 2.3596 | 2.4573 | 2.7500 |
| 31 | 1.6955 | 1.8100 | 1.8767 | 2.0395 | 2.3556 | 2.4528 | 2.7440 |
| 32 | 1.6939 | 1.8081 | 1.8746 | 2.0369 | 2.3518 | 2.4487 | 2.7385 |
| 33 | 1.6924 | 1.8063 | 1.8726 | 2.0345 | 2.3483 | 2.4448 | 2.7333 |
| 34 | 1.6909 | 1.8046 | 1.8708 | 2.0322 | 2.3451 | 2.4411 | 2.7284 |
| 35 | 1.6896 | 1.8030 | 1.8691 | 2.0301 | 2.3420 | 2.4377 | 2.7238 |
| 36 | 1.6883 | 1.8015 | 1.8674 | 2.0281 | 2.3391 | 2.4345 | 2.7195 |
| 37 | 1.6871 | 1.8001 | 1.8659 | 2.0262 | 2.3363 | 2.4314 | 2.7154 |
| 38 | 1.6860 | 1.7988 | 1.8644 | 2.0244 | 2.3337 | 2.4286 | 2.7116 |
| 39 | 1.6849 | 1.7975 | 1.8630 | 2.0227 | 2.3313 | 2.4258 | 2.7079 |
| 40 | 1.6839 | 1.7963 | 1.8617 | 2.0211 | 2.3289 | 2.4233 | 2.7045 |
| 41 | 1.6829 | 1.7952 | 1.8605 | 2.0195 | 2.3267 | 2.4208 | 2.7012 |
| 42 | 1.6820 | 1.7941 | 1.8593 | 2.0181 | 2.3246 | 2.4185 | 2.6981 |
| 43 | 1.6811 | 1.7931 | 1.8582 | 2.0167 | 2.3226 | 2.4163 | 2.6951 |
| 44 | 1.6802 | 1.7921 | 1.8571 | 2.0154 | 2.3207 | 2.4141 | 2.6923 |
| 45 | 1.6794 | 1.7911 | 1.8561 | 2.0141 | 2.3189 | 2.4121 | 2.6896 |
| 50 | 1.6759 | 1.7870 | 1.8516 | 2.0086 | 2.3109 | 2.4033 | 2.6778 |
| 55 | 1.6730 | 1.7836 | 1.8479 | 2.0040 | 2.3044 | 2.3961 | 2.6682 |
| 60 | 1.6706 | 1.7808 | 1.8448 | 2.0003 | 2.2990 | 2.3901 | 2.6603 |
| 65 | 1.6686 | 1.7785 | 1.8423 | 1.9971 | 2.2945 | 2.3851 | 2.6536 |
| 70 | 1.6669 | 1.7765 | 1.8401 | 1.9944 | 2.2906 | 2.3808 | 2.6479 |

## B.5 THE NORMAL DISTRIBUTION TABLE

This table gives the area under the normal distribution curve between a *Z*-value of 0.00 and some selected value for the normal deviate. This is seen in the accompanying graph. For example, given *Z* = 1.96, the area is 0.4750.

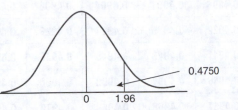

| Z-Value | 0.0 | 0.01 | 0.02 | 0.03 | 0.04 | 0.05 | 0.06 | 0.07 | 0.08 | 0.09 |
|---|---|---|---|---|---|---|---|---|---|---|
| 0.0 | 0.0000 | 0.0040 | 0.0080 | 0.0120 | 0.0160 | 0.0199 | 0.0239 | 0.0279 | 0.0319 | 0.0359 |
| 0.1 | 0.0398 | 0.0438 | 0.0478 | 0.0517 | 0.0557 | 0.0596 | 0.0636 | 0.0675 | 0.0714 | 0.0753 |
| 0.2 | 0.0793 | 0.0832 | 0.0871 | 0.0910 | 0.0948 | 0.0987 | 0.1026 | 0.1064 | 0.1103 | 0.1141 |
| 0.3 | 0.1179 | 0.1217 | 0.1255 | 0.1293 | 0.1331 | 0.1368 | 0.1406 | 0.1443 | 0.1480 | 0.1517 |
| 0.4 | 0.1554 | 0.1591 | 0.1628 | 0.1664 | 0.1700 | 0.1736 | 0.1772 | 0.1808 | 0.1844 | 0.1879 |
| 0.5 | 0.1915 | 0.1950 | 0.1985 | 0.2019 | 0.2054 | 0.2088 | 0.2123 | 0.2157 | 0.2190 | 0.2224 |
| 0.6 | 0.2257 | 0.2291 | 0.2324 | 0.2357 | 0.2389 | 0.2422 | 0.2454 | 0.2486 | 0.2517 | 0.2549 |
| 0.7 | 0.2580 | 0.2611 | 0.2642 | 0.2673 | 0.2704 | 0.2734 | 0.2764 | 0.2794 | 0.2823 | 0.2852 |
| 0.8 | 0.2881 | 0.2910 | 0.2939 | 0.2967 | 0.2995 | 0.3023 | 0.3051 | 0.3078 | 0.3106 | 0.3133 |
| 0.9 | 0.3159 | 0.3186 | 0.3212 | 0.3238 | 0.3264 | 0.3289 | 0.3315 | 0.3340 | 0.3365 | 0.3389 |
| 1 | 0.3413 | 0.3438 | 0.3461 | 0.3485 | 0.3508 | 0.3531 | 0.3554 | 0.3577 | 0.3599 | 0.3621 |
| 1.1 | 0.3643 | 0.3665 | 0.3686 | 0.3708 | 0.3729 | 0.3749 | 0.3770 | 0.3790 | 0.3810 | 0.3830 |
| 1.2 | 0.3849 | 0.3869 | 0.3888 | 0.3907 | 0.3925 | 0.3944 | 0.3962 | 0.3980 | 0.3997 | 0.4015 |
| 1.3 | 0.4032 | 0.4049 | 0.4066 | 0.4082 | 0.4099 | 0.4115 | 0.4131 | 0.4147 | 0.4162 | 0.4177 |
| 1.4 | 0.4192 | 0.4207 | 0.4222 | 0.4236 | 0.4251 | 0.4265 | 0.4279 | 0.4292 | 0.4306 | 0.4319 |
| 1.5 | 0.4332 | 0.4345 | 0.4357 | 0.4370 | 0.4382 | 0.4394 | 0.4406 | 0.4418 | 0.4429 | 0.4441 |
| 1.6 | 0.4452 | 0.4463 | 0.4474 | 0.4484 | 0.4495 | 0.4505 | 0.4515 | 0.4525 | 0.4535 | 0.4545 |
| 1.7 | 0.4554 | 0.4564 | 0.4573 | 0.4582 | 0.4591 | 0.4599 | 0.4608 | 0.4616 | 0.4625 | 0.4633 |
| 1.8 | 0.4641 | 0.4649 | 0.4656 | 0.4664 | 0.4671 | 0.4678 | 0.4686 | 0.4693 | 0.4699 | 0.4706 |
| 1.9 | 0.4713 | 0.4719 | 0.4726 | 0.4732 | 0.4738 | 0.4744 | 0.4750 | 0.4756 | 0.4761 | 0.4767 |

| 2 | 0.4772 | 0.4778 | 0.4783 | 0.4788 | 0.4793 | 0.4798 | 0.4803 | 0.4808 | 0.4812 | 0.4817 |
|-----|--------|--------|--------|--------|--------|--------|--------|--------|--------|--------|
| 2.1 | 0.4821 | 0.4826 | 0.4830 | 0.4834 | 0.4838 | 0.4842 | 0.4846 | 0.4850 | 0.4854 | 0.4857 |
| 2.2 | 0.4861 | 0.4864 | 0.4868 | 0.4871 | 0.4875 | 0.4878 | 0.4881 | 0.4884 | 0.4887 | 0.4890 |
| 2.3 | 0.4893 | 0.4896 | 0.4898 | 0.4901 | 0.4904 | 0.4906 | 0.4909 | 0.4911 | 0.4913 | 0.4916 |
| 2.4 | 0.4918 | 0.4920 | 0.4922 | 0.4925 | 0.4927 | 0.4929 | 0.4931 | 0.4932 | 0.4934 | 0.4936 |
| 2.5 | 0.4938 | 0.4940 | 0.4941 | 0.4943 | 0.4945 | 0.4946 | 0.4948 | 0.4949 | 0.4951 | 0.4952 |
| 2.6 | 0.4953 | 0.4955 | 0.4956 | 0.4957 | 0.4959 | 0.4960 | 0.4961 | 0.4962 | 0.4963 | 0.4964 |
| 2.7 | 0.4965 | 0.4966 | 0.4967 | 0.4968 | 0.4969 | 0.4970 | 0.4971 | 0.4972 | 0.4973 | 0.4974 |
| 2.8 | 0.4974 | 0.4975 | 0.4976 | 0.4977 | 0.4977 | 0.4978 | 0.4979 | 0.4979 | 0.4980 | 0.4981 |
| 2.9 | 0.4981 | 0.4982 | 0.4982 | 0.4983 | 0.4984 | 0.4984 | 0.4985 | 0.4985 | 0.4986 | 0.4986 |
| 3 | 0.4987 | 0.4987 | 0.4987 | 0.4988 | 0.4988 | 0.4989 | 0.4989 | 0.4989 | 0.4990 | 0.4990 |
| 3.1 | 0.4990 | 0.4991 | 0.4991 | 0.4991 | 0.4992 | 0.4992 | 0.4992 | 0.4992 | 0.4993 | 0.4993 |
| 3.2 | 0.4993 | 0.4993 | 0.4994 | 0.4994 | 0.4994 | 0.4994 | 0.4994 | 0.4995 | 0.4995 | 0.4995 |
| 3.3 | 0.4995 | 0.4995 | 0.4995 | 0.4996 | 0.4996 | 0.4996 | 0.4996 | 0.4996 | 0.4996 | 0.4997 |
| 3.4 | 0.4997 | 0.4997 | 0.4997 | 0.4997 | 0.4997 | 0.4997 | 0.4997 | 0.4997 | 0.4997 | 0.4998 |
| 3.5 | 0.4998 | 0.4998 | 0.4998 | 0.4998 | 0.4998 | 0.4998 | 0.4998 | 0.4998 | 0.4998 | 0.4998 |
| 3.6 | 0.4998 | 0.4998 | 0.4999 | 0.4999 | 0.4999 | 0.4999 | 0.4999 | 0.4999 | 0.4999 | 0.4999 |
| 3.7 | 0.4999 | 0.4999 | 0.4999 | 0.4999 | 0.4999 | 0.4999 | 0.4999 | 0.4999 | 0.4999 | 0.4999 |
| 3.8 | 0.4999 | 0.4999 | 0.4999 | 0.4999 | 0.4999 | 0.4999 | 0.4999 | 0.4999 | 0.4999 | 0.4999 |
| 3.9 | 0.5000 | 0.5000 | 0.5000 | 0.5000 | 0.5000 | 0.5000 | 0.5000 | 0.5000 | 0.5000 | 0.5000 |

# NOTES

## CHAPTER 1

1.  As a statute of the 1978 Bankruptcy Reform Act, Chapter 11 is a form of bankruptcy that involves a reorganization of a debtor's business affairs and assets. It is generally filed by corporations which require time to restructure their debts. It covers the specific proceedings and provisions regarding reorganization and the execution of such a plan of an individual, partnership, corporation, or municipality. Under Chapter 11, unless the court rules otherwise, the debtor remains in control of the business and its operations. Debtor and creditors are allowed to work together, thus making possible the restructuring of debt and the rescheduling of payments.

2.  Named after Carl Friedrich Gauss (1777–1855), a German mathematician. The graph of a Gaussian is a characteristic symmetric "bell curve" shape that quickly falls off toward plus/minus infinity. In its general form it appears as

$$f(x) = ae^{-\frac{(x-b)^2}{2c^2}}$$

    for some real constants $a$, $b$, $c > 0$, and $e \approx 2.718281828$ (Euler's number). The parameter $a$ is the height of the curve's peak, $b$ is the position of the center of the peak, and $c$ controls the width of the "bell." Gaussian functions are widely used in statistics, where they describe the normal distributions. They also arise by applying the exponential function to a general quadratic function. The Gaussian functions are thus those functions whose logarithm is a quadratic function.

## CHAPTER 2

1.  Developed by Carl Friedrich Gauss and Andrei Markov. Proof of the theorem can be found at: http://elsa.berkeley.edu/GMTheorem/node14.html#appGaussMarkov_proof and http://emlab.berkeley.edu/GMTheorem/index.html

2.  If it's called Total Sum of Squares, why isn't it TSS? Probably because it was originally called the Sum of the Squares of the Total Deviation—since that's what it is—but the term "deviation" was dropped, since it was understood that we are dealing with deviations, and we are left with SST.

3.  It might more accurately be called "Okun's rule of thumb" because it is primarily an empirical observation rather than a result derived from theoretical testing.

## CHAPTER 3

1. Like most legends, this one bends the truth a touch. Actually, Gosset was an agro-chemist with a special knack for statistics. It was his job to select the highest-yielding varieties of barley used in the brewing process. Guinness prohibited employees from publishing any work that might be of benefit to competitors. When Gosset developed the $t$-distribution he convinced his employer that it could not be useful to other brewers so he was allowed to present his findings to the public. But he had to do so under the name of Student to pacify other staff workers who were not allowed publication rights.

2. The $Z$-values derived from Equation (3.3.1) will take on a mean of zero because of the symmetry. If the null hypothesis is true and $\beta_1$ is zero, one-half of the $Z$-values will be positive and one-half will be negative. They will therefore average out to zero.

3. Realistically, it is unlikely that inflation in any one month would impact trade levels during that same month. It would be necessary to "lag" the data so that inflation in one month might affect trade in a later month. However, lagged variables will be discussed in a subsequent chapter, so we will dispense with this issue until later.

## CHAPTER 5

1. Remember, in a simple regression model the $F$-value is equal to the $t$-value squared, so it doesn't matter which statistic is used to make the determination.

2. R. F. Engle (1982) "A General Approach to Lagrangian Multiplier Diagnostics," *Annals of Econometrics*, pp. 83–104.

## CHAPTER 6

1. As noted in Chapter 4, this is referred to as the "restricted" model because by not including the RHS variables in the model and using only the intercept we are restricting the betas of those RHS variables to zero.

## CHAPTER 7

1. John Maynard Keynes (1936) *The General Theory of Employment, Interest and Money*, New York: Harcourt, Brace and Company. (First published by Macmillan and Cambridge University Press for the Royal Economic Society.)

2. R. E. Park (1966) "Estimation with Heteroscedastic Error Terms," *Econometrica*, 34(4), p. 888.

3. The subscript $i$ is added to the symbol to recognize that the variances are different at different values of $X$, which is the nature of heteroscedasticity.

4. H. Glejser (1969) "A New Test for Heteroscedasticity," *Journal of the American Statistical Association*, 64, pp. 316–23.

5. H. White (1980) "A Heteroscedasticity-Consistent Covariance Matrix Estimator and a Direct Test for Heteroscedasticity," *Econometrica*, 48, pp. 817–38.

6. S. M. Goldfeld and R. E. Quandt (1965) "Some Tests for Homoskedasticity," *Journal of the American Statistical Association*, 60, pp. 539–47.

7. The European Union is composed of 27 sovereign Member States: Austria, Belgium, Bulgaria, Cyprus, the Czech Republic, Denmark, Estonia, Finland, France, Germany, Greece, Hungary, Ireland, Italy, Latvia, Lithuania, Luxembourg, Malta, the Netherlands, Poland, Portugal, Romania, Slovakia, Slovenia, Spain, Sweden, and the United Kingdom. It grew from six original founding states: Belgium, France, (then-West) Germany, Italy, Luxembourg, and the Netherlands.

8. Remember, the suspect variable, $X$ in this case, does not have to be an explanatory variable used in the model. It may be a variable not included in the model. For this reason, some sources refer to the suspect variable as $Z$.

9. Sir John Richard Hicks (April 8, 1904 to May 20, 1989) was a British economist and one of the most important and influential economists of the twentieth century. The most familiar of his many contributions in the field of economics was his statement of general equilibrium and value in his 1939 book *Value and Capital* (Oxford: Clarendon Press). This grand opus significantly extended general-equilibrium and value theory. The compensated demand function is named the Hicksian demand function in his honor. In 1972 he received the Nobel Memorial Prize in Economic Sciences (jointly) for his pioneering contribution to general equilibrium theory and welfare theory.

10. In 1927, Paul Douglas and Charles Cobb formulated a production function of the form specified here. See C. W. Cobb and P. H. Douglas (1928) "A Theory of Production," *American Economic Review*, 18(Suppl), pp. 139–65.

# CHAPTER 8

1. J. Durbin and G. S. Watson (1950) "Testing for Serial Correlation in Least Squares Regression, I," *Biometrika*, 37, pp. 409–28; (1951) "Testing for Serial Correlation in Least Squares Regression, II," *Biometrika*, 38, pp. 159–79.

2. T. S. Breusch (1979) "Testing for Autocorrelation in Dynamic Linear Models," *Australian Economic Papers*, 17, pp. 334–55.
L. G. Godfrey (1978) "Testing Against General Autoregressive and Moving Average Error Models when the Regressors Include Lagged Dependent Variables," *Econometrica*, 46, pp. 1293–302.

3. J. Durbin (1970) "Testing for Serial Correlation in Least Squares Regression When Some of the Regressors Are Lagged Dependent Variables," *Econometrica*, 38, pp. 420–21.

4. J. von Neumann (1941) "Distribution of the Ratio of the Mean Square Successive Difference to the Variance," *Annals of Mathematical Statistics*, 12, pp. 367–95.

5. T. Breusch (1978) "Testing for Autocorrelation in Dynamic Linear Models," *Australian Economic Papers*, 17, pp. 334–55.

6. L. Godfrey (1978) "Testing for Higher Order Serial Correlation in Regression Equations When the Regressors Include Lagged Dependent Variables," *Econometrica*, 46, pp. 1303–10.

7. D. Cochrane and G. H. Orcutt (1949) "Applications of Least Squares Regressions to Relationships Containing Autocorrected Error Terms," *Journal of the American Statistical Association*, 44, pp. 32–61.

8. S. J. Prais and C. B. Winsten (1954) Cowles Commission Discussion Paper: Statistics #383, "Trend Estimators and Serial Correlation," February 24. At: http://cowles.econ.yale.edu/P/ccdp/st/s-0383.pdf

9. G. S. Maddala (2001) *Introduction to Econometrics*. 3rd edition, New York: John Wiley and Sons, pp. 231–32.

## CHAPTER 9

1.  It may seem strange to refer to a model with the highest power of 2 as a quadratic, since we normally think of a quad as referencing "four." But in Latin, "quad" (or quadrangle) referred to a *square* plot of land surrounded by buildings.

2.  The Cartesian coordinates were first prescribed by the seventeenth-century French philosopher and mathematician René Descartes. The creation revolutionized mathematics by providing the first systematic link between Euclidean geometry and algebra. His Latinized name was *Cartesius*, hence the term Cartesian coordinates. He also gave us the familiar phrase *I think, therefore I am*, or, in the Latin, *Cogito ergo sum*.

3.  http://www.thepigsite.com/swinenews/7082/the-costs-and-benefits-of-farm-assurance-to-livestock-producers-in-england

4.  Some sources refer to this as a *log-linear* model, but this can be a bit confusing given the lexicon associated with logarithmic transformations. Thus, the term *double-log* model will be used when variables on both sides of the equal sign are expressed as logarithms.

5.  C. W. Cobb and P. H. Douglas (1928) "A Theory of Production," *American Economic Review*, 18 (Suppl), pp. 139–65.

6.  Data available upon request.

7.  The reader is reminded that in this text the term "log-linear" is reserved for models in which the dependent variable is taken in its logarithms and the independent variables enter the model in their absolute form. Some sources use the term log-linear to imply the log-log or double-log model just discussed above.

8.  For a general review of the literature see M. Francesconi, H. Sutherland, and F. Zantomio (2011) "A Comparison of Earnings Measures from Longitudinal and Cross-Sectional Surveys: Evidence from the UK," *Journal of the Royal Statistical Society: Series A (Statistics in Society)*, 174(2), pp. 297–326; and S. W. Polachek (2008) "Earnings Over the Life Cycle: The Mincer Earnings Function and Its Applications," *Foundations and Trends in Microeconomics*, 4(3), pp. 165–272.

## CHAPTER 10

1.  John Maynard Keynes (1936) *The General Theory of Employment, Interest and Money*, New York: Harcourt, Brace and Company.

2.  J. Durbin (1954) "Errors in Variables," *Review of the International Statistical Institute*, 22, pp. 23–32.
    J. A. Hausman (1978) "Specification Tests in Econometrics," *Econometrica*, 46, pp. 1251–71.
    D. Wu (1973) "Alternative Tests of Independence Between Stochastic Regressors and Disturbances," *Econometrica*, 41, pp. 733–50.

## CHAPTER 11

1.  L. M. Koyck (1954) *Distributed Lags and Investment Analysis*, New York: North-Holland.

2.  http://www.bea.gov/national/nipaweb/TableView.asp?SelectedTable=58&ViewSeries=NO&Java=no&Request3Place=N&3Place=N&FromView=YES&Freq=Year&FirstYear=1970&LastYear=2010&3Place=N&Update=Update&JavaBox=no

3.  Recall that in the test for autocorrelation a Durbin–Watson at or near 2 leads us to not reject the null that the correlation is zero (no autocorrelation).

4. J. Durbin (1970) "Testing for Serial Correlation in Least Squares Regression When Some of the Regressors Are Lagged Dependent Variables," *Econometrica*, 38, pp. 420–21.

5. D. Dickey and W. Fuller (1979) "Distribution of Estimators for Autoregressive Time Series with a Unit Root," *Journal of the American Statistical Association*, 74(June), pp. 427–31.

6. W. Enders (2004) *Applied Econometric Time Series*. 2nd edition, New York: John Wiley & Sons. J. J. Dolado, T. Jenkinson, and S. Sosvilla-Rivero (1990) "Cointegration and Unit Roots," *Journal of Economic Surveys*, 4(3), pp. 249–73. J. Elder and P. E. Kennedy (2001) "Testing for Unit Roots: What Should Students Be Taught?," *Journal of Economic Education*, 32(2), pp. 137–46.

7. S. Almon (1965) "The Distributed Lag Between Capital Appropriations and Expenditures," *Econometrica*, 33(1), pp. 178–96.

8. C. W. J. Granger (1969) "Investigating Causal Relations by Econometric Models and Cross-Spectral Methods," *Econometrica*, 37(3), pp. 424–38.

9. A *weighted* moving average can be used to overcome this drawback but exponential smoothing accomplishes the same purpose and is a bit easier to administer.

10. C. Holt (1957) "Forecasting Seasonals and Trends by Exponentially Weighted Averages," *Office of Naval Research Memorandum*, 52. (Reprinted 2004 in *International Journal of Forecasting*, 20(1), pp. 5–10.)

11. G. Box and G. Jenkins (1970) *Time Series Analysis: Forecasting and Control*, San Francisco: Holden-Day.

# INDEX